CENGAGE LEARNING'S
GLOBAL ECONOMIC WATCH
GLOBAL ECONOMIC CRISIS RESOURCE CENTER

The credit collapse. Tumbling markets. Bailouts and bankruptcies. Surging unemployment. Political debate. Today's financial turmoil transforms academic theory into breaking news that affects every family and business sector — from Wall Street to Shanghai.

Cengage Learning's Global Economic Watch brings these pivotal current events into the classroom. It helps you answer the key questions of the day, including: "How did we get here?" and "Where do we go from here?"

The Watch, a first of its kind resource, stimulates discussion and understanding of the global downturn with easy-to-integrate learning solutions:

- **A content-rich blog** of breaking news, expert analysis and commentary — updated multiple times daily — plus links to many other blogs

- **A powerful real-time database** of hundreds of relevant and vetted journal, newpaper and periodical articles, videos, and podcasts — updated four times every day

- **A thorough overview and timeline of events** leading up to the global economic crisis

- **Student forums** for sharing questions, ideas, and opinions

History is happening now. Experience it in the classroom.

For more information on the power of The Watch, please visit **www.cengage.com/thewatch**.

10TH EDITION

ORGANIZATIONAL BEHAVIOR

MANAGING PEOPLE AND ORGANIZATIONS

RICKY W. GRIFFIN

Texas A&M University

GREGORY MOORHEAD

Arizona State University

SOUTH-WESTERN
CENGAGE Learning™

Australia • Brazil • Japan • Korea • Mexico • Singapore • Spain • United Kingdom • United States

SOUTH-WESTERN
CENGAGE Learning

Organizational Behavior: Managing People and Organizations, Tenth Edition
Ricky W. Griffin and Gregory Moorhead

Vice President of Editorial, Business:
   Jack W. Calhoun

Executive Editor: Scott Person

Senior Developmental Editor: Julia Chase

Editorial Assistant: Ruth Belanger

Marketing Manager: Jonathan Monahan

Senior Content Project Manager: Holly Henjum

Media Editor: Rob Ellington

Buyer: Arethea L. Thomas

Marketing Communications Manager: Jim
   Overly

Production Service: S4Carlisle Publishing
   Services

Sr. Art Director: Tippy McIntosh

Cover and Internal Design: Joe Devine, Red
   Hanger Design LLC

Cover Image: © Eric Isselée, Shutterstock

Rights Acquisitions Specialist/Images: John Hill

For product information and technology assistance,
contact us at **Cengage Learning Customer &
Sales Support, 1-800-354-9706**

For permission to use material from this text or product,
submit all requests online at **www.cengage.com/permissions**

Further permissions questions can be emailed to
permissionrequest@cengage.com

Library of Congress Control Number: 2010940502

Student Edition ISBN-13: 978-0-538-47813-7
Student Edition ISBN-10: 0-538-47813-6

South-Western
5191 Natorp Boulevard
Mason, OH 45040
USA

Cengage Learning products are represented in Canada by Nelson Education, Ltd.

For your course and learning solutions, visit www.cengage.com

Purchase any of our products at your local college store or at our preferred online store **www.CengageBrain.com**

Printed in Canada
1 2 3 4 5 6 7 14 13 12 11 10

BRIEF CONTENTS

CONTENTS

PART 2   INDIVIDUAL PROCESSES IN ORGANIZATIONS   61

3 Foundations of Individual Behavior   61

4 Motivation in Organizations   87

7 Managing Stress and the Work-Life Balance   175

8 Decision Making and Problem Solving   202

PART 3 INTERPERSONAL PROCESSES IN ORGANIZATIONS 234

11 Communication in Organizations   292

12 Traditional Models for Understanding Leadership   322

13 Contemporary Views of Leadership in Organizations   349

14 Power, Politics, and Organizational Justice   372

15 Conflict and Negotiation in Organizations   402

PART 4 ORGANIZATIONAL PROCESSES AND CHARACTERISTICS 430

PREFACE

The last ten years have produced some of the most challenging conditions ever faced by organizations and the people who comprise them. Organizations are contending with the longest and deepest economic recession since the Great Depression; wars and military skirmishes continue throughout the world; the pace of global technology innovation is increasing faster than ever; and natural and human-caused disasters seem to occur more frequently—all putting more and different kinds of pressure on organizations: first to survive, and, second, to develop new methods and processes, to develop new products and services, and to seek out new markets. While money, research, technological development, new marketing campaigns, and favorable political or governmental relations can be applied to provide some relief, the most important contributor to long-term organizational survival and success is in how an organization manages its people. The commitment and dedication of all of those who toil in the trenches and do the core work of the organization are the key elements in an organization's drive to change and evolve in order to confront the unprecedented challenges it faces. All facets of the field of organizational behavior contribute to the creation of a high performing organization, including motivational practices, key leadership processes, organization structure, high performing groups and teams, and the organization's culture.

It is the behavior of humans in organizations that creates and enacts the changes necessary for those organizations to survive and thrive in these challenging times. Now more than ever, managers need a comprehensive and sophisticated understanding of the assets, tools, and resources they can draw upon to compete most effectively. And understanding the people who comprise organizations—the operating employees, managers, engineers, support staff, sales representatives, decision makers, professionals, maintenance workers, and administrative employees—is critical for any manager who aspires to understand not only change but also how his or her organization needs to respond to that change.

As we prepared this edition of *Organizational Behavior: Managing People and Organizations*, we once again relied on a fundamental assumption that has helped this book remain a market leader since the publication of its first edition more than two decades ago: we must equip today's students (and tomorrow's managers) with a solid and grounded perspective on managing people that allows them to innovate, interpret, judge, imagine, and build behaviors and relationships. This perspective requires students to gain a firm grasp of the fundamentals of human behavior in organizations—the basic foundations of behavior—so that they can develop new answers to the new problems they encounter. As new challenges are thrust upon us from around the world by economic recession, natural and human-caused disasters, global competition, new technologies, newer and faster information processes, new world-wide uncertainties, and customers who demand the best in quality and service, the next generation of managers will need to go back to basics—the fundamentals—and then combine those basics with new developments in the field of Organizational Behavior as well as with valid new experiences in a complex world, and ultimately develop innovative new solutions, processes, products, or services to gain competitive advantage.

THE TEXT THAT MEETS THE CHALLENGE

This edition of *Organizational Behavior: Managing People and Organizations* takes on that challenge by providing the basics in each area, bolstered by the latest research in the field, and infused with examples of what companies are doing in each area. We open each chapter with an introduction and a new opening vignette that provides an immediate example of how the topic of the chapter is relevant to today's organizations. So that students become involved with the opening incident and begin to think about the topics in the chapter, we provide two questions following the opening incident asking students what they think about some of the issues in the incident. Chapter outlines and learning objectives are also presented at the beginning of each chapter. We continue to build and reinforce learning techniques at the end of each chapter in order to provide more opportunities to work with the chapter content. In addition to a brand-new end-of-chapter case, experiential exercise, and self-assessment exercise, we have added an opportunity for students to build their own managerial skills with the Building Managerial Skills exercise. We have also kept the in-depth running case that is presented at the end of each part of the book. This edition's all-new running case features Netflix, Inc.

Organizational Behavior: Managing People and Organizations prepares and energizes managers of the future for the complex and challenging tasks of the new century while it preserves the past contributions of the classics. It is comprehensive in its presentation of practical perspectives, backed up by the research and learning of the experts. We expect each reader to be inspired by the most exciting task of the new century: managing people in organizations.

CONTENT AND ORGANIZATION

The tenth edition of *Organizational Behavior: Managing People and Organizations* retains the same basic overall organization that has worked so well for over 20 years. But within that framework, we also continue several exciting and innovative changes that were initiated in the ninth edition and further enhanced the book's usefulness. We have also integrated the latest research and managerial practice throughout the book.

Part 1 discusses the managerial context of organizational behavior. In Chapter 1 we introduce the basic concepts of the field, discuss the importance of the study of organizational behavior, and relate organizational behavior to the broader field of management. Chapter 2 focuses on the changing environment of organizations. The key topics addressed in this chapter are globalization, diversity, technology, ethics and corporate governance, and new employment relationships.

Part 2 includes six chapters that focus on the fundamental individual processes in organizations: individual behavior, motivation, employee performance, work stress, and decision making. Chapter 3 presents the foundations for understanding individual behavior in organizations by discussing the psychological nature of people, elements of personality, individual attitudes, perceptual processes, and workplace behavior. Coverage of emotional intelligence, added to this chapter in the ninth edition, was well received and has been retained. Chapter 4 focuses on the two primary categories of motivation theories: need-based approaches and process-based approaches. Chapters 5 and 6, meanwhile, move away from theory per se and describe some of the more important methods and techniques used by organizations to actually implement the theories of motivation, with Chapter 5 discussing work-related methods for motivating employees and Chapter 6 addressing reward-based approaches to motivation. Work stress, another important element of individual behavior in organizations, is covered in Chapter 7. Finally, Chapter 8 is devoted to decision making and problem solving.

In Part 3 we move from the individual aspects of organizational behavior to the more interpersonal aspects of the field, including communication, groups and teams, leadership and influence processes, power and politics, and conflict and negotiations. Chapters 9 and 10 are a two-chapter sequence on groups and teams in organizations. We believe there is too much important material to have only one chapter on these topics. Therefore, we present the basics of understanding the dynamics of small group behavior in Chapter 9 and discuss the more applied material on teams in Chapter 10. In this manner readers get to understand the more basic processes first before attacking the more complex issues in developing teams in organizations. Chapter 11 describes the behavioral aspects of communication in organizations. We present leadership in a two-chapter sequence, examining models and concepts in Chapter 12 and contemporary views in Chapter 13. We believe users will especially enjoy Chapter 13, with its coverage of strategic, ethical, and virtual leadership, as well as gender and cross-cultural impacts on leadership. Closely related to leadership are the concepts of power, politics, and workplace justice. This material is covered in Chapter 14. Part 3 closes with Chapter 15, devoted to conflict and negotiations in organizations.

In Part 4 we address more macro and system-wide aspects of organizational behavior. Chapter 16, the first of a two-chapter sequence on organization structure and design, presents the classical view of organizations and then describes the basic building blocks of organizations—division of labor, specialization, centralization, formalization, responsibility, and authority. Chapter 17 describes more about the factors and the process through which the structure of an organization is matched to fit the demands of change, new technology, and expanding competition, including global issues. Chapter 18 moves on to the important concept of organizational culture, describing the key elements of culture and how it is created and changed. The final chapter, Chapter 19, could really be the cornerstone of every chapter, because it presents the classical and contemporary views of organizational change. Due to the demands on organizations today, as stated earlier and by every management writer alive, change is the order of the day, the year, the decade, and the new century.

FEATURES OF THE BOOK

This edition of *Organizational Behavior: Managing People and Organizations* is guided by our continuing devotion to the preparation of the next generation of managers. This is reflected in four key elements of the book which we believe stem from this guiding principle: a strong student orientation; contemporary content; a real world, applied approach; and effective pedagogy.

Student Orientation

We believe that students, instructors, and other readers will agree with our students' assessment of the book as being easy and even enjoyable to read with its direct and active style. We have tried to retain the comprehensive nature of the book while writing in a style that is active and lively and geared to the student reader. We want students to enjoy reading the book while they learn from it. The cartoons and their content-rich captions tie the humorous intent of the cartoons to the concepts in the text. Thought-provoking questions bring the student into the opening incident, drawing them into the topics in each chapter. All of the figures include meaningful captions, again to tie the figure directly to the concepts. The end-of-chapter features retain the popular experiential exercises and the diagnostic questionnaires, or self-assessments, and the real-world cases that show how the chapter material relates to actual practice. A third of these exercises are new to this edition and all of the cases' boxed inserts are brand new.

Contemporary Content Coverage

This edition continues our tradition of presenting the most modern management approaches as expressed in the popular press and the academic research. The basic structure of the book remains the same, but you will find new coverage that represents the most recent research in many areas of the book.

Real World, Applied Approach

The organizations cited in the opening incidents, examples, cases, and boxed features throughout this edition represent a blend of large, well-known and smaller, less well-known organizations so that students will see the applicability of the material in a variety of organizational settings. Each chapter opens and closes with concrete examples of relevant topics from the chapter. The running end-of-part case about Netflix provides a more in-depth case for class discussion. Each chapter also contains two boxes, selected from the five types of boxed features included in this edition. Each box has a unique, identifying icon that distinguishes it and makes it easier for students to identify.

As in the ninth edition, and completely unlike other books, we have achieved a very exciting form of integration with the boxed inserts in this edition. One box in the chapter continues the story from the opening case and then ties it to one of the thematic concepts described below:

- Each "Technology" box describes how a company uses advances in computer and information technology to improve its business.
- Each "Change" box shows an organization rethinking its methods of operation to respond to changes in the business climate.
- Each "Globalization" box describes an organization meeting the needs of its increasingly complex global environment.
- Each "Diversity" box shows an organization dealing with its increasingly diverse work force.
- Each "Ethics" box shows an organization's ethical perspective when making decisions or dealing with complicated situations.

Effective Pedagogy

Our guiding intent continues to be to put together a package that enhances student learning. The package includes several features of the book, many of which have already been mentioned:

- Each chapter begins with a Chapter Outline and Objectives and ends with a Synopsis.
- "Discussion Questions" at the end of each chapter stimulate interaction among students and provide a guide to complete studying of the chapter concepts.

- Following the Opening Incident in each chapter are two thought-provoking questions in a "What Do You Think?" section that draw the students into the incident and then into the topics in the chapter.

- "Experiencing Organizational Behavior" exercises at the end of each chapter, (many new to this edition), help students make the transition from textbook learning to real world applications. The end-of-chapter case, "Organizational Behavior Case for Discussion," also assists in this transition.

- A "Self Assessment Exercise" activity at the end of each chapter gives students the opportunity to apply a concept from the chapter to a brief self-assessment or diagnostic activity.

- The "Building Managerial Skills" activity provides an opportunity for students to "get their hands dirty" and really use something discussed in the chapter.

- The Opening and Closing Cases—all of which are brand new to this edition—and accompanying boxed inserts—one half of which are new—illustrate chapter concepts with real life applications.

- The brand-new Integrative Running Case at the end of each part focuses on Netflix and provides an opportunity for students to discuss an actual ongoing management situation with significant organizational behavior facets.

- Figures, tables, photographs, and cartoons offer visual and humorous support for the text content. Explanatory captions to figures, photographs, and cartoons enhance their pedagogical value.

- A running marginal glossary and a complete glossary found on the textbook website provide additional support for identifying and learning key concepts.

A new design reflects this edition's content, style, and pedagogical program. The colors remain bold to reflect the dynamic nature of the behavioral and managerial challenges facing managers today, and the interior photographs in this edition have been specially selected to highlight the dynamic world of organizational behavior.

But why zebras on the cover? Well, for one thing, they present an attractive image. But more seriously, if we look a bit closer we can see that while all zebras look similar to one another, in reality the marking and patterns on each is unique. They are social animals that live and travel in groups. Within each group there is a well-defined hierarchy based on power and status, and each group has a leader. And the group itself works with certain other groups (such as impalas and wildebeests) to protect themselves from other groups (most notably lions). When you have finished reading and studying this book, you will come to understand that like zebras, each of us as human beings has certain things in common with all other humans, but each of us is also unique. We are social, live and travel in groups, have hierarchies and leaders, and both collaborate and compete with others. So, what can managers learn from zebras? Probably more than you think, and they are still wonderful creatures to watch!

We would like to hear from you about your experiences in using the book. We want to know what you like and what you do not like about it. Please write to us via e-mail to tell us about your learning experiences. You may contact us at:

Ricky Griffin
rgriffin@tamu.edu

Greg Moorhead
greg.moorhead@asu.edu

ACKNOWLEDGEMENTS

Although this book bears our two names, numerous people have contributed to it. Through the years we have had the good fortune to work with many fine professionals who helped us to sharpen our thinking about this complex field and to develop new and more effective ways of discussing it. Their contributions were essential to the development of this edition. Any and all errors of omission, interpretation, and emphasis remain the responsibility of the authors.

Several reviewers made essential contributions to the development of this and previous editions. We would like to express a special thanks to them for taking the time to provide us with their valuable assistance:

Abdul Aziz
College of Charleston

Steve Ball
Cleary College

Brendan Bannister
Northeastern University

Greg Baxter
Southeastern Oklahoma State University

Jon W. Beard
Purdue University

Mary-Beth Beres
Mercer University Atlanta

Ronald A. Bigoness
Stephen F. Austin State University

Allen Bluedorn
University of Missouri Columbia

Ken Butterfield
Washington State University

Bryan Bonner
University of Utah

Wayne Boss
University of Colorado-Boulder

Murray Brunton
Central Ohio Technical College

John Bunch
Kansas State University

Mark Butler
San Diego State University

Richard R. Camp
Eastern Michigan University

Anthony Chelte
Western New England College

Anne Cooper
St. Petersburg Community College

John L. Cotton
Marquette University

Dan R. Dalton
Indiana University Bloomington

Carla L. Dando
Idaho State University

T. K. Das
Baruch College

George deLodzia
University of Rhode Island

Ronald A. DiBattista
Bryant College

Harry Domicone
California Lutheran University

Thomas W. Dougherty
University of Missouri Columbia

Cathy Dubois
Kent State University

Earlinda Elder-Albritton
Detroit College of Business

Stanley W. Elsea
Kansas State University

Jan Feldbauer
Austin Community College

Maureen J. Fleming
The University of Montana—Missoula

Joseph Forest
Georgia State University

Eliezer Geisler
Northeastern Illinois University

Robert Giacalone
University of Richmond

Bob Goddard
Appalachian State University

Lynn Harland
*University of Nebraska
at Omaha*

Stan Harris
Lawrence Tech University

Nell Hartley
Robert Morris College

Peter Heine
Stetson University

William Hendrix
Clemson University

John Jermier
University of South Florida

Avis L. Johnson
University of Akron

Bruce Johnson
Gustavus Adolphus College

Gwen Jones
Bowling Green State University

Kathleen Johnson
Keene State College

Robert T. Keller
University of Houston

Michael Klausner
University of Pittsburgh at Bradford

Stephen Kleisath
University of Wisconsin

Barbara E. Kovatch
Rutgers University

David R. Lee
University of Dayton

Richard Leifer
Rensselaer Polytechnic Institute

Robert W. Leonard
Lebanon Valley College

Fengru Li
University of Montana

Peter Lorenzi
University of Central Arkansas

Joseph B. Lovell
*California State University,
San Bernardino*

Patricia Manninen
North Shore Community College

Edward K. Marlow
Eastern Illinois University

Edward Miles
Georgia State University

C. W. Millard
University of Puget Sound

Alan N. Miller
University of Nevada Las Vegas

Herff L. Moore
University of Central Arkansas

Robert Moorman
West Virginia University

Stephan J. Motowidlo
Pennsylvania State University

Richard T. Mowday
University of Oregon

Margaret A. Neale
Northwestern University

Christopher P. Neck
Virginia Tech

Linda L. Neider
University of Miami

Mary Lippitt Nichols
University of Minnesota Minneapolis

Ranjna Patel
Bethune-Cookman College

Robert J. Paul
Kansas State University

John Perry
Pennsylvania State University

Pamela Pommerenke
Michigan State University

James C. Quick
University of Texas at Arlington

Richard Raspen
Wilkes University

Elizabeth Rawlin
University of South Carolina

Gary Reinke
University of Maryland

Joan B. Rivera
West Texas A&M University

Bill Robinson
Indiana University of Pennsylvania

Hannah Rothstein
CUNY—Baruch College

Carol S. Saunders
University of Oklahoma

Daniel Sauers
Winona State University

Constance Savage
Ashland University

Mary Jane Saxton
University of Colorado at Denver

Ralph L. Schmitt
Macomb Community College

Randall S. Schuler
Rutgers University

Amit Shah
Frostburg State University

Gary Shields
Wayne State University

Randall G. Sleeth
Virginia Commonwealth University

Dayle Smith
University of San Francisco

Rieann Spence-Gale
Northern Virginia Community College (Alexandria)

William R. Stevens
Missouri Southern State College

Dianna L. Stone
University of Texas at San Antonio

Nareatha Studdard
Arkansas State University

Christy Suciu
Boise State University

Steve Taylor
Boston College

Donald Tompkins
Slippery Rock University

Ahmad Tootoonchi
Frostburg State University

Matthew Valle
Troy State University at Dothan

Linn Van Dyne
Michigan State University

David D. Van Fleet
Arizona State University West

Bobby C. Vaught
Southwest Missouri State University

Sean Valentine
University of Wyoming

Jack W. Waldrip
American Graduate School of International Management

John P. Wanous
The Ohio State University

Judith Y. Weisinger
Northeastern University

Joseph W. Weiss
Bentley College

Albert D. Widman
Berkeley College

The tenth edition could never have been completed without the support of Texas A&M University and Arizona State University, whose leadership teams facilitated our work by providing the environment that encourages scholarly activities and contributions to the field. Several assistants and graduate and undergraduate assistants were also involved in the development of the tenth edition.

We would also like to acknowledge the outstanding team of professionals at Cengage Learning who helped us prepare this book. Julia Chase has been steadfast in her commitment to quality and her charge to us to raise quality throughout the book. Holly Henjum has been a master of professionalism. Melissa Acuna, Scott Person, Clinton Kernen, Jonathan Monahan, Rob Ellington, Tippy McIntosh, and Ruth Belanger were also key players in planning the book and supplements package. Ron Librach made important substantive contributions by helping research case material and revising the end-of-chapter exercises.

Finally, we would like to acknowledge the role of change in our own lives. One of us has successfully fought cancer and the other has had a complete lower leg reconstruction. The techniques that led us to where we are today did not exist when we wrote the first edition of this book. Hence, change has touched the two of us in profound ways. We also continue to be mindful of the daily reminders that we get from our families about the things that really matter in life. Without the love and support of our families, our lives would be far less enriched and meaningful. It is with all of our love that we dedicate this book to them.

R.W.G.
G.M.

For my daughter Ashley, a rock star at work but still her daddy's sweet and shining star.

—R.W.G.

For my family: Linda, Alex, and Lindsay.

—G.M.

CHAPTER 1

An Overview of Organizational Behavior

CHAPTER LEARNING OBJECTIVES

After studying this chapter you should be able to:

- Define organizational behavior.
- Identify the functions that comprise the management process and relate them to organizational behavior.
- Relate organizational behavior to basic managerial roles and skills.
- Describe contemporary organizational behavior characteristics.
- Discuss contextual perspectives on organizational behavior.
- Describe the role of organizational behavior in managing for effectiveness.

No Company for Old-Fashioned Management

"Anything that requires knowledge and service gives us a reason to be."

—DANNY WEGMAN, CEO OF WEGMANS FOOD MARKETS

If you're looking for the best Parmesan cheese for your chicken parmigiana recipe, you might try Wegmans, especially if you happen to live in the vicinity of Pittsford, New York. Cheese department manager Carol Kent will be happy to recommend the best brand because her job calls for knowing cheese as well as managing

Wegmans' reputation as a great place to work has helped the firm build a committed and motivated workforce. These Wegmans employees are having a team meeting before their store opens.

RICHARD A. LIPSKI/THE WASHINGTON POST/GETTY IMAGES

1

some 20 employees. Kent is a knowledgeable employee, and knowledgeable employees, says Wegmans CEO Danny Wegman, are "something our competitors don't have and our customers couldn't get anywhere else."

Wegmans Food Markets, a family-owned East Coast chain with more than 70 outlets in five states, prides itself on its commitment to customers, and it shows: It (U of C, 6.64) ranks at the top of the latest *Consumer Reports* survey of the best national and regional grocery stores. Wegmans rates especially high on service, and although such amenities as sushi stations, crab-cake counters, kosher delis, and Thai and Indian buffets drive up costs, the chain also keeps a close eye on prices. In fact, back in November 2008, as the economy continued to sink into the recession, Wegmans announced what amounted to a price war with itself by promising to cut prices on many of its products: Bread went down by 17 percent and pork by 26 percent, and Wegmans claims to have saved customers $20 million. "During difficult times like these," explains Danny Wegman, "it's okay with us if we make a little less money."

But commitment to customers is only half of Wegmans' overall strategy, which calls for reaching its customers through its employees. "How do we differentiate ourselves?" asks Wegman, who then proceeds to answer his own question: "If we can sell products that require knowledge in terms of how you use them, that's our strategy. Anything that requires knowledge and service gives us a reason to be." That's the logic behind one of Carol Kent's recent assignments—one that she understandably regards as a perk: Wegmans sent her to Italy to conduct a personal study of Italian cheese. "We sat with the families" that make the cheeses, she recalls, and "broke bread with them. It helped me understand that we're not just selling a piece of cheese. We're selling a tradition, a quality."

Kent and the employees in her department also enjoy the best benefits package in the industry, including fully paid health insurance. And that includes part-timers, who make up about two-thirds of the company's workforce of more than 37,000. In part, the strategy of extending benefits to this large segment of the labor force is intended to make sure that stores have enough good workers for crucial peak periods, but there's no denying that the costs of employee-friendly policies can mount up. At 15 to 17 percent of sales, for example, Wegmans' labor costs are well above the 12 percent figure for most supermarkets. But according to one company HR executive, holding down labor costs isn't necessarily a strategic priority: "We would have stopped offering free health insurance [to part-timers] a long time ago," she admits, "if we tried to justify the costs."

Besides, employee turnover at Wegmans is about 6 percent—a mere fraction of an industry average that hovers around 19 percent (and that, for part-timers, can approach 100 percent). And this is an industry in which total turnover costs have been known to outstrip total annual profits by 40 percent. Wegmans employees tend to be knowledgeable because about 20 percent of them have been with the company for at least 10 years, and many have logged at least a quarter century. Says one 19-year-old college student who works at an upstate–New York Wegmans while pursuing a career as a high school history teacher: "I love this place. If teaching doesn't work out, I would so totally work at Wegmans." Edward McLaughlin, who directs the Food Industry Management Program at Cornell University, understands this sort of attitude: "When you're a 16-year-old kid, the last thing you want to do is wear a geeky shirt and work for a supermarket," but at Wegmans, he explains, "it's a badge of honor. You're not a geeky cashier. You're part of the social fabric."

In 2009, Wegmans placed fifth in *Fortune* magazine's annual list of "100 Best Companies to Work For"—down from number 1 in 2006 and number 3 in 2008 but good for twelve consecutive years on the list and five straight top-5 finishes. "It says that we're doing something right," says a company spokesperson, "and that there's no better way to take care of our customers than to be a great place for our employees to work." In addition to its healthcare package, Wegmans has been cited for such perks as fitness center discounts, compressed workweeks, telecommuting, and domestic-partner benefits (which extend to same-sex partners). For eight weeks in the summer of 2009, and again for a six-week period from Thanksgiving to New Year's, the company offered employees 10 percent discounts to help with grocery purchases during economic crunch times. "With a challenging economy," reasons Danny Wegman, "being a great place to work is the best way we can take care of our customers."

What Do You Think?

1. Why don't more firms adopt the kind of management practices that have contributed to Wegmans' success?

2. Under what circumstances might Wegmans be forced to change its approach to dealing with its employees?

References: Jon Springer, "Danny Wegman," *Supermarket News*, July 14, 2009, http://supermarketnews.com on January 19, 2010; Michael A. Prospero, "Employee Innovator: Wegmans," *Fast Company*, October 2004, www.fastcompany.com on January 19, 2010; "Survey: Wegmans, Trader Joe's and Publix among the Best of 59 Grocery Chains," *ConsumerReports.org*, http://pressroom.consumerreports.org on January 19, 2010; Dan Mitchell, "Wegmans Price War against Itself," *The Big Money*, November 2, 2009, www.thebigmoney.com on January 19, 2010; Sharon Linstedt, "Wegmans Ranked Fifth-Best Place to Work by *Fortune* Magazine," *The Buffalo News*, January 23, 2009, www.buffalonews.com on January 19, 2010; Business Civic Leadership Center, "Wegmans," *2009 Corporate Citizenship Awards* (U.S. Chamber of Commerce, 2009), www.uschamber.com on January 19, 2010.

In many ways a Wegmans store may not look substantially different from a large national chain store. But its dual emphasis on both customer and employee satisfaction had paid big dividends as the firm continues to thrive through good times and bad. Regardless of their size, scope, or location, all organizations have at least one thing in common—they are comprised of people. And it is these people who make decisions about the strategic direction of a firm, it is they who acquire the resources the firm uses to create new products, and it is they who sell those products; people manage a firm's corporate headquarters, its warehouses, and its information technology; and it is people who clean up at the end of the day. No matter how effective a manager might be, all organizational successes—and failures—are the result of the behaviors of many people. Indeed, no manager can succeed without the assistance of others.

Thus, any manager—whether responsible for a big business like Google, Abercrombie & Fitch, General Electric, Apple, Starbucks, or British Airways; for a niche business like the Boston Celtics basketball team or the Mayo Clinic; or for a local Pizza Hut restaurant or neighborhood dry cleaning establishment—must strive to understand the people who work in the organization. This book is about those people. It is also about the organization itself and the managers who operate it. The study of organizations and the study of the people who work in them together constitute the field of organizational behavior. Our starting point in exploring this field begins with a more detailed discussion of its meaning and its importance to managers.

WHAT IS ORGANIZATIONAL BEHAVIOR?

What exactly is meant by the term "organizational behavior"? And why should it be studied? Answers to these two fundamental questions will both help establish our foundation for discussion and analysis and help you better appreciate the rationale as to how and why understanding the field can be of value to you in the future.

The Meaning of Organizational Behavior

Organizational behavior (OB) is the study of human behavior in organizational settings, of the interface between human behavior and the organization, and of the organization itself.[1] Although we can focus on any one of these three areas, we must also remember that all three are ultimately necessary for a comprehensive understanding of organizational behavior. For example, we can study individual behavior without explicitly considering the organization. But because the organization influences and is influenced by the individual, we cannot fully understand the individual's behavior without learning something about the organization. Similarly, we can study organizations without focusing explicitly on the people within them. But again, we are looking at only a portion of the puzzle. Eventually we must consider the other pieces, as well as the whole.

Figure 1.1 illustrates this view of organizational behavior. It shows the linkages among human behavior in organizational settings, the individual–organization interface, the organization itself, and the environment surrounding the organization. Each individual brings to an organization a unique set of personal characteristics as well as a unique personal background and set of experiences from other organizations. Therefore, in considering the people who work in their organizations, managers must look at the unique perspective each individual brings to the work setting. For example, suppose managers at The Home Depot realize that employee turnover within the firm is gradually but consistently increasing. Further suppose that they hire a consultant to help them better understand the problem. As a starting point, the consultant might analyze the types of people the company usually hires. The goal would be to learn as much as possible about the nature of the company's workforce as individuals—their expectations, their personal goals, and so forth.

𝓕𝒾𝑔𝓊𝓇𝑒 1.1   THE NATURE OF ORGANIZATIONAL BEHAVIOR

The field of organizational behavior attempts to understand human behavior in organizational settings, the organization itself, and the individual–organization interface. As illustrated here, these areas are highly interrelated. Thus, although it is possible to focus on only one of these areas at a time, a complete understanding of organizational behavior requires knowledge of all three areas.

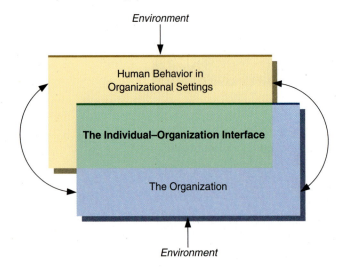

Environment

Human Behavior in Organizational Settings

The Individual–Organization Interface

The Organization

Environment

Organizational behavior is the study of human behavior in organizational settings, the interface between human behavior and the organization, and the organization itself.

But individuals do not work in isolation. They come in contact with other people and with the organization in a variety of ways. Points of contact include managers, co-workers, the formal policies and procedures of the organization, and various changes implemented by the organization. In addition, over time, individuals change, as a function of personal experiences and maturity as well as work experiences and organizational developments. The organization, in turn, is affected by the presence and eventual absence of the individual. Clearly, then, managers must also consider how the individual and the organization interact. Thus, the consultant studying turnover at The Home Depot might next look at the orientation procedures and initial training for newcomers to the organization. The goal of this phase of the study would be to understand some of the dynamics of how incoming individuals are introduced to and interact with the broader organizational context.

An organization, of course, exists before a particular person joins it and continues to exist after he or she leaves. Thus, the organization itself represents a crucial third perspective from which to view organizational behavior. For instance, the consultant studying turnover would also need to study the structure and culture of The Home Depot. An understanding of factors such as a firm's performance evaluation and reward systems, its decision-making and communication patterns, and the structure of the firm itself can provide added insight into why some people choose to leave a company and others elect to stay.

Clearly, then, the field of organizational behavior is both exciting and complex. Myriad variables and concepts accompany the interactions just described, and together these factors greatly complicate the manager's ability to understand, appreciate, and manage others in the organization. They also provide unique and important opportunities to enhance personal and organizational effectiveness.

The Importance of Organizational Behavior

The importance of organizational behavior may now be clear, but we should nonetheless take a few moments to make it even more explicit. Most people are raised and educated in organizations, acquire most of their material possessions from organizations, and die as members of organizations. Many of our activities are regulated by the various organizations that make up our governments. And most adults spend the better part of their lives working in organizations. Because organizations influence our lives so powerfully, we have every reason to be concerned about how and why those organizations function.

In our relationships with organizations, we may adopt any one of several roles or identities. For example, we can be consumers, employees, suppliers, competitors, owners, or investors. Since most readers of this book are either present or future managers, we will adopt a managerial perspective throughout our discussion. The study of organizational behavior can greatly clarify the factors that affect how managers manage. Hence, the field attempts to describe the complex human context of organizations and to define the opportunities, problems, challenges, and issues associated with that realm.

The value of organizational behavior is that it isolates important aspects of the manager's job and offers specific perspectives on the human side of management: people as organizations, people as resources, and people as people. To further underscore the importance of organizational behavior to managers, we should consider this simple fact: Year-in and year-out, most of the firms on *Fortune*'s list of the world's most admired companies have impeccable reputations for valuing and respecting the people who work for them.[2] Clearly, then, an understanding of organizational behavior can play a vital role in managerial work. To most effectively use the knowledge provided by this

JIN LEE/BLOOMBERG/GETTY IMAGES

People represent the essence of an organization, regardless of the size of the organization or the technology it uses. Apple, for example, relies on creative people to help generate new business ideas and then translate those ideas into business practice. While most Apple products are assembled and shipped using automated technology, without people neither Apple products nor the technology used to make and distribute them would exist. These Apple employees are celebrating the launch of the iPad, one of the most successful new products to be introduced in business history.

field, managers must thoroughly understand its various concepts, assumptions, and premises. To provide this foundation, we next tie organizational behavior even more explicitly to management and then turn to a more detailed examination of the manager's job itself.

Organizational Behavior and Management

Virtually all organizations have managers with titles such as chief financial officer, marketing manager, director of public relations, vice president for human resources, and plant manager. But probably no organization has a position called "organizational behavior manager." The reason for this is simple: Organizational behavior is not a defined business function or area of responsibility similar to finance or marketing. Rather, an understanding of organizational behavior is a perspective that provides a set of insights and tools that all managers can use to carry out their jobs more effectively.[3]

An appreciation and understanding of organizational behavior helps managers better understand why others in the organization behave as they do.[4] For example, most managers in an organization are directly responsible for the work-related behaviors of a certain set of other people—their immediate subordinates. Typical managerial activities in this realm include motivating employees to work harder, ensuring that employees' jobs are properly designed, resolving conflicts, evaluating performance, and helping workers set goals to achieve rewards. The field of organizational behavior abounds with models and research relevant to each of these activities.[5]

Unless they happen to be chief executive officers (CEOs), managers also report to others in the organization (and even the CEO reports to the board of directors). In dealing with these individuals, an understanding of basic issues associated with leadership, power and political behavior, decision making, organization structure and design, and organization culture can be extremely beneficial. Again, the field of organizational behavior provides numerous valuable insights into these processes.

Managers can also use their knowledge of organizational behavior to better understand their own needs, motives, behaviors, and feelings, which will help them improve decision-making capabilities, control stress, communicate better, and comprehend how career dynamics unfold. The study of organizational behavior provides insights into all of these concepts and processes.

Managers interact with a variety of colleagues, peers, and coworkers inside the organization. An understanding of attitudinal processes, individual differences, group dynamics, intergroup dynamics, organization culture, and power and political behavior can help managers handle such interactions more effectively. Organizational behavior provides a variety of practical insights into these processes. Virtually all of the insights into behavioral processes already mentioned are also valuable in interactions with people outside the organization—suppliers, customers, competitors, government officials, representatives of citizens' groups, union officials, and potential joint-venture partners. In addition, a special understanding of the environment, technology, and global issues is valuable. Again, organizational behavior offers managers many different insights into how and why things happen as they do.

Finally, these patterns of interactions hold true regardless of the type of organization. Whether a business is large or small, domestic or international, growing or stagnating, its managers perform their work within a social context. And the same can be said of managers in health care, education, and government, as well as in student organizations such as fraternities, sororities, and professional clubs. We see, then, that it is essentially impossible to understand and practice management without considering the numerous areas of organizational behavior. Further, as more and more organizations hire managers from other countries, the processes of understanding human behavior in organizations will almost certainly grow increasingly complex. We now address the nature of the manager's job in more detail before returning to our primary focus on organizational behavior.

ORGANIZATIONAL BEHAVIOR
AND THE MANAGEMENT PROCESS

Managerial work is fraught with complexity and unpredictability and enriched with opportunity and excitement. However, in characterizing managerial work most educators and other experts find it useful to conceptualize the activities performed by managers as reflecting one or more of four basic functions. These functions are generally referred to as *planning*, *organizing*, *leading*, and *controlling*. While these functions are often described in a sequential manner, in reality, of course, most managerial work involves all four functions simultaneously.

Similarly, organizations use many different resources in the pursuit of their goals and objectives. As with management functions, though, these resources can also generally be classified into four groups: *human*, *financial*, *physical*, and/or *information* resources. As illustrated in Figure 1.2, managers combine these resources through the four basic functions, with the ultimate purpose of efficiently and effectively attaining the goals of the organization. That is, the figure shows how managers apply the basic functions across resources to advance the organization toward its goals.

Figure 1.2　**BASIC MANAGERIAL FUNCTIONS**

Managers engage in the four basic functions of planning, organizing, leading, and controlling. These functions are applied to human, financial, physical, and information resources with the ultimate purpose of efficiently and effectively attaining organizational goals.

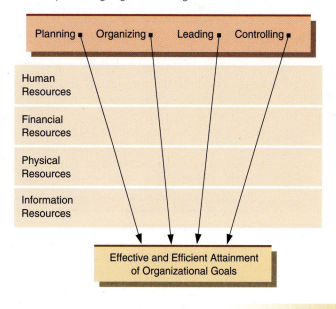

Planning, the first managerial function, is the process of determining the organization's desired future position and deciding how best to get there. The planning process at Sears, for example, includes studying and analyzing the environment, deciding on appropriate goals, outlining strategies for achieving those goals, and developing tactics

Planning is the process of determining an organization's desired future position and the best means of getting there.

CHANGE

Microsoft Recruits to Win

There's a battle waging to recruit top technical talent. In 2006, just 10,000 computer science degrees were awarded in the United States, yet Microsoft needed 11,000 new workers. The competition to hire the best and brightest is tough, highlighting fierce industry rivalry. On-campus interviews aren't sufficient to generate the number of applicants needed.

Unfortunately for Microsoft, Google is the current favorite. The stock is rising rapidly, making stock-option compensation very attractive. While basic compensation and benefits are average, Google offers a wealth of "creature comforts." Employees get unlimited free gourmet beverages, meals, and snacks. Doctors, massage therapists, and auto mechanics make on-site visits. The list goes on and on. Microsoft, on the other hand, has a stagnant stock price that makes options unrewarding. The company offers above-average pay and basic benefits, but less pampering.

What then can Microsoft do to compete? The company is doing a better job of publicizing its advantages. The recruiting center has been updated into a Google-style lounge with concierge service, food, and Guitar Hero. Aggressive recruiting from competitors and more H1-B visas for skilled foreign workers are

> *"While it takes super leadership to rise up and push for the change, it takes extraordinary fantastic leadership to realize big change day-to-day from here forward."*
> —ANONYMOUS MICROSOFT EMPLOYEE AND BLOGGER

two more tactics. When these still fall short, Microsoft tries new recruiting methods.

One of the most interesting new techniques is the use of online programming competitions run by TopCoder, Inc. The best algorithm wins. Winners can earn cash prizes—some top competitors clear $500,000. Job offers follow, too, from companies such as Yahoo!, Google, and eBay, as well as Microsoft. The method is completely free from biases related to age, race, or gender. It also provides a global reach at little cost.

The changes are difficult, but worthwhile. An anonymous blogger at Microsoft says, "While it takes super leadership to rise up and push for the change, it takes extraordinary fantastic leadership to realize big change day-to-day from here forward." For Microsoft to finally close the recruiting gap with younger, hipper companies like Google, it must sustain these changes.

References: Michelle Conlin and Jay Greene, "How to Make a Microserf Smile," *BusinessWeek*, September 10, 2007, www.businessweek.com on January 29, 2010; "Microsoft's Mini-Me Susses Brummel," *BusinessWeek*, September 10, 2007, www.businessweek.com on January 29, 2010; Benjamin J. Romano, "Under Pressure, Microsoft Fights to Keep Its Workers," *Seattle Times*, May 19, 2006, www.seattletimes.nwsource.com on January 29, 2010; Benjamin J. Romano, "Microsoft Exec Puts Her Stamp on Human Resources," *Seattle Times*, October 9, 2006, www.seattletimes.nwsource.com on January 29, 2010.

---

to help execute the strategies. Behavioral processes and characteristics pervade each of these activities. Perception, for instance, plays a major role in environmental scanning, and creativity and motivation influence how managers set goals, strategies, and tactics for their organization. Larger corporations such as General Motors and Starbucks usually rely on their top management teams to handle most planning activities. In smaller firms, the owner usually takes care of planning.

The second managerial function is **organizing**—the process of designing jobs, grouping jobs into manageable units, and establishing patterns of authority among jobs and

Organizing is the process of designing jobs, grouping jobs into units, and establishing patterns of authority between jobs and units.

groups of jobs. This process produces the basic structure, or framework, of the organization. For large organizations such as Apple and Toyota, that structure can be extensive and complicated. The structure includes several hierarchical layers and spans myriad activities and areas of responsibility. Smaller firms can often function with a relatively simple and straightforward form of organization. As noted earlier, the processes and characteristics of the organization itself are a major theme of organizational behavior.

Leading, the third major managerial function, is the process of motivating members of the organization to work together toward the organization's goals. An Abercrombie & Fitch store manager, for example, must hire people, train them, and motivate them. Major components of leading include motivating employees, managing group dynamics, and the actual process of leadership itself. These are all closely related to major areas of organizational behavior. All managers, whether they work in a huge multinational corporation spanning dozens of countries or in a small neighborhood business serving a few square city blocks, must understand the importance of leading.

The *Change* box on page 8 shows how the leadership at Microsoft made the changes necessary to compete with Google in the battle to recruit top talent in the computer science market.

The fourth managerial function, controlling, is the process of monitoring and correcting the actions of the organization and its people to keep them headed toward their goals. A manager at Best Buy has to control costs, inventory, and so on. Again, behavioral processes and characteristics are a key part of this function. Performance evaluation, reward systems, and motivation, for example, all apply to control. Control is of vital importance to all businesses, but it may be especially critical to smaller ones. Wal-Mart, for example, can withstand with relative ease a loss of several thousand dollars due to poor control; but an equivalent loss may be devastating to a small firm.

ORGANIZATIONAL BEHAVIOR AND THE MANAGER'S JOB

As they engage in the basic management functions previously described, managers often find themselves playing a variety of different roles. Moreover, in order to perform the functions most effectively and to be successful in their various roles, managers must also draw upon a set of critical skills. This section first introduces the basic managerial roles and then describes the core skills necessary for success in an organization.

Basic Managerial Roles

In an organization, as in a play or a movie, a role is the part a person plays in a given situation. Managers often play a number of different roles. In general, as summarized in Table 1.1, there are ten basic managerial roles which cluster into three general categories.[6]

Interpersonal Roles   The interpersonal roles are primarily social in nature; that is, they are roles in which the manager's main task is to relate to other people in certain ways. The manager sometimes may serve as a *figurehead* for the organization. Taking visitors to dinner and attending ribbon-cutting ceremonies are part of the figurehead role. In the role of *leader*, the manager works to hire, train, and motivate employees. Finally, the *liaison* role consists of relating to others outside the group or organization. For example, a manager at Intel might be responsible for handling all price negotiations with a key supplier of microchips. Obviously, each of these interpersonal roles involves behavioral processes.

Leading is the process of getting the organization's members to work together toward the organization's goals.

Controlling is the process of monitoring and correcting the actions of the organization and its members to keep them directed toward their goals.

Key **interpersonal roles** are the figurehead, the leader, and the liaison.

Table 1.1 IMPORTANT MANAGERIAL ROLES

Category	Role	Example
Interpersonal	Figurehead	Attend employee retirement ceremony
	Leader	Encourage workers to increase productivity
	Liaison	Coordinate activities of two committees
Informational	Monitor	Scan *Business Week* for information about competition
	Disseminator	Send out memos outlining new policies
	Spokesperson	Hold press conference to announce new plant
Decision-Making	Entrepreneur	Develop idea for new product and convince others of its merits
	Disturbance handler	Resolve dispute
	Resource allocator	Allocate budget requests
	Negotiator	Settle new labor contract

Informational Roles   The three informational roles involve some aspect of information processing. The *monitor* actively seeks information that might be of value to the organization in general or to specific managers. The manager who transmits this information to others is carrying out the role of *disseminator*. The *spokesperson* speaks for the organization to outsiders. A manager chosen by Dell Computer to appear at a press conference announcing a new product launch or other major deal, such as a recent decision to undertake a joint venture with Microsoft or Amazon, would be serving in this role. Again, behavioral processes are part of each of these roles, because information is almost always exchanged between people.

Decision-Making Roles   Finally, there are also four decision-making roles. The *entrepreneur* voluntarily initiates change—such as innovations or new strategies— within the organization. The *disturbance handler* helps settle disputes between various parties, such as other managers and their subordinates. The *resource allocator* decides who will get what—how resources in the organization will be distributed among various individuals and groups. The *negotiator* represents the organization in reaching agreements with other organizations, such as contracts between management and labor unions. Again, behavioral processes clearly are crucial in each of these decisional roles.

Critical Managerial Skills

Another important element of managerial work is mastery of the skills necessary to carry out basic functions and fill fundamental roles. In general, most successful managers have a strong combination of technical, interpersonal, conceptual, and diagnostic skills.[7]

Technical Skills   Technical skills are skills necessary to accomplish specific tasks within the organization. Designing a new computer for Hewlett-Packard, developing a new formula for a frozen-food additive for Conagra, or writing a press release for Halliburton all require technical skills. Hence, these skills are generally associated with the operations employed by the organization in its production processes. For example, David Packard and Bill Hewlett, founders of Hewlett-Packard, started out their careers

Key **informational roles** are the monitor, the disseminator, and the spokesperson.

Important **decision-making roles** are the entrepreneur, the disturbance handler, the resource allocator, and the negotiator.

Technical skills are the skills necessary to accomplish specific tasks within the organization.

as engineers. Other examples of managers with strong technical skills include H. Lee Scott (president and CEO of Wal-Mart, who started his career as a store manager) and Eric Molson (CEO of Molson Coors Brewing, who began his career as a brewmaster). The CEOs of the Big Four accounting firms also began their careers as accountants.

Interpersonal Skills   The manager uses interpersonal skills to communicate with, understand, and motivate individuals and groups. As we have noted, managers spend a large portion of their time interacting with others, so it is clearly important that they get along well with other people. For instance, David Novak is CEO of YUM! Brands, the firm that owns KFC, Pizza Hut, and Taco Bell. Novak is able to relate to employees throughout the firm. He is also known to his employees as a caring, compassionate, and honest person. These qualities inspire others throughout the firm and help motivate them to work hard to help Novak work toward the firm's goals.

Conceptual Skills   Conceptual skills are the manager's ability to think in the abstract. A manager with strong conceptual skills is able to see the "big picture." That is, she or he can see opportunity where others see roadblocks or problems. For example, after Steve Wozniak and Steve Jobs built a small computer of their own design in a garage, Wozniak essentially saw a new toy that could be tinkered with. Jobs, however, saw far more and convinced his partner that they should start a company to make and sell the computers. The result? Apple Computer. More recently Jobs has also used his conceptual skills to identify the potential in digital media technologies, leading to the introduction of such products as the iPod, iPhone, iTunes, and iPad as well as his overseeing the creation of Pixar Animation Studios.

Diagnostic Skills   Most successful managers also bring diagnostic skills to the organization. Diagnostic skills allow managers to better understand cause-and-effect relationships and to recognize the optimal solutions to problems. For instance, as chairman and CEO of SBC Communications, Ed Whitacre recognized that, while his firm was performing well in the consumer market, it lacked strong brand identification in the business environment. He first carefully identified and then implemented an action to remedy the firm's shortcoming—SBC would buy AT&T (for $16 billion), acquiring in the process the very name recognition that his company needed. Hence, after the acquisition was completed, the firm changed its corporate name from SBC to AT&T. And it was his diagnostic skills that pulled it all together.[8] Indeed, his legacy of strong diagnostic skills led to him being asked to lead the corporate turnaround at General Motors in 2009.

Of course, not every manager has an equal measure of these four basic types of skills. Nor are equal measures critical. As shown in Figure 1.3, for example, the optimal skills mix tends to vary with the manager's level in the organization. First-line managers generally need to depend more on their technical and interpersonal skills and less on their conceptual and diagnostic skills. Top managers tend to exhibit the reverse combination—more emphasis on conceptual and diagnostic skills and less dependence on technical and interpersonal skills. Middle managers require a more even distribution of skills. Similarly, the mix of needed skills can vary depending on economic circumstances. One recent survey suggested that during very tough economic times, the most important skills for a CEO are that he or she be an effective communicator and motivator, be decisive, and be a visionary.[9] While these skills certainly are always important, during times of economic prosperity other skills may be even more critical.

The *Ethics* box on page 13 describes a form of managerial behavior that, to put it as tactfully as possible, reflects a breakdown in interpersonal skills.

The manager uses **interpersonal skills** to communicate with, understand, and motivate individuals and groups.

The manager uses **conceptual skills** to think in the abstract.

The manager uses **diagnostic skills** to understand cause-and-effect relationships and to recognize the optimal solutions to problems.

𝒥igure 1.3   MANAGERIAL SKILLS AT DIFFERENT ORGANIZATIONAL LEVELS

Most managers need technical, interpersonal, conceptual, and diagnostic skills, but the importance of these skills varies by level in the organization. As illustrated here, conceptual and diagnostic skills are usually more important for top managers in organizations, whereas technical and interpersonal skills may be more important for first-line managers.

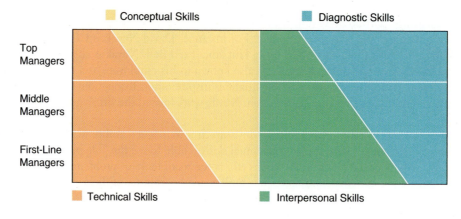

CONTEMPORARY ORGANIZATIONAL BEHAVIOR

Now, with this additional understanding of managerial work, we can return to our discussion of organizational behavior. We first introduce two fundamental characteristics of contemporary organizational behavior that warrant special discussion; we then identify the particular set of concepts that are generally accepted as defining the field's domain.

Characteristics of the Field

Managers and researchers who use concepts and ideas from organizational behavior must recognize that it has an interdisciplinary focus and a descriptive nature; that is, it draws from a variety of other fields and it attempts to describe behavior (rather than to predict how behavior can be changed in consistent and predictable ways).

An Interdisciplinary Focus   In many ways, organizational behavior synthesizes several other fields of study. Perhaps the greatest contribution is from psychology, especially organizational psychology. Psychologists study human behavior, whereas organizational psychologists deal specifically with the behavior of people in organizational settings. Many of the concepts that interest psychologists, such as individual differences and motivation, are also central to students of organizational behavior. These concepts are covered in Chapters 3–8.

Sociology, too, has had a major impact on the field of organizational behavior. Sociologists study social systems such as families, occupational classes, and organizations. Because a major concern of organizational behavior is the study of organization structures, the field clearly overlaps with areas of sociology that focus on the organization as a social system. Chapters 16–19 reflect the influence of sociology on the field of organizational behavior.

ETHICS

Do You Feel Like You Have "Kick Me" Tattooed on Your Forehead?

Have you ever encountered a bully? If you've ever worked in an organizational setting, there's a pretty good chance—75 percent, says one study—that you've at least witnessed bullying behavior. In fact, according to the Workplace Bullying Institute, 37 percent of the U.S. labor force—that's 54 million people—have actually been the object of bullying at some point during their work lives. "Anything that affects 37 percent of the public," says Institute director Gary Namie, "is an epidemic, but it's a silent epidemic," he adds, largely because victims tend to confide their experiences to close friends rather than to the higher-ups who might be expected to take some kind of action.

What is *bullying*? For one thing, it's a form of *aggression*—it's intended to intimidate, offend, or degrade a particular person or group of people. For another, it's a *pattern* of aggression—it involves repeated incidents or instances of behavior. And because it works through repetition, it often takes subtle forms and may, according to one expert, "include behaviors that don't appear obvious to others." Physical abuse or the threat of it are clearly forms of bullying, as are tampering with someone's personal property or workplace equipment and yelling at someone or using profanity. Other less overt examples include:

- Spreading rumors or gossip about someone
- Excluding someone socially
- Undermining or impeding someone's work
- Intruding on someone's privacy by pestering or spying

"Targets of severe workplace bullying are suffering from physical and psychological conditions that would drive even the strongest of us into the ground."

—DAVID C. YAMADA, DIRECTOR OF THE NEW WORKPLACE INSTITUTE

Work-related bullying may also take the following forms:

- Removing areas of responsibility without cause
- Constantly changing work guidelines
- Establishing impossible deadlines
- Assigning unreasonable duties or workload
- Assigning too little work (to foster a sense of uselessness)

You don't have to look too closely at the items on the second list to recognize actions that can be taken by superiors in order to bully subordinates. Granted, there can be a fine line between strong management techniques and bullying tactics, but upon closer inspection, the line isn't quite *that* fine. Human resource professionals, for example, characterize "tough bosses" as objective, performance focused, and organizationally oriented. But "with a bully," says one HR veteran, "there's no goal orientation. There's nothing to do with your job. There's nothing to do with the company. . . . It's simply something that's irritated the individual. It's maddened him to the point that he's driven to make a person's life miserable." HR managers point to the misuse of power and authority as the most common sign of workplace bullying, and psychologists observe that people who are prone to bullying display bullying behavior once they've achieved positions of power and influence.

How does bullying affect its victims? They report feeling "beaten," "abused," "broken," "maimed," "eviscerated," and "character assassinated," and many describe the

Continued

sensation of having been reduced to a level of vulnerability associated with children, prisoners, and slaves. "I feel like I have 'kick me' tattooed on my forehead," admits one victim. According to a psychologist who's studied the effects of workplace bullying, "There's no question that unrelenting, daily hostilities" in the workplace, "... can be on a par with torture" and that "repeated and severe bullying can cause psychological trauma." Adds another researcher: "Targets of severe workplace bullying are suffering from physical and psychological conditions that would drive even the strongest of us into the ground."

For more about counterproductive emotions in the workplace, see the *Organizational Behavior Case for Discussion*, "What to Do When the Boss Unleashes His Inner Toddler," on page 23.

References: Steve Opperman, "Workplace Bullying: Psychological Violence?" *FedSmith.com*, December 3, 2009, www.workplacebullying.org on January 25, 2010; Jeanna Bryner, "Workplace Bullying 'Epidemic' Worse Than Sexual Harassment," *LiveScience*, March 8, 2008, www.livescience.com on January 25, 2010; Jan Aylsworth, "Sociopaths and Bullying in the Workplace," *WorkplaceViolenceNews.com*, July 28, 2009, http://workplaceviolencenews.com on January 25, 2010; Jeanna Bryner, "Study: Office Bullies Create Workplace 'Warzone,'" *LiveScience*, October 31, 2006, www.livescience.com on January 26, 2010; Teresa A. Daniel, "Tough Boss or Workplace Bully?" *SHRM*, June 1, 2009, www.shrm.org on January 26, 2010.

Anthropology is concerned with the interactions between people and their environments, especially their cultural environment. Culture is a major influence on the structure of organizations and on the behavior of people in organizations. Culture is discussed in Chapters 2 and 18.

Political science also interests organizational behaviorists. We usually think of political science as the study of political systems such as governments. But themes of interest to political scientists include how and why people acquire power and such topics as political behavior, decision making, conflict, the behavior of interest groups, and coalition formation. These are also major areas of interest in organizational behavior, as is reflected in Chapters 9–15.

Economists study the production, distribution, and consumption of goods and services. Students of organizational behavior share the economist's interest in areas such as labor market dynamics, productivity, human resource planning and forecasting, and cost-benefit analysis. Chapters 2, 5, and 6 most strongly illustrate these issues.

Engineering has also influenced the field of organizational behavior. Industrial engineering in particular has long been concerned with work measurement, productivity measurement, work flow analysis and design, job design, and labor relations. Obviously these areas are also relevant to organizational behavior and are discussed in Chapters 2, 5, and 10.

Most recently, medicine has come into play in connection with the study of human behavior at work, specifically in the area of stress. Increasingly, research is

Stress has emerged as an important individual-level outcome in many organizations. Organizational factors can both cause and be affected by stress among the firm's workers. While few employees may actually exhibit the stress levels shown here, many firms do actively seek ways to help people better cope with stress. (We discuss stress more fully in Chapter 7.)

showing that controlling the causes and consequences of stress in and out of organizational settings is important for the well-being of both the individual and the organization. Chapter 7 is devoted to stress.

A Descriptive Nature A primary goal of studying organizational behavior is to describe relationships between two or more behavioral variables. The theories and concepts of the field, for example, cannot predict with certainty that changing a specific set of workplace variables will improve an individual employee's performance by a certain amount.[10] At best, the field can suggest that certain general concepts or variables tend to be related to one another in particular settings. For instance, research might indicate that in one organization, employee satisfaction and individual perceptions of working conditions are positively related. However, we may not know if better working conditions lead to more satisfaction, or if more-satisfied people see their jobs differently than dissatisfied people, or if both satisfaction and perceptions of working conditions are actually related through other intervening variables. Also, the relationship between satisfaction and perceptions of working conditions observed in one setting may be considerably stronger, weaker, or nonexistent in other settings.

Organizational behavior is descriptive for several reasons: the immaturity of the field, the complexities inherent in studying human behavior, and the lack of valid, reliable, and accepted definitions and measures. Whether the field will ever be able to make definitive predictions and prescriptions is still an open question. But even if it never succeeds in these endeavors, the value of studying organizational behavior is firmly established. Because behavioral processes pervade most managerial functions and roles, and because the work of organizations is done primarily by people, the knowledge and understanding gained from the field can significantly help managers in many ways.[11]

Basic Concepts of the Field

The central concepts of organizational behavior can be grouped into three basic categories: (1) individual processes, (2) interpersonal processes, and (3) organizational processes and characteristics. As Figure 1.4 shows, these categories provide the basic framework for this book.

This chapter and the next develop a managerial perspective on organizational behavior and link the core concepts of organizational behavior with actual management for organizational effectiveness. Chapter 2 describes the changing environment of organizations, especially relating to diversity, globalization, and similar trends and issues. Together, the two chapters in Part I provide a fundamental introduction to organizational behavior.

The six chapters of Part II cover individual processes in organizations. Chapter 3 explores key individual differences in such characteristics as personality and attitudes. Chapter 4 provides an introduction to and discussion of basic models useful for understanding employee work motivation. Chapters 5 and 6 are devoted to various methods and strategies that managers can use to enhance employee motivation and performance. Chapter 7 covers the causes and consequences of stress in the workplace. Finally, Chapter 8 explores decision making, problem solving, and creativity.

Part III is devoted to interpersonal processes in organizations. Chapter 9 introduces the foundations of interpersonal behavior through its coverage of group dynamics. Chapter 10 describes how managers are using teams in organizations today, while Chapter 11 explores communications processes in organizations. Chapter 12 discusses leadership models and concepts, while Chapter 13 describes contemporary views of leadership in organizations. Power, politics, and workplace justice are covered in Chapter 14. Chapter 15 covers conflict and negotiation processes in organizations.

Figure 1.4 THE FRAMEWORK FOR UNDERSTANDING ORGANIZATIONAL BEHAVIOR

Organizational behavior is an exciting and complex field of study. The specific concepts and topics that constitute the field can be grouped into three categories: individual, interpersonal, and organizational processes and characteristics. Here these concepts and classifications are used to provide an overall framework for the organization of this book.

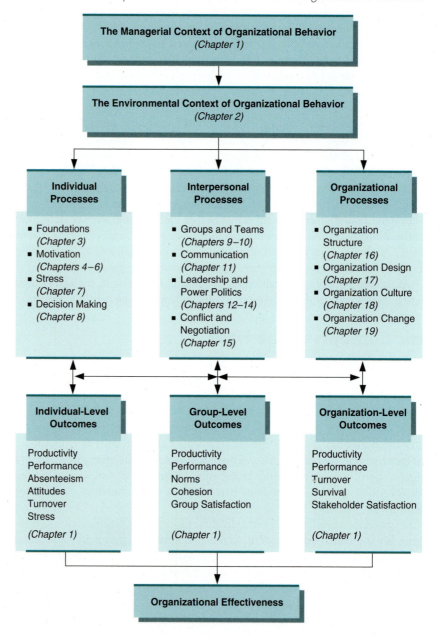

Part IV is devoted to organizational processes and characteristics. Chapter 16 sets the stage with its coverage of the foundations of organization structure; Chapter 17 is an in-depth treatment of organization design. Organizational culture is discussed in Chapter 18. Organizational change and development are covered in Chapter 19. Finally, research methods in organizational behavior and the field's historical development are covered in Appendices A and B.

CONTEXTUAL PERSPECTIVES ON ORGANIZATIONAL BEHAVIOR

Several contextual perspectives—most notably the systems and contingency perspectives and the interactional view—also influence our understanding of organizational behavior. Many of the concepts and theories discussed in the chapters that follow reflect these perspectives; they represent basic points of view that influence much of our contemporary thinking about behavior in organizations. In addition, they allow us to more clearly see how managers use behavioral processes as they strive for organizational effectiveness.

Systems and Situational Perspectives

The systems and situational perspectives share related viewpoints on organizations and how they function. Each is concerned with interrelationships among organizational elements and between organizational and environmental elements.

The Systems Perspective   The systems perspective, or the theory of systems, was first developed in the physical sciences, but it has been extended to other areas, such as management.[12] A **system** is an interrelated set of elements that function as a whole. Figure 1.5 shows a general framework for viewing organizations as systems.

According to this perspective, an organizational system receives four kinds of inputs from its environment: material, human, financial, and informational (note that this is consistent with our earlier description of management functions). The organization's managers then combine and transform these inputs and return them to the environment in the form of products or services, employee behaviors, profits or losses, and additional information. Then the system receives feedback from the environment regarding these outputs.

Figure 1.5   THE SYSTEMS APPROACH TO ORGANIZATIONS

The systems approach to organizations provides a useful framework for understanding how the elements of an organization interact among themselves and with their environment. Various inputs are transformed into different outputs, with important feedback from the environment. If managers do not understand these interrelations, they may tend to ignore their environment or to overlook important interrelationships within their organizations.

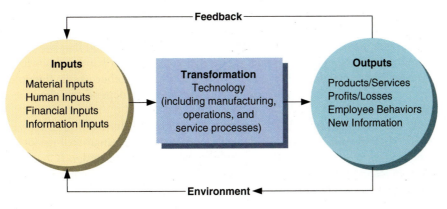

A **system** is a set of interrelated elements functioning as a whole.

As an example, we can apply systems theory to the Shell Oil Company. Material inputs include pipelines, crude oil, and the machinery used to refine petroleum. Human inputs are oil field workers, refinery workers, office staff, and other people employed by the company. Financial inputs take the form of money received from oil and gas sales, stockholder investment, and so forth. Finally, the company receives information inputs from forecasts about future oil supplies, geological surveys on potential drilling sites, sales projections, and similar analyses.

Through complex refining and other processes, these inputs are combined and transformed to create products such as gasoline and motor oil. As outputs, these products are sold to the consuming public. Profits from operations are fed back into the environment through taxes, investments, and dividends; losses, when they occur, hit the environment by reducing stockholders' incomes. In addition to having on-the-job contacts with customers and suppliers, employees live in the community and participate in a variety of activities away from the workplace, and their behavior is influenced in part by their experiences as Shell workers. Finally, information about the company and its operations is also released into the environment. The environment, in turn, responds to these outputs and influences future inputs. For example, consumers may buy more or less gasoline depending on the quality and price of Shell's product, and banks may be more or less willing to lend Shell money based on financial information released about the company.

The systems perspective is valuable to managers for a variety of reasons. First, it underscores the importance of an organization's environment. For instance, failing to acquire the appropriate resources and failing to heed feedback from the environment can be disastrous. The systems perspective also helps managers conceptualize the flow and interaction of various elements of the organization itself as they work together to transform inputs into outputs.

The Situational Perspective Another useful viewpoint for understanding behavior in organizations comes from the **situational perspective**. In the earlier days of management studies, managers searched for universal answers to organizational questions. They sought prescriptions, the "one best way" that could be used in any organization under any conditions, searching, for example, for forms of leadership behavior that would always lead employees to be more satisfied and to work harder. Eventually, however, researchers realized that the complexities of human behavior and organizational settings make universal conclusions virtually impossible. They discovered that in organizations, most situations and outcomes are contingent; that is, the precise relationship between any two variables is likely to be situational—i.e., dependent on other variables.[13]

Figure 1.6 distinguishes the universal and situational perspectives. The universal model, shown at the top of the figure, presumes a direct cause-and-effect linkage between variables. For example, it suggests that whenever a manager encounters a certain problem or situation (such as motivating employees to work harder), a universal approach exists (such as raising pay or increasing autonomy) that will lead to the desired outcome. The situational perspective, on the other hand, acknowledges that several other variables alter the direct relationship. In other words, the appropriate managerial action or behavior in any given situation depends on elements of that situation.

The field of organizational behavior gradually has shifted from a universal approach in the 1950s and early 1960s to a situational perspective. The situational perspective is especially strong in the areas of motivation (Chapter 4), job design (Chapter 5), leadership (Chapters 12 and 13), and organizational design (Chapter 17), but it is becoming increasingly important throughout the entire field.

The **situational perspective** suggests that in most organizations situations and outcomes are influenced by other variables.

Figure 1.6 UNIVERSAL VERSUS SITUATIONAL APPROACH

Managers once believed that they could identify the "one best way" of solving problems or reacting to situations. Here we illustrate a more realistic view, the situational approach. The situational approach suggests that approaches to problems and situations are contingent on elements of the situation.

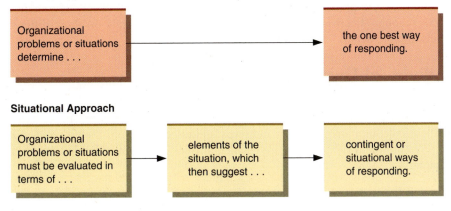

Universal Approach

Organizational problems or situations determine . . . → the one best way of responding.

Situational Approach

Organizational problems or situations must be evaluated in terms of . . . → elements of the situation, which then suggest . . . → contingent or situational ways of responding.

Interactionalism: People and Situations

Interactionalism is another useful perspective to help better understand behavior in organizational settings. First presented in terms of interactional psychology, this view assumes that individual behavior results from a continuous and multidirectional interaction between characteristics of the person and characteristics of the situation. More specifically, interactionalism attempts to explain how people select, interpret, and change various situations.[14] Figure 1.7 illustrates this perspective. Note that the individual and the situation are presumed to interact continuously. This interaction is what determines the individual's behavior.

The interactional view implies that simple cause-and-effect descriptions of organizational phenomena are not enough. For example, one set of research studies may suggest that job changes lead to improved employee attitudes. Another set of studies may propose that attitudes influence how people perceive their jobs in the first place. Both positions probably are incomplete: Employee attitudes may influence job perceptions, but these perceptions may in turn influence future attitudes. Because interactionalism is a fairly recent contribution to the field, it is less prominent in the chapters that follow than the systems and contingency theories. Nonetheless, the interactional view appears to offer many promising ideas for future development.

Figure 1.7 THE INTERACTIONIST PERSPECTIVE ON BEHAVIOR IN ORGANIZATIONS

When people enter an organization, their own behaviors and actions shape that organization in various ways. Similarly, the organization itself shapes the behaviors and actions of each individual who becomes a part of it. This interactionist perspective can be useful in explaining organizational behavior.

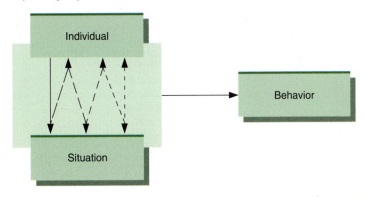

Individual

Situation

Behavior

Interactionalism suggests that individuals and situations interact continuously to determine individuals' behavior.

MANAGING FOR EFFECTIVENESS

Earlier in this chapter we noted that managers work toward various goals. We are now in a position to elaborate on the nature of these goals in detail. In particular, as shown in Figure 1.8, goals—or outcomes—exist at three specific levels in an organization: individual-level outcomes, group-level outcomes, and organizational-level outcomes. Of course, it may sometimes be necessary to make trade-offs among these different kinds of outcomes, but, in general, each is seen as a critical component of organizational effectiveness. The sections that follow elaborate on these different levels in more detail.

Individual-Level Outcomes

Several different outcomes at the individual level are important to managers. Given the focus of the field of organizational behavior, it should not be surprising that most of these outcomes are directly or indirectly addressed by various theories and models. (We provide a richer and more detailed analysis of individual-level outcomes in Chapter 3.)

Individual Behaviors   First, several individual behaviors result from a person's participation in an organization. One important behavior is productivity. A person's productivity is an indicator of his or her efficiency and is measured in terms of the products or services created per unit of input. For example, if Bill makes 100 units of a product in a day and Sara makes only 90 units in a day, then, assuming that the units are of the same quality and that Bill and Sara make the same wages, Bill is more productive than Sara.

Performance, another important individual-level outcome variable, is a somewhat broader concept. It is made up of all work-related behaviors. For example, even though

Figure 1.8   MANAGING FOR EFFECTIVENESS

Managers work to optimize a variety of individual-level, group-level, and organization-level outcomes. It is sometimes necessary to make trade-offs among the different types and levels of outcomes, but each is an important determinant of organizational effectiveness.

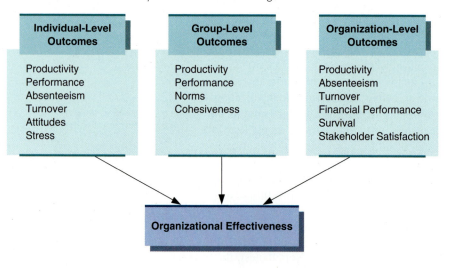

Bill is highly productive, it may also be that he refuses to work overtime, expresses negative opinions about the organization at every opportunity, and will do nothing unless it falls precisely within the boundaries of his job. Sara, on the other hand, may always be willing to work overtime, is a positive representative of the organization, and goes out of her way to make as many contributions to the organization as possible. Based on the full array of behaviors, then, we might conclude that Sara actually is the better performer.

Two other important individual-level behaviors are absenteeism and turnover. Absenteeism is a measure of attendance. Although virtually everyone misses work occasionally, some people miss far more than others. Some look for excuses to miss work and call in sick regularly just for some time off; others miss work only when absolutely necessary. Turnover occurs when a person leaves the organization. If the individual who leaves is a good performer or if the organization has invested heavily in training the person, turnover can be costly.

Individual Attitudes and Stress   Another set of individual-level outcomes influenced by managers consists of individual attitudes. (We discuss attitudes more fully in Chapter 3.) Levels of job satisfaction or dissatisfaction, organizational commitment, and organizational involvement all play an important role in organizational behavior. Stress, discussed more fully in Chapter 7, is another important individual-level outcome variable. Given its costs, both personal and organizational, it should not be surprising that stress is becoming an increasingly important topic for both researchers in organizational behavior and practicing managers.

Group- and Team-Level Outcomes

Another set of outcomes exists at the group and team level. Some of these outcomes parallel the individual-level outcomes just discussed. For example, if an organization makes extensive use of work teams, team productivity and performance are important outcome variables. On the other hand, even if all the people in a group or team have the same or similar attitudes toward their jobs, the attitudes themselves are individual-level phenomena. Individuals, not groups, have attitudes.

But groups or teams can also have unique outcomes that individuals do not share. For example, as we will discuss in Chapter 9, groups develop norms that govern the behavior of individual group members. Groups also develop different levels of cohesiveness. Thus, managers need to assess both common and unique outcomes when considering the individual and group levels.

Group- and team-level outcomes are becoming increasingly important to all organizations. Because so much work today is done by groups and teams, managers need to understand how to effectively create a team, how to direct and motivate that team, and then how to assess the team's performance. In this team, one member is presenting a proposal for how to complete a project to his five teammates. The team as a whole will then decide whether to accept the proposal, modify it, or start over looking for a new approach.

JACOB WACKERHAUSEN/ISTOCKPHOTO.COM

Organization-Level Outcomes

Finally, a set of outcome variables exists at the organization level. As before, some of these outcomes parallel those at the individual and group levels, but others are unique. For example, we can measure and compare organizational productivity. We can also develop organization-level indicators of absenteeism and turnover. But profitability is generally assessed only at the organizational level.

Organizations are also commonly assessed in terms of financial performance: stock price, return on investment, growth rates, and so on. They are also evaluated in terms of their ability to survive and the extent to which they satisfy important stakeholders such as investors, government regulators, employees, and unions.

Clearly, then, the manager must balance different outcomes across all three levels of analysis. In many cases, these outcomes appear to contradict one another. For example, paying workers high salaries can enhance satisfaction and reduce turnover, but it also may detract from bottom-line performance. Similarly, exerting strong pressure to increase individual performance may boost short-term profitability but increase turnover and job stress. Thus, the manager must look at the full array of outcomes and attempt to balance them in an optimal fashion. The manager's ability to do this is a major determinant of the organization's success.

SYNOPSIS

Organizational behavior is the study of human behavior in organizational settings, the interface between human behavior and the organization, and the organization itself. The study of organizational behavior is important because organizations have a powerful influence over our lives. It also directly relates to management in organizations. Indeed, by its very nature, management requires an understanding of human behavior, to help managers better comprehend those behaviors at different levels in the organization, those at the same level, those in other organizations, and those in themselves.

The manager's job can be characterized in terms of four functions. These basic managerial functions are planning, organizing, leading, and controlling. Planning is the process of determining the organization's desired future position and deciding how best to get there. Organizing is the process of designing jobs, grouping jobs into manageable units, and establishing patterns of authority among jobs and groups of jobs. Leading is the process of motivating members of the organization to work together toward the organization's goals. Controlling is the process of monitoring and correcting the actions of the organization and its people to keep them headed toward their goals.

Managerial work involves ten basic roles and requires the use of four skills. The roles consist of three interpersonal roles (figurehead, leader, and liaison), three informational roles (monitor, disseminator, and spokesperson), and four decision-making roles (entrepreneur, disturbance handler, resource allocator, and negotiator). The four basic skills necessary for effective management are technical, interpersonal, conceptual, and diagnostic skills.

Contemporary organizational behavior attempts to describe, rather than prescribe, behavioral forces in organizations. Ties to psychology, sociology, anthropology, political science, economics, engineering, and medicine make organizational behavior an interdisciplinary field. The basic concepts of the field are divided into three categories: individual processes, interpersonal processes, and organizational processes and characteristics. Those categories form the framework for the organization of this book.

Important contextual perspectives on the field of organizational behavior are the systems and situational perspectives and interactionalism. There are also a number of very important individual-, group-, and organizational-level outcomes related to organizational effectiveness.

DISCUSSION QUESTIONS

1. Some people have suggested that understanding human behavior at work is the single most important requirement for managerial success. Do you agree or disagree with this statement? Why?

2. In what ways is organizational behavior comparable to functional areas such as finance, marketing, and production? In what ways is it different from these areas? Is it similar to statistics in any way?

3. Identify some managerial jobs that are highly affected by human behavior and others that are less so. Which would you prefer? Why?

4. The text identifies four basic managerial functions. Based on your own experiences or observations, provide examples of each function.

5. Which managerial skills do you think are among your strengths? Which are among your weaknesses? How might you improve the latter?

6. Suppose you have to hire a new manager. One candidate has outstanding technical skills but poor interpersonal skills. The other has exactly the opposite mix of skills. Which would you hire? Why?

7. Some people believe that individuals working in an organization have basic human rights to satisfaction with their work and to the opportunity to grow and develop. How would you defend this position? How would you argue against it?

8. Many universities offer a course in industrial or organizational psychology. The content of those courses is quite similar to the content of this one. Do you think that behavioral material is best taught in a business or in a psychology program, or is it best to teach it in both?

9. Do you believe the field of organizational behavior has the potential to become prescriptive as opposed to descriptive? Why or why not?

10. Are the notions of systems, situationalism, and interactionalism mutually exclusive? If not, describe ways in which they are related.

11. Get a recent issue of a popular business magazine such as *Business Week* or *Fortune* and scan its major articles. Do any of them reflect concepts from organizational behavior? Describe.

12. Do you read Dilbert? Do you think it accurately describes organization life? Are there other comic strips that reflect life and work in contemporary organizations?

ORGANIZATIONAL BEHAVIOR CASE FOR DISCUSSION

WHAT TO DO WHEN THE BOSS RELEASES HIS INNER TODDLER

Put yourself in the following scenario:

You're one of 10 VPs at a small chain of regional clothing stores, where you're in charge of the women's apparel department. One of your jobs is to review each month's performance at a meeting of all 10 department heads and the company president. Like your fellow VPs, you prepare a Power-Point presentation showing the results for the previous month and your projections for the upcoming month, and during your presentation, you take the podium and lead the discussion from the front of the room.

> **"Most tantrums don't involve things being thrown across the room."**
> —ORGANIZATIONAL CONSULTANT LYNN TAYLOR, ON TOTS

On the whole, the meeting is part of a pretty sound overall strategy that allows everyone to know what's going on and what to expect across the board. Typically, the only drawback to an informative and productive session is the president's apparent inability to deal with bad news. He gets irritable and likes to lambaste "underperformers," and as a result, you and your colleagues always enter the meeting with stomachs in knots and leave it with full-blown gastric distress. The president himself thinks he's fostering open and honest discussion, but everyone else in the room knows plain old-fashioned bullying when they see it.

As luck would have it, you now find yourself at the front of the room, looking up at the floor-to-ceiling screen on which are emblazoned, in what looks to you like 500-point font (red, of course), your less than stellar monthly numbers. Sweating profusely, you're attempting to explain some disappointing sales figures when you hear a noise—a sort of thudding and rattling—against the wall behind you. Startled, you spin around toward the room and are surprised to see that everyone seems to be looking for something on the floor or checking the weather through the windows on one side of the room. Finally you glance toward the wall behind you, where you discover a bent meeting-room chair lying on the floor, and as you look up again, you see that the president is standing, his arms crossed and his face scowling. "The next time you show me numbers like those," he snarls, "I won't miss!"

Believe it or not, this is a true story (although we've changed a few details—very few—in the interest of plausibility and dramatic impact). It's told by John McKee, a consultant to professionals and businesspeople who want to move up the ladder as quickly—and, presumably, with as little violence—as possible. McKee was actually an eyewitness to the episode, and although he admits that it's "the clearest example of a boss behaving badly" that he's ever seen, he hastens to add that he won't be the least bit surprised when someone comes up with an even better one.

Consultant Lynn Taylor, who specializes in the development of work and management teams, calls bosses like the one in our scenario *Terrible Office Tyrants*, or *TOTs*—managers who can't control their behavior when they're placed under stress. Taylor believes that the characterization is apt in light of research showing that bosses like the one we've described actually "return to their misbehaving 'inner toddler' to handle unwieldy pressures." In other words, they revert to the kind of behavior that produced "self-serving results" when they were children. In the adult workplace, explains Taylor, they "occasionally find that their ability to master the world is limited, as it is with most mortal beings. This revelation, on top of their inability to communicate clearly in the moment, makes them furious and frustrated."

According to Taylor, there are 20 "core, parallel traits [shared by] TOTs and toddlers." The following, which are fairly aggressive, she catalogs under "Bratty Behavior":

- Bragging
- Bullying
- Demanding
- Ignoring
- Impulsiveness
- Lying
- Self-centeredness
- Stubbornness
- Tantrums
- Territorialism
- Whining

"Most tantrums," Taylor assures us, "don't involve things being thrown across the room," and TOT behavior, especially in its less aggressive forms—fickleness, mood swings, neediness—can be "proactively managed" by employees who don't care to be treated as emotional punching bags. She recommends "humor, common sense, rational thinking, and setting limits to bad behavior." And remember, she adds, "You are the parent with the proverbial cookie jar when it comes to managing a TOT."

Taylor's approach to understanding and dealing with bad bosses isn't entirely metaphorical, and she does suggest that beleaguered employees translate her general advice into some concrete coping techniques. When confronted by managerial neediness, for example, a good "pacifier" might be a reply such as: "It'll be the first thing on my to-do list tomorrow." If you're looking for a handy toolbox of effective techniques, you can find dozens on the Internet, most of them posted by psychologists and organizational consultants. The following was compiled by Karen Burns, *U.S. News & World Report* columnist and specialist on career advice for women:

- *Put everything in writing.* Write and date progress reports. When you get verbal instructions, summarize them in a reply email.

- *Be a star performer.* Beyond just being a good employee, maintain a positive demeanor; it's hard for some to ambush you when you're doing your job and smiling in the process.

- *Pick your moments.* Rather than simply avoiding your boss, study her patterns. Steer clear when she's a nutcase and schedule interactions for times when she's stabilized.

- *Seek community.* Anchor your sanity in ties to coworkers and other managers. Find a mentor inside the workplace and someone outside to talk (and vent) to.

- *Control what you can.* You can't control your boss's irrational behavior, so control what you can— namely, the way you respond to it. Ignore the cranky tone of voice and respond to the substance of what she says. Also, eat right, exercise, get enough sleep, and spend the rest of your time with sane people.

- *Know your rights.* If you want to take your griev- ance to the HR department (or further), be sure that you've documented your problem and your efforts to resolve it, and be specific about the remedy you're asking for (transfer, severance package, etc.).

- *Identify the exits.* Come up with a plan, and don't be bullied into taking action before you're ready.

CASE QUESTIONS

1. How might the episode described in the scenario be explained from the *situational perspective* on organizational behavior? From the *interactionalist perspective*?

2. How do you suppose the executive described in the scenario got to be president of the company?

3. Have you ever encountered anyone who behaved in ways that can be compared to the behavior of the president in the scenario—either in the workplace or in any other context? As you think back on your experience, how well does Taylor's TOT framework help to explain the individual's behavior?

4. Of the items on Burns's list of recommended coping techniques, which do you think would be most helpful to the employees of the company in the scenario? Which would *you* be most likely to adopt? Can you think of any potentially effective techniques that aren't on Burns's list?

REFERENCES

John McKee, "Worst Boss Ever," *TechRepublic*, February 8, 2007, http://blogs.techrepublic.com on January 20, 2009; Lynn Taylor, "Why Bad Bosses Act Like Toddlers," *Psychology Today*, August 27, 2009, www.psychologytoday.com on January 20, 2009; Lynn Taylor, "10 Ways to Manage Bad Bosses," *CNN.com*, December 15, 2009, www.cnn.com on January 20, 2009; Karen Burns, "How to Survive a Bad Boss," *U.S. News & World Report*, November 4, 2009, www .usnews.com on January 20, 2009.

EXPERIENCING ORGANIZATIONAL BEHAVIOR

Relating OB and Popular Culture

Purpose   This exercise will help you appreciate the importance and pervasiveness of organizational behav- ior concepts and processes in both contemporary orga- nizational settings and popular culture.

Format   Your instructor will divide the class into groups of three to five members. Each group will be assigned a specific television program to watch before the next class meeting.

Procedure   Arrange to watch the program as a group. Each person should have a pad of paper and a pencil handy. As you watch the show, jot down examples of individual behavior, interpersonal dynamics, organiza- tional characteristics, and other concepts and processes relevant to organizational behavior. After the show, spend a few minutes comparing notes. Compile one list for the entire group. (It is advisable to turn off the television set during this discussion!)

During the next class meeting, have someone in the group summarize the plot of the show and list the concepts it illustrated. The following television shows are especially good for illustrating behavioral concepts in organizational settings:

The Big Bang Theory	N.C.I.S.
American Chopper	C. S. I.(any version)
The Office	Star Trek
Grey's Anatomy	Lost
The Deadliest Catch	Glee
Pawn Stars	30 Rock

Follow-up Questions

1. What does this exercise illustrate about the per- vasiveness of organizations in our contemporary society?

2. What recent or classic movies might provide simi- lar kinds of examples?

3. Do you think television programs from countries other than the United States would provide more or fewer examples of shows set in organizations?

BUILDING MANAGERIAL SKILLS

Exercise Overview It's important for managers to have a reasonably good idea of what they do in various situations, how they do it, and what the consequences usually are. In short, they need a certain degree of self-knowledge. When it comes to building skills, however, just "knowing" ourselves isn't enough: The vast majority of us have room for improvement, and improvement generally means acquiring *new* knowledge about ourselves. The purpose of this exercise is to combine two good ways of gathering new self-knowledge:

- Taking self-assessment inventories like the one in the previous "Self-Assessment Exercise"
- Getting feedback from other people

Exercise Background Fill in the questionnaire in the "Self-Assessment Exercise" for this chapter. Add up your scores and be prepared to share your results.

Exercise Task Your instructor will divide the class into small groups of five to seven members. Once your group has been formed, do the following:

1. Each group member should spend about 5 minutes drawing up two lists: (a) a list of his or her interpersonal strengths and weaknesses; (b) a list of his or her most noteworthy accomplishments.

2. Each member will take about 3 minutes to introduce himself or herself to the group. Be sure to give some background about yourself and to mention your career goals and your most noteworthy accomplishments; finally, briefly describe your strengths and weaknesses.

3. Now comes a round of self-disclosure and feedback. One member volunteers to be the "focus" of the group's discussion: That person will share his or her scores from the "Self-Assessment Exercise" and then say what he or she thinks about its accuracy. Then it's the group's turn: One person at a time, members will provide feedback by comparing the scores from the "Self-Assessment Exercise" with the information provided by the "focus" member in Steps 1 and 2 of this exercise. Finally, the "focus" member will provide a brief summary of the feedback that he or she has received during the round.

4. Each member of the group volunteers in turn to be the "focus" member, and the process is repeated until everyone has had a turn as "focus."

SELF-ASSESSMENT EXERCISE

Assessing Your Own Management Skills

The following questions are intended to provide insights into your confidence about your capabilities regarding the management skills discussed in this chapter. Answer each question by circling the scale value that best reflects your feelings.

1. I generally do well in quantitative courses like math, statistics, accounting, and finance.

5	4	3	2	1
Strongly Agree	Agree	Neither Agree Nor Disagree	Disagree	Strongly Disagree

2. I get along well with most people.

5	4	3	2	1
Strongly Agree	Agree	Neither Agree Nor Disagree	Disagree	Strongly Disagree

3. It is usually easy for me to see how material in one of my classes relates to material in other classes.

5	4	3	2	1
Strongly Agree	Agree	Neither Agree Nor Disagree	Disagree	Strongly Disagree

4. I can usually figure out why a problem occurred.

5	4	3	2	1
Strongly Agree	Agree	Neither Agree Nor Disagree	Disagree	Strongly Disagree

5. When I am asked to perform a task or to do some work, I usually know how to do it or else can figure it out pretty quickly.

5	4	3	2	1
Strongly Agree	Agree	Neither Agree Nor Disagree	Disagree	Strongly Disagree

6. I can usually understand why people behave as they do.

5	4	3	2	1
Strongly Agree	Agree	Neither Agree Nor Disagree	Disagree	Strongly Disagree

7. I enjoy classes that deal with theories and concepts.

5	4	3	2	1
Strongly Agree	Agree	Neither Agree Nor Disagree	Disagree	Strongly Disagree

8. I usually understand why things happen as they do.

5	4	3	2	1
Strongly Agree	Agree	Neither Agree Nor Disagree	Disagree	Strongly Disagree

9. I like classes that require me to "do things"—write papers, solve problems, research new areas, and so forth.

5	4	3	2	1
Strongly Agree	Agree	Neither Agree Nor Disagree	Disagree	Strongly Disagree

10. Whenever I work in a group, I can usually get others to accept my opinions and ideas.

5	4	3	2	1
Strongly Agree	Agree	Neither Agree Nor Disagree	Disagree	Strongly Disagree

11. I am much more interested in understanding the "big picture" than in dealing with narrow, focused issues.

5	4	3	2	1
Strongly Agree	Agree	Neither Agree Nor Disagree	Disagree	Strongly Disagree

12. When I know what I am supposed to do, I can usually figure out how to do it.

5	4	3	2	1
Strongly Agree	Agree	Neither Agree Nor Disagree	Disagree	Strongly Disagree

Instructions: Add up your point values for questions 1, 5, and 9; this total reflects your assessment of your technical skills. The point total for questions 2, 6, and 10 reflects interpersonal skills; the point total for questions 3, 7, and 11 reflects conceptual skills; the point total for questions 4, 8, and 12 reflects diagnostic skills. Higher scores indicate stronger confidence in that realm of management.

Note: This brief instrument has not been scientifically validated and is to be used for classroom discussion only.

The Changing Environment of Organizations

CHAPTER LEARNING OBJECTIVES

After studying this chapter you should be able to:

- Discuss the emergence of international management and its impact on organizations.
- Describe the nature of diversity in organizations and identify and explain key dimensions of diversity.
- Discuss the changing nature of technology and its impact on business.
- Describe emerging perspectives on ethics and corporate governance.
- Discuss the key issues in new employment relationships.

Capital Adventures in Social Entrepreneuring

"We function much as venture capitalists do in the private sector. You could say we're social VCs."

—NEAL KENY–GUYER, CEO OF MERCY CORPS

In the aftermath of the devastating earthquake that struck the island nation of Haiti on January 12, 2010, Oregon-based Mercy Corps arrived with a team of emergency-response experts from around the world. Focusing on immediate

Mercy Corps helps people in times of crisis. These Mercy Corps staff members, Cassandra Nelson and Gene Kunze, are developing action plans for helping survivors cope with the aftermath of the devastating earthquake that hit Haiti in 2010.

AP PHOTO/GREG WAHL-STEPHENS

humanitarian needs, the team delivered food to overwhelmed hospitals and set up services to provide clean water. Mercy Corps also initiated a work-for-cash program that paid survivors to aid in clearing debris and restoring buildings, thus providing them with a little dignity along with the means to purchase supplies for their families and jump-start the local economy. In addition, the organization set up trauma centers for children, using counseling methods that it had helped to develop in the wake of the 9/11 terrorist attacks in New York City.

Obviously, Mercy Corps isn't a newcomer to the enterprise of providing humanitarian aid. Founded in 1979 as Save the Refugees Fund, a task force to help victims of famine and genocide in Cambodia, it expanded in 1982, becoming Mercy Corps International to reflect its broader mission. Since 1979, Mercy Corps has provided $1.7 billion in assistance to people in 107 countries and currently reaches nearly 17 million people in about 40 nations. As a nongovernmental organization (NGO), it gets most of its money from government grants and in-kind donations of food, medical, and other types of supplies and services. Its current budget is almost $300 million, and it employs 3,700 people worldwide.

Mercy Corps, however, is more than an immediate responder and supplier of emergency relief services. According to its mission statement:

> In 25 years of experience on the ground, Mercy Corps has learned that communities recovering from war or social upheaval must be the agents of their own transformation for change to endure. It's only when communities set their own agendas, raise their own resources, and implement programs themselves that the first successes result in the renewed hope, confidence, and skills to continue their development independently.

Mercy Corps thus works to establish "sustainable community development that integrates agriculture, health, housing and infrastructure, economic development, education and environment, and local management," as well as "initiatives that promote citizen participation, accountability, conflict management, and the rule of law."

In India, for example, Mercy Corps has taught small-scale tea farmers sustainable ways to grow organic teas and get fair prices for them. On plantations owned by big tea companies, it's helped not only to improve living and economic conditions in worker villages but also to form self-governing Community Initiative Groups to manage ongoing community needs in education, infrastructure, and employment. In southern Sudan, which has been torn by Africa's longest civil war, Mercy Corps has built networks of local organizations to provide such essential services as adult literacy, orphan care, and HIV/AIDS counseling; other programs have helped to build roads and community centers and electrify villages.

In Indonesia, where sanitation is a major area of concern, Mercy Corps has launched a long-term Hygiene Promotion Program. On Hand Washing Day, for instance, community representatives take to the streets with colorful buckets and teach children how to wash their hands with soap and water; similarly equipped hand-washing stations have been set up in neighborhoods throughout the capital of Djakarta. (Dirty hands cause diarrhea, which kills 2 million children under the age of 5 every year.) Other programs focus on education and equipment for harvesting rain water and removing solid waste from residential neighborhoods.

Most of Indonesia's problems can be traced to poverty—110 million Indonesians live on less than $2 a day. About 20 percent of the population depends on micro and small businesses to earn a living, but only a quarter of the country's 40 million microenterprises have access to credit from standard lending institutions. To support entrepreneurs and small businesses that have little means of raising cash, more than 50,000 microfinance institutions (MFIs) provide some form of service to the poorest sectors of the economy—but the industry is both crowded and fractured. Mercy Corps entered the country's microfinance field in May 2008 because, as CEO Neal Keny-Guyer puts it, "We wanted real impact." The idea was to buy a bank and turn it into a "bank of banks"—a commercial bank that would partner with other MFIs in the country. It's an innovative idea, although the strategy of finding financial solutions to social problems is certainly nothing new at Mercy Corps: The organization had already built a worldwide network of 12 MFIs through which it had distributed microloans worth $1.09 billion. "We function much as venture capitalists do in the private sector," explains Keny-Guyer. "You could say we're social VCs. As such, we're committed to bringing economic opportunity, through financial services, to low-income businesspeople and entrepreneurs around the world."

Mercy Corps' MAXIS program (for Maximizing Financial Access and Innovation at Scale) was launched in 2008 with funding of $33 million. The target bank was a local commercial bank in the island province of Bali. PT Bank Sri Partha had been servicing some 40,000 customers directly with average loans of about $650, but Mercy Corps turned it into a wholesale bank: Rather than providing direct loans, the new Bank Andara provides financial services and products to reliable MFIs. Working through MICRA (Microfinance Innovation Center for Resources and Alternatives), a foundation established by Mercy Corps to direct its efforts in the Indonesian microfinance sector, Bank Andara furnishes such products as microloans, savings accounts, microinsurance, mortgage financing, and mobile-phone banking. In the first three years, it reached more than 3 million microentrepreneurs and low-income borrowers through a network of 620 MFI clients.

For more on Mercy Corps and microfinancing as a form of social entrepreneuring, see the *Change* box entitled "Capital Adventures in Microfinancial Outreach" on page 33.

What Do You Think?

1. What environmental events and forces have led to the existence of organizations such as Mercy Corps?

2. In what ways does Mercy Corps interact with its environment in order to fulfill its mission?

References: "What We're Doing in Haiti," *Mercy Corps*, January 23, 2010, www.mercycorps.org on January 27, 2010; "Mercy Corps," *GuideStar*, 2009, www.guidestar.org on January 27, 2010; Roger Burks, "Change Brewing in the Tea Lands," *Mercy Corps*, April 9, 2008, www.mercycorps.org on January 27, 2010; "Sudan," *Mercy Corps*, 2009, www.mercycorps.org on January 27, 2010; Mercy Corps Indonesia, 2009, http://indonesia.mercycorps.org on January 27, 2010; Jennifer Vilaga, "Mercy Corps: The Bank of Banks," *Fast Company.com*, November 25, 2008, www.fastcompany.com on January 27, 2010; Ipek Kuran, "Microcapital Story: Mercy Corps Buys a Commercial Bank in Bali to Service the Microfinance Sector in Indonesia," *Microcapital*, June 23, 2008, www.microcapital.org on January 27, 2010; Steve Hamm, "Social Entrepreneurs Turn Business Sense to Good," *Next Billion*, December 3, 2008, www.nextbillion.net on January 27, 2010; Bija Gutoff, "Neal Keny-Guyer-Social Entrepreneurship at Mercy Corps," *Global Envision*, December 11, 2007, www.globalenvision.org on January 27, 2010.

The environment of all organizations is changing at an unprecedented rate. The growth of microfinancing and the rise of social entrepreneuring by organizations such as Mercy Corps represent only two perspectives on environmental change. Indeed, in some industries, such as consumer electronics, popular entertainment, and information technology, the speed and magnitude of change are truly breathtaking. Even industries characterized by what have been staid and predictable environments, such as traditional retailing and heavy manufacturing, also face sweeping environmental changes today. Understanding and addressing the environment of a business has traditionally been the purview of top managers. But the effects of today's changing environment permeate the entire organization. Hence, to truly understand the behavior of people in organizational settings, it is also necessary to understand the changing environment of business.[1] This chapter is intended to provide the framework for such understanding. Specifically, we introduce and examine five of the central environmental forces for change faced by today's organizations: globalization, diversity, technology, ethics and corporate governance, and new employment relationships. An understanding of these forces will then set the stage for our in-depth discussion of contemporary organizational behavior.

GLOBALIZATION AND BUSINESS

Perhaps the most significant source of change impacting many organizations today is the increasing **globalization** of organizations and management. Of course, in many ways, international management is nothing new. Centuries ago, the Roman army was forced to develop a management system to deal with its widespread empire.[2] Moreover, many notable early explorers like Christopher Columbus and Magellan were not seeking new territory but instead were looking for new trade routes to boost international trade. Likewise, the Olympic Games, the Red Cross, and other organizations have international roots. From a business standpoint, however, widespread concerns about, and the effects from, international management are relatively new, at least in the United States.

The Growth of International Business

In 2010, the volume of international trade in current dollars was over fifty times greater than the amount in 1960. What led to this dramatic increase? As Figure 2.1 shows, four major factors account for much of the momentum.

First, communication and transportation have advanced dramatically over the past several decades. Telephone service has improved, communication networks span the globe and can interact via satellite, and once-remote areas have become routinely accessible. Telephone service in some developing countries is now almost entirely by cellular phone technology rather than land-based wired telephone service. Fax machines and electronic mail allow managers to send documents around the world in seconds as opposed to the days it took just a few years ago. And new applications like text messaging and Skype have made global communication even easier. In short, it is simply easier to conduct international business today.

Second, businesses have expanded internationally to increase their markets. Companies in smaller countries, such as Nestlé in Switzerland and Heineken in the Netherlands, recognized long ago that their domestic markets were too small to sustain much growth and therefore moved into the international arena. Many U.S. firms, on the other hand, only found it advantageous to enter foreign markets in

Globalization is the internationalization of business activities and the shift toward an integrated global economy.

Figure 2.1 FORCES THAT HAVE INCREASED INTERNATIONAL BUSINESS

Movement along the continuum from domestic to international business is due to four forces. Businesses subject to these forces are becoming more international.

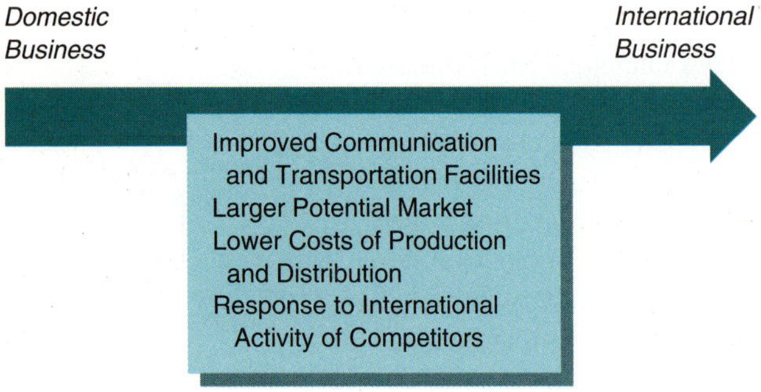

Domestic Business

International Business

Improved Communication and Transportation Facilities
Larger Potential Market
Lower Costs of Production and Distribution
Response to International Activity of Competitors

the last half century. Now, though, most mid-size and even many small firms routinely buy and/or sell products and services in other countries.

The *Change* box on page 33 continues the story of Mercy Corps' mission to extend its global impact through innovations in its approach to sustainable development.

Third, more and more firms are moving into international markets to control costs, especially to reduce labor costs. Plans to cut costs in this way do not always work out as planned, but many firms are successfully using inexpensive labor in Asia and Mexico.[3] In searching for lower labor costs, some companies have discovered well-trained workers and built more efficient plants that are closer to international markets. India, for instance, has emerged as a major force in the high-tech sector. And many foreign automakers have built plants in the United States.

Finally, many organizations have become international in response to competition. If an organization starts gaining strength in international markets, its competitors often must follow suit to avoid falling too far behind in sales and profitability. Exxon Mobil Corporation and Chevron realized they had to increase their international market share to keep pace with foreign competitors such as BP and Royal Dutch Shell.

Cross-Cultural Differences and Similarities

Since the primary concern of this book is human behavior in organizational settings, we now turn our attention to differences and similarities in behavior across cultures. While there is relatively little research in this area, interesting findings are beginning to emerge.[4]

General Observations At one level, it is possible to make several general observations about similarities and differences across cultures. For one thing, cultural and national boundaries do not necessarily coincide. Some areas of Switzerland are very much like Italy, other parts like France, and still other parts like Germany. Similarly, within the United States there are large cultural differences across, say, Southern California, Texas, and the East Coast.[5]

Given this basic assumption, one major review of the literature on international management reached five basic conclusions.[6] First, behavior in organizational settings does indeed vary across cultures. Thus, employees in companies based in Japan, the United States, and Germany are likely to have different attitudes and patterns of behavior. The behavior patterns are also likely to be widespread and pervasive within an organization.

Second, culture itself is one major cause of this variation. **Culture** is the set of shared values, often taken for granted, that help people in a group, organization, or society understand which actions are considered acceptable and which are deemed unacceptable (we use this same definition to frame our discussion of organizational culture in Chapter 18). Thus, although the behavioral differences just noted may be caused in part by different standards of living, different geographical conditions, and so forth, culture itself is a major factor apart from other considerations.

Culture is the set of shared values, often taken for granted, that help people in a group, organization, or society understand which actions are considered acceptable and which are deemed unacceptable.

CHANGE

Capital Adentures in Microfinancial Outreach

Mercy Corps, a nongovernmental, nonprofit organization that's provided humanitarian aid and development assistance to countries around the world for nearly 30 years, made *Fast Company* magazine's 2009 list of the ten best Social Enterprises of the Year. Other companies on the list include OneWorld Health, a pharmaceuticals maker built on a no-profit/no-loss business model to develop drugs for treating targeted diseases among the poor, and Husk Power Systems, which has developed a system to electrify Indian villages by burning discarded rice husks in miniature power plants.

> *"Traditional ways of doing things haven't produced the kind of progress we all hoped for. So we're trying to come up with new approaches that are fully transformational."*
>
> —NEAL KENY–GUYER, CEO OF MERCY CORPS

Each of these organizations is a *social business enterprise (SBE)*—a business designed to address a social objective in such areas as health, education, poverty, or the environment. An SBE is a *non-loss/non-dividend company*: It strives for sustainability in its activities, but investors do not take profits, which are instead used to expand the company and extend its efforts to achieve its goals. The idea originated with Muhammad Yunus, a Bangladeshi economist and banker who's also responsible for the concept of *microcredit*—the principle of extending small loans (called *microloans*) to entrepreneurs who can't meet the minimal qualifications for credit through traditional sources.

Today, microcredit is actually one form of *microfinance*, which refers to the practice of providing a broad range of financial services to the same clientele. Mercy Corps has long been active in providing immediate-response assistance in crisis situations, such as the Indian Ocean tsunami that killed 230,000 people in 14 countries and left 1.5 million homeless in December 2004 and the earthquake that killed and displaced similar numbers of people in Haiti in January 2010. Since the mid-1990s, however, Mercy Corps has concentrated more of its resources on sustainable financial assistance as a means of effecting durable change. "Traditional ways of doing things," says CEO Neal Keny-Guyer, "haven't produced the kind of progress we all hoped for. So we're trying to come up with new approaches that are fully transformational." In 2008, for example, Mercy Corps launched Bank Andara in Indonesia to provide financial services and products to reliable microfinance institutions (MFIs) which, in turn, make direct microloans to entrepreneurs and small businesses.

Keny-Guyer likens his organization's financial focus to that of venture capital companies. "You could say we're social VCs," he says, and he hopes to exercise financial strength in the public sphere in much the same way that VCs leverage it in the private sector—"by bringing economic opportunity, through financial services, to low-income businesspeople." In the business world, he explains, "the infrastructure is aligned to support innovation and entrepreneurship," but "in the public sphere, we haven't had the financial infrastructure to support innovation."

He's convinced, however, that things are changing in the world of SBEs and that "new paradigms for creating social value are emerging." Bank Andara, for example, along with other initiatives in microfinancial outreach, put Mercy Corps on what Keny-Guyer calls "the edge of . . . prudent risk." It's an important step

Continued

in SBE strategy, he insists, because undeveloped economies

don't need more well-funded retail institutions. What's needed is to develop MFI as a real industry that's integrated with the commercial banks, so there will be a seamless web of financial institutions that serve everyone, from the poorest borrower to the richest, with a full range of products and services. That's the real home run. It's the kind of social

innovation that's making Mercy Corps a leader in social entrepreneurship.

References: "The 10 Best Social Enterprises of 2009," *Fast Company,* November 25, 2008, www.fastcompany.com on January 27, 2010; Jennifer Vilaga, "Mercy Corps: The Bank of Banks," *Fast Company.com,* November 25, 2008, www.fastcompany.com on January 27, 2010; Bija Gutoff, "Neal Keny-Guyer-Social Entrepreneurship at Mercy Corps," *Global Envision,* December 11, 2007, www.globalenvision .org on January 27, 2010; Steve Hamm, "Social Entrepreneurs Turn Business Sense to Good," *Next Billion,* December 3, 2008, www.nextbillion.net on January 27, 2010; Ipek Kuran, "Microcapital Story: Mercy Corps Buys a Commercial Bank in Bali to Service the Microfinance Sector in Indonesia," *Microcapital,* June 23, 2008, www.microcapital.org on January 27, 2010.

KLAUS TIEDGE/GETTY IMAGES

Cultural diversity plays an increasingly important role in businesses today. Managers must be comfortable in interacting with colleagues and other business associates from all parts of the globe and all walks of life. The managers shown here, for example, are part of an international project team working on a construction facility in South America. Their diverse backgrounds and perspectives help bring different and novel perspectives to the project.

Third, although the causes and consequences of behavior within organizational settings remains quite diverse across cultures, organizations and the way they are structured appear to be growing increasingly similar. Hence, managerial practices at a general level may be becoming more and more alike, but the people who work within organizations still differ markedly.

Fourth, the same individual behaves differently in different cultural settings. A manager may adopt one set of behaviors when working in one culture but change those behaviors when moved to a different culture. For example, Japanese executives who come to work in the United States may slowly begin to act more like U.S. managers and less like Japanese managers. This, in turn, may be source of concern for them when they are transferred back to Japan.

Finally, cultural diversity can be an important source of synergy in enhancing organizational effectiveness. More and more organizations are coming to appreciate the virtues of diversity, but they still know surprisingly little about how to manage it. Organizations that adopt a multinational strategy can—with effort—become more than a sum of their parts. Operations in each culture can benefit from operations in other cultures through an enhanced understanding of how the world works.[7]

Specific Cultural Issues Geert Hofstede, a Dutch researcher, studied workers and managers in sixty countries and found that specific attitudes and behaviors differed significantly because of the values and beliefs that characterized those countries.[8] Table 2.1 shows how Hofstede's categories help us summarize differences for several countries.

The two primary dimensions that Hofstede found are the individualism/collectivism continuum and power distance. **Individualism** exists to the extent that people in a

Individualism exists to the extent that people in a culture define themselves primarily as individuals rather than as part of one or more groups or organizations.

Table 2.1   WORK-RELATED DIFFERENCES IN 10 COUNTRIES

Country	Individualism/ Collectivism	Power Distance	Uncertainty Avoidance	Masculinity	Long-Term Orientation
CANADA	H	M	M	M	L
GERMANY	M	M	M	M	M
ISRAEL	M	L	M	M	(no data)
ITALY	H	M	M	H	(no data)
JAPAN	M	M	H	H	H
MEXICO	H	H	H	M	(no data)
PAKISTAN	L	M	M	M	L
SWEDEN	H	M	L	L	M
UNITED STATES	H	M	M	M	L
VENEZUELA	L	H	M	H	(no data)

Note: H = high; M = moderate; L = low. These are only ten of the more than sixty countries that Hofstede and others have studied.

References: Adapted from Geert Hofstede and Michael Harris Bond, "The Confucius Connection: From Cultural Roots to Economic Growth," *Organizational Dynamics,* Spring 1988, pp. 5–21; Geert Hofstede, "Motivation, Leadership, and Organization: Do American Theories Apply Abroad?" *Organizational Dynamics,* Summer 1980, pp. 42–63.

culture define themselves primarily as individuals rather than as part of one or more groups or organizations. At work, people from more individualistic cultures tend to be more concerned about themselves as individuals than about their work group, individual tasks are more important than relationships, and hiring and promotion are usually based on skills and rules. **Collectivism**, on the other hand, is characterized by tight social frameworks in which people tend to base their identities on the group or organization to which they belong. At work, this means that employee–employer links are more like family relationships, relationships are more important than individuals or tasks, and hiring and promotion are based on group membership. In the United States, a very individualistic culture, it is important to perform better than others and to stand out from the crowd. In Japan, a more collectivist culture, an individual tries to fit in with the group, strives for harmony, and prefers stability.

Power distance, which can also be called **orientation to authority**, is the extent to which people accept as normal an unequal distribution of power. In countries such as Mexico and Venezuela, for example, people prefer to be in a situation in which authority is clearly understood and lines of authority are never bypassed. On the other hand, in countries such as Israel and Denmark, authority is not as highly respected and employees are quite comfortable circumventing lines of authority to accomplish something. People in the United States tend to be mixed, accepting authority in some situations but not in others.

Hofstede also identified other dimensions of culture. **Uncertainty avoidance**, which can also be called **preference for stability**, is the extent to which people feel threatened by unknown situations and prefer to be in clear and unambiguous situations. People in Japan and Mexico prefer stability to uncertainty, whereas uncertainty is normal and accepted in Sweden, Hong Kong, and the United Kingdom. **Masculinity**, which might more accurately called **assertiveness** or **materialism**, is the extent to which

Collectivism is characterized by tight social frameworks in which people tend to base their identities on the group or organization to which they belong.

Power distance, which can also be called **orientation to authority**, is the extent to which people accept as normal an unequal distribution of power.

Uncertainty avoidance, which can also be called **preference for stability**, is the extent to which people feel threatened by unknown situations and prefer to be in clear and unambiguous situations.

Masculinity, which might more accurately called **assertiveness** or **materialism**, is the extent to which the dominant values in a society emphasize aggressiveness and the acquisition of money and other possessions as opposed to concern for people, relationships among people, and overall quality of life.

Figure 2.3 WORKFORCE COMPOSITION 1990–2014

In the period between 1990 and 2014 all workforce segments are expected to increase as a percentage of the total workforce except the white male segment, which is has declined from 47.4% in 1990 to 43.2% in 2010 and is expected to decline further to 41.5 % by 2014.

Note: the percentages for each year exceed 100 because of the number of individuals who report dual or multiple ethnicities.

Source: Bureau of Labor Statistics, Labor Force Projections to 2014: Retiring Boomers, http://www.bls.gov/opub/mlr/2010/11/art3full.pdf

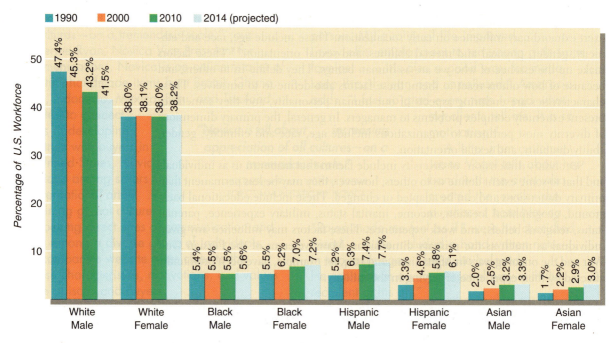

Global Workforce Diversity

Similar statistics on workforce diversity are found in other countries. In Canada, for instance, minorities are the fastest-growing segment of the population and the workforce. In addition, women make up two-thirds of the growth in the Canadian workforce, increasing from 35 percent in the 1970s to over 50 percent in 2010. These changes have initiated a workforce revolution in offices and factories throughout Canada. Managers and employees are learning to adapt to changing demographics. One study found that 81 percent of the organizations surveyed by the Conference Board of Canada include diversity management programs for their employees.[16]

Increasing diversity in the workplace is even more dramatic in Europe, where employees have been crossing borders for many years. In fact, in 1991 more than 2 million Europeans were living in one country and working in another. When the European Union further eased border crossings for its citizens in 1992, this number increased significantly. It was expected that opening borders among the European community members primarily would mean relaxing trade restrictions so that goods and services could move more freely among the member countries. In addition, however, workers were also freer to move, and they have taken advantage of the opportunity. It is clear that diversity in the workforce is more than a U.S. phenomenon. Many German factories now have a very diverse workforce that includes many workers from Turkey. Several of the emerging economies in Central Europe are encountering increasing diversity in their workforce. Poland, Hungary, and the Czech Republic, for

Figure 2.4   PROJECTED WORKFORCE GROWTH BY SEGMENT FROM 2004 TO 2014

As this figure illustrates, while the overall workforce is expected to grow by 1% between 2004 and 2014, the smallest growth will occur in the white male and female categories, while the largest growth will occur in the Asian female category.

Source: Bureau of Labor Statistics, Labor Force Projections to 2014; http://www.bls.gov/opub/mlr/2005/11/art3full.pdf

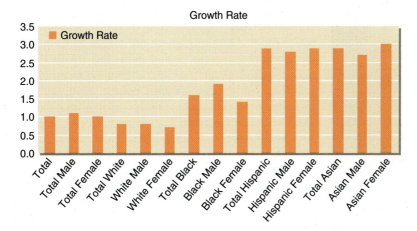

instance, have experienced a steady influx of workers from the Ukraine, Afghanistan, Sri Lanka, China, and Somalia.[17]

Companies throughout Europe are learning to adjust to the changing workforce. Amadeus Global Travel Distribution serves the travel industry, primarily in Europe, but its staff of 650 is composed of individuals from thirty-two different countries. Amadeus developed a series of workshops to teach managers how to lead multicultural teams. Such seminars also teach them how to interact better with peers, subordinates, and superiors who come from a variety of countries. Other companies experiencing much the same phenomenon in Europe and doing something about it include Mars, Hewlett-Packard Spain, Fujitsu Spain, and BP. Companies in Asia are also encountering increasing diversity. In Thailand, where there is a shortage of skilled and unskilled workers because of rapid industrialization and slow population growth, there is a growing demand for foreign workers to fill the gap, which creates problems integrating local and foreign workers.[18] Thus, the issue of workforce diversity is not limited to only the United States.

The Value of Diversity

The United States has historically been seen as a "melting pot" of people from many different countries, cultures, and backgrounds. For centuries, it was assumed that people who came from other countries should assimilate themselves into the existing cultural context they were entering. Although equal employment opportunity and accompanying affirmative action legislation have had significant effects on diversifying workplaces, they sometimes focused on bringing into the workplace people from culturally different groups and fully assimilating them into the existing organization. In organizations, however, integration proved to be difficult to implement. Members of the majority were slow to adapt and usually resistant to the change. Substantive career advancement opportunities rarely materialized for those who were "different."

The issue of workforce diversity has become increasingly more important in the last few years as employees, managers, consultants, and the government finally realized that the composition of the workforce affects organizational productivity. Today, instead of a melting pot, the workplace in the United States might be regarded as more of a 'tossed salad' made up of a mosaic of different flavors, colors, and textures. Rather than trying to assimilate those who are different into a single organizational culture, the current view holds that organizations need to celebrate the differences and utilize the variety of talents, perspectives, and backgrounds of all employees.[19]

Assimilation Assimilation is the process through which members of a minority group are forced to learn the ways of the majority group. In organizations this entails hiring people from diverse backgrounds and attempting to mold them to fit into the existing organizational culture. One way that companies attempt to make people fit in is by requiring that employees speak only one language. For instance, Carlos Solero was fired after he refused to sign a work agreement that included a policy of English-only at a suburban manufacturing plant near Chicago. Management said the intent of the English-only policy was to improve communication among workers at the plant. In response, Solero and seven other Spanish speakers filed lawsuits against the plant. Attempts to assimilate diverse workers by imposing English-only rules can lead to a variety of organizational problems. Most organizations develop systems such as performance evaluation and incentive programs that reinforce the values of the dominant group. (Chapter 18 discusses organizational culture as a means of reinforcing the organizational values and affecting the behavior of workers.) By universally applying the values of the majority group throughout the organization, assimilation tends to perpetuate false stereotypes and prejudices. Workers who are different are expected to meet the standards for dominant group members.[20]

Dominant groups tend to be self-perpetuating. Majority group members may avoid people who are "different" simply because they find communication difficult. Moreover, informal discussions over coffee and lunch and during after-hours socializing tend to be limited to people in the dominant group. As a result, those who are not in the dominant group miss out on the informal communication opportunities in which office politics, company policy, and other issues are often discussed in rich detail. Subsequently, employees not in the dominant group often do not understand the more formal communications and may not be included in necessary actions taken in response. The dominant group likewise remains unaware of opinions from the "outside."

Similarly, since the dominant group makes decisions based on their values and beliefs, the minority group has little say in decisions regarding compensation, facility location, benefit plans, performance standards, and other work issues that pertain directly to all workers. Workers who differ from the majority very quickly get the idea that to succeed in such a system, one must be like the dominant group in terms of values and beliefs, dress, and most other characteristics. Since success depends on assimilation, differences are driven underground.

Most organizations have a fairly predictable dominant group. Table 2.2 shows the results of interviews with members of several organizations who were asked to list the attributes reinforced by their organization's culture. Typically, white men in

© ED QUINN/CORBIS

Diversity training is a common method used in businesses today to better enable their employees to accept and value differences. These Pilgrim Health Care workers, for instance, are participating in a role-playing exercise as part of a diversity training program. Various individuals wear labels branding themselves as "complainer," "rookie-new hire," "opposed to change," "overweight," and so forth. As they interact with one another, they begin to see how labels affect their interactions with others at work.

Assimilation is the process through which members of a minority group are forced to learn the ways of the majority group.

Table 2.2 ATTRIBUTES REINFORCED BY THE CULTURE IN TYPICAL ORGANIZATIONS

Rational, linear thinker	Ages 35–49
Impersonal management style	Competitive
Married with children	Protestant or Jewish
Quantitative	College graduate
Adversarial	Tall
Careerist	Heterosexual
Individualistic	Predictable
Experience in competitive team sports	Excellent physical condition
In control	Willing to relocate
Military veteran	

Reference: Marilyn Loden and Judy B. Rosener, *Workforce America! Managing Employee Diversity as a Vital Resource* (Homewood, IL: Business One Irwin, 1991), p. 43. Copyright © 1991 by permission of The McGraw-Hill Companies.

organizations view themselves as quite diverse. However, others in the organizations view them as quite homogeneous, having attributes similar to those listed. Also, typically those who work in these dominant groups tend to be less aware of the problems that homogeneity can cause. Generally, those not in the dominant group feel the effects more keenly.

Not paying attention to diversity can be very costly to the organization. In addition to blocking minority involvement in communication and decision making, it can result in tensions among workers, lower productivity, increased costs due to increasing absenteeism, increased employee turnover, increased equal employment opportunity and harassment suits, and lower morale among the workers.

Benefits of Valuing Diversity   Valuing diversity means putting an end to the assumption that everyone who is not a member of the dominant group must assimilate. This is not easily accomplished in most organizations. Truly valuing diversity is not merely giving lip service to an ideal, putting up with a necessary evil, promoting a level of tolerance for those who are different, or tapping into the latest fad. It is an opportunity to develop and utilize all of the human resources available to the organization for the benefit of the workers as well as the organization.

Valuing diversity is not just the right thing to do for workers; it is the right thing to do for the organization, both financially and economically. One of the most important benefits of diversity is the richness of ideas and perspectives that it makes available to the organization. Rather than relying on one homogeneous dominant group for new ideas and alternative solutions to increasingly complex problems, companies that value diversity have access to more perspectives of a problem. These fresh perspectives may lead to development of new products, opening of new markets, or improving service to existing customers.[22]

Overall, the organization wins when it truly values diversity. Worker who recognize that the organization truly values them are likely to be more creative, motivated, and productive. Valued workers in diverse organizations experience less interpersonal

Valuing diversity means putting an end to the assumption that everyone who is not a member of the dominant group must assimilate.

conflict because the employees understand each other. When employees of different cultural groups, backgrounds, and values understand each other, they have a greater sense of teamwork, a stronger identification with the team, and a deeper commitment to the organization and its goals.

TECHNOLOGY AND BUSINESS

Technology refers to the methods used to create products, including both physical goods and intangible services. Technological change has become a major driver for other forms of organization change. Moreover, it also has widespread effects on the behaviors of people inside an organization. Three specific areas of technology worth noting here are: (1) the shift toward a service-based economy, (2) the growing use of technology for competitive advantage, and (3) mushrooming change in information technology.[23]

Manufacturing and Service Technologies

Manufacturing is a form of business that combines and transforms resources into tangible outcomes that are then sold to others. The Goodyear Tire and Rubber Company is a manufacturer because it combines rubber and chemical compounds and uses blending equipment and molding machines to create tires. Broyhill is a manufacturer because it buys wood and metal components, pads, and fabric and then combines them into furniture.

Manufacturing was once the dominant technology in the United States. During the 1970s, manufacturing entered a long period of decline, primarily because of foreign competition. U.S. firms had grown lax and sluggish, and new foreign competitors came onto the scene with better equipment and much higher levels of efficiency. For example, steel companies in the Far East were able to produce high-quality steel for much lower prices than U.S. companies such as Bethlehem Steel and U.S. Steel (now USX Corporation). Faced with a battle for survival, many companies underwent a long and difficult period of change by eliminating waste and transforming themselves into leaner and more efficient and responsive entities. They reduced their workforces dramatically, closed antiquated or unnecessary plants, and modernized their remaining plants. Since around 1990 their efforts have started to pay dividends as U.S. manufacturing has regained its competitive position in many different industries.

During the decline of the manufacturing sector, a tremendous growth in the service sector kept the overall U.S. economy from declining at the same rate. A **service organization** is one that transforms resources into an intangible output and creates time or place utility for its customers. For example, Merrill Lynch makes stock transactions for its customers, Avis leases cars to its customers, and your local hairdresser cuts your hair. In 1947, the service sector was responsible for less than half of the U.S. gross national product (GNP). By 1975, however, this figure reached 65 percent, and by 2006 had surpassed 75 percent. The service sector has been responsible for almost 90 percent of all new jobs created in the United States since 1990. Moreover, service-providing industries are expected to create approximately 14.5 million new wage and salary jobs by 2018.[24]

Managers have come to see that many of the tools, techniques, and methods that are used in a factory are also useful to a service firm. For example, managers of automobile plants and hair salons each have to decide how to design their facility, identify the best location for it, determine optimal capacity, make

---

Technology refers to the methods used to create products, including both physical goods and intangible services.

Manufacturing is a form of business that combines and transforms resources into tangible outcomes that are then sold to others.

A **service organization** is one that transforms resources into an intangible output and creates time or place utility for its customers.

decisions about inventory storage, set procedures for purchasing raw materials, and set standards for productivity and quality. At the same time, though, service-based firms must hire and train employees based on a different skill set than is required by most manufacturers. For instance, consumers seldom come into contact with the Toyota employee who installs the seats in their car, so that person can be hired based on technical skills. But Avis must recruit people who not only know how to do a job but who can also effectively interface with a variety of consumers.

Technology and Competition

Technology is the basis of competition for some firms, especially those whose goals include being the technology leaders in their industries. A company, for example, might focus its efforts on being the lowest-cost producer or on always having the most technologically advanced products on the market. But because of the rapid pace of new developments, keeping a leadership position based on technology is becoming increasingly challenging. Another challenge is meeting constant demands to decrease cycle time (the time that it takes a firm to accomplish some recurring activity or function from beginning to end).

Businesses have increasingly found that they can be more competitive if they can systematically decrease cycle times. Many companies, therefore, now focus on decreasing cycle times in areas ranging from developing products

The U.S. economy has moved from one based largely on manufacturing to one based on service. This hairdresser, for example, is providing a service for his client—cutting and styling her hair. But services and manufacturing are often interrelated. For example, the tools and equipment the stylist uses to provide service were created by manufacturers. Managers need to understand both the differences and the similarities in leading service versus manufacturing businesses.

JACK HOLLINGSWORTH/BRAND X PICTURES/JUPITERIMAGES

to making deliveries and collecting credit payments. Twenty years ago, it took a carmaker about five years from the decision to launch a new product until it was available in dealer showrooms. Now most companies can complete the cycle in less than two years. The speedier process allows them to more quickly respond to changing economic conditions, consumer preferences, and new competitor products while recouping more quickly their product-development costs. Some firms compete directly on how quickly they can get things done for consumers. In the early days of personal computers, for instance, getting a made-to-order system took six to eight weeks. Today, firms such as Dell can usually ship exactly what the customer wants in a matter of days.

Information Technology

Most people are very familiar with advances in information technology. Cellular telephones, electronic books, smart phones like the iPhone and Blackberry, the iPad, and digital cameras, as well as technologically based social networking sites such as Facebook, are just a few of the many recent innovations that have changed how people live and work.[25] Breakthroughs in information technology have resulted in leaner organizations, more flexible operations, increased collaboration among employees, more flexible work sites, and improved management processes and systems. On the other hand, they have also resulted in less personal communication, less "down time" for managers and employees, and an increased sense of urgency vis-à-vis decision making and communication—changes that have not necessarily always been beneficial. We discuss information technology and its relationship to organizational behavior in more detail in Chapter 11.

ETHICS AND CORPORATE GOVERNANCE

While **ethics** have long been of relevance to businesses, what seems like an epidemic of ethical breaches in recent years has placed ethics in the mainstream of managerial thought today. One special aspect of business ethics, corporate governance, has also taken on increased importance. Ethics also increasingly relate to information technology.

Contemporary Ethical Issues

A central issue today revolves around the fact that rapid changes in business relationships, organizational structures, and financial systems pose unsurpassed difficulties in keeping accurate track of a company's financial position. The public—as well as current and potential investors—often get blurred pictures of a firm's competitive health. However, stakeholders—employees, stockholders, consumers, unions, creditors, and government—are all entitled to a fair accounting so they can make enlightened personal and business decisions. Even the American Institute for Certified Public Accountants (AICPA) admits that keeping up with today's increasingly fast-paced business activities is putting a strain on the accounting profession's traditional methods for auditing, financial reporting, and time-honored standards for professional ethics.

The Enron scandal, for example, involved extended enterprises using fast-moving financial transactions among layers of subsidiary firms, some domestic and many offshore, with large-scale borrowing from some of the world's largest financial institutions. The flood of electronic transactions that drove financial flows through a vast network of quickly formed and rapidly dissolved partnerships among energy brokers and buyers was so complex that Enron's accounting reports completely failed to reflect the firm's disastrous financial and managerial condition. In a blatant display of unethical conduct, Enron's public reports concealed many of its partnerships with (and obligations to) other companies, thus hiding its true operating condition.

Furthermore, why did Arthur Andersen, the accounting firm that audited Enron's finances, not catch its client's distorted reports? Auditors are supposed to provide an objective and independent assessment of the accuracy of financial information reported by corporations to key stakeholders, such as investors and governmental agencies. Indeed, publicly traded corporations are legally required to use an external auditor for just this purpose. The answer to this question reveals a further illustration

8. **Ethics** are a person's beliefs regarding what is right or wrong in a given situation.

of the hazards faced by today's extended firm. Andersen, like other major accounting firms, had expanded from auditing into more lucrative non-accounting areas such as management consulting. Reports suggest that Andersen's desire for future high-revenue consulting services with Enron may have motivated the CPA's auditors to turn a blind eye on questionable practices that eventually turned up during audits of Enron's finances.

Beyond these large-scale issues, other contemporary ethical concerns involve such areas as executive compensation, environmental protection, working conditions in foreign factories, pricing policies, and pressures to balance profits against costs as businesses continue to globalize. We discuss ethical issues in several places later in this book, including Chapter 8 (decision making) and Chapter 13 (contemporary views of leadership).

Ethical Issues in Corporate Governance

A related area of emerging concern relates to ethical issues in **corporate governance**—the oversight of a public corporation by its board of directors. The board of a public corporation is expected to ensure that the business is being properly managed and that the decisions made by its senior management are in the best interests of shareholders and other stakeholders. But in far too many cases the recent ethical scandals alluded to previously have actually started with a breakdown in the corporate governance structure. For instance, in a now-classic ethical scandal involving governance issues, WorldCom's board approved a personal loan to the firm's CEO, Bernard Ebbers, for $366 million when there was little evidence that he could repay it. Likewise, Tyco's board approved a $20 million bonus for one of its own members for helping with the acquisition of a firm owned by that individual (this bonus was in addition to the purchase price!).

But boards of directors are also being increasingly criticized even when they are not directly implicated in wrongdoing. The biggest complaint here often relates to board independence. Disney, for instance, has faced this problem. Several key members of the firm's board of directors are from companies that do business with Disney, and others are long-time friends with senior Disney executives. While board members need to have some familiarity with both the firm and its industry in order to function effectively, they also need to have sufficient independence as might be necessary to carry out their oversight function.[26]

Ethical Issues in Information Technology

Another set of issues that have emerged in recent times involves information technology. Among the specific questions in this area are individual rights to privacy and the potential abuse of information technology by companies. Indeed, online privacy has become a hot issue as companies sort out the related ethical and management issues. DoubleClick, an online advertising network, is one of the firms at the center of the privacy debate. The company has collected data on the habits of millions of Web surfers, recording which sites they visit and which ads they click on. DoubleClick insists that the profiles are anonymous and are used to better match surfers with appropriate ads. However, after the company announced a plan to add names and addresses to its database, it was forced to back down because of public concerns over invasion of online privacy.

DoubleClick isn't the only firm gathering personal data about people's Internet activities. People who register at Yahoo! are asked to list date of birth, among other

Corporate governance refers to the oversight of a public corporation by its board of directors.

RICK WILKING/REUTERS/LANDOV

DoubleClick, an online advertising network, has been the focus of discussion about individual privacy. DoubleClick has collected data on the habits of millions of Web surfers, recording which sites they visit and which ads they click on. The firm argues that these data are confidential and only used to better match surfers with appropriate ads. But when it announced a plan to add names and addresses to its database, public backlash forced DoubleClick to drop the idea.

details. Amazon.com, eBay, and other sites also ask for personal information. As Internet usage increases, however, surveys show that people are troubled by the amount of information being collected and who gets to see it.

One way management can address these concerns is by posting a privacy policy on its website. The policy should explain exactly what data the company collects and who gets to see the data. It should also allow people a choice about having their information shared with others and indicate how people can opt out of data collection. Disney, IBM, and other companies support this position by refusing to advertise on websites that have no posted privacy policies.

In addition, companies can offer Web surfers the opportunity to review and correct information that has been collected, especially medical and financial data. In the off-line world, consumers are legally allowed to inspect credit and medical records. In the online world, this kind of access can be costly and cumbersome, because data are often spread across several computer systems. Despite the technical difficulties, government agencies are already working on Internet privacy guidelines; this means, in turn, that companies will also need internal guidelines, training, and leadership to ensure compliance.

NEW EMPLOYMENT RELATIONSHIPS

A final significant area of environmental change that is particularly relevant for businesses today involves what we call new employment relationships. While we discuss employment relationships from numerous perspectives in Part 2 of this book, two particularly important areas today involve the management of knowledge workers and the outsourcing of jobs to other businesses, especially when those businesses are in other countries.

The Management of Knowledge Workers

Knowledge workers are those employees who add value in an organization simply because of what they know.

Traditionally, employees added value to organizations because of what they did or because of their experience. However, during today's "information age," many employees add value simply because of what they know.[27] These employees are often referred to as **knowledge workers**. How well these employees are managed is seen as a major factor in determining which firms will be successful in the future.[28] Knowledge workers include computer scientists, physical scientists, engineers, product designers, and video game developers. They tend to work in high technology firms, and are usually experts in some abstract knowledge base. They often believe they have the right to work in an autonomous fashion, and they identify more strongly with their profession than with any organization—even to the extent of defining performance primarily in terms recognized by other members of their profession.[29]

As the importance of information-driven jobs grows, the need for knowledge workers will grow as well. But these employees require extensive and highly specialized training, and not everyone is willing to make the human capital investments necessary to move into these jobs. In fact, even after knowledge workers are on the job, retraining and training updates are critical so that their skills do not become obsolete. It has been suggested, for example, that the "half-life" for a technical education in engineering is about three years. Further, the failure to update the required skills will not only result in the organization losing competitive advantage but will also increase the likelihood that the knowledge worker will go to another firm that is more committed to updating those skills.[30]

Compensation and related policies for knowledge workers must also be specially tailored. For example, in many high-tech organizations, engineers and scientists have the option of entering a technical career path that parallels a management career path. This allows the knowledge worker to continue to carry out specialized work without taking on large management responsibilities, while at the same time offering that worker compensation that is equivalent to that available to management. But in other high-tech firms, the emphasis is on pay for performance, with profit sharing based on projects or products developed by the knowledge workers. In addition, in most firms employing these workers there has been a tendency to reduce the number of levels of the organization to allow the knowledge workers to react more quickly to the external environment by reducing the need for bureaucratic approvals.[31]

Outsourcing

Outsourcing is the practice of hiring other firms to do work previously performed by the organization itself. It is an increasingly popular strategy because it helps firms focus on their core activities and avoid getting sidetracked onto secondary activities. The snack bar at a large commercial bank may be important to employees and some customers, but running it is not the bank's main line of business and expertise. Bankers need to focus on money management and financial services, not food-service operations. That's why most banks outsource snack bar operations to food-service management companies whose main line of business includes cafeterias. The result, ideally, is more attention to banking by bankers, better food service for snack bar customers, and formation of a new supplier–client relationship (food-service company/bank). Firms today often outsource numerous activities, including payroll, employee training, facility maintenance, and research and development.

Up to a point, at least, outsourcing makes good business sense in areas that are highly unrelated to a firm's core business activities. However, it has attracted considerable more attention in recent years because of the growing trend toward outsourcing abroad in order to lower labor costs; this practice is often called *offshoring*. One recent estimate suggests that 3.3 million white-collar jobs currently being performed in the United States will likely be moved abroad by 2015; this same study suggests that 1 out of 10 IT jobs once held by U.S. workers will be handled by non-U.S. workers by that same date.[32]

Many software firms, for example, have found that there is an abundance of talented programmers in India who are willing to work for much lower salaries than their American counterparts. Likewise, many firms that operate large call centers find that

Outsourcing is the practice of hiring other firms to do work previously performed by the organization itself; when this work is moved overseas it is often called *offshoring*.

they can handle those operations for much lower costs from other parts of the world. As a result domestic jobs may be lost. And some firms attract additional criticism when they require their domestic workers—soon to be out of jobs—to train their newly hired foreign replacements! Clearly, there are numerous behavioral and motivational issues involved in practices such as these.

Temp and Contingency Workers

Another trend that has impacted employment relationships in business involves the use of contingent or temporary workers. Indeed, recent years have seen an explosion in the use of such workers by organizations. A **contingent worker** is a person who works for an organization on something other than a permanent or full-time basis. Categories of contingent workers include independent contractors, on-call workers, temporary employees (usually hired through outside agencies), and contract and leased employees. Another category is part-time workers. The financial services giant Citigroup, for example, makes extensive use of part-time sales agents to pursue new clients. About 10 percent of the U.S. workforce currently uses one of these alternative forms of employment relationships. Experts suggest, however, that this percentage is increasing at a consistent pace.

Managing contingent workers is not always straightforward, however, especially from a behavioral perspective. Expecting too much from such workers, for example, is a mistake that managers should avoid. An organization with a large contingent workforce must make some decisions about the treatment of contingent workers relative to the treatment of permanent, full-time workers. Should contingent workers be invited to the company holiday party? Should they have the same access to such employee benefits as counseling services and childcare? There are no right or wrong answers to such questions. Managers must understand that they need to develop a strategy for integrating contingent workers according to some sound logic and then follow that strategy consistently over time.[33]

Tiered Workforce

A final emerging issue dealing with new employment relationships is what we might call the tiered workforce. A **tiered workforce** exists when one group of an organization's workforce has a contractual arrangement with the organization objectively different from that of another group performing the same jobs. For example, Harley-Davidson recently negotiated a new agreement with its labor union for wages and job security at its large factory in York, Pennsylvania. The change was needed to help the plant remain competitive and to prevent Harley from moving York jobs to other factories. Under terms of the new agreement, the lowest-paid production worker currently on staff would earn $24.10 an hour. All new employees hired for that same job in the future, however, will earn $19.28 an hour. Yet another group of employees, called "casual" workers, will work on an "as needed" basis and will earn $16.75 an hour.[34] Similarly, under a new contract with the United Auto Workers, new hires at Ford, General Motors, and Chrysler will earn a lower hourly wage and reduced benefits when compared to workers already on the payroll when the agreement was signed.[35]

These and other arrangements will pose challenges in the future. For instance, newly hired workers may come to feel resentment towards their more senior colleagues who are doing the same work but getting paid more for that work. Likewise, when the job market improves and workers have more options, firms may face higher turnover among their lower-paid employees.

A **contingent worker** is a person who works for an organization on something other than a permanent or full-time basis.

A **tiered workforce** exists when one group of an organization's workforce has a contractual arrangement with the organization objectively different from another group performing the same jobs.

SYNOPSIS

Globalization is playing a major role in the environment of many firms today. The volume of international trade has grown significantly and continues to grow at a very rapid pace. There are four basic reasons for this growth: (1) communication and transportation have advanced dramatically over the past several decades; (2) businesses have expanded internationally to increase their markets; (3) firms are moving into international markets to control costs, especially to reduce labor costs; and (4) many organizations have become international in response to competition. There are numerous cross-cultural differences and similarities that affect behavior within organizations.

A second major environmental shift in recent years has been the increased attention devoted to the concept of diversity. Workforce diversity refers to the important similarities and differences among the employees of organizations. Unfortunately, many people tend to stereotype others in organizations. Stereotypes can lead to the even more dangerous process of prejudice toward others. Managers should be cognizant of both primary and secondary dimensions of diversity, as well as the wide array of benefits to be derived from having a diverse workforce.

Technology refers to the methods used to create products, including both physical goods and intangible services. Technological change has become a major driver for other forms of organization change. Moreover, it also has widespread effects on the behaviors of people inside an organization. Three specific areas of technology relevant to the study of organizational behavior are: (1) the shift toward a service-based economy, (2) the growing use of technology for competitive advantage, and (3) mushrooming change in information technology.

While ethics have long been of relevance to businesses, what seems like an epidemic of ethical breaches in recent years has placed ethics in the mainstream of managerial thought today. One special aspect of business ethics, corporate governance, has also taken on increased importance. Ethics also increasingly relate to information technology. A central issue today revolves around the fact that rapid changes in business relationships, organizational structures, and financial systems pose unsurpassed difficulties in keeping accurate track of a company's financial position.

Another significant area of environmental change that is particularly relevant for businesses today involves new employment relationships. Knowledge workers are those who add value to an organization because of what they know. How well these employees are managed is seen as a major factor in determining which firms will be successful in the future. Outsourcing is the practice of hiring other firms to do work previously performed by the organization itself. It is an increasingly popular strategy because it helps firms focus on their core activities and avoid getting sidetracked onto secondary activities. However, it grows controversial when the jobs being outsourced are really being exported to foreign countries in ways that reduce domestic job opportunities. Contingent and temporary workers and the creation of a tiered workforce also pose special challenges. These challenges center around the treatment of various groups (such as contingent or lower-tier workers) compared to other groups (such as permanent or higher-tier employees).

DISCUSSION QUESTIONS

1. Identify ways in which the internationalization of business affects businesses in your community.
2. What would you imagine to be the major differences among working for a domestic firm inside the United States, working for a foreign company's operations inside the United States, and working for an American firm's operations abroad?
3. Why do organizations need to be interested in managing diversity? Is it a legal or moral obligation, or does it have some other purpose?
4. Summarize in your own words what the statistics tell us about the workforce of the future.
5. All things considered, do you think people from diverse cultures are more alike or more different? Explain the reasons for your answer.
6. What role does changing technology play in your daily activities?
7. How concerned are you regarding Internet security? Are your concerns increasing? Why or why not?

8. Do you think concerns regarding ethics will remain central in managerial thinking, or will these concerns eventually become less important? Why?

9. Do you anticipate becoming a "knowledge worker"? How do you think this will shape your own thinking regarding your employer, compensation, and so forth?

10. What are your personal opinions about the use of international outsourcing?

11. Does multiculturalism contribute to competitive advantage for an organization?

ORGANIZATIONAL BEHAVIOR CASE FOR DISCUSSION

LOST IN AEROSPACE

For seven years, two organizations had battled for a lucrative U.S. Air Force contract. One is the American firm Boeing, the world's largest aerospace company. The other is an American–European partnership between Northrop Grumman, the world's number-three defense contractor, and the European Aeronautic Defense and Space Company (EADS), parent of Airbus, Boeing's rival for the top spot in the commercial-aircraft market. At stake was (and, as of this writing, still is) a contract to replace 179 planes in the Air Force's aging fleet of jet tankers—planes that refuel other military aircraft in midair. In February 2008, the Pentagon stunned the industry by awarding the $35 billion contract—which could eventually be worth $100 billion over several decades—to the Northrop–EADS partnership, putting an abrupt end to Boeing's 50-year grip on the jet tanker franchise. The Pentagon not only rejected Boeing's argument that it would create more U.S. jobs, but bypassed congressional (U of C 8.67) sentiment in Boeing's favor.

How had this sudden reversal of Boeing's fortunes come about? Some observers believe that the respective ethics of the competing organizations—particularly those of Boeing—may have entered into the decision. Writing in *Ethics Newsline*, Rushworth M. Kidder suggested that the Air Force's decision was merely the latest episode in "the parable of Boeing as a morality play about the relationship of ethics and the bottom line." Kidder was hardly alone in his assessment, but to evaluate his judgment, we need to examine this so-called "morality play" a little more closely. Some background:

> *"I think the culture morphed in dysfunctional ways. There are elements of our culture that I think we all would like to change."*
> —BOEING CEO W. JAMES MCNERNEY JR.

- In 2001, a $20 billion deal between Boeing and the Air Force is aborted because of congressional investigation into ethical and legal violations at the aerospace company. ("Every time we turn over a rock," reports U.S. Senator John McCain, "something really unpleasant crawls out.")

- In 2003, two Boeing employees are indicted in a federal court for conspiring to steal trade secrets from archrival Lockheed Martin. The Air Force bars Boeing from bidding on certain systems for 20 months. Boeing also admits that it has possession of numerous Lockheed documents, upping its original estimate from a boxful to 30,000 pages.

- Later in the year, McCain's investigation reveals that Boeing's CFO and the Pentagon's number-two procurement officer had conspired to trade jobs for inflated jet tanker prices. Boeing's Michael Sears and the Pentagon's Darleen Druyun are fired, fined, and sent to prison, and Boeing CEO Philip Condit decides it's time to step down.

- In 2004, new CEO Harry Stonecipher states that "my No. 1 priority will be to restore our credibility with the huge customer called the U.S. government." He then makes all of Boeing's 155,000 employees sign a companywide code of conduct, assuring the media that the firm's problem "is not the culture; it's acts by individuals."

- In 2005, Stonecipher is forced to step down after initiating an affair with a female manager at the firm's executive retreat. The incident is memorialized in company lore as the "Palm Springs fling."

- Two months later, Boeing escapes criminal charges in the jet tanker and Lockheed investigations but is required to pay a fine of $615 million, the largest ever levied against a military contractor.

- In July 2005, 3M chief executive W. James McNerney Jr. becomes the first outsider to head Boeing since World War II. "We wanted a change agent," explains a board member, "someone who could communicate a commitment to ethics."

- At an executive retreat in January 2006, McNerney introduces chief legal officer Douglas Bain, who puts up a PowerPoint slide featuring the convict numbers of Sears and Druyun. "These are not Zip codes," says Bain, admonishing the assembled executives that federal prosecutors still regard Boeing as "rotten to the core." In March, McNerney tells an interviewer, "I think the culture morphed in dysfunctional ways. There are elements of our culture that I think we all would like to change."

- A year later, McNerney tells Boeing employees, "We'd rather have you not deliver what you've promised . . . than cut corners. [We] have to be willing to take a business hit if it's the right thing to do." He warns them that another episode of ethical malfeasance could kill the company's chances at the latest Air Force contract for jet tankers—along with all the jobs that the deal would keep secure. "You have to fight it every day," he reminds them, "whether you've had corruption or not. . . .The temptation to cut corners is always there."

Which brings us back again to February 2008, when McNerney gets the news that the Air Force has awarded the jet tanker contract to the Northrop–EADS partnership. "Did [its] prior ethics lapses lose Boeing the contract?" asks ethicist Kidder. "Better to say," he concludes, "that a slow drip of public uneasiness with Boeing's integrity made politicians and Pentagon officials just that much more open to alternatives."

The jury, however, is still out in the jet tanker case. In July 2008, Boeing persuaded the Pentagon to delay the award of the jet tanker contract by protesting that the military's competition had been unfair. The Government Accounting Office—which investigates the spending of federal tax dollars—agreed, and the Air Force opened a new competition for the contract in 2009. Who's the favorite? Many observers suggest that the likely outcome will be a split down the middle, with each company getting half the contract. "Given the amount of money and jobs at stake," opined the

New York Times in October 2009, "we fear neither side will ever accept a decision that lets the other win." In fact, both sides seem ready to accept a draw. One aerospace investment analyst has likened the potential compromise to "kindergarten sports day: everyone has to have a prize so they don't cry."

On a more sober note, the *Times* warned that, after "two bungled attempts . . . another unresolved competition is definitely not in the country's interest." The newspaper also reminded its readers that, in the midst of two wars and countless other military engagements around the globe, the U.S. military continues to refuel planes with tankers built in the 1950s.

CASE QUESTIONS

1. Is McNerney's approach to the company's ethical problems likely to improve ethical practices at Boeing? If your answer is yes, explain why. If it's no, propose some actions that would be effective.

2. In October 2010, Boeing announced a record charge of $1 billion related to delays in delivering its new 747-8 jet. As an investor with a good knowledge of the company's past record, to what extent do you attribute its performance problems to problems in its corporate governance?

3. Let's say that you're a member of Boeing's board of directors—and thus a representative of its shareholders. Boeing's stock price stood at $60 at the beginning of 2009 (down from a high of $105 a little more than year earlier). By October, it had dropped to just over $29, although it again topped $60 at the beginning of 2010. What's your current thinking about McNerney's performance as CEO?

REFERENCES

Leslie Wayne, "Pentagon Gives Boeing New Chance at Contract," *New York Times*, July 10, 2008, www.nytimes.com on January 29, 2010; Rushworth M. Kidder, "Boeing's $40 Billion Ethics Bill," *Ethics Newsline*, March 3, 2008, www.globalethics.org on January 29, 2010; "Two Former Boeing Managers Charged in Plot to Steal Trade Secrets from Lockheed Martin," U.S. Department of Justice, June 25, 2003, www.justice.gov on January 29, 2010; Stanley Holmes, "Cleaning Up Boeing," *BusinessWeek*, March 13, 2006, www.businessweek .com on January 29, 2010; Caroline Brothers, "Boeing and Airbus Prepare (Again) for Tanker Battle," *New York Times*, June 17, 2009, www.nytimes.com on January 29, 2010; Christopher Drew, "$35 Billion Tanker Contract Opens," *New York Times*, September 25, 2009, www.nytimes.com on January 29, 2010; "The Tanker Saga, Continued," *New York Times*, editorial, October 8, 2009, www.nytimes.com on January 29, 2010; Jon Talton, "Boeing's Troubles Reach to the Top," *Seattle Times*, October 6, 2009, http://seattletimes.nwsource .com on January 30, 2010.

EXPERIENCING ORGANIZATIONAL BEHAVIOR

Understanding Your Own Stereotypes about Others

Purpose   This exercise will help you better understand your own stereotypes and attitudes toward others.

Format   You will be asked to evaluate a situation and the assumptions you make in doing so. Then you will compare your results with those of the rest of the class.

Procedure

1. Read the following description of the situation to yourself, and decide who it is that is standing at your door and why you believe it to be that person. Make some notes that explain your rationale for eliminating the other possibilities and selecting the one that you did. Then answer the follow-up questions.
2. Working in small groups or with the class as a whole, discuss who might be standing at your door and why you believe it to be that person. Record the responses of your class members.
3. In class discussion, reflect on the stereotypes used to reach a decision and consider the following:
   a. How hard was it to let go of your original belief once you had formed it?
   b. What implications do first impressions of people have concerning how you treat them, what you expect of them, and your assessment of whether the acquaintance is likely to go beyond the initial stage?
   c. What are the implications of your responses to these questions concerning how you, as a manager, might treat a new employee? What will the impact be on that employee?
   d. What are the implications of your answers for yourself in terms of job hunting?

Situation   You have just checked into a hospital room for some minor surgery the next day. When you get to your room, you are told that the following people will

be coming to speak with you within the next several hours.

1. The surgeon who will do the operation
2. A nurse
3. The secretary for the department of surgery
4. A representative of the company that supplies televisions to the hospital rooms
5. A technician who does laboratory tests
6. A hospital business manager
7. The dietitian

[Note: You have never met any of these people before and do not know what to expect.]

About half an hour after your arrival, a woman who seems to be of Asian ancestry appears at your door dressed in a straight red wool skirt, a pink-and-white-striped polyester blouse with a bow at the neck, and red medium-high-heeled shoes that match the skirt. She is wearing gold earrings, a gold chain necklace, a gold wedding band, and a white hospital laboratory coat. She is carrying a clipboard.

Follow-up Questions

1. Of the seven people listed, which of them is standing at your door? How did you reach this conclusion?
2. If the woman had not been wearing a white hospital laboratory coat, how might your perceptions of her have differed? Why?
3. If you find out that she is the surgeon who will be operating on you in the morning, and you thought initially that she was someone else, how confident do you now feel in her ability as a surgeon? Why?
4. What implications can you draw from this exercise regarding the management of knowledge workers?

BUILDING MANAGERIAL SKILLS

Exercise Overview   Communications skills refer to your ability to convey ideas and information to other people. The task, of course, is easier when the person to whom you're communicating is familiar with the same language as you are; but in an increasingly diverse business environment, you won't always have the luxury of expressing yourself strictly on your own terms. This

exercise asks you to communicate information by carefully crafting the terms in which you express yourself.

Exercise Background   You're the owner of a store that sells unfinished furniture made of fine woods. Customers, both individual consumers and retailers, buy your furniture and finish the pieces themselves, usually with oil-based finishes. One of your best customers is the owner of a small furniture store catering to the members of a local ethnic community. She is not a native speaker of English. She has learned that waste rags used in the application of oil-based finishes have been known to explode—a phenomenon known as "spontaneous combustion"—and has become worried, both about the safety of her customers and about her own liability. You need to send her a letter reassuring her that the problem, while real, can be dealt with easily and safely. You also need to tell her what to tell her customers.

Exercise Task   Now do the following:

1. Review the following sampling of guidelines for "internationalizing" the English language. It's designed to help you write clear messages to nonnative speakers and to reduce the possibility of creating a misunderstanding between you and a person from a different culture. (You can also follow the same guidelines when communicating to another native speaker of English.)*

   - Use the most common words in the language (there are 3,000 to 4,000 to choose from).
   - Use only the most common meaning of words that have multiple meanings (the word "high" has 20 meanings, the word "expensive" only one).
   - Avoid sports terms ("ballpark figure") and words that require mental pictures ("red tape").
   - Use words only in the most common way (don't make verbs out of nouns, as in "*faxing* a letter").
   - Don't create or use new words; avoid slang.
   - Avoid two-word verbs (use "apply" instead of "put on").
   - Use more short, simple sentences than you normally would.
   - Avoid acronyms ("ASAP"), emoticons (:-o), and shorthand ("4" for "for").
   - Adopt a formal tone and use maximum punctuation for the greatest clarity.

2. Go online to locate a manufacturer of oil-based finishes. Find out what the maker of the product has to say about dealing with the problem of spontaneous combustion.
3. Write a letter to your nonnative-speaking customer. Explain the problem of spontaneous combustion, tell her what the manufacturer recommends, and sum up your own advice.

*List adapted from D.I. Riddle and Z.D. Lanham, "Internationalizing Written Business English: 20 Propositions for Native English Speakers," *Journal of Language for International Business*, vol. 1 (1984–1985), 1–11.

SELF-ASSESSMENT EXERCISE

Cross-Cultural Awareness

The following questions are intended to provide insights into your awareness of other cultures. Please indicate the best answers to the questions listed below. There is no passing or failing answer. Use the following scale, recording it in the space before each question.

1 = definitely no

2 = not likely

3 = not sure

4 = likely

5 = definitely yes

____ 1. I can effectively conduct business in a language other than my native language.

____ 2. I can read and write a language other than my native language with great ease.

____ 3. I understand the proper protocol for conducting a business card exchange in at least two countries other than my own.

____ 4. I understand the role of the *keiretsu* in Japan or the *chaebol* in Korea.

____ 5. I understand the differences in manager-subordinate relationships in two countries other than my own.

____ 6. I understand the differences in negotiation styles in at least two countries other than my own.

____ 7. I understand the proper protocols for gift giving in at least three countries.

____ 8. I understand how a country's characteristic preference for individualism versus collectivism can influence business practices.

____ 9. I understand the nature and importance of demographic diversity in at least three countries.

____ 10. I understand my own country's laws regarding giving gifts or favors while on international assignments.

____ 11. I understand how cultural factors influence the sales, marketing, and distribution systems of different countries.

____ 12. I understand how differences in male-female relationships influence business practices in at least three countries.

____ 13. I have studied and understand the history of a country other than my native country.

____ 14. I can identify the countries of the European Union without looking them up.

____ 15. I know which gestures to avoid using overseas because of their obscene meanings.

____ 16. I understand how the communication styles practiced in specific countries can influence business practices.

____ 17. I know in which countries I can use my first name with recent business acquaintances.

____ 18. I understand the culture and business trends in major countries in which my organization conducts business.

____ 19. I regularly receive and review news and information from and about overseas locations.

____ 20. I have access to and utilize a cultural informant before conducting business at an overseas location.

____ = Total Score

When you have finished, add up your score and compare it with those of others in your group. Discuss the areas of strength and weakness of the group members.

[Note: This brief instrument has not been scientifically validated and is to be used for classroom discussion purposes only.]

Reference: Neal R. Goodman, "Cross-Cultural Training for the Global Executive," in Richard W. Brislin and Tomoko Yoshida (eds.), *Improving Intercultural Interactions*, pp. 35–36, copyright © 1994 by Sage Publications, Inc. Reprinted by permission of Sage Publications, Inc.

PART 1
INTEGRATIVE RUNNING CASE

THE JOY OF QUEUING AND OTHER REASONS WHY NETFLIX WORKS

Back in 1997, Reed Hastings, a California entrepreneur between startup ventures, incurred a $40 late fee at Blockbuster for the movie *Apollo 13*. "It was six weeks late," he admits. "I had misplaced the cassette [and] I didn't want to tell my wife. . . . I was embarrassed about it . . .[but] I said to myself, 'I'm going to compromise the integrity of my marriage over a late fee?'" So the next day he dropped off the VHS cassette and paid his late fee on his way to the gym. In the middle of his work-out, he recalls, "I realized [the gym] had a much better business model. You could pay $30 or $40 a month and work out as little or as much as you wanted."

Thus was born the idea for Netflix, although Hastings's immediate inspiration—the idea of signing up customers on a subscription basis—wasn't actually part of his original business plan. When Netflix launched in April 1998, its only innovations involved the convenience of ordering movies over the Internet and receiving and returning them by mail: Netflix simply rented movies for $4 apiece plus $2 for postage (and, yes, it charged late fees). Basically, the customer base consisted of people who wanted to watch movies without having to get off the couch.

The rental-by-mail model, admits Hastings, "worked more like Blockbuster. Some people liked it, but it wasn't very popular"; and in 1999, CEO Hastings and cofounder Marc Randolph decided to test a subscription-based model—unlimited rentals by mail for a flat fee and, perhaps most importantly, no due dates (and thus no late fees). Current customers were first offered the opportunity to shift from their pay-per-rental plans to subscription plans on a free-trial basis and then given the chance to renew the subscription plan on a paid basis. "We knew it wouldn't be terrible," says Hastings, "but we didn't know if it would be great." In the first month, however, 80 percent of Netflix users who'd tried the no-cost subscription plan had renewed on a paid basis. Today, the same offer enjoys a renewal rate of 90 percent—and that's among a considerably larger customer base of more than 12 million.

"Having unlimited due dates and no late fees," says Hastings, "has worked in a powerful way and now seems obvious, but at that time, we had no idea if cus-tomers would even build and use an online queue." The "queue," as any Netflix user will tell you, is the list of movies that the customer wants to watch. Netflix maintains your queue, follows your online directions in keeping it up to date, and automatically sends you the next movie you want each time you send back one that you've already watched. "We call it the queue obsession," says Hastings, "and about a third of our customers have it. They visit their lists three or more times a week and look at them the way they look at their stocks. 'What's on the list?' 'What should I move around?' Honestly, I've heard of people who have more than 400 films on their queues. . . . The number-one request we get for enhancing the service," he adds, "is to find a way to protect the queue from a spouse changing it."

The queue, contends a writer for the *New York Times* who's also a dedicated Netflix customer, is "how Netflix gets you. I can't recall any previous service that allowed movie lovers to quantify their fixation with such detail." Another *Times* writer observes that the queue "inspires almost cult-like enthusiasm" among Netflix users, helping to give the company a "level of brand-name familiarity that most companies can only yearn for." For example, when the satirical newspaper the *Onion* ran a story under the headline "Boyfriend Not to Be Trusted with Netflix Queue," the editors didn't bother to identify Netflix or explain "Queue": They fully expected readers to get the reference and appreciate the issue simply by drawing on their store of pop-cultural knowledge.

In part, "queuing" movies to rent is so appealing because it's a little like shopping without spending any money—or, perhaps more accurately, it's like using a gift certificate (one that, admittedly, you've bought for yourself). The big difference, of course, is that your spending limit depends on the calendar rather than on your bank account. For a set fee—say, $8.99 a month (plus tax)—you can rent a movie, watch it at your leisure, and return it when you're ready. Once you've sent it back, you'll receive the next movie on your queue in about one business day, and (assuming that your monthly fee is paid up) you can repeat this process as often as you want throughout the month, always watching and returning movies at your own con-venience. (There was a time when you could hold on to as many as eight movies at once, but that policy has been replaced for reasons that we'll discuss in detail in Part IV of this case.)

The essence of queuing—and of the Netflix business model—is clearly convenience, and although the ability to enhance customer convenience, even when combined with cost savings, often gives a company a competitive advantage in its industry, it doesn't necessarily have the industry-wide effect that it's had in the case of Netflix. Marketing consultant Sally Aaron reminds us that Netflix has "revolutionized how people rent movies," and in so doing, she explains, its impact on the movie-rental industry has been that of a *disruptive innovation*: Not only did the Netflix subscriber model improve the service provided by the industry in an unexpected way, but ultimately it also weakened the competitive positions of companies already doing business in the industry. In 2002, for example, Blockbuster, which had dominated the move-rental business since the late 1980s, controlled about 40 percent of the market, with the competition consisting mainly of small independent and regional outfits. Netflix had gone public in May of that year, opening at $15 a share, but by October, after both Blockbuster and Wal-Mart had entered the field with their own rental-by-mail plans, its price had dropped to less than $5 a share. At the time, Netflix was saddled with accumulated deficits of $140 million and wasn't expected to show a profit for another year.

Now flash-forward to the period 2008–2010. For fiscal 2008, Blockbuster's revenues were $700 million less than they had been in 2003, while revenues at Netflix were more than $1 billion higher. A year later, Blockbuster reported losses of nearly $200 million for fiscal 2009; and its stock, which had been trading at $29 in 2002, was worth 40 cents a share. At the same time, Netflix reported an increase in profits of 22 percent (to $116 million) and a 40 percent increase in revenue (to $1.67 billion). Its shares were trading at $61. As of this writing, Blockbuster's market capitalization stands at $59.1 million, while Netflix is worth $6.08 billion. At this point, in other words, Netflix is worth more than 100 times what Blockbuster is worth.

How did this stunning reversal of fortunes come about? Not without some anxious moments at Netflix headquarters in Los Gatos, California. Head-to-head competition between Netflix and Blockbuster started in earnest in 2004, the same year that Blockbuster spun off from the entertainment giant Viacom. Granted, Blockbuster's profits were already being drained not only by Netflix but by sales of DVDs at mass-retail outlets: The rental chain had lost $1.6 billion in 2002 and another $1 billion in 2003, and it would lose yet another $1.2 billion in 2004. Blockbuster, however, had more than 7,000 stores throughout the United States

and an active customer base of 20 million (compared to Netflix's subscriber base of 2.1 million). It continued to regard online rentals as a niche market; and—besides an aggressive expansion into videogames—the brick-and-mortar giant announced a strategy designed to integrate online and in-store rentals. At the time, analysts thought it was a good idea. "Blockbuster," explained Sandy Brasher of Rice Voelker, a New Orleans-based research firm, "has the real estate. The average Joe who lives in Plano, Texas, and has a $50 DVD player from Wal-Mart is not going to spend $22 a month . . . at some subscription place." In the wake of Blockbuster's entry into the rental-by-mail market, Netflix stock plunged by 20 percent, to under $20, in just two days.

By October, Netflix shares were down by 68 percent from a high of $73 in January, and Hastings, anticipating the entry of Amazon into the market as well, announced that he was cutting the basic Netflix subscription fee from $21.99 to $17.99. Foreseeing a steep drop in the firm's income, eight of nine analysts who covered Netflix downgraded its stock on the same day. "It was like all our beliefs in the Netflix growth strategy were shattered," said Derek L. Brown of Pacific Growth Equities. Five years later, when asked to reveal the secrets of his success, Hastings was quick to include "Never underestimate the competition." In 2004, he explained, "we erroneously concluded that Blockbuster probably wasn't going to launch a competitive effort 'when they hadn't by 2003. Then, in 2004, they did. We thought, 'Well, they won't put much money behind it.' Over the past four years [2004 to 2009], they've invested more than $500 million against us."

It wasn't until December 2004, however, that Blockbuster came to the same realization that Reed Hastings had come to seven years earlier: "In no-late-fees test markets," said a company statement, "the increased rental transactions and retail sales offset the lower level of revenues resulting from eliminating late fees." Blockbuster thus replaced its late-fee policy with a plan, eventually known as Total Access, involving grace periods, automatic purchase payments, and restocking fees. The resulting loss in late-fee revenue cut profits by about 15 percent in 2005; and, although the company's financial performance showed signs of improvement in 2006, by 2007 it was becoming clear that Blockbuster's Total Access strategy was a classic example of too little, too late. In the first quarter of 2007, for example, Blockbuster gained market share on Netflix by signing up 800,000 new subscribers and bringing its total user base to nearly 3 million. In the process, however, it lost $46 million on revenue of about $1.5 billion—substantially more than in the first quarter of 2006, when it had lost only $2 million on comparable revenue. And Netflix still had nearly 7 million subscribers.

Blockbuster was learning the truth of something that had been observed a few years before by Mike Schuh of Foundation Capital, an early Netflix supporter: "The barriers to entry in this market," said Schuh back in 2002, "are low, but the barriers to profitability are extremely high." To stop the bleeding, Blockbuster had actually resorted to tactics for *discouraging* unprofitable subscribers (and thus managed to show a profit in the last two quarters of 2008)—but like the introduction of Total Access, its retooling seems to have amounted to too little, too late: In March 2010, after losses of $435 million in the fourth quarter of 2009, the company warned that it might have to declare bankruptcy. Shares fell to 28 cents, their value as of this writing.

And Netflix? Netflix continues to grow, and in much the same way as it always has—"virally," according to Motley Fool's Rick Munarriz. "Word of mouth. Office water-cooler envy." It also continues to spend heavily on marketing, especially on the Internet and especially when it comes to new customers ("Like a pro bono law firm," quips Munarriz, "Netflix lives for free trials"). In the fourth quarter of 2009—the same period in which Blockbuster suffered losses of $435 million—Netflix reported profits of $31 million, up 36 percent over the fourth quarter of 2008. At $445 million, revenues were up by 24 percent. Perhaps most amazing, however, was the surge in the number of subscribers: Over the three-month period at the end of 2009, Netflix added 1.1 million subscribers—a 10 percent bump in its total user base, which had climbed to 12.3 million. (It took Netflix four years—from 1999 to 2003—to sign up its first million subscribers.) The company expected to have more than 16 million users by the end of fiscal 2010, for which it forecast revenues of over $2 billion.

> *"Having unlimited due dates and no late fees has worked in a powerful way and now seems obvious, but at that time, we had no idea if customers would even build and use an online queue."*
>
> —REED HASTINGS, COFOUNDER AND CEO OF NETFLIX

Case Questions

1. In general, how in your opinion did Netflix manage to put itself in the enviable position that it occupied at the outset of fiscal 2010? More specifically, how would you account for the sudden—and very big—bounce in subscriptions that Netflix enjoyed during the fourth quarter of 2009? (*Hint for second question*: Check the Netflix website.)

2. Use the *situational perspective* on organizational behavior to describe the growth strategies developed by Netflix and the competitive strategies adopted by both Netflix and Blockbuster. Explain how these competitive strategies have contributed to *organization-level outcomes* at each company.

3. An organization's *environment* includes all the elements that lie outside its own boundaries—everything from human beings to economic phenomena. What can *psychology* tell us about the environment in which Netflix competes? What can *sociology* tell us? How about *anthropology*?

4. Discuss the role of *technology* both in the nature of the service that Netflix provides and in the environment in which it competes. Feel free to expand by drawing on any personal knowledge you may have of the movie-rental business and movie-rental plans.

5. *Take the consumer challenge.* You currently subscribe to Netflix, which allows you to rent 3 movies per week by mail; you can keep out 1 movie at a time, and the monthly charge is $16.99. Blockbuster now makes you the following offer: You can rent 3 movies per week by mail, plus you can take out 5 movies per month from any Blockbuster store; you can keep out 1 movie at a time, and the monthly charge is $19.99. Assuming that you can afford either plan, which is the better plan *from a strictly financial point of view*? Which is the better plan *for you*? (*Hint:* You'll have to do some math, but that's often the case for cost-conscious consumers.)

References

"How Netflix Got Started," *CNNMoney.com*, January 28, 2009, http://money.cnn.com on June 16, 2010; Amy Zipkin, "Out of Africa, Onto the Web," *New York Times*, December 17, 2006, www.nytimes.com on June 16, 2010; Laurie J. Flynn, "One Man's Two Challenges," *New York Times*, June 3, 2003, www.nytimes.com on June 16, 2010; Peter Wayner, "DVD's Have Found an Unexpected Route to a Wide Public: Snail Mail," *New York Times*, September 23, 2002, www.nytimes.com on June 16, 2010; Reed Hastings, "How I Did It: Reed Hastings, Netflix," *Inc.com*, December 1, 2005, www.inc.com on June 16, 2010; Sally Aaron, "Netflix Script Spells Disruption," *Harvard Business School Working Knowledge*, March 22, 2004, http://hbswk.hbs.edu on June 16, 2010; Craig Tomashoff, "You Are What You Queue," *New York Times*, March 2, 2003, www.nytimes.com on June 16, 2010; Gary Rivlin, "Does the Kid Stay in the Picture?" *New York Times*, February 22, 2005, www.nytimes.com on June 16, 2010; Geraldine Fabrikant, "Showdown Begins in Movie-Rental Business: Blockbuster Tries a Remake," *New York Times*, July 26, 2004, www.nytimes.com on June 16, 2010; Greg Sandoval, "Netflix Has Blockbuster on the Ropes," *CNET News*,

February 9, 2010, http://news.cnet.com on June 22, 2010; "Blockbuster Sales Fall on Chapter 11 Warning," *New York Times*, February 17, 2010, www.nytimes.com on June 16, 2010; "Blockbuster Drops Late Fees," *CNNMoney.com*, December 14, 2004, http://money.cnn.com on June 23, 2010; Carneades, "Blockbuster Could Collapse in 2010," *Seeking Alpha*, September 8, 2009, http://seekingalpha.com on June 22, 2009; Rick Aristotle Munarriz, "Netflix: A Blockbuster?" *The Motley Fool*, October 14, 2002, http://www.fool.com on June 22, 2010; Lance Whitney, "1.1 Million New Subscribers Boost Netflix Earnings," *CNET News*, January 28, 2010, http://news.cnet.com on June 25, 2010; "The Lowdown on Blockbuster Total Access Plan Changes," *Knowzy*, February 24, 2009, www.knowzy.com on June 24, 2010.

FOUNDATIONS OF INDIVIDUAL BEHAVIOR

CHAPTER LEARNING OBJECTIVES

After studying this chapter you should be able to:

- Explain the nature of the individual–organization relationship.

- Define personality and describe personality attributes that affect behavior in organizations.

- Discuss individual attitudes in organizations and how they affect behavior.

- Describe basic perceptual processes and the role of attributions in organizations.

- Explain how workplace behaviors can directly or indirectly influence organizational effectiveness.

The Creepy Genius

"[Steve Jobs] has a great ability to get others excited about fulfilling a vision. This has more to do with Apple's success than yelling and screaming."

—LEANDER KAHNEY, AUTHOR OF *INSIDE STEVE'S BRAIN*

Apple CEO Steve Jobs is a personality with an interesting personality. He's the public face of an extremely successful company who some people see as an inspiring visionary and others as "one of Silicon Valley's leading egomaniacs" (in the words of *Newsweek*). The bottom line is that his complex and often contradictory

AP PHOTO/PAUL SAKUMA

Steve Jobs is one of the most successful entrepreneurs in history. His complex personality has attracted many devoted followers but also alienated others.

personality is clearly a factor in the remarkable success of a business venture notable for high-tech breakthroughs and marketing savvy. Here's a little background:

In 1976, 21-year-old Jobs and an ex-electronics hacker named Steve Wozniak started Apple Computer to commercialize a personal computer designed by Wozniak. A mere four years later, the company's initial public offering had made millionaires of Jobs, Wozniak, and a lot of other people. As CEO, Jobs marshaled his idealistic vision and high standards to push the company on to further success, but as rapid expansion put more pressure on his managerial skills, the company hired an experienced executive, PepsiCo CEO John Sculley, to take over in 1983. Jobs continued to oversee the development of a new computer called the Macintosh, but he clashed continually with Sculley until the Apple board forced him to resign in 1985. In that same year Jobs launched NeXT Computer to market a technologically advanced workstation. The venture wasn't entirely successful, but 10 years later, when Apple purchased the company, Jobs came along with it. In 1997, after several years of strategic miscalculations, product flops, and declining market share and stock prices, the board removed Sculley's successor, Gilbert F. Amelio, and named Jobs "interim CEO" (or "iCEO," as Jobs put it).

In his second go-round at Apple, Jobs focused on marketing and rejuvenating the company's image, while also giving personal attention to its new-product pipeline. One result of his efforts was a desktop computer called the iMac, which Forbes declared an "industry-altering success." More innovative new products followed during the course of the decade, including the iPhone, MacBook, and iPod, and Jobs's company was once more a juggernaut in the high-tech industry. Apple, he declared, "leads when it expresses its vision through its products, exciting you and making you proud to own a Mac. . . . The same focus and passion that brings these products to market has also made us a healthier company." Jobs may be (as his critics claim) an erratic self-absorbed control freak with unrealistically high standards and a bad temper, but since his return to the top spot, the value of Apple's shares has gone up more than 38-fold. (By comparison, Microsoft shares have only doubled in value over the same stretch of time.)

Because of Apple's success, Steve Jobs is a well-researched personality—there are nearly 30 books about him out there, plus countless articles—and journalists, tech-industry specialists, and psychologists continue to probe Jobs's brain. Daniel Okrent, a former editor at the *New York Times* and Time Inc., divides the media perception of Jobs according to the three stages of his career:

Jobs as Genius. Books and articles on the first stage, from the early 1980s to the 1990s, says Okrent, may "skate lightly over Jobs the professional bully, sticking instead to the man's business skills." They regard his "manic attention to detail" as a strength and applaud his "unshakable conviction that customer research stifles innovation." When advised, for example, that people wouldn't want an all-in-one computer like the iMac that he envisioned, Jobs replied, "I know what I want, and I know what they want." Proponents of the Jobs-the-Genius image argue that such arrogance goes hand in hand with solid business sense, and the market, they say, has proved Jobs right over and over again.

Jobs as Creep. According to Okrent, books and articles on this stage, which focus on Apple's sinking fortunes and Jobs's ouster in the 1990s, tend to "concentrate heavily on his perceived personality flaws." One book, for instance, cites his unwillingness to listen to customers as a major factor in his downfall. It's interesting to note, however, that at the time of Jobs's firing, insiders harbored a more balanced perspective on the split in his personality: "People in the company had very mixed feelings about it," admits chief scientist Larry Tesler. "Everyone had been terrorized by Steve Jobs at some point or another, and so there was a certain relief that the terrorist would be gone. On the other hand, I think there was incredible respect for Steve Jobs by the very same people, and we were all very worried what would happen to this company without the visionary, without the founder, without the charisma."

Jobs as Creepy Genius. As we've seen, such ominous foreboding was well grounded, and Okrent observes that material devoted to this stage of Jobs's career centers squarely on the extraordinary turnaround that he engineered when he returned to the struggling company. Not surprisingly, for example, assessments of Jobs's antipathy to consumer research have come full circle: "Perhaps no other company," writes Leander Kahney, author of *Inside Steve's Brain*, "has been as good at giving customers what they want before they know they want it."

Apple's remarkable recovery has hinged on a steady-stream of new-product introductions, and much of its success in marketing these new products has been a function of its ability to project a certain mystique and generate buzz—a strategy to which Jobs himself has been crucial. "He's really the face of the company," explains Kendall Whitehouse of the University of Pennsylvania's Wharton School of business. "When you speak to Apple employees, there's always a lot of talk about Steve and what Steve wants. It's palpable.... Jobs [has been] the centerpiece for refocusing the company and brand." Jobs, adds Kahney, "has a great ability to get others excited about fulfilling a vision. This has more to do with Apple's success than yelling and screaming."

What Do You Think?

1. Why do you think Steve Jobs has been so successful?

2. Would you want to work for someone like Steve Jobs? Why or why not?

References: Daniel Okrent, "The Books of Jobs," CNNMoney.com, November 5, 2009, http://money.cnn.com on February 1, 2010; Leander Kahney, *Inside Steve's Brain, Expanded Edition* (New York: Portfolio, 2008); Dan Schwabel, "Steve Jobs' Personal Brand Is Finally Revealed," Personal Branding Blog, June 2, 2008, http://personalbrandingblog.wordpress.com on February 1, 2010; Leander Kahney, "Leander Kahney vs. Fake Steve Jobs," *Wired*, March 18, 2008, www.wired.com on February 2, 2010; Michael Maccoby, "Steve Jobs Is Not Dull: Why Context Matters in CEO Success," *Washington Post*, May 22, 2009, http://views.washingtonpost.com on February 1, 2010.

Think about human behavior as a jigsaw puzzle. Puzzles consist of various pieces that fit together in precise ways. And of course, no two puzzles are exactly alike. They have different numbers of pieces, the pieces are of different sizes and shapes, and they fit together in different ways. The same can be said of human behavior and its determinants. Each of us is a whole picture, like a fully assembled jigsaw puzzle, but the puzzle pieces that define us and the way those pieces fit together are unique. Steve Jobs, for instance, is different from every other person. Similarly, every person in an organization is fundamentally different from everyone else. To be successful, managers must recognize that these differences exist and attempt to understand them.

Psychological contracts play an important role in the relationship between an organization and its employees. As long as both parties agree that the contributions provided by an employee and the inducements provided by the organization are balanced, both parties are satisfied and will likely maintain their relationship. But if a serious imbalance occurs, one or both parties may attempt to change the relationship. As illustrated here, for example, an employee who feels sufficiently dissatisfied may even resort to using company assets for his or her own personal gain.
Dilbert: © Scott Adams/Distributed by United Feature Syndicate

In this chapter we explore some of the key characteristics that differentiate people from one another in organizations. We first investigate the psychological nature of individuals in organizations. We then look at elements of people's personalities that can influence behavior and consider individual attitudes and their role in organizations. Next, we examine the role of perception in organizations. We close this chapter with an examination of various kinds of workplace behaviors that affect organizational performance.

PEOPLE IN ORGANIZATIONS

As a starting point for understanding the behavior of people in organizations, we first examine the basic nature of the individual–organization relationship. Understanding this relationship helps us appreciate the nature of individual differences. That is, these differences play a critical role in determining various important workplace behaviors of special relevance to managers.

Psychological Contracts

Whenever we buy a car or sell a house, both buyer and seller sign a contract that specifies the terms of the agreement—who pays what to whom, when it's paid, and so forth. A psychological contract resembles a standard legal contract in some ways, but is less formal and less well defined. Specifically, a **psychological contract** is a person's overall set of expectations regarding what he or she will contribute to the organization and what the organization will provide in return.[1] Thus, unlike any other kind of business contract, a psychological contract is not written on paper, nor are all of its terms explicitly negotiated.

Figure 3.1 illustrates the essential nature of a psychological contract. The individual makes a variety of **contributions** to the organization—such things as effort, skills, ability, time, and loyalty. Jill Henderson, a branch manager for Merrill Lynch, uses her knowledge of financial markets and investment opportunities to help her clients

A **psychological contract** is a person's set of expectations regarding what he or she will contribute to the organization and what the organization, in return, will provide to the individual.

An individual's **contributions** to an organization include such things as effort, skills, ability, time, and loyalty.

make profitable investments. Her MBA in finance, coupled with hard work and motivation, have allowed her to become one of the firm's most promising young managers. The firm believed she had these attributes when it hired her, of course, and expected that she would do well.

In return for these contributions, the organization provides **inducements** to the individual. Some inducements, such as pay and career opportunities, are tangible rewards. Others, such as job security and status, are more intangible. Jill Henderson started at Merrill Lynch at a very competitive salary and has received an attractive salary increase each of the six years she has been with the firm. She has also been promoted twice and expects another promotion—perhaps to a larger office—in the near future.

In this instance, both Jill Henderson and Merrill Lynch apparently perceive that the psychological contract is fair and equitable. Both will be satisfied with the relationship and will do what they can to continue it. Henderson is likely to continue to work hard and effectively, and Merrill Lynch is likely to continue to increase her salary and give her promotions. In other situations, however, things might not work out as well. If either party sees an inequity in the contract, that party may initiate a change. The employee might ask for a pay raise or promotion, put forth less effort, or look for a better job elsewhere. The organization can also initiate change by training the worker to improve his skills, by transferring him to another job, or by firing him.

All organizations face the basic challenge of managing psychological contracts. They want value from their employees, and they need to give employees the right inducements. For instance, underpaid employees may perform poorly or leave for better jobs elsewhere. Similarly, an employee may even occasionally start to steal organizational resources as a way to balance the psychological contract. Overpaying employees who contribute little to the organization, though, incurs unnecessary costs.

Recent trends in downsizing and cutbacks have complicated the process of managing psychological contracts, especially during the recession of 2008–10. For example, many organizations used to offer at least reasonable assurances of job permanence as a fundamental inducement to employees. Now, however, job permanence is less likely, so alternative inducements may be needed.[2] Among the new forms of inducements that some companies are providing are such incentives as additional training opportunities and increased flexibility in working schedules.

Increased globalization of business also complicates the management of psychological contracts. For example, the array of inducements that employees deem to be of value varies across cultures. U.S. workers tend to value individual rewards and recognition, but Japanese workers are more likely to value group-based rewards and recognition. Workers in Mexico and Germany highly value leisure time and may thus prefer more time off from work, whereas workers in China may place a lower premium on time off. The Lionel Train Company, maker of toy electric trains, once moved its operations to Mexico to capitalize on cheaper labor. The firm encountered problems, however, when it could not hire enough motivated employees to maintain quality standards and ended up making a costly move back to the United States.

A related problem faced by international businesses is the management of psychological contracts for expatriate managers. In some ways, this process is more like

Figure 3.1 THE PSYCHOLOGICAL CONTRACT

Psychological contracts govern the basic relationship between people and organizations. Individuals contribute such things as effort and loyalty. Organizations, in turn, offer such inducements as pay and job security.

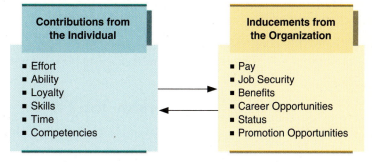

Organizations provide **inducements** to individuals in the form of tangible and intangible rewards.

a formal contract than are other employment relationships. Managers selected for a foreign assignment, for instance, are usually given some estimate of the duration of the assignment and receive various adjustments in their compensation package, including cost-of-living adjustments, education subsidies for children, reimbursement of personal travel expenses, and so forth. When the assignment is over, the manager must then be integrated back into the domestic organization. During the time of the assignment, however, the organization itself may have changed in many ways—new managers, new coworkers, new procedures, new business practices, and so forth. Thus, returning managers may very well come back to an organization that is quite different from the one they left and to a job quite different from what they expected.[3]

The Person-Job Fit

One specific aspect of managing psychological contracts is management of the **person-job fit.** A good person-job fit is one in which the employee's contributions match the inducements the organization offers. In theory, each employee has a specific set of needs to be fulfilled and a set of job-related behaviors and abilities to contribute. If the organization can take perfect advantage of those behaviors and abilities and exactly fulfill the employee's needs, it will have achieved a perfect person-job fit.

Of course, such a precise person-job fit is seldom achieved. For one thing, hiring procedures are imperfect. Managers can estimate employee skill levels when making hiring decisions and can improve them through training, but even simple performance dimensions are hard to measure objectively and validly. For another thing, both people and organizations change. An employee who finds a new job stimulating and exciting to begin with may find the same job boring and monotonous a few years later. An organization that adopts new technology needs new skills from its employees. Finally, each person is unique. Measuring skills and performance is difficult enough. Assessing attitudes and personality is far more complex. Each of these individual differences makes matching individuals with jobs a difficult and complex process.[4]

Individual Differences

As already noted, every individual is unique. **Individual differences** are personal attributes that vary from one person to another. Individual differences may be physical, psychological, and emotional. The individual differences that characterize a specific person make that person unique. As we see in the sections that follow, basic categories of individual differences include personality, attitudes, perception, and creativity. First, however, we need to note the importance of the situation in assessing the individual's behavior.

Are the specific differences that characterize a given person good or bad? Do they contribute to or detract from performance? The answer, of course, is that it depends on the circumstances. One person may be dissatisfied, withdrawn, and negative in one job setting but satisfied, outgoing, and positive in another. Working conditions, coworkers, and leadership are just a few of the factors that affect how a person performs and feels about a job. Thus, whenever a manager attempts to assess or account for individual differences among her employees, she must also be sure to consider the situation in which behavior occurs.

Since managers need to establish effective psychological contracts with their employees and achieve optimal fits between people and jobs, they face a major challenge in attempting to understand both individual differences and contributions in relation to inducements and contexts. A good starting point in developing this understanding is to appreciate the role of personality in organizations.

Person-job fit is the extent to which the contributions made by the individual match the inducements offered by the organization.

Individual differences are personal attributes that vary from one person to another.

PERSONALITY AND ORGANIZATIONS

Personality is the relatively stable set of psychological attributes that distinguish one person from another. A longstanding debate among psychologists—often expressed as "nature versus nurture"—concerns the extent to which personality attributes are inherited from our parents (the "nature" argument) or shaped by our environment (the "nurture" argument). In reality, both biological and environmental factors play important roles in determining our personalities.[5] Although the details of this debate are beyond the scope of our discussion here, managers should strive to understand basic personality attributes and how they can affect people's behavior in organizational situations, not to mention their perceptions of and attitudes toward the organization.

The "Big Five" Personality Traits

Psychologists have identified literally thousands of personality traits and dimensions that differentiate one person from another. But in recent years, researchers have identified five fundamental personality traits that are especially relevant to organizations.[6] These traits, illustrated in Figure 3.2, are now commonly called the **"big five" personality traits**.

Agreeableness refers to a person's ability to get along with others. Agreeableness causes some people to be gentle, cooperative, forgiving, understanding, and good-natured in their dealings with others. But lack of it results in others being irritable, short-tempered, uncooperative, and generally antagonistic toward other people. Researchers have not yet fully investigated the effects of agreeableness, but it seems likely that highly agreeable people are better at developing good working relationships with coworkers, subordinates, and higher-level managers, whereas less agreeable people are not likely to have particularly good working relationships. The same pattern might extend to relationships with customers, suppliers, and other key organizational constituents.

Conscientiousness refers to the number of goals on which a person focuses. People who focus on relatively few goals at one time are likely to be organized, systematic, careful, thorough, responsible, and self-disciplined; they tend to focus on a small number of goals at one time. Others, however, tend to pursue a wider array of goals, and, as a result, tend to be more disorganized, careless, and irresponsible, as well as less thorough and self-disciplined. Research has found that more conscientious people tend to be higher performers than less conscientious people in a variety of different jobs. This pattern seems logical, of course, since conscientious people take

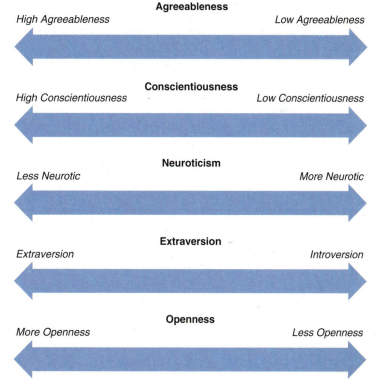

Figure 3.2   **THE "BIG FIVE" PERSONALITY FRAMEWORK**

The "big five" personality framework is currently very popular among researchers and managers. These five dimensions represent fundamental personality traits presumed to be important in determining the behaviors of individuals in organizations. In general, experts agree that personality traits closer to the left end of each dimension are more positive in organizational settings whereas traits closer to the right are less positive.

Agreeableness
High Agreeableness — Low Agreeableness

Conscientiousness
High Conscientiousness — Low Conscientiousness

Neuroticism
Less Neurotic — More Neurotic

Extraversion
Extraversion — Introversion

Openness
More Openness — Less Openness

The **personality** is the relatively stable set of psychological attributes that distinguish one person from another.

The **"big five" personality traits** are a set of fundamental traits that are especially relevant to organizations.

Agreeableness is the ability to get along with others.

Conscientiousness refers to the number of goals on which a person focuses.

TETRA IMAGES/PHOTOLIBRARY

Personality traits can play an important role in the kinds of jobs a person gravitates to. For instance, an individual who is an extrovert may be attracted to a job that is based on personal relationships and that involves frequent interactions with other people. This salesperson, for example, seems to be genuinely enjoying his interactions with his customer.

their jobs seriously and approach their jobs in a highly responsible fashion.

The third of the "big five" personality dimensions is **neuroticism**. People who are relatively more neurotic tend to experience unpleasant emotions such as anger, anxiety, depression, and feelings of vulnerability more often than do people who are relatively less neurotic. People who are less neurotic are relatively poised, calm, resilient, and secure; people who are relatively more neurotic are more excitable, insecure, reactive, and subject to extreme mood swings. People with less neuroticism might be expected to better handle job stress, pressure, and tension. Their stability might also lead them to be seen as being more reliable than their less-stable counterparts.

Extraversion reflects a person's comfort level with relationships. Extroverts are sociable, talkative, assertive, and open to establishing new relationships. Introverts are much less sociable, talkative, and assertive, and more reluctant to begin new relationships. Research suggests that extroverts tend to be higher overall job performers than introverts, and that they are more likely to be attracted to jobs based on personal relationships, such as sales and marketing positions.

Finally, **openness** reflects a person's rigidity of beliefs and range of interests. People with high levels of openness are willing to listen to new ideas and to change their own ideas, beliefs, and attitudes in response to new information. They also tend to have broad interests and to be curious, imaginative, and creative. On the other hand, people with low levels of openness tend to be less receptive to new ideas and less willing to change their minds. Further, they tend to have fewer and narrower interests and to be less curious and creative. People with more openness might be expected to be better performers due to their flexibility and the likelihood that they will be better accepted by others in the organization. Openness may also encompass a person's willingness to accept change; people with high levels of openness may be more receptive to change, whereas people with little openness may resist change.

The "big five" framework continues to attract the attention of both researchers and managers. The potential value of this framework is that it encompasses an integrated set of traits that appear to be valid predictors of certain behaviors in certain situations. Thus, managers who can both understand the framework and assess these traits in their employees are in a good position to understand how and why they behave as they do. On the other hand, managers must be careful to not overestimate their ability to assess the "big five" traits in others. Even assessment using the most rigorous and valid measures is likely to be somewhat imprecise. Another limitation of the "big five" framework is that it is primarily based on research conducted in the United States. Thus, its generalizability to other cultures presents unanswered questions. Even within the United States a variety of other factors and traits are also likely to affect behavior in organizations.

Neuroticism is characterized a person's tendency to experience unpleasant emotions such as anger, anxiety, depression, and feelings of vulnerability.

Extraversion is the quality of being comfortable with relationships; the opposite extreme, introversion, is characterized by more social discomfort.

Openness is the capacity to entertain new ideas and to change as a result of new information.

The Myers-Briggs Framework

Another interesting approach to understanding personalities in organizations is the Myers-Briggs framework. This framework, based on the classical work of Carl Jung, differentiates people in terms of four general dimensions: sensing, intuiting, judging, and perceiving. Higher and lower positions in each of the dimensions are used to classify people into one of sixteen different personality categories.

The Myers-Briggs Type Indicator (MBTI) is a popular questionnaire some organizations use to assess personality types. Indeed, it is among the most popular selection instruments used today, with as many as 2 million people taking it each year. Research suggests that the MBTI is a useful method for determining communication styles and interaction preferences. In terms of personality attributes, however, questions exist about both the validity and the stability of the MBTI.

Emotional Intelligence [10]

The concept of emotional intelligence has been identified in recent years and provides some interesting insights into personality. **Emotional intelligence**, or **EQ**, refers to the extent to which people are self-aware, can manage their emotions, can motivate themselves, express empathy for others, and possess social skills.[7] (EQ is used to parallel the traditional term IQ, which of course stands for "intelligence quotient.") These various dimensions can be described as follows:

- *Self-awareness* This is the basis for the other components. It refers to a person's capacity for being aware of how they are feeling. In general, more self-awareness allows a person to more effectively guide their own lives and behaviors.

- *Managing Emotions* This refers to a person's capacities to balance anxiety, fear, and anger so that they do not overly interfere with getting things accomplished.

- *Motivating Oneself* This dimension refers to a person's ability to remain optimistic and to continue striving in the face of setbacks, barriers, and failure.

- *Empathy* Empathy refers to a person's ability to understand how others are feeling even without being explicitly told.

- *Social Skill* This refers to a person's ability to get along with others and to establish positive relationships.

Preliminary research suggests that people with high EQs may perform better than others, especially in jobs that require a high degree of interpersonal interaction and that involve influencing or directing the work of others. Moreover, EQ appears to be something that isn't biologically based but instead can be developed.[8]

Other Personality Traits at Work

Besides these complex models of personality, several other specific personality traits are also likely to influence behavior in organizations. Among the most important are locus of control, self-efficacy, authoritarianism, Machiavellianism, self-esteem, and risk propensity.

Locus of control is the extent to which people believe that their behavior has a real effect on what happens to them.[9] Some people, for example, believe that if they work hard they will succeed. They may also believe that people who fail do so because they lack ability or motivation. People who believe that individuals are in control of their lives are said to have an internal locus of control. Other people think that fate, chance, luck, or other people's behavior determines what happens to them.

Emotional intelligence or **(EQ)** is the extent to which people are self-aware, can manage their emotions, can motivate themselves, express empathy for others, and possess social skills.

A person's **locus of control** is the extent to which he believes his circumstances are a function of either his own actions or of external factors beyond his control.

For example, an employee who fails to get a promotion may attribute that failure to a politically motivated boss or just bad luck, rather than to her or his own lack of skills or poor performance record. People who think that forces beyond their control dictate what happens to them are said to have an external locus of control.

Self-efficacy is a related but subtly different personality characteristic. A person's self-efficacy is that person's belief about his or her capabilities to perform a task. People with high self-efficacy believe that they can perform well on a specific task, but people with low self-efficacy tend to doubt their ability to perform a specific task. Self-assessments of ability contribute to self-efficacy, but so does the individual's personality. Some people simply have more self-confidence than others. This belief in their ability to perform a task effectively results in their being more self-assured and better able to focus their attention on performance.[10]

Another important personality characteristic is **authoritarianism**, the extent to which a person believes that power and status differences are appropriate within hierarchical social systems such as organizations.[11] For example, a person who is highly authoritarian may accept directives or orders from someone with more authority purely because the other person is "the boss." On the other hand, a person who is not highly authoritarian, although she or he may still carry out reasonable directives from the boss, is more likely to question things, express disagreement with the boss, and even refuse to carry out orders if they are for some reason objectionable.

A highly authoritarian manager may be relatively autocratic and demanding, and highly authoritarian subordinates are more likely to accept this behavior from their leader. On the other hand, a less authoritarian manager may allow subordinates a bigger role in making decisions, and less authoritarian subordinates might respond more positively to this behavior.

Machiavellianism is another important personality trait. This concept is named after Niccolo Machiavelli, a sixteenth-century author. In his book *The Prince*, Machiavelli explained how the nobility could more easily gain and use power. The term "Machiavellianism" is now used to describe behavior directed at gaining power and controlling the behavior of others. Research suggests that the degree of Machiavellianism varies from person to person. More Machiavellian individuals tend to be rational and nonemotional, may be willing to lie to attain their personal goals, put little emphasis on loyalty and friendship, and enjoy manipulating others' behavior. Less Machiavellian individuals are more emotional, less willing to lie to succeed, value loyalty and friendship highly, and get little personal pleasure from manipulating others. By all accounts, Dennis Kozlowski, the indicted former CEO of Tyco International, had a high degree of Machiavellianism. He apparently came to believe that his position of power in the company gave him the right to do just about anything he wanted with company resources.[12]

Self-esteem is the extent to which a person believes that he or she is a worthwhile and deserving individual. A person with high self-esteem is more likely to seek higher-status jobs, be more confident in his or her ability to achieve higher levels of performance, and derive greater intrinsic satisfaction from his or her accomplishments. In contrast, a person with less self-esteem may be more content to remain in a lower-level job, be less confident of his or her ability, and focus more on extrinsic rewards (extrinsic rewards are tangible and observable rewards like a paycheck, job promotion, and so forth). Among the major personality dimensions, self-esteem is the one that has been most widely studied in other countries. Although more research is clearly needed, the published evidence suggests that self-esteem as a personality trait does indeed exist in a variety of countries and that its role in organizations is reasonably important across different cultures.

A person's **self-efficacy** is that person's beliefs about his or her capabilities to perform a task.

Authoritarianism is the belief that power and status differences are appropriate within hierarchical social systems such as organizations.

People who possess the personality trait of **Machiavellianism** behave to gain power and control the behavior of others.

A person's **self-esteem** is the extent to which that person believes he or she is a worthwhile and deserving individual.

Risk propensity is the degree to which a person is willing to take chances and make risky decisions. A manager with a high risk propensity, for example, might experiment with new ideas and gamble on new products. Such a manager might also lead the organization in new and different directions. This manager might be a catalyst for innovation, or on the other hand, might jeopardize the continued well-being of the organization if the risky decisions prove to be bad ones. A manager with low risk propensity might lead an organization to stagnation and excessive conservatism, or might help the organization successfully weather turbulent and unpredictable times by maintaining stability and calm. Thus, the potential consequences of a manager's risk propensity depend heavily on the organization's environment.

RICHARD LEVINE/ALAMY

Risk propensity refers to a person's willingness to take chances and make risky decisions. Senior executives at Apple have fostered a culture that encourages risk and rewards; this culture, in turn, attracts people with a high degree of risk propensity. This customer is leaving the Apple store in Manhattan after buying her new iPad, one of the riskiest new products launched in the last few years. But the product was an immediate success, further reinforcing the risk-oriented culture at Apple.

ATTITUDES IN ORGANIZATIONS

People's attitudes also affect their behavior in organizations. **Attitudes** are complexes of beliefs and feelings that people have about specific ideas, situations, or other people. Attitudes are important because they are the mechanism through which most people express their feelings. An employee's statement that he feels underpaid by the organization reflects his feelings about his pay. Similarly, when a manager says that she likes the new advertising campaign, she is expressing her feelings about the organization's marketing efforts.

The *Technology* box on page 72 shows how one restaurant chain in Boston has used automated systems to complement traditional means of training personnel in the art of superior customer service.

How Attitudes Are Formed

Attitudes are formed by a variety of forces, including our personal values, our experiences, and our personalities. For example, if we value honesty and integrity, we may form especially favorable attitudes toward a manager who we believe to be very honest and moral. Similarly, if we have had negative and unpleasant experiences with a particular coworker, we may form an unfavorable attitude toward that person. Any of the "big five" or individual personality traits may also influence our attitudes. Understanding the basic structure of an attitude helps us see how attitudes are formed and can be changed.

Attitude Structure Attitudes are usually viewed as stable dispositions to behave toward objects in a certain way. For any number of reasons, a person might decide that he or she does not like a particular political figure or a certain restaurant

A person's **risk propensity** is the degree to which he or she is willing to take chances and make risky decisions.

Attitudes are a person's complexes of beliefs and feelings about specific ideas, situations, or other people.

TECHNOLOGY

High-Tech Customer Service at Finagle a Bagel

Boston restaurant chain Finagle a Bagel, owned by Laura Trust and Alan Litchman, competes for customers against coffeehouses, doughnut stores, groceries, full-service diners, fast-food eateries, and more. In order to beat that competition, their stores must offer something unique. "We provide an outstanding product at a good price point in a clean environment with a high level of customer service," says Trust. She offers this criticism of competing food providers: "Customer service is almost nonexistent. If you're lucky, it's horrendous."

Finagle a Bagel uses traditional methods to increase customer service, including staff training, incentives for performance, and so on. Customers, says Trust, "just want to know that you're going to take care of them. That you appreciate their business. That you're happy they're there. That you can talk to them in a polite manner. That you can understand their questions and concerns." In the never-ending search for better service, the firm has also turned to a less obvious solution: automated technology.

Marketing manager Heather Robertson has always answered the phone in person to handle customer questions or feedback. She handwrites apology letters when a customer is dissatisfied. Yet when management wanted to know how

"[Customers] just want to know that you're going to take care of them."
—LAURA TRUST, OWNER AND CO-PRESIDENT, FINAGLE A BAGEL

many customers had complained about a particular server, for example, Robertson couldn't answer, but she didn't stop there. She felt such a strong sense of organizational commitment that she went out of her way to find a novel solution, establishing a customer comment database to track messages. As a result, Finagle a Bagel has retrained personnel, offered new products, and changed management policies, all resulting in more loyal customers.

Another automated system manages the Frequent Finaglers cards, which can be used as gift or prepaid cards and which can also track frequent buyer rewards. Customers can conveniently check their point balances or load dollars onto their card online. At the same time, the cards provide valuable information to the company about customer spending patterns. "The program...helps us to drive sales. It also gives us a way to manage our promotions, understand our guests, and provide our vendors information," says co-president Trust.

References: "Finagle Knows Bagels," Finagle a Bagel website, www.finagleabagel.com on February 2, 2010; Paytronix Systems Inc., "Customer Testimonials," www.paytronix.com on February 28, 2005; Jennifer deJong, "Turbocharging Customer Service," *Inc.*, June 1995, www.inc.com on February 2, 2010; "Zero Stage Capital Commits $3 Million to Fund Rapid Gazelle Growth," *Encyclopedia.com*, www.encyclopedia.com on February 2, 2010.

(a disposition). We would expect that person to express consistently negative opinions of the candidate or restaurant and to maintain the consistent, predictable intention of not voting for the political candidate or not eating at the restaurant. In this view, attitudes contain three components: affect, cognition, and intention.

A person's **affect** is his or her feelings toward something. In many ways, affect is similar to emotion—it is something over which we have little or no conscious control. For example, most people react to words such as "love," "hate," "sex," and "war" in a manner that reflects their feelings about what those words convey. Similarly, you may like one of your classes, dislike another, and be indifferent

A person's **affect** is his or her feelings toward something.

toward a third. If the class you dislike is an elective, you may not be particularly concerned. But if it is the first course in your chosen major, your affective reaction may cause you considerable anxiety.

Cognition is the knowledge a person presumes to have about something. You may believe you like a class because the textbook is excellent, the class meets at your favorite time, the instructor is outstanding, and the workload is light. This "knowledge" may be true, partially true, or totally false. For example, you may intend to vote for a particular candidate because you think you know where the candidate stands on several issues. In reality, depending on the candidate's honesty and your understanding of his or her statements, the candidate's thinking on the issues may be exactly the same as yours, partly the same, or totally different. Cognitions are based on perceptions of truth and reality, and, as we note later, perceptions agree with reality to varying degrees.

Intention guides a person's behavior. If you like your instructor, you may intend to take another class from him or her next semester. Intentions are not always translated into actual behavior, however. If the instructor's course next semester is scheduled for 8:00 A.M., you may decide that another instructor is just as good. Some attitudes, and their corresponding intentions, are much more central and significant to an individual than others. You may intend to do one thing (take a particular class) but later alter your intentions because of a more significant and central attitude (fondness for sleeping late).

Cognitive Dissonance   When two sets of cognitions or perceptions are contradictory or incongruent, a person experiences a level of conflict and anxiety called cognitive dissonance. Cognitive dissonance also occurs when people behave in a fashion that is inconsistent with their attitudes. For example, a person may realize that smoking and overeating are dangerous yet continue to do both. Because the attitudes and behaviors are inconsistent with each other, the person probably will experience a certain amount of tension and discomfort and may try to reduce these feelings by changing the attitude, altering the behavior, or perceptually distorting the circumstances. For example, the dissonance associated with overeating might be resolved by continually deciding to go on a diet "next week."

Cognitive dissonance affects people in a variety of ways. We frequently encounter situations in which our attitudes conflict with each other or with our behaviors. Dissonance reduction is the way we deal with these feelings of discomfort and tension. In organizational settings, people contemplating leaving the organization may wonder why they continue to stay and work hard. As a result of this dissonance, they may conclude that the company is not so bad after all, that they have no immediate options elsewhere, or that they will leave "soon."

Attitude Change   Attitudes are not as stable as personality attributes. For example, new information may change attitudes. A manager may have a negative attitude about a new colleague because of his lack of job-related experience. After working with the new person for a while, however, the manager may come to realize that he is actually very talented and subsequently develop a more positive attitude. Likewise, if the object of an attitude changes, a person's attitude toward that object may also change. Suppose, for example, that employees feel underpaid and, as a result, have negative attitudes toward the company's reward system. A big salary increase may cause these attitudes to become more positive.

Attitudes can also change when the object of the attitude becomes less important or less relevant to the person. For example, suppose an employee has a negative attitude about his company's health insurance. When his spouse gets a new job with

A person's **cognitions** constitute the knowledge a person presumes to have about something.

An **intention** is a component of an attitude that guides a person's behavior.

Cognitive dissonance is the anxiety a person experiences when simultaneously possessing two sets of knowledge or perceptions that are contradictory or incongruent.

an organization that has outstanding insurance benefits, his attitude toward his own insurance may become more moderate simply because he no longer has to worry about it. Finally, as noted earlier, individuals may change their attitudes as a way to reduce cognitive dissonance.

Deeply rooted attitudes that have a long history are, of course, resistant to change. For example, over a period of years a former airline executive named Frank Lorenzo developed a reputation in the industry of being antiunion and for cutting wages and benefits. As a result, employees throughout the industry came to dislike and distrust him. When he took over Eastern Airlines, its employees had such a strong attitude of distrust toward him that they could never agree to cooperate with any of his programs or ideas. Some of them actually cheered months later when Eastern went bankrupt, even though it was costing them their own jobs!

Key Work-Related Attitudes

People in an organization form attitudes about many different things. Employees are likely to have attitudes about their salary, their promotion possibilities, their boss, employee benefits, the food in the company cafeteria, and the color of the company softball team uniforms. Of course, some of these attitudes are more important than others. Especially important attitudes are job satisfaction and organizational commitment.

Job Satisfaction   Job satisfaction reflects the extent to which people find gratification or fulfillment in their work. Extensive research on job satisfaction shows that personal factors such as an individual's needs and aspirations determine this attitude, along with group and organizational factors such as relationships with coworkers and supervisors and working conditions, work policies, and compensation.[13]

A satisfied employee tends to be absent less often, to make positive contributions, and to stay with the organization.[14] In contrast, a dissatisfied employee may be absent more often, may experience stress that disrupts coworkers, and may be continually looking for another job. Contrary to what a lot of managers believe, however, high levels of job satisfaction do not necessarily lead to higher levels of productivity.[15] One survey indicated that, also contrary to popular opinion, Japanese workers are less satisfied with their jobs than their counterparts in the United States.[16]

Organizational Commitment   Organizational commitment, sometimes called job commitment, reflects an individual's identification with and attachment to the organization. A highly committed person will probably see herself as a true member of the firm (for example, referring to the organization in personal terms such as "we make high-quality products"), overlook minor sources of dissatisfaction, and see herself remaining a member of the organization. In contrast, a less committed person is more likely to see herself as an outsider (for example, referring to the organization in less personal terms such as "they don't pay their employees very well"), to express more dissatisfaction about things, and to not see herself as a long-term member of the organization.[17]

Organizations can do few definitive things to promote satisfaction and commitment, but some specific guidelines are available. For one thing, if the organization treats its employees fairly and provides reasonable rewards and job security, its employees are more likely to be satisfied and committed. Allowing employees to have a say in how things are done can also promote these attitudes. Designing jobs so that they are stimulating can enhance both satisfaction and commitment. Research suggests that Japanese workers may be more committed to their organizations than are U.S. workers.[18] Other

Job satisfaction is the extent to which a person is gratified or fulfilled by his or her work.

Organizational commitment is a person's identification with and attachment to an organization.

research suggests that some of the factors that may lead to commitment, including extrinsic rewards, role clarity, and participative management, are the same across different cultures.[19]

Affect and Mood in Organizations

Researchers have recently started to renew their interest in the affective component of attitudes. Recall from our previous discussion that the affective component of an attitude reflects our emotions. Managers once believed that emotion and feelings varied among people from day to day, but research now suggests that although some short-term fluctuation does indeed occur, there are also underlying stable predispositions toward fairly constant and predictable moods and emotional states.[20]

Some people, for example, tend to have a higher degree of **positive affectivity**. This means that they are relatively upbeat and optimistic, that they have an overall sense of well-being, and that they usually see things in a positive light. Thus, they always seem to be in a good mood. People with more **negative affectivity** are just the opposite. They are generally downbeat and pessimistic and they usually see things in a negative way. They seem to be in a bad mood most of the time.

Of course, as noted above, short-term variations can occur among even the most extreme types. People with a lot of positive affectivity, for example, may still be in a bad mood if they have just been passed over for a promotion, gotten extremely negative performance feedback, or have been laid off or fired, for instance. Similarly, those with negative affectivity may be in a good mood—at least for a short time—if they have just been promoted, received very positive performance feedback, or had other good things befall them. After the initial impact of these events wears off, however, those with positive affectivity generally return to their normal positive mood, whereas those with negative affectivity gravitate back to their normal bad mood.[21]

Most managers recognize the importance of rewarding good performance. When people feel that their efforts are appreciated and rewarded, they generally feel more satisfied with their jobs and their employer and develop more organizational commitment. This manager, for instance, is giving a plaque to one of his subordinates to recognize her accomplishments as the top sales representative in the region. She will hang this plaque in her office and feel a sense of accomplishment every time she sees it.

PERCEPTION IN ORGANIZATIONS

Perception—the set of processes by which an individual becomes aware of and interprets information about the environment—is another important element of workplace behavior. If everyone perceived everything the same way, things would be a lot simpler (and a lot less exciting!). Of course, just the opposite is true: People perceive the same things in very different ways.[22] Moreover, people often assume that reality is objective and that we all perceive the same things in the same way.

People who possess **positive affectivity** are upbeat and optimistic, have an overall sense of well-being, and see things in a positive light.

People characterized by **negative affectivity** are generally downbeat and pessimistic, see things in a negative way, and seem to be in a bad mood.

Perception is the set of processes by which an individual becomes aware of and interprets information about the environment.

Figure 3.3 BASIC PERCEPTUAL PROCESSES

Perception determines how we become aware of information from our environment and how we interpret it. Selective perception and stereotyping are particularly important perceptual processes that affect behavior in organizations.

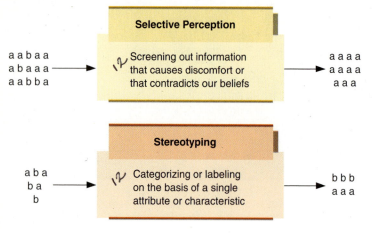

To test this idea, we could ask students at the University of Missouri and the University of Kansas to describe the most recent basketball game between their schools. We probably would hear two conflicting stories. These differences would arise primarily because of perception. The fans "saw" the same game but interpreted it in sharply contrasting ways.

Since perception plays a role in a variety of workplace behaviors, managers should understand basic perceptual processes. As implied in our definition, perception actually consists of several distinct processes. Moreover, in perceiving we receive information in many guises, from spoken words to visual images of movements and forms. Through perceptual processes, the receiver assimilates the varied types of incoming information for the purpose of interpreting it.[23]

Basic Perceptual Processes

Figure 3.3 shows two basic perceptual processes that are particularly relevant to managers—selective perception and stereotyping.

Selective Perception Selective perception is the process of screening out information that we are uncomfortable with or that contradicts our beliefs. For example, suppose a manager is exceptionally fond of a particular worker. The manager has a very positive attitude about the worker and thinks he is a top performer. One day the manager notices that the worker seems to be goofing off. Selective perception may cause the manager to quickly forget what he observed. Similarly, suppose a manager has formed a very negative image of a particular worker. She thinks this worker is a poor performer who never does a good job. When she happens to observe an example of high performance from the worker, she may quickly forget it. In one sense, selective perception is beneficial because it allows us to disregard minor bits of information. Of course, the benefit occurs only if our basic perception is accurate. If selective perception causes us to ignore important information, however, it can become quite detrimental.

Stereotyping Stereotyping is categorizing or labeling people on the basis of a single attribute. Certain forms of stereotyping can be useful and efficient. Suppose, for example, that a manager believes that communication skills are important for a particular job and that speech communication majors tend to have exceptionally good communication skills. As a result, whenever he interviews candidates for jobs he pays especially close attention to speech communication majors. To the extent that communication skills truly predict job performance and that majoring in speech communication does indeed provide those skills, this form of stereotyping can be beneficial. Common attributes from which people often stereotype are race and sex. Of course, stereotypes along these lines are inaccurate and can be harmful. For

Selective perception is the process of screening out information that we are uncomfortable with or that contradicts our beliefs.

Stereotyping is the process of categorizing or labeling people on the basis of a single attribute.

Figure 3.4   THE ATTRIBUTION PROCESS

The attribution process involves observing behavior and then attributing causes to it. Observed behaviors are interpreted in terms of their consensus, their consistency, and their distinctiveness. The interpretations result in behavior being attributed to either internal or external causes.

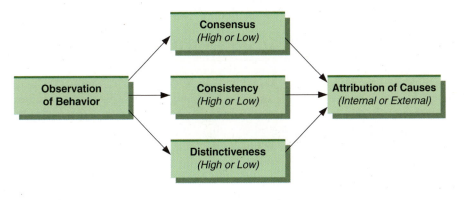

example, suppose a human resource manager forms the stereotype that women can only perform certain tasks and that men are best suited for other tasks. To the extent that this affects the manager's hiring practices, he or she is (1) costing the organization valuable talent for both sets of jobs, (2) violating federal law, and (3) behaving unethically.

Perception and Attribution

Attribution theory has extended our understanding of how perception affects behavior in organizations.[24] Attribution theory suggests that we observe behavior and then attribute causes to it. That is, we attempt to explain why people behave as they do. The process of attribution is based on perceptions of reality, and these perceptions may vary widely among individuals.

Figure 3.4 illustrates the basic attribution theory framework. To start the process, we observe behavior, either our own or someone else's. We then evaluate that behavior in terms of its degrees of consensus, consistency, and distinctiveness. Consensus is the extent to which other people in the same situation behave in the same way. Consistency is the degree to which the same person behaves in the same way at different times. Distinctiveness is the extent to which the same person behaves in the same way in different situations. We form impressions or attributions as to the causes of behavior based on various combinations of consensus, consistency, and distinctiveness. We may believe the behavior is caused internally (by forces within the person) or externally (by forces in the person's environment).

For example, suppose you observe one of your subordinates being rowdy, disrupting others' work, and generally making a nuisance of himself. If you can understand the causes of this behavior, you may be able to change it. If the employee is the only one engaging in the disruptive behavior (low consensus), if he behaves like this several times each week (high consistency), and if you have seen him behave like this in other settings (low distinctiveness), a logical conclusion would be that internal factors are causing his behavior.

Attribution theory suggests that we attribute causes to behavior based on our observations of certain characteristics of that behavior.

Suppose, however, that you observe a different pattern: Everyone in the person's work group is rowdy (high consensus); and although the particular employee often is rowdy at work (high consistency), you have never seen him behave this way in other settings (high distinctiveness). This pattern indicates that something in the situation is causing the behavior—that is, that the causes of the behavior are external.

TYPES OF WORKPLACE BEHAVIOR

Now that we have looked closely at how individual differences can influence behavior in organizations, let's turn our attention to what we mean by workplace behavior. **Workplace behavior** is a pattern of action by the members of an organization that directly or indirectly influences the organization's effectiveness. One way to talk about workplace behavior is to describe its impact on performance and productivity, absenteeism and turnover, and organizational citizenship. Unfortunately, employees can exhibit dysfunctional behaviors as well.

Performance Behaviors

Performance behaviors are the total set of work-related behaviors that the organization expects the individual to display. You might think of these as the "terms" of the psychological contract. For some jobs, performance behaviors can be narrowly defined and easily measured. For example, an assembly-line worker who sits by a moving conveyor and attaches parts to a product as it passes by has relatively few performance behaviors. He or she is expected to remain at the workstation and correctly attach the parts. Performance can often be assessed quantitatively by counting the percentage of parts correctly attached.

For many other jobs, however, performance behaviors are more diverse and much more difficult to assess. For example, consider the case of a research-and-development scientist at Merck. The scientist works in a lab trying to find new scientific breakthroughs that have commercial potential. The scientist must apply knowledge learned in graduate school and experience gained from previous research. Intuition and creativity are also important. And the desired breakthrough may take months or even years to accomplish. Organizations rely on a number of different methods to evaluate performance. The key, of course, is to match the evaluation mechanism with the job being performed.

Dysfunctional Behaviors

Some work-related behaviors are dysfunctional in nature. That is, **dysfunctional behaviors** are those that detract from, rather than contribute to, organizational performance. Two of the more common ones are absenteeism and turnover. **Absenteeism** occurs when an employee does not show up for work. Some absenteeism has a legitimate cause, such as illness, jury duty, or a death or illness in the family. At other times, the employee may report a feigned legitimate cause that's actually just an excuse to stay home. When an employee is absent, legitimately or not, her or his work does not get done at all or a substitute must be hired to do it. In either case, the quantity or quality of actual output is likely to suffer. Obviously,

Workplace behavior is a pattern of action by the members of an organization that directly or indirectly influences organizational effectiveness.

Performance behaviors are all of the total set of work-related behaviors that the organization expects the individual to display.

Dysfunctional behaviors are those that detract from organizational performance.

Absenteeism occurs when an individual does not show up for work.

some absenteeism is expected, but organizations strive to minimize feigned absenteeism and reduce legitimate absences as much as possible.

Turnover occurs when people quit their jobs. An organization usually incurs costs in replacing workers who have quit, and if turnover involves especially productive people, it is even more costly. Turnover seems to result from a number of factors, including aspects of the job, the organization, the individual, the labor market, and family influences. In general, a poor person-job fit is also a likely cause of turnover. People may also be prone to leave an organization if its inflexibility makes it difficult to manage family and other personal matters and may be more likely to stay if an organization provides sufficient flexibility to make it easier to balance work and nonwork considerations.[25] One Chick-fil-A operator in Texas has cut the turnover rate in his stores by offering flexible work schedules, college scholarships, and such perks as free bowling trips.[26]

Other forms of dysfunctional behavior may be even more costly for an organization.[27] Theft and sabotage, for example, result in direct financial costs for an organization. Sexual and racial harassment also cost an organization, both indirectly (by lowering morale, producing fear, and driving off valuable employees) and directly (through financial liability if the organization responds inappropriately). Workplace violence is also a growing concern in many organizations. Violence by disgruntled workers or former workers results in dozens of deaths and injuries each year.[28]

The *Change* box on page 80 entitled "Disturbance in the Workforce" discusses the possible role of the current economic downturn as a contributing factor in workplace violence.

Organizational Citizenship

Managers strive to minimize dysfunctional behaviors while trying to promote organizational citizenship. Organizational citizenship refers to the behavior of individuals who make a positive overall contribution to the organization.[29] Consider, for example, an employee who does work that is acceptable in terms of both quantity and quality. However, she refuses to work overtime, won't help newcomers learn the ropes, and is generally unwilling to make any contribution beyond the strict performance of her job. This person may be seen as a good performer, but she is not likely to be seen as a good organizational citizen.

Another employee may exhibit a comparable level of performance. In addition, however, he always works late when the boss asks him to, he takes time to help newcomers learn their way around, and he is perceived as being helpful and committed to the organization's success. He is likely to be seen as a better organizational citizen.

A complex mosaic of individual, social, and organizational variables determines organizational citizenship behaviors. For example, the personality, attitudes, and needs (discussed in Chapter 4) of the individual must be consistent with citizenship behaviors. Similarly, the social context, or work group, in which the individual works must facilitate and promote such behaviors (we discuss group dynamics in Chapter 9). And the organization itself, especially its culture, must be capable of promoting, recognizing, and rewarding these types of behaviors if they are to be maintained. The study of organizational citizenship is still in its infancy, but preliminary research suggests that it may play a powerful role in organizational effectiveness.

Turnover occurs when people quit their jobs.

A person's degree of **organizational citizenship** is the extent to which his or her behavior makes a positive overall contribution to the organization.

EXPERIENCING ORGANIZATIONAL BEHAVIOR

Matching Jobs and Personalities

Purpose   This exercise is designed to give you some insight into the importance of matching personalities both to workplaces and to specific jobs. It should also give you a good idea of how hard it is to perform this task well.

Format   The exercise asks you to perform two tasks:

- Match personality traits with specific jobs.
- Develop a series of questions to assess personality traits in job applicants.

Procedure   Read each of the following job descriptions:

Page   Conducts visitors on tours of radio and television station facilities and explains duties of staff, operation of equipment, and methods of broadcasting. Utilizes general knowledge of various phases of radio and television station operations. Runs errands within studio. May relieve telephone switchboard operator. May perform general clerical duties such as taking messages, filing, and typing.

Young-Adult Librarian   Plans and conducts library program to provide special services for young adults. Selects books and audiovisual materials of interest to young adults to be acquired by library. Assists young adults in selecting materials. Plans and organizes young-adult activities, such as film programs, chess clubs, creative writing clubs, and photography contests. Delivers talks on books to stimulate reading. Compiles lists of library materials of interest to young adults. Confers with parents, teachers, and community organizations to assist in developing programs to stimulate reading and develop communication skills.

Mortgage Loan Interviewer   Interviews applicants applying for mortgage loans to document income, debt, and credit history. Requests documents for verification, such as income tax returns, bank account numbers, purchase agreements, and property descriptions. Determines if applicant meets establishment standards for further consideration, following the manual and using a calculator. Informs applicant of closing costs, such as appraisal, credit report, and notary fees. Answers applicant's questions and asks for signature on information authorization forms. Submits application forms for verification of application information. Calls applicant or other persons to resolve discrepancies,

such as credit report showing late payment history. Informs applicant of loan denial or acceptance.

Park Ranger   Enforces laws, regulations, and policies in state or national park. Registers vehicles and visitors, collects fees, and issues parking and use permits. Provides information pertaining to park use, safety requirements, and points of interest. Directs traffic, investigates accidents, and patrols area to prevent fires, vandalism, and theft. Cautions, evicts, or apprehends violators of laws and regulations. Directs or participates in first-aid and rescue activities. May compile specified park-use statistics, keep records, and prepare reports of area activities. May train and supervise park workers and concession attendants.

Headwaiter/Headwaitress   Supervises and coordinates activities of dining room personnel to serve food aboard ship. Assigns duties, work stations, and responsibilities to personnel and directs their performances. Inspects dining tables and work areas for cleanliness. Greets patrons and shows them to dining tables. Requisitions supplies, such as glassware, china, and silverware. Authorizes personnel to work overtime. May suggest entrees, dinner courses, and wines to guests.

Exercise Task   Working alone, you need to prepare by doing two things:

1. Select any **three** of these jobs, and for each, determine a personality trait that you think is especially important for a person performing the job (i.e., 3 jobs = 3 personality traits).
2. For each of the three jobs that you've analyzed, write up a series of five questions that will help you assess how an applicant for the job scores on the trait that you've selected for it. Make sure that your questions can be answered on a five-point scale (i.e., *strongly agree, agree, neither agree nor disagree, disagree, strongly disagree*).

After you've finished these preparatory steps, do the following:

1. Exchange your lists of questions with one of your classmates. You'll pretend to be a job applicant, and your partner will pretend to be a job interviewer. He or she will choose one of your lists and ask those questions to you, and you will provide honest and truthful answers.

2. Repeat the process with you taking the role of the interviewer and your partner taking the role of the applicant.

3. When you've finished the role-playing part of the exercise, discuss the experience with one another. First, each of you should reveal the trait that you had in mind when you drew up the list of five questions that you were asked in your "interview." Second, you should discuss how well each of your question sets measured the trait that you had in mind when you compiled them. If you have time remaining, you can have the same discussion about one or more of your remaining lists of questions.

BUILDING MANAGERIAL SKILLS

Exercise Overview   Interpersonal skills refer to the ability to communicate with, understand, and motivate individuals and groups. Implicit in this definition is the notion that a manager should try to understand important characteristics of others, including their personalities. This exercise will give you insights into both the importance of personality in the workplace as well as some of the difficulties associated with assessing personality traits.

Exercise Background   You will first try to determine which personality traits are most relevant for different jobs. You will then write a series of questions that you think may help assess or measure those traits in prospective employees. First, read each of the following job descriptions:

Sales representative: This position involves calling on existing customers to ensure that they are happy with the firm's products. It also requires the sales representative to work to get customers to increase the quantity of your products they are buying, as well as to attract new customers. A sales representative must be aggressive, but not pushy.

Office manager: The office manager oversees the work of a staff of twenty secretaries, receptionists, and clerks. The manager hires them, trains them, evaluates their performance, and sets their pay. The manager also schedules working hours and, when necessary, disciplines or fires workers.

Warehouse worker: Warehouse workers unload trucks and carry shipments to shelves for storage. They also pull customer orders from shelves and take products for packing. The job requires workers to follow orders precisely and has little room for autonomy or interaction with others during work.

Exercise Task   Working alone, identify a single personality trait that you think is especially important for a person to be able to effectively perform each of these three jobs. Next, write five questions, which, when answered by a job applicant, will help you assess how that applicant scores on that particular trait. These questions should be of the type that can be answered on a five-point scale (for example, *strongly agree, agree, neither agree or disagree, disagree, strongly disagree*).

Exchange questions with a classmate. Pretend you are a job applicant. Provide honest and truthful answers to each question. Discuss the traits each of you identified for each position. How well you think your classmate's questions actually measure those traits?

Conclude by addressing the following questions:

1. How easy is it to measure personality?
2. How important do you believe it is for organizations to consider personality in hiring decisions?
3. Do perception and attitudes affect how people answer personality questions?

SELF-ASSESSMENT EXERCISE

Assessing Your Locus of Control

Read each pair of statements and indicate whether you agree more with statement A or with statement B. There are no right or wrong answers. In some cases, you may agree somewhat with both statements; choose the one with which you agree more.

_____ 1. A. Making a lot of money is largely a matter of getting the right breaks.
    B. Promotions are earned through hard work and persistence.

_____ 2. A. There is usually a direct correlation between how hard I study and the grades I get.
    B. Many times the reactions of teachers seem haphazard to me.

_____ 3. A. The number of divorces suggests that more and more people are not trying to make their marriages work.
    B. Marriage is primarily a gamble.

_____ 4. A. It is silly to think you can really change another person's basic attitudes.
    B. When I am right, I can generally convince others.

_____ 5. A. Getting promoted is really a matter of being a little luckier than the next person.
    B. In our society, a person's future earning power is dependent upon her or his ability.

_____ 6. A. If one knows how to deal with people, they are really quite easily led.
    B. I have little influence over the way other people behave.

_____ 7. A. The grades I make are the result of my own efforts; luck has little or nothing to do with it.
    B. Sometimes I feel that I have little to do with the grades I get.

_____ 8. A. People like me can change the course of world affairs if we make ourselves heard.
    B. It is only wishful thinking to believe that one can readily influence what happens in our society at large.

_____ 9. A. A great deal that happens to me probably is a matter of chance.
    B. I am the master of my life.

_____ 10. A. Getting along with people is a skill that must be practiced.
    B. It is almost impossible to figure out how to please some people.

Instructions: Give yourself 1 point each if you chose the following answers: 1B, 2A, 3A, 4B, 5B, 6A, 7A, 8A, 9B, 10A.

Sum your scores and interpret them as follows:

8–10	=	high internal locus of control
6–7	=	moderate internal locus of control
5	=	mixed internal/external locus of control
3–4	=	moderate external locus of control
1–2	=	high external locus of control

Note: This is an abbreviated version of a longer instrument. The scores obtained here are only an approximation of what your score might be on the complete instrument.

Reference: Adapted from J. B. Rotter, "External Control and Internal Control," _Psychology Today_, June 1971, p. 42. Reprinted with permission from _Psychology Today Magazine_. Copyright © 1971 Sussex Publishers, Inc.

4

CHAPTER

MOTIVATION IN ORGANIZATIONS

CHAPTER LEARNING OBJECTIVES

After studying this chapter you should be able to:

- Characterize the nature of motivation, including its importance and basic historical perspectives.
- Identify and describe the need-based perspectives on motivation.
- Identify and describe the major process-based perspectives on motivation.
- Describe learning-based perspectives on motivation.

The NetApp Approach to Net Satisfaction

"Funny, no one mentions wanting free M&Ms."

—CONSULTANT GEORGE BRYMER ON WHAT NETAPP EMPLOYEES DO AND DON'T WANT

NetApp, a computer storage and data-management company headquartered in Sunnyvale, California, is no stranger to best-places-to-work lists. Since 2005, it's been ranked among the top-15 employers in Europe, Australia, Germany, India, France, and the Netherlands. In 2009, it was named the fourth-best place to work, and best overall among tech companies, in the United Kingdom; and in the same year, it came in seventh on *Fortune* magazine's list of the "100 Best Companies to Work For" in the United States—a drop from No. 1 the previous year, but its eighth consecutive appearance on the list.

AP PHOTO/PAUL SAKUMA

NetApp is considered to be a great place to work. Rather than providing lots of free "goodies" to employees, though, NetApp has achieved this distinction by creating a culture that truly values its employees.

NetApp likes to cite employee-survey scores as a key reason for its regular selection to the list by *Fortune* and the Great Place to Work® Institute. According to the company's website, worker surveys reflect "our employees' experiences and opinions about our culture and values, trust in leadership, integrity and fairness, teamwork, and camaraderie." High on the list of things that keep workers satisfied and motivated seems to be a culture that encourages employee input and the sharing of ideas. The "most impressive thing...about the company," says one engineer, "is the open-door culture. I can approach any other engineer with technical issues, product marketing with new ideas, and anyone in management with any questions." Also highly satisfying appears to be the collaborative approach to work processes. "Cooperation is the...actual norm," reports one worker. "This company is unique in my experience for avoiding the politics and empire building typical in growing companies." "The focus is on the issues," adds another employee, "and in most cases, you find that the issues aren't owned by one particular function. The focus is on team problem solving."

Most of all, NetApp employees seem happy with the level of freedom that they're given in the pursuit of both organizational and personal objectives. In particular, says one worker, "I have...lots of freedom to implement my ideas to make things better, and [I'm] also able to make decisions in order to get the job done." Another employee thinks that "the most unique thing about NetApp...is that they give us a lot of the free stuff—*free* as in *freedom*, not 'free beer.'" Granted, he adds, "there's a lot of 'free beer' here—free gifts, goodies, lunches. But I think giving 'free beer' to keep employees happy works only as long as the company is [riding] high. Freedom lasts forever." Or at least as long as it's imbued in the company culture, according to George Brymer, founder and president of All Square Inc., a provider of managerial training programs. Brymer, who's also the author of *Vital Integrities: How Values-Based Leaders Acquire and Preserve Their Credibility*, contrasts the role of "free beer" at NetApp with its more highly publicized counterpart at Google. "Among the perks enjoyed by Google employees," he writes,

> are onsite haircuts, free laundry facilities, workout and massage rooms, in-house childcare, and car washes. And then there's the free food. The campus has eleven cafeterias serving everything from gourmet meals to M&Ms....
>
> Unlike Google, which got to the top [of the *Fortune* list of "100 Best Companies to Work For" in 2007] largely by providing employees with lots of goodies, NetApp earned [its] spot because of its culture of trust. NetApp's leaders promote an atmosphere of openness and honesty, and they go out of their way to proactively share information with workers....
>
> For their part, NetApp employees say they appreciate how easy it is to share ideas, get answers to questions, meet with senior leaders, and find opportunities to take responsibility. Funny, no one mentions wanting free M&Ms.

In placing NetApp on its 2009 lists of the "UK's 50 Best Workplaces" and "100 Best Workplaces in Europe," the Great Places to Work Institute cited employees' opinions that company management is approachable and easy to talk to, is forthcoming with straight answers to reasonable questions, and keeps workers informed about important issues and changes.

In addition, the principle of trust at NetApp seems to go beyond management's confidence in the ability of informed employees to make good operational decisions. Apparently it also applies to management's confidence that satisfied employees will live up to item number six on the company's list of "living values"—namely, that they'll "Get Things Done!" "What I appreciate most about NetApp," says one worker, *is that I'm respected—[allowed] to manage my time, my day, my workload. No one's telling me to be at my desk by a certain time or gives me a strange look if I'm leaving the office early. It's expected that you get your work done, and if you do that late at night or early in the morning, that's your choice. . . . No one's watching your movements. It's about performance, achieving goals. . . .*

When things get done—when individuals and teams perform and achieve goals—NetApp has a number of programs in place to recognize them. The SHARE Rewards program, for instance, offers incentives for knowledge sharing; a program called Total Customer Experience Champions offers rewards for enhancing customer views of the company; and the NetApp Patent Award program distributes up to $15,000 to employees involved on projects that produce patents. NetApp is also ranked among *Fortune*'s list of "25 Top-Paying Companies." In order to recruit and retain top talent, it regularly monitors the competitiveness of its pay rates among high-tech companies, and in 2009, 98 percent of all employees received incentive bonuses totaling $47 million.

Finally, NetApp supports what one employee calls "a true sense of spirit and 'family.'" Consider the case of marketing director J.P. Gallagher, who was diagnosed with stomach cancer after two years with the company: "My wife was 8½ months pregnant," reports Gallagher,

and the employees on my team set up a night nanny and six months of dinners delivered to our home. The company kept my job for me and raised $30,000 in my name for the American Cancer Society. . . . [W]hen I came back [after several months] . . . my job was there, plus the company let me ease back in. I was part time for about six months and then went full time. Now I'm back on my original growth trajectory. I've used my volunteer time off to . . . start a foundation to help other cancer patients fight this disease. NetApp has helped me build a database of gastric-cancer patients around the country and made a significant contribution of equipment to our foundation.

Just how much control do companies have over the conditions that foster worker satisfaction and workplace productivity? The *Change* box on page 113, entitled "The NetApp Approach to Net Jobs," shows that, even at the highest-ranked companies, the external environment imposes limits on management's ability to establish and communicate workplace policy.

What Do You Think?

1. In what ways is NetApp similar to and different from Wegmans, as discussed at the beginning of Chapter 1?

2. Would you want to want for NetApp? Why or why not?

References: "100 Best Companies to Work For," *Fortune*, January 21, 2010, http://money.cnn.com on February 8, 2010; "25 Top-Paying Companies," *Fortune*, January 21, 2010, http://money.cnn.com on February 11, 2010; Amy Lyman, "NetApp: Culture—Values—Leadership," Great Place to Work Institute, 2009, http://resources.greatplacetowork.com on February 11, 2010; "A Great Place to Work," *News@NetApp*, www.netapp.com on February 11, 2010; George Brymer, "NetApp: A Great Place to Work," *Vital Integrities*, April 2009, http://allsquareinc.blogspot.com on February 11, 2010; "NetApp Named Best Technology Company to Work For in the UK," *News@NetApp*, www.netapp.com on February 11, 2010; J.P. Gallagher, "I Work for One of the 10 Best Companies," *Fortune*, January 21, 2010, http://money.cnn.com on February 11, 2010.

Given the complex array of individual differences discussed in Chapter 3, it should be obvious that people work for a wide variety of different reasons. Some people want money, some want challenge, and some want power. What people in an organization want from work and how they think they can achieve it plays an instrumental role in determining their motivation to work. As we see in this chapter, motivation is vital to all organizations. Indeed, the difference between highly effective organizations and less effective ones often lies in the motivations of their members (as evidenced by NetApp at the beginning of this chapter). Thus, managers need to understand the nature of individual motivation, especially as it applies to work situations. In this chapter we first explore various need-based perspectives on motivation. We then turn our attention to the more sophisticated process-based perspectives. We conclude with a discussion of learning-based perspectives on motivation.[1]

THE NATURE OF MOTIVATION

Motivation is the set of forces that causes people to engage in one behavior rather than some alternative behavior.[2] Students who stay up all night to ensure that their term papers are the best they can be, salespeople who work on Saturdays to get ahead, and doctors who make follow-up phone calls to patients to check on their conditions are all motivated people. Of course, students who avoid the term paper by spending the day at the beach, salespeople who go home early to escape a tedious sales call, and doctors who skip follow-up calls to have more time for golf are also motivated, but their goals are different. From the manager's viewpoint, the objective is to motivate people to behave in ways that are in the organization's best interest.[3]

The Importance of Motivation

Managers strive to motivate people in the organization to perform at high levels. This means getting them to work hard, to come to work regularly, and to make positive contributions to the organization's mission. But job performance depends on ability and environment as well as motivation. This relationship can be stated as follows:

$$P = M + A + E$$

with
P = performance, M = motivation,
A = ability, and E = environment.

To reach high levels of performance, an employee must want to do the job well (motivation), must be able to do the job effectively (ability), and must have the materials, resources, equipment, and information required to do the job (environment). A deficiency in any one of these areas hurts performance. A manager should thus strive to ensure that all three conditions are met.[4]

In most settings motivation is the most difficult of these factors to manage. If an employee lacks the ability to perform, she or he can be sent to training programs to learn new job skills. If the person cannot learn those skills, she or he can be transferred to a simpler job and replaced with a more skilled worker. If an employee lacks materials, resources, equipment, and/or information, the manager can take steps to provide them. For example, if a worker cannot complete a project without sales forecast data from marketing, the manager can contact marketing and request that information. But if motivation is deficient, the manager faces the more complex situation of determining what will motivate the employee to work harder.[5]

Motivation is the set of forces that leads people to behave in particular ways.

The Motivational Framework

We can start to understand motivation by looking at need deficiencies and goal-directed behaviors. Figure 4.1 shows the basic motivational framework we use to organize our discussion. A need—something an individual requires or wants—is the starting point.[6] Motivated behavior usually begins when a person has one or more important **needs**. Although a need that is already satisfied may also motivate behavior (for example, the need to maintain a standard of living one has already achieved), unmet needs usually result in more intense feelings and behavioral changes. For example, if a person has yet to attain the standard of living she desires, this unmet need may stimulate her to action.

Figure 4.1 MOTIVATIONAL FRAMEWORK

This framework provides a useful way to see how motivational processes occur. When people experience a need deficiency, they seek ways to satisfy it, which results in a choice of goal-directed behaviors. After performing the behavior, the individual experiences rewards or punishments that affect the original need deficiency.

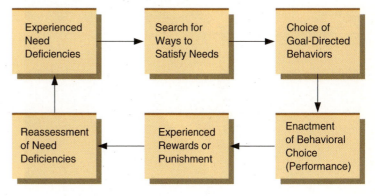

A need deficiency usually triggers a search for ways to satisfy it. Consider a person who feels her salary and position are deficient because they do not reflect the importance to the organization of the work she does and because she wants more income. She may feel she has three options: to simply ask for a raise and a promotion, to work harder in the hope of earning a raise and promotion, or to look for a new job with a higher salary and a more prestigious title.

Next comes a choice of goal-directed behaviors. Although a person might pursue more than one option at a time (such as working harder while also looking for another job), most effort is likely to be directed at one option. In the next phase, the person actually carries out the behavior chosen to satisfy the need. She will probably begin putting in longer hours, working harder, and so forth. She will next experience either rewards or punishment as a result of this choice. She may perceive her situation to be punishing if she ends up earning no additional recognition and not getting a promotion or pay raise. Alternatively, she may actually be rewarded by getting the raise and promotion because of her higher performance.

Finally, the person assesses the extent to which the outcome achieved fully addresses the original need deficiency. Suppose the person wanted a 10 percent raise and a promotion to vice president. If she got both, she should be satisfied. On the other hand, if she got only a 7 percent raise and a promotion to associate vice president, she will have to decide whether to keep trying, to accept what she got, or to choose one of the other options considered earlier. (Sometimes, of course, a need may go unsatisfied altogether, despite the person's best efforts.)

Historical Perspectives on Motivation

Historical views on motivation, although not always accurate, are of interest for several reasons. For one thing, they provide a foundation for contemporary thinking about motivation. For another, because they generally were based on common sense and intuition, an appreciation of their strengths and weaknesses can help managers gain useful insights into employee motivation in the workplace (we discuss these historical perspectives more fully in Appendix B).

A **need** is anything an individual requires or wants.

© ROGER-VIOLLET / THE IMAGE WORKS. REPRODUCED BY PERMISSION

Frederick Taylor, the so-called father of scientific management, studied work and motivation in the early years of the 20th century. He came to believe that people are motivated almost exclusively by money. Using this assumption as the basis for his other work, Taylor urged managers to structure jobs so that workers could increase their earnings by producing at a higher level. While later research revealed that motivation is much more complex than this simple argument, Taylor's work on work design and incentives still has relevance today.

The Traditional Approach One of the first writers to address work motivation—over a century ago—was Frederick Taylor. Taylor developed a method for structuring jobs that he called scientific management. As one basic premise of this approach, Taylor assumed that employees are economically motivated and work to earn as much money as they can.[7] Hence, he advocated incentive pay systems. He believed that managers knew more about the jobs being performed than did workers, and he assumed that economic gain was the primary thing that motivated everyone. Other assumptions of the traditional approach were that work is inherently unpleasant for most people, and that the money they earn is more important to employees than the nature of the job they are performing. Hence, people could be expected to perform any kind of job if they were paid enough. Although the role of money as a motivating factor cannot be dismissed, proponents of the traditional approach took too narrow a view of the role of monetary compensation and also failed to consider other motivational factors.

The Human Relations Approach The human relations approach supplanted scientific management in the 1930s.[8] The human relation approach assumed that employees want to feel useful and important, that employees have strong social needs, and that these needs are more important than money in motivating employees. Advocates of the human relations approach advised managers to make workers feel important and to allow them a modicum of self-direction and self-control in carrying out routine activities. The illusion of involvement and importance were expected to satisfy workers' basic social needs and result in higher motivation to perform. For example, a manager might allow a work group to participate in making a decision, even though he had already determined what the decision would be. The symbolic gesture of seeming to allow participation was expected to enhance motivation, even though no real participation took place.

The **scientific management approach** assumes that employees are motivated by money.

The **human relations approach** to motivation suggests that favorable employee attitudes result in motivation to work hard.

The **human resource approach** to motivation assumes that people want to contribute and are able to make genuine contributions.

The Human Resource Approach The human resource approach to motivation carries the concepts of needs and motivation one step farther. Whereas the human relationists believed that the illusion of contribution and participation would enhance motivation, the human resource view, which began to emerge in the 1950s, assumes that the contributions themselves are valuable to both individuals and organizations. It assumes that people want to contribute and are able to make genuine contributions. Management's task, then, is to encourage participation and to create a work environment that makes full use of the human resources available. This philosophy guides most contemporary thinking about employee motivation. At Ford, Westinghouse, Texas Instruments, and Hewlett-Packard, for example, work teams are being called upon to solve a variety of problems and to make substantive contributions to the organization.

NEED-BASED PERSPECTIVES ON MOTIVATION

Need-based perspectives represent the starting point for most contemporary thought on motivation, although these theories also attracted critics.[9] The basic premise of **need-based theories** and models, consistent with our motivation framework introduced earlier, is that humans are motivated primarily by deficiencies in one or more important needs or need categories. Need theorists have attempted to identify and categorize the needs that are most important to people.[10] (Some observers call these "content theories" because they deal with the content, or substance, of what motivates behavior.) The best-known need theories are the hierarchy of needs and the ERG theory.

The Hierarchy of Needs

The hierarchy of needs, developed by psychologist Abraham Maslow in the 1940s, is the best-known need theory.[11] Influenced by the human relations school, Maslow argued that human beings are "wanting" animals: They have innate desires to satisfy a given set of needs. Furthermore, Maslow believed that these needs are arranged in a hierarchy of importance, with the most basic needs at the foundation of the hierarchy.

Figure 4.2 shows **Maslow's hierarchy of needs**. The three sets of needs at the bottom of the hierarchy are called *deficiency needs*, because they must be satisfied for the individual to be fundamentally comfortable. The top two sets of needs are termed *growth needs* because they focus on personal growth and development.

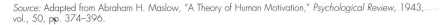

𝒥igure 4.2   THE HIERARCHY OF NEEDS

Maslow's hierarchy of needs consists of five basic categories of needs. This figure illustrates both general and organizational examples of each type of need. Of course, each individual has a wide variety of specific needs within each category.

Source: Adapted from Abraham H. Maslow, "A Theory of Human Motivation," *Psychological Review,* 1943, vol., 50, pp. 374–396.

Need-based theories of motivation assume that need deficiencies cause behavior.

Maslow's hierarchy of needs theory assumes that human needs are arranged in a hierarchy of importance.

The most basic needs in the hierarchy are *physiological needs*. They include the needs for food, sex, and air. Next in the hierarchy are *security needs*: things that offer safety and security, such as adequate housing and clothing and freedom from worry and anxiety. *Belongingness needs*, the third level in the hierarchy, are primarily social. Examples include the need for love and affection and the need to be accepted by peers. The fourth level, *esteem needs*, actually encompasses two slightly different kinds of needs: the need for a positive self-image and self-respect and the need to be respected by others. At the top of the hierarchy are *self-actualization needs*. These involve a person's realizing his or her full potential and becoming all that he or she can be.

Maslow believed that each need level must be satisfied before the level above it can become important. Thus, once physiological needs have been satisfied, their importance diminishes, and security needs emerge as the primary sources of motivation. This escalation up the hierarchy continues until the self-actualization needs become the primary motivators. Suppose, for example, that Jennifer Wallace earns all the money she needs and is very satisfied with her standard of living. Additional income may have little or no motivational impact on her behavior. Instead, Jennifer will strive to satisfy other needs, such as a desire for higher self-esteem.

However, if a previously satisfied lower-level set of needs becomes deficient again, the individual returns to that level. For example, suppose that Jennifer unexpectedly loses her job. At first, she may not be too worried because she has savings and confidence that she can find another good job. As her savings dwindle, however, she will become increasingly motivated to seek new income. Initially, she may seek a job that both pays well and satisfies her esteem needs. But as her financial situation grows increasingly worse, she may lower her expectations regarding esteem and instead focus almost exclusively on simply finding a job with a reliable paycheck.

In most businesses, physiological needs are probably the easiest to evaluate and to meet. Adequate wages, toilet facilities, ventilation, and comfortable temperatures and working conditions are measures taken to satisfy this most basic level of needs. Security needs in organizations can be satisfied by such things as job continuity (no layoffs), a grievance system (to protect against arbitrary supervisory actions), and an adequate insurance and retirement system (to guard against financial loss from illness and to ensure retirement income).

Most employees' belongingness needs are satisfied by family ties and group relationships both inside and outside the organization. In the workplace, people usually develop friendships that provide a basis for social interaction and can play a major role in satisfying social needs. Managers can help satisfy these needs by fostering a sense of group identity and interaction among employees. At the same time, managers can be sensitive to the probable effects on employees (such as low performance and absenteeism) of family problems or lack of acceptance by coworkers. Esteem needs in the workplace are met at least partially by job titles, choice offices, merit pay increases, awards, and other forms of recognition. Of course, to be sources of long-term motivation, tangible rewards such as these must be distributed equitably and be based on performance.

Self-actualization needs are perhaps the hardest to understand and the most difficult to satisfy. For example, it is difficult to assess how many people completely meet their full potential. In most cases, people who are doing well on Maslow's hierarchy will have satisfied their esteem needs and will be moving toward self-actualization. Working toward self-actualization, rather than actually achieving it, may be the ultimate motivation for most people. In recent years there has been a pronounced trend toward people leaving well-paying but less fulfilling jobs to take lower-paying but more fulfilling jobs such as nursing and teaching. This might indicate that they are actively working toward self-actualization.[12]

Research shows that the need hierarchy does not generalize very well to other countries. For example, in Greece and Japan, security needs may motivate employees more than self-actualization needs. Likewise, belongingness needs are especially important in Sweden, Norway, and Denmark. Research has also found differences in the relative importance of different needs in Mexico, India, Peru, Canada, Thailand, Turkey, and Puerto Rico.[13]

Maslow's needs hierarchy makes a certain amount of intuitive sense. And because it was the first motivation theory to become popular, it is also one of the best known among practicing managers. However, research has revealed a number of deficiencies in the theory. For example, five levels of needs are not always present; the actual hierarchy of needs does not always conform to Maslow's model; and need structures are more unstable and variable than the theory would lead us to believe.[14] And sometimes managers are overly clumsy or superficial in their attempts to use a theory such as this one. Thus, the theory's primary contribution seems to lie in providing a general framework for categorizing needs.

ERG Theory

The ERG theory, developed by Yale psychologist Clayton Alderfer, is another historically important need theory of motivation.[15] In many respects, ERG theory extends and refines Maslow's needs hierarchy concept, although there are also several important differences between the two. The E, R, and G stand for three basic need categories: existence, relatedness, and growth. *Existence needs*—those necessary for basic human survival—roughly correspond to the physiological and security needs of Maslow's hierarchy. *Relatedness needs*—those involving the need to relate to others—are similar to Maslow's belongingness and esteem needs. Finally, *growth needs* are analogous to Maslow's needs for self-esteem and self-actualization.

In contrast to Maslow's approach, ERG theory suggests that more than one kind of need, for example, both relatedness and growth needs, may motivate a person at the same time. A more important difference from Maslow's hierarchy is that ERG theory includes a satisfaction-progression component and a frustration-regression component. The satisfaction-progression concept suggests that after satisfying one category of needs, a person progresses to the next level. On this point, the need hierarchy and ERG theory agree. The need hierarchy, however, assumes the individual remains at the next level until the needs at that level are satisfied. In contrast, the frustration-regression component of ERG theory suggests that a person who is frustrated by trying to satisfy a higher level of needs eventually will regress to the preceding level.[16]

Suppose, for instance, that Nick Hernandez has satisfied his basic needs at the relatedness level and now is trying to satisfy his growth needs. That is, he has many friends and social relationships and is now trying to learn new skills and advance in his career. For a variety of reasons, such as organizational constraints (i.e., few challenging jobs, a glass ceiling, etc.) and the lack of opportunities to advance, he is unable to satisfy those needs. No matter how hard he tries, he seems stuck in his current position. According to ERG theory, frustration of his growth needs will cause Nick's relatedness needs to once again become dominant as motivators. As a result, he will put renewed interest into making friends and developing social relationships.

The **ERG theory** describes existence, relatedness, and growth needs.

The **dual-structure theory** identifies motivation factors, which affect satisfaction, and hygiene factors, which determine dissatisfaction.

The Dual-Structure Theory

Another important need-based theory of motivation is the dual-structure theory, which is in many ways similar to the need theories just discussed. This theory was originally called the "two-factor theory," but the more contemporary name used here

Figure 4.3 **THE DUAL-STRUCTURE THEORY OF MOTIVATION**

The traditional view of satisfaction suggested that satisfaction and dissatisfaction were opposite ends of a single dimension. Herzberg's dual-structure theory found evidence of a more complex view. In this theory, motivation factors affect one dimension, ranging from satisfaction to no satisfaction. Other workplace characteristics, called "hygiene factors," are assumed to affect another dimension, ranging from dissatisfaction to no dissatisfaction.

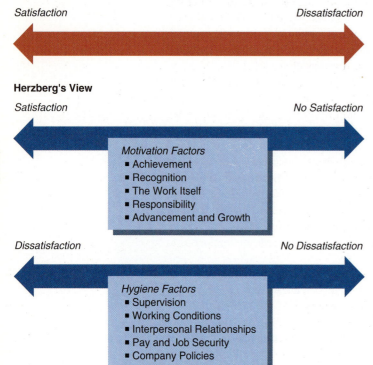

The Traditional View

Satisfaction   Dissatisfaction

Herzberg's View

Satisfaction   No Satisfaction

Motivation Factors
- Achievement
- Recognition
- The Work Itself
- Responsibility
- Advancement and Growth

Dissatisfaction   No Dissatisfaction

Hygiene Factors
- Supervision
- Working Conditions
- Interpersonal Relationships
- Pay and Job Security
- Company Policies

is more descriptive. This theory has played a major role in managerial thinking about motivation, and even though few researchers today accept the theory, it is nevertheless widely known and accepted among practicing managers.

Development of the Theory Frederick Herzberg and his associates developed the dual-structure theory in the late 1950s and early 1960s.[17] Herzberg began by interviewing approximately two hundred accountants and engineers in Pittsburgh. He asked them to recall times when they felt especially satisfied and motivated by their jobs and times when they felt particularly dissatisfied and unmotivated. He then asked them to describe what caused the good and bad feelings. The responses to the questions were recorded by the interviewers and later subjected to content analysis. (In a content analysis, the words, phrases, and sentences used by respondents are analyzed and categorized according to their meanings.)

To his surprise, Herzberg found that entirely different sets of factors were associated with the two kinds of feelings about work. For example, a person who indicated "low pay" as a source of dissatisfaction would not necessarily identify "high pay" as a source of satisfaction and motivation. Instead, people associated entirely different causes, such as recognition or achievement, with satisfaction and motivation. The findings led Herzberg to conclude that the prevailing thinking about satisfaction and motivation was incorrect. As Figure 4.3 shows, at the time, job satisfaction was being viewed as a single construct ranging from satisfaction to dissatisfaction. If this were the case, Herzberg reasoned, one set of factors should therefore influence movement back and forth along the continuum. But because his research had identified differential influences from two different sets of factors, Herzberg argued that two different dimensions must be involved. Thus, he saw motivation as a dual-structured phenomenon.

Figure 4.3 also illustrates the dual-structure concept that there is one dimension ranging from satisfaction to no satisfaction and another ranging from dissatisfaction to no dissatisfaction. The two dimensions must presumably be associated with the two sets of factors identified in the initial interviews. Thus, this theory proposed, employees might be either satisfied or not satisfied and, at the same time, dissatisfied or not dissatisfied.[18]

In addition, Figure 4.3 lists the primary factors identified in Herzberg's interviews. **Motivation factors** such as achievement and recognition were often cited by people as primary causes of satisfaction and motivation. When present in a job, these factors apparently could cause satisfaction and motivation; when they were absent, the result was feelings of no satisfaction rather than dissatisfaction. The other set of factors,

Motivation factors are intrinsic to the work itself and include factors such as achievement and recognition.

hygiene factors, came out in response to the questions about dissatisfaction and lack of motivation. The respondents suggested that pay, job security, supervisors, and working conditions, if seen as inadequate, could lead to feelings of dissatisfaction. When these factors were considered acceptable, however, the person still was not necessarily satisfied; rather, he or she was simply not dissatisfied.[19]

To use the dual-structure theory in the workplace, Herzberg recommended a two-stage process. First, the manager should try to eliminate situations that cause dissatisfaction, which Herzberg assumed to be the more basic of the two dimensions. For example, suppose that Susan Kowalski wants to use the dual-structure theory to enhance motivation in the group of seven technicians she supervises. Her first goal would be to achieve a state of no dissatisfaction by addressing hygiene factors. Imagine, for example, that she discovers that their pay is a bit below market rates and that a few of them are worried about job security. Her response would be to secure a pay raise for them and to allay their concerns about job security.

According to the theory, once a state of no dissatisfaction exists, trying to further improve motivation through hygiene factors is a waste of time.[20] At that point, the motivation factors enter the picture. Thus, when Susan Kowalski is sure that she has adequately dealt with hygiene issues, she should try to increase opportunities for achievement, recognition, responsibility, advancement, and growth. As a result, she would be helping her subordinates feel satisfied and motivated.

Unlike many other theorists, Herzberg described explicitly how managers could apply his theory. In particular, he developed and described a technique called "job enrichment" for structuring employee tasks.[21] (We discuss job enrichment in Chapter 5.) Herzberg tailored this technique to his key motivation factors. This unusual attention to application may explain the widespread popularity of the dual-structure theory among practicing managers.

Evaluation of the Theory   Because it gained popularity so quickly, the dual-structure theory has been scientifically scrutinized more than almost any other organizational behavior theory.[22] The results have been contradictory, to say the least. The initial study by Herzberg and his associates supported the basic premises of the theory, as did a few follow-up studies.[23] In general, studies that use the same methodology as Herzberg did (content analysis of recalled incidents) tend to support the theory. However, this methodology has itself been criticized, and studies that use other methods to measure satisfaction and dissatisfaction frequently obtain results quite different from Herzberg's.[24] If the theory is "method bound," as it appears to be, its validity is therefore questionable.

Several other criticisms have been directed against the theory. Critics say the original sample of accountants and engineers may not represent the general working population. Furthermore, they maintain that the theory fails to account for individual differences. Also, subsequent research has found that a factor such as pay may affect satisfaction in one sample and dissatisfaction in another and that the effect of a given factor depends on the individual's age and organizational level. In addition, the theory does not define the relationship between satisfaction and motivation.

Research has also suggested that the dual-structure framework varies across cultures. Only limited studies have been conducted, but findings suggest that employees in New Zealand and Panama assess the impact of motivation and hygiene factors differently than U.S. workers.[25] It is not surprising, then, that the dual-structure theory is no longer held in high esteem by organizational behavior researchers. Indeed, the field has since adopted far more complex and valid conceptualizations of motivation, most of which we discuss in Chapter 6. But because of its initial popularity and its specific guidance for application, the dual-structure theory merits a special place in the history of motivation research.

Hygiene factors are extrinsic to the work itself and include factors such as pay and job security.

Other Important Needs

Each theory discussed so far describes interrelated sets of important individual needs within specific frameworks. Several other key needs have been identified; but these needs are not allied with any single integrated theoretical perspective. The three most frequently mentioned are the needs for achievement, affiliation, and power.

The Need for Achievement The need for achievement is most frequently associated with the work of David McClelland.[26] This need arises from an individual's desire to accomplish a goal or task more effectively than in the past. Individuals who have a high need for achievement tend to set moderately difficult goals and to make moderately risky decisions. Suppose, for example, that Mark Cohen, a regional manager for a national retailer, sets a sales increase goal for his stores of either 1 percent or 50 percent. The first goal is probably too easy, and the second is probably impossible to reach; either would suggest a low need for achievement. But a mid-range goal of, say, 15 percent might present a reasonable challenge but also be within reach. Setting this goal might more accurately reflect a high need for achievement.

High-need achievers also want immediate, specific feedback on their performance. They want to know how well they did something as quickly after finishing it as possible. For this reason, high-need achievers frequently take jobs in sales, where they get almost immediate feedback from customers, and avoid jobs in areas such as research and development, where tangible progress is slower and feedback comes at longer intervals. If Mark Cohen only asks his managers for their sales performance on a periodic basis, he might not have a high need for achievement. But if he is constantly calling each store manager in his territory to ask about their sales increases, this activity indicates a high need for achievement on his part.

Preoccupation with work is another characteristic of high-need achievers. They think about it on their way to the workplace, during lunch, and at home. They find it difficult to put their work aside, and they become frustrated when they must stop working on a partly completed project. If Cohen seldom thinks about his business in the evening, he may not be a high-need achiever. However, if work is always on his mind, he might indeed be a high-need achiever.

Finally, high-need achievers tend to assume personal responsibility for getting things done. They often volunteer for extra duties and find it difficult to delegate part of a job to someone else. Accordingly, they derive a feeling of accomplishment when they have done more work than their peers without the assistance of others. Suppose Mark Cohen visits a store one day and finds that the merchandise is poorly displayed, that the floor is dirty, and that sales clerks don't seem motivated to help customers. If he has a low need for achievement, he might point the problems out to the store manager and then leave. But if his need for achievement is high, he may very well stay in the store for a while, personally supervising the changes that need to be made.

Although high-need achievers tend to be successful, they often do not achieve top management posts. The most common explanation is that although high need for achievement helps these people advance quickly through the ranks, the traits associated with the need often conflict with the requirements of high-level management positions. Because of the amount of work they are expected to do, top executives must be able to delegate tasks to others. In addition, they seldom receive immediate feedback, and they often must make decisions that are either more or less risky than those with which a high-need achiever would be comfortable.[27] High-need achievers tend to do well as individual entrepreneurs with little or no group reinforcement. Steve Jobs, the cofounder of Apple Computer, and Bill Gates, the cofounder of Microsoft, are both recognized as being high-need achievers.

The **need for achievement** is the desire to accomplish a task or goal more effectively than was done in the past.

The Need for Affiliation Individuals also experience the **need for affiliation**—the need for human companionship.[28] Researchers recognize several ways that people with a high need for affiliation differ from those with a lower need. Individuals with a high need tend to want reassurance and approval from others and usually are genuinely concerned about others' feelings. They are likely to act and think as they believe others want them to, especially those with whom they strongly identify and desire friendship. As we might expect, people with a strong need for affiliation most often work in jobs with a lot of interpersonal contact, such as sales and teaching positions.

For example, suppose that Watanka Jackson is seeking a job as a geologist or petroleum field engineer, a job that will take her into remote areas for long periods of time with little interaction with co-workers. Aside from her academic training, one reason for the nature of her job search might be that she has a low need for affiliation. In contrast, a class-

The need for affiliation is the basic need that many people have for the companionship of others. People who have a strong need for affiliation will seek out opportunities to interact with others, while people with a low need for affiliation are comfortable spending time alone. These managers are enjoying a working lunch to... completing this project as a team may have been drive... demands, they could have handled the project via ema... they enjoy each other's company, they decided to mee...

COMSTOCK IMAGES/JUPITER IMAGES

mate of hers, William Pfeffer, may be seeking a job in the corporate headquarters of a petroleum company. His preferences might be dictated, at least in part, by a desire to be around other people in the workplace; thus he has a higher need for affiliation. A recent Gallup survey suggests that people who have at least one good friend at work are much more likely to be highly engaged with their work and to indicate higher levels of job satisfaction.[29]

The Need for Power A third major individual need is the **need for power**—the desire to control one's environment, including financial, material, informational, and human resources.[30] People vary greatly along this dimension. Some individuals spend much time and energy seeking power; others avoid power if at all possible. People with a high need for power can be successful managers if three conditions are met. First, they must seek power for the betterment of the organization rather than for their own interests. Second, they must have a fairly low need for affiliation because fulfilling a personal need for power may well alienate others in the workplace. Third, they need plenty of self-control to curb their desire for power when it threatens to interfere with effective organizational or interpersonal relationships.[31]

PROCESS-BASED PERSPECTIVES ON MOTIVATION

Process-based perspectives are concerned with how motivation occurs. Rather than attempting to identify motivational stimuli, process perspectives focus on why people choose certain behavioral options to satisfy their needs and how they evaluate their

The **need for affiliation** is the need for human companionship.

The **need for power** is the desire to control the resources in one's environment.

The **process-based perspectives on motivation** focus on how people behave in their efforts to satisfy their needs.

STEVE LABADASSA

The equity theory of motivation suggests that people compare themselves with others in terms of their inputs to their organization relative to their outcomes. But in these days of high-stress jobs and overworked employees, equity perceptions may be about as stable as a house of cards. Take Sherri Stoddard, for example. Stoddard is a registered nurse. Efforts to lower healthcare costs have caused nurses to take on ever-growing patient loads. In addition, they often have mandatory overtime requirements and mountains of paperwork. While their compensation has grown slightly, many nurses like Stoddard are feeling that they are being asked to do too much for what they are paid.

satisfaction after they have attained these goals. Three useful process perspectives on motivation are the equity, expectancy, and goal-setting theories.

The Equity Theory of Motivation

The **equity theory** of motivation is based on the relatively simple premise that people in organizations want to be treated fairly.[32] The theory defines **equity** as the belief that we are being treated fairly in relation to others and inequity as the belief that we are being treated unfairly compared with others. Equity theory is just one of several theoretical formulations derived from social comparison processes. Social comparisons involve evaluating our own situation in terms of others' situations. In this chapter, we focus mainly on equity theory because it is the most highly developed of the social comparison approaches and the one that applies most directly to the work motivation of people in organizations.

Forming Equity Perceptions   People in organizations form perceptions of the equity of their treatment through a four-step process. First, they evaluate how they are being treated by the firm. Second, they form a perception of how a "comparison-other" is being treated. The comparison-other might be a person in the same work group, someone in another part of the organization, or even a composite of several people scattered throughout the organization.[33] Third, they compare their own circumstances with those of the comparison-other and then use this comparison as the basis for forming an impression of either equity or inequity. Fourth, depending on the strength of this feeling, the person may choose to pursue one or more of the alternatives discussed in the next section.

Equity theory describes the equity comparison process in terms of an input-to-outcome ratio. Inputs are an individual's contributions to the organization—such factors as education, experience, effort, and loyalty. Outcomes are what the person receives in return—pay, recognition, social relationships, intrinsic rewards, and similar things. In effect, then, this part of the equity process is essentially a personal assessment of one's psychological contract. A person's assessments of inputs and outcomes for both self and others are based partly on objective data (for example, the person's own salary) and partly on perceptions (such as the comparison-other's level of recognition). The equity comparison thus takes the following form:

$$\frac{\text{Outcome (self)}}{\text{Inputs (self)}} \text{ compared with } \frac{\text{Outcomes (other)}}{\text{Inputs (other)}}$$

Equity theory focuses on people's desire to be treated with what they perceive as equity and to avoid perceived inequity.

Equity is the belief that we are being treated fairly in relation to others; inequity is the belief that we are being treated unfairly in relation to others.

If the two sides of this psychological equation are comparable, the person experiences a feeling of equity; if the two sides do not balance, a feeling of inequity results. We should stress, however, that a perception of equity does not require that the perceived outcomes and inputs be equal, but only that their ratios be the same. A person may believe that his comparison-other deserves to make more money because she works harder, thus making her outcomes (higher pay) acceptable because it is proportional to her higher input (harder work). Only if the other person's outcomes seem disproportionate to her inputs does the comparison provoke a perception of inequity.

Responses to Equity and Inequity   Figure 4.4 summarizes the results of an equity comparison. If a person feels equitably treated, she is generally motivated to maintain the status quo. For example, she will continue to provide the same level of input to the organization as long as her outcomes do not change and the ratio of inputs and outcomes of the comparison-other do not change. But a person who is experiencing inequity—real or imagined—is motivated to reduce it. Moreover, the greater the inequity, the stronger the level of motivation.

People may use one of six common methods to reduce inequity.[34] First, we may change our own inputs. Thus, we may put more or less effort into the job, depending on which way the inequity lies, as a way to alter our ratio. If we believe we are being underpaid, for example, we may decide not to work as hard.

Second, we may change our own outcomes. We might, for example, demand a pay raise, seek additional avenues for growth and development, or even resort to stealing as a way to "get more" from the organization. Or we might alter our perceptions of the value of our current outcomes, perhaps by deciding that our present level of job security is greater and more valuable than we originally thought.

A third, more complex response is to alter our perceptions of ourselves and our behavior. After perceiving an inequity, for example, we may change our original self-assessment and decide that we are really contributing less but receiving more than we originally believed. For example, we might decide that we are not really working as many hours as we had first thought—admitting, perhaps, that some of our time spent in the office is really just socializing and not actually contributing to the organization.

Fourth, we may alter our perception of the comparison-other's inputs or outcomes. After all, much of our assessment of other people is based on perceptions, and perceptions can be changed. For example, if we feel underrewarded, we may decide that our comparison-other is working more hours than we originally believed—say by coming in on weekends and taking work home at night.

Fifth, we may change the object of comparison. We may conclude, for instance, that the current comparison-other is the boss's personal favorite, is unusually lucky, or has special skills and abilities. A different person would thus provide a more valid basis for comparison. Indeed, we might change comparison-others fairly often.

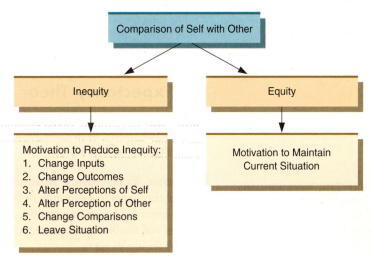

Figure 4.4   **RESPONSES TO PERCEPTIONS OF EQUITY AND INEQUITY**

People form equity perceptions by comparing their situation with that of someone else. If they experience equity, they are motivated to maintain the current situation. If they experience inequity, they are motivated to use one or more of the strategies shown here to reduce the inequity.

Comparison of Self with Other

Inequity | Equity

Motivation to Reduce Inequity:
1. Change Inputs
2. Change Outcomes
3. Alter Perceptions of Self
4. Alter Perception of Other
5. Change Comparisons
6. Leave Situation

Motivation to Maintain Current Situation

𝓕*igure 4.5*   THE EXPECTANCY THEORY OF MOTIVATION

The expectancy theory is the most complex model of employee motivation in organizations. As shown here, the key components of expectancy theory are effort-to-performance expectancy, performance-to-outcome expectancy, and outcomes, each of which has an associated valence. These components interact with effort, the environment, and the ability to determine an individual's performance.

Then she comes across an advertisement for a management training position with a large company known for being an excellent place to work. No experience is necessary, the primary requirement is a college degree, and the starting salary is $37,000. She will probably apply for this position because (1) she wants it, and (2) she thinks she has a reasonable chance of getting it. (Of course, this simple example understates the true complexity of most choices. Job-seeking students may have strong geographic preferences, have other job opportunities, and also be considering graduate school. Most decisions of this type, in fact, are quite complex.)

Figure 4.5 summarizes the basic expectancy model. The model's general components are effort (the result of motivated behavior), performance, and outcomes. Expectancy theory emphasizes the linkages among these elements, which are described in terms of expectancies and valences.

Effort-to-Performance Expectancy   **Effort-to-performance expectancy** is a person's perception of the probability that effort will lead to successful performance. If we believe our effort will lead to higher performance, this expectancy is very strong, perhaps approaching a probability of 1.0, where 1.0 equals absolute certainty that the outcome will occur. If we believe our performance will be the same no matter how much effort we make, our expectancy is very low—perhaps as low as 0, meaning that there is no probability that the outcome will occur. A person who thinks there is a moderate relationship between effort and subsequent performance—the normal circumstance—has an expectancy somewhere between 1.0 and 0. Mia Hamm, a star soccer player who believes that when she puts forth maximum effort she has a great chance of scoring higher than any opponent, clearly sees a link between her effort and performance.

Performance-to-Outcome Expectancy   **Performance-to-outcome expectancy** is a person's perception of the probability that performance will lead to certain other outcomes. If a person thinks a high performer is certain to get a pay raise, this expectancy is close to 1.0. At the other extreme, a person who believes raises are entirely independent of performance has an expectancy close to 0. Finally, if a person thinks performance has some bearing on the prospects for a pay raise, his or her expectancy is somewhere between 1.0 and 0. In a work setting, several performance-to-outcome expectancies are relevant because, as Figure 4.5 shows, several outcomes might

Effort-to-performance expectancy is a person's perception of the probability that effort will lead to performance.

Performance-to-outcome expectancy is the individual's perception of the probability that performance will lead to certain outcomes.

logically result from performance. Each outcome, then, has its own expectancy. Philadelphia's quarterback Donovan McNabb may believe that if he plays aggressively all the time (performance), he has a great chance of leading his team to the playoffs. Playing aggressively may win him individual honors like the Most Valuable Player award, but he may also experience more physical trauma and throw more interceptions. (All three anticipated results are outcomes.)

Outcomes and Valences An **outcome** is anything that might potentially result from performance. High-level performance conceivably might produce such outcomes as a pay raise, a promotion, recognition from the boss, fatigue, stress, or less time to rest, among others. The **valence** of an outcome is the relative attractiveness or unattractiveness—the value—of that outcome to the person. Pay raises, promotions, and recognition might all have positive valences whereas fatigue, stress, and less time to rest might all have negative valences.

The strength of outcome valences varies from person to person. Work-related stress may be a significant negative factor for one person but only a slight annoyance to another. Similarly, a pay increase may have a strong positive valence for someone desperately in need of money, a slight positive valence for someone interested mostly in getting a promotion, or—for someone in an unfavorable tax position—even a negative valence!

The basic expectancy framework suggests that three conditions must be met before motivated behavior occurs. First, the effort-to-performance expectancy must be well above zero. That is, the worker must reasonably expect that exerting effort will produce high levels of performance. Second, the performance-to-outcome expectancies must be well above zero. Thus, the person must believe that performance will realistically result in valued outcomes. Third, the sum of all the valences for the potential outcomes relevant to the person must be positive. One or more valences may be negative as long as the positives outweigh the negatives. For example, stress and fatigue may have moderately negative valences, but if pay, promotion, and recognition have very high positive valences, the overall valence of the set of outcomes associated with performance will still be positive.

Conceptually, the valences of all relevant outcomes and the corresponding pattern of expectancies are assumed to interact in an almost mathematical fashion to determine a person's level of motivation. Most people do assess likelihoods of and preferences for various consequences of behavior, but they seldom approach them in such a calculating manner.

The Porter-Lawler Model The original presentation of expectancy theory placed it squarely in the mainstream of contemporary motivation theory. Since then, the model has been refined and extended many times. Most modifications have focused on identifying and measuring outcomes and expectancies. An exception is the variation of expectancy theory developed by Porter and Lawler. These researchers used expectancy theory to develop a novel view of the relationship between employee satisfaction and performance.[38] Although the conventional wisdom was that satisfaction leads to performance, Porter and Lawler argued the reverse: If rewards are adequate, high levels of performance may lead to satisfaction.

The Porter-Lawler model appears in Figure 4.6. Some of its features are quite different from the original version of expectancy theory. For example, the extended model includes abilities, traits, and role perceptions. At the beginning of the motivational cycle, effort is a function of the value of the potential reward for the employee (its valence) and the perceived effort-reward probability (an expectancy). Effort then combines with abilities, traits, and role perceptions to determine actual performance.

An **outcome** is anything that results from performing a particular behavior.

Valence is the degree of attractiveness or unattractiveness a particular outcome has for a person.

Figure 4.6 THE PORTER-LAWLER MODEL

The Porter and Lawler expectancy model provides interesting insights into the relationships between satisfaction and performance. As illustrated here, this model predicts that satisfaction is determined by the perceived equity of intrinsic and extrinsic rewards for performance. That is, rather than satisfaction causing performance, which many people might predict, this model argues that it is actually performance that eventually leads to satisfaction.

Reference: Figure from Lyman W. Porter and Edward E. Lawler, *Managerial Attitudes and Performance.* Copyright © 1968. McGraw-Hill, Inc. Used by permission of Lyman W. Porter.

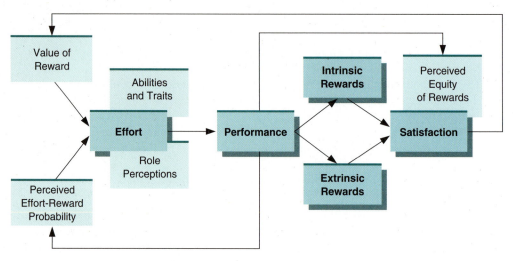

Performance results in two kinds of rewards. Intrinsic rewards are intangible—a feeling of accomplishment, a sense of achievement, and so forth. Extrinsic rewards are tangible outcomes such as pay and promotion. The individual judges the value of his or her performance to the organization and uses social comparison processes (as in equity theory) to form an impression of the equity of the rewards received. If the rewards are regarded as equitable, the employee feels satisfied. In subsequent cycles, satisfaction with rewards influences the value of the rewards anticipated, and actual performance following effort influences future perceived effort-reward probabilities.

Evaluation and Implications Expectancy theory has been tested by many different researchers in a variety of settings and using a variety of methods.[39] As noted earlier, the complexity of the theory has been both a blessing and a curse.[40] Nowhere is this double-edged quality more apparent than in the research undertaken to evaluate the theory. Several studies have supported various parts of the theory. For example, both kinds of expectancy and valence have been found to be associated with effort and performance in the workplace.[41] Research has also confirmed expectancy theory's claims that people will not engage in motivated behavior unless they (1) value the expected rewards, (2) believe their efforts will lead to performance, and (3) believe their performance will result in the desired rewards.[42]

However, expectancy theory is so complicated that researchers have found it quite difficult to test. In particular, the measures of various parts of the model may lack validity, and the procedures for investigating relationships among the variables have often been less scientific than researchers would like. Moreover, people are seldom as rational and objective in choosing behaviors as expectancy theory implies. Still, the logic of the model, combined with the consistent, albeit modest, research support for it, suggests that the theory has much to offer.

Research has also suggested that expectancy theory is more likely to explain motivation in the United States than in other countries. People from the United States tend to be very goal oriented and tend to think that they can influence their own success. Thus, under the right combinations of expectancies, valences, and outcomes, they will be highly motivated. But different patterns may exist in other countries. For example, many people from Muslim countries think that God determines the outcome of every behavior, so the concept of expectancy is not applicable.[43]

Because expectancy theory is so complex, it is difficult to apply directly in the workplace. A manager would need to figure out what rewards each employee wants and how valuable those rewards are to each person, measure the various expectancies, and finally adjust the relationships to create motivation. Nevertheless, expectancy theory offers several important guidelines for the practicing manager. The following are some of the more fundamental guidelines:

1. Determine the primary outcomes each employee wants.
2. Decide what levels and kinds of performance are needed to meet organizational goals.
3. Make sure the desired levels of performance are possible.
4. Link desired outcomes and desired performance.
5. Analyze the situation for conflicting expectancies.
6. Make sure the rewards are large enough.
7. Make sure the overall system is equitable for everyone.[44]

LEARNING-BASED PERSPECTIVES ON MOTIVATION

Learning is another key component in employee motivation. In any organization, employees quickly learn which behaviors are rewarded and which are ignored or punished. Thus, learning plays a critical role in maintaining motivated behavior. **Learning** is a relatively permanent change in behavior or behavioral potential that results from direct or indirect experience. For example, we can learn to use a new software application program by practicing and experimenting with its various functions and options.

How Learning Occurs

The Traditional View: Classical Conditioning   The most influential historical approach to learning is classical conditioning, developed by Ivan Pavlov in his famous experiments with dogs.[45] **Classical conditioning** is a simple form of learning in which a conditioned response is linked with an unconditioned stimulus. In organizations, however, only simple behaviors and responses can be learned in this manner. For example, suppose an employee receives very bad news one day from his boss. It's possible that the employee could come to associate, say, the color of the boss's suit that day with bad news. Thus, the next time the boss wears that same suit to the office, the employee may experience dread and foreboding.

But this form of learning is obviously simplistic and not directly relevant to motivation. Learning theorists soon recognized that although classical conditioning offered some interesting insights into the learning process, it was inadequate as an explanation of human learning. For one thing, classical conditioning relies on simple cause-and-effect relationships between one stimulus and one response; it cannot deal

Learning is a relatively permanent change in behavior or behavioral potential resulting from direct or indirect experience.

Classical conditioning is a simple form of learning that links a conditioned response with an unconditioned stimulus.

with the more complex forms of learned behavior that typify human beings. For another, classical conditioning ignores the concept of choice; it assumes that behavior is reflexive, or involuntary. Therefore, this perspective cannot explain situations in which people consciously and rationally choose one course of action from among many. Because of these shortcomings of classical conditioning, theorists eventually moved on to other approaches that seemed more useful in explaining the processes associated with complex learning.

The Contemporary View: Learning as a Cognitive Process   Although it is not tied to a single theory or model, contemporary learning theory generally views learning as a cognitive process; that is, it assumes that people are conscious, active participants in how they learn.[46]

First, the cognitive view suggests that people draw on their experiences and use past learning as a basis for their present behavior. These experiences represent knowledge, or cognitions. For example, an employee faced with a choice of job assignments will use previous experiences in deciding which one to accept. Second, people make choices about their behavior. The employee recognizes that she has two alternatives and chooses one. Third, people recognize the consequences of their choices. Thus, when the employee finds the job assignment rewarding and fulfilling, she will recognize that the choice was a good one and will understand why. Finally, people evaluate those consequences and add them to prior learning, which affects future choices. Faced with the same job choices next year, the employee will probably be motivated to choose the same one. As implied earlier, several perspectives on learning take a cognitive view. Perhaps foremost among them is reinforcement theory. Although reinforcement theory per se is not really new, it has only been applied to organizational settings in the last few years.

Reinforcement Theory and Learning

Reinforcement theory (also called "operant conditioning") is generally associated with the work of B. F. Skinner.[47] In its simplest form, **reinforcement theory** suggests that behavior is a function of its consequences.[48] Behavior that results in pleasant consequences is more likely to be repeated (the employee will be motivated to repeat the current behavior), and behavior that results in unpleasant consequences is less likely to be repeated (the employee will be motivated to engage in different behaviors). Reinforcement theory also suggests that in any given situation, people explore a variety of possible behaviors. Future behavioral choices are affected by the consequences of earlier behaviors. Cognitions, as already noted, also play an important role. Therefore, rather than assuming the mechanical stimulus-response linkage suggested by the traditional classical view of learning, contemporary theorists believe that people consciously explore different behaviors and systematically choose those that result in the most desirable outcomes.

Suppose a new employee at Monsanto in St. Louis wants to learn the best way to get along with his boss. At first, the employee is very friendly and informal, but the boss responds by acting aloof and, at times, annoyed. Because the boss does not react positively, the employee is unlikely to continue this behavior. In fact, the employee next starts acting more formal and professional and finds the boss much more receptive to this posture. The employee will probably continue this new set of behaviors because they have resulted in positive consequences.

Reinforcement theory is based on the idea that behavior is a function of its consequences.

Reinforcements are the consequences of behavior.

Types of Reinforcement in Organizations   The consequences of behavior are called **reinforcement**. Managers can use various kinds of reinforcement to affect employee behavior. There are four basic forms of reinforcement—positive reinforcement, avoidance, extinction, and punishment.

Positive reinforcement is a reward or other desirable consequence that follows behavior. Providing positive reinforcement after a particular behavior motivates employees to maintain or increase the frequency of that behavior. A compliment from the boss after an employee has completed a difficult job and a salary increase following a worker's period of high performance are examples of positive reinforcement. This type of reinforcement has been used at Corning's ceramics factory in Virginia, where workers receive bonuses for pulling blemished materials from assembly lines before they go into more expensive stages of production. Intuit has started a program of giving relatively small but relatively frequent rewards when workers perform well. So, for example, rather than getting one large bonus at the end of the year, a high performer may get several smaller ones throughout the year.[49]

Avoidance, also known as **negative reinforcement**, is another means of increasing the frequency of desirable behavior. Rather than receiving a reward following a desirable behavior, the person is given the opportunity to avoid an unpleasant consequence. For example, suppose that a boss habitually criticizes employees who dress casually. To avoid criticism, an employee may routinely dress to suit the supervisor's tastes. The employee is thus motivated to engage in desirable behavior (at least from the supervisor's viewpoint) to avoid an unpleasant, or aversive, consequence.

Extinction decreases the frequency of behavior, especially behavior that was previously rewarded. If rewards are withdrawn for behaviors that were previously reinforced, the behaviors will probably become less frequent and eventually die out. For example, a manager with a small staff may encourage frequent visits from subordinates as a way of keeping in touch with what is going on. Positive reinforcement might include cordial conversation, attention to subordinates' concerns, and encouragement to come in again soon. As the staff grows, however, the manager may find that such unstructured conversations make it difficult to get her own job done. She then might begin to brush off casual conversation and reward only to-the-point "business" conversations. Withdrawing the rewards for casual chatting will probably extinguish that behavior. We should also note that if managers, inadvertently or otherwise, stop rewarding valuable behaviors such as good performance, those behaviors also may become extinct.

Punishment, like extinction, also tends to decrease the frequency of undesirable behaviors. Punishment is an unpleasant, or aversive, consequence of a behavior.[50] Examples of punishment are verbal or written reprimands, pay cuts, loss of privileges, layoffs, and termination. Many experts question the value of punishment and believe that managers use it too often and use it inappropriately. In some situations, however, punishment may be an appropriate tool for altering behavior. Many instances of

HARLEY SCHWADRON/SCHWADRON CARTOONS

ENCOURAGING PATS ON THE BACK 50¢

Positive reinforcement, of course, can be a powerful force in organizations and can help sustain motivated behaviors. But in order to really work, reinforcement should be of value to the individual and conform to one of the five schedules, as discussed in the text. However, if someone is truly desperate for a pat on the back, a simple device such as the one shown here might have some hidden market potential!

Positive reinforcement is a reward or other desirable consequence that a person receives after exhibiting behavior.

Avoidance, or **negative reinforcement**, is the opportunity to avoid or escape from an unpleasant circumstance after exhibiting behavior.

Extinction decreases the frequency of behavior by eliminating a reward or desirable consequence that follows that behavior.

Punishment is an unpleasant, or aversive, consequence that results from behavior.

Table 4.1
SCHEDULES OF REINFORCEMENT

Schedule of Reinforcement	Nature of Reinforcement
Command Groups	Task Groups
Continuous	Behavior is reinforced every time it occurs.
Fixed-Interval	Behavior is reinforced according to some predetermined, constant schedule based on time.
Variable-Interval	Behavior is reinforced after periods of time, but the time span varies from one time to the next.
Fixed-Ratio	Behavior is reinforced according to the number of behaviors exhibited, with the number of behaviors needed to gain reinforcement held constant.
Variable-Ratio	Behavior is reinforced according to the number of behaviors exhibited, but the number of behaviors needed to gain reinforcement varies from one time to the next.

life's unpleasantness teach us what to do by means of punishment. Falling off a bike, drinking too much, or going out in the rain without an umbrella all lead to punishing consequences (getting bruised, suffering a hangover, and getting wet), and we often learn to change our behavior as a result. Furthermore, certain types of undesirable behavior may have far-reaching negative effects if they go unpunished. For instance, an employee who sexually harasses a coworker, a clerk who steals money from the petty cash account, and an executive who engages in illegal stock transactions all deserve punishment.

Schedules of Reinforcement in Organizations
Should the manager try to reward every instance of desirable behavior and punish every instance of undesirable behavior? Or is it better to apply reinforcement according to some plan or schedule? As you might expect, it depends on the situation. Table 4.1 summarizes five basic schedules of reinforcement that managers can use.

Continuous reinforcement rewards behavior every time it occurs. Continuous reinforcement is very effective in motivating desirable behaviors, especially in the early stages of learning. When reinforcement is withdrawn, however, extinction sets in very quickly. But continuous reinforcement poses serious difficulties because the manager must monitor every behavior of an employee and provide effective reinforcement. This approach, then, is of little practical value to managers. Offering partial reinforcement according to one of the other four schedules is much more typical.

Fixed-interval reinforcement is reinforcement provided on a predetermined, constant schedule. The Friday-afternoon paycheck is a good example of a fixed-interval reinforcement. Unfortunately, in many situations the fixed-interval schedule does not necessarily maintain high performance levels. If employees know the boss will drop by to check on them every day at 1:00 P.M., they may be motivated to work hard at that time, hoping to gain praise and recognition or to avoid the boss's wrath. At other times of the day, the employees probably will not work as hard because they have learned that reinforcement is unlikely except during the daily visit.

Variable-interval reinforcement also uses time as the basis for applying reinforcement, but it varies the interval between reinforcements. This schedule is inappropriate for paying wages, but it can work well for other types of positive reinforcement, such

Schedules of reinforcement indicate when or how often managers should reinforce certain behaviors.

With **continuous reinforcement**, behavior is rewarded every time it occurs.

Fixed-interval reinforcement provides reinforcement on a fixed time schedule.

Variable-interval reinforcement varies the amount of time between reinforcements.

as praise and recognition, and for avoidance. Consider again the group of employees just described. Suppose that instead of coming by at exactly 1:00 P.M. every day, the boss visits at a different time each day: 9:30 A.M. on Monday, 2:00 P.M. on Tuesday, 11:00 A.M. on Wednesday, and so on. The following week, the times change. Because the employees do not know exactly when to expect the boss, they may be motivated to work hard for a longer period—until her visit. Afterward, though, they may drop back to lower levels because they have learned that she will not be back until the next day.

The fixed- and variable-ratio schedules gear reinforcement to the number of desirable or undesirable behaviors rather than to blocks of time. With **fixed-ratio reinforcement**, the number of behaviors needed to obtain reinforcement is constant. Assume, for instance, that a work group enters its cumulative performance totals into the firm's computer network every hour. The manager of the group uses the network to monitor its activities. He might adopt a practice of dropping by to praise the group every time it reaches a performance level of five hundred units. Thus, if the group does this three times on Monday, he stops by each time; if it reaches the mark only once on Tuesday, he stops by only once. The fixed-ratio schedule can be fairly effective in maintaining desirable behavior. Employees may acquire a sense of what it takes to be reinforced and may be motivated to maintain their performance.

With **variable-ratio reinforcement**, the number of behaviors required for reinforcement varies over time. An employee performing under a variable-ratio schedule is motivated to work hard because each successful behavior increases the probability that the next one will result in reinforcement. With this schedule, the exact number of behaviors needed to obtain reinforcement is not crucial; what is important is that the intervals between reinforcement not be so long that the worker gets discouraged and stops trying. The supervisor in the fixed-ratio example could reinforce his work group after it reaches performance levels of 325, 525, 450, 600, and so on. A variable-ratio schedule can be quite effective, but it is difficult and cumbersome to use when formal organizational rewards, such as pay increases and promotions, are the reinforcers. A fixed-interval system is the best way to administer these rewards.

Social Learning in Organizations

In recent years, managers have begun to recognize the power of social learning. **Social learning** occurs when people observe the behaviors of others, recognize their consequences, and alter their own behavior as a result. A person can learn to do a new job by observing others or by watching videotapes. Or an employee may learn to avoid being late by seeing the boss chew out fellow workers. Social learning theory, then, suggests that individual behavior is determined by a person's cognitions and social environment. More specifically, people are presumed to learn behaviors and attitudes at least partly in response to what others expect of them.

Several conditions must be met to produce an appropriate environment for social learning. First, the behavior being observed and imitated must be relatively simple. Although we can learn by watching someone else how to push three or four buttons to set specifications on a machine or to turn on a computer, we probably cannot learn a complicated sequence of operations for the machine or how to run a complex software package without also practicing the various steps ourselves. Second, social learning usually involves observed and imitated behavior that is concrete, not intellectual. We can learn by watching others how to respond to the different behaviors of a particular manager or how to assemble a few component parts into a final assembled product. But we probably cannot learn through simple observation how to write computer software, how to write complicated text, how to conceptualize, or how to think abstractly.

Fixed-ratio reinforcement provides reinforcement after a fixed number of behaviors.

Variable-ratio reinforcement varies the number of behaviors between reinforcements.

Social learning occurs when people observe the behaviors of others, recognize their consequences, and alter their own behavior as a result.

Finally, for social learning to occur, we must possess the physical ability to imitate the behavior observed. Most of us, even if we watch televised baseball games or tennis matches every weekend, cannot hit a fastball like Alex Rodriguez or execute a backhand like Venus Williams.

Social learning influences motivation in a variety of ways. Many of the behaviors we exhibit in our daily work lives are learned from others. Suppose a new employee joins an existing work group. She already has some basis for knowing how to behave from her education and previous experience. However, the group provides a set of very specific cues she can use to tailor her behavior to fit her new situation. The group may indicate how the organization expects its members to dress, how people are "supposed" to feel about the boss, and so forth. Hence, the employee learns how to behave in the new situation partly in response to what she already knows and partly in response to what others suggest and demonstrate.

As we showed in our opening vignette on NetApp, social learning can be a significant factor in developing a satisfying workplace. In continuing our discussion of NetApp, the *Change* box on page 113 shows that, under certain adverse conditions, even the most successful motivational techniques have limitations.

Organizational Behavior Modification

Learning theory alone has important implications for managers, but organizational behavior modification has even more practical applications. Organizational behavior modification is an important application of reinforcement theory some managers use to enhance motivation and performance.

Behavior Modification in Organizations   Organizational behavior modification, or OB mod, is the application of reinforcement theory to people in organizational settings.[51] Reinforcement theory says that we can increase the frequency of desirable behaviors by linking those behaviors with positive consequences and decrease undesirable behaviors by linking them with negative consequences. OB mod characteristically uses positive reinforcement to encourage desirable behaviors in employees. Figure 4.7 illustrates the basic steps in OB mod.

The first step is to identify performance-related behavioral events—that is, desirable and undesirable behaviors. A manager of an electronics store might decide that the most important behavior for salespeople working on commission is to greet customers warmly and show them the exact merchandise they came in to see. Note in Figure 4.7 that three kinds of organizational activity are associated with this behavior: the behavioral event itself, the performance that results, and the organizational consequences that befall the individual.

Next, the manager measures baseline performance—the existing level of performance for each individual. This usually is stated in terms of a percentage frequency across different time intervals. For example, the electronics store manager may observe that a particular salesperson presently is greeting around 40 percent of the customers each day as desired. Performance management techniques, described in Chapter 6, are used for this purpose.

The third step is to identify the existing behavioral contingencies, or consequences, of performance; that is, what happens now to employees who perform at various levels? If an employee works hard, does he or she get a reward or just get tired? The electronics store manager may observe that when customers are greeted warmly and assisted competently, they buy something 40 percent of the time whereas customers who are not properly greeted and assisted make a purchase only 20 percent of the time.

Organizational behavior modification, or **OB mod**, is the application of reinforcement theory to people in organizational settings.

CHANGE

The NetApp Approach to Net Jobs

In January 2009, when they placed NetApp at the top of their 2008 list of the "100 Best Companies to Work For," the editors at *Fortune* magazine noted that the storage and data-management company "has gained market share during the slump, hasn't had layoffs, and has more than $2 billion in cash on hand to help it ride out the global financial crisis." A month later—on Monday, February 11, to be precise—NetApp announced that it was taking "a number of steps to better align our resources with the business outlook. This restructuring includes a reduction of about 6 percent of the global workforce, as well as the reallocation of other resources to initiatives designed to increase operating efficiency and build a foundation for additional market-share gains."

Dan Warmenhoven, who holds the title of Executive Chairman, told a reporter that he'd gone online to find some scrap of optimistic economic news with which to soften the blow for remaining employees. "I spent about an hour," he said, "and I couldn't find a single thing. Nothing." About 530 of the firm's more than 8,000 global employees were laid off, either as a result of the lingering recession or "restructuring." In any case, blogged one employee, "for 6 percent of the staff, it's no longer the best place to work."

As it happens, the announcement of the layoff, coupled with some optimistic analyst previews (the storage segment promised to be stronger than the rest of the IT market), gave NetApp a pre-earnings-report boost, as its stock price rose by 16 cents, or nearly 10 percent, per share. In addition, the aforementioned restructuring, which also involved reductions in the numbers of contractors and outside services, had saved the company $30 million in the third quarter of 2009.

> *"Well, for 6 percent of the staff, it's no longer the best place to work."*
> —NETAPP EMPLOYEE ON THE COMPANY'S 2009 LAYOFFS

The next day, however—February 12—NetApp announced a decline in sales of 16 percent for the quarter and a loss of $75 million. CFO Steve Gomo attributed the decline to "a shift away from our larger software-rich systems which we believe has been driven by customer frugality."

When it was revealed during the same month that Warmenhoven had recently taken delivery of a $3 million Phenom-100 jet, NetApp was quick to inform interested parties that the plane was for Warmenhoven's private use and had been on order for two years. "The global economy," explained VP for corporate relations Eric Brown, "was in a very healthy spot two years ago." Brown added that Warmenhoven

was personally committed to making sure NetApp employees around the world got severance packages that would go beyond what even the most generous packages typically include—in line with his own ethics and our commitment to be a model company. As an example, all U.S. employees will be paid their annual bonus pro-rated for the first three quarters of the year along our bonus-accrual guidelines. That's extremely rare in severance payouts.

"I hope this example shows," concluded Brown, "that we as a company and Dan in particular as our [chairman] and as a compassionate man do not take a reduction in force as something trivial."

In characterizing the firm as the number-one U.S. company to work for, the Great Place to Work Institute had attributed "the quality of the workplace at NetApp" to its "high trust culture." NetApp leaders, said Amy Lyman, the Institute's director of corporate research, "reach out to employees, sharing information, support, and time

Continued

in a variety of ways." She reported that, as the recession deepened through 2008, the company took steps to ensure that all employees were "kept well informed of changes in projections with frequent communications from senior leaders." A Vice President's Forum, for example, convened every two weeks to share economic information and find out what was on employees' minds. To help managers respond to questions, recognize signs of stress, and involve employees in discussions of issues facing the company, NetApp distributed a kit entitled "Communicating with Employees During Tough Times."

The goal of such programs is twofold: to let people know that the company will provide support and to help them understand the effect of the economic downturn on the decisions being made by its leadership. "Right now," admits Warmenhoven, "we can't predict our future. We don't know if it's going up or down," but he's not optimistic about immediate prospects for growth. He won't rule out modest growth per quarter, but he also points out that it will take years for NetApp to get back to the levels that it enjoyed as recently as the fall of 2008.

"Not surprising," replied one worker whose response indicates how difficult it is for any company to juggle messages that employees often (and sometimes rightly) perceive as motivated less by the desire to reveal information than to conceal it. "Over the previous quarter," continued the anonymous employee, "Warmenhoven and [CEO Tom] Georgens slowly changed their tune from 'belt-tightening, no layoffs,' to 'we'll only do layoffs if we absolutely to have to,' to 'gee, things are looking really bad, we don't know what will happen.'"

References: "100 Best Companies to Work For," *Fortune*, February 2, 2009, http://money.cnn.com on February 13, 2010; Joseph F. Kovar, "NetApp Layoffs, Analyst Report Prompt Stock Increase," *ChannelWeb*, February 9, 2009, www.crn.com on February 13, 2010; Chris Mellor, "NetApp Restructures after $75M Loss," *Channel Register*, February 12, 2009, www.channelregister.co.uk on February 13, 2010; Chris Mellor, "NetApp Boss Flying High on Phenom?" *Channel Register*, February 11, 2009, www.channelregister.co.uk on February 13, 2010; Amy Lyman, "NetApp: Culture—Values—Leadership," Great Place to Work Institute, 2009, http://resources.greatplacetowork.com on February 11, 2010; Peter Burrows, "NetApp Rethinks the Future," *BusinessWeek*, February 11, 2009, www.businessweek.com on February 13, 2010.

At this point, the manager develops and applies an appropriate intervention strategy. In other words, some element of the performance-reward linkage—structure, process, technology, groups, or task—is changed to make high-level performance more rewarding. Various kinds of positive reinforcement are used to guide employee behavior in desired directions. The electronics store manager might offer a sales commission plan whereby salespeople earn a percentage of the dollar amount taken in by each sale. The manager might also compliment salespeople who give appropriate greetings and ignore those who do not. This reinforcement helps shape the behavior of salespeople. In addition, an individual salesperson who does not get reinforced may imitate the behavior of more successful salespersons. In general, this step relies on the reward system in the organization, as discussed previously.

After the intervention step, the manager again measures performance to determine whether the desired effect has been achieved. If not, the manager must redesign the intervention strategy or repeat the entire process. For instance, if the salespeople in the electronics store are still not greeting customers properly, the manager may need to look for other forms of positive reinforcement—perhaps a higher commission.

If performance has increased, the manager must try to maintain the desirable behavior through some schedule of positive reinforcement. For example, higher commissions might be granted for every other sale, for sales over a certain dollar amount, and so forth. (As we saw earlier, a reinforcement schedule defines the interval at which reinforcement is given.)

Finally, the manager looks for improvements in individual employees' behavior. Here the emphasis is on offering significant longer-term rewards, such as promotions and salary adjustments, to sustain ongoing efforts to improve performance.

𝒥igure 4.7   STEPS IN ORGANIZATIONAL BEHAVIOR MODIFICATION

Organizational behavior modification involves using reinforcement theory to motivate employee behavior. By employing the steps shown here, managers can often isolate behaviors they value and then link specific rewards to those behaviors. As a result, employees will be more likely to engage in those behaviors in the future.

Reference: "Steps in Organizational Behavior Modification" from *Personnel,* July–August 1974. Copyright © 1974 American Management Association. Reprinted by permission.

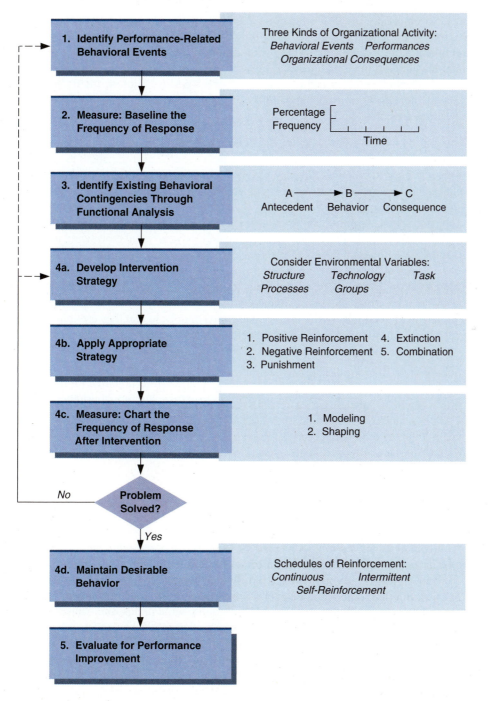

The Effectiveness of OB Mod   Since the OB mod approach is relatively simple, it has been used by many types of organizations, with varying levels of success.[52] A program at Emery Air Freight prompted much of the initial enthusiasm for OB mod, and other success stories have caught the attention of practicing managers.[53] B. F. Goodrich increased productivity over 300 percent and Weyerhaeuser increased productivity by at least 8 percent in three different work groups.[54] These results suggest that OB mod is a valuable method for improving employee motivation in many situations.

OB mod also has certain drawbacks. For one thing, not all applications have worked. A program at Standard Oil of Ohio was discontinued because it failed to meet its objectives; another program at Michigan Bell was only modestly successful. In addition, managers frequently have only limited means for providing meaningful reinforcement for their employees. Furthermore, much of the research testing OB mod has gone on in laboratories and thus is hard to generalize to the real world. And even if OB mod works for a while, the impact of the positive reinforcement may wane once the novelty has worn off, and employees may come to view it as a routine part of the compensation system.[55]

The Ethics of OB Mod   Although OB mod has considerable potential for enhancing motivated behavior in organizations, its critics raise ethical issues about its use. The primary ethical argument is that use of OB mod compromises individual freedom of choice. Managers may tend to select reinforcement contingencies that produce advantages for the organization with little or no regard for what is best for the individual employee. Thus, workers may be rewarded for working hard, producing high-quality products, and so forth. Behaviors that promote their own personal growth and development or that reduce their level of personal stress may go unrewarded.

An element of manipulation is also involved in OB mod. Indeed, its very purpose is to shape the behaviors of others. Thus, rather than giving employees an array of behaviors from which to choose, managers may continually funnel employee efforts through an increasingly narrow array of behavioral options so that they eventually have little choice but to select the limited set behaviors approved of by managers.

These ethical issues are, of course, real concerns that should not be ignored. At the same time, many other methods and approaches used by managers have the same goal of shaping behavior. Thus, OB mod is not really unique in its potential for misuse or misrepresentation. The keys are for managers to recognize and not abuse their ability to alter subordinate behavior and for employees to maintain control of their own work environment to the point that they are fully cognizant of the behavioral choices they are making.

SYNOPSIS

Motivation is the set of forces that cause people to behave as they do. Motivation starts with a need. People search for ways to satisfy their needs and then behave accordingly. Their behavior results in rewards or punishment. To varying degrees, an outcome may satisfy the original need. Scientific management asserted that money is the primary human motivator in the workplace. The human relations view suggested that social factors are primary motivators.

According to Abraham Maslow, human needs are arranged in a hierarchy of importance, from physiological to security to belongingness to esteem and, finally, to self-actualization. The ERG theory is a refinement of Maslow's original hierarchy that includes a frustration-regression component. In Herzberg's dual-structure theory, satisfaction and dissatisfaction are two distinct dimensions instead of opposite ends of the same dimension. Motivation factors are presumed to affect satisfaction and hygiene factors are presumed to affect dissatisfaction. Herzberg's theory is well known among managers but has several deficiencies. Other important individual needs include the needs for achievement, affiliation, and power.

The equity theory of motivation assumes that people want to be treated fairly. It hypothesizes that people compare their own input-to-outcome ratio in the organization with the ratio of a comparison-other. If they feel their treatment has been inequitable, they take steps to reduce the inequity. Expectancy theory, a somewhat more complicated model, follows from the assumption that people are motivated to work toward a goal if they want it and think that they have a reasonable chance of achieving it. Effort-to-performance expectancy is the belief that effort will lead to performance. Performance-to-outcome expectancy is the belief that performance will lead to certain outcomes. Valence is the desirability to the individual of the various possible outcomes of performance. The Porter-Lawler version of

expectancy theory provides useful insights into the relationship between satisfaction and performance. This model suggests that performance may lead to a variety of intrinsic and extrinsic rewards. When perceived as equitable, these rewards lead to satisfaction.

Learning also plays a role in employee motivation. Various kinds of reinforcement provided according to different schedules can increase or decrease motivated behavior. People are affected by social learning processes. Organizational behavior modification is a strategy for using learning and reinforcement principles to enhance employee motivation and performance. This strategy relies heavily on the effective measurement of performance and the provision of rewards to employees after they perform at a high level.

DISCUSSION QUESTIONS

1. Is it possible for someone to be unmotivated, or is all behavior motivated?
2. When has your level of performance been directly affected by your motivation? By your ability? By the environment?
3. Identify examples from your own experience that support, and others that refute, Maslow's hierarchy of needs theory.
4. Do you agree or disagree with the basic assumptions of Herzberg's dual-structure theory? Why?
5. How do you evaluate yourself in terms of your needs for achievement, affiliation, and power?
6. Have you ever experienced inequity in a job or a class? How did it affect you?
7. Which is likely to be a more serious problem— perceptions of being underrewarded or perceptions of being overrewarded?

8. What are some managerial implications of equity theory beyond those discussed in the chapter?
9. Do you think expectancy theory is too complex for direct use in organizational settings? Why or why not?
10. Do the relationships between performance and satisfaction suggested by Porter and Lawler seem valid? Cite examples that both support and refute the model.
11. Think of occasions on which you experienced each of the four types of reinforcement.
12. Identify the five types of reinforcement that you receive most often. On what schedule do you receive each of them?
13. What is your opinion about the ethics of OB mod?

ORGANIZATIONAL BEHAVIOR CASE FOR DISCUSSION

ARE YOU HAPPILY PRODUCTIVE OR PRODUCTIVELY HAPPY?

Sara Caputo is the founder and owner of Radiant Organizing, a training and coaching firm located in Santa Barbara, California. As a productivity consultant, her work includes both one-on-one sessions with clients and speaking on how to get things done in the workplace. One day, she recalls, as she was in the middle of a presentation at a professional conference, "I just felt myself really loving what I do.... This got me thinking,"

she says. "What comes first—happiness in your work or productivity in your work? Are we *more productive* in our jobs and at work because we enjoy what we do and [because] that in itself is a motivator? Or are we *happier* in our jobs and at work because we're productive?"

At first, Caputo admits, she was willing to accept the likelihood that her question came down to "sort of a chicken/egg dilemma." Upon further reflection, however, she decided that happiness probably comes first. "At one point in your life," she reasons,

> you had a calling to do what you're doing right now. Then time goes by, and what gets in the way? All the "other stuff." At the end of the day, if you're not happy doing what you do on a daily basis, you'll have a hard time sustaining your productivity because you'll just be getting things done for the sake of getting things done.

One rather suspects that Caputo's workplace experience has been somewhat happier than average, but her bottom-line perspective on the cause-and-effect relationship between happiness and productivity is pretty much in keeping with most thinking on the subject. "If you want to get more done at work…you should start by liking what you do," advises Alexander Kierulf, founder and CHO ("Chief Happiness Officer") of Spoing!, a Danish consulting firm. "…[T]he productivity gurus out there, he warns,

> *"If you're not happy doing what you do on a daily basis, you'll just be getting things done for the sake of getting things done."*
> —PRODUCTIVITY CONSULTANT SARA CAPUTO

> will tell you that it's all about having the right system. You need to prioritize your tasks, you must keep detailed logs of how you spend your time, to-do lists are of course essential, you must learn to structure your calendar, and much, much more.…[But] no system, no tool or methodology in the world can beat the productivity boost you get from really, really enjoying your work.

Happiness at work, says Kjerulf, "is the #1 productivity booster," and he cites a number of reasons why: Happy people work better with others, fix problems rather than complain about them, and make better decisions; they're optimistic and "way more motivated," and they have more energy and get sick less often.

Kjerulf admits that there's still a "question of causation"—the chicken-or-the-egg issue of which came first, happiness or productivity. "The link," he concludes, "goes both ways," but "the link is strongest from happiness to productivity—which means that if you want to be more productive, the very best thing you can do is focus on being happy with what you do."

Not everyone, however, sees the happiness-productivity link from the same perspective. For Paul Larson, a veteran of operations management in a variety of industries, the "legend that happy workers are productive employees has been a part of our organizational thinking for so long that many just take

for granted that it has to be true." Larson, founder and president of The Myrddin Group, a Texas-based consultancy specializing in organizational design and development, agrees that "productive workers do seem to be happier." But that, he suggests, is "where the confusion is coming from.…[P]roductivity leads to satisfaction and happiness," he argues, "not the other way around. People who do a good job tend to feel intrinsically good about it." To boost productivity, Larson advises, companies should train and support managers "in their efforts to keep the troops fully engaged. It's that engagement that provides the venues for achievement and recognition."

Charles Kerns, a behavioral psychologist at Pepperdine University's Graziado School of Business and Management, agrees with Larson that engagement is the best goal for a manager who wants "to influence the happiness level of his or her employees." He's not quite so sure, however, that enhancing either personal or organizational productivity hinges on solving the chicken-or-egg dilemma. "Job satisfaction researchers," he points out, "have had a long-standing debate as to whether employees are happy first and performers second, or performers first and happy second," and he doesn't seem to think that the matter is going to be resolved any time soon. For practical purposes, he suggests, "both happiness and job performance need to be addressed."

This where *engagement* comes in. On the one hand, according to Kerns, managers should probably resign themselves to the fact that improving engagement is about the best they can hope for. On the other hand, improving an employee's engagement with his or her work is no small achievement. Engagement can be measured by the extent to which an individual has *more happy or positive experiences than negative ones*, and the key to increasing positive experiences, says Kerns, is engaging an employee's strengths: "An employee's level of engagement…and subsequent happiness," he contends, "is likely boosted when he or she has the opportunity to do what he or she does best at work: Utilizing one's strengths is a positive experience." With engagement as a starting point, Kerns thinks that the happiness-productivity equation can be formulated in more practical terms: Happiness, he explains, "comes from work experiences that yield positive emotions [and] positive thoughts," and "people who approach tasks with positivity [are] more productive."

CASE QUESTIONS

1. How might the relationship between happiness and productivity be approached by each of the major motivational theories discussed in the chapter?
2. What factors help you to engage you in a task? What factors tend to contribute to "positivity" when you're working on a task? What factors tend to make your attitude negative?
3. Paul Larson says that "people tend to join a company but leave their supervisor." Do you agree or disagree? Explain your answer.
4. According to Alexander Kjerulf, there are two things that you can do enhance happiness in your work life: (1) get happy in the job you have or (2) get another job. In your opinion, which of these options is most likely to be successful? Personally, which option appeals to you more? If you must accept option (1), what steps would you take to make yourself happier in a job?

REFERENCES

Sara Caputo, "Which Comes First: Happiness or Productivity?" *Toolbox for HR*, April 15, 2009, http://hr.toolbox.com on February 15, 2010; Alexander Kjerulf, "Top 10 Reasons Why Happiness at Work Is the Ultimate Productivity Booster," *PositiveSharing.com*, March 27, 2007, http://positivesharing.com on February 15, 2010; Paul Larson, "Do Happy Employees Make Productive Employees?" *Suite101.com*, May 4, 2009, http://human-resources-management.suite101.com on February 14, 2010; Charles Kerns, "Both Job Performance and the Employee's Level of Happiness Impact the Potential of Success for an Organization," *Graziado Business Report*, vol. 11 (2008), http://gbr.pepperdine.edu on February 14, 2010.

EXPERIENCING ORGANIZATIONAL BEHAVIOR

Understanding the Dynamics of Expectancy Theory

Purpose: This exercise will help you recognize both the potential value and the complexity of expectancy theory.

Format: Working alone, you will be asked to identify the various aspects of expectancy theory that are pertinent to your class. You will then share your thoughts and results with some of your classmates.

Procedure: Considering your class as a workplace and your effort in the class as a surrogate for a job, do the following:

1. Identify six or seven things that might happen as a result of good performance in your class (for example, getting a good grade or a recommendation from your instructor). Your list must include at least one undesirable outcome (for example, a loss of free time).
2. Using a value of 10 for "extremely desirable," -10 for "extremely undesirable," and 0 for "complete neutrality," assign a valence to each outcome. In other words, the valence you assign to each outcome should be somewhere between 10 and -10, inclusive.
3. Assume you are a high performer. On that basis, estimate the probability of each potential outcome. Express this probability as a percentage.
4. Multiply each valence by its associated probability and add the results. This total is your overall valence for high performance.
5. Assess the probability that if you exert effort, you will be a high performer. Express that probability as a percentage.
6. Multiply this probability by the overall valence for high performance calculated in step 4. This score reflects your motivational force—that is, your motivation to exert strong effort.

Now form groups of three or four. Compare your scores on motivational force. Discuss why some scores differ widely. Also, note whether any group members had similar force scores but different combinations of factors leading to those scores.

Follow-up Questions

1. What does this exercise tell you about the strengths and limitations of expectancy theory?
2. Would this exercise be useful for a manager to run with a group of subordinates? Why or why not?

BUILDING MANAGERIAL SKILLS

Exercise Overview   Interpersonal skills refer to the ability to communicate with, understand, and motivate individuals and groups, and communication skills refer to the ability to send and receive information effectively. This exercise is designed to demonstrate the essential roles played in employee motivation by an understanding of what motivates people and an ability to communicate that understanding.

Exercise Background   One implication of reinforcement theory is that both positive reinforcement (reward) and punishment can be effective in altering employee behavior. The use of punishment, however, may result in resentment on the employee's part, and over the long term, the resentment can diminish the effectiveness of the punishment. By and large, positive reinforcement is more effective over time.

Exercise Task   Your instructor will ask for volunteers to perform a demonstration in front of the class. Consider volunteering, but if you don't want to participate, observe the behavior of the volunteers closely. When the demonstration is over, respond to the following questions:

1. Based on what you saw, which is more effective— positive reinforcement or punishment?
2. How did positive reinforcement and punishment affect the "employee" in the demonstration? How did it affect the "boss"?
3. What, in your opinion, are the likely long-term consequences of positive reinforcement and punishment?

REFERENCE

Ricky W. Griffin, *Management*, 10th ed. (Mason, OH: South Western Educational Publishing, 2010).

SELF-ASSESSMENT EXERCISE

Assessing Your Equity Sensitivity

The questions that follow are intended to help you better understand your equity sensitivity. Answer each question on the scales by circling the number that best reflects your personal feelings.

1. I think it is important for everyone to be treated fairly.

5	4	3	2	1
Strongly Agree	Agree	Neither Agree Nor Disagree	Disagree	Strongly Disagree

2. I pay a lot of attention to how I am treated in comparison to how others are treated.

5	4	3	2	1
Strongly Agree	Agree	Neither Agree Nor Disagree	Disagree	Strongly Disagree

3. I get really angry if I think I'm being treated unfairly.

5	4	3	2	1
Strongly Agree	Agree	Neither Agree Nor Disagree	Disagree	Strongly Disagree

4. It makes me uncomfortable if I think someone else is not being treated fairly.

5	4	3	2	1
Strongly Agree	Agree	Neither Agree Nor Disagree	Disagree	Strongly Disagree

5. If I thought I was being treated unfairly, I would be very motivated to change things.

5	4	3	2	1
Strongly Agree	Agree	Neither Agree Nor Disagree	Disagree	Strongly Disagree

6. It doesn't really bother me if someone else gets a better deal than I do.

5	4	3	2	1
Strongly Agree	Agree	Neither Agree Nor Disagree	Disagree	Strongly Disagree

7. It is impossible for everyone to be treated fairly all the time.

5	4	3	2	1
Strongly Agree	Agree	Neither Agree Nor Disagree	Disagree	Strongly Disagree

8. When I'm a manager, I'll make sure that all of my employees are treated fairly.

5	4	3	2	1
Strongly Agree	Agree	Neither Agree Nor Disagree	Disagree	Strongly Disagree

9. I would quit my job if I thought I was being treated unfairly.

5	4	3	2	1
Strongly Agree	Agree	Neither Agree Nor Disagree	Disagree	Strongly Disagree

10. Short-term inequities are okay because things all even out in the long run.

5	4	3	2	1
Strongly Agree	Agree	Neither Agree Nor Disagree	Disagree	Strongly Disagree

Instructions: Add up your total points (note that some items have a "reversed" numbering arrangement). If you scored 35 or higher, you are highly sensitive to equity and fairness; 15 or lower, you have very little sensitivity to equity and fairness; between 35 and 15, you have moderate equity sensitivity.

5

CHAPTER

MOTIVATING EMPLOYEE PERFORMANCE THROUGH WORK

CHAPTER LEARNING OBJECTIVES

After studying this chapter you should be able to:

- Relate motivation and employee performance.
- Discuss work design, including its evolution and alternative approaches.
- Relate employment involvement in work and motivation.
- Identify and describe key flexible work arrangements.

Orchestrating Outcomes

"[T]hey feel empowered. They don't have anyone telling them what to do. They walk into the rehearsal hall and it's their opportunity to influence [and] shape music."

—EXECUTIVE DIRECTOR GRAHAM PARKER ON THE MUSICIANS OF THE ORPHEUS CHAMBER ORCHESTRA

Reviewing a recent concert by the Orpheus Chamber Orchestra, *New York Times* music critic Vivien Schweitzer wrote that the orchestra played Robert Schumann's

The Orpheus Chamber Orchestra performs without a conductor. The musicians rely on their own individual motivation—and much practice—to work together as they create beautiful music.

Symphony No. 2 "with remarkable coordination"; the "balance among strings, winds, and brass," she added, "was impressively well proportioned."

Was Schweitzer, as we sometimes say, damning with faint praise? Isn't a *symphony*, which means "harmony of sounds," *supposed* to be played with remarkable coordination? Aren't the various sections of the orchestra *supposed* to be well balanced? Had the conductor, whose job is to ensure a consummate performance of the music, achieved little more than coordination and balance? Actually, New York-based Orpheus doesn't play with a conductor, and Schweitzer was remarking on the fact the orchestra had "bravely—and successfully—attempted" such a complex work without the artistic and managerial leadership of someone who directs rehearsals and stands at a podium waving an authoritative baton.

"For us at Orpheus," explains current executive director Graham Parker, "it's the *way* we make the music that's the difference." Orpheus holds to the principle that its product—the music performed for audiences—is of the highest quality when its workers—the musicians—are highly satisfied with their jobs. All professional orchestra musicians, of course, are highly trained, skilled, and experienced, but make no mistake about it: A lot of them are not very happy workers. J. Richard Hackman, an organizational psychologist at Harvard, surveyed workers in 13 different occupational categories, including orchestra players, to determine relative levels of job motivation and satisfaction. On the one hand, musicians ranked at the top in motivation, "fueled by their own pride and professionalism," according to Hackman. But when it came to general satisfaction with their jobs, orchestra players ranked seventh (just below federal prison guards and slightly above beer sales and delivery teams). On the question of satisfaction with growth opportunities, they ranked ninth (again, below prison guards, although a little higher than OR nurses and hockey players).

It's this disconnect between motivation and satisfaction—and between motivation and product quality—that Orpheus was conceived to rectify, and the first principle in what's now known as the "Orpheus Process" is: "Put power in the hands of the people doing the work." "If you ask any musician in the orchestra why they love playing with Orpheus," says Parker, "it's because they feel empowered. They don't have anyone telling them what to do. They walk into the rehearsal hall and it's their opportunity to influence [and] shape music, to make music with all their experience, all their training coming together."

Ask double-bass player Don Palma, for instance. Palma took a sabbatical after one year with Orpheus to play with the Los Angeles Philharmonic. "I just hated it," he says. "I didn't like to be told what to do all the time, being treated like I wasn't really worth anything other than to be a good soldier and just sit there and do as I was told. I felt powerless to affect things. . . . I felt frustrated, and there was nothing I could . . . do to help make things better." By contrast, says Palma, "Orpheus keeps me involved. I have some measure of participation in the direction the music is going to take. I think that's why a lot of us have stayed involved so long."

In most orchestras, the conductor makes more or less autocratic decisions about what will be played and how. The input of musicians is neither sought nor welcomed, and unsolicited advice may be sharply rebuffed—and may, in fact, serve as grounds for dismissal. At Orpheus, says Parker, "we have a completely different structure to the way we approach rehearsal": A core team of players selected by the orchestra from each instrument section plans and leads rehearsals for a given piece of music.

To assist in meeting the inevitable challenges posed by its democratic structure, Orpheus recruited Harvard's Hackman to its board of trustees in 2007, and he immediately helped the orchestra organize itself around two leadership groups. An *artistic planning group* consists of two staff members and three "artistic directors." The executive director serves as a sort of moderator for group discussions, and the general manager keeps everyone posted on market-related events and initiatives. The three artistic directors, who are members of the orchestra, work with other members to find out what they're interested in working on and to convey their ideas to the planning group. They also serve on a *senior leadership team* with the executive director, the general manager, and the directors of finance, marketing, and operations. This team determines the best ways to do things—given the organization's commitment to democratic structure, leadership, and roles—such as the best way to develop artistic agendas, to choose players, soloists, and composers, and to make the team accountable for its own artistic decisions.

It's important to remember, however, that neither the Orpheus Process nor the Orpheus two-team structure is any guarantee of organizational effectiveness. As in any organizational endeavor, execution is the difference between success and failure, and a study of the Orpheus approach to management has revealed a variety of reasons for the effectiveness of teamwork within the ensemble. Every member, for example, clearly understands the group's purpose and mission; every member's role is clearly stated and agreed upon; and all members perform an equal amount of work in meeting the group's objectives.

In the *Change* box entitled "How to Work in Concert" on page 135, we explore the Orpheus Process in more detail.

What Do You Think?

1. In what ways is motivating professional musicians similar to and different from motivating workers in more "traditional" job settings?

2. What other occupational groups, if any, might have motivational profiles similar to those of the professional musicians in Orpheus?

References: Vivien Schweitzer, "Players with No Conductor and, Increasingly, with No Fear," *New York Times*, May 7, 2007, www.nytimes.com on February 4, 2010; Jennifer Higgs, "Orpheus Chamber Orchestra Embodies Democratic Principles," *Axiom News*, October 28, 2008, www.axiomnews.ca on February 4, 2010; Amanda Gordon, "Self-Governing Orpheus Chamber Orchestra Has Broader Lessons to Offer, Says Banking and Civic Leader John Whitehead," *New York Sun*, April 25, 2009, www.nysun.com on February 4, 2010; Harvey Seifter, "The Conductor-Less Orchestra," *Leader to Leader*, no. 21 (Summer 2001), http://docs.google.com on February 4, 2010; J. Richard Hackman, *Leading Teams: Setting the Stage for Great Performances* (Cambridge: Harvard Business School Press, 2002), http://books.google.com on February 4, 2010.

Managers determine what jobs will be performed in their organizations and how those jobs will be performed. But managers must also determine how to motivate people and how to optimize their performance. The long-term key to success in business is to create jobs that optimize the organization's requirements for productivity and efficiency while simultaneously motivating and satisfying the employees who perform those jobs. As people and organizations change, and as we continue to learn more about management, it is important to look back occasionally at those jobs and make whatever changes are necessary to improve them.

This chapter is the first of two that address the strategies managers use to optimize the performance of their employees. We begin with a discussion of work design, starting with a look at historical approaches. Then we discuss an important contemporary perspective on jobs, the job characteristics theory. Next, we review the importance of employee involvement through participation in their work. Finally, we discuss flexible work arrangements that can be used to enhance motivation and performance. To begin, we will introduce a general framework that can guide managers as they attempt to put into practice various theories and models of motivation.

MOTIVATION AND EMPLOYEE PERFORMANCE

Chapter 4 described a variety of perspectives on motivation. But no single theory or model completely explains motivation—each covers only some of the factors that actually result in motivated behavior. Moreover, even if one theory were applicable in a particular situation, a manager might still need to translate that theory into operational terms. Thus, while using the actual theories as tools, managers need to understand various operational procedures, systems, and methods for enhancing motivation and performance.

Figure 5.1 illustrates a basic framework for relating various theories of motivation to potential and actual motivation and to operational methods for translating this potential and actual motivation into performance. The left side of the figure illustrates

Figure 5.1   ENHANCING PERFORMANCE IN ORGANIZATIONS

Managers can use a variety of methods to enhance performance in organizations. The need- and process-based perspectives on motivation explain some of the factors involved in increasing the potential for motivated behavior directed at enhanced performance. Managers can then use such means as goal setting, job design, flexible work arrangements, performance management, rewards, and organizational behavior motivation to help translate this potential into actual enhanced performance.

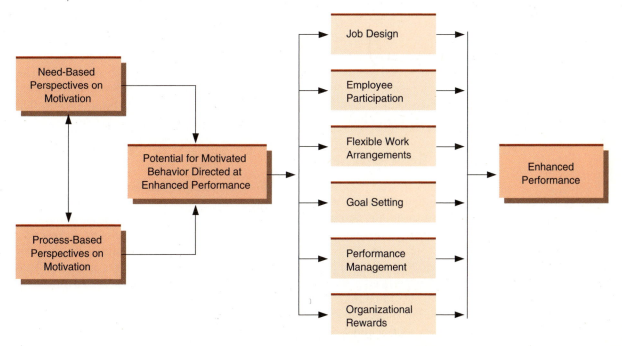

that motivated behavior can be induced by need-based or process-based circumstances. That is, people may be motivated to satisfy various specific needs or through various processes such as perceptions of inequity, expectancy relationships, and reinforcement contingencies.

These need-, process-, and learning-based concepts result in the situation illustrated in the center of the figure—a certain potential exists for motivated behavior directed at enhanced performance. For example, suppose that an employee wants more social relationships—that is, he wants to satisfy belongingness, relatedness, or affiliation needs. This means that there is potential for the employee to want to perform at a higher level if he thinks that higher performance will satisfy those social needs. Likewise, if an employee's high performance in the past was followed by strong positive reinforcement, there is again a potential for motivation directed at enhanced performance.

But managers may need to take certain steps to translate the potential for motivation directed at enhanced performance into real motivation and real enhanced performance. In some cases, these steps may be tied to the specific need or process that has created the existing potential. For example, providing more opportunities for social interaction contingent on improved performance might capitalize on an employee's social needs. More typically, however, a manager needs to go further to help translate potential into real performance.

The right side of Figure 5.1 names some of the more common methods used to enhance performance. This chapter covers the first three—job design, employee participation and empowerment, and flexible work arrangements. The other three—goal setting, performance management, and organizational rewards—are discussed in Chapter 6.

WORK DESIGN IN ORGANIZATIONS

Work design is an important method managers can use to enhance employee performance.[1] When work design is addressed at the individual level, it is most commonly referred to as **job design**; it can be defined as how organizations define and structure jobs. As we will see, properly designed jobs can have a positive impact on the motivation, performance, and job satisfaction of those who perform them. On the other hand, poorly designed jobs can impair motivation, performance, and job satisfaction. The first widespread model of how individual work should be designed was job specialization. For example, a worker who applies safety decals to a piece of equipment as that equipment moves down an assembly line is performing a specialized job.

Job Specialization

Frederick Taylor, the chief proponent of **job specialization**, argued that jobs should be scientifically studied, broken down into small component tasks, and then standardized across all workers doing those jobs.[2] Taylor's view grew from the historical writings about division of labor advocated by Scottish economist Adam Smith. In practice, job specialization generally brought most, if not all, of the advantages its advocates claimed. Specialization paved the way for large-scale assembly lines and was at least partly responsible for the dramatic gains in output U.S. industry achieved for several decades after the turn of the century.

On the surface, job specialization appears to be a rational and efficient way to structure jobs. The jobs in many factories, for instance, are highly specialized and

Job design is how organizations define and structure jobs.

Job specialization, as advocated by scientific management, can help improve efficiency, but it can also promote monotony and boredom.

are often designed to maximize productivity. In practice, however, performing those jobs can cause problems, foremost among them the extreme monotony of highly specialized tasks. Consider the job of assembling toasters. A person who does the entire assembly may find the job complex and challenging, albeit inefficient. If the job is specialized so that the worker simply inserts a heating coil into the toaster as it passes along on an assembly line, the process may be efficient, but it is unlikely to interest or challenge the worker. A worker numbed by boredom and monotony may be less motivated to work hard and more inclined to do poor-quality work or to complain about the job. For these reasons, managers began to search for job design alternatives to specialization.

Traditional assembly line work can be routine, boring, and monotonous. As a result, workers can quickly become dissatisfied with their jobs. Dissatisfaction, in turn, can lead to increased absenteeism and cause workers to look for better jobs elsewhere. This Goodyear inspector is doing a final check on a run of automobile tires before they are delivered to a nearby auto assembly plant. To counter the effects of boredom and monotony, the Goodyear inspectors rotate across a number of different inspection points throughout the day.

One of the primary catalysts for this search was a famous study of jobs in the automobile industry. The purpose of this study was to assess how satisfied automobile workers were with various aspects of their jobs.[3] The workers indicated that they were reasonably satisfied with their pay, working conditions, and the quality of their supervision. However, they expressed extreme dissatisfaction with the actual work they did. The plants were very noisy, and the moving assembly line dictated a rigid, grueling pace. Jobs were highly specialized and standardized.

The workers complained about six facets of their jobs: mechanical pacing by an assembly line, repetitiveness, low skill requirements, involvement with only a portion of the total production cycle, limited social interaction with others in the workplace, and lack of control over the tools and techniques used in the job. These sources of dissatisfaction were a consequence of the job design prescriptions of scientific management. Thus, managers began to recognize that although job specialization might lead to efficiency, if carried too far, it would have a number of negative consequences.[4]

Early Alternatives to Job Specialization

In response to the automobile plant study, other reported problems with job specialization, and a general desire to explore ways to create less monotonous jobs, managers began to seek alternative ways to design jobs. Managers initially formulated two alternative approaches: job rotation and job enlargement.

Job Rotation   Job rotation involves systematically shifting workers from one job to another to sustain their motivation and interest. Under specialization, each task is broken down into small parts. For example, assembling fine writing pens such as those made by Mont Blanc or Cross might involve four discrete steps: testing the ink cartridge, inserting the cartridge into the barrel of the pen, screwing the cap onto the barrel, and inserting the assembled pen into a box. One worker might perform step one, another step two, and so forth.

Job rotation is systematically moving workers from one job to another in an attempt to minimize monotony and boredom.

MICHAEL L. ABRAMSON/TIME LIFE PICTURES/GETTY IMAGES

When job rotation is introduced, the tasks themselves stay the same. However, the workers who perform them are systematically rotated across the various tasks. Jones, for example, starts out with task 1 (testing ink cartridges). On a regular basis—perhaps weekly or monthly—she is systematically rotated to task 2, to task 3, to task 4, and back to task 1. Gonzalez, who starts out on task 2 (inserting cartridges into barrels), rotates ahead of Jones to tasks 3, 4, 1, and back to 2.

Numerous firms have used job rotation, including American Cyanamid, Baker Hughes, Ford, and Prudential Insurance. Job rotation did not entirely live up to its expectations, however.[5] The problem again was narrowly defined, routine jobs. That is, if a rotation cycle takes workers through the same old jobs, the workers simply experience several routine and boring jobs instead of just one. Although a worker may begin each job shift with a bit of renewed interest, the effect usually is short-lived.

Rotation may also decrease efficiency. For example, it clearly sacrifices the proficiency and expertise that grow from specialization. At the same time, job rotation is an effective training technique because a worker rotated through a variety of related jobs acquires a larger set of job skills. Thus, there is increased flexibility in transferring workers to new jobs. Many U.S. firms now use job rotation for training or other purposes, but few rely on it to motivate workers. For instance, Pilgrim's Pride, one of the largest chicken-processing firms in the United States, uses job rotation, but not for motivation. Because workers in a chicken-processing plant are subject to cumulative trauma injuries such as carpel tunnel syndrome, managers at Pilgrim's believe that rotating workers across different jobs can reduce these injuries.

Job Enlargement   Job enlargement, or horizontal job loading, is expanding a worker's job to include tasks previously performed by other workers. For instance, if job enlargement were introduced at a Cross pen plant, the four tasks noted above might be combined into two "larger" ones. Hence, one set of workers might each test cartridges and then insert them into barrels (old steps one and two); another set of workers might then attach caps to the barrels and put the pens into boxes (old steps three and four). The logic behind this change is that the increased number of tasks in each job reduces monotony and boredom.

Maytag was one of the first companies to use job enlargement.[6] In the assembly of washing machine water pumps, for example, jobs done sequentially by six workers at a conveyor belt were modified so that each worker completed an entire pump alone. Other organizations that implemented job enlargement included AT&T, the U.S. Civil Service, and Colonial Life Insurance Company.

Unfortunately, job enlargement also failed to have the desired effects. Generally, if the entire production sequence consisted of simple, easy-to-master tasks, merely doing more of them did not significantly change the worker's job. If the task of putting two bolts on a piece of machinery was "enlarged" to putting on three bolts and connecting two wires, for example, the monotony of the original job essentially remained.

Job Enrichment

Job rotation and job enlargement seemed promising but eventually disappointed managers seeking to counter the ill effects of extreme specialization. They failed partly because they were intuitive, narrow approaches rather than fully developed, theory-driven methods. Consequently, a new, more complex approach to task design—job enrichment—was developed. Job enrichment is based on the dual-structure theory of motivation, which is discussed in Chapter 4. That theory contends that employees can be motivated by positive job-related experiences such as feelings of achievement,

Job enlargement involves giving workers more tasks to perform.

Job enrichment entails giving workers more tasks to perform and more control over how to perform them.

responsibility, and recognition. To achieve these, job enrichment relies on vertical job loading—not only adding more tasks to a job, as in horizontal loading, but also giving the employee more control over those tasks.]

AT&T, Texas Instruments, IBM, and General Foods have all used job enrichment. For example, AT&T utilized job enrichment in a group of eight people who were responsible for preparing service orders. Managers believed turnover in the group was too high and performance too low. Analysis revealed several deficiencies in the work. The group worked in relative isolation, and any service representative could ask them to prepare work orders. As a result, they had little client contact or responsibility, and they received scant feedback on their job performance. The job enrichment program focused on creating a process team. Each member of the team was paired with a service representative, and the tasks were restructured: Ten discrete steps were replaced with three more complex ones. In addition, the group members began to get specific feedback on performance, and their job titles were changed to reflect their greater responsibility and status. As a result of these changes, the number of orders delivered on time increased from 27 percent to 90 percent, accuracy improved, and turnover decreased significantly.[8]

One of the first published reports on job enrichment told how Texas Instruments had used this technique to improve janitorial jobs. The company had given janitors more control over their schedules and let them sequence their own cleaning jobs and purchase their own supplies. As a direct result, turnover dropped, cleanliness improved, and the company reported estimated initial cost savings of approximately $103,000.[9]

At the same time, we should note that many job enrichment programs have failed. Some companies have found job enrichment to be cost ineffective, and others believe that it simply did not produce the expected results.[10] Several programs at Prudential Insurance, for example, were abandoned because managers believed they were benefiting neither employees nor the firm. Some of the criticism is associated with the dual-structure theory of motivation on which job enrichment is based: The theory confuses employee satisfaction with motivation, is fraught with methodological flaws, ignores situational factors, and is not convincingly supported by research.

Because of these and other problems, job enrichment recently has fallen into disfavor among managers. Yet some valuable aspects of the concept can be salvaged. The efforts of managers and academic theorists ultimately have led to more complex and sophisticated viewpoints. Many of these advances are evident in the job characteristics theory, which we consider next.

The Job Characteristics Theory

The **job characteristics theory**[focuses on the specific motivational properties of jobs. The theory, diagrammed in Figure 5.2, was developed by Hackman and Oldham.[11] At the core of the theory is the idea of critical psychological states. These states are presumed to determine the extent to which characteristics of the job enhance employee responses to the task.]The three critical psychological states are:

1. *Experienced meaningfulness of the work*—the degree to which the individual experiences the job as generally meaningful, valuable, and worthwhile

2. *Experienced responsibility for work outcomes*—the degree to which individuals feel personally accountable and responsible for the results of their work

3. *Knowledge of results*—the degree to which individuals continuously understand how effectively they are performing the job

If employees experience these states at a sufficiently high level, they are likely to feel good about themselves and to respond favorably to their jobs. Hackman and

The **job characteristics theory** identifies five motivational properties of tasks and three critical psychological states of people.

Figure 5.2 THE JOB CHARACTERISTICS THEORY

The job characteristics theory is an important contemporary model of how to design jobs. By using five core job characteristics, managers can enhance three critical psychological states. These states, in turn, can improve a variety of personal and work outcomes. Individual differences also affect how the job characteristics affect people.

Reference: Reprinted from *Organizational Behavior and Human Performance,* vol. 16, J. R. Hackman and G. R. Oldham, "Motivation Through the Design of Work: Test of a Theory," pp. 250–279. Copyright 1976, with permission from Elsevier.

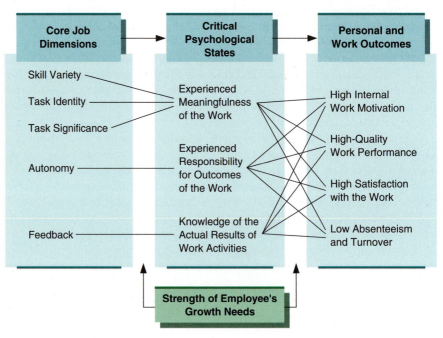

Oldham suggest that the three critical psychological states are triggered by the following five characteristics of the job, or core job dimensions:

1. *Skill variety*—the degree to which the job requires a variety of activities that involve different skills and talents

2. *Task identity*—the degree to which the job requires completion of a "whole" and an identifiable piece of work; that is, the extent to which a job has a beginning and an end with a tangible outcome

3. *Task significance*—the degree to which the job affects the lives or work of other people, both in the immediate organization and in the external environment

4. *Autonomy*—the degree to which the job allows the individual substantial freedom, independence, and discretion to schedule the work and determine the procedures for carrying it out

5. *Feedback*—the degree to which the job activities give the individual direct and clear information about the effectiveness of his or her performance

Figure 5.2 shows that these five job characteristics, operating through the critical psychological states, affect a variety of personal and work outcomes: high internal work motivation (that is, intrinsic motivation), high-quality work performance, high satisfaction with the work, and low absenteeism and turnover. The figure also suggests that individual differences play a role in job design. People with strong needs for personal growth and development will be especially motivated by the five core job characteristics. On the other hand, people with weaker needs for personal growth and development are less likely to be motivated by the core job characteristics.

Figure 5.3 expands the basic job characteristics theory by incorporating general guidelines to help managers implement it.[12] Managers can use such means as forming natural work units (that is, grouping similar tasks together), combining existing tasks into more complex ones, establishing direct relationships between workers and clients, increasing worker autonomy through vertical job loading, and opening feedback channels. Theoretically, such actions should enhance the motivational properties of each task. Using these guidelines, sometimes in adapted form, several firms, including 3M, Volvo, AT&T, Xerox, Texas Instruments, and Motorola, have successfully implemented job design changes.[13]

Much research has been devoted to this approach to job design.[14] This research has generally supported the theory, although performance has seldom been found to correlate with job characteristics.[15] Several apparent weaknesses in the theory have also come to light. First, the measures used to test the theory are not always as valid and reliable as they should be. Further, the role of individual differences frequently has not been supported by research. Finally, guidelines for implementation are not specific, so managers usually tailor them to their own particular circumstances. Still, the theory remains a popular perspective on studying and changing jobs.[16]

The *Diversity* box on page 132 shows that one of the problems in making workers as happy and productive as possible is the fact the workforce has always consisted of people from different walks of life.

Figure 5.3 IMPLEMENTING THE JOB CHARACTERISTICS THEORY

Managers should use a set of implementation guidelines if they want to apply the job characteristics theory in their organization. This figure shows some of these guidelines. For example, managers can combine tasks, form natural work units, establish client relationships, vertically load jobs, and open feedback channels.

Reference: From J. R. Hackman, G. R. Oldham, R. Janson, and K. Purdy, "A New Stage for Job Enrichment." Copyright © 1975 by The Regents of the University of California. Reprinted from *California Management Review*, vol. 17, no. 4. By permission of The Regents.

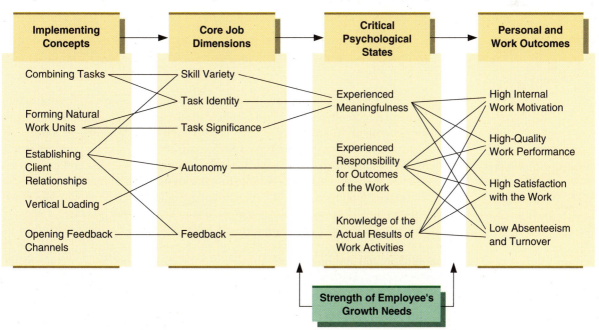

DIVERSITY

Happiness

To increase happiness, white-collar workers have options, but what about low-skill workers? In the *New York Times*, journalist Daniel Akst wrote an article titled, "White-Collar Stress? Stop the Whining." Akst points out that workplace unhappiness "is not a new phenomenon. Work is not a picnic. It's always tough for people." Akst admonishes his readers, "If you find the modern, air-conditioned workplace stressful—all that email!—just think back to the work most Americans used to do." Contrast today's modern office work with farming, the most common occupation a century ago. Farmers at that time performed hard outdoor labor seven days per week, for uncertain pay, in social isolation, and with no benefits or retirement plans.

Just as a focus on the past shows us how fortunate middle-class workers truly are, so too does a comparison of middle- and working-class employees. The Bureau of Labor Statistics reports that in 2006, 5.9 million U.S. managers earned an average salary of $91,900, while 11 million food-service workers earned only $18,400. The disparity is even greater when benefits and other rewards are considered.

Organizations face a stiff challenge in designing jobs for low-skill workers that are richer and more rewarding. Even if pay were greater, motivation theory theorizes that repetitive, routine jobs with little autonomy will not create worker happiness or motivation. Innovative job design for barbers, grounds workers, fishing crews, and nursing aides seems very difficult, yet could affect tens of millions of individuals nationwide.

> *"White-collar stress? Stop the whining."*
> —DANIEL AKST, JOURNALIST, *NEW YORK TIMES*

References: Daniel Akst, "White-Collar Stress? Stop the Whining," *New York Times*, September 19, 2004, www.nytimes.com on February 7, 2010; Lisa Belkin, "Take This Job and Hug It," *New York Times*, February 13, 2005, www.nytimes.com on February 7, 2010; "National Cross-Industry Estimates of Employment and Mean Annual Wage for Major Occupational Groups," Bureau of Labor Statistics, August 2007, www.bls.gov on January 28, 2008.

EMPLOYEE INVOLVEMENT AND MOTIVATION

Participation entails giving employees a voice in making decisions about their own work.

Empowerment is the process of enabling workers to set their own work goals, make decisions, and solve problems within their sphere of responsibility and authority.

Employee involvement in their work can also play an important role in motivation. Involvement is most often enhanced through what are called participative management and empowerment. In most cases managers who use these techniques are attempting to enhance employee motivation. In a sense, participation and empowerment are extensions of job design because each fundamentally alters how employees in an organization perform their jobs. **Participation** occurs when employees have a voice in decisions about their own work. (One important model that can help managers determine the optimal level of employee participation, Vroom's decision tree approach, is discussed in Chapter 13.) **Empowerment** is the process of enabling workers to set their own work goals, make decisions, and solve problems within their spheres of responsibility and authority. Thus, empowerment is a somewhat broader concept that promotes participation in a wide variety of areas, including but not limited to work itself, work context, and work environment.[17]

Early Perspectives on Employee Involvement

The human relations movement in vogue from the 1930s through the 1950s assumed that employees who are happy and satisfied will work harder. This view stimulated management interest in having workers participate in a variety of organizational activities. Managers hoped that if employees had a chance to participate in decision making concerning their work environment, they would be satisfied, and this satisfaction would supposedly result in improved performance. However, managers tended to see employee participation merely as a way to increase satisfaction, not as a source of potentially valuable input. Eventually, managers began to recognize that employee input was useful in itself, apart from its presumed effect on satisfaction. In other words, they came to see employees as valued human resources who can contribute to organizational effectiveness.[18]

© COURTESY OF CHAPARRAL STEEL

The role of participation and empowerment in motivation can be expressed in terms of both the need-based perspectives and the expectancy theory discussed in Chapter 4. Employees who participate in decision making may be more committed to executing decisions properly. Furthermore, successfully making a decision, executing it, and then seeing the positive consequences can help satisfy one's need for achievement, provide recognition and responsibility, and enhance self-esteem. Simply being asked to participate in organizational decision making may also enhance an employee's self-esteem. In addition, participation should help clarify expectancies; that is, by participating in decision making, employees may better understand the linkage between their performance and the rewards they want most.

Areas of Employee Involvement

At one level, employees can participate in addressing questions and making decisions about their own jobs. Instead of just telling them how to do their jobs, for example, managers can ask employees to make their own decisions about how to do them. Based on their own expertise and experience with their tasks, workers might be able to improve their own productivity. In many situations, they might also be well qualified to make decisions about what materials to use, which tools to use, and so forth.

Chaparral Steel, a small steel producer near Dallas, allows its workers considerable autonomy in how they perform their jobs. For example, when the firm recently needed a new rolling mill lathe, it budgeted $1 million for its purchase, and then put the purchase decision in the hands of an operating machinist. This machinist, in turn, investigated various options, visited other mills

Employee involvement in their work and the opportunity to make important decisions about how that work is performed can be powerful factors in employee motivation. Chaparral steel, for example, allows its workers a great deal of autonomy in how they perform their jobs. As a result of Chaparral's approach to employee involvement, it has very low turnover and is among the most productive and efficient steel producers in the industry.

in Japan and Europe, and then recommended an alternative piece of machinery costing less than half of the budgeted amount. The firm also helped pioneer an innovative concept called "open-book management"—any employee at Chaparral can see any company document, record, or other piece of information at any time and for any reason.

It might also help to let workers make decisions about administrative matters, such as work schedules. If jobs are relatively independent of one another, employees might decide when to change shifts, take breaks, go to lunch, and so forth. A work group or team might also be able to schedule vacations and days off for all of its members. Furthermore, employees are getting increasing opportunities to participate in broader issues of product quality. Involvement of this type has become a hallmark of successful Japanese and other international firms, and many U.S. companies have followed suit.

Techniques and Issues in Employee Involvement

In recent years many organizations have actively sought ways to extend employee involvement beyond the traditional areas. Simple techniques such as suggestion boxes and question-and-answer meetings allow a certain degree of participation, for example. The basic motive has been to better capitalize on the assets and capabilities inherent in all employees. Thus, many managers today prefer the term "empowerment" to "participation" because it implies a more comprehensive level of involvement.

One method some firms use to empower their workers is the use of work teams. This method grew out of early attempts to use what Japanese firms call "quality circles." A *quality circle* is a group of employees who voluntarily meet regularly to identify and propose solutions to problems related to quality. Quality circles quickly evolved into a broader and more comprehensive array of work groups, now generally called "work teams." These teams are collections of employees empowered to plan, organize, direct, and control their own work. Their supervisor, rather than being a traditional "boss," plays more the role of a coach. We discuss work teams more fully in Chapter 10.

The other method some organizations use to facilitate employee involvement is to change their overall method of organizing. The basic pattern is for an organization to eliminate layers from its hierarchy, thereby becoming much more decentralized. Power, responsibility, and authority are delegated as far down the organization as possible, so control of work is squarely in the hands of those who actually do it.

Regardless of the specific technique used, however, empowerment only enhances organizational effectiveness if certain conditions exist. First, the organization must be sincere in its efforts to spread power and autonomy to lower levels of the organization. Token efforts to promote participation in just a few areas are unlikely to succeed. Second, the organization must be committed to maintaining participation and empowerment. Workers will be resentful if they are given more control only to later have it reduced or taken away altogether. Third, the organization must be systematic and patient in its efforts to empower workers. Turning over too much control too quickly can spell disaster. Finally, the organization must be prepared to increase its commitment to training. Employees being given more freedom concerning how they work are likely to need additional training to help them exercise that freedom most effectively.

The *Change* box on page 135, entitled "How to Work in Concert," examines the process by which a renowned orchestra empowers the musicians who comprise its workforce.

CHANGE

How to Work in Concert

Harvey Seifter, current director of Creativity Connection, which helps U.S. corporations enhance creativity and develop organizational-learning programs, served as executive director of the Orpheus Chamber Orchestra from 1998 to 2002. His book *Leadership Ensemble* draws on his experiences with "the World-Famous Conductorless Orchestra" to show for-profit organizations how to emulate the orchestra's remarkable success with democratic structure and work processes based on multiple levels of teamwork.

Seifter calls the orchestra's overall approach the "Orpheus Process," which consists of "five key elements":

1. *Choosing Leaders.* For each piece of music that the orchestra decides to perform, members select a leadership team composed of five to seven musicians. This "core team" then leads rehearsals and serves as a conduit for members' input. It's also responsible for seeing that the final performance reflects "a unified vision."

2. *Developing Strategies.* Prior to rehearsals, the core team decides how a piece of music will be played. Its ultimate goal is to ensure "an overall interpretive approach to the music," and it works to meet this goal by trying out various approaches during rehearsals with the full orchestra.

3. *Developing the Product.* Once an interpretive approach has been chosen, rehearsals are geared toward refining it. At this point, players make suggestions and critique the playing of their colleagues. It is, of course, a highly collaborative stage in the process, and its success depends upon mutual respect. "We're all specialists—that's the

> **"When I talk to...another musician in the group, it's on an equal level. It's absolutely crucial that we have that attitude."**
>
> —MARTHA CAPLIN, VIOLINIST WITH THE ORPHEUS CHAMBER ORCHESTRA

beginning of the discussion," says violinist Martha Caplin. "When I talk to...another musician in the group, it's on an equal level. It's absolutely crucial that we have that attitude." Violist Nardo Poy admits that "there are times in rehearsal [when], because of the way we work—the intensity, the directness—often we do get pretty emotional, angry at each other. And yet," he adds, "when rehearsal is over, that's pretty much it."

When disagreements arise, everyone works toward a consensus, and if a consensus can't be reached, the issue is settled by a vote. Violinist Eriko Sato also emphasizes that the process of collaborative input works best when members focus their contributions on outcomes of the highest possible quality: "Fundamentally," she says, "I don't think everybody's opinion should be addressed at all times. There are certain places and times for certain things to be said. The appropriate moment. Everybody knows what's wrong, everybody can feel what's wrong. But do you have a *solution*? Do you know how to solve a *problem*?"

4. *Perfecting the Product.* Just before each concert, a couple of members take seats in the hall to listen to the performance from the audience's perspective. Then they report to the full ensemble and may suggest some final adjustments.

5. *Delivering the Product.* The final performance is the ultimate result of the Orpheus Process, but it isn't the last step. When the concert is over, members get together to share their impressions of the performance and make suggestions for even further refinements.

Continued

The Orpheus Process, says Seifter, not only has served the ensemble for more than three decades, but "continues to evolve to meet the needs of the orchestra and its customers: the listening public.... The result," he concludes in a businesslike manner, "is a better product, increased customer satisfaction, and a healthier bottom line."

References: Orpheus Chamber Orchestra, "History," www .orpheusnyc.com on February 7, 2010; Harvey Seifter and Peter Economy, *Leadership Ensemble: Lessons in Collaborative Management from the World-Famous Conductorless Orchestra* (New York: Henry Holt & Co., 2001); Harvey Seifter, "The Conductor-Less Orchestra," *Leader to Leader*, no. 21 (Summer 2001), http://docs.google.com on February 4, 2010; Stevens Institute of Technology, "Orpheus Chamber Orchestra Offers Unique Business Lessons and Two Musical Events at Stevens Institute of Technology," *University Communications*, June 6, 2006, www.stevens.edu on February 4, 2010.

FLEXIBLE WORK ARRANGEMENTS

Beyond the actual redesigning of jobs and the use of employee involvement, many organizations today are experimenting with a variety of flexible work arrangements. These arrangements are generally intended to enhance employee motivation and performance by giving workers more flexibility about how and when they work. Among the more popular flexible work arrangements are variable work schedules, flexible work schedules, extended work schedules, job sharing, and telecommuting.[19]

Variable Work Schedules

There are many exceptions, of course, but the traditional work schedule in the United States has long been days that start at 8:00 or 9:00 in the morning and end at 5:00 in the evening, five days a week (and, of course, managers and other professionals often work many additional hours outside of these times). Although the exact starting and ending times vary, most companies in other countries have also used a well-defined work schedule. But such a schedule makes it difficult for workers to attend to routine personal business—going to the bank, seeing a doctor or dentist for a checkup, having a parent-teacher conference, getting an automobile serviced, and so forth. Employees locked into this work schedule may find it necessary to take a sick or vacation day to handle these activities. On a more psychological level, some people may feel so powerless and constrained by their job schedules that they grow resentful and frustrated.

To help counter these problems, one alternative some businesses use is a **compressed work schedule**.[20] An employee following a compressed work week schedule works a full forty-hour week in fewer than the traditional five days. Most typically, this schedule involves working ten hours a day for four days, leaving an extra day off. Another alternative is for employees to work slightly less than ten hours a day but to complete the forty hours by lunchtime on Friday. And a few firms have tried having employees work twelve hours a day for three days, followed by four days off. Firms that have used these forms of compressed workweeks include John Hancock, British Petroleum, and R. J. Reynolds. One problem with this schedule is that if everyone in the organization is off at the same time, the firm may have no one on duty to handle problems or deal with outsiders on the off day. On the other hand, if a company staggers days off across the workforce, people who don't get the more desirable days off (Monday and Friday, for most people) may be jealous or resentful. Another problem is that when employees put in too much time in a single day, they tend to get tired and perform at a lower level later in the day.

A popular schedule some organizations are beginning to use is called a "nine-eighty" schedule. Under this arrangement, an employee works a traditional schedule one week

In a **compressed work schedule**, employees work a full forty-hour week in fewer than the traditional five days.

and a compressed schedule the next, getting every other Friday off. That is, they work eighty hours (the equivalent of two weeks of full-time work) in nine days. By alternating the regular and compressed schedules across half of its workforce, the organization is staffed at all times but still gives employees two additional full days off each month. Shell Oil and Amoco Chemicals are two businesses that currently use this schedule.

Flexible Work Schedules

Another promising alternative work arrangement is **flexible work schedules**, sometimes called **flextime**. The compressed work schedules previously discussed give employees time off during "normal" working hours, but they must still follow a regular and defined schedule on the days when they do work. Flextime, however, usually gives employees less say about what days they work but more personal control over the times when they work on those days.[21]

Figure 5.4 illustrates how flextime works. The workday is broken down into two categories: flexible time and core time. All employees must be at their workstations during core time, but they can choose their own schedules during flexible time. Thus, one employee may choose to start work early in the morning and leave in mid-afternoon, another to start in the late morning and work until late afternoon, and a third to start early in the morning, take a long lunch break, and work until late afternoon.

The major advantage of this approach, as already noted, is that workers get to tailor their workday to fit their personal needs. A person who needs to visit the dentist in the late afternoon can just start work early. A person who stays out late one night can start work late the next day. And the person who needs to run some errands during lunch can take a longer midday break. On the other hand, flextime is more difficult to manage because others in the organization may not be sure when a person will be available for meetings other than during the core time. Expenses such as utilities will also be higher since the organization must remain open for a longer period each day.

Some organizations have experimented with a plan in which workers set their own hours but then must follow that schedule each day. Others allow workers to modify their own schedule each day. Organizations that have used the flexible work schedule method for arranging work include Control Data Corporation, DuPont, Metropolitan Life, Chevron Texaco, and some offices in the U.S. government. One recent survey found that as many as 43 percent of U.S. workers have the option to modify their work schedules; most of those who choose to do so start earlier than normal so as to get off work earlier in the day.[22]

$\mathcal{F}igure$ 5.4   FLEXIBLE WORK SCHEDULES

Flexible work schedules are an important new work arrangement used in some organizations today. All employees must be at work during "core time." In the hypothetical example shown here, core time is from 9 to 11 A.M. and 1 to 3 P.M. The other time, then, is flexible—employees can come and go as they please during this time, as long as the total time spent at work meets organizational expectations.

6:00 A.M.	9:00 A.M. – 11:00 A.M.		1:00 P.M. – 3:00 P.M.	6:00 P.M.
Flexible Time	Core Time	Flexible Time	Core Time	Flexible Time

Flexible work schedules, or **flextime**, give employees more personal control over the hours they work each day.

Extended Work Schedules

In certain cases some organizations use another type of work scheduling called an **extended work schedule**. An extended work schedule is one that requires relatively long periods of work followed by relatively long periods of paid time off. These schedules are most often used when the cost of transitioning from one worker to another is high and there are efficiencies associated with having a small workforce.

For instance, KBR is a large defense contractor that manages U.S. military installations in foreign countries, including Iraq and Afghanistan. KBR's civilian employees handle maintenance, logistics, and communications, as well as food, laundry, and mail services, among other things. The typical work schedule for a KBR employee is 12 hours a day, 7 days a week. Extended schedules such as this allow the firm to function with a smaller workforce than would be the case under a more traditional approach to work scheduling. In order to motivate employees to accept and maintain this kind of schedule, the firm pays them a compensation premium plus provides them with 16 days of paid vacation and an airline ticket to any major destination in the world after every 120-day work period.

Other work settings that are conducive to this kind of extended work schedule include offshore petroleum-drilling platforms, transoceanic cargo ships, research labs in distant settings such as the South Pole, and movie crews filming in remote locations. While the specific number of hours, days, and vacation time varies, most of these job settings are characterized by long periods of work followed by an extended vacation plus premium pay.

Job Sharing

Yet another potentially useful alternative work arrangement is job sharing. In **job sharing**, two part-time employees share one full-time job. Job sharing may be desirable for people who only want to work part time or when job markets are tight. For its part, the organization can accommodate the preferences of a broader range of employees and may benefit from the talents of more people. Perhaps the simplest job-sharing arrangement to visualize is that of a receptionist. To share this job, one worker would staff the receptionist's desk from, say, 8:00 A.M. to noon each day; the office might close from noon to 1:00 P.M., and a second worker would staff the desk from 1:00 P.M. in the afternoon until 5:00 P.M. To the casual observer or visitor to the office, the fact that two people serve in one job is essentially irrelevant. The responsibilities of the job in the morning and responsibilities in the afternoon are not likely to be interdependent. Thus, the position can easily be broken down into two or perhaps even more components.

Organizations sometimes offer job sharing as a way to entice more workers to the organization. If a particular kind of job is difficult to fill, a job-sharing arrangement might make it more attractive to more people. There are also cost benefits for the organization. Since the employees may be working only part-time, the organization does not have to give them the same benefits that full-time employees receive. The organization can also tap into a wider array of skills when it provides job-sharing arrangements. The firm gets the advantage of the two sets of skills from one job.

Some workers like job sharing because it gives them flexibility and freedom. Certain workers, for example, may only want part-time work. Stepping into a shared job may also give them a chance to work in an organization that otherwise only wants to hire full-time employees. When the job sharer isn't working, she or he may attend school, take care of the family, or simply enjoy leisure time.

An **extended work schedule** is one that requires relatively long periods of work followed by relatively long periods of paid time off.

In **job sharing**, two or more part-time employees share one full-time job.

Job sharing does not work for every organization, and it isn't attractive to all workers, but it has produced enough success stories to suggest that it will be around for a long time. Among the organizations that are particularly committed to job-sharing programs are the Bank of Montreal, United Airlines, and the National School Board Association. Each of these organizations, and dozens more like them, report that job sharing has become a critically important part of its human resource system. Although job sharing has not been scientifically evaluated, it appears to be a useful alternative to traditional work scheduling.[23]

Telecommuting

Another approach to alternative work arrangements that is surging in popularity is **telecommuting**—allowing employees to spend part of their time working off-site, usually at home. By using email, web interfaces, and other technology, many employees can maintain close contact with their organization and do as much

Telecommuting is an alternative work arrangement that allows employees to spend some of their time working off-site, usually at home. This manager, for example, is working from the comfort of her home office. She spends 2-3 days each week working from home, going into her company office whenever she needs to meet with her boss or her own subordinates. But modern technology allows her to stay on top of her own work as well as what's going on in the office regardless of where she is.

work at home as they could in their offices. The increased power and sophistication of modern communication technology—laptops and smart phones, among others—is making telecommuting easier and easier.[24] (Other terms used to describe this concept are e-commuting and working from home.)

On the plus side, many employees like telecommuting because it gives them added flexibility. By spending one or two days a week at home, for instance, they have the same kind of flexibility to manage personal activities as is afforded by flextime or compressed schedules. Some employees also feel that they get more work done by staying at home because they are less likely to be interrupted. Organizations may benefit for several reasons as well: (1) they can reduce absenteeism and turnover since employees will need to take less "formal" time off, and (2) they can save on facilities such as parking spaces, because fewer people will be at work on any given day. There are also environmental benefits, given that fewer cars are on the highways.

On the other hand, although many employees thrive under this arrangement, others do not. Some feel isolated and miss the social interaction of the workplace. Others simply lack the self-control and discipline to walk away from the breakfast table to their desk and start working. Managers may also encounter coordination difficulties in scheduling meetings and other activities that require face-to-face contact.

Another issue with telecommuting involves workplace safety. In 2000, the Department of Labor, operating under the Occupational Safety and Health Act, began to require employers to take a proactive stance on home safety. Among other things, employers had to inspect workers' homes to ensure that all safety requirements were being met. For example, the employer had to verify that there were two external exits, that no lead paint had been used on the walls, that the employee's chairs were ergonomically sound, and that the indoor air quality met OSHA standards. This stipulation led

Telecommuting is a work arrangement in which employees spend part of their time working off-site.

CARTOONBANK.COM

Rini

Flexible work arrangements have led to a blurring of the lines between work and non-work. Many people today routinely take care of work-related issues that pop up while at home or traveling; similarly, people also have more freedom to address personal issues while working. This busy manager, for example, has brought her child to work, but in a most unusual manner!

to somewhat absurd decisions, such as corporations allowing their employees to use home telephones but not home computers if the employees' monitors did not meet low-radiation requirements. The employer could also be held accountable for employees' unsafe behaviors, such as plugging too many electrical devices into one power outlet or standing on a chair rather than on a ladder to change a light bulb. Employers complained that the requirements were too burdensome, especially as more workers began telecommuting. Employees, too, objected to the requirements as being too intrusive, invading the privacy of their homes.

So, in 2001, the ruling was lifted. However, there are still lingering legal issues and some firms still find it best to take at least some role in assessing home safety for their telecommuting employees. And there is now a new area of growing concern—cybercrime. Is a company liable if a client's confidential information is stolen because an employee's home computer didn't have hacker protection? What if the employee uses a home computer for business and also peddles online pornography? Given the trends and pressures toward telecommuting and the associated legal issues, there will no doubt continue to be significant changes in this area in the future.[25]

SYNOPSIS

Managers seek to enhance employee performance by capitalizing on the potential for motivated behavior to improve performance. Methods often used to translate motivation into performance involve work design, participation and empowerment, alternative work arrangements, performance management, goal setting, and rewards.

The essence of work design is job design—how organizations define and structure jobs. Historically, there was a general trend toward increasingly specialized jobs, but more recently the movement has consistently been away from extreme specialization. Two early alternatives to specialization were job rotation and job enlargement. Job enrichment approaches stimulated considerable interest in job design.

The job characteristics theory grew from early work on job enrichment. One basic premise of this theory is that jobs can be described in terms of a specific set of

motivational characteristics. Another is that managers should work to enhance the presence of those motivational characteristics in jobs but should also take individual differences into account.

Employee involvement using participative management and empowerment can help improve employee motivation in many business settings. New management practices such as the use of various kinds of work teams and of flatter, more decentralized methods of organizing are intended to empower employees throughout the organization. Organizations that want to empower their employees need to understand a variety of issues as they go about promoting participation.

Flexible work arrangements are commonly used today to enhance motivated job performance. Among the more popular alternative arrangements are compressed workweeks, flexible work schedules, extended work schedules, job sharing, and telecommuting.

DISCUSSION QUESTIONS

1. What are the primary advantages and disadvantages of job specialization? Were they the same in the early days of mass production?
2. Under what circumstances might job enlargement be especially effective? Especially ineffective? How about job rotation?
3. Do any trends today suggest a return to job specialization?
4. What are the strengths and weaknesses of job enrichment? When might it be useful?
5. Do you agree or disagree that individual differences affect how people respond to their jobs? Explain.

6. What are the primary similarities and differences between job enrichment and the approach proposed by job characteristics theory?
7. What are the motivational consequences of increased employee involvement from the frame of reference of expectancy and equity theories?
8. What motivational problems might result from an organization's attempt to set up work teams?
9. Which form of a flexible work schedule might you prefer?
10. How do you think you would like telecommuting?

ORGANIZATIONAL BEHAVIOR CASE FOR DISCUSSION

THE LAW OF DIMINISHING MOTIVATION

The enrollment of women in U.S. law schools took off after 1970, and women have been graduating at the same rate as men for more than 25 years. Today, however, the census of American law firms still counts relatively few women *partners*—typically, the veteran lawyers who are joint owners and directors. Currently, for example, 34.4 percent of all lawyers are women, yet only 17.8 percent of law-firm partners are women. Most female lawyers are *associates*—paid employees with the prospect of becoming partners. Moreover, the further up the law-firm ladder you look, the greater the disparity. According to the National Association of Women Lawyers, 92 percent of all managing partners (partners who run the business end of a firm) are men; men occupy 85 percent of the seats on the governing committees that control a firm's policies, and they hold 84 percent of all equity partnerships (which come with ownership and profit sharing). At this rate, women will achieve parity with male colleagues in approximately 2088.

So what happens between the time women get job offers and the time firms hand out partnerships and promotions? Bettina B. Plevan, an employment-law

> *"You have a given population of people who were significantly motivated to go through law school with a certain career goal in mind. What de-motivates them to want to continue working in the law?"*
>
> —ATTORNEY BETTINA B. PLEVAN

specialist and partner in the Manhattan firm of Proskauer Rose, believes that, somewhere along the way, female lawyers lose the kind of motivation necessary to get ahead in a law office. "You have a given population of people," she observes, "who were significantly motivated to go through law school with a certain career goal in mind. What de-motivates them," she asks, "to want to continue working in the law?"

The problem, says Karen M. Lockwood, a partner in the Washington DC firm Howrey LLP, is neither discrimination nor lack of opportunity. "Law firms," she says, "are way beyond discrimination. Problems with advancement and retention are grounded in biases, not discrimination." In part, these biases stem from institutional inertia. Lauren Stiller Rikleen, a partner in the Worcester, Massachusetts, firm of Bowditch & Dewey, points out that most law firms are "running on an institutional model that's about 200 years old." Most of them, she adds, "do a horrible job of managing their personnel, in terms of training them and communicating with them." Such problems, of course, affect men as well as women, but because of lingering preconceptions about women's attitudes, values, and goals, women bear the brunt of these workplace burdens. In practical terms, they face less adequate mentoring, poorer networking opportunities, lower-grade case assignments, and unequal access to positions of committee control.

To all of these barriers to success Lockwood adds the effect of what she calls the "maternal wall": Male partners, she says, assume that women who return to the firm after having children will be less willing to work hard and less capable of dedicating themselves to their jobs when they return. As a result, men get the choice assignments and senior positions. Jane DiRenzo Pigott, a onetime law-firm partner who now owns a consultancy firm, agrees but thinks the issues run deeper than maternity leave. "People explain it simply as the fact that women have children," she explains,

> but so many other factors play into it. Women self-promote in a different way than men, and because women don't get their success acknowledged in the same way as men who more aggressively self-promote, it creates a high level of professional dissatisfaction for women. Saying these two words "I want" is not something women are used to doing. They're not saying, "I want the top bonus" or "I want that position."...[W]omen need to learn how to be comfortable saying "I want" and how to say it effectively.

The fact remains that, according to a 2009 study of "Women in Law" conducted by Catalyst, a New York research firm, 1 in 8 female lawyers work only part time, compared to just 1 in 50 males. Why? According to Plevan, most female attorneys would prefer to work and raise children at the same time but find that they can't do both effectively. "I organized my personal life so I was able to move toward my goals," she says, but she also admits that it helped to have a gainfully employed spouse (also a lawyer), dual incomes sufficient to hire household help, and nearby relatives to pick up the slack in home-life responsibilities. In most cases, of course, although dual incomes are an advantage to a household, it's difficult for either spouse to devote time to child rearing when they're both working. The Catalyst study shows that only 44 percent of male lawyers have spouses who are employed full time—and are thus unavailable for such household duties as attending to children. Among women, however, nearly twice as many—84 percent—have spouses with full-time jobs.

Like firms in many other industries, law firms have experimented with such options as flexible scheduling and parental leave. More and more, however, they report that such measures have not been as effective as they'd hoped. Says Edith R. Matthai, who founded with her husband the Los Angeles firm Robie & Matthai: "We're very accommodating with leaves and flexible schedules, and even with that we still lose women...." She adds, "[The] pressures on women from spouses, family, peers, schools, and others is huge." The situation has improved over the last 30 years, but "we have a long way to go.... I think the real solution is a reassessment of the role that women play in the family. One thing we need is a sense of shared responsibilities for the household and, most importantly, shared responsibilities for taking care of the kids."

CASE QUESTIONS

1. How would you characterize the type of worker discussed in the case? In what ways is your own situation, either as a current or future worker, similar to that of these workers? In what ways is it dissimilar?

2. Among the various approaches to enhancing workplace satisfaction and productivity discussed in the chapter, which ones might you take under the circumstances described in the case? Why are some of the other approaches less likely to be effective (or even relevant)?

3. What about your own values when it comes to balancing your home and work life? Assume that you're about to graduate from law school and about to get married to a fiancé(e) who's also about to graduate from law school. When you sit down with your future husband/wife to discuss your plans for married life ever after, what do you want to do about raising a family? What kind of adjustments will you propose if it turns out that your fiancé(e)'s ideas on the matter are more or less the opposite of your own? Be sure to consider such factors as the debt you've racked up while in law school and the standard of living that you'd like to achieve.

REFERENCES

Patricia Gillette, "Lack of Self-Promotion Hurts Women in Large Firms," *Law.com*, July 9, 2009, www.law.com on February 8, 2010; Lizz O'Donnell, "Women in Law Firms: Stuck in the Middle," *The Glass Hammer*, July 23, 2009, www.theglasshammer.com on February 8, 2010; Timothy L. O'Brien, "Why Do So Few Women Reach the Top of Big Law Firms?" *New York Times*, March 19, 2006, www.nytimes.com on February 8, 2010; Catalyst, "Women in Law," 2009, www.catalyst.org on February 8, 2010; Lynne Marek, "Women Lawyers Find Their Own Paths as Law Firms Struggle to Keep Them," *Law.com*, June 25, 2007, www.law.com on February 8, 2010.

EXPERIENCING ORGANIZATIONAL BEHAVIOR

Learning About Job Design

Purpose: This exercise will help you assess the processes involved in designing jobs to make them more motivating.

Format: Working in small groups, you will diagnose the motivating potential of an existing job, compare its motivating potential to that of other jobs, suggest ways to redesign the job, and then assess the effects of your redesign suggestions on other aspects of the workplace.

Procedure: Your instructor will divide the class into groups of three or four people each. In assessing the characteristics of jobs, use a scale value of 1 ("very little") to 7 ("very high").

1. Using the scale values, assign scores on each core job dimension used in the job characteristics theory (see below) to the following jobs: secretary, professor, food server, auto mechanic, lawyer, short-order cook, department store clerk, construction worker, and newspaper reporter.
2. Researchers often assess the motivational properties of jobs by calculating their motivating potential score (MPS). The usual formula for MPS is

$$\frac{(\text{Variety} + \text{Identity} + \text{Significance})}{3}$$
$$\times \text{ Autonomy} \times \text{Feedback}$$

Use this formula to calculate the MPS for each job in step 1.
3. Your instructor will now assign your group one of the jobs from the list. Discuss how you might reasonably go about enriching the job.
4. Calculate the new MPS score for the redesigned job, and check its new position in the rank ordering.
5. Discuss the feasibility of your redesign suggestions. In particular, look at how your recommended changes might necessitate changes in other jobs, in the reward system, and in the selection criteria used to hire people for the job.
6. Briefly discuss your observations with the rest of the class.

Follow-up Questions

1. How might your own preexisting attitudes explain some of your own perceptions in this exercise?
2. Are some jobs simply impossible to redesign?

BUILDING MANAGERIAL SKILLS

Exercise Overview   Communication skills are your ability to convey ideas and information to other people. They also involve the ways in which you receive ideas and information conveyed *to you*. This exercise puts you on the receiving end of an email which directs you to motivate others but which may not be very effective in motivating you to perform the task. As a result, you may be called upon to exercise not only your own communication skills but other managerial skills as well.

Exercise Background   Albert Q. Fixx, the founder and CEO of your company, a small manufacturer of auto parts, has long been committed to the continuous improvement of the firm's management practices through the application of modern management techniques. It seems that Mr. Fixx spent the past weekend at a seminar conducted by a nationally respected consultant on management effectiveness. The principal speaker and the group sessions focused squarely on the use of employee participation as means of improving company-wide productivity and enhancing employees' commitment to their jobs.

So inspired was Mr. Fixx by his weekend experience that he went straight back to his office on Sunday night, where he composed and sent an email that all managers would find in their inboxes bright and early on Monday morning. After recapping his eye-opening weekend, he wrote the following:

I am convinced that participative management is the key to improving productivity at this company. Because you did not have the advantage of attending the same seminar that I did, I am attaching copies of all the handouts that were given to participants. They explain everything you need to know about practicing participative management, and I expect all of you to begin putting these principles into practice, starting this week. As of now, both I myself and this company are committed to participative management. Those of you who do not undertake the application of participative-management principles in your departments will find it very difficult to remain with a forward-looking company like A.Q. Fixx.

Exercise Task Your instructor will divide the class into groups of four to seven people. Each member of the group will pretend to be a manager at A.Q. Fixx, and your group of "managers" will discuss each of the following issues. Be prepared to discuss the group's thinking on each issue, even if the group doesn't reach a consensus.

1. What are the chances that Mr. Fixx's email will spur effective participative management at the company? Are the odds better or worse than 50–50?
2. How has each individual manager responded to the email? Is your response consistent with that of most group members, or do you find yourself taking a stance that's different, even if only slightly so? If you've taken a different stance, do you think it worthwhile trying to convince the group to come around to your way of thinking? Why or why not?
3. What is the group's opinion of Mr. Fixx's approach to implementing participative management at the company? If you don't regard his approach as the best way of implementing participative practices— or his email as the best means of introducing the subject—discuss some ways in which he could he have improved his approach.

SELF-ASSESSMENT EXERCISE

The Job Characteristics Inventory

The following questionnaire was developed to measure the central concepts of the job characteristics theory. Answer the questions in relation to the job you currently hold or the job you most recently held.

Skill Variety

1. How much *variety* is there in your job? That is, to what extent does the job require you to do many different things at work, using a variety of your skills and talents?

1	2	3	4	5	6	7
Very little; the job requires me to do the same routine things over and over again.			Moderate variety			Very much; the job requires me to do many different things, using a number of different skills and talents.

2. The job requires me to use a number of complex or high-level skills.

How accurate is the statement in describing your job?

1	2	3	4	5	6	7
Very inaccurate	Mostly inaccurate	Slightly inaccurate	Uncertain	Slightly accurate	Mostly accurate	Very accurate

3. The job is quite simple and repetitive.*

How accurate is the statement in describing your job?

1	2	3	4	5	6	7
Very inaccurate	Mostly inaccurate	Slightly inaccurate	Uncertain	Slightly accurate	Mostly accurate	Very accurate

Task Identity

1. To what extent does your job involve doing a *"whole" and identifiable piece of work*? That is, is the job a complete piece of work that has an obvious beginning and end? Or is it only a small *part* of the overall piece of work, which is finished by other people or by automatic machines?

1	2	3	4	5	6	7

My job is only a tiny part of the overall piece of work; the results of my activities cannot be seen in the final product or service.	My job is a moderate-sized "chunk" of the overall piece of work; my own contribution can be seen in the final outcome.	My job involves doing the whole piece of work, from start to finish; the results of my activities are easily seen in the final product or service.

2. The job provides me a chance to completely finish the pieces of work I begin.

How accurate is the statement in describing your job?

1	2	3	4	5	6	7
Very inaccurate	Mostly inaccurate	Slightly inaccurate	Uncertain	Slightly accurate	Mostly accurate	Very accurate

3. The job is arranged so that I do *not* have the chance to do an entire piece of work from beginning to end.*

How accurate is the statement in describing your job?

1	2	3	4	5	6	7
Very inaccurate	Mostly inaccurate	Slightly inaccurate	Uncertain	Slightly accurate	Mostly accurate	Very accurate

Task Significance

1. In general, how significant or important is your job? That is, are the results of your work likely to significantly affect the lives or well-being of other people?

1	2	3	4	5	6	7

Not very significant; the outcomes of my work are *not* likely to have important effects on other people.	Moderately significant	Highly significant; the outcomes of my work can affect other people in very important ways.

2. This job is one in which a lot of people can be affected by how well the work gets done.

How accurate is the statement in describing your job?

1	2	3	4	5	6	7
Very inaccurate	Mostly inaccurate	Slightly inaccurate	Uncertain	Slightly accurate	Mostly accurate	Very accurate

3. The job itself is *not* very significant or important in the broader scheme of things.*

How accurate is the statement in describing your job?

1	2	3	4	5	6	7
Very inaccurate	Mostly inaccurate	Slightly inaccurate	Uncertain	Slightly accurate	Mostly accurate	Very accurate

Autonomy

1. How much *autonomy* is there in your job? That is, to what extent does your job permit you to decide *on your own* how to go about doing your work?

1	2	3	4	5	6	7

Very little; the job gives me almost no personal "say" about how and when the work is done.	Moderate autonomy; many things are standardized and not under my control, but I can make some decisions about the work.	Very much; the job gives me almost complete responsibility for deciding how and when the work is done.

2. The job gives me considerable opportunity for independence and freedom in how I do the work.

How accurate is the statement in describing your job?

1	2	3	4	5	6	7
Very inaccurate	Mostly inaccurate	Slightly inaccurate	Uncertain	Slightly accurate	Mostly accurate	Very accurate

3. The job denies me any chance to use my personal initiative or judgment in carrying out the work.*

How accurate is the statement in describing your job?

1	2	3	4	5	6	7
Very inaccurate	Mostly inaccurate	Slightly inaccurate	Uncertain	Slightly accurate	Mostly accurate	Very accurate

Feedback

1. To what extent does *doing the job itself* provide you with information about your work performance? That is, does the actual *work itself* provide clues about how well you are doing—aside from any "feedback" coworkers or supervisors may provide?

1	2	3	4	5	6	7
Very little; the job itself is set up so I could work forever without finding out how well I am doing.			Moderately; sometimes doing the job provides "feedback" to me; sometimes it does not.			Very much; the job is set up so that I get almost constant "feedback" as I work about how well I am doing.

2. Just doing the work required by the job provides many chances for me to figure out how well I am doing.

How accurate is the statement in describing your job?

1	2	3	4	5	6	7
Very inaccurate	Mostly inaccurate	Slightly inaccurate	Uncertain	Slightly accurate	Mostly accurate	Very accurate

3. The job itself provides very few clues about whether or not I am performing well.*

How accurate is the statement in describing your job?

1	2	3	4	5	6	7
Very inaccurate	Mostly inaccurate	Slightly inaccurate	Uncertain	Slightly accurate	Mostly accurate	Very accurate

Scoring: Responses to the three items for each core characteristic are averaged to yield an overall score for that characteristic. Items marked with an asterisk (*) should be scored as follows: $1 = 7$; $2 = 6$; $3 = 5$; $6 = 2$; $7 = 1$

Once you have calculated the score for each core characteristic, calculate the motivating potential score (MPS) of your job using this formula:

$$\text{MPS} = \frac{(\text{Skill variety} + \text{Task identity} + \text{Task significance})}{3} \times \text{Autonomy} \times \text{Feedback}$$

Finally, compare your MPS with those of your classmates and discuss why some scores are higher or lower than others.

CHAPTER 6

MOTIVATING EMPLOYEE PERFORMANCE THROUGH REWARDS

CHAPTER LEARNING OBJECTIVES

After studying this chapter you should be able to:

- Describe goal setting and relate it to motivation.
- Discuss performance management in organizations.
- Identify the key elements in understanding individual rewards in organizations.
- Describe the issues and processes involved in managing reward systems.

The Benefits of Survival

"Eddie Bauer is a good company with a great brand and a bad balance sheet."

—CEO NEIL FISKE

Let's say that back in 1972, when you graduated from high school, you took a job stocking shelves at your local Eddie Bauer outlet. Despite your menial starting position (and paycheck), you found that you not only liked working for the company (which specializes in sportswear and accessories) but decided that

TIM BOYLE/GETTY IMAGES

Venerable retailer Eddie Bauer has struggled in recent years. Its story highlights both some of the excesses of executive compensation and the importance of long-term rewards for all employees.

147

retail clothing might be the right line of work for you. So you stayed on at the Eddie Bauer store, working full time while you pursued a college degree in marketing (with a specialty in fashion merchandising). Before long, you were advancing steadily in the ranks, from sales clerk to store manager, to district manager, to your current position as an assistant VP for merchandising and planning at corporate headquarters in Bellevue, Washington.

Along the way, you survived the 2003 bankruptcy of the parent company, catalog retailer Spiegel, and still had a job when Eddie Bauer Holdings Inc. emerged as a stand-alone publicly traded company in 2005. Moreover, you still had your benefits and pension because the new company had assumed its predecessor's compensation plans (along with its debt). You also survived a 15 percent cut in nonretail personnel in 2008, and although your salary was frozen, you were gratified to see that the company also reduced compensation paid to the board of directors and cut CEO Neil Fiske's pay by 10 percent. After all, you remembered when, just a year earlier, the previous CEO had agreed to step down after the company's stock had dropped from over $30 to about $9 a share (thus wiping out most of the value of your stock options). The company had lost $300 million in the previous three quarters, but Fabian Mansson walked away with $6 million in "separation benefits," bonuses totaling nearly $1.5 million, and another two years' worth of salary (plus benefits) amounting to more than $1 million a year.

That's when Fiske and his new management team took over and worked to engineer a turnaround. By early 2009, however, the $300 million debt that Eddie Bauer had assumed when it came out of the Spiegel bankruptcy in 2005 was still at $285.9 million, and you knew that the firm was spending 50 cents of every dollar in revenue to pay it down. And then, of course, there was the recession. With sales down 15 percent, there wasn't much revenue to pay off the debt or do much of anything else to improve the company's fortunes. The firm had lost $165 million in 2008, bringing the three-year total to $487 million, and in the first quarter of 2009, things continued to go downhill, with another $44.5 million in losses.

For a week, the stock in your option plan had been trading for about 25 cents a share, leaving your stock options worthless, and you were prepared for the bankruptcy filing that came in June of 2009. Even then, however, you had to give Fiske credit for planning ahead. Not only had he lined up bank financing of $100 million to cover operations during the bankruptcy period, but he'd arranged to sell the company to a private equity firm called CCMP Capital Advisors, which had made a bid of just over $200 million.

More importantly—at least from your point of view—CCMP intended to keep Eddie Bauer up and running. "We're not looking to liquidate the company or close most of the stores," said a CCMP executive. "We're trying to help 8,000 employees save an iconic American brand." As one of those 8,000 employees, you were glad to hear that Eddie Bauer's stores, websites, and catalog unit would stay open for business and that the firm would even be honoring customer gift cards, loyalty-program points, and returns. Neil Fiske insisted that "Eddie Bauer is a good company with a great brand and a bad balance sheet" and promised that the bankruptcy process "will allow the business to emerge with far less debt, positioned for growth as the economy recovers and as our new products gain traction."

Fiske also announced that he expected the process "to be completed very quickly, protecting our employees and critical vendor partners every step of the way." Sure enough, the sale of the company was finalized in the first week in August, although the buyer wasn't CCMP. As it turns out, Golden Gate Capital, another private equity firm, bid $286 million to beat out CCMP and seven other would-be buyers. Golden State also took on hundreds of millions in liabilities and promised to keep open at least 300 of the firm's 370 stores. "A very good result in this economy," observed one lawyer involved in the proceedings. The buyer and sale price (which had to be okayed by a federal judge) also meant that eight (unidentified) Eddie Bauer executives would split $2.5 million in bonus money (as compensation for their extra work in the months leading up to the sale). According to your math, that came to $312,000 apiece (if they split it evenly); and you also learned that 39 key VPs and managers—all of them just a notch above you in the corporate pecking order—would split another $1.25 million in bonuses.

As the deal was discussed in the press and company announcements, you also couldn't help but notice one other item: Among the liabilities that Golden Gate Capital did *not* pick up was responsibility for the company's pension plan. "Essentially, the company liquidated," explained a government spokesman, "and the purchasers of its assets were under no obligation to assume the old plan or create a new one." Doing a little research, you discovered that while the company's pension plan held $29.8 million in assets, it was obligated to pay out a total of $51.4 million to 1,800 workers and retirees who (like you) were with the company back in its days as Spiegel. Thus, as 2010 rolled around and the stock that your option plan was based on was worth somewhere between 2 and 3 cents a share, you naturally found yourself wondering how the firm's pension-plan shortfall of $21.7 million might impact your retirement plans.

As you now know, this chapter in your career life story has a reasonably happy ending. In January 2010, the federal Pension Benefit Guaranty Corporation (PBGC) announced that it had assumed responsibility for your company's underfunded pension plan. Because your plan, which came to an abrupt end in August 2009, was only 58 percent funded, it failed to meet federal minimum requirements and thus fell under the provisions of the PBGC, which protects 44 million workers and retirees who went—and still go—to work under the assumption that their pensions will be paid as per agreement with their employers. Hence, the notification you received from PBGC informing you that the maximum guaranteed pension at age 65 for workers in plans ending in 2009 is $54,000 a year.

So here you are, pushing 60, and you still have a job at Eddie Bauer, and at least company morale isn't completely shot. In fact, in the middle of one slow afternoon at your office in Bellevue, your curiosity is piqued and you log on to a website dedicated to the anonymous sharing of employees' opinions about their workplaces. Searching "Eddie Bauer," you find a couple of recent postings that catch your eye. "I believe that Mr. Fiske is an awesome leader & a great match for EB," says one of your coworkers. "In time and with some luck, he'll make it happen!" Another colleague is optimistic in a little more detail (interestingly, it could be you): "I have been with the company for many years and have seen the ups and downs. Currently, 2009, we have recently survived a huge economic crash and bankruptcy and are doing great. Our CEO has taken the company in a very promising direction and the future is bright."

For another interesting story from the annals of PBGC, see the *Ethics* box on p. 163 entitled "'Legalized Crime' or Just 'Fundamentally Wrong'?"

What Do You Think?

1. What can you learn about organizational rewards and reward systems from your "hypothetical" career at Eddie Bauer?

2. What examples of goals and goal setting can you identify in this case?

References: Stephanie Rosenbloom and Michael J. de la Merced, "Eddie Bauer Files for Bankruptcy," *New York Times*, June 18, 2009, www.nytimes.com on February 16, 2010; Greg Lamm, "Eddie Bauer Declares Bankruptcy," *Puget Sound Business Journal*, June 17, 2009, http://seattle.bizjournals.com on February 16, 2010; Chantal Todé, "Eddie Bauer Cuts Corporate Staff by 16%," *DMNews*, January 30, 2008, www.dmnews.com on February 16, 2010; Monica Soto Ouchi, "Ex-CEO Still Got a Hefty Check," *Seattle Times*, February 16, 2007, http://seattletimes .nwsource.com on February 16, 2010; Rachel Feintzeig and Kerry Grace Benn, "Golden Gate Capital Prevails at Auction for Eddie Bauer with $286 Million Offer," *Wall Street Journal*, http://online.wsj.com on February 16, 2010; Greg Lamm, "Eddie Bauer Execs Get Sales Bonuses," *Puget Sound Business Journal*, July 23, 2009, http://seattle .bizjournals.com on February 16, 2010; Amy Martinez, "Government Takes Over Legacy Spiegel Obligations from Eddie Bauer," *Seattle Times*, January 7, 2010, http://seattletimes.nwsource.com on February 16, 2010; "PBGC Protects Eddie Bauer Pension Plan," PBGC Public Affairs, January 6, 2010, www.pbgc.gov on February 16, 2010.

For decades management experts have advocated the importance of providing meaningful rewards for employees. Most managers initially focused on pay as the basic reward offered to employees. But now many people understand that employees actually seek and respond to a variety of rewards from their work. As we established at the beginning of Chapter 5, managers, in order to capitalize on the potential for motivated behavior, can use a number of strategies directed at enhanced performance in order to transform that potential into actual enhanced performance. Subsequent discussions in that chapter identified various work-related elements that can help with that transformation.

In this chapter we examine several other organizational methods and elements that can promote enhanced performance. We begin with a discussion of goals and how they relate to both motivation and performance. Next, we describe performance management per se, as well as how performance relates to total quality management. Individual rewards are then introduced and related to motivated performance. Finally, we conclude with a discussion of a variety issues that affect the management of reward systems.

GOAL SETTING AND MOTIVATION

Goal setting is a very useful method of enhancing employee performance.[1] From a motivational perspective, a **goal** is a meaningful objective. Goals are used for two purposes in most organizations. First, they provide a useful framework for managing motivation. Managers and employees can set goals for themselves and then work toward them. Thus, if the organization's overall goal is to increase sales by 10 percent, a manager can use individual goals to help attain that organizational goal. Second, goals are an effective control device (control meaning the monitoring by management of how well the organization is performing). Comparing people's short-term performances with their goals can be an effective way to monitor the organization's longer-term performance.

Social learning theory perhaps best describes the role and importance of goal setting in organizations.[2] This perspective suggests that feelings of pride or shame

A goal is a desirable objective.

A s
with to
goals f
goals l
employ
collabo
the ove
everyon
with ea
meetin
unit go
two tog
dinate
effectiv
selor ar
nate de
For exa
5 perce
of "doir
ager ar
subordi
to reac
process
ordinat
her own
goals.
initial g
through

− Dur
periodic
modify
some of
evaluati
nate ass
the ann
rewards
setting

Evalu

Goal-se
strated f
perform
have bee
tance ar
become
on the s
howevei
into actu

Fron
Tennec

about performance are a function of the extent to which people achieve their goals. A person who achieves a goal will be proud of having done so whereas a person who fails to achieve a goal will feel personal disappointment, and perhaps even shame. People's degree of pride or disappointment is affected by their **self-efficacy**, the extent to which they feel that they can still meet their goals even if they failed to do so in the past.

Goal-Setting Theory

Social learning theory provides insights into why and how goals can motivate behavior. It also helps us understand how different people cope with failure to reach their goals. The research of Edwin Locke and his associates most clearly established the utility of goal-setting theory in a motivational context.[3]

Locke's goal-setting theory of motivation assumes that behavior is a result of conscious goals and intentions. Therefore, by setting goals for people in the organization, a manager should be able to influence their behavior. Given this premise, the challenge is to develop a thorough understanding of the processes by which people set their goals and then work to reach them. In the original version of goal-setting theory, two specific goal characteristics—goal difficulty and goal specificity—were expected to shape performance.

Goal Difficulty   Goal difficulty is the extent to which a goal is challenging and requires effort. If people work to achieve goals, it is reasonable to assume that they will work harder to achieve more difficult goals. But a goal must not be so difficult that it is unattainable. If a new manager asks her sales force to increase sales by 300 percent, the group may ridicule her charge as laughable because they regard it as impossible to reach. A more realistic but still difficult goal—perhaps a 20 percent increase in sales—would probably be a better incentive.

A substantial body of research supports the importance of goal difficulty.[4] In one study, managers at Weyerhaeuser set difficult goals for truck drivers hauling loads of timber from cutting sites to wood yards. Over a nine-month period, the drivers increased the quantity of wood they delivered by an amount that would have required $250,000 worth of new trucks at the previous per-truck average load.[5] Reinforcement also fosters motivation toward difficult goals. A person who is rewarded for achieving a difficult goal will be more inclined to strive toward the next difficult goal than will someone who received no reward for reaching the first goal.

Goal Specificity   Goal specificity is the clarity and precision of the goal. A goal of "increasing productivity" is not very specific, whereas a goal of "increasing productivity by 3 percent in the next six months" is quite specific. Some goals, such as those involving costs, output, profitability, and growth, can easily be stated in clear and precise terms. Other goals, such as improving employee job satisfaction and morale, company image and reputation, ethical behavior, and social responsibility, are much harder to state in specific terms.

Like difficulty, specificity has been shown to be consistently related to performance. The study of timber truck drivers previously mentioned also examined goal specificity. The initial loads the truck drivers were carrying were found to be 60 percent of the maximum weight each truck could haul. The managers set a new goal for drivers of 94 percent, which the drivers were soon able to reach. Thus, the goal was quite specific as well as difficult.

Locke's theory attracted much widespread interest and research support from both researchers and managers; so Locke, together with Gary Latham, eventually

Our **self-efficacy** is the extent to which we believe we can accomplish our goals even if we failed to do so in the past.

Goal difficulty is the extent to which a goal is challenging and requires effort.

Goal specificity is the clarity and precision of a goal.

Figu

The goal
here, app
in turn, h

Reference: F
with permiss

G
Dif

G
Spe

meaning or worth. A salary increase of 5 percent, for example, means that an individual has 5 percent more spending power than before whereas a promotion, on the surface, means new duties and responsibilities. But managers must recognize that rewards also carry **symbolic value**. If a person gets a 3 percent salary increase when everyone else gets 5 percent, one plausible meaning is that the organization values other employees more. But if the same person gets 3 percent and all others get only 1 percent, the meaning may be just the opposite—the individual is seen as the most valuable employee. Thus, rewards convey to people not only how much they are valued by the organization but also their importance relative to others. Managers need to tune in to the many meanings rewards can convey—not only to the surface messages but to the symbolic messages as well.

Types of Rewards

Most organizations use several different types of rewards. The most common are base pay (wages or salary), incentive systems, benefits, perquisites, and awards. These rewards are combined to create an individual's **compensation package**.

Base Pay For most people, the most important reward for work is the pay they receive. Obviously, money is important because of the things it can buy, but as we just noted, it can also symbolize an employee's worth. Pay is very important to an organization for a variety of reasons. For one thing, an effectively planned and managed pay system can improve motivation and performance. For another, employee compensation is a major cost of doing business—as much as 50 to 60 percent in many organizations—so a poorly designed system can be an expensive proposition. Finally, since pay is considered a major source of employee dissatisfaction, a poorly designed system can result in problems in other areas such as turnover and low morale.

Incentive Systems Incentive systems are plans in which employees can earn additional compensation in return for certain types of performance. Examples of incentive programs include the following:

1. *Piecework programs*, which tie a worker's earnings to the number of units produced
2. *Gain-sharing programs*, which grant additional earnings to employees or work groups for cost-reduction ideas
3. *Bonus systems*, which provide managers with lump-sum payments from a special fund based on the financial performance of the organization or a unit
4. *Long-term compensation*, which gives managers additional income based on stock price performance, earnings per share, or return on equity
5. *Merit pay plans*, which base pay raises on the employee's performance
6. *Profit-sharing plans*, which distribute a portion of the firm's profits to all employees at a predetermined rate
7. *Employee stock option plans*, which set aside stock in the company for employees to purchase at a reduced rate

Plans oriented mainly toward individual employees may cause increased competition for the rewards and some possibly disruptive behaviors, such as sabotaging a coworker's performance, sacrificing quality for quantity, or fighting over customers. A group incentive plan, on the other hand, requires that employees trust one another and work together. Of course, all incentive systems have advantages and disadvantages.

Long-term compensation for executives is particularly controversial because of the large sums of money involved and the basis for the payments. Indeed, executive compensation is one of the more controversial subjects that U.S. businesses have had to face in recent years. News reports and the popular press seem to take great joy in telling stories about how this or that executive has just received a huge windfall from his or her organization. Clearly, successful top managers deserve significant rewards. The job of a senior executive, especially a CEO, is grueling and stressful and takes talent and decades of hard work to reach. Only a small handful of managers ever attain a top position in a major corporation. The question is whether some companies are overrewarding such managers for their contributions to the organization.[15]

When a firm is growing rapidly, and its profits are also growing rapidly, relatively few objections can be raised to paying the CEO well. However, objections arise when an organization is laying off workers, its financial performance is perhaps less than might be expected, and the CEO is still earning a huge amount of money. It is these situations that dictate that a company's board of directors take a closer look at the appropriateness of its executive compensation decisions.[16]

Indirect Compensation   Another major component of the compensation package is **indirect compensation**, also commonly referred to as the employee benefits plan. Typical **benefits** provided by businesses include the following:

1. *Payment for time not worked*, both on and off the job. On-the-job free time includes lunch, rest, coffee breaks, and wash-up or get-ready time. Off-the-job time not worked includes vacation, sick leave, holidays, and personal days.

2. *Social Security contributions*. The employer contributes half the money paid into the system established under the Federal Insurance Contributions Act (FICA). The employee pays the other half.

3. *Unemployment compensation*. People who have lost their jobs or are temporarily laid off get a percentage of their wages from an insurance-like program.

4. *Disability and workers' compensation benefits*. Employers contribute funds to help workers who cannot work due to occupational injury or ailment.

5. *Life and health insurance programs*. Most organizations offer insurance at a cost far below what individuals would pay to buy insurance on their own.

6. *Pension or retirement plans*. Most organizations offer plans to provide supplementary income to employees after they retire.

A company's Social Security, unemployment, and workers' compensation contributions are set by law. But deciding how much to contribute for other kinds of benefits is up to each company. Some organizations contribute more to the cost of these benefits than others. Some companies pay the entire cost; others pay a percentage of the cost of certain benefits, such as health insurance, and bear the entire cost of other benefits. Offering benefits beyond wages became a standard component of compensation during World War II as a way to increase employee compensation when wage controls were in effect. Since then, competition for employees and employee demands (expressed, for instance, in union bargaining) have caused companies to increase these benefits. In many organizations today, benefits now account for 30 to 40 percent of the payroll.

The burden of providing employee benefits is growing heavier for firms in the United States than it is for organizations in other countries, especially among unionized firms. For example, consider the problem that General Motors faces. Long-time workers at GM's brake factory in Dayton, Ohio, earn an average of $27 an hour in wages. They also earn another $16 an hour in benefits, including full healthcare coverage with no deductibles, full pension benefits after thirty years of service, life and

Indirect compensation, or **benefits**, are an important element in most compensation plans.

to copresident and COO Walter Robb, is "customers first, then team members, balanced with what's good for other stakeholders. . . . If I put our mission in simple terms," Robb continues, "it would be, No. 1, to change the way the world eats and, No. 2, to create a workplace based on love and respect." Adds founder, ex-chairman and current co-CEO John Mackey: "The beauty . . . of capitalism is that it has a harmony of interests. All . . . stakeholders are important. It's important that the owners and workers cooperate to provide value for the customer. That's what all business is about, and I'd say that's a beautiful thing."

WFM made *Fortune* magazine's very first list of the "100 Best Companies to Work For" in 1998 and is one of 13 organizations to have made it every year since. The 2010 award cited the company's growth (which means more jobs), salary cap limits (the top earner gets no more than 19 times the average hourly wage of $16.98), and generous health plan. The structure of the company's current health-care program, which revolves around high deductibles and so-called *health savings accounts (HSAs)*, was first proposed in 2003. Under such a plan, an employee (a "team member" in WFM parlance) pays a deductible before his or her expenses are covered. Meanwhile, the employer funds a special account (an HSA) for each employee, who can spend the money to cover health-related expenditures. The previous WFM plan had covered 100 percent of all expenses, and when some employees complained about the proposed change, the company decided to put it to a vote. Nearly 90 percent of the workforce went to the polls, with 77 percent voting for the new plan. In 2006, employees voted to retain the plan, which now carries a deductible of around $1,300; HSAs may go as high as $1,800 (and accrue for future use). The company pays 100 percent of the premiums for eligible employees (about 89 percent of the workforce).

High-deductible plans save money for the employer (the higher the deductible, the lower the premium), and more importantly—at least according to co-CEO Mackey—they also make employees more responsible consumers. When the first $1,300 of their medical expenses comes out of their own pockets (or their own HSAs), he argues, people "start asking how much things cost. Or they get a bill and say, 'Wow, that's expensive.' They begin to ask questions. They may not want to go to the emergency room if they wake up with a

> *"There's way more going on here than 'health insurance.'"*
>
> —ANONYMOUS FORMER EXECUTIVE AT WHOLE FOODS MARKET

hangnail in the middle of the night. They may schedule an appointment now." WFM marketing director Mary Ann Buttros agrees: Before she was enrolled in the new plan, she admits, she never asked medical providers what anything cost "because it didn't matter. Now it matters to me because it's my money."

Mackey believes that "the individual is the best judge of what's right for the individual," and he's so convinced of the value of plans like the one offered by his company that, in August 2009, he wrote an op-ed article in the *Wall Street Journal* in which he recommended "The Whole Foods Alternative to ObamaCare." Healthcare, he wrote, "is a service that we all need, but just like food and shelter, it is best provided through voluntary and mutually beneficial market exchanges." Going a step further, Mackey argued against an "intrinsic right to healthcare," and on this point, he stirred up a reaction among his customers that ran the gamut from surprise to boycotting. "I'm boycotting [Whole Foods]," said one customer who'd been shopping WFM several times a week, "because all Americans need healthcare. While Mackey is worried about healthcare and stimulus spending, he doesn't seem too worried about expensive wars and tax breaks for the wealthy and big businesses such as his own that contribute to the [national] deficit."

One ex-employee calls Mackey's statement "idiotic and harmful" and adds that, "the latest outrage aside, WFM has both good and bad about it." "The bad," according to some observers, includes WFM's health-care plan. "High-deductible plans for low-wage workers," says Judy Dugan, research director of Consumer Watchdog, "are the next best thing to being uninsured: The upfront costs are so high that workers have to weigh getting healthcare against paying the rent (to the detriment of their health)." A former WFM executive points out, for example, that the firm's plan entails "astronomical deductibles and co-pays." The $1,300 deductible, he explains,

> *means that you, minimum-wage-earning worker, must pay $1,300 of your own money before you get any coverage applied for medical services. After that, for in-network visits, the rate is 20/80, up to a maximum of $4,600 out of pocket for the year. This means that if you get charged $10,000 for a special hospital test . . . you are still liable for . . . $2,000!*

As for the HSA, it has to cover all co-pays and all expenses not covered by the plan (such as mental-health care). "There's way more going on here than 'health insurance,'" concludes the anonymous former exec. ". . . [The] system has massive hidden charges that routinely threaten and undermine the financial stability and, ultimately, [the] well-being of the employees."

Responding to the backlash against Mackey's *WSJ* piece, the WFM Customer Communications Team hastened to point out that "our team members vote on our plan . . . to make sure they continue to have a voice in our benefits." Mackey's intent, said the press release, "was to express his personal opinions—not those of Whole Foods Market team members or our company as a whole." The release also offered an apology for having "offended some of our customers," but for many onetime WFM loyalists, the apology was too little too late. "I will no longer be shopping at Whole Foods," announced one New Jersey shopper, explaining that "a CEO should take care that if he speaks about politics, his beliefs reflect at least the majority of his clients." In fact, WFM had become, in the words of one reporter, "the granola set's chain of choice," and much of its customer base consists of people whose opinions on such issues as healthcare reform are quite different from Mackey's. His *WSJ* article, declared a contributor to the company's online forum, was "an absolute slap in the face to the millions of progressive-minded consumers that have made [Whole Foods] what it is today."

The potential repercussions weren't lost on the WFM board. In late August, following the appearance of the *WSJ* op-ed piece, shareholder activists called for Mackey's removal. The CEO, they charged, had "attempted to capitalize on the brand reputation of Whole Foods to champion his personal political views but has instead deeply offended a key segment of Whole Foods consumer base." The company's stock had also slipped 30 percent over the previous five-year period, and in December, the board compromised by convincing Mackey to step down as chairman of the board.

CASE QUESTIONS

1. If you worked at WFM, how would you vote when the company's current healthcare plan came up for an employee vote? Explain your reasoning.
2. To underscore WFM's relatively high prices, some sceptics add "Whole Paycheck" to the company's motto of "Whole Foods, Whole People, Whole Planet"; they also point out that, despite discounts of 15 percent or more, many of the firm's employees can't afford to shop where they work. If you were a team member at WFM, how would this fact affect your attitude toward the company? How would it affect your attitude toward your job?
3. John Mackey now takes $1 a year in pay. In the last year in which he received a regular paycheck as CEO, his pay package totalled $436,000—about 14 times the average WFM worker's salary of $32,000 and relatively low for the industry. In the same year, however, he exercised nearly $2 million in stock options, bringing his total earnings to about $2.5 million. The company acknowledges that Mackey also holds more money in vested stock options but prefers to publicize its worker-friendly pay cap. If you were a team member at WFM, would this fact affect your attitude toward the company? How about your attitude toward your job?

REFERENCES

"100 Best Companies to Work For," *Fortune*, January 21, 2010, http://money.cnn.com on February 8, 2010; John Stossel et al., "Health Savings Accounts: Putting Patients in Control," *ABC News*, September 14, 2007, http://abcnews.go.com on February 9, 2010; John Mackey, "The Whole Foods Alternative to ObamaCare," *Wall Street Journal*, August 11, 2009, http://online.wsj.com on February 9, 2010; Jill Richardson, "A Former Whole Foods Employee's View of Whole Foods," *La Vida Locavore*, August 15, 2009, www.lavidalocavore.org on February 8, 2010; Judy Dugan, "Whole Foods' Crummy Insurance: What John Mackey Means by 'Choice,'" *Consumer Watchdog*, August 20, 2009, www.consumerwatchdog.org on February 10, 2010; Emily Friedman, "Health Care Stirs Up Whole Foods CEO John Mackey, Customers Boycott Organic Grocery Store," *ABC News*, August 14, 2009, http://abcnews.go.com on February 9, 2010; "Whole Foods CEO John Mackey Stepping Down as Chairman," *Huffington Post*, December 25, 2009, www.huffingtonpost.com on February 10, 2010.

EXPERIENCING ORGANIZATIONAL BEHAVIOR

Using Compensation to Motivate Workers

Purpose   The purpose of this exercise is to illustrate how compensation can be used to motivate employees.

Format   You will be asked to review eight managers and make salary adjustments for each.

Procedure   Listed below are your notes on the performance of eight managers who work for you. You (either individually or as a group, depending on your instructor's choice) have to recommend salary increases for eight managers who have just completed their first year with the company and are now to be considered for their first annual raise. Keep in mind that you may be setting precedents and that you need to keep salary costs down. However, there are no formal company restrictions on the kind of raises you can give. Indicate the sizes of the raise that you would like to give each manager by writing a percentage next to each name.

Variations   The instructor might alter the situation in one of several ways. One way is to assume that all of the eight managers entered the company at the same salary, say $30,000, which gives a total salary expense of $240,000. If upper management has allowed a salary raise pool of 10 percent of the current salary expenses, then you as the manager have $24,000 to give out as raises. In this variation, students can deal with actual dollar amounts rather than just percentages for the raises. Another interesting variation is to assume that all of the managers entered the company at different salaries, averaging $30,000. (The instructor can create many interesting possibilities for how these salaries might vary.) Then, the students can suggest salaries for the different managers.

_____ % Abraham McGowan. Abe is not, as far as you can tell, a good performer. You have checked your view with others, and they do not feel that he is effective either. However, you happen to know he has one of the toughest work groups to manage. His subordinates have low skill levels, and the work is dirty and hard. If you lose him, you are not sure whom you could find to replace him.

_____ % Benjy Berger. Benjy is single and seems to live the life of a carefree bachelor. In general, you feel that his job performance is not up to par, and some of his "goofs" are well known to his fellow employees.

_____ % Clyde Clod. You consider Clyde to be one of your best subordinates. However, it is obvious that other people do not consider him to be an effective manager. Clyde has married a rich wife, and as far as you know, he does not need additional money.

_____ % David Doodle. You happen to know from your personal relationship with "Doodles" that he badly needs more money because of certain personal problems he is having. As far as you are concerned, he also happens to be one of the best of your subordinates. For some reason, your enthusiasm is not shared by your other subordinates, and you have heard them make joking remarks about his performance.

_____ % Ellie Ellesberg. Ellie has been very successful so far in the tasks she has undertaken. You are particularly impressed by this since she has a hard job. She needs money more than many of the other people, and you are sure that they respect her because of her good performance.

_____ % Fred Foster. Fred has turned out to be a very pleasant surprise to you. He has done an excellent job and it is generally accepted among the others that he is one of the best people. This surprises you because he is generally frivolous and does not seem to care very much about money and promotion.

_____ % Greta Goslow. Your opinion is that Greta is just not cutting the mustard. Surprisingly enough, however, when you check to see how others feel about her, you discover that her work is very highly regarded. You also know that she badly needs a raise. She was just recently widowed and is finding it extremely difficult to support her household and her young family of four.

_____ % Harry Hummer. You know Harry personally, and he just seems to squander his money continually. He has a fairly easy job assignment, and your view is that he does not do it particularly well. You are, therefore, quite surprised to find that several of the other new managers think that he is the best of the new group.

After you have made the assignments for the eight people, you will have a chance to discuss them either in groups or in the larger class.

Follow-up Questions

1. Is there a clear difference between the highest and lowest performer? Why or why not?
2. Did you notice differences in the types of information that you had available to make the raise decisions? How did you use the different sources of information?
3. In what ways did your assignment of raises reflect different views of motivation?

Reference: Edward E. Lawler III, "Motivation Through Compensation," adapted by D. T. Hall, in *Instructor's Manual for Experiences in Management and Organizational Behavior* (New York: John Wiley & Sons, 1975). Reprinted by permission of the author.

BUILDING MANAGERIAL SKILLS

Exercise Overview   Communication skills refer to your ability to convey ideas and information to other people. In this exercise, you'll get some practice communicating effective goals to someone who, if not exactly a "subordinate," is willing to work with you in achieving the objectives that you develop.

Exercise Background   You'll need to review the section on "Goal Setting and Motivation" in this chapter, especially the subsections on *management by objectives*, or *MBO* ("Broader Perspectives on Goal Setting") and "Evaluation and Implications." In addition, you'll need to consider the following material—a series of sequential steps that will help you get the best results from your goal-setting project:

1. *Integrate goals and overall objectives.* Goals for every individual should be coordinated with overall organizational objectives and strategy. They should also be compatible with the goals of everyone else whose activities may be affected by them.
2. *Be sure that goals are specific.* Explain what each individual should accomplish and describe the tasks needed to accomplish his or her goals. Also be sure to explain the level of performance that you expect of each individual.
3. *Get people to commit to the goals you set for them.* Appeal to each individual's values and needs. Show how achieving organizational goals will help the individual achieve his or her personal goals.
4. *Prioritize goals.* When more than one goal is involved, rank them in order of importance. Encourage individuals to devote the most time and energy to the goals with the biggest payoffs.
5. *Explain how you'll measure performance.* Standards can be quantitative (e.g., units of production) or measured in terms of time (e.g., meeting schedules).
6. *Provide feedback.* Individuals must know whether or not they're on the right track. The best time to provide feedback is while individuals are in the process of working toward goals. Feedback can take the form of memos, charts, reports, or personal interaction.

Exercise Task   Once you've considered the material above, your instructor will divide the class into groups of five or six members each. Then do the following:

1. Spend a few minutes discussing the nature of your instructor's job. What does he or she do? What do you think constitutes a good performance in his or her job? What factors contribute to a good performance in the job?
2. Now develop a series of five goals that, in the group's opinion, could be used to develop an MBO program for classes in the business curriculum at your college. Try to select goals that are most critical in the performance of your instructor's job. [*Note:* As your chapter says, the most effective MBO goals are usually set in collaboration between "superiors" and "subordinates." For the sake of convenience, we're bypassing this part of the process.]
3. Select a group leader to share the group's list of goals with the whole class.
4. One group at a time, the class will then discuss the goals presented to it. The focus should be on the following criteria:
   - specificity
   - measurability
   - importance
   - motivational qualities
5. When the goals of all groups have been discussed, your instructor will share his or her opinions.

Reference

Phillip L. Hunsaker, *Management: A Skills Approach*, 2nd ed. (Upper Saddle River, NJ: Prentice Hall, 2005), pp. 169–71, 179.

SELF-ASSESSMENT EXERCISE

Diagnosing Poor Performance and Enhancing Motivation

Introduction Formal performance appraisal and feedback are part of assuring proper performance in an organization. The following assessment is designed to help you understand how to detect poor performance and overcome it.

Procedure Please respond to the following statements by writing a number from the following rating scale in the left-hand column. Your answers should reflect your attitudes and behaviors as they are *now*.

Strongly agree   = 6
Agree   = 5
Slightly agree   = 4
Slightly disagree = 3
Disagree   = 2
Strongly disagree = 1

When another person needs to be motivated,

_____ 1. I always approach a performance problem by first establishing whether it is caused by a lack of motivation or ability.

_____ 2. I always establish a clear standard of expected performance.

_____ 3. I always offer to provide training and information, without offering to do the task myself.

_____ 4. I am honest and straightforward in providing feedback on performance and assessing advancement opportunities.

_____ 5. I use a variety of rewards to reinforce exceptional performance.

_____ 6. When discipline is required, I identify the problem, describe its consequences, and explain how it should be corrected.

_____ 7. I design task assignments to make them interesting and challenging.

_____ 8. I determine what rewards are valued by the person and strive to make those available.

_____ 9. I make sure that the person feels fairly and equitably treated.

_____ 10. I make sure that the person gets timely feedback from those affected by task performance.

_____ 11. I carefully diagnose the causes of poor performance before taking any remedial or disciplinary actions.

_____ 12. I always help the person establish performance goals that are challenging, specific, and time-bound.

_____ 13. Only as a last resort do I attempt to reassign or release a poorly performing individual.

_____ 14. Whenever possible, I make sure that valued rewards are linked to high performance.

_____ 15. I consistently discipline when effort is below expectations and capabilities.

_____ 16. I try to combine or rotate assignments so that the person can use a variety of skills.

_____ 17. I try to arrange for the person to work with others in a team, for the mutual support of all.

_____ 18. I make sure that the person is using realistic standards for measuring fairness.

_____ 19. I provide immediate compliments and other forms of recognition for meaningful accomplishments.

_____ 20. I always determine if the person has the necessary resources and support to succeed in the task.

Reference: David A. Whetten and Kim S. Cameron, *Developing Management Skills*, 2nd ed., pp. 336–337. Copyright © 1991 by HarperCollins. Reprinted by permission of Pearson Education, Inc., Upper Saddle River, NJ.

7

CHAPTER

MANAGING STRESS AND THE WORK-LIFE BALANCE

The Balance of Trade-offs

"In order to retain the best and the brightest, we have to be flexible in how, when, and where the work gets done."

—KRISTEN PIERSOL-STOCKTON, REGIONAL DIRECTOR OF WORKPLACE SOLUTIONS, KPMG

The good news is that 60 percent of HR executives are satisfied with the work-life services that their companies offer employees. The bad news is that only 16 percent of their employees agree with them.

CHAPTER LEARNING OBJECTIVES

After studying this chapter you should be able to:

- Define and describe the nature of stress.
- Identify basic individual differences related to stress.
- Identify and describe common causes of stress.
- Discuss the central consequences of stress.
- Describe various ways that stress can be managed.
- Discuss work-life linkages and their relation to stress.

KPMG, an Atlanta-based tax and audit consultancy, has benefitted from providing substantial workplace flexibility for its professional employees.

According to a 2009 study conducted by the Corporate Executive Board (CEB), a global network of business professionals, the disconnect results from the fact that HR managers tend to value services differently than employees do. They tend to assume, for example, that expensive, high-profile services such as on-site gyms and healthcare options are the kinds of things that employees want in a workplace that promotes a good work-life balance. In reality, only about 20 percent of employees place any value at all on such services.

So, what *do* employees—managers and subordinates alike—really want? The answer seems to be *time*—or, more precisely, *more control over time*. More than 60 percent of the 50,000 workers polled in the CEB study specified *flexible schedules* as the single most important work-life benefit that an employer can offer. Flexible scheduling—or "flextime"—allows employees to adjust the time and/or place for completing their work (see Chapter 5). For example, Best Buy, the country's largest electronics retailer, calls its flextime program "ROWE," for Results Only Work Environment. Employees at corporate headquarters work when and where they want, and all meetings are optional. What are the results of this focus on Results Only? Productivity is up 35 percent, while turnover is down 90 percent. And Best Buy is by no means alone in realizing productivity gains from systematic efforts to help employees strike better balances in their work and home lives. Research shows, for example, that comparable initiatives have increased productivity by $195 million at Cisco Systems, the country's largest supplier of networking equipment; similarly, the tax and financial advisory firm Deloitte estimates that it has saved $41.5 million in turnover costs since implementing a program of flexible-work options.

Another company that's happy with the results of its flexible-work program is KPMG, an Atlanta-based tax and audit consultancy. KPMG is in an industry in which turnover is traditionally higher for women than for men. The numbers in the financial industry, however, also reflect broader trends in the U.S. workforce. According to a survey reported by the *Harvard Business Review*, for instance, 24 percent of male executives take a career "off-ramp" at some point—that is, they voluntarily leave their careers for a period of time. When it comes to women, however, the figure is 37 percent; for women with children, it's 43 percent. Among the men, 12 percent have interrupted their careers to take care of children or elders; among the women, it's the reason cited by 44 percent.

Because of similar data, KPMG launched a campaign in 2002 to transform itself into an "employer of choice" by offering employees a range of options for balancing work and home life. Family-friendly policies fall into such categories as *flexibility* (flextime, telecommuting, and job sharing) and *family resources* (backup childcare and eldercare, and discounts at childcare centers). Now, according to Barbara Wankoff, director of Workplace Solutions, 70 percent of KPMG employees work flexible hours. "Our employees," she says, "tend to be ambitious and career oriented. They want to develop professionally and build a career, but they also have lives as parents, sons or daughters, and spouses. So at KPMG we're promoting a culture of flexibility to help them manage the complexities of work and life." In one recent year, KPMG managed to improve retention of female employees by 10 percent and to increase the total number of women in its workforce by 15 percent. KPMG also says that if it hadn't offered flexible scheduling to female employees with young children, it would have lost about two-thirds of them.

Obviously, many women choose to stay in their jobs rather than take the off-ramp when faced with home-life pressures such as raising children. And with good reason: Research shows that although women leave their careers for an average of only 2.2 years, those two-plus years cost them 18 percent of their earning power (and 38 percent if they're out of the workforce for three years or more). That's why flexibility and family-resource options are so important to the third of all working women who choose to stay on the job and look for ways to balance professional and personal responsibilities. It's also one reason why companies like KPMG are willing to make concessions to women's needs for flexibility and family resources. "In order to retain the best and the brightest," says Kristen Piersol-Stockton, one of Barbara Wankoff's regional directors, "we have to be flexible in how, when, and where the work gets done." Tammy Hunter, a partner at KPMG and mother of three, maintains that flexible scheduling is what makes work-home balance possible. "I struggled," she explains, "when I thought I could be great only if I was at home 100 percent of the time or at work. Now that I have a balance, I feel like I spend enough time at home *and* enough time at work."

Hunter, who not only keeps her own flexible schedule but encourages her subordinates to do likewise, sees the advantages of adjustable scheduling from the perspectives of both employee and manager. For one thing, she's convinced that flextime programs work only if the company's commitment is top-down, with managers actively supporting participation by employees at all levels. She also knows firsthand what more and more studies now confirm: Trying to find time for children is particularly stressful for many employees. The results are increased absenteeism (which costs many companies nearly $1 million a year) and decreased productivity. Conversely, employees who manage their own schedules have lower stress levels, focus better on their tasks, and (according to the CEB study) work 21 percent harder than those who don't. It makes sense to Hunter: "When you enjoy your work environment and you aren't stressed out about getting other things done," she says, "you're more productive."

We continue this discussion in the *Diversity* box on p. 194, which identifies a few of the reasons why finding a balance between their professional and personal lives is often difficult for professional women.

What Do You Think?

1. How important will factors such as work flexibility and opportunities for work-life balance be to you when you begin your career, especially when selecting your first job?

2. How do you currently manage stress in your life? Do you think this will change when you finish school?

References: Corporate Executive Board, "The Increasing Call for Work-Life Balance," *BusinessWeek*, March 27, 2009, www.businessweek.com on February 18, 2010; Lori K. Long, "How to Negotiate a Flexible Work Schedule," *CIO.com*, August 29, 2007, www.cio.com on February 18, 2010; Georgetown University Law Center, "Flexible Work Arrangements: Selected Case Studies," *Workplace Flexibility 2010*, www.law.georgetown.edu on February 18, 2010; "Implementing a Results-Only Workplace," *Jerm*, January 20, 2010, www.jerm.com on February 18, 2010; Network of Executive Women, "Balancing Acts: People-Friendly Policies That Build Productivity," 2007, http://workforceexcellence.com on February 18, 2010; Emily Schmitt, "How a Flexible Work Schedule Can Help You Strike the Balance," *Forbes*, March 16, 2009, www.forbes.com on February 18, 2010.

In several of our earlier chapters we discussed motivational forces and organizational methods that might lead people to be more motivated. However, there are also dark sides to these same perspectives. Many people today work long hours, face constant deadlines, and are subject to pressure to produce more and more. Organizations and the people who run them are under constant pressure to increase income while keeping costs in check. To do things faster and better—but with fewer people—is the goal of many companies today. An unfortunate effect of this trend is to put too much pressure on people—operating employees, other managers, and oneself. The results can indeed be increased performance, higher profits, and faster growth. But stress, burnout, turnover, aggression, and other unpleasant side effects can also occur.

In this chapter, we examine how and why stress occurs in organizations and how to better understand and control it. First, we explore the nature of stress. Then we look at such important individual differences as Type A and Type B personality profiles and their role in stress. Next, we discuss a number of causes of stress and consider the potential consequences of stress. We then highlight several things people and organizations can do to manage stress at work. We conclude by discussing an important factor related to stress—linkages between work and nonwork parts of people's lives.

THE NATURE OF STRESS

Many people think of stress as a simple problem. In reality, however, stress is complex and often misunderstood.[1] To learn how job stress truly works, we must first define it and then describe the process through which it develops.

Stress Defined

Stress has been defined in many ways, but most definitions say that stress is caused by a stimulus, that the stimulus can be either physical or psychological, and that the individual responds to the stimulus in some way.[2] Therefore, we define stress as a person's adaptive response to a stimulus that places excessive psychological or physical demands on him or her.

Given the underlying complexities of this definition, we need to examine its components carefully. First is the notion of adaptation. As we discuss presently, people may adapt to stressful circumstances in any of several ways. Second is the role of the stimulus. This stimulus, generally called a *stressor*, is anything that induces stress. Third, stressors can be either psychological or physical. Finally, the demands the stressor places on the individual must be excessive for stress to actually result. Of course, what is excessive for one person may be perfectly tolerable for another. The point is simply that a person must perceive the demands as excessive or stress will not actually be present.

There has been a marked increase in stress reported by airline workers in the last few years. A combination of increased pressure for salary and benefit reductions, threats to pensions, demotions, layoffs, and heavier workloads have all become more pronounced since September 11. And today's rising energy prices are likely to increase these pressures. As a result, more airline workers than ever before are seeking counseling services; turnover and absenteeism are also on the rise.[3]

Stress is a person's adaptive response to a stimulus that places excessive psychological or physical demands on that person.

The Stress Process

Much of what we know about stress today can be traced to the pioneering work of Dr. Hans Selye.[4] Among Selye's most important contributions were his identification of the general adaptation syndrome and the concepts of *eustress* and *distress*.

General Adaptation Syndrome

Figure 7.1 graphically shows the **general adaptation syndrome (GAS)**. According to this model, each of us has a normal level of resistance to stressful events. Some of us can tolerate a great deal of stress and others much less, but we all have a threshold at which stress starts to affect us.

The GAS begins when a person first encounters a stressor. The first stage is called "alarm." At this point, the person may feel some degree of panic and begin to wonder how to cope. The individual may also have to resolve a "fight-or-flight" question: "Can I deal with this, or should I run away?" For example, suppose a manager is assigned to write a lengthy report overnight. Her first reaction may be, "How will I ever get this done by tomorrow?"

If the stressor is too extreme, the person may simply be unable to cope with it. In most cases, however, the individual gathers his or her strength (physical or emotional) and begins to resist the negative effects of the stressor. The manager with the long report to write may calm down, call home to tell her kids that she's working late, roll up her sleeves, order out for dinner, and get to work. Thus, at stage 2 of the GAS, the person is resisting the effects of the stressor.

Often, the resistance phase ends the GAS. If the manager completes the report earlier than she expected, she may drop it in her briefcase, smile to herself, and head home tired but happy. On the other hand, prolonged exposure to a stressor without resolution may bring on phase 3 of the GAS: exhaustion. At this stage, the person literally gives up and can no longer fight the stressor. For example, the manager may fall asleep at her desk at 3 A.M. and fail to finish the report.

Distress and Eustress

Selye also pointed out that the sources of stress need not be bad. For example, receiving a bonus and then having to decide what to do with the money can be stressful. So can getting a promotion, making a speech as part of winning a major award, getting married, and similar "good" things. Selye called this type of stress **eustress**. As we will see later, eustress can lead to a number of positive outcomes for the individual. Of course, there is also negative stress. Called **distress**, this is what most people think of when they hear the word *stress*. Excessive pressure, unreasonable demands on our time, and bad news all fall into this category. As the term suggests, this form of stress generally results in negative consequences for the individual. For purposes of simplicity, we will continue to use the simple term *stress* throughout this chapter. But as you read and study the chapter, remember that stress can be either good or bad. It can motivate and stimulate us, or it can lead to any number of dangerous side effects.

Figure 7.1 THE GENERAL ADAPTATION SYNDROME

The general adaptation syndrome (GAS) perspective describes three stages of the stress process. The initial stage is called alarm. As illustrated here, a person's resistance often dips slightly below the normal level during this stage. Next comes actual resistance to the stressor, usually leading to an increase above the person's normal level of resistance. Finally, in stage 3, exhaustion may set in, and the person's resistance declines sharply below normal levels.

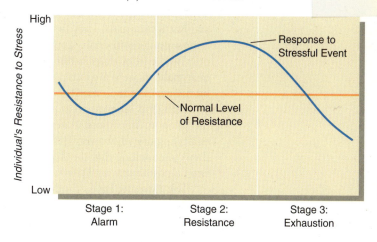

The **general adaptation syndrome (GAS)** identifies three stages of response to a stressor: alarm, resistance, and exhaustion.

Eustress is the pleasurable stress that accompanies positive events.

Distress is the unpleasant stress that accompanies negative events.

INDIVIDUAL DIFFERENCES AND STRESS

We have already alluded to the fact that stress can affect different people in different ways. Given our earlier discussion of individual differences back in Chapter 3, of course, this should come as no surprise.[5] The most fully developed individual difference relating specifically to stress is the distinction between Type A and Type B personality profiles.

Type A and B Personality Profiles

Type A and Type B profiles were first observed by two cardiologists, Meyer Friedman and Ray Rosenman.[6] They first got the idea when a worker repairing the upholstery on their waiting-room chairs commented on the fact that many of the chairs were worn only on the front. After further study, the two cardiologists realized that many of their heart patients were anxious and had a hard time sitting still—they were literally sitting on the edges of their seats!

Using this observation as a starting point, Friedman and Rosenman began to study the phenomenon more closely. They eventually concluded that their patients were exhibiting one of two very different types of behavior patterns. Their research also led them to conclude that the differences were based on personality. They labeled these two behavior patterns Type A and Type B.

The extreme **Type A** individual is extremely competitive, very devoted to work, and has a strong sense of time urgency. Moreover, this person is likely to be aggressive, impatient, and highly work oriented. He or she has a lot of drive and motivation and wants to accomplish as much as possible in as short a time as possible.

The extreme **Type B** person, in contrast, is less competitive, is less devoted to work, and has a weaker sense of time urgency. This person feels less conflict with either people or time and has a more balanced, relaxed approach to life. He or she has more confidence and is able to work at a constant pace.

A commonsense expectation might be that Type A people are more successful than Type B people. In reality, however, this is not necessarily true—the Type B person is not necessarily any more or less successful than the Type A. There are several possible explanations for this. For example, Type A people may alienate others because of their drive and may miss out on important learning opportunities in their quest to get ahead. Type B's, on the other hand, may have better interpersonal reputations and may learn a wider array of skills.

Friedman and Rosenman pointed out that most people are not purely Type A or Type B; instead, people tend toward one or the other type. For example, an individual might exhibit marked Type A characteristics much of the time but still be able to relax once in a while and even occasionally forget about time. Likewise, even the most laid-back Type B person may occasionally spend some time obsessing about work.

Friedman and Rosenman's initial research on the Type A and Type B profile differences yielded some alarming findings. In particular, they suggested that Type A's were much more likely to get coronary heart disease than were Type B's. In recent years, however, follow-up research by other scientists has suggested that the relationship between Type A behavior and the risk of coronary heart disease is not all that straightforward.

Although the reasons are unclear, recent findings suggest that Type A's are much more complex than originally believed. For example, in addition to the characteristics already noted, they are also more likely to be depressed and hostile. Any one of these characteristics or a combination of them can lead to heart problems. Moreover, different approaches to measuring Type A tendencies have yielded different results.

Finally, in one study that found Type A's to actually be less susceptible to heart problems than Type B's, the researchers offered an explanation consistent with earlier

Type A people are extremely competitive, highly committed to work, and have a strong sense of time urgency.

Type B people are less competitive, less committed to work, and have a weaker sense of time urgency.

thinking: Because Type A's are relatively compulsive, they may seek treatment earlier and are more likely to follow their doctors' orders![7]

Hardiness and Optimism

Two other important individual differences related to stress are hardiness and optimism. Research suggests that some people have what are termed *hardier* personalities than others.[8] **Hardiness** is a person's ability to cope with stress. People with hardy personalities have an internal locus of control, are strongly committed to the activities in their lives, and view change as an opportunity for advancement and growth. Such people are seen as relatively unlikely to suffer illness if they experience high levels of pressure and stress. On the other hand, people with low hardiness may have more difficulties in coping with pressure and stress.

Another potentially important individual difference is optimism. **Optimism** is the extent to which a person sees life in positive or negative terms. A popular expression used to convey this idea concerns the glass "half filled with water." A person with a lot of optimism will tend to see it as half full, whereas a person with less optimism (a pessimist) will often see it as half empty. Optimism is also related to positive and negative affectivity, as discussed earlier in Chapter 3. In general, optimistic people tend to handle stress better. They will be able to see the positive characteristics of the situation and recognize that things may eventually improve. In contrast, less optimistic people may focus more on the negative characteristics of the situation and expect things to get worse, not better.

Hardiness is a person's ability to cope with stress. Hardiness is especially important when people work in high-stress occupations. Take this doctor, for example. She has to work long hours and must help her patients make complex medical decisions that have long-lasting effects. She also must deal with an increasingly complex legal system and new health care reforms. Her demeanor, a partial reflection of hardiness, suggests she has the capacity to handle these pressures.

Cultural differences also are important in determining how stress affects people. For example, research suggests that American executives may experience less stress than executives in many other countries, including Japan and Brazil. The major causes of stress also differ across countries. In Germany, for example, major causes of stress are time pressure and deadlines. In South Africa, long work hours more frequently lead to stress. And in Sweden, the major cause of stress is the encroachment of work on people's private lives.[9]

Other research suggests that women are perhaps more prone to experience the psychological effects of stress, whereas men may report more physical effects.[10] Finally, some studies suggest that people who see themselves as complex individuals are better able to handle stress than people who view themselves as relatively simple.[11] We should add, however, that the study of individual differences in stress is still in its infancy. It would therefore be premature to draw rigid conclusions about how different types of people handle stress.

COMMON CAUSES OF STRESS

Many things can cause stress. Figure 7.2 shows two broad categories: organizational stressors and life stressors. It also shows three categories of stress consequences: individual consequences, organizational consequences, and burnout.

Hardiness is a person's ability to cope with stress.

Optimism is the extent to which a person sees life in relatively positive or negative terms.

Figure 7.2   CAUSES AND CONSEQUENCES OF STRESS

The causes and consequences of stress are related in complex ways. As shown here, most common causes of stress can be classified as either organizational stressors or life stressors. Similarly, common consequences include individual and organizational consequences, as well as burnout.

Reference: Adapted from James C. Quick and Jonathan D. Quick, *Organizational Stress and Preventive Management* (McGraw-Hill, 1984) pp. 19, 44, and 76. Used by permission of James C. Quick.

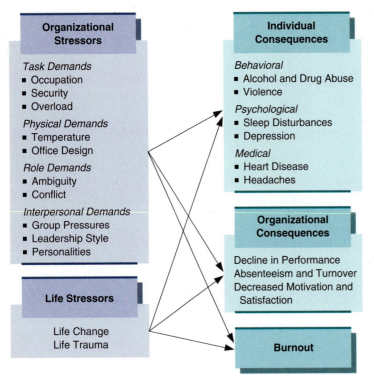

Organizational Stressors

Organizational stressors are various factors in the workplace that can cause stress. Four general sets of organizational stressors are task demands, physical demands, role demands, and interpersonal demands.

Task Demands   **Task demands** are stressors associated with the specific job a person performs. Some occupations are by nature more stressful than others. Table 7.1 lists a representative sample of relative high and low stress jobs, based on one study. As you can see, the jobs of surgeon and commercial airline pilot are among the most stressful, while the jobs of actuary and dietitian are among the least stressful jobs.

Beyond specific task-related pressures, other aspects of a job may pose physical threats to a person's health. Unhealthy conditions exist in occupations such as coal mining and toxic waste handling. Lack of job security is another task demand that can cause stress. Someone in a relatively secure job is not likely to worry unduly about losing that position; however, threats to job security can increase stress dramatically. For example, stress generally increases throughout an organization during a period of layoffs or immediately after a merger with another firm. This has been observed at a number of organizations, including AT&T, Safeway, and Digital Equipment.

Table 7.1   MOST AND LEAST STRESSFUL JOBS

Top Most Stressful Jobs	Top Least Stressful Jobs
1. Surgeon	1. Actuary
2. Commercial Airline Pilot	2. Dietitian
3. Photojournalist	3. Computer Systems Analyst
4. Advertising Account Executive	4. Statistician
5. Real Estate Agent	5. Astronomer
6. Physician (General Practice)	6. Mathematician
7. Reporter (Newspaper)	7. Historian
8. Physician Assistant	8. Software Engineer

Source: www.careercast.com/jobs/content/StressfulJobs_page1, accessed on April 5, 2010.

Task demands are stressors associated with the specific job a person performs.

A final task demand stressor is overload. Overload occurs when a person simply has more work than he or she can handle. The overload can be either quantitative (the person has too many tasks to perform or too little time to perform them) or qualitative (the person may believe he or she lacks the ability to do the job). We should note that the opposite of overload may also be undesirable. As Figure 7.3 shows, low task demands can result in boredom and apathy just as overload can cause tension and anxiety. Thus, a moderate degree of workload-related stress is optimal, because it leads to high levels of energy and motivation.

To see how task demands can be affected by available technology—and can add to the pressure on workers performing certain technology-related tasks—see the *Technology* box on p. 184.

Figure 7.3 WORKLOAD, STRESS, AND PERFORMANCE

Too much stress is clearly undesirable, but too little stress can also lead to unexpected problems. For example, too little stress may result in boredom and apathy and be accompanied by low performance. And although too much stress can cause tension, anxiety, and low performance, for most people there is an optimal level of stress that results in high energy, motivation, and performance.

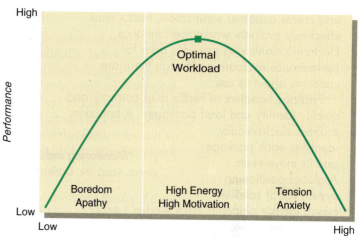

Physical Demands The **physical demands** of a job are its physical requirements on the worker; these demands are a function of the physical characteristics of the setting and the physical tasks the job involves. One important element is temperature. Working outdoors in extreme temperatures can result in stress, as can working in an improperly heated or cooled office. Strenuous labor such as loading heavy cargo or lifting packages can lead to similar results. Office design also can be a problem. A poorly designed office can make it difficult for people to have privacy or promote too much or too little social interaction. Too much interaction may distract a person from his or her task, whereas too little may lead to boredom or loneliness. Likewise, poor lighting, inadequate work surfaces, and similar deficiencies can create stress. And shift work can cause disruptions for people because of the way it affects their sleep and leisure-time activities.

Role Demands Role demands also can be stressful to people in organizations. A **role** is a set of expected behaviors associated with a particular position in a group or organization. As such, it has both formal (i.e., job-related and explicit) and informal (i.e., social and implicit) requirements. People in an organization or work group expect a person in a particular role to act in certain ways. They transmit these expectations both formally and informally. Individuals perceive role expectations with varying degrees of accuracy, and then attempt to enact that role. However, "errors" can creep into this process, resulting in stress-inducing problems called role ambiguity, role conflict, and role overload.

Role ambiguity arises when a role is unclear. If your instructor tells you to write a term paper but refuses to provide more information, you will probably experience ambiguity. You do not know what the topic is, how long the paper should be, what format to use, or when the paper is due. In work settings, role ambiguity can stem from poor job descriptions, vague instructions from a supervisor, or unclear cues from coworkers. The result is likely to be a subordinate who does not know what to do. Role ambiguity can thus be a significant source of stress.

Physical demands are stressors associated with the job's physical setting, such as the adequacy of temperature and lighting and the physical requirements the job makes on the employee.

Role demands are stressors associated with the role a person is expected to play.

A **role** is a set of expected behaviors associated with a particular position in a group or organization.

Role ambiguity arises when a role is unclear.

affects you. For example, do exams cause stress because you delay studying?

2. Develop a strategy for using time more efficiently in relation to each stressor that relates to time.

3. Note interrelationships among different kinds of stressors and time. For example, financial pressures may cause you to work, but work may interfere with school. Can any of these interrelationships be more effectively managed vis-a-vis time?

4. Assess how you manage the stress in your life. Is it possible to manage stress in a more time-effective manner?

SELF-ASSESSMENT EXERCISE

Are You Type A or Type B?

This test will help you develop insights into your own tendencies toward Type A or Type B behavior patterns. Answer the questions honestly and accurately about either your job or your school, whichever requires the most time each week. Then calculate your score according to the instructions that follow the questions. Discuss your results with a classmate. Critique each other's answers and see if you can help each other develop a strategy for reducing Type A tendencies.

Choose from the following responses to answer the questions that follow:

a. Almost always true

b. Usually true

c. Seldom true

d. Never true

_____ 1. I do not like to wait for other people to complete their work before I can proceed with mine.

_____ 2. I hate to wait in most lines.

_____ 3. People tell me that I tend to get irritated too easily.

_____ 4. Whenever possible, I try to make activities competitive.

_____ 5. I have a tendency to rush into work that needs to be done before knowing the procedure I will use to complete the job.

_____ 6. Even when I go on vacation, I usually take some work along.

_____ 7. When I make a mistake, it is usually because I have rushed into the job before completely planning it through.

_____ 8. I feel guilty about taking time off from work.

_____ 9. People tell me I have a bad temper when it comes to competitive situations.

_____ 10. I tend to lose my temper when I am under a lot of pressure at work.

_____ 11. Whenever possible, I will attempt to complete two or more tasks at once.

_____ 12. I tend to race against the clock.

_____ 13. I have no patience with lateness.

_____ 14. I catch myself rushing when there is no need.

Score your responses according to the following key:

• *An intense sense of time urgency* is a tendency to race against the clock, even when there is little reason to. The person feels a need to hurry for hurry's sake alone, and this tendency has appropriately been called hurry sickness. Time urgency is measured by items 1, 2, 8, 12, 13, and 14. Every *a* or *b* answer to these six questions scores one point.

• *Inappropriate aggression and hostility* reveal themselves in a person who is excessively competitive and who cannot do anything for fun. This inappropriately aggressive behavior easily evolves into frequent displays of hostility, usually at the slightest provocation or frustration. Competitiveness and hostility are measured by items 3, 4, 9, and 10. Every *a* or *b* answer scores one point.

• *Polyphasic behavior* refers to the tendency to undertake two or more tasks simultaneously at inappropriate times. It usually results in wasted time because of an inability to complete the tasks. This behavior is measured by items 6 and 11. Every *a* or *b* answer scores one point.

• *Goal directedness without proper planning* refers to the tendency of an individual to rush into work without really knowing how to accomplish the desired result. This usually results in incomplete work or work with many errors, which in turn leads to wasted time, energy, and money. Lack of planning is measured by items 5 and 7. Every *a* or *b* response scores one point.

TOTAL SCORE ___

If your score is 5 or greater, you may possess some basic components of the Type A personality.

Reference: "Are You Type A or Type B?" p. 94 from *Controlling Stress and Tension*, 6th ed. By Daniel A. Girdano, George S. Everly Jr., and Dorothy E. Dusek, Copyright © 2001 by Allyn & Bacon. Reprinted by permission of Pearson Education, Inc.

DECISION MAKING AND PROBLEM SOLVING

CHAPTER LEARNING OBJECTIVES

After studying this chapter you should be able to:

- Describe the nature of decision making and distinguish it from problem solving.
- Discuss the decision-making process from a variety of perspectives.
- Identify and discuss related behavioral aspects of decision making.
- Discuss the nature of creativity and relate it to decision making and problem solving.

The Creative Imprint at Bigfoot

"What was I going to do—buy more boats, buy more houses? I discovered there's a creative side in me."

—MICHAEL GLEISSNER, FOUNDER OF BIGFOOT ENTERTAINMENT

Have you seen *Midnight Movie*? You wouldn't have caught it in a theater because it went straight to DVD, but that doesn't prevent hardcore horror-film fans from tracking it down—after all, it was selected as the Best Feature Film at the 10th Annual Chicago Horror Film Festival. A blogger on HorrorNews.net called

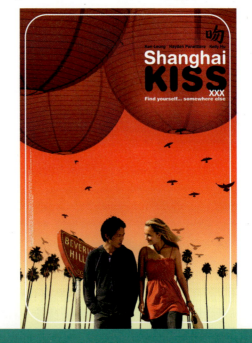

Bigfoot Entertainment has used an effective blend of decision making and creativity to make a splash in the entertainment industry. Shanghai Kiss was the firm's second movie.

it "the most original horror film I've seen this year," and a contributor to Movieweb.com declared it "a true modern day horror classic." It also found an audience outside the United States, with producer Bigfoot selling distribution rights in such countries as Germany, Greece, Thailand, and Japan.

How about *3 Needles*, a Canadian-made movie about the worldwide AIDS crisis? It wasn't a blockbuster, but while it was in theaters, it earned about $50,000 for AIDS charities. It was endorsed by the United Nations and did well enough at international film festivals to find distributors in such countries as Australia, New Zealand, and Brazil. Bigfoot CEO Kacy Andrews was pleased with the film's reception: "The positive response from critics and audiences," she said, ". . . once again affirms our conviction to promote independent filmmakers."

Bigfoot Entertainment is responsible for a host of independently produced films, many of which follow similar distribution paths to venues and audiences around the world. The company, says Andrews, "is dedicated to the community of filmmakers who possess the vision and passion to create critically acclaimed independent films." It was founded in 2004 by a German serial entrepreneur named Michael Gleissner, who is in some ways a model for the sort of creative individual that Bigfoot likes to back. He was certainly the model for the hero of *Hui Lu*, a 2007 Bigfoot film that Gleissner wrote and directed about a young entrepreneur who sells his company but finds himself pushed to the edge despite his millions. "What was I going to do," he replied when asked about his unusual career move, "—buy more boats, buy more houses? I discovered there's a creative side in me."

Gleissner was an e-commerce pioneer in Germany, where he founded Telebook, Germany's number-one online bookstore, and WWW-Service GmbH, the country's first, and one of its most successful, Web-hosting companies. In 1998, he sold Telebook to Amazon.com, where he served two years as a VP before cashing in and, in 2001, moving to Asia as a base for a new round of entrepreneurial activities. When he bought Bigfoot, it was an email-management firm, but Gleissner quickly re-created it as an international entertainment company whose main business, according to its mission statement, is producing and financing "innovative entertainment content, including independent feature films, television series, and reality shows." As head of Bigfoot, Gleissner served as executive producer on *Midnight Movie* and *3 Needles*, as well as on *Irreversi*, his second effort at writing and directing, and on *Shanghai Kiss*, in which he also tried his hand at acting.

Bigfoot maintains offices in Los Angeles and a small production facility in Venice, California, but the centerpiece of its operations is Bigfoot Studios, which opened in 2004 on the island of Mactan, in Cebu, home to Cebu City, the second-largest city in the Philippines. The state-of-the-art facility features six large soundstages, fully equipped editing suites and sound-mixing studios, and the latest in high-tech cameras and other equipment. In 2007, under the auspices of Bigfoot Properties, Gleissner expanded Bigfoot Studios as the first phase of Bigfoot Center, a complex that will eventually house not only film- and TV-production facilities but also the Bigfoot Executive Hotel; an array of restaurants, boutiques, and sidewalk shops; and an 11-story office build-ing (home to Bigfoot Outsourcing, which specializes in business-process services). The Bigfoot Center in the Philippines, by the way, should not be confused with the 26-story Bigfoot Centre in Hong Kong, where Bigfoot Properties is headquartered.

Gleissner's goal is to turn Cebu into a destination of choice for filmmakers who want to cut costs by shooting and finishing movies outside the United States. When

Bigfoot Entertainment finds a film suitable for financing and development, the deal usually requires the director to do some production work at the Cebu facility. By the time the studio opened in 2004, the Philippines were already an attractive location for animators looking for cheap post-production help. Unfortunately, however, the pool of talent available for work on live-action films was quite small. Gleissner's solution? He founded the International Academy of Film and Television (IAFT), not only to staff Bigfoot Studios but to train what executive director Keith Sensing calls "the next generation of global filmmakers." IAFT, says Sensing, looks for creative people who "have a desire for adventure" and "an education that will set them apart from people who have a strictly Hollywood background." IAFT enrollment is currently 60 percent international and 40 percent Filipino, but "all of our students," says Sensing, "have the opportunity to participate in real projects going on at Bigfoot Studios. . . . Many IAFT graduates," he adds, "have gone on to write, produce, and direct their own films" and often follow in Bigfoot's steps by finding distribution for their independent features on the international festival circuit.

Meanwhile, three recent graduates landed jobs on Michael Gleissner's latest project, a Philippines-set thriller starring Vietnamese actress Bebe Pham as a professional diver. Gleissner not only cowrote and directed *Deep Gold* but drew on his experience as an underwater photographer to shoot key scenes in Bigfoot's specially designed 170,000-gallon Underwater Studio.

What Do You Think?

1. What can we learn from Bigfoot about the tensions between creativity and innovation on the one hand and budgets and control on the other?

2. When you make decisions do you tend to lean more toward the creative side or the conservative side? Why do you think this is the case?

References: Kellen Merrill, "The Big Imprint in the Film Industry," *inmag.com*, 2010, www.inmag.com on February 24, 2010; Stephanie N. Mehta, "Hollywood, South Pacific-Style," *CNNMoney.com*, June 8, 2006, http://money.cnn .com on February 24, 2010; Bigfoot Entertainment, "Bigfoot Entertainment Breaks Ground at Cebu City's SRP," press release, May 8, 2007, www.bigfootstudios.com on February 24, 2010; Marlene Rodriguez, "Bigfoot Entertainment's International Academy of Film and Television in Mactan Island, Cebu," *NEDA Knowledge Emporium*, November 5, 2007, www.neda.gov.ph on February 24, 2010; Josh Elmets with Rebecca Pahle, "International Academy of Film and TV Flourishes in the Philippines," *MovieMaker*, January 29, 2010, www.moviemaker.com on February 24, 2010; Bigfoot Entertainment, "Bigfoot Underwater Studio Ends Its Stunt with a Bang," press release, 2008, http:// uw-studios.com on February 24, 2010.

Managers routinely make both tough and easy decisions. Regardless of which decisions are made, though, it is almost certain that some observers will criticize and others will applaud. Indeed, in the rough-and-tumble world of business, there are few simple or easy decisions to make. Some managers claim to be focused on the goal of what is good for the company in the long term and make decisions accordingly. Others clearly focus on the here and now. Some decisions deal with employees, some with investors, and others with dollars and cents. But all require careful thought and consideration.

This chapter describes many different perspectives of decision making. We start by examining the nature of decision making and distinguishing it from problem solving.

Next, we describe several different approaches to understanding the decision-making process. We then identify and discuss related behavioral aspects of decision making. Finally, we discuss creativity, a key ingredient in many effective decisions.

THE NATURE OF DECISION MAKING

Decision making is choosing one alternative from among several. Consider a game of football, for example. The quarterback can run any of perhaps a hundred plays. With the goal of scoring a touchdown always in mind, he chooses the play that seems to promise the best outcome. His choice is based on his understanding of the game situation, the likelihood of various outcomes, and his preference for each outcome.

Problem solving, on the other hand, involves finding the answer to a question. Suppose after running a play the quarterback sees that a referee has thrown a flag to signal a rules infraction. The referee explains to the quarterback that the defensive team committed a foul, and that the offense has the choice of accepting the play that was just run without a sanction against the defense or else they can impose the sanction and then run the play again. If the play resulted in a 30-yard gain, whereas the penalty would mean only 5 yards, the answer is to refuse the penalty and take the play. But if the play had resulted in a big loss, the penalty would be accepted.

Note that in some situations decision making and problem solving start out alike. Suppose the issue is to identify the best location for a new plant. If after evaluating each of the primary locations only one viable choice remains, then there is really no decision left to make. But if three locations each meet the firm's basic requirements and have different relative strengths, the manager will then have to make a decision from among the options. Most of our interest relates to decision making. However, we will identify implications for problem solving as relevant.

Figure 8.1 shows the basic elements of decision making. A decision maker's actions are guided by a goal. Each of several alternative courses of action is linked with various outcomes. Information is available on the alternatives, on the likelihood that each outcome will occur, and on the value of each outcome relative to the goal. The decision maker chooses one alternative on the basis of his or her evaluation of the information.

Decisions made in organizations can be classified according to frequency and to information conditions. In a decision-making context, frequency is how often a particular decision situation recurs, and information conditions describe how much information is available about the likelihood of various outcomes.

Types of Decisions

The frequency of recurrence determines whether a decision is programmed or nonprogrammed. A **programmed decision** recurs often enough for decision rules to be developed. A **decision rule** tells decision makers which alternative to choose once they have predetermined information about the decision situation. The appropriate decision rule is used whenever the same situation is encountered. Programmed decisions usually are highly structured; that is, the goals are clear and well known, the decision-making procedure is already established, and the sources and channels of information are clearly defined.[1]

Airlines use established procedures when an airplane breaks down and cannot be used on a particular flight. Passengers may not view the issue as a programmed decision because they experience this situation relatively infrequently. But the airlines

Decision making is the process of choosing from among several alternatives.

Problem solving is finding the answer to a question.

A **programmed decision** is a decision that recurs often enough for a decision rule to be developed.

A **decision rule** is a statement that tells a decision maker which alternative to choose based on the characteristics of the decision situation.

Figure 8.1 ELEMENTS OF DECISION MAKING

A decision maker has a goal, evaluates the outcomes of alternative courses of action in terms of the goal, and selects one alternative to be implemented.

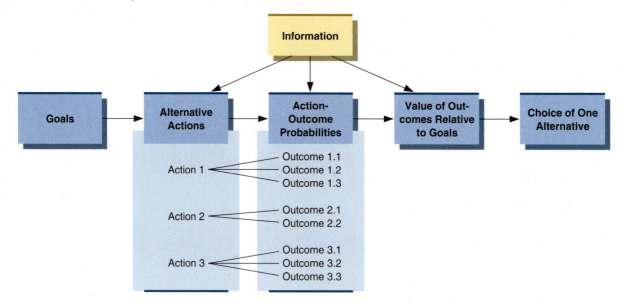

know that equipment problems that render a plane unfit for service arise regularly. Each airline has its own set of clear and defined procedures to use in the event of equipment problems. A given flight may be delayed, canceled, or continued on a different plane, depending on the nature of the problem and other circumstances (such as the number of passengers booked, the next scheduled flight for the same destination, and so forth).

When a problem or decision situation has not been encountered before, however, a decision maker cannot rely on previously established decision rules. Such a decision is called a **nonprogrammed decision**, and it requires problem solving. **Problem solving** is a special form of decision making in which the issue is unique—it requires developing and evaluating alternatives without the aid of a decision rule. Nonprogrammed decisions are poorly structured because information is ambiguous, there is no clear procedure for making the decision, and the goals are often vague. Many of the decisions that had to be made by government, military, and business leaders in the wake of the events of September 11, 2001, were clearly this type. One key element of nonprogrammed decisions is that they require good judgment on the part of leaders and decision makers.[2]

A **nonprogrammed decision** is a decision that recurs infrequently and for which there is no previously established decision rule.

Problem solving is a form of decision making in which the issue is unique and alternatives must be developed and evaluated without the aid of a programmed decision rule.

Table 8.1 summarizes the characteristics of programmed and nonprogrammed decisions. Note that programmed decisions are more common at the lower levels of the organization; whereas a primary responsibility of top management is to make the difficult, nonprogrammed decisions that determine the organization's long-term effectiveness. By definition, the strategic decisions for which top management is responsible are poorly structured, nonroutine, and have far-reaching consequences.[3] Programmed decisions, then, can be made according to previously tested rules and procedures. Nonprogrammed decisions generally require that the decision maker exercise judgment and creativity. In other words, all problems require a decision, but not all decisions require problem solving.

Table 8.1   CHARACTERISTICS OF PROGRAMMED AND NONPROGRAMMED DECISIONS

Characteristics	Programmed Decisions	Nonprogrammed Decisions
Type of Decision	Well structured	Poorly structured
Frequency	Repetitive and routine	New and unusual
Goals	Clear, specific	Vague
Information	Readily available	Not available, unclear channels
Consequences	Minor	Major
Organizational Level	Lower levels	Upper levels
Time for Solution	Short	Relatively long
Basis for Solution	Decision rules, set procedures	Judgment and creativity

Information Required for Decision Making

Decisions are made to bring about desired outcomes, but the information available about those outcomes varies. The range of available information can be considered as a continuum whose endpoints represent complete certainty—when all alternative outcomes are known—and complete uncertainty, when all alternative outcomes are unknown. Points between the two extremes create risk—the decision maker has some information about the possible outcomes and may be able to estimate the probability of their occurrence.

Different information conditions present different challenges to the decision maker.[4] For example, suppose the marketing manager of PlayStation is trying to determine whether to launch an expensive promotional effort for a new video game (see Figure 8.2). For simplicity, assume there are only two alternatives: to promote the game or not to promote it. Under a **condition of certainty**, the manager knows the outcomes of each alternative. If the new game is promoted heavily, the company will realize a $10 million profit. Without promotion, the company will realize only a $2 million profit. Here the decision is simple: Promote the game. (Note: These figures are created for the purposes of this example and are not actual profit figures for any company.)

Under a **condition of risk**, the decision maker cannot know with certainty what the outcome of a given action will be but has enough information to estimate the probabilities of various outcomes. Thus, working from information gathered by the market research department, the marketing manager in our example can estimate the likelihood of each outcome in a risk situation. In this case, the alternatives are defined by the size of the market. The probability for a large video game market is 0.6, and the probability for a small market is 0.4. The manager can calculate the expected value of the promotional effort based on these probabilities and the expected profits associated with each. To find the expected value of an alternative, the manager multiplies each outcome's value by the probability of its occurrence. The sum of these calculations for all possible outcomes represents that alternative's expected value. In this case, the expected value of alternative 1—to promote the new game—is as follows:

$$0.6 \times \$10,000,000 = \$6,000,000$$
$$+ \ 0.4 \times \$2,000,000 = \$800,000$$
$$\text{Expected value of alternative 1} = \$6,800,000$$

The expected value of alternative 2—not to promote the new game—is $1,400,000 (see Figure 8.2). The marketing manager should choose the first alternative, because its expected value is higher. The manager should recognize, however, that although

Under the **condition of certainty**, the manager knows the outcomes of each alternative.

Under the **condition of risk**, the decision maker cannot know with certainty what the outcome of a given action will be but has enough information to estimate the probabilities of various outcomes.

Figure 8.2 ALTERNATIVE OUTCOMES UNDER DIFFERENT INFORMATION CONDITIONS

The three decision-making conditions of certainty, risk, and uncertainty for the decision about whether to promote a new video game to the market.

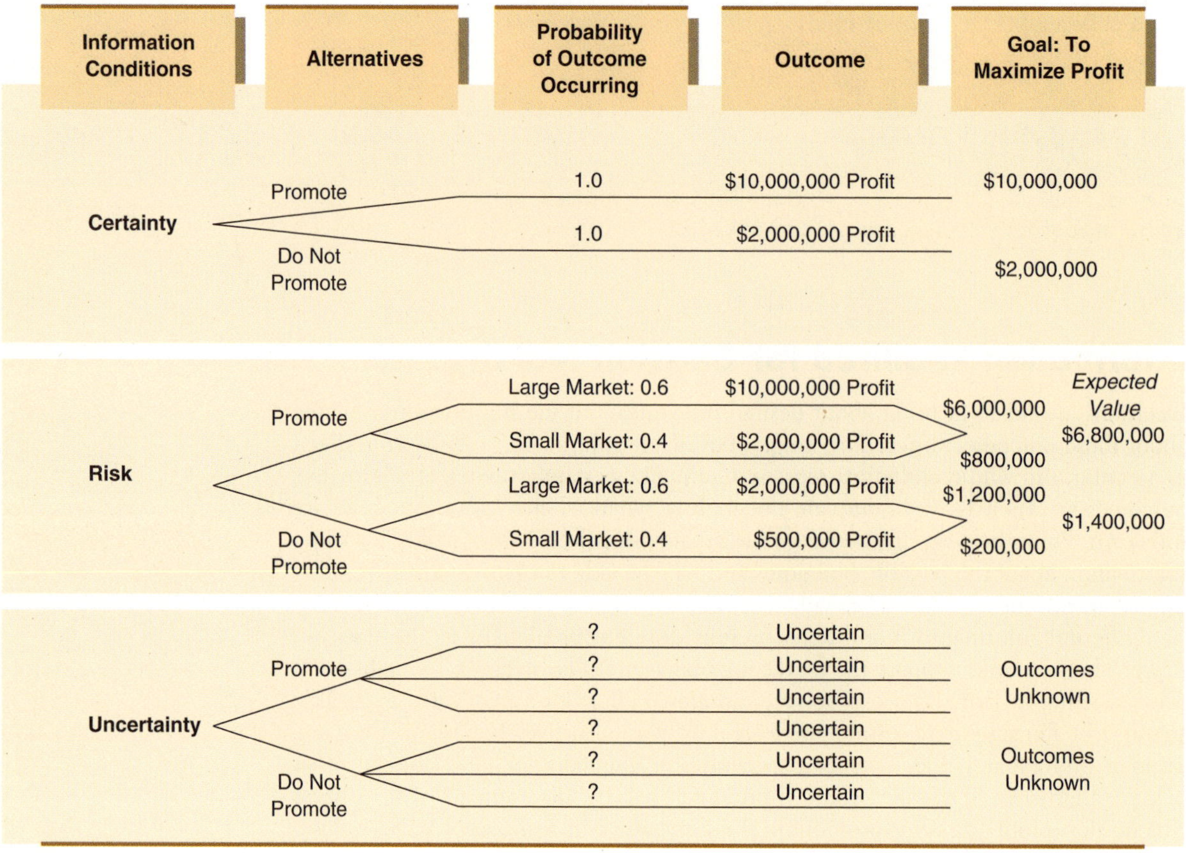

Information Conditions	Alternatives	Probability of Outcome Occurring	Outcome	Goal: To Maximize Profit
Certainty	Promote	1.0	$10,000,000 Profit	$10,000,000
	Do Not Promote	1.0	$2,000,000 Profit	$2,000,000
Risk	Promote	Large Market: 0.6	$10,000,000 Profit	$6,000,000 — Expected Value $6,800,000
		Small Market: 0.4	$2,000,000 Profit	$800,000
	Do Not Promote	Large Market: 0.6	$2,000,000 Profit	$1,200,000 — $1,400,000
		Small Market: 0.4	$500,000 Profit	$200,000
Uncertainty	Promote	?	Uncertain	Outcomes Unknown
		?	Uncertain	
		?	Uncertain	
	Do Not Promote	?	Uncertain	Outcomes Unknown
		?	Uncertain	
		?	Uncertain	

the numbers look convincing, they are based on incomplete information and are only estimates of probability.

The decision maker who lacks enough information to estimate the probability of outcomes (or perhaps even to identify the outcomes at all) faces a **condition of uncertainty**. In the PlayStation example, this might be the case if sales of video games had recently collapsed, and it was not clear whether the precipitous drop was temporary or permanent, or when information to clarify the situation would be available. Under such circumstances, the decision maker may wait for more information to reduce uncertainty or rely on judgment, experience, and intuition to make the decision. Of course, it is also important to remember that decision making is not always so easy to classify in terms of certainty, risk, and uncertainty.

THE DECISION-MAKING PROCESS

Under the **condition of uncertainty**, the decision maker lacks enough information to estimate the probability of possible outcomes.

Several approaches to decision making offer insights into the process by which managers arrive at their decisions. The rational approach is appealing because of its logic and economy. Yet these very qualities raise questions about this approach because actual decision making often is not a wholly rational process. The behavioral approach, meanwhile, attempts to account for the limits on rationality in decision making. The practical approach combines features of the rational and behavioral approaches. Finally, the personal approach focuses on the decision-making processes individuals use in difficult situations.

The Rational Approach

The rational decision-making approach assumes that managers follow a systematic, step-by-step process. It further assumes the organization is dedicated to making logical choices and doing what makes the most sense economically and managed by decision makers who are entirely objective and have complete information.[5] Figure 8.3 identifies the steps of the process, starting with stating a goal and running logically through the process until the best decision is made, implemented, and controlled.

© 2005 Charles Barsotti from cartoonbank.com. All rights reserved.

Risk propensity refers to the extent that a person is willing to gamble when making a decision. Those with lower risk propensity often struggle to reach a decision because they may worry too much about the risk associated with various options. This executive, for example, is clearly having trouble deciding on an option, perhaps because he has a low propensity for risk.

State the Situational Goal   The rational decision-making process begins with the statement of a situational goal—that is, a goal for a particular situation. The goal of a marketing department, for example, may be to obtain a certain market share by the end of the year. (Some models of decision making do not start with a goal. We include it, however, because it is the standard used to determine whether there is a decision to be made.)

Identify the Problem   The purpose of problem identification is to gather information that bears on the goal. If there is a discrepancy between the goal and the actual state, action may be needed. In the marketing example, the group may gather information about the company's actual market share and then compare it with the desired market share. A difference between the two represents a problem that necessitates a decision. Reliable information is very important in this step. Inaccurate information can lead to an unnecessary decision or no decision when one is required.

Determining Decision Type   Next, the decision makers must determine if the problem represents a programmed or a nonprogrammed decision. If a programmed decision is needed, the appropriate decision rule is invoked, and the process moves on to the choice among alternatives. A programmed marketing decision may be called for if analysis reveals that competitors are outspending the company on print advertising. Because creating print advertising and buying space for it are well-established functions of the marketing group, the problem requires only a programmed decision.

Although it may seem simple to diagnose a situation as programmed, apply a decision rule, and arrive at a solution, mistakes can still occur. Choosing the wrong decision rule or assuming the problem calls for a programmed decision when a

The **rational decision-making approach** is a systematic, step-by-step process for making decisions.

𝒻igure 8.3 THE RATIONAL DECISION-MAKING APPROACH

The rational model follows a systematic, step-by-step approach from goals to implementation, measurement, and control.

nonprogrammed decision actually is required can result in poor decisions. The same caution applies to the determination that a nonprogrammed decision is called for. If the situation is wrongly diagnosed, the decision maker wastes time and resources seeking a new solution to an old problem, or "reinventing the wheel."

Generate Alternatives   The next step in making a nonprogrammed decision is to generate alternatives. The rational process assumes that decision makers will generate all the possible alternative solutions to the problem. However, this assumption is unrealistic because even simple business problems can have scores of possible solutions. Decision makers may rely on education and experience as well as knowledge of the situation to generate alternatives. In addition, they may seek information from other people such as peers, subordinates, and supervisors. Decision makers may analyze the symptoms of the problem for clues or fall back on intuition or judgment to develop alternative solutions.[6] If the marketing department in our example determines that a nonprogrammed decision is required, it will need to generate alternatives for increasing market share.

Evaluate Alternatives   Evaluation involves assessing all possible alternatives in terms of predetermined decision criteria. The ultimate decision criterion is "Will this alternative bring us nearer to the goal?" In each case, the decision maker must examine each alternative for evidence that it will reduce the discrepancy between the desired state and the actual state. The evaluation process usually includes (1) describing the anticipated outcomes (benefits) of each alternative, (2) evaluating the anticipated costs of each alternative, and (3) estimating the uncertainties and risks associated with each alternative.[7] In most decision situations, the decision maker does not have perfect information regarding the outcomes of all alternatives. At one extreme, as shown earlier in Figure 8.2, outcomes may be known with certainty; at the other, the decision maker has no information whatsoever, so the outcomes are entirely uncertain. But risk is the most common situation.

Choose an Alternative   Choosing an alternative is usually the most crucial step in the decision-making process. Choosing consists of selecting the alternative with the highest possible payoff, based on the benefits, costs, risks, and uncertainties of all alternatives. In the PlayStation promotion example, the decision maker evaluated the two alternatives by calculating their expected values. Following the rational approach, the manager would choose the alternative with the largest expected value.

Even with the rational approach, however, difficulties can arise in choosing an alternative. First, when two or more alternatives have equal payoffs, the decision maker must obtain more information or use some other criterion to make the choice. Second, when no single alternative will accomplish the objective, some combination of two or three alternatives may have to be implemented. Finally, if no alternative or combination of alternatives will solve the problem, the decision maker must obtain more information, generate more alternatives, or change the goals.[8]

An important part of the choice phase is the consideration of **contingency plans**—alternative actions that can be taken if the primary course of action is unexpectedly disrupted or rendered inappropriate.[9] Planning for contingencies is part of the transition between choosing the preferred alternative and implementing it. In developing contingency plans, the decision maker usually asks such questions as "What if something unexpected happens during the implementation of this alternative?" or "If the economy goes into a recession, will the choice of this alternative ruin the company?" or "How can we alter this plan if the economy suddenly rebounds and begins to grow?"

Implement the Plan   Implementation puts the decision into action. It builds on the commitment and motivation of those who participated in the decision-making process (and may actually bolster individual commitment and motivation). To succeed, implementation requires the proper use of resources and good management skills. Following the decision to promote the new PlayStation game heavily, for example, the marketing manager must implement the decision by assigning the project to a work group or task force. The success of this team depends on the leadership, the reward structure, the communications system, and group dynamics. Sometimes the decision

Contingency plans are alternative actions to take if the primary course of action is unexpectedly disrupted or rendered inappropriate.

When Nissan first introduced its upscale brand Infiniti, decision makers in the firm's marketing department commissioned a series of Zen-like ads featuring ponds, rocks, and sand—but few images of the car itself. Meanwhile, Toyota was also introducing its upscale brand Lexus with ads highlighting the car's styling, performance, and luxury features. As a result, Infiniti's launch was sluggish. Decision makers at Nissan quickly scrapped the original ad campaign and began to concentrate more on the product itself. But Infiniti's poor product launch gave Lexus a jump on grabbing market share. And while Infiniti has held its own in recent years, it still trails Lexus and other premium brands in market share.

maker begins to doubt a choice already made. This doubt is called *post-decision dissonance*, or more generally, **cognitive dissonance**.[10] To reduce the tension created by the dissonance, the decision maker may seek to rationalize the decision further with new information.

Control: Measure and Adjust In the final stage of the rational decision-making process, the outcomes of the decision are measured and compared with the desired goal. If a discrepancy remains, the decision maker may restart the decision-making process by setting a new goal (or reiterating the existing one). The decision maker, unsatisfied with the previous decision, may modify the subsequent decision-making process to avoid another mistake. Changes can be made in any part of the process, as Figure 8.3 illustrates by the arrows leading from the control step to each of the other steps. Decision making therefore is a dynamic, self-correcting, and ongoing process in organizations.

Suppose a marketing department implements a new print advertising campaign. After implementation, it constantly monitors market research data and compares its new market share with the desired market share. If the advertising has the desired effect, no changes will be made in the promotion campaign. If, however, the data indicate no change in the market share, additional decisions and implementation of a contingency plan may be necessary. For example, when Nissan introduced its Infiniti luxury car line, it relied on a Zen-like series of ads that featured images of rocks, plants, and water—but no images of the car. At the same time, Toyota was featuring close-up pictures of its own luxury car line, Lexus, which quickly established itself as a market leader. When Infiniti managers realized their mistake, they quickly pulled the old ads and started running new ones centered on images of their car.[11]

Strengths and Weaknesses of the Rational Approach The rational approach has several strengths. It forces the decision maker to consider a decision in a logical, sequential manner, and the in-depth analysis of alternatives enables the decision maker to choose on the basis of information rather than emotion or social pressure. But the rigid assumptions of this approach often are unrealistic.[12] The amount of information available to managers usually is limited by either time or cost constraints, and most decision makers have limited ability to process information about the alternatives. In addition, not all alternatives lend themselves to quantification in terms that will allow for easy comparison. Finally, because they cannot predict the future, it is unlikely that decision makers will know all possible outcomes of each alternative.

The Behavioral Approach

Cognitive dissonance is doubt about a choice that has already been made.

Whereas the rational approach assumes that managers operate logically and rationally, the behavioral approach acknowledges the role and importance of human behavior in the decision-making process. In particular, a crucial assumption of the behavioral approach is that decision makers operate with bounded rationality rather than with the perfect rationality assumed by the rational approach. **Bounded rationality** is the idea that although individuals may seek the best solution to a problem, the demands of processing all the information bearing on the problem, generating all possible solutions, and choosing the single best solution are beyond the capabilities of most decision makers. Thus, they accept less-than-ideal solutions based on a process that is neither exhaustive nor entirely rational. For example, one recent study found that under time pressure, groups usually eliminate all but the two most favorable alternatives and then process the remaining two in great detail.[13] Thus, decision makers operating with bounded rationality limit the inputs to the decision-making process and base decisions on judgment and personal biases as well as on logic.[14]

The **behavioral approach** is characterized by (1) the use of procedures and rules of thumb, (2) suboptimizing, and (3) satisficing. Uncertainty in decision making can initially be reduced by relying on procedures and rules of thumb. If, for example, increasing print advertising has increased a company's market share in the past, that linkage may be used by company employees as a rule of thumb in decision making. When the previous month's market share drops below a certain level, the company might increase its print advertising expenditures by 25 percent during the following month.

Suboptimizing is knowingly accepting less than the best possible outcome. Frequently it is not feasible to make the ideal decision in a real-world situation given organizational constraints. The decision maker often must suboptimize to avoid unintended negative effects on other departments, product lines, or decisions.[15] An automobile manufacturer, for example, can cut costs dramatically and increase efficiency if it schedules the production of one model at a time. Thus, the production group's optimal decision is single-model scheduling. But the marketing group, seeking to optimize its sales goals by offering a wide variety of models, may demand the opposite production schedule: short runs of entirely different models. The groups in the middle—design and scheduling—may suboptimize the benefits the production and marketing groups seek by planning long runs of slightly different models. This is the practice of the large auto manufacturers such as General Motors and Ford, which make multiple body styles in different models on the same production line.

The final feature of the behavioral approach is **satisficing**: examining alternatives only until a solution that meets minimal requirements is found and then ceasing to look for a better one.[16] The search for alternatives usually is a sequential process guided by procedures and rules of thumb based on previous experiences with similar problems. The search often ends when the first minimally acceptable choice is encountered. The resulting choice may narrow the discrepancy between the desired and the actual states, but it is not likely to be the optimal solution. As the process is repeated, incremental improvements slowly reduce the discrepancy between the actual and desired states.

The decision-making process is supposed to be logical and rational but is instead often affected by behavioral, practical, and personal considerations. Consider, for example, Gabrielle Melchionda. Ms. Melchionda is a Maine entrepreneur whose skin-care product business is booming. She was recently offered a lucrative contract to begin exporting her products to Turkey. But she turned it down when she learned that the exporter also sold weapons. Had rational decision making prevailed, she would have jumped on the idea. But her own personal values kept her focused on what was important to her as a person—and it wasn't just the money!

© COURTESY OF MAD GABS

Bounded rationality is the idea that decision makers cannot deal with information about all the aspects and alternatives pertaining to a problem and therefore choose to tackle some meaningful subset of it.

The **behavioral approach** uses rules of thumb, suboptimizing, and satisficing in making decisions.

Figure 8.4 PRACTICAL APPROACH TO DECISION MAKING WITH BEHAVIORAL GUIDELINES

The practical model applies some of the conditions recognized by the behavioral approach to the rational approach to decision making. Although similar to the rational model, the practical approach recognizes personal limitations at each point (or step) in the process.

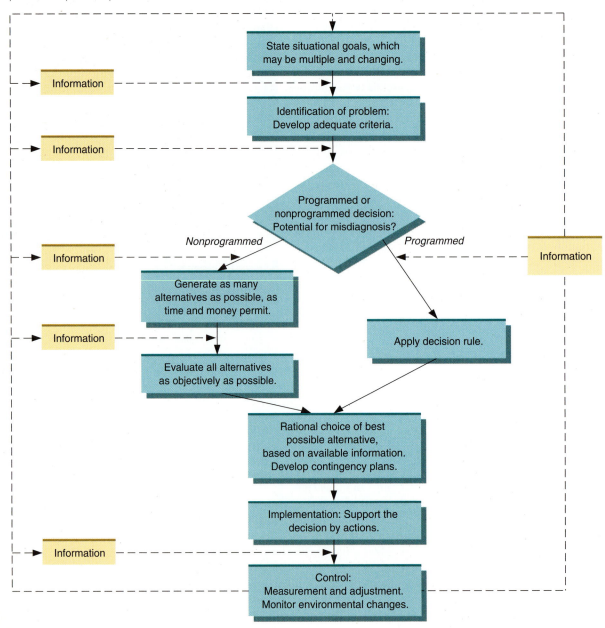

The Practical Approach

Suboptimizing is knowingly accepting less than the best possible outcome to avoid unintended negative effects on other aspects of the organization.

Because of the unrealistic demands of the rational approach and the limited, short-term orientation of the behavioral approach, neither is entirely satisfactory. However, the worthwhile features of each can be combined into a practical approach to decision making, shown in Figure 8.4. The steps in this process are the same as in the rational approach; however, the conditions recognized by the behavioral approach are added to provide a more realistic process. For example, the **practical approach** suggests that rather than generating all alternatives, the decision maker should try to go beyond rules of thumb and satisficing limitations and generate as many alternatives as time, money, and other practicalities of the situation allow. In this synthesis of the two other approaches, the rational approach provides an analytical framework for making decisions whereas the behavioral approach provides a moderating influence.

In practice, decision makers use some hybrid of the rational, behavioral, and practical approaches to make the tough, day-to-day decisions in running organizations. Some decision makers use a methodical process of gathering as much information as possible, developing and evaluating alternatives, and seeking advice from knowledgeable people before making a decision. Others fly from one decision to another, making seemingly hasty decisions and barking out orders to subordinates. The second group would seem not to use much information or a rational approach to making decisions. Recent research, however, has shown that managers who make decisions very quickly probably are using just as much, or more, information and generating and evaluating as many alternatives as slower, more methodical decision makers.[17]

The Personal Approach

Although the models just described have provided significant insight into decision making, they do not fully explain the processes people engage in when they are nervous, worried, and agitated over making a decision that has major implications for them, their organization, or their families. In short, they still do not reflect the conditions under which many decisions are made. One attempt to provide a more realistic view of individual decision making is the model presented by Irving Janis and Leon Mann.[18] The Janis-Mann concept, called the **conflict model**, is based on research in social psychology and individual decision processes and is a very personal approach to decision making. Although the model may appear complex, if you examine it one step at a time and follow the example in this section, you should easily understand how it works. The model has five basic characteristics:

1. It deals only with important life decisions—marriage, schooling, career, and major organizational decisions—that commit the individual or the organization to a certain course of action following the decision.

2. It recognizes that procrastination and rationalization are mechanisms by which people avoid making difficult decisions and coping with the associated stress.

3. It explicitly acknowledges that some decisions probably will be wrong and that the fear of making an unsound decision can be a deterrent to making any decision at all.

4. It provides for **self-reactions**—comparisons of alternatives with internalized moral standards. Internalized moral standards guide decision making as much as economic and social outcomes do. A proposed course of action may offer many economic and social rewards, but if it violates the decision maker's moral convictions, it is unlikely to be chosen.

5. It recognizes that at times the decision maker is ambivalent about alternative courses of action; in such circumstances, it is very difficult to make a wholehearted commitment to a single choice. However, major life decisions seldom allow compromise; usually they are either-or decisions that require commitment to one course of action.

Satisficing is examining alternatives only until a solution that meets minimal requirements is found.

The **practical approach** to decision making combines the steps of the rational approach with the conditions in the behavioral approach to create a more realistic approach for making decisions in organizations.

The **conflict model** is a very personal approach to decision making because it deals with the personal conflicts that people experience in particularly difficult decision situations.

Self-reactions are comparisons of alternatives with internalized moral standards.

The Janis-Mann conflict model of decision making is shown in Figure 8.5. A concrete example will help explain each step. Suppose Richard is a thirty-year-old engineer with a working wife and two young children. Richard has been employed at a large manufacturing company for eight years. He keeps abreast of his career progress

Figure 8.5   JANUS-MANN CONFLICT MODEL OF DECISION MAKING

A decision maker answering "yes" to all four questions will engage in vigilant information processing.

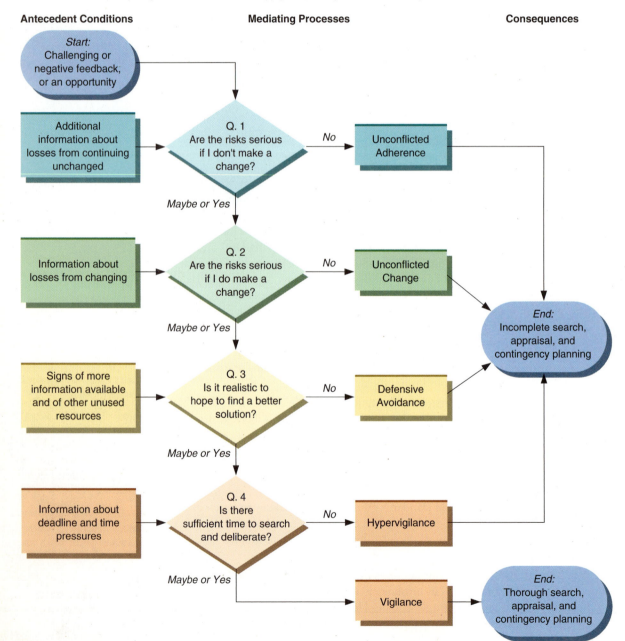

through visits with peers at work and in other companies, through feedback from his manager and others regarding his work and future with the firm, through the alumni magazine from his university, and through other sources.

At work one morning, Richard learns that he has been passed over for a promotion for the second time in a year. He investigates the information, which can be considered negative feedback, and confirms it. As a result, he seeks out other information regarding his career at the company, the prospect of changing employers, and the possibility of going back to graduate school to get an MBA. At the same time, he asks himself, "Are the risks serious if I do not make a change?" If the answer is "no," Richard will continue his present activities. In the model's terms, this option is called **unconflicted adherence**. If instead the answer is "yes" or "maybe," Richard will move to the next question in the model.

The second step asks, "Are the risks serious if I do make a change?" If Richard goes on to this step, he will gather information about potential losses from making a change. He may, for example, find out whether he would lose health insurance and pension benefits if he changed jobs or went back to graduate school. If he believes that changing presents no serious risks, Richard will make the change, called an **unconflicted change**. Otherwise, Richard will move on to the next step.

But suppose Richard has determined that the risks are serious whether or not he makes a change. He believes he must make a change because he will not be promoted further in his present company; yet serious risks are also associated with making a change—perhaps loss of benefits, uncertain promotion opportunities in another company, or lost income from going to graduate school for two years. In the third step, Richard wonders, "Is it realistic to hope to find a better solution?" He continues to look for information that can help him make the decision. If the answer to this third question is "no," Richard may give up hope of finding anything better and opt for what Janis and Mann call **defensive avoidance**; that is, he will make no change and avoid any further contact with the issue. A positive response, however, will move Richard onward to the next step.

Here the decision maker, who now recognizes the serious risks involved yet expects to find a solution, asks, "Is there sufficient time to search and deliberate?" Richard now asks himself how quickly he needs to make a change. If he believes that he has little time to deliberate, perhaps because of his age, he will experience what Janis and Mann call **hypervigilance**. In this state, he may suffer severe psychological stress and engage in frantic, superficial pursuit of some satisficing strategy. (This might also be called "panic"!) If, on the other hand, Richard believes that he has two or three years to consider various alternatives, he will undertake vigilant information processing, in which he will thoroughly investigate all possible alternatives, weigh their costs and benefits before making a choice, and develop contingency plans.

Negative answers to the questions in the conflict model lead to responses of unconflicted adherence, unconflicted change, defensive avoidance, and hypervigilance. All are coping strategies that result in incomplete search, appraisal, and contingency planning. A decision maker who gives the same answer to all the questions will always engage in the same coping strategy. However, if the answers change as the situation changes, the individual's coping strategies may change as well. The decision maker who answers "yes" to each of the four questions is led to **vigilant information processing**, a process similar to that outlined in the rational decision-making model. The decision maker objectively analyzes the problem and all alternatives, thoroughly searches for information, carefully evaluates the consequences of all alternatives, and diligently plans for implementation and contingencies.

Unconflicted adherence entails continuing with current activities if doing so does not entail serious risks.

Unconflicted change involves making decisions in present activities if doing so presents no serious risks.

Defensive avoidance entails making no changes in present activities and avoiding further contact with associated issues because there appears to be no hope of finding a better solution.

Hypervigilance is the frantic, superficial pursuit of some satisficing strategy.

Vigilant information processing involves thoroughly investigating all possible alternatives, weighing their costs and benefits before making a decision, and developing contingency plans.

RELATED BEHAVIORAL ASPECTS
OF DECISION MAKING

The behavioral, practical, and personal approaches each have behavioral components, but the manager should also be aware of other behavioral aspects of decision making as well. These include political forces, intuition, escalation of commitment, risk propensity, and ethics.

Political Forces in Decision Making

Political forces can play a major role in how decisions are made. We cover political behavior in Chapter 14, but one major element of politics, coalitions, is especially relevant to decision making. A **coalition** is an informal alliance of individuals or groups formed to achieve a common goal. This common goal is often a preferred decision alternative. For example, coalitions of stockholders frequently band together to force a board of directors to make a certain decision. Indeed, many of the recent power struggles between management and dissident shareholders at Disney Corporation have relied on coalitions as each side tried to gain the upper hand against the other.[19]

The impact of coalitions can be either positive or negative. They can help astute managers get the organization on a path toward effectiveness and profitability, or they can strangle well-conceived strategies and decisions. Managers must recognize when to use coalitions, how to assess whether coalitions are acting in the best interests of the organization, and how to constrain their dysfunctional effects.[20]

Intuition

Intuition is an innate belief about something without conscious consideration. Managers sometimes decide to do something because it "feels right" or they have a hunch. This feeling is usually not arbitrary, however. Rather, it is based on years of experience and practice in making decisions in similar situations. An inner sense may help managers make an occasional decision without going through a full-blown rational sequence of steps. The recent best-selling book by Malcolm Gladwell entitled *Blink: The Power of Thinking Without Thinking* made strong arguments that intuition is both used more commonly and results in better decisions than had previously been believed. On the other hand, some experts challenge this view and suggest that underlying understanding and experience make intuition mask the true processes used to make quick decisions.[21]

A few years ago the New York Yankees called three major sneaker manufacturers, Nike, Reebok, and Adidas, and informed them that they were looking to make a sponsorship deal. While Nike and Reebok were carefully and rationally assessing the possibilities, managers at Adidas quickly realized that a partnership with the Yankees made a lot of sense for them. They responded very quickly to the idea, and ended up hammering out a contract while the competitors were still analyzing details.[22] Of course, all managers, but most especially inexperienced ones, should be careful not to rely on intuition too heavily. If rationality and logic are continually flaunted for what "feels right," the odds are that disaster will strike one day.

A **coalition** is an informal alliance of individuals or groups formed to achieve a common goal.

Intuition is innate belief about something without conscious consideration.

Escalation of Commitment

Another important behavioral process that influences decision making is **escalation of commitment** to a chosen course of action. In particular, decision makers sometimes make decisions and then become so committed to the course of action suggested by that decision that they stay with it, even when it appears to have been wrong.[23] For example, when people buy stock in a company, they sometimes refuse to sell it even after repeated drops in price. They chose a course of action—buying the stock in anticipation of making a profit—and then stay with it even in the face of increasing losses.

For years Pan American World Airways ruled the skies and used its profits to diversify into real estate and other businesses. But with the advent of deregulation, Pan Am began to struggle and lose market share to other carriers. When Pan Am managers finally realized how ineffective the airline operations had become, the "rational" decision would have been, as experts today point out, to sell off the remaining airline operations and concentrate on the firm's more profitable businesses. But because they still saw the company as being first and foremost an airline, they instead began to slowly sell off the firm's profitable holdings to keep the airline flying. Eventually, the company was left with nothing but an ineffective and inefficient airline, and then had to sell off its more profitable routes before eventually being taken over by Delta. Had Pan Am managers made the more rational decision years earlier, chances are the firm could still be a profitable enterprise today, albeit one with no involvement in the airline industry.[24]

Thus, decision makers must walk a fine line. On the one hand, they must guard against sticking with an incorrect decision too long. To do so can bring about financial decline. On the other hand, managers should not bail out of a seemingly incorrect decision too soon, as did Adidas several years ago. Adidas once dominated the market for professional athletic shoes. It subsequently entered the market for amateur sports shoes and did well there also. But managers incorrectly interpreted a sales slowdown as a sign that the boom in athletic shoes was over. They thought that they had made the wrong decision and ordered drastic cutbacks. The market took off again with Nike at the head of the pack, and Adidas could not recover. Fortunately, a new management team has changed the way Adidas makes decisions and, as illustrated earlier, the firm is again on its way to becoming a force in the athletic shoe and apparel markets.

Risk Propensity and Decision Making

The behavioral element of **risk propensity** is the extent to which a decision maker is willing to gamble when making a decision. (Recall that we introduced risk propensity back in Chapter 3.) Some managers are cautious about every decision they make. They try to adhere to the rational model and are extremely conservative in what they do. Such managers are more likely to avoid mistakes, and they infrequently make decisions that lead to big losses. Other managers are extremely aggressive in making decisions and are willing to take risks.[25] They rely heavily on intuition, reach decisions quickly, and often risk big investments on their decisions. As in gambling, these managers are more likely than their conservative counterparts to achieve big successes with their decisions; they are also more likely to incur greater losses.[26] The organization's culture is a prime ingredient in fostering different levels of risk propensity.

Escalation of commitment occurs when a decision maker stays with a decision even when it appears to be wrong.

Risk propensity is the extent to which a decision maker is willing to gamble in making a decision.

ETHICS

Death by Email

When the Starwood Hotels board of directors fired CEO Steven J. Heyer, they hit hard. "Issues with regard to his management style have led us to lose confidence in his leadership," said Stephen Quazzo, the director who prepared the statement.

Heyer was a strong advocate for change, and was called "supportive" and "inspirational" by some employees. Starwood's net income doubled during his short tenure. His innovative marketing strategy is still driving the firm's decisions. He could also be critical when dissatisfied and that alienated many longtime Starwood managers. *Forbes* writer Evelyn M. Rusli says, "While Heyer's aggressive approach and his larger-than-life personality may have beefed up the company's bottom line, it was also rumored to turn board members against him."

However, *Wall Street Journal* reporters became suspicious when Heyer forfeited $35 million severance pay. Why walk away from that much money? An investigation uncovered the truth. An anonymous letter sent to Starwood's board in February 2007 claimed that Heyer created a hostile work environment for women. A search

> *"Most of these executives have blind spots, and they do not appreciate that what they're doing is inappropriate."*
> —MICHAEL USEEM, MANAGEMENT PROFESSOR, WHARTON

turned up a large number of sexually suggestive emails to and from Heyer, who is married, and younger, unmarried female employees. The terms of his employment contract allowed the directors to fire him without compensation for "gross negligence or willful misconduct."

Heyer isn't the only one, of course. Other business and political leaders have been ostracized or ousted following the discovery of provocative emails. How is it that intelligent, experienced folks make such poor decisions? "When smart people turn out to be dumb, they have a lapse of judgment," says Michael Useem, a Wharton management professor. "In this area [of sexual misconduct], they still seem to be tone-deaf. Most of these executives have blind spots, and they do not appreciate that what they're doing is inappropriate."

References: Mike Beirne, "Starwood's Heyer Told: Here's Your Hat; What's Your Hurry?" *The Gourmet Retailer*, April 2, 2007, www.gourmetretailer.com on February 25, 2010; Roger Matus, "Was Starwood's CEO Caught by Email, Too?" *Death by Email*, May 30, 2007, www.deathbyemail.com on February 25, 2010; Marcus Baram, "Misconduct in the Corner Office," April 11, 2007, *ABC News*, www.abcnews.go.com on February 25, 2010; Evelyn M. Rusli, "Heyer Checks Out of Starwood," *Forbes*, April 3, 2007, www.forbes.com on February 25, 2010.

Ethics and Decision Making

Ethics are a person's beliefs about what constitutes right and wrong behavior. Ethical behavior is that which conforms to generally accepted social norms; unethical behavior does not conform to generally accepted social norms. Some decisions made by managers may have little or nothing to do with their own personal ethics, but many other decisions are influenced by the manager's ethics. For example, decisions involving such disparate issues as hiring and firing employees, dealing with customers and suppliers, setting wages and assigning tasks, and maintaining one's expense account are all subject to ethical influences. And, of course, managers can make fatal personal decisions simply because they choose to ignore the difference between right and wrong. Such is the case recounted in the *Ethics* box entitled "Death by Email."

Ethics are a person's beliefs about what constitutes right and wrong behavior.

In general, ethical dilemmas for managers may center on direct personal gain, indirect personal gain, or simple personal preferences. Consider, for example, a top executive contemplating a decision about a potential takeover. His or her stock option package may result in enormous personal gain if the decision goes one way, even though stockholders may benefit more if the decision goes the other way. An indirect personal gain may result when a decision does not directly add value to a manager's personal worth but does enhance her or his career. Or the manager may face a choice about relocating a company facility in which one of the options is closest to his or her residence.

The *Ethics* box on page 222 entitled "The Heartbreak of Polluted Processes" concerns an accountant who smelled cooked books when he sniffed around for the recipe for success at a very large, well-known company.

Managers should carefully and deliberately consider the ethical context of every one of their decisions. The goal, of course, is for the manager to make the decision that is in the best interest of the firm, as opposed to the best interest of the manager. Doing this requires personal honesty and integrity. Managers also find it helpful to discuss potential ethical dilemmas with colleagues. Others can often provide an objective view of a situation that may help a manager avoid unintentionally making an unethical decision.

MICHAEL NEWMAN / PHOTOEDIT

Creativity—the ability to generate new ideas or new perspectives on existing ideas—plays a big role in decision making and problem solving. Charles Grant is a gifted California artist who developed a unique style based on traditional African motifs. He made a decision to start his own shop, a combination gift shop and gallery in Pasadena. His shop carries both inexpensive souvenirs like coffee mugs, post cards, and scarves while also carrying more upscale items such as limited edition prints and original oil paintings. With the African motif as the unifying thread, his business appeals to both tourists looking for trinkets to take home and serious collectors who buy the paintings and prints.

CREATIVITY, PROBLEM SOLVING, AND DECISION MAKING

Creativity is an important individual difference variable that exists in everyone. However, rather than discuss it with other individual-level concepts in Chapter 3, we describe it here because it plays such a central role in both decision making and problem solving. **Creativity** is the ability of an individual to generate new ideas or to conceive of new perspectives on existing ideas. Hence, creativity can play a role in how a problem or decision situation is defined, what alternatives are identified, and how each is evaluated. Creativity can also enable a manager to identify a new way of looking at things.

What makes a person creative? How does the creative process work? Although psychologists have not yet discovered complete answers to these questions, examining a few general patterns can help us understand the sources of individual creativity within organizations and the processes through which creativity emerges.[27]

The Creative Individual

Numerous researchers have focused their efforts on attempting to describe the common attributes of creative individuals. These attributes generally fall into three categories: background experiences, personal traits, and cognitive abilities.

Background Experiences and Creativity   Researchers have observed that many creative individuals were raised in an environment in which creativity was nurtured. Mozart was raised in a family of musicians and began composing and

Creativity is a person's ability to generate new ideas or to conceive of new perspectives on existing ideas.

at this warehouse, you have signed a confidentiality agreement that you will not divulge its location."

Employees—which Netflix, like a lot of contemporary organizations, calls "associates"—enter the building "through a less than obvious door," with the first shift beginning at 3 A.M. There are about 40 workers and, as far as Borrelli can tell, no more than seven computers in the 28,500-square-foot building. Most of these employees have been hired as "DVD inspectors." The job description specifies "Ability to work independently in a fast-paced environment" and "Ability to handle repetitive actions for extended periods of time, while maintaining a high degree of speed and accuracy." Applicants are advised that they'll have only "limited outside contact during work hours."

As the job title suggests, DVD inspectors inspect DVD discs. Discs that customers have returned by mail are delivered to the warehouse in cartons, which are then distributed at the feet of inspectors seated at workstations aligned in wide rows. To begin the process, explains a veteran inspector (who wishes to remain anonymous), "we log in to the computer to time us. . . . [Then] we check the DVDs real fast and must do it accurately. After that we log out to finish timing us." During the "checking" process, each inspector rips open every returned envelope, removes the disc from its sleeve, and makes sure that the title on the disc matches the title on the sleeve. Each disc is then inspected for cracks and scratches and each sleeve for coffee stains or other signs of wear and tear. Next, the disc is cleaned and reinserted in its sleeve and, depending on whether or not it's damaged, placed in one of two cartons. All of this must be done very quickly—"Every second counts," says the anonymous inspector, "since we're being timed." Veteran inspectors are expected to process a minimum of 650 discs an hour, and our anonymous inspector reports that, "when I'm in a good mood," he can process up to 950, assuring skeptics that "it's really possible to do." At rates like these, the Chicago warehouse ships 60,000 discs daily.

At the same time, of course, accuracy is critical—particularly when it comes to putting the right disc in the right sleeve—and Borrelli reports that during his tour of the Chicago warehouse, he was asked "not to disturb [the inspectors'] groove and hit them up with questions." ("There's no worse experience," explains Steve Swasey, Netflix VP of corporate communications, "than sitting down on the sofa to watch *Goodfellas*, putting your feet up, and seeing that you have a copy of *Peter Pan*.") Currently, a facility like the Chicago warehouse processes discs with 99.5 percent accuracy, but according to CEO Hastings, this rate "is horribly inefficient

compared to how we want it to be and where it will be in three years." He says that he has a plan in place (it's still "top secret") to "move from 99.5 percent correct to 99.9 percent correct. That may sound easy," he adds, "but it isn't."

Meanwhile, our anonymous inspector reports that "after working at Netflix for a while, it starts to get boring, and it really brings your emotions down since there aren't that many interactions with your fellow coworkers. . . . [W]e can talk very, very little . . . because we need to concentrate on inspecting the DVDs at a fast pace." Entry-level jobs like DVD inspector are filled by employment agencies and start out as temp positions. Borrelli notes that the Chicago warehouse workforce includes "a disproportionate number of local grandparents," but he's also quick to point out that employees get 40-hour workweeks and full medical benefits. They can also earn as much as $31,000 a year and $34,000 if they move up to the job of quality inspector. Once a new employee successfully passes a three-month probation period, he or she also receives a free Netflix subscription and a free DVD player.

Of approximately 2,500 employees, about 2,000, including site managers, work at distribution hubs like the one visited by Borrelli in Chicago. Another 500 salaried employees, almost all of them working out of company headquarters in Los Gatos, California, develop and coordinate operations. At this level, Hastings calls his approach to managing people a matter of "freedom and responsibility." How does it work? Hastings, says *Business Week*'s Michelle Conlin, "pays his people lavishly, gives them unlimited vacations, and lets them structure their own compensation packages. In return, he expects ultra-high performance." "We're unafraid to pay high," says Hastings—and Netflix is known to dispense salaries well above the industry average. Each business unit maintains what Conlin likens to "an internal boutique headhunting firm," and salaries are tied to job-market value. Even employees who don't make it benefit from Hastings's desire to keep good managers and keep them happy. "At most companies," says the CEO, "average performers get an average raise. At Netflix, they get a generous severance package." Why? Hastings, it seems, wants to spare his managers the guilt of firing people.

Employees decide for themselves what portion of their compensation they want in cash and what portion in stock, and in one recent year, 47 percent of employee compensation was tied at least in part to the company's profitability. (It's a fairly risky choice, of course: As we saw in Part 1, Netflix stock has had a pretty bumpy ride in the last decade.) The "freedom" aspect of Hastings's HR approach is also reflected in the company's vacation policy and tracking: "There is no policy or tracking," says the company's *Reference Guide to Our Freedom & Responsibility Culture*, because Netflix employees can take all the vacation time they want—or, more precisely, all the time they're afforded by the progress of their workloads.

"We don't think of it as a perk," says one Netflix engineer. "It's just emblematic of the way we work here," and HR head Patty McCord (her actual title is Chief Talent Officer) hastens to add that unlimited vacation time is possible at Netflix because "we place a high value on adult behavior—people here have important jobs and 'own' a lot." In other words, Netflix depends upon its culture to guide employees in taking responsible actions, and as we suggested earlier, it also depends on its culture to ensure that the company as a whole remains focused on its highest priority—its strategies for offering the highest possible level of customer satisfaction. We'll examine the Netflix culture in more detail in Part 3, where we'll have more to say about its strategies for customer satisfaction, and in Part 4, where we'll focus on its role in keeping the company ready to respond to changes in its organizational environment.

Case Questions

1. What *individual differences, personality traits,* and *attitudes* might contribute to a reasonable *person-job fit* for the position of DVD inspector at a Netflix warehouse? What steps might Netflix take to improve the attitudes of a worker like the anonymous inspector cited in the case? What might the company do in terms of *work design*? In terms of *employee involvement*? In terms of *flexible work arrangements*? Given the wage rates in your local area, what kind of hourly wage would you want in order to work as a Netflix DVD inspector?

2. What perspectives on motivation are reflected in the fact that the work of DVD inspectors at Netflix warehouses is carefully timed? Which type of motivational process seems to be most important at these facilities—*need based, process based,* or *learning based*? In your opinion, which of these processes would be the most effective in improving performance? Would *OB mod* be very helpful? Why or why not?

3. The marketing term *churn* refers to the rate at which customers abandon a product or service. Netflix has a very good *churn rate* of around 4 percent annually—that is, the company loses about 4 in every 100 subscribers each year. How important are the company's hourly workers, such as the employees at its warehouses, in maintaining a good churn rate? What sort of things might salaried employees, such as a Senior Software Engineer, do to contribute to a good churn rate? (*Hint:* Check out Netflix job descriptions at http://jobs.netflix.com.)

4. A spokesperson for Yahoo! doesn't think that Netflix's unlimited-vacation time policy would work at her company: "We're a grown-up company with over 12,000 employees," she says, "and you have to have some semblance of process and procedure." As Netflix grows, will CEO Hastings and other top managers have to make adjustments in this feature of the company's incentive plan? If so, what principles should guide them in making these adjustments? What sort of problems are they likely to encounter?

References

Laurie J. Flynn, "One Man's Two Challenges," *New York Times*, June 3, 2003, www.nytimes.com on June 16, 2010; Peter Zaballos, "A Blockbuster Closing," *Open Ambition*, July 9, 2009, http://openambition.com on June 21, 2010; Mike Sachoff, "Netflix Scores High in Customer Satisfaction," *WebProNews*, February 16, 2010, www.webpronews.com on June 25, 2010; "The Lowdown on Blockbuster Total Access Plan Changes," *Knowzy*, February 24, 2009, www.knowzy.com on June 24, 2010; Lindsay Hunt, "Netflix: MarketBuster," *RGM*, February 2, 2005, http://ritamcgrath.com on June 21, 2010; Tracy V. Wilson, "How Netflix Works" (2007), *HowStuffWorks*, 1998–2010, http://electronics.howstuffworks.com on June 30, 2010; Christopher Borrelli, "How Netflix Gets Your Movies to Your Mailbox So Fast," *Chicago Tribune*, August 4, 2009, www.chicagotribune.com on June 16, 2010; Jefferson Graham, "Netflix Looks to Future but Still Going Strong with DVD Rentals," *USA Today*, July 1, 2009, www.usatoday.com on July 1, 2010; Etan Horowitz, "Netflix Distribution Centers: A Portrait of Speed and Efficiency," *The Seattle Times*, August 20, 2009, http://seattletimes.nwsource.com on June 30, 2010; "Working for Netflix at a Shipping Center," *Hacking Netflix*, February 15, 2007, www.hackingnetflix.com on July 1, 2010; Michelle Conlin, "Netflix: Flex to the Max," *BusinessWeek*, September 24, 2007, www.businessweek.com on July 2, 2010; Ryan Blitstein, "Work Zone: A Bottomless Well of Vacation Time," *Pittsburgh Post-Gazette*, April 2, 2007, www.post-gazette.com on July 2, 2010; Kira Busch, "Trust Begins at Home—Netflix's Approach to Building Customer Relationships," *Leading Practices in Business Ethics* (Business Roundtable, Institute for Corporate Ethics, 2009), www.darden.virginia.edu on July 2, 2010; "Netflix—Interview with a Hiring Professional," *San Francisco Chronicle*, August 21, 2005, www.engr.sjsu.edu[MCK1] on July 2, 2010; "Netflix's Autonomous Workforce," *Fast Company.com*, March 27, 2007, www.fastcompany.com on July 2, 2010.

9

CHAPTER

CHAPTER LEARNING OBJECTIVES

After studying this chapter you should be able to:

- Discuss the interpersonal nature of organizations.
- Define a group and illustrate their importance in organizations.
- Identify and discuss the types of groups commonly found in organizations.
- Describe the general stages of group development.
- Discuss the major group performance factors.
- Discuss intergroup dynamics.
- Describe group decision making in organizations.

FOUNDATIONS OF INTERPERSONAL AND GROUP BEHAVIOR

Managing by Clowning Around

"It's difficult to be creative in isolation."

—LYN HEWARD, FORMER PRESIDENT OF CIRQUE DU SOLEIL'S CREATIVE CONTENT DIVISION

Fourteen-year-old Guy Laliberté dropped out of high school in Québec, Canada, because he wanted to see the world. "I decided to go into street performing because it was a traveling job," he recalls, and although his skills were limited

Guy Laliberte has made widespread use of groups and teams to catapult Cirque de Soleil into a global entertainment powerhouse.

to playing the accordion and telling stories, they were enough to get him to London by the time he was 18. From there he not only extended his travels to Europe but broadened his repertoire to include fire breathing, juggling, magic, and stilt walking. "It was just an adventure," he admits, "and I was planning to go back to school and have a regular life," but his nearly decade-long adventure had only deepened his passion for street performing. When he returned to Canada, he joined a stilt-walking troupe, and in 1984, when he was 23 years old, Laliberté partnered with another high school dropout to form their own street-performance company. Today, he's still head of that company and, as CEO of Cirque du Soleil, one of the richest people in Canada.

Cirque du Soleil, which is French for *circus of the sun* ("The sun," explains Laliberté, "stands for energy and youth, which is what I thought the circus should be about"), has completely transformed the traditional three-ring spectacle replete with trapeze artists, clowns, and lion tamers. Laliberté calls Cirque a "transdisciplinary experience"—an amalgam of breathtaking stunt work, dazzling stagecraft, surreal costumes, and pulsing music. There are currently 20 different Cirque shows, each developed around a distinctive theme and story arc, such as "the urban experience in all its myriad forms" (*Saltimbanco*) and "a tribute to the nomadic soul" (*Varekai*). Headquartered in Montreal, Canada, the company now employs 4,000 people, including more than 1,000 artists, and its shows have been seen by nearly 90 million spectators. Revenues for 2009 were reportedly $810 million.

The key to this success, according to Laliberté, is creativity: "I believe that the profits will come from the quality of your creative products," he says. "Since the beginning, I've always wanted to develop a self-feeding circle of creative productions: the positive financial returns from one show would be used to develop and create a new show, and so on." He's also convinced that his job is providing a working environment that fosters collective creativity: "I believe in nurturing creativity and offering a haven for creators, enabling them to develop their ideas to the fullest. With more and more talented creators being drawn to Cirque in an environment that fulfills them, these [conditions] are ideal to continue developing great new shows."

Lyn Heward, former president of Cirque's Creative Content Division, calls the company's process of training and integrating talented people "creative transformation": "Everyone," she says, "when they come to Cirque as an employee, even an accountant, comes there because it's a creative and admired company, and they want to be able to contribute something creatively." From her experience at Cirque, Heward drew up a nine-point guide to "creative transformation," and at the heart of her list is a commitment to the value of teamwork. In fact, item #5 on her list says, "Practice teamwork. True creativity requires stimulation and collaboration. It's difficult to be creative in isolation." Item #6 picks up the same theme: "Keep creativity fresh with hard-working bosses who constantly encourage and receive employees' ideas and feedback and accept that there are often different ways of getting the same end result."

"No matter what your product," Heward argues, "whether it's computers, cars, or anything else, your results [depend on] having a passionate strong team of people." In any workplace, she explains, "our most natural resource is the people we work with—the people we build our product with. Unless there's a strong commitment to teambuilding, passionate leadership, and creativity, even at Cirque it would not happen." Heward is willing to admit that "incredible freedom is a problem for most people because it requires us to think differently," but she's also confident that getting people committed to teamwork is the best way to get them to develop their creativity. Take Igor Jijikine, a Russian-born acrobat-actor who helped to train performers for *Mystère*, Cirque's permanent show at Las Vegas's Treasure Island Hotel and Casino. "[T]he really challenging thing," he says,

> is to change the mentality of the performers I work with. Many of our performers are former competitive gymnasts. Gymnastics is essentially an individual sport. Gymnasts never have to think creatively or be a part of a true team. They got here by being strong individuals. So, right from the start, we really challenge ourselves to erase the lines between athletics and artistry, between individuals and the group. We need to transform an individual into a team player everyone else can count on, literally with their lives.

Finally, Heward acknowledges that you can't imbue employees with the Cirque du Soleil culture and "then tell them to go work in their cubicles." The space in which they work, she says, "has to reflect [Cirque's] values and vision." All Cirque du Soleil productions are created and developed by teams working at the Montreal facility which the company calls "the Studio" and describes as "a full-fledged creation, innovation, and training laboratory." In addition to administrative space— "eight floors of uniquely designed office spaces and relaxation areas conducive to inspiration"—the complex boasts acrobatic, dance, and theatrical studios, and the effect of the whole, says Heward, is that of "a fantastical playground": Creativity, she explains,

> is fostered in work groups where people first get to know each other and then learn to trust one another. And in this playground, we recognize that a good idea can emerge from anywhere in the organization or from within a team. We make our shows from this collective creativity.

Daniel Lamarre, Cirque president and COO, has a succinct way of explaining the company's success: "We let the creative people run it." As for the CEO, Laliberté, too, is content to trust his creative people—an instinct, he says, that he learned in his days as a street performer: "In the street, you have to develop that instinct of trusting people and reading people because that instinct is your life saver." He lists himself as "Artistic Guide" in production notes and tries "not to be too involved in the beginning and during the process," the better to keep his perspective "fresh" and to "be able to give constructive recommendation on the final production." He also wants to do the same thing that he wanted to do when he was 14: "I still want to travel, I still want to entertain, and I most certainly still want to have fun."

To appreciate how technology can also be a life saver in the world of Cirque du Soleil, see the *Technology* box on "Teaming Technology and Artistry" on page 248.

What Do You Think?

1. One key to success at Cirque seems to be the blend of creativity and delegation. How easy or difficult do you think it is to keep maintain both of these conditions?

2. If Cirque moved away from the use of teams, what would you expect to happen?

References: "Stick to Your Dream—Guy Laliberté," *Young Entrepreneur*, July 8, 2008, www.youngentrepreneur.com on February 28, 2010; "Business Lessons from Poker—Guy Laliberté," *Young Entrepreneur*, July 8, 2008, www .youngentrepreneur.com on February 28, 2010; "Laliberté, Guy," *Contemporary Musicians*, eNotes.com, 2006, www.enotes.com on February 28, 2010; Lyn Heward and John U. Bacon, *Spark: Igniting the Creative Fire That Lives within Us All* (Toronto: Doubleday Canada, 2006), http://books.google.com on February 28, 2010; Arupa Tesolin, "Igniting the Creative Spark at Cirque du Soleil," *Self-Growth.com*, September 12, 2007, www.selfgrowth .com on February 28, 2010; Cirque du Soleil, "About Cirque du Soleil," "The International Headquarters," www .cirquedusoleil.com on March 1, 2010; Geoff Keighly, "The Phantasmagoria Factory," *CNNMoney.com*, January 1, 2004, http://money.cnn.com on March 1, 2010; Glenn Collins, "Run Away to the Circus? No Need. It's Staying Here," *New York Times*, April 29, 2009, www.nytimes.com on March 1, 2010.

In Chapter 1 we noted the pervasiveness of human behavior in organizations and the importance of interactions among people as critical to achieving important outcomes for organizations. Indeed, a great deal of all managerial work involves interacting with other people, both directly and indirectly and both inside and outside the organization. This chapter is the first of seven that deal primarily with interpersonal processes in organizations. We begin by reinforcing the interpersonal nature of organizations. We then introduce and describe numerous elements of one important aspect of interpersonal relations, group dynamics. In subsequent chapters we discuss such other forms of interpersonal activity in organizations as work teams (Chapter 10), interpersonal communication (Chapter 11), leadership (Chapters 12 and 13), power, politics, and workplace justice (Chapter 14), and conflict and negotiation in organizations (Chapter 15).

THE INTERPERSONAL NATURE OF ORGANIZATIONS

The schedule that follows is a typical day for the president of a Houston-based company, part of a larger firm headquartered in California. He kept a log of his activities for several different days so you could better appreciate the nature of managerial work.

- 7:45–8:15 A.M. Arrive at work; review hard-copy mail sorted by assistant; review and respond to email; discuss day's schedule with assistant.
- 8:15–8:30 A.M. Scan *The Wall Street Journal* and online financial news sources.
- 8:30–9:00 A.M. Meet with labor officials and plant manager to resolve minor labor disputes.
- 9:00–9:30 A.M. Review internal report; read and respond to new email.
- 9:30–10:00 A.M. Meet with two marketing executives to review advertising campaign; instruct them to fax approvals to advertising agency.
- 10:00–11:30 A.M. Meet with company executive committee to discuss strategy, budgetary issues, and competition (this committee meets weekly).
- 11:30 A.M.–12:00 P.M. Send several emails; read and respond to new email.
- 12:00–1:15 P.M. Lunch with the financial vice president and two executives from another subsidiary of the parent corporation. Primary topic of discussion is the Houston Rockets basketball team. Place three business calls from Blackberry en route to lunch, and receive one business call en route back to office. Received and read four emails on Blackberry during lunch.

RYAN MCVAY/PHOTODISC/JUPITER IMAGES

Group norms are standards of behavior that define appropriate behavior for members of the group. The two group members in the background are hard at work on a major project, while the group member in the foreground is relaxing. One possible explanation for these behaviors is that the group's norms allow a member to take a few minutes to relax when she or he has been putting in extra hours on a project. Another possibility is that he is violating group norms and will subsequently be sanctioned by other group members.

the group. Group norms are enforced, however, only for actions that are important to group members. For example, if the office norm is for employees to wear suits to convey a professional image to clients, a staff member who wears blue jeans and a sweatshirt violates the group norm and will hear about it quickly. But if the norm is that dress is unimportant because little contact with clients occurs in the office, the fact that someone wears blue jeans may not even be noticed.

Norms serve four purposes in organizations. First, they help the group survive. Groups tend to reject deviant behavior that does not help meet group goals or contribute to the survival of the group if it is threatened. Accordingly, a successful group that is not under threat may be more tolerant of deviant behavior. Second, they simplify and make more predictable the behaviors expected of group members. Because they are familiar with norms, members do not have to analyze each behavior and decide on a response. Members can anticipate the actions of others on the basis of group norms, usually resulting in increased productivity and goal attainment. Third, norms help the group avoid embarrassing situations. Group members often want to avoid damaging other members' self-images and are likely to avoid certain subjects that might hurt a member's feelings. And finally, norms express the central values of the group and identify the group to others. Certain clothes, mannerisms, or behaviors in particular situations may be a rallying point for members and may signify to others the nature of the group.[24]

Group Cohesiveness

Group cohesiveness is the extent to which a group is committed to remaining together; it results from forces acting on the members to remain in the group. The forces that create cohesiveness are attraction to the group, resistance to leaving the group, and the motivation to remain a member of the group.[25] As shown in Figure 9.3, group cohesiveness is related to many aspects of group dynamics that we have already discussed—maturity, homogeneity, manageable size, and frequency of interactions.

The figure also shows that group cohesiveness can be increased by competition or by the presence of an external threat. Either factor can focus members' attention on a clearly defined goal and increase their willingness to work together. Finally, successfully reaching goals often increases the cohesiveness of a group because people are proud to be identified with a winner and to be thought of as competent and successful. This may be one reason behind the popular expression "Success breeds success." A group that is successful may become more cohesive and hence possibly even more successful. Of course, other factors can get in the way of continued success, such as personal differences, egos, and the lure of more individual success in other activities.

Group cohesiveness is the extent to which a group is committed to staying together.

Research on group performance factors has focused on the relationship between cohesiveness and group productivity.[26] Highly cohesive groups appear to be more effective at achieving their goals than groups that are low in cohesiveness, especially in research and development groups in U.S. companies.[27] However, highly cohesive groups will not necessarily be more productive in an organizational sense than groups with low cohesiveness. As Figure 9.4 illustrates, when a group's goals are compatible with the organizational goals, a cohesive group probably will be more productive than one that is not cohesive. In other words, if a highly cohesive group has the goal of contributing to the good of the organization, it is very likely to be productive in organizational terms. But if such a group decides on a goal that has little to do with the business of the organization, it will probably achieve its own goal even at the expense of any organizational goal. In a study of group characteristics and productivity, group cohesiveness was the only factor that was consistently related to high performance for research and development engineers and technicians.

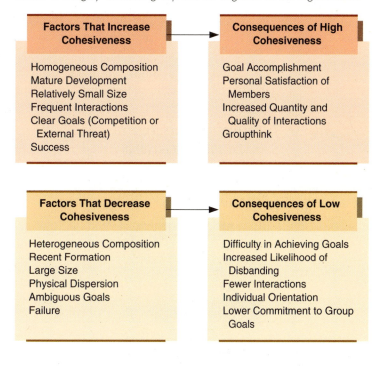

Figure 9.3   FACTORS THAT AFFECT GROUP COHESIVENESS AND CONSEQUENCES OF GROUP COHESIVENESS

The factors that increase and decrease cohesiveness and the consequences of high and low cohesiveness indicate that although it is often preferable to have a highly cohesive group, in some situations the effects of a highly cohesive group can be negative for the organization.

Factors That Increase Cohesiveness

Homogeneous Composition
Mature Development
Relatively Small Size
Frequent Interactions
Clear Goals (Competition or External Threat)
Success

Consequences of High Cohesiveness

Goal Accomplishment
Personal Satisfaction of Members
Increased Quantity and Quality of Interactions
Groupthink

Factors That Decrease Cohesiveness

Heterogeneous Composition
Recent Formation
Large Size
Physical Dispersion
Ambiguous Goals
Failure

Consequences of Low Cohesiveness

Difficulty in Achieving Goals
Increased Likelihood of Disbanding
Fewer Interactions
Individual Orientation
Lower Commitment to Group Goals

Figure 9.4   GROUP COHESIVENESS, GOALS, AND PRODUCTIVITY

This figure shows that the best combination is for the group to be cohesive and for the group's goals to be congruent with the organization's goals. The lowest potential group performance also occurs with highly cohesive groups when the group's goals are not consistent with the organization's goals.

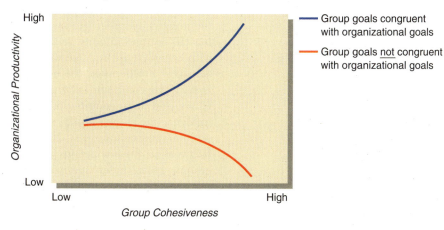

Group goals congruent with organizational goals

Group goals not congruent with organizational goals

Groupthink is a mode of thinking that occurs when members of a group are deeply involved in a cohesive in-group, and the desire for unanimity offsets their motivation to appraise alternative courses of action.

Cohesiveness may also be a primary factor in the development of certain problems for some decision-making groups. An example is **groupthink**, which occurs when a group's overriding concern is a unanimous decision rather than critical analysis of alternatives.[28] (We discuss groupthink later in this chapter.) These problems, together with the evidence regarding group cohesiveness and productivity, mean that a manager must carefully weigh the pros and cons of fostering highly cohesive groups.

INTERGROUP DYNAMICS

A group's contribution to an organization depends on its interactions with other groups as well as on its own productivity. Many organizations are expanding their use of cross-functional teams to address more complex and increasingly more important organizational issues. The result has been heightened emphasis on the teams' interactions with other groups. Groups that actively interact with other groups by asking questions, initiating joint programs, and sharing their team's achievements are usually the most productive.

Interactions are the key to understanding intergroup dynamics. The orientation of the groups toward their goals takes place under a highly complex set of conditions that determine the relationships among the groups. The most important of these factors are presented in the model of intergroup dynamics in Figure 9.5. The model emphasizes three primary factors that influence intergroup interactions: group characteristics, organizational setting, and task and situational bases of interaction.

First, we must understand the key characteristics of the interacting groups. Each group brings to the interaction its own unique features. As individuals become a part of a group, they tend to identify so strongly with the group that their views of other groups become biased, so harmonious relationships with other groups may be difficult to achieve.[29] Furthermore, the individuals in the group contribute to the group processes, and these contributions in turn influence the group's norms, size, composition, and cohesiveness; all of these factors affect the interactions with other groups. Thus, understanding the individuals in the group and the key characteristics of the group can help managers monitor intergroup interactions.

Figure 9.5 **FACTORS THAT INFLUENCE INTERGROUP INTERACTIONS**

The nature of the interactions between groups depends on the characteristics of the groups involved, the organizational setting, and the task and situational setting for the interaction.

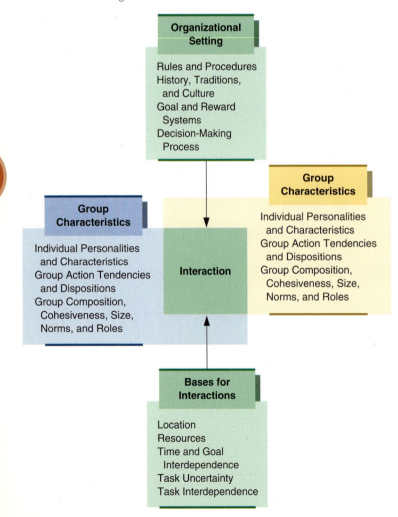

Organizational Setting

Rules and Procedures
History, Traditions, and Culture
Goal and Reward Systems
Decision-Making Process

Group Characteristics

Individual Personalities and Characteristics
Group Action Tendencies and Dispositions
Group Composition, Cohesiveness, Size, Norms, and Roles

Group Characteristics

Individual Personalities and Characteristics
Group Action Tendencies and Dispositions
Group Composition, Cohesiveness, Size, Norms, and Roles

Interaction

Bases for Interactions

Location
Resources
Time and Goal Interdependence
Task Uncertainty
Task Interdependence

Second, the organizational setting in which the groups interact can have a powerful influence on intergroup interactions. The organization's structure, rules and procedures, decision-making processes, and goals and reward systems all affect interactions. For example, organizations in which frequent interactions occur and strong ties among groups exist usually are characterized as low-conflict organizations.[30] Third, the task and situational bases of interactions focus attention on the working relationships among the interacting groups and on the reasons for the interactions. As Figure 9.5 shows, five factors affect intergroup interactions: location, resources, time and goal interdependence, task uncertainty, and task interdependence. These factors both create the interactions and determine their characteristics, such as the frequency of interaction, the volume of information exchange among groups, and the type of coordination the groups need to interact and function. For example, if two groups depend heavily on each other to perform a task about which much uncertainty exists, they need a great deal of information from each other to define and perform the task.

GROUP DECISION MAKING IN ORGANIZATIONS

People in organizations work in a variety of groups—formal and informal, permanent and temporary. Most of these groups make decisions that affect the welfare of the organization and the people in it. Here we discuss several issues surrounding how groups make decisions: group polarization, groupthink, and group problem solving.

Group Polarization

Members' attitudes and opinions with respect to an issue or a solution may change during group discussion. Some studies of this tendency have showed the change to be a fairly consistent movement toward a more risky solution, called "risky shift."[31] Other studies and analyses have revealed that the group-induced shift is not always toward more risk; the group is just as likely to move toward a more conservative view.[32] Generally, group polarization occurs when the average of the group members' post-discussion attitudes tends to be more extreme than average pre-discussion attitudes.[33]

Several features of group discussion contribute to polarization. When individuals discover during group discussion that others share their opinions, they may become more confident about their opinions, resulting in a more extreme view. Persuasive arguments also can encourage polarization. If members who strongly support a particular position are able to express themselves cogently in the discussion, less avid supporters of the position may become convinced that it is correct. In addition, members may believe that because the group is deciding, they are not individually responsible for the decision or its outcomes. This diffusion of responsibility may enable them to accept and support a decision more radical than those they would make as individuals.

Polarization can profoundly affect group decision making. If group members are known to lean toward a particular decision before a discussion, it may be expected that their post-decision position will be even more extreme. Understanding this phenomenon may be useful for one who seeks to affect their decision.

Groupthink

As discussed earlier, highly cohesive groups and teams often are very successful at meeting their goals, although they sometimes have serious difficulties as well. One problem that can occur is groupthink. According to Irving L. Janis, groupthink is "a

Group polarization is the tendency for a group's average post-discussion attitudes to be more extreme than its average pre-discussion attitudes.

mode of thinking that people engage in when they are deeply involved in a cohesive in-group, when the members' strivings for unanimity override their motivation to realistically appraise alternative courses of action."[34] When groupthink occurs, then, the group unknowingly makes unanimity rather than the best decision its goal. Individual members may perceive that raising objections is not appropriate. Groupthink can occur in many decision-making situations in organizations. The current trend toward increasing use of teams in organizations may increase instances of groupthink because of the susceptibility of self-managing teams to this type of thought.[35]

Symptoms of Groupthink The three primary conditions that foster the development of groupthink are cohesiveness, the leader's promotion of his or her preferred solution, and insulation of the group from experts' opinions. Based on analysis of the disaster associated with the explosion of the space shuttle *Challenger* in 1986, the original idea of groupthink symptoms was enhanced to include the effects of increased time pressure and the role of the leader in not stimulating critical thinking in developing the symptoms of groupthink.[36] Figure 9.6 outlines the revised groupthink process.

A group in which groupthink has taken hold exhibits eight well-defined symptoms:

1. An *illusion of invulnerability*, shared by most or all members, that creates excessive optimism and encourages extreme risk taking

2. *Collective efforts to rationalize or discount warnings* that might lead members to reconsider assumptions before recommitting themselves to past policy decisions

3. An *unquestioned belief in the group's inherent morality*, inclining members to ignore the ethical and moral consequences of their decisions

4. *Stereotyped views of "enemy" leaders* as too evil to warrant genuine attempts to negotiate or as too weak or stupid to counter whatever risky attempts are made to defeat their purposes

5. *Direct pressure on a member* who expresses strong arguments against any of the group's stereotypes, illusions, or commitments, making clear that such dissent is contrary to what is expected of loyal members

Figure 9.6 THE GROUPTHINK PROCESS

Groupthink can occur when a highly cohesive group with a directive leader is under time pressure; it can result in a defective decision process and low probability of successful outcomes.

Reference: Gregory Moorhead, Richard Ference, and Chris P. Neck, "Group Decision Fiascoes Continue: Space Shuttle *Challenger* and a Revised Groupthink Framework," *Human Relations,* 1991, vol. 44, pp. 539–550.

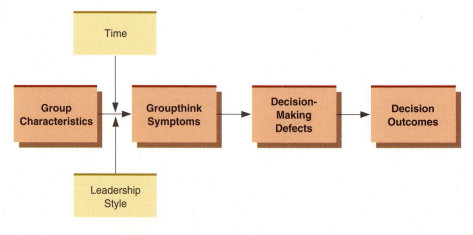

6. *Self-censorship of deviations* from the apparent group consensus, reflecting each member's inclination to minimize the importance of his or her doubts and counterarguments

7. A *shared illusion of unanimity*, resulting partly from self-censorship of deviations, augmented by the false assumption that silence means consent[37]

8. *The emergence of self-appointed "mindguards,"* members who protect the group from adverse information that might shatter their shared complacency about the effectiveness and morality of their decisions[38]

Janis contends that the members of the group involved in the Watergate cover-up during President Richard Nixon's administration and reelection campaign—Nixon himself, H. R. Haldeman, John Ehrlichman, and John Dean—may have been victims of groupthink. Evidence of most of the groupthink symptoms can be found in the unedited transcripts of the group's deliberations.[39]

Decision-Making Defects and Decision Quality   When groupthink dominates group deliberations, the likelihood increases that decision-making defects will occur. The group is less likely to survey a full range of alternatives and may focus on only a few (often one or two). In discussing a preferred alternative, the group may fail to examine it for nonobvious risks and drawbacks. The group may not reexamine previously rejected alternatives for nonobvious gains or some means of reducing apparent costs, even when they receive new information. The group may reject expert opinions that run counter to its own views and may choose to consider only information that supports its preferred solution. The decision to launch the space shuttle *Challenger* in January 1986 may have been a product of groupthink because due to the increased time pressure to make a decision and the leaders' style, negative information was ignored by the group that made the decision. (Unfortunately, this same pattern apparently occurred again prior to the ill-fated launch of the shuttle *Columbia* in 2003.) Finally, the group may not consider any potential setbacks or countermoves by competing groups and therefore may fail to develop contingency plans. It should be noted that Janis contends that these defects may arise from other common problems as well: fatigue, prejudice, inaccurate information, information overload, and ignorance.[40]

Defects in decision making do not always lead to bad outcomes or defeats. Even if its own decision-making processes are flawed, one side can win a battle because of the poor decisions made by the other side's leaders. Nevertheless, decisions produced by defective processes are less likely to succeed. Although the arguments for the existence of groupthink are convincing, the hypothesis has not been subjected to rigorous empirical examination. Research supports parts of the model but leaves some questions unanswered.[41]

Prevention of Groupthink   Several suggestions have been offered to help managers reduce the probability of groupthink in group decision making. Summarized in Table 9.2, these prescriptions fall into four categories, depending on whether they apply to the leader, the organization, the individual, or the process. All are designed to facilitate the critical evaluation of alternatives and discourage the single-minded pursuit of unanimity.

Participation

A major issue in group decision making is the degree to which employees should participate in the process. Early management theories, such as those of the scientific management school, advocated a clear separation between the duties of managers and workers: Management was to make the decisions, and employees were to implement

Table 9.2 PRESCRIPTIONS FOR PREVENTING GROUPTHINK

A. Leader prescriptions
1. Assign everyone the role of critical evaluator.
2. Be impartial; do not state preferences.
3. Assign the devil's advocate role to at least one group member.
4. Use outside experts to challenge the group.
5. Be open to dissenting points of view.

B. Organizational prescriptions
1. Set up several independent groups to study the same issue.
2. Train managers and group leaders in groupthink prevention techniques.

C. Individual prescriptions
1. Be a critical thinker.
2. Discuss group deliberations with a trusted outsider; report back to the group.

D. Process prescriptions
1. Periodically break the group into subgroups to discuss the issues.
2. Take time to study external factors.
3. Hold second-chance meetings to rethink issues before making a commitment.

them.[42] Other approaches have urged that employees be allowed to participate in decisions to increase their ego involvement, motivation, and satisfaction.[43] Numerous research studies have shown that whereas employees who seek responsibility and challenge on the job may find participation in the decision-making process to be both motivating and enriching, other employees may regard such participation as a waste of time and a management imposition.[44]

Whether employee participation in decision making is appropriate depends on the situation. In tasks that require an estimation, a prediction, or a judgment of accuracy—usually referred to as "judgmental tasks"—groups typically are superior to individuals simply because more people contribute to the decision-making process. However, one especially capable individual may make a better judgment than a group.

In problem-solving tasks, groups generally produce more and better solutions than do individuals. But groups take far longer than individuals to develop solutions and make decisions. An individual or very small group may be able to accomplish some things much faster than a large, unwieldy group or organization. In addition, individual decision making avoids the special problems of group decision making such as groupthink or group polarization. If the problem to be solved is fairly straightforward, it may be more appropriate to have a single capable individual concentrate on solving it. On the other hand, complex problems are more appropriate for groups. Such problems can often be divided into parts and the parts assigned to individuals or small groups who bring their results back to the group for discussion and decision making.

An additional advantage of group decision making is that it often creates greater interest in the task. Heightened interest may increase the time and effort given to the task, resulting in more ideas, a more thorough search for solutions, better evaluation of alternatives, and improved decision quality.

The Vroom decision tree approach to leadership (discussed in Chapter 12) is one popular way of determining the appropriate degree of subordinate participation.[45] The model includes decision styles that vary from "decide" (the leader alone makes the decision) to "delegate" (the group makes the decision, with each member having an equal say). The choice of style rests on seven considerations that concern the characteristics of the situation and the subordinates.

Participation in decision making is also related to organizational structure. For example, decentralization involves delegating some decision-making authority throughout the organizational hierarchy. The more decentralized the organization, the more its employees tend to participate in decision making. Whether one views participation in decision making as pertaining to leadership, organization structure, or motivation, it remains an important aspect of organizations that continues to occupy managers and organizational scholars.[46]

Group Problem Solving

A typical interacting group may have difficulty with any of several steps in the decision-making process. One common problem arises in the generation-of-alternatives phase: The search may be arbitrarily ended before all plausible alternatives have been identified. Several types of group interactions can have this effect. If members immediately express their reactions to the alternatives as they are first proposed, potential contributors may begin to censor their ideas to avoid embarrassing criticism from the group. Less confident group members, intimidated by members who have more experience, higher status, or more power, also may censor their ideas for fear of embarrassment or punishment. In addition, the group leader may limit idea generation by enforcing requirements concerning time, appropriateness, cost, feasibility, and the like. To improve the generation of alternatives, managers may employ any of three techniques to stimulate the group's problem-solving capabilities: brainstorming, the nominal group technique, or the Delphi technique.

Brainstorming   Brainstorming is most often used in the idea-generation phase of decision making and is intended to solve problems that are new to the organization and have major consequences. In brainstorming, the group convenes specifically to generate alternatives. The members present ideas and clarify them with brief explanations. Each idea is recorded in full view of all members, usually on a flip chart. To avoid self-censoring, no attempts to evaluate the ideas are allowed. Group members are encouraged to offer any ideas that occur to them, even those that seem too risky or impossible to implement. (The absence of such ideas, in fact, is evidence that group members are engaging in self-censorship.) In a subsequent session, after the ideas have been recorded and distributed to members for review, the alternatives are evaluated.

The intent of brainstorming is to produce totally new ideas and solutions by stimulating the creativity of group members and encouraging them to build on the contributions of others. Brainstorming does not provide the resolution to the problem, an evaluation scheme, or the decision itself. Instead, it should produce a list of alternatives that is more innovative and comprehensive than one developed by the typical interacting group.

Brainstorming is a technique used in the idea-generation phase of decision making that assists in development of numerous alternative courses of action.

SPENCER GRANT / PHOTOEDIT

Brainstorming is often used in the idea generation phase of decision making to help come up with new and novel solutions. These people are members of an advertising agency. Their group was charged with developing an advertising campaign for a client's new product. The group used brainstorming to identify several possible new ideas. After thoroughly discussing each one, they narrowed their ideas to the best three. One group member is shown here presenting how one of the possible ideas would translate to a print and mail advertising campaign.

The Nominal Group Technique   The nominal group technique is another means of improving group decision making. Whereas brainstorming is used primarily to generate alternatives, this technique may be used in other phases of decision making, such as identification of the problem and of appropriate criteria for evaluating alternatives. To use this technique, a group of individuals convenes to address an issue. The issue is described to the group, and each individual writes a list of ideas; no discussion among the members is permitted. Following the five-to-ten-minute idea-generation period, individual members take turns reporting their ideas, one at a time, to the group. The ideas are recorded on a flip chart, and members are encouraged to add to the list by building on the ideas of others. After all ideas have been presented, the members may discuss them and continue to build on them or proceed to the next phase. This part of the process can also be carried out without a face-to-face meeting or by mail, telephone, or computer. A meeting, however, helps members develop a group feeling and puts interpersonal pressure on the members to do their best in developing their lists.

After the discussion, members privately vote on or rank the ideas or report their preferences in some other agreed-upon way. Reporting is private to reduce any feelings of intimidation. After voting, the group may discuss the results and continue to generate and discuss ideas. The generation-discussion-vote cycle can continue until an appropriate decision is reached.

The nominal group technique has two principal advantages. It helps overcome the negative effects of power and status differences among group members, and it can be used to explore problems to generate alternatives, or to evaluate them. Its primary disadvantage lies in its structured nature, which may limit creativity.

The Delphi Technique   The Delphi technique was originally developed by Rand Corporation as a method to systematically gather the judgments of experts for use in developing forecasts. It is designed for groups that do not meet face to face. For instance, the product development manager of a major toy manufacturer might use the Delphi technique to probe the views of industry experts to forecast developments in the dynamic toy market.

The manager who wants the input of a group is the central figure in the process. After recruiting participants, the manager develops a questionnaire for them to complete. The questionnaire is relatively simple in that it contains straightforward questions that deal with the issue, trends in the area, new technological developments, and other factors the manager is interested in. The manager summarizes the responses and reports back to the experts with another questionnaire. This cycle may be repeated as many times as necessary to generate the information the manager needs.

The Delphi technique is useful when experts are physically dispersed, anonymity is desired, or the participants are known to have trouble communicating with one another because of extreme differences of opinion. This method also avoids the intimidation problems that may exist in decision-making groups. On the other hand, the technique eliminates the often fruitful results of direct interaction among group members.

With a **nominal group technique** group members follow a generate-discussion-vote cycle until they reach a decision.

The **Delphi technique** is a method of systematically gathering judgments of experts for use in developing forecasts.

SYNOPSIS

Interpersonal dynamics are a pervasive element of all organizations. Interpersonal relations can vary from positive to negative and from personal to professional. Numerous outcomes can result from various forms of interpersonal relations, including different levels of need satisfaction, social support, synergy, performance, and conflict.

A group is two or more people who interact so as to influence one another. It is important to study groups because they can profoundly affect individual behavior and because the behavior of individuals in a group is key to the group's success or failure. The work group is the primary means by which managers coordinate individual behavior to achieve organizational goals. Individuals form or join groups because they expect to satisfy personal needs.

Groups may be differentiated on the bases of relative permanence and degree of formality. The three types of formal groups are command, task, and affinity groups. Friendship and interest groups are the two types of informal groups. Command groups are relatively permanent work groups established by the organization and usually are specified on an organization chart. Task groups, although also established by the organization, are relatively temporary and exist only until the specific task is accomplished. Affinity groups are formed by the organization, are composed of employees at the same level and doing similar jobs, and come together regularly to share information and discuss organizational issues. In friendship groups, the affiliation among members arises from close social relationships and the enjoyment that comes from being together. The common bond in interest groups is the activity in which the members engage.

Groups develop in four stages: mutual acceptance, communication and decision making, motivation and productivity, and control and organization. Although the stages are sequential, they may overlap. A group that does not fully develop within each stage will not fully mature as a group, resulting in lower group performance.

Four additional factors affect group performance: composition, size, norms, and cohesiveness. The homogeneity of the people in the group affects the interactions that occur and the productivity of the group. The effect of increasing the size of the group depends on the nature of the group's tasks and the people in the group. Norms help people function and relate to one another in predictable and efficient ways. Norms serve four purposes:

They facilitate group survival, simplify and make more predictable the behaviors of group members, help the group avoid embarrassing situations, and express the central values of the group and identify the group to others.

To comprehend intergroup dynamics, we must understand the key characteristics of groups: that each group is unique, that the specific organizational setting influences the group, and that the group's task and setting have an effect on group behavior. Interactions among work groups involve some of the most complex relationships in organizations. They are based on five factors: location, resources, time and goal interdependence, task uncertainty, and task interdependence. The five bases of intergroup interactions determine the characteristics of the interactions among groups, including their frequency, how much information is exchanged, and what type of interaction occurs. Being physically near one another naturally increases groups' opportunities for interactions. If groups use the same or similar resources, or if one group can affect the availability of the resources needed by another group, the potential for frequent interactions increases. The nature of the tasks that groups perform—including time and goal orientation, the uncertainties of group tasks, and group interdependencies—influences how groups interact.

Group decision making involves problems as well as benefits. One possible problem is group polarization, the shift of members' attitudes and opinions to a more extreme position following group discussion. Another difficulty is groupthink, a mode of thinking in which the urge toward unanimity overrides the critical appraisal of alternatives. Yet another concern involves employee participation in decision making. The appropriate degree of participation depends on the characteristics of the situation.

DISCUSSION QUESTIONS

1. Why is it useful for a manager to understand group behavior? Why is it useful for an employee?
2. Our definition of a group is somewhat broad. Would you classify each of the following collections of people as a group? Explain why or why not.
   a. Seventy thousand people at a football game
   b. Students taking this course
   c. People in an elevator
   d. People on an escalator
   e. Employees of IBM
   f. Employees of your local college bookstore

3. List four groups to which you belong. Identify each as formal or informal.
4. Explain why each group you listed in question 3 formed. Why did you join each group? Why might others have decided to join each group?
5. In which stage of development is each of the four groups listed in question 3? Did any group move too quickly through any of the stages? Explain.
6. Analyze the composition of two of the groups to which you belong. How are they similar in composition? How do they differ?

7. Are any of the groups to which you belong too large or too small to get their work done? If so, what can the leader or the members do to alleviate the problem?

8. List two norms each for two of the groups to which you belong. How are these norms enforced?

9. Discuss the following statement: "Group cohesiveness is the good, warm feeling we get from working in groups and is something that all group leaders should strive to develop in the groups they lead."

10. Consider one of the groups to which you belong and describe the interactions that group has with another group.

11. Recall a situation in which you may have encountered or observed groupthink (either as member of a group or as a target or as a simple observer).

ORGANIZATIONAL BEHAVIOR CASE FOR DISCUSSION

THE VERDICT ON GROUPTHINK

In the 1957 movie *Twelve Angry Men*, Henry Fonda plays a mild-mannered architect who's been selected to serve on a jury with 11 other white, middle-class, middle-aged men. Within the confines of the claustrophobic jury room, attitudes and preconceptions gradually begin to harden and the group's decision seems increasingly like a foregone conclusion—finding a young man guilty in a case of capital murder. Fonda, however, has his doubts and starts to suggest alternative interpretations of the case until, by movie's end, he's steered the group to a more cogently considered decision. "My favorite part of a trial," reports one Texas attorney, "is when the judge ... tells the jurors that deliberations should involve discussions, the questioning of their beliefs, and a willingness to change their minds. I really want jurors to do that," he says, but "I don't think they do." Like many lawyers, he doubts very seriously if the kind of deliberative decision making extolled in *Twelve Angry Men* goes on in many real jury rooms.

So do David A. Mitchell and Daniel Eckstein, authors of "Jury Dynamics and Decision-Making: A Prescription for Groupthink." They characterize a jury as "a unique variety of an autonomous work group"—"one in which group members are chosen, essentially at random, to perform a function of great importance for which they generally have no direct training." It's a prescription, they suggest, for "group dynamics that are not conducive to quality decision making." The problem, they argue, is *groupthink*, and they agree with Irving Janis, who conducted early studies on the phenomenon, that it

"[T]he structure of the jury system may not only be conducive but often helps create the occurrence of groupthink."
—PSYCHOLOGISTS DAVID H. MITCHELL AND DANIEL ECKSTEIN

infects groups whose members let their "strivings for unanimity override their motivation to realistically appraise alternative courses of action."

Mitchell (a clinical psychologist) and Eckstein (a psychologist and consultant on leadership development) focus on Janis's seven "antecedent conditions" for groupthink—factors that make groupthink more likely—in order to show how "the conditions under which juries operate" add up to "a substantial risk of jury decisions being tainted by groupthink."

- *Cohesiveness.* A number of factors combine to ensure that the jury is a cohesive group. From the moment that jurors are selected, for example, they're "treated as a unit [and] their individual identities become submerged in the group identity." They eat together and often spend a great deal of time together prior to deliberations, and because they're not supposed to discuss the case during the trial itself, they often talk about such topics as the shared experience of being on a jury.

- *Insulation.* Once it's impaneled, the jury is isolated from other individuals and groups; jurors are physically separated from other people in the courthouse and sometimes even kept under guard to ensure their isolation.

- *Lack of a tradition of impartial leadership.* The only leadership in the group comes from the foreperson, who typically has an opinion on the case and therefore can't really be impartial in relating to other members.

- *Lack of norms requiring methodical procedures.* Juries have no set rules for how to proceed in arriving at a decision. In fact, the only specific requirement—to reach a unanimous decision—increases the likelihood of faulty decision making.

- *Homogeneity of social background and ideology.* Juries are rarely valid cross sections of the community. Desirable jury members, for example, share certain qualities that lawyers look for, and because lawyers try to seat jurors who share qualities favorable to their cases, juries often tend toward homogeneity on those qualities.

- *High stress from external threats / Low hope of a solution better than the leader's.* This factor basically underscores the fact that stress—and the desire to avoid it—contribute to groupthink, and it reflects two hypotheses: (1) that jurors find that having to choose among unpleasant or complicated alternatives increases stress, especially if the group leader is authoritarian or tends to promote a particular decision; and (2) that jurors are more likely to agree with the leader's decision if they feel that opposing it will increase stress among group members.

- *Temporarily low self-esteem induced by situational factors.* The more difficult it becomes to sort out alternatives and reach a decision, the lower a juror's sense of *self-efficacy* may become (see Chapter 3); in other words, as jurors lose their confidence in their ability to perform the task at hand, they may try to alleviate the feeling by taking refuge in conformity and consensus.

Mitchell and Eckstein acknowledge that none of these seven conditions by itself "is sufficient to cause . . . groupthink," but they hasten to point out that "the greater the number of these conditions that exist, the greater the propensity toward" groupthink. They also admit that any group is susceptible to groupthink but emphasize that "the structure of the jury system places juries at particularly high risk. ... Considering the regularity with which many of the above antecedent conditions occur in juries," they argue, "the structure of the jury system may not only be conducive but often helps create the occurrence of groupthink." Finally, they observe that different types of groups make different types of errors, but caution that groupthink "increases the risk that all types of decision-making errors will occur."

CASE QUESTIONS

1. In your experience, have you found that decision-making groups tend toward groupthink? If so, what factors contributed to this tendency? If not, what factors helped to prevent it?
2. The text discusses four group performance factors— *group composition, group size, group norms,* and *group cohesiveness.* How does each of these factors affect "the conditions under which juries operate"? How might each contribute to "a substantial risk of jury decisions being tainted by groupthink"?
3. A recent study found that racially mixed juries "deliberated longer, raised more facts, and conducted broader and more wide-ranging deliberations" than either all-white or all-black juries. Why do you think this was so? Do you think that "mixed" juries are more likely to avoid groupthink than racially homogeneous juries? Explain your reasoning.

REFERENCES

Twelve Angry Men (United Artists, 1957); David H. Mitchell and Daniel Eckstein, "Jury Dynamics and Decision-Making: A Prescription for Groupthink," *International Journal of Academic Research,* vol. 1 (September 2009), www.ijar.lit.az/pdf on March 3, 2010; Irving L. Janis, *Groupthink,* 2nd ed. (Boston: Houghton Mifflin, 1972); Michael P. Maslanka, "The Dirty Realities of Group-Think," *Texas Lawyer,* December 23, 2009, http://texaslawyer.typepad.com on March 3, 2010; Samuel R. Sommers, "On Racial Diversity and Group Decision Making: Identifying Multiple Effects of Racial Composition on Jury Deliberations," *Journal of Personality and Social Psychology,* vol. 90, no. 4 (2006), www.apa.org on March 4, 2010.

EXPERIENCING ORGANIZATIONAL BEHAVIOR

Learning the Benefits of a Group

Purpose   This exercise demonstrates the benefits a group can bring to a task.

Format   You will be asked to do the same task both individually and as part of a group.

Procedure   You will need a pen or pencil and full-size sheet of paper. Working alone, do the following:

Part 1

1. Write the letters of the alphabet in a vertical column down the left side of the paper: A–Z.
2. Your instructor will randomly select a sentence from any written document and read out loud the first twenty-six letters in that sentence. Write these letters in a vertical column immediately to the right of the alphabet column. Everyone should have an identical set of twenty-six two-letter combinations.
3. Working alone, think of a famous person whose initials correspond to each pair of letters, and write the name next to the letters—for example, "MT Mark Twain." You will have ten minutes. Only one name per set is allowed. One point is awarded for each legitimate name, so the maximum score is twenty-six points.
4. After time expires, exchange your paper with another member of the class and score each other's work. Disputes about the legitimacy of names will be settled by the instructor. Keep your score for use later in the exercise.

Part 2

Your instructor will divide the class into groups of five to ten people. All groups should have approximately the same number of members. Each group now follows the procedure given in Part 1. Again write the letters of the alphabet down the left side of the sheet of paper, this time in reverse order: Z–A. Your instructor will dictate a new set of letters for the second column. The time limit and scoring procedure are the same. The only difference is that the groups will generate the names.

Part 3

Each team identifies the group member who came up with the most names. The instructor places these "best" students into one group. Then all groups repeat Part 2, but this time the letters from the reading will be in the first column and the alphabet letters will be in the second column.

Part 4

Each team calculates the average individual score of its members on Part 1 and compares it with the team score from Parts 2 and 3, kept separately. Your instructor will put the average individual score and team scores from each part of each group on the board.

Follow-up Questions

1. Are there differences in the average individual scores and the team scores? What are the reasons for the differences, if any?
2. Although the team scores in this exercise usually are higher than the average individual scores, under what conditions might individual averages exceed group scores?

Reference: Adapted from *The Handbook for Group Facilitators*, pp. 19–20, by John E. Jones and J. William Pfeiffer (eds.), Copyright © 1979 Pfeiffer. This material is used by permission of Pfeiffer/Jossey-Bass, Inc., a subsidiary of John Wiley & Sons, Inc.

BUILDING MANAGERIAL SKILLS

Exercise Overview   A manager's interpersonal skills refer to her or his ability to understand how to motivate individuals and groups. Clearly, then, interpersonal skills play a major role in determining how well a manager can interact with others in a group setting. This exercise will allow you to practice your interpersonal skills in relation to just such a setting.

Exercise Background   You have just been transferred to a new position supervising a group of five employees. The business you work for is fairly small and has few rules and regulations. Unfortunately, the lack of rules and regulations is creating a problem that you must now address.

Specifically, two of the group members are non-smokers. They are becoming increasingly more vocal about the fact that two other members of the group smoke at work. These two workers feel that the secondary smoke in the workplace is endangering their health and want to establish a no-smoking policy like those of many large businesses today.

The two smokers, however, argue that since the firm did not have such a policy when they started working there, it would be unfair to impose such a policy now. One of them, in particular, says that he turned down an attractive job with another company because he wanted to work in a place where he could smoke.

The fifth worker is also a nonsmoker bu says that she doesn't care if others smoke. Her husband smokes at home anyway, she says, so she is used to being around smokers. You suspect that if the two vocal nonsmokers are not appeased, they may leave. At the same time, you also think that the two smokers will leave if you mandate a no-smoking policy. All five workers do good work, and you do not want any of them to leave.

Exercise Task   With this information as context, do the following:

1. Explain the nature of the conflict that exists in this work group.
2. Develop a course of action for dealing with the situation.

Reference

Ricky W. Griffin, *Management*, 10th ed. (Cengage Learning, 2011), 605.

SELF-ASSESSMENT EXERCISE

Group Cohesiveness

Introduction   You are probably a member of many different groups: study groups for school, work groups, friendship groups within a social club such as a fraternity or sorority, and interest groups. You probably have some feel for how tightly knit or cohesive each of those groups is. This exercise will help you diagnose the cohesiveness of one of those groups.

Instructions   First, pick one of the small groups to which you belong for analysis. Be sure that it is a small group, say between three and eight people. Next, rate on the following scale of 1 (poorly) to 5 (very well) how well you feel the group works together.

1	2	3	4	5
Poorly	Not Very Well	About Average	Pretty Well	Very Well

How well does this group work together?

Now answer the following six questions about the group. Put a check in the blank next to the answer that best describes how you feel about each question.

1. How many of the people in your group are friendly toward each other?
   ____ (5) All of them
   ____ (4) Most of them
   ____ (3) Some of them
   ____ (2) A few of them
   ____ (1) None of them
2. How much trust is there among members of your group?
   ____ (1) Distrust
   ____ (2) Little trust
   ____ (3) Average trust
   ____ (4) Considerable trust
   ____ (5) A great deal of trust

3. How much loyalty and sense of belonging is there among group members?
   ____ (1) No group loyalty of sense of belonging
   ____ (2) A little loyalty and sense of belonging
   ____ (3) An average sense of belonging
   ____ (4) An above-average sense of belonging
   ____ (5) A strong sense of belonging
4. Do you feel that you are really a valuable part of your group?
   ____ (5) I am really a part of my group.
   ____ (4) I am included in most ways.
   ____ (3) I am included in some ways but not others.
   ____ (2) I am included in a few ways but not many.
   ____ (1) I do not feel I really belong.
5. How friendly are your fellow group members toward each other?
   ____ (1) Not friendly
   ____ (2) Somewhat friendly
   ____ (3) Friendly to an average degree
   ____ (4) Friendlier than average
   ____ (5) Very friendly
6. If you had a chance to work with a different group of people doing the same task, how would you feel about moving to another group?
   ____ (1) I would want very much to move.
   ____ (2) I would rather move than stay where I am.
   ____ (3) It would make no difference to me.
   ____ (4) I would rather stay where I am than move.
   ____ (5) I would want very much to stay where I am.

Now add up the numbers you chose for all six questions and divide by 6. Total from all six questions = /6 =. This is the group cohesiveness score for your group.

Compare this number with the one you checked on the scale at the beginning of this exercise about how well you feel this group works together. Are they about the same, or are they quite different? If they are about the same, then you have a pretty good feel for the group and how it works. If they are quite different, then you probably need to analyze what aspects of the group functioning you misunderstood. (This is only part of a much longer instrument; it has not been scientifically validated in this form and is to be used for class discussion purposes only.)

Reference: The six questions were taken from the Groupthink Assessment Inventory by John R. Montanari and Gregory Moorhead, "Development of the Groupthink Assessment Inventory," *Educational and Psychological Measurement*, 1999, vol. 39, pp. 209–219. Reprinted by permission of Gregory Moorhead.

10

Using Teams in Organizations

CHAPTER LEARNING OBJECTIVES

After studying this chapter you should be able to:

- Differentiate teams from groups.
- Identify and discuss the benefits and costs of teams in organizations.
- Identify and describe various types of teams.
- Describe how organizations implement the use of teams.
- Discuss other essential team issues.

On the One Hand (or the Other Hand)

"Every time one of these kinds of things happens, [our] commitment is just made stronger."

—A HOSPITAL ADMINISTRATOR ON THE FACILITY'S EFFORTS TO CUT DOWN ON SURGICAL ERRORS

All of the following operating-room mishaps occurred in hospitals in the state of Rhode Island:

- A surgeon drilled into the wrong side of a patient's head in a procedure to drain blood.
- A surgeon operated on the wrong knee of a patient undergoing arthroscopic surgery.

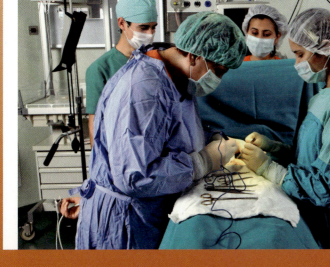

Hospitals rely on a variety of different teams to identify and address patient needs.

- A surgeon operated on the wrong side of a child's mouth during surgery to correct a cleft palate.
- A surgeon anesthetized the wrong eye of a patient about to undergo eye surgery.
- A surgeon operated on the wrong finger of a patient during hand surgery.

The last instance of so-called "wrong-site surgery"—an operation conducted on a body part other than the one intended by patient and surgeon—took place at Rhode Island Hospital, the state's largest and the main teaching hospital of prestigious Brown University. According to the chief quality officer of the hospital's parent company, Lifespan, the incident served to underscore how difficult it is to prevent such errors. The hospital, said Mary Reich Cooper, is committed to safety, and "every time one of these kinds of things happens, that commitment is just made stronger." There's apparently some question, however, about how many times such errors have to happen before a hospital's commitment is strong enough. Only two years earlier, the state department of health had fined Rhode Island Hospital $50,000 for the occurrence of three wrong-site surgical errors in a one-year span—all of them involving procedures in which doctors drilled into the wrong side of a patient's head. "Frustrating—in capital letters—is probably the best way to describe the mood here," said department director David R. Gifford after the wrong-finger incident. Asked if there might be some fundamental flaw in the hospital's procedural system, Gifford replied, "I'm wondering that myself."

All the incidents of wrong-site surgery on our list occurred in one state during a period of just over two years, and the Joint Commission on Accreditation of Healthcare Organizations, which evaluates more than 15,000 healthcare facilities and programs in the United States, estimates that wrong-site surgery occurs about 40 times a week around the country. A study in Pennsylvania conducted by the state's Patient Safety Authority added "near misses" into the mix and found that an "adverse event" (i.e., wrong-site surgery) or a "near miss" occurred every other day at Pennsylvania healthcare facilities. "To be frank," says Dr. Stan Mullens, VP of the Authority's board of directors, "wrong-site surgeries in Pennsylvania should never occur," but he hastens to add, "we're not alone. Wrong-site surgeries are no more common in Pennsylvania than they are in other states."

The Joint Commission has spent 15 years looking for ways to reduce the number of wrong-site surgical errors, but the results so far haven't been very promising; in fact, the rate of occurrence is the same as it was 15 years ago. So what's the underlying problem? According to the Commission, it's *communications breakdown*, and some studies show that communications failure is a factor in two-thirds of all surgical mishaps resulting in serious patient harm or death. Surgery, of course, is performed by *teams*, and the typical surgical team has at least three core members: the surgeon, who performs the operation and leads the team; the anesthesiologist, whose responsibility is pain management and patient safety; and the operating nurse, who provides comprehensive care, assistance, and pain management at every stage of the operation. Perhaps the most logical question to start with, therefore, is: What are the barriers to communication among the core members of a surgical team?

According to some researchers, the most serious barrier results from team members' different perceptions about the nature and quality of the group's teamwork and communications. According to a study commissioned by the Department of Veterans Affairs, the "most common pattern" of differing perceptions reflects a disparity between the perceptions of nurses and anesthesiologists on the one hand, and those of the surgeons on the other. In particular, surgeons tend to believe that both teamwork and communications are more effective than nurses and anesthesiologists do. One item on the research questionnaire, for example, asked team members to respond to the statement "I am comfortable intervening in a procedure if I have concerns about what is occurring." While surgeons reported that the OR environment did indeed support intervention, nurses and anesthesiologists generally did not. The same disparity appeared in response to the item "During surgical and diagnostic procedures, everyone on the team is aware of what is happening." Surgeons were also more likely to report that "morale on our team is high." In assessing such results as these, the authors of the study wonder, "If surgical team members have disparate perceptions about how well they are communicating or collaborating with each other, how is it possible for them to be collaborating optimally with other members of the surgical team for the care of their patients?"

When the results of a study at Johns Hopkins revealed a similar disparity in perceptions, the lead researcher, who is also a surgeon, admitted that "the study is somewhat humbling to me. . . . We need to balance out the captain-of-the-ship doctrine," suggested Dr. Martin A. Makary. Makary believes that a standardized OR briefing program is one way to improve surgical-team communication and has helped to make brief two-minute "team meetings" a regular step in surgical procedures at Johns Hopkins and other university hospitals. During the meeting, which is conducted just after anesthesia is administered, all members of the OR team state their names and roles and the surgeon verifies the critical aspects of the procedure, including the correct site. Where the policy had been adopted, according to Makary, researchers have observed an increase in "the awareness of OR personnel with regard to the site and procedure and their perceptions of operating room safety." Without such a policy, Makary points out, many surgeons simply walk into the OR and start operating without even asking the names of the other medical personnel in the room.

Such measures as team meetings hold some promise in the effort to reduce surgical error, as do checklists and "time outs," both of which require periodic confirmation of the critical components of a procedure. But "the unfortunate truth," cautions Dr. Mark R. Chassin, president of the Joint Commission, "is that no hospital today . . . can guarantee that [surgical errors] will never happen. We do not know how to perfect our processes. . . ." In some hospitals, he admits, the Commission has even encountered "denial or serious avoidance of the potential for real problems," and he recommends that patients everywhere ask surgeons in advance what steps will be taken to prevent errors while they're in the OR.

If you're wondering what wonders surgical teams can perform if they're communicating effectively, see the *Technology* box on page 278 entitled "When the Surgeon Asks for a Joystick Instead of a Scalpel."

What Do You Think?

1. How might team complexity in hospitals be generalized to other work settings?

2. In general, do you prefer to work as an individual or as part of a team? Why?

References: Felice J. Freyer, "Another Wrong-Site Surgery at R.I. Hospital," *Providence Journal*, October 28, 2009, www .projo.com on March 4, 2010; "Wrong-Site Surgery Problems Common: Study," *Philadelphia Business Journal*, June 26, 2007, www.bizjournals.com on March 4, 2010; Stephen Smith, "Hospital Tells of Surgery on Wrong Side," *Boston Globe*, July 4, 2008, www.boston.com on March 4, 2010; Steven Reinberg, "Errors in Surgical Procedure Persist," *HealthDay*, November 19, 2009, www.healthday.com on March 4, 2010; Peter Mills, Julia Neily, and Ed Dunn, "Teamwork and Communication in Surgical Teams: Implications for Patient Safety," *Journal of the American College of Surgeons*, vol. 206 (January 2008), www.surgicalpatientsafety.facs.org on March 5, 2010; Johns Hopkins Medicine, "RX for Wrong-Site Surgery: Two Minutes of Conversation," press release, January 23, 2007, www.hopkinsmedicine.org on March 4, 2010.

Teams are an integral part of the management process in many organizations today. But the notion of using teams as a way of organizing work is not new. Neither is it an American or Japanese innovation. Indeed, one of the earliest uses and analyses of teams was the work of the Tavistock Institute in the late 1940s in the United Kingdom.[1] Major companies such as Hewlett-Packard, Xerox, Procter & Gamble, General Motors, and General Mills have been using teams as a primary means of accomplishing tasks for many years. The popular business press, such as *Fortune*, *Business Week*, *Forbes*, and the *Wall Street Journal*, regularly reports on the use of teams in businesses around the world. The use of teams is not a fad of the month or some new way to manipulate workers into producing more at their own expense to enrich owners. Managers and experts agree that using teams can be among the best ways to organize and manage successfully in the twenty-first century.

This chapter presents a summary of many of the current issues involving teams in organizations. First, we define what "team" means and differentiate teams from normal work groups. We then discuss the rationale for using teams, including both the benefits and the costs. Next, we describe six types of teams in use in organizations today. Then we present the steps involved in implementing teams. Finally, we take a brief look at two essential issues that must be addressed.

DIFFERENTIATING TEAMS FROM GROUPS

Teams have been used, written about, and studied under many names and organizational programs: self-directed teams, self-managing teams, autonomous work groups, participative management, and many other labels. Groups and teams are not exactly the same thing, however, although the two words are often used interchangeably in popular usage. A brief look at a dictionary shows that "group" usually refers to an assemblage of people or objects gathered together whereas "team" usually refers to people or animals organized to work together. Thus, a "team" places more emphasis on concerted action than a "group" does. In common, everyday usage, however, terms such as "committee," "group," "team," and "task force" are often used interchangeably.

In organizations, teams and groups are also quite different. As we noted in Chapter 9, a group is two or more persons who interact with one another such that each person influences and is influenced by each other person. We specifically noted that individuals interacting and influencing each other need not have a common goal. The collection of people who happen to report to the same supervisor or manager in an organization can be called a "work group." Group members may be satisfying their own needs in the group and have little concern for a common objective. This is where a team and a group differ. In a team, all team members are committed to a common goal.

We could therefore simply say that a team is a group with a common goal. But teams differ from groups in other ways, too, and most experts are a bit more specific in defining teams. A more complete definition is "A **team** is a small number of people with complementary skills who are committed to a common purpose, performance goals, and approach for which they hold themselves mutually accountable."[2] Several facets of this definition need further explanation. A team typically includes few people because the interaction and influence processes needed for the team to function can only occur when the number of members is small. When many people are involved, they have difficulty interacting and influencing each other, utilizing their complementary skills, meeting goals, and holding themselves accountable. Regardless of the name, by our definition, mature, fully developed teams are self-directing, self-managing, and autonomous. If they are not, then someone from outside the group must be giving directions, so the group cannot be considered a true team.[3]

A **team** is a small number of people with complementary skills who are committed to a common purpose, common performance goals, and an approach for which they hold themselves mutually accountable.

Teams include people with a mix of skills appropriate to the tasks to be done. Three types of skills are usually required in a team. First, the team needs to have members with the technical or functional skills to do the jobs. Some types of engineering, scientific, technological, legal, or business skills may be necessary. Second, some team members need to have problem-solving and decision-making skills to help the team identify problems, determine priorities, evaluate alternatives, analyze trade-offs, and make decisions about the direction of the team. Third, members need interpersonal skills to manage communication flow, resolve conflict, direct questions and discussion, provide support, and recognize the interests of all members of the team. Not all members will have all of the required skills, especially when the team first convenes; different members will have different skills. However, as the team grows, develops, and matures, team members will come to have more of the necessary skills.[4]

Teams function most effectively if they have a common purpose and common performance goals. These team members are raising money for a Miami program intended to reduce drug abuse among children and teenagers. Their common purpose helped energize them as they planned their fundraiser and their common performance goals helped them set an ambitious but attainable goal for how much money they wanted to raise.

Having a common purpose and common performance goals sets the tone and direction of the team. A team comes together to take action to pursue a goal, unlike a work group, in which members merely report to the same supervisor or work in the same department. The purpose becomes the focus of the team, which makes all decisions and takes all actions in pursuit of the goal. Teams often spend days or weeks establishing the reason for their existence, an activity that builds strong identification and fosters commitment to the team. This process also helps team members develop trust in one another.[5] Usually, the defining purpose comes first, followed by development of specific performance goals.

For example, a team of local citizens, teachers, and parents may come together for the purpose of making the local schools the best in the state. The team then establishes specific performance goals to serve as guides for decision making, to maintain the focus on action, to differentiate this team from other groups who may want to improve schools, and to challenge people to commit themselves to the team. One study looked at more than thirty teams and found that demanding, high-performance goals often challenge members to create a real team—as opposed to being merely a group—because when goals are truly demanding, members must pull together, find resources within themselves, develop and use the appropriate skills, and take a common approach to reach the goals.[6]

Agreeing on a common approach is especially important for teams because it is often the approach that differentiates one team from others. The team's approach usually covers how work will be done, social norms regarding dress, attendance at meetings, tardiness, norms of fairness and ethical behavior, and what will and will not be included in the team activities.

Finally, the definition states that teams hold themselves mutually accountable for results—rather than merely meeting a manager's demands for results, as in the traditional approach. If the members translate accountability to an external manager into internal, or mutual, accountability, the group moves toward acting like a team. Mutual accountability is essentially a promise that members make to each other to do everything possible to achieve their goals, and it requires the commitment and trust of all members. It is the promise of each member—to hold herself or himself accountable for the team's goals—that earns each individual the right to express her or his views and expect them to get a fair and constructive hearing. With this promise, members maintain and strengthen the trust necessary for the team to succeed. The clearly stated high-performance goals and the common approach serve as the standards to which the team holds itself. Because teams are mutually accountable for meeting performance goals, three other differences between groups and teams become important: job categories, authority, and reward systems. The differences for traditional work groups and work teams are shown in Table 10.1.

Job Categories

The work of conventional groups is usually described in terms of highly specialized jobs that require minimal training and moderate effort. Tens or even hundreds of people may have similar job descriptions and see little relationship between their effort and the end result or finished product. In teams, on the other hand, members have many different skills that fit into one or two broad job categories. Neither workers nor management worries about who does what job as long as the team puts out the finished product or service and meets its performance goals.[7]

Authority

As shown in Table 10.1, in conventional work groups, the supervisor directly controls the daily activities of workers. In teams, the team discusses what activities need to be done and determines for itself who in the team has the necessary skills and who will do each task. The team, rather than the supervisor, makes the decisions. If a "supervisor" remains on the team, that person's role usually changes to that of coach, facilitator, or one who helps the team make decisions, rather than remaining the traditional role of decision maker and controller.

Reward Systems

How employees are rewarded is vital to the long-term success of an organization. The traditional reward and compensation systems suitable for individual motivation (discussed in Chapter 4) are simply not appropriate in a team-based organization. In conventional settings, employees are usually rewarded on the basis of their individual performance, their seniority, or their job classification. In a team-based situation, team members are rewarded for mastering a range of skills needed to meet team performance goals, and rewards are sometimes based on team performance. Such a pay system tends to promote the flexibility that teams need to be responsive to changing envi-

Table 10.1   DIFFERENCES BETWEEN TEAMS AND TRADITIONAL WORK GROUPS

Issue	Conventional Work Groups	Teams
JOB CATEGORIES	Many narrow categories	One or two broad categories
AUTHORITY	Supervisor directly controls daily activities	Team controls daily activities
REWARD SYSTEM	Depends on the type of job, individual performance, and seniority	Based on team performance and individual breadth of skills

Reference: Adapted from Jack D. Osburn, Linda Moran, and Ed Musselwhite, with Craig Perrin, *Self-Directed Work Teams: The New American Challenge* (Homewood, IL: Business One Irwin, 1990), p. 11.

ronmental factors. Three types of reward systems are common in a team environment: skill-based pay, gain-sharing systems, and team bonus plans.

Skill-Based Pay Skill-based pay systems require team members to acquire a set of the core skills needed for their particular team plus additional special skills, depending on career tracks or team needs. Some programs require all members to acquire the core skills before any member receives additional pay. Usually employees can increase their base compensation by some fixed amount, say $0.50 per hour for each additional skill acquired, up to some fixed maximum. Companies using skill-based pay systems include Eastman Chemical Company, Colgate-Palmolive Company, and Pfizer.

Whole Foods credits much of its success to its employees. The company uses teams in virtually every area of its operations. A team of bakery employees, for example, developed a system for allowing customers to sample fresh bakery products at minimal costs to the store. Whole Foods uses both skill-based pay to incent employees to develop and refine new job skills and team bonus plans to reward those teams that contribute new ideas and procedures.

BROOKS KRAFT/CORBIS NEWS/CORBIS

Gain-Sharing Systems Gain-sharing systems usually reward all team members from all teams based on the performance of the organization, division, or plant. Such a system requires a baseline performance that must be exceeded for team members to receive some share of the gain over the baseline measure. Westinghouse gives equal one-time, lump-sum bonuses to everyone in the plant based on improvements in productivity, cost, and quality. Employee reaction is usually positive because when employees work harder to help the company, they share in the profits they helped generate. On the other hand, when business conditions or other factors beyond their control make it impossible to generate improvements over the preset baseline, employees may feel disappointed and even disillusioned with the process.

Team Bonus Plans Team bonus plans are similar to gain-sharing plans except that the unit of performance and pay is the team rather than a plant, a division, or the entire organization. Each team must have specific performance targets or baseline measures that the team considers realistic for the plan to be effective. Companies using team bonus plans include Milwaukee Insurance Company, Colgate-Palmolive, and Harris Corporation.

Changes in an organizational compensation system can be traumatic and threatening to most employees. However, matching the reward system to the way that work is organized and accomplished can have very positive benefits. The three types of team-based reward systems presented can be used in isolation for simplicity or in some combination to address different types of issues for each organization.

BENEFITS AND COSTS OF TEAMS IN ORGANIZATIONS

With the popularity of teams increasing so rapidly around the world, it is possible that some organizations are starting to use teams simply because everyone else is doing it—which is obviously the wrong reason. The reason for a company to create teams should be that teams make sense for that particular organization. The best reason to start teams in any organization is to recap the positive benefits that can result from a team-based environment: enhanced performance, employee benefits, reduced costs, and organizational enhancements. Four categories of benefits and some examples are shown in Table 10.2.

Enhanced Performance

Enhanced performance can come in many forms, including improved productivity, quality, and customer service. Working in teams enables workers to avoid wasted effort, reduce errors, and react better to customers, resulting in more output for each unit of employee input. Such enhancements result from pooling of individual efforts in new ways and from continuously striving to improve for the benefit of the team.[8] For example, a General Electric plant in North Carolina experienced a 20 percent increase in productivity after team implementation.[9] K Shoes reported a 19 percent increase in productivity and significant reductions in rejects in the manufacturing process after it started using teams.

Table 10.2 BENEFITS OF TEAMS IN ORGANIZATIONS

Type of Benefit	Specific Benefit	Organizational Examples
ENHANCED PERFORMANCE	Increased productivity	Ampex: On-time customer delivery rose 98%.
	Improved quality	K Shoes: Rejects per million dropped from 5,000 to 250.
	Improved customer service	Eastman: Productivity rose 70%.
EMPLOYEE BENEFITS	Quality of work life	Milwaukee Mutual: Employee assistance program usage dropped to 40% below industry average.
	Lower stress	
REDUCED COSTS	Lower turnover, absenteeism	Kodak: Reduced turnover to one-half the industry average.
	Fewer injuries	Texas Instruments: Reduced costs more than 50%.
		Westinghouse: Costs down 60%.
ORGANIZATIONAL ENHANCEMENTS	Increased innovation, flexibility	IDS Mutual Fund Operations: Improved flexibility to handle fluctuations in market activity. Hewlett-Packard: Innovative order-processing system.

References: Adapted from Richard S. Wellins, William C. Byham, and George R. Dixon, *Inside Teams* (San Francisco: Jossey-Bass, 1994); Charles C. Manz and Henry P. Sims Jr., *Business Without Bosses* (New York: Wiley, 1993).

Employee Benefits

Employees tend to benefit as much as organizations in a team environment. Much attention has been focused on the differences between the baby-boom generation and the "postboomers" in their attitudes toward work, its importance to their lives, and what they want from it. In general, younger workers tend to be less satisfied with their work and the organization, tend to have lower respect for authority and supervision, and tend to want more than a paycheck every week. Teams can provide the sense of self-control, human dignity, identification with work, and sense of self-worth and self-fulfillment for which current workers seem to strive. Rather than relying on the traditional, hierarchical, manager-based system, teams give employees the freedom to grow and to gain respect and dignity by managing themselves, making decisions about their work, and really making a difference in the world around them.[10] As a result, employees have a better work life, face less stress at work, and make less use of employee assistance programs.

Reduced Costs

As empowered teams reduce scrap, make fewer errors, file fewer worker compensation claims, and reduce absenteeism and turnover, organizations based on teams are showing significant cost reductions. Team members feel that they have a stake in the outcomes, want to make contributions because they are valued, and are committed to their team and do not want to let it down. Wilson Sporting Goods reported saving $10 million per year for five years thanks to its teams. Colgate-Palmolive reported that technician turnover was extremely low—more than 90 percent of technicians were retained after five years—once it changed to a team-based approach.

Organizational Enhancements

Other improvements in organizations that result from moving from a hierarchically based, directive culture to a team-based culture include increased innovation, creativity, and flexibility.[11] Use of teams can eliminate redundant layers of bureaucracy and flatten the hierarchy in large organizations. Employees feel closer and more in touch with top management. Employees who think their efforts are important are more likely to make significant contributions. In addition, the team environment constantly challenges teams to innovate and solve problems creatively. If the "same old way" does not work, empowered teams are free to throw it out and develop a new way. With increasing global competition, organizations must constantly adapt to keep abreast of changes. Teams provide the flexibility to react quickly. One of Motorola's earliest teams challenged a long-standing, top-management policy regarding supplier inspections in order to reduce the cycle times and improve delivery of crucial parts.[12] After several attempts, management finally allowed the team to change the system and consequently reaped the expected benefits.

Sometimes, of course, organizational enhancements and adaptive measures don't work out as well as planned and organizations find that they must "re-adapt." The *Change* box on "backsourcing" on page 274 deals with one area in which some U.S. companies have been obliged to do just that.

CHANGE

"Backsourcing" Improves Teamwork

Many organizations use outsourcing effectively but some do not. The IRS outsources some debt collections even though using that funding for more internal collection staff efforts could save up to $81 million annually. Many U.S. airlines outsource plane maintenance to foreign, uncertified airports that are of unknown quality.

Outsourcing took another blow with the controversy surrounding H-1B visas. India-based outsourcers use the temporary work visas to train foreign workers here in the United States. The number of visas granted has fallen two-thirds over the last several years due to concerns about employment for American workers.

> *"I wouldn't trust an outside team to innovate for me. . . . You simply can't outsource your success to others."*
> —VIVEK WADHWA, HIGH-TECH ENTREPRENEUR AND FELLOW, HARVARD LAW SCHOOL

Even the much-publicized cost savings associated with outsourcing are questionable. For example, an American programmer makes $50 hourly while an Indian programmer makes $10. However, there are additional costs associated with the supervision, communications, and quality assurance demands created by outsourcing. Also, one manager notes that after outsourcing, "We didn't pick up technologies that would give us a competitive advantage." Perhaps most importantly, organizations that outsource typically experience low morale, diminished productivity, and less teamwork.

In response, some U.S. companies are "backsourcing," returning work in-house that was formerly outsourced overseas. The state of Indiana planned to outsource unemployment claims processing to Tata Consulting, an Indian firm. The deal was canceled when voters protested the irony of their state using foreign workers to process Indiana's unemployment claims. A U.S. credit card company backsourced billing services when it found that Indian workers could not effectively handle delicate communications situations, such as delinquent bill collection. Dell found that Indian workers had difficulty answering technical support questions so it backsourced its customer support function. For most companies today, programming jobs can often be effectively outsourced, but not core tasks. Vivek Wadhwa, a high-tech entrepreneur with outsourcing experience, says, "I wouldn't trust an outside team to innovate for me. . . . You simply can't outsource your success to others."

References: Vivek Wadhwa, "Why Small Tech Companies Aren't Outsourcing," *BusinessWeek*, July 20, 2007, www.businessweek .com on March 9, 2010; Andy McCue, "More Firms Setting Up Own Offshoring," *BusinessWeek*, July 13, 2007, www.businessweek .com on March 9, 2010; Lynley Browning, "Taxpayer Advocate Says Outsourcing at IRS Is Inept," *New York Times*, March 14, 2008, www .nytimes.com on March 9, 2010; Joe Sharkey, "Airplane Maintenance: Maybe Not a Place to Skimp," *New York Times*, April 1, 2008, www.nytimes.com on March 9, 2010; Compass Bank, "Reversal of Fortune: Outsourcing Is Out, Backsourcing Is In," *Compass on Business*, Spring 2006, www.compassbank.com on March 9, 2010; Stephanie Overby, "Outsourcing—and Backsourcing—at JP Morgan Chase," *CIO*, September 1, 2005, www.cio.com on March 9, 2010.

Costs of Teams

The costs of teams are usually expressed in terms of the difficulty of changing to a team-based organization. Managers have expressed frustration and confusion about their new roles as coaches and facilitators, especially if they developed their managerial skills under the old traditional hierarchical management philosophy. Some managers have felt as if they were working themselves out of a job as they turned over more and more of their old directing duties to a team.[13]

Employees may also feel like losers during the change to a team culture. Some traditional staff groups, such as technical advisory staffs, may feel that their jobs are in jeopardy as teams do more and more of the technical work formerly done by technicians. New roles and pay scales may need to be developed for the technical staff in these situations. Often, technical people have been assigned to a team or a small group of teams and become members who fully participate in team activities.

Another cost associated with teams is the slowness of the process of full team development. As discussed elsewhere in this chapter, it takes a long time for teams to go through the full development cycle and become mature, efficient, and effective. If top management is impatient with the slow progress, teams may be disbanded, returning the organization to its original hierarchical form with significant losses for employees, managers, and the organization.

Probably the most dangerous cost is premature abandonment of the change to a team-based organization. If top management gets impatient with the team change process and cuts it short, never allowing teams to develop fully and realize benefits, all the hard work of employees, middle managers, and supervisors is lost. As a result, employee confidence in management in general and in the decision makers in particular may suffer for a long time.[14] The losses in productivity and efficiency will be very difficult to recoup. Management must therefore be fully committed before initiating a change to a team-based organization.

TYPES OF TEAMS

Many different types of teams exist in organizations today. Some evolved naturally in organizations that permit various types of participative and empowering management programs. Others have been formally created at the suggestion of enlightened management. One easy way to classify teams is by what they do; for example, some teams make or do things, some teams recommend things, and some teams run things. The most common types of teams are quality circles, work teams, and problem-solving teams; management teams are also quite common.

Quality Circles

Quality circles (QCs) are small groups of employees from the same work area who meet regularly (usually weekly or monthly) to discuss and recommend solutions to workplace problems.[15] QCs were the first type of team created in U.S. organizations, becoming most popular during the 1980s in response to growing Japanese competition. QCs had some success in reducing rework and cutting defects on the shop floors of many manufacturing plants. Some attempts have been made to use QCs in offices and service operations, too. They exist alongside the traditional management structure and are relatively permanent. The role of QCs is to investigate a variety of quality problems that might come up in the workplace. They do not replace the work group or make decisions about how the work is done. The usage of QCs has declined in recent years, although many companies still have them.[16] QCs are teams that make recommendations.

Work Teams

Work teams tend to be permanent, like QCs, but they are, rather than auxiliary committees, the teams that do the daily work.[17] The nurses, orderlies, and various technicians responsible for all patients on a floor or wing in a hospital comprise a work team. Rather than investigate a specific problem, evaluate alternatives, and recommend a solution or change, a work team does the actual daily work of the unit. The difference between a traditional work group of

Quality circles are small groups of employees from the same work area who regularly meet to discuss and recommend solutions to workplace problems.

Work teams include all the people working in an area, are relatively permanent, and do the daily work, making decisions regarding how the work of the team is done.

Crisis teams are problem-solving teams created to help address real-time issues that arise during a crisis. They are usually comprised of people from many different areas and function only for the duration of the crisis. Recent examples of situations where crisis teams were used included the BP oil spill in the Gulf of Mexico, the devastating earthquake in Haiti, and a natural gas pipeline explosion in California.

nurses and the patient care team is that the latter has the authority to decide how the work is done, in what order, and by whom; the entire team is responsible for all patient care. When the team decides how the work is to be organized or done, it becomes a self-managing team, to which accrue all of the benefits described in this chapter. Work teams are teams that make or do things.

Problem-Solving Teams

Problem-solving teams are temporary teams established to attack specific problems in the workplace. Teams can use any number of methods to solve the problem, as discussed in Chapter 9. After solving the problem, the team is usually disbanded, allowing members to return to their normal work. One survey found that 91 percent of U.S. companies utilize problem-solving teams regularly.[18] High-performing problem-solving teams are often cross-functional, meaning that team members come from many different functional areas. Crisis teams are problem-solving teams created only for the duration of an organizational crisis and are usually composed of people from many different areas. Problem-solving teams are teams that make recommendations for others to implement.

Management Teams

Management teams, consisting of managers from various areas, coordinate work teams. They are relatively permanent because their work does not end with the completion of a particular project or the resolution of a problem. Management teams must concentrate on the teams that have the most impact on overall corporate performance. The primary job of management teams is to coach and counsel other teams to be self-managing by making decisions within the team. The second most important task of management teams is to coordinate work between work teams that are interdependent in some manner. Digital Equipment Corporation abandoned its team matrix structure because the matrix of teams was not well organized and coordinated. Team members at all levels reported spending hours and hours in meetings trying to coordinate among teams, leaving too little time to get the real work done.[19]

Top-management teams may have special types of problems. First, the work of the top-management team may not be conducive to teamwork. Vice presidents or heads of divisions may be in charge of different sets of operations that are not related and do not need to be coordinated. Forcing that type of top-management group to be a team may be inappropriate. Second, top managers often have reached high levels in the organization because they have certain characteristics or abilities to get things done. For successful managers to alter their style, to pool resources, and to sacrifice their independence and individuality can be very difficult.[20]

Product Development Teams

Product development teams are combinations of work teams and problem-solving teams that create new designs for products or services that will satisfy customer needs. They are

Problem-solving teams are temporary teams established to attack specific problems in the workplace.

Management teams consist of managers from various areas; they coordinate work teams.

Product development teams are combinations of work teams and problem-solving teams that create new designs for products or services that will satisfy customer needs.

similar to problem-solving teams because when the product is fully developed and in production, the team may be disbanded. As global competition and electronic information storage, processing, and retrieving capabilities increase, companies in almost every industry are struggling to cut product development times. The primary organizational means of accomplishing this important task is the "blue-ribbon" cross-functional team. Boeing's team that developed the 787 commercial airplane and the platform teams of Chrysler are typical examples. The rush to market with new designs can lead to numerous problems for product development teams. The primary problems of poor communication and poor coordination of typical product development processes in organizations can be rectified by creating self-managing, cross-functional product development teams.[21]

Virtual Teams

Virtual teams are teams that may never actually meet together in the same room—their activities take place on the computer via teleconferencing and other electronic information systems. Engineers in the United States can directly connect audibly and visually with counterparts all around the globe, sharing files via Internet, electronic mail, and other communication utilities. All participants can look at the same drawing, print, or specification, so decisions are made much faster. With electronic communication systems, team members can move in or out of a team or a team discussion as the issues warrant.

The *Technology* box on page 278, entitled "When the Surgeon Asks for a Joystick Instead of a Scalpel," discusses a special kind of virtual team that depends on cutting-edge technology.

IMPLEMENTING TEAMS IN ORGANIZATIONS

Implementing teams in organizations is not easy; it takes a lot of hard work, time, training, and patience. Changing from a traditional organizational structure to a team-based structure is much like other organizational changes (which we discuss in Chapter 19). It is really a complete cultural change for the organization. Typically, the organization is hierarchically designed in order to provide clear direction and control. However, many organizations need to be able to react quickly to a dynamic environment. Team procedures artificially imposed on existing processes are a recipe for disaster. In this section we present several essential elements peculiar to an organizational change to a team-based situation.

Planning the Change

The change to a team-based organization requires a lot of analysis and planning before it is implemented; the decision cannot be made overnight and then quickly implemented. It is such a drastic departure from the traditional hierarchy and authority-and-control orientation that significant planning, preparation, and training are prerequisites. The planning actually takes place in two phases, the first leading to the decision about whether to move to a team-based approach and the second while preparing for implementation.

Making the Decision   Prior to making the decision, top management needs to establish the leadership for the change, develop a steering committee, conduct a feasibility study, and then make the go/no-go decision. Top management must be sure that the team culture is consistent with its strategy, as we discuss in Chapter 18. Quite

Virtual teams work together by computer and other electronic communication utilities; members move in and out of meetings and the team itself as the situation dictates.

When the Surgeon Asks for a Joystick Instead of a Scalpel

In September 2001, surgeons removed the gall bladder of a 68-year-old woman in Strasbourg, France. Gall-bladder removal is a pretty routine procedure, and the standard of care is the use of "minimally invasive surgery." Such surgery is made possible by the laparoscope—a thin, lighted tube that allows doctors to see what they're doing with remote-controlled instruments inserted into the patient's body through small incisions. The patient in Strasbourg left the hospital after 48 hours and had an uneventful recovery. The only noteworthy aspect of the operation was the fact that the surgeon wasn't in Strasbourg. In fact, he wasn't even in a hospital: He was in the U.S. offices of France Télécom in New York, 4,300 miles away. The operation was the first complete "remote surgery" performed on a human patient—the result of a hands-on collaboration (so to speak) among Dr. Jacques Marescaux, director of the European Institute of Telesurgery; Computer Motion Inc., a maker of medical devices located in California; France Télécom, the biggest telecommunications company in France; and surgeons at Strasbourg's Hôpitaux Universitaires.

This particular operation wasn't necessarily a qualitative leap forward from conventional laparoscopic surgery. Surgeons had been performing computer-assisted procedures since the mid-1990s, though always in the same theaters with their patients. *Remote surgery*, or *telesurgery*, simply adds the technology that allows surgeons and patients to be in different places, and the breakthrough made in the 2001 New York–Strasbourg procedure was largely a matter of distance. In demonstrating "the feasibility of a transatlantic procedure," said

> *"Having a world expert from the United States looking over our shoulder . . . greatly enhanced our comfort level and provided the best care for the patient."*
>
> —AN ARGENTINE SURGEON WHO PERFORMED TRANSCONTINENTAL TELESURGERY

Marescaux, his team had achieved merely "a richly symbolic milestone."

Even so, the benefits of remote surgery—say, having a world-class surgeon perform an operation on one patient in Europe in the morning and on another in South America in the afternoon—are fairly obvious. Some doctors also refer to a related benefit that Marescaux calls "telecompanionship"—the opportunity for surgeons to hone their skills and learn new ones by watching acknowledged experts at work. Dr. Louis Kavoussi, for example, pioneered new techniques in minimally invasive surgery for urologic diseases in the 1990s but soon found that he was spending more of his time demonstrating his innovations to other surgeons than putting them to use in the OR. "I became involved in telesurgery," he says, "because my department felt I was doing too much traveling in teaching these new techniques." Kavoussi, currently of New York University School of Medicine, now communicates his specialized knowledge to fellow surgeons through a system that uses ISDN phone lines, cameras, X-ray images, and other technologies in conjunction with an OR-based robot.

Similarly, in mid-2007, Dr. Alex Gandsas, a surgeon at Sinai Hospital in Baltimore, used a telesurgery system to enable physicians in Argentina to perform a procedure for the treatment of obesity. Dr. Sergio Cantarelli had originally contacted Gandsas about the possibility of coming to the United States to learn the procedure. "He had never done this type of surgery before," recalls Gandas, but "in practice, it wasn't possible for him to come over and train here." That's when Gandsas got the idea of mentoring Cantarelli remotely, and for nearly three months, Cantarelli and a colleague, Dr. Gabriel Egidi, studied the procedure by participating in surgeries performed in the United States. At the end of the training period, Cantarelli and Egidi performed the operation in Argentina by means of a "remote-presence robot" that allowed Gandsas, controlling a joystick in Baltimore, to monitor the procedure and mentor the surgeons in the actual OR 5,400 miles away. "During the surgery," explains Gandsas, "the robot allowed me to zoom in on the patient and the monitors to assess the situation" while the Argentine doctors actually operated on the patient, a 39-year-old woman. Meanwhile, Cantarelli and Egidi,

who had never met their American colleague personally, reported that the long-distance collaboration benefited everyone involved. "Having a world expert from the United States looking over our shoulder," said Cantarelli, "... greatly enhanced our comfort level and provided the best care for the patient."

References: J[acques] Marescaux, "Code Name: Lindbergh Operation," *WebSurg*, January 2002, www.websurg.com on March 9, 2010; Sharon Kay, "Light Speed," *Innovation Online* (2004), www.pbs.org on March 9, 2010; Vicki Brower, "The Cutting Edge in Surgery," *EMBO Reports*, vol. 3 (2002), www.nature.com on March 9, 2010; "Remote Surgery between U.S. and Argentina," *The Medical News*, October 4, 2007, www.news-medical.net on March 8, 2010; Matthew Knight, "Virtual Surgery Becoming a Reality," *CNN.com*, October 18, 2007, http://edition.cnn.com on March 9, 2010; "Robot Teaches World's First Remote Surgery," *Physorg.com*, October 3, 2007, www.physorg.com on March 9, 2010.

often the leadership for the change is the chief executive officer, the chief operating officer, or another prominent person in top management. Regardless of the position, the person leading the change needs to (1) have a strong belief that employees want to be responsible for their own work, (2) be able to demonstrate the team philosophy, (3) articulate a coherent vision of the team environment, and (4) have the creativity and authority to overcome obstacles as they surface.

The leader of the change needs to put together a steering committee to help explore the organization's readiness for the team environment and lead it through the planning and preparation for the change. The steering committee can be of any workable size, from two to ten people who are influential and know the work and the organization. Members may include plant or division managers, union representatives, human resource department representatives, and operational-level employees. The work of the steering committee includes visits to sites that might be candidates for utilizing work teams, visits to currently successful work teams, data gathering and analysis, low-key discussions, and deliberating and deciding whether to use a consultant during the change process.

A feasibility study is a necessity before making the decision to use teams. The steering committee needs to know if the work processes are conducive to team use; if the employees are willing and able to work in a team environment; if the managers in the unit to be converted are willing to learn and apply the hands-off managerial style necessary to make teams work; if the organization's structure and culture are ready to accommodate a team-based organization; if the market for the unit's products or services is growing or at least stable enough to absorb the increased productive capacity that teams will be putting out; and if the community will support the transition teams. Without answers to these questions, management is merely guessing and hoping that teams will work—and may be destined for many surprises that could doom the effort.

After the leadership has been established, the steering committee has been set up, and a feasibility study has been conducted, the go/no-go decision can be made. The committee and top management will need to decide jointly to go ahead if conditions are right. On the other hand, if the feasibility study indicates that questions exist as to whether the organizational unit is ready, the committee can decide to postpone implementation while changes are made in personnel, organizational structure, and

© ROBERT BOREA/AP PHOTOS

W. L. Gore, best known for its Gore-Tex fabric, uses a team organization approach to business. The firm has no job titles or fixed hierarchies, and workers (called "associates") collaborate in small teams. W. L Gore believes this model fuels creativity and innovation. Potential new employees are carefully screened to ensure they fit the Gore culture. Associates are responsible to one another for the success of their projects.

organizational policies, or until market conditions improve. The committee could also decide to implement training and acculturation for employees and managers in the unit in preparation for later implementation.

Preparing for Implementation

Once the decision is made to change to a team-based organization, much needs to be done before implementation can begin. Preparation consists of the following five steps: clarifying the mission, selecting the site for the first work teams, preparing the design team, planning the transfer of authority, and drafting the preliminary plan.

The mission statement is simply an expression of purpose that summarizes the long-range benefits the company hopes to gain by moving to a team environment. It must be consistent with the organization's strategy as it establishes a common set of assumptions for executives, middle managers, support staff, and the teams. In addition, it sets the parameters or boundaries within which the change will take place. It may identify which divisions or plants will be involved or what levels will be converted to teams. The mission statement attempts to stimulate and focus the energy of those people who need to be involved in the change. The mission can focus on continuous improvement, employee involvement, increasing performance, competition, customer satisfaction, and contributions to society. The steering committee should involve many people from many different areas to foster fuller involvement in the change.

Once the mission is established, the steering committee needs to decide where teams will be implemented first. Selection of the first site is crucial because it sets the tone for the success of the total program. The best initial site would be one that includes workers from multiple job categories, one where improving performance or reaching the targets set in the mission is feasible, and one where workers accept the idea of using teams. Also valuable are a tradition or history of success and a staff that is receptive to training, especially training in interpersonal skills. One manufacturing company based its choice of sites for initial teams not on criteria such as these but on the desire to reward the managers of successful divisions or to "fix" areas performing poorly. Team implementation in that company consequently was very slow and not very successful.[22] Initial sites must also have a local "champion" of the team concept.

Once the initial sites have been identified, the steering committee needs to set up the team that will design the other teams. The design team is a select group of employees, supervisors, and managers who will work out the staffing and operational details to make the teams perform well. The design team selects the initial team members, prepares members and managers for teams, changes work processes for use with the team design, and plans the transition from the current state to the new self-managed teams. The design team usually spends the first three months learning from the steering committee, visiting sites where teams are being used successfully, and spending a significant amount of time in classroom training. Considering the composition of the teams is one of the most important decisions the design team has to make.

Planning the transfer of authority from management to teams is the most important phase of planning the implementation. It is also the most distinctive and difficult part of moving to a team-based organization. It is difficult because it is so different from the traditional, hierarchical organization management system. It is a gradual process, one that takes from two to five years in most situations. Teams must learn new skills and make new decisions related to their work, all of which take time. It is, essentially, a cultural change for the organization.

The last stage of planning the implementation is to write the tentative plan for the initial work teams. The draft plan combines the work of the steering and design committees and becomes the primary working document that guides the continuing work of the design teams and the first work teams. The draft plan (1) recommends a process for selecting the people who will be on the first teams; (2) describes roles and responsibilities for all the people who will be affected (team members, team leaders, facilitators, support teams, managers, and top management); (3) explains what training the several groups will need; (4) identifies specifically which work processes will be involved; (5) describes what other organizational systems will be affected; and (6) lays out a preliminary master schedule for the next two to three years. Once the steering committee and top management approve the preliminary plan, the organization is ready to start the implementation.

Phases of Implementation

Implementation of self-managing work teams is a long and difficult process, often taking two to five years. During this period, the teams go through a number of phases (Figure 10.1); these phases are not, however, readily apparent at the times the team is going through them.

Phase 1: Start-Up   In phase 1, team members are selected and prepared to work in teams so that the teams have the best possible chance of success. Much of the initial training is informational or "awareness" training that sends the message that top management is firmly committed to teams and that teams are not experimental. The steering committee usually starts the training at the top, and the training and information are passed down the chain to the team members.

Figure 10.1   PHASES OF TEAM IMPLEMENTATIONS

Implementation of teams in organizations is a long and arduous process. After the decision is made to initiate teams, the steering committee develops the plans for the design team, which plans the entire process. The goal is for teams to become self-managing. The time it takes for each stage varies with the organization.

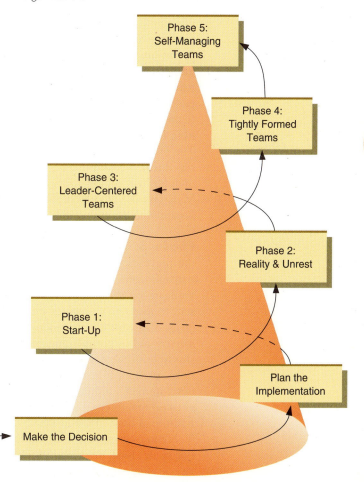

Training covers the rationale for moving to a team-based organization, how teams were selected, how they work, the roles and responsibilities of teams, compensation, and job security. In general, training covers the technical skills necessary to do the work of the team, the administrative skills necessary for the team to function within the organization, and the interpersonal skills necessary to work with people in the team and throughout the organization. Sometimes the interpersonal skills are important. Perhaps most important is establishing the idea that teams are not "unmanaged" but are "differently managed." The difference is that the new teams manage themselves. Team boundaries are also identified, and the preliminary plan is adjusted to fit the particular team situations. Employees typically feel that much is changing during the first few months, enthusiasm runs high, and the anticipation of employees is quite positive. Performance by teams increases at start-up because of this initial enthusiasm for the change.

Phase 2: Reality and Unrest   After perhaps six to nine months, team members and managers report frustration and confusion about the ambiguities of the new situation. For employees, unfamiliar tasks, more responsibility, and worry about job security replace hope for the opportunities presented by the new approach. All of the training and preparation, as important as it is, is never enough to prepare for the storm and backlash. Cummins Engine Company held numerous "prediction workshops" in an effort to prepare employees and managers for the difficulties that lay ahead, all to no avail. Its employees reported the same problems that employees of other companies did. The best advice is to perform phase 1 very well and then make managers very visible, continue to work to clarify the roles and responsibilities of everyone involved, and reinforce the positive behaviors that do occur.

Some managers make the mistake of staying completely away from the newly formed teams, thinking that the whole idea is to let teams manage themselves. In reality, managers need to be very visible to provide encouragement, to monitor team performance, to act as intermediaries between teams, to help teams acquire needed resources, to foster the right type of communication, and sometimes to protect teams from those who want to see them fail. Managers, too, feel the unrest and confusion. The change they supported results in more work for them. In addition, there is the real threat, at least initially, that work will not get done, projects may not get finished, or orders will not get shipped on time and that they will be blamed for the problems.[23] Managers also report that they still have to intervene and solve problems for the teams because the teams do not know what they are doing.

Phase 3: Leader-Centered Teams   As the discomfort and frustrations of the previous phase peak, teams usually long for a system that resembles the old manager-centered organizational structure (see Figure 10.1). However, members are learning about self-direction and leadership from within the team and usually start to focus on a single leader in the team. In addition, the team begins to think of itself as a unit as members learn to manage themselves. Managers begin to get a sense of the positive possibilities of organizing in teams and begin to withdraw slowly from the daily operation of the unit to begin focusing on standards, regulations, systems, and resources for the team.[24] This phase is not a setback to team development—although it may seem like one—because development of and reliance on one internal leader is a move away from focusing on the old hierarchy and traditional lines of authority.

The design and steering committees need to be sure that two things happen during this phase. First, they need to encourage the rise of strong internal team leaders. The new leaders can either be company appointed or team appointed. Top management sometimes prefers the additional control they get from appointing the team leaders, assuming that production will continue through the team transition. On the other hand, if the company-appointed leaders are the former managers, team members have trouble believing that anything has really changed. Team-appointed leaders can be a problem if the leaders are not trained properly and oriented toward team goals.

If the team-appointed leader is ineffective, the team usually recognizes the problem and makes the adjustments necessary to get the team back on track. Another possibility for team leadership is a rotating system in which the position changes every quarter, month, week, or even day. A rotating system fosters professional growth of all members of the team and reinforces the strength of the team's self-management.

The second important issue for this phase is to help each team develop its own sense of identity. Visits to observe mature teams in action can be a good step

NISHAN AKGULIAN/IMAGES.COM/CORBIS

Leader-centered teams start to look to a team member for leadership. While this may sometimes seem to be a setback, in reality most teams are really moving away from the old hierarchical view of leadership and authority and instead adopting a self-management perspective. If the emergent leader is effective, the team can then readily progress to the next phase of development as it becomes a tightly formed team.

for newly formed teams. Recognizing teams and individuals for good performance is always powerful, especially when the teams choose the recipients. Continued training in problem-solving steps, tools, and techniques is imperative. Managers need to push as many problem-solving opportunities as possible down to the team level. Finally, as team identity develops, teams develop social activities and display T-shirts, team names, logos, and other items that show off their identity. All of these are a sure sign that the team is moving into phase 4.

Phase 4: Tightly Formed Teams   The fourth phase of team implementation is when teams become tightly formed to the point that their internal focus can become detrimental to other teams and to the organization as a whole. Such teams are usually extremely confident of their ability to do everything. They are solving problems, managing their schedule and resources, and resolving internal conflicts. However, communication with external teams begins to diminish, the team covers up for underperforming members, and interteam rivalries can turn sour, leading to unhealthy competition.

To avoid the dangers of the intense team loyalty and isolation inherent in phase 4, managers need to make sure that teams continue to do the things that have enabled them to prosper thus far. First, teams need to keep the communication channels with other teams open through councils of rotating team representatives who meet regularly to discuss what works and what does not; teams who communicate and cooperate with other teams should be rewarded. At the Digital Equipment plant in Connecticut, team representatives meet weekly to share successes and failures so that all can avoid problems and improve the ways their teams operate.[25] Second, management needs to provide performance feedback through computer terminals in the work area that give up-to-date information on performance, or via regular feedback meetings. At TRW plants, management introduced peer performance appraisal at this stage of the team implementation process. It found that in phase 4, teams were ready to take on this administrative task but needed significant training in how to perform and communicate appraisals. Third, teams need to follow the previously developed plan to transfer authority and responsibility to the teams and to be sure that all team members have followed the plan to get training in all of the skills necessary to do the work of the team. By the end of phase 4, the team should be ready to take responsibility for managing itself.

Phase 5: Self-Managing Teams   Phase 5 is the end result of the months or years of planning and implementation. Mature teams are meeting or exceeding their performance goals. Team members are taking responsibility for team-related leadership functions. Managers and supervisors have withdrawn from the daily operations and are planning and providing counseling for teams. Probably most important, mature teams are flexible—taking on new ideas for improvement; making changes as needed to membership, roles, and tasks; and doing whatever it takes to meet the strategic objectives of the organization. Although the teams are mature and functioning quite well, several things need to be done to keep them on track. First and foremost, individuals and teams need to continue their training in job skills and team and interpersonal skills. Second, support systems need to be constantly improved to facilitate team development and productivity. Third, teams always need to improve their internal customer and supplier relationships within the organization. Partnerships among teams throughout the organization can help the internal teams continue to meet the needs of external customers.

ESSENTIAL TEAM ISSUES

This chapter has described the many benefits of teams and the process of changing to a team-based organization. Teams can be utilized in small and large organizations, on the shop floor and in offices, and in countries around the world. Teams must be initiated for performance-based business reasons, and proper planning and implementation strategies must be used. In this section we discuss two essential issues that cannot be overlooked as organizations move to a team-based setup: team performance and starting at the top. Another interesting team issue, norm conformity, which is relevant in professional sports, is discussed in the "Business of Ethics" box.

Team Performance

Organizations typically expect too much too soon when they implement teams. In fact, things often get worse before they get better.[26] Figure 10.2 shows how, shortly after implementation, team performance often declines and then rebounds to rise to the original levels and above. Management at Investors Diversified Services, a financial services firm in Minneapolis, Minnesota (and now a part of American Express), expected planning for team start-up to take three or four months. The actual planning took eight and a half months.[27] It often takes a year or more before performance levels return to at least their before-team levels. If teams are implemented without proper planning, their performance may never return to prior levels. The long lead time for improving performance can be discouraging to managers who reacted to the fad for teams and expected immediate returns.

The phases of implementation discussed in the previous sections correspond to key points on the team performance curve. At the start-up, performance is at its normal levels, although sometimes the anticipation of, and enthusiasm for, teams cause a slight increase in performance. In phase 2, reality and unrest, teams are often confused and frustrated with the training and lack of direction from top management to the point that actual performance may decline. In phase 3, leader-centered teams become more comfortable with the team idea and refocus on the work of the team. They once again have established leadership, although it is with an internal leader rather than an external manager or supervisor. Thus, their performance usually returns to at least their former levels. In phase 4, teams are beginning to experience the real potential of teamwork and are producing above their prior levels. Finally, in phase 5, self-managing teams are mature, flexible, and usually setting new records for performance.

Organizations changing to a team-based arrangement need to recognize the time and effort involved in making such a change. Hopes for immediate, positive results can lead to disappointment. The most rapid increases in performance occur between the leader-centered phase and the team-centered phase because teams have managed to get past the difficult, low-performance stages, have had a lot of training, and are ready to utilize their independence and freedom to make decisions about their own work. Team members are deeply committed to each other and to the success of the team. In phase 5, management needs to make sure that teams are focused on the strategic goals of the organization.

Figure 10.2 PERFORMANCE AND IMPLEMENTATION OF TEAMS

The team performance curve shows that performance initially drops as reality sets in, and team members experience frustration and unrest. However, performance soon increases and rises to record levels as the teams mature and become self-managing.

Reference: Reprinted by permission of Harvard Business School Press. From *The Wisdom of Teams: Creating the High Performance Organization* by Jon R. Katzenbach and Douglas K. Smith. Boston, MA, 1993, p. 84. Copyright by the Harvard Business School Publishing Corporation; all rights reserved.

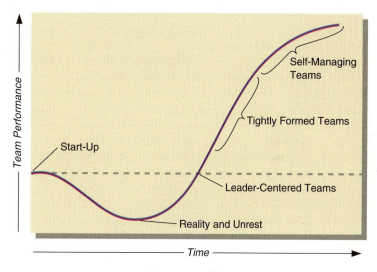

Start at the Top

The question of where to start in team implementation is really no issue at all. Change starts at the top in every successful team implementation. Top management has three important roles to play. First, top management must decide to go to a team-based organization for sound business performance-related reasons. A major cultural change cannot be made because it is the fad, because the boss went to a seminar on teams, or because a quick fix is needed. Second, top management is instrumental in communicating the reasons for the change to the rest of the organization. Third, top management has to support the change effort during the difficult periods. As discussed previously, performance usually goes down in the early phases of team implementation. Top-management support may involve verbal encouragement of team members, but organizational support systems for the teams are also needed. Examples of support systems for teams include more efficient inventory and scheduling systems, better hiring and selection systems, improved information systems, and appropriate compensation systems.

SYNOPSIS

Groups and teams are not the same. A team is a small number of people with complementary skills who are committed to a common purpose, common performance goals, and a common approach for which they hold themselves mutually accountable. Teams differ from traditional work groups in their job categories, authority, and reward systems.

Teams are used because they make sense for a specific organization. Organizational benefits include enhanced performance, employee benefits, and reduced costs, among others.

Many different types of teams exist in organizations. Quality circles are small groups of employees from the same work area who meet regularly to discuss and recommend solutions to workplace problems. Work teams perform the daily operations of the organization and make decisions about how to do the work. Problem-solving teams are temporarily established to solve a particular problem. Management teams consist of managers from various areas; these teams are relatively permanent and coach and counsel the new teams. Product development teams are teams assigned the task of developing a new product or service for the organization. Members of virtual teams usually meet via teleconferencing, may never actually sit in the same room together, and often have a fluid membership.

Planning the change entails all the activities leading to the decision to utilize teams and then preparing the organization for the initiation of teams. Essential steps include establishing leadership for the change, creating a steering committee, conducting a feasibility study, and making the go/no-go decision. After the decision to utilize teams has been made, preparations include clarifying the mission of the change, selecting the site for the first teams, preparing the design team, planning the transfer of authority, and drafting the preliminary plan.

Implementation includes five phases: start-up, reality and unrest, leader-centered teams, tightly formed teams, and self-managing teams. Implementation of teams is really a cultural change for the organization.

For teams to succeed, the change must start with top management, who must decide why the change is needed, communicate the need for the change, and support the change. Management must not expect too much too soon because team performance tends to decrease before it returns to prior levels and then increases to record levels.

DISCUSSION QUESTIONS

1. Why is it important to make a distinction between "group" and "team"? What kinds of behaviors might be different in these assemblages?
2. How are other organizational characteristics different for a team-based organization?
3. Some say that changing to a team-based arrangement "just makes sense" for organizations. What are the four primary reasons why this might be so?
4. If employees are happy working in the traditional boss-hierarchical organization, why should a manager even consider changing to a team-based organization?
5. How are the six types of teams related to each other?

6. Explain the circumstances under which a cross-functional team is useful in organizations.
7. Which type of team is the most common in organizations? Why?
8. Why is planning the change important in the implementation process?
9. What can happen if your organization prematurely starts building a team-based organization by clarifying the mission and then selecting the site for the first work teams?
10. What are two of the most important issues facing team-based organizations?

ORGANIZATIONAL BEHAVIOR CASE FOR DISCUSSION

TRACKING CARBON FOOTPRINTS ACROSS SCIENTIFIC BORDERS

If you're one of the world's 700 million richest people, you're probably a "high emitter" living a "carbon-intensive" lifestyle (at least statistically speaking). In plain English, because your lifestyle probably includes air travel, the use of a car, and a house to heat and cool, you're probably responsible for releasing more than your share of CO_2—carbon dioxide—into the earth's atmosphere. "We estimate that...half the world's emissions come from just 700 million people," explains Shoibal Chakravarty, lead author of a 2009 study conducted by researchers at Princeton University. "It's mischievous," admits coauthor Robert Socolow, "but it's meant to be a logjam-breaking concept," and the proposals for cutting CO_2 emissions offered by the Princeton team have been widely praised for the fairness that they inject into a debate that's been stalemated for nearly 20 years.

It all has to do with individual "carbon footprints" and the relative responsibilities of industrialized and developing nations in regulating individual emissions among their citizens. *Time* magazine named the "personal carbon footprint"—the team's metaphor for each individual's impact on climate through the release of CO_2 into the atmosphere—one of "The 50 Best Inventions of 2009," but for the purposes of this case, we want to focus less on the "invention" itself than on the process that produced it.

The research team's report, entitled "Sharing Global CO_2 Emission Reductions among One Billion High Emitters," appeared in the July 2009 *Proceedings of the National Academy of Sciences* under the names of six coauthors. Shoibal Chakravarty, a physicist specializing in CO_2 emissions, is a research associate at the Princeton Environmental Institute (PEI), an interdisciplinary center for environmental research and education. Also associated with PEI is Massimo Tavoni, an economist who studies international policies on climate change. Stephen Pacala, who's the director of PEI, is a professor of ecology and evolutionary biology who focuses on the interactions of climate and the global biosphere. Robert Socolow, a professor of mechanical and aerospace engineering, studies global carbon management. Ananth Chikkatur, of Harvard's Belfer Center for Science and International Affairs, is a physicist who specializes in energy policy and technology innovation.

> *"If you think of universities as trying to address problems, then it's natural that they should be engaged in broad, multidisciplinary research."*
> —ROBERTO PECCEI, VICE CHANCELLOR FOR RESEARCH, UCLA

Heleen de Coninck, a chemist, works on international climate policy and technology at the Energy Research Centre of the Netherlands.

Needless to say, the carbon footprint team was a diverse group in terms of academic discipline (not to mention nationality). Its innovative approach to the problem of CO_2 emissions—one which shows that it's possible to cut emissions and reduce poverty at the same time—resulted from an approach to high-level scientific problem solving that's typically called *interdisciplinary* or *multidisciplinary research*. Since at least the 1990s, the model of interdisciplinary collaboration among professional researchers has replaced the fanciful model of the lone scientist conducting arcane experiments in a laboratory located somewhere in the upper reaches of an old castle (or even an ivory tower). The global footprint study, says Pacala, "is an example of what Princeton does best. It represents a collaboration among young people from disparate disciplines—physics, economics, political science. ... The team," he stresses, "worked together to formulate a novel approach to a long-standing and intractable problem," and its interdisciplinary approach to that problem reflects the prevailing model for the study of today's most complex and daunting issues, such as AIDS, terrorism, and global climate change. "For any problem that has some importance today," explains Roberto Peccei, vice chancellor for research at UCLA,

> you find that, really, it doesn't fit neatly into biology or into chemistry or into law. It tends to have many ramifications. If you think of universities as trying to address problems, then it's natural that they should be engaged in broad, multidisciplinary research.

To determine the extent to which team-based research has supplanted individual research among academics, a group at Northwestern University examined nearly 20 million papers published over a period of five decades. They found that

> teams increasingly dominate solo authors in the production of knowledge. Research is increasingly done in teams across virtually all fields. Teams typically produce more highly cited research than

individuals do, and this advantage is increasing over time. Teams now also produce the exceptionally high-impact research, even where that distinction was once the domain of solo authors.

Not surprisingly, the shift from the individual to the team-based model of research has been most significant in the sciences, where there's been, says the Northwestern study, "a substantial shift toward collective research." One reason for the shift, suggest the authors, may be "the increasing capital intensity of research" in laboratory sciences, where the growth of collaboration has been particularly striking. The increasing tendency toward specialization may be another reason. As knowledge grows in a discipline, scientists tend to devote themselves to specialty areas, the discipline itself becomes fragmented into "finer divisions of labor," and studies of larger issues in the discipline thus require greater collaboration.

And what about collaboration that extends beyond the confines of academia? As it happens, Robert Socolow and Stephen Pacala, in addition to working on the carbon footprint team, are codirectors of the Carbon Mitigation Initiative (CMI), a partnership among Princeton, Ford, and BP, the world's third-largest oil company. BP picks up 75 percent of the tab for research whose goal, according to CMI's mission statement, is "a compelling and sustainable solution of the carbon and climate change problem." CMI seeks "a novel synergy across fundamental science, technological development, and business principles that accelerates the pace of discovery," and collaboration is essential to its work because it crosses the borders between scientific, technological, and business interests.

It's also crucial because CMI's research is geared toward what Socolow calls a "whole system" approach to the problem of reducing carbon emissions. "If BP takes a whole system view of the problem," explains Socolow, "and as a supplier pays attention to the use of its products and finds ways of improving their efficiency during the use phase, that may be the most important thing this company can do over the next 10 years to save carbon." A whole system approach, for example, may include research into a process called CCS, for *carbon capture and storage*, which involves capturing CO_2 emissions from a major source, such as a power plant, and storing it somewhere away from the atmosphere, perhaps in a deep geological formation, such as an oil field or a seam of coal. Accordingly, CMI is divided into research groups, including the Capture Group, which works on technologies for capturing emissions from fossil fuels, and the Storage Group, which investigates the potential risks of injecting CO_2 underground. Working through CMI, BP has been able to launch a CCS trial at a gas-development facility in Algeria.

Not surprisingly, research in such areas as CCS also requires that CMI itself be organized as a complex network of collaboration and teamwork. In addition to the Capture and Storage Groups, CMI maintains a Science Group to study and collect data on natural sources of carbon and the probable impact of emissions on climate in the future, and an Integration Group, which synthesizes the organization's findings and explores strategies for further research and development. CMI now supports more than 60 researchers from Princeton's faculties in geosciences, ecology and evolutionary biology, and civil and mechanical engineering, all of whom work with networks of international collaborators.

CASE QUESTIONS

1. In what sense was the carbon footprint team a *work team*? A *problem-solving team*? A *management team*? A *virtual team*?
2. In what sense is the Carbon Mitigation Initiative (CMI) a *group*, and in what sense is it better characterized as a *team*?
3. What's your experience with teamwork? Have you ever undertaken a solo project which, in retrospect, would have benefited from a team-based approach? If you've ever been part of a work or problem-solving team, explain why, in your opinion, it succeeded (or failed) at its appointed task(s).
4. Some researchers are wary about the nature of collaborations between academic and industry organizations, such as CMI. Why do you suppose this is so? What potential problems do you see? How can they best be avoided?

REFERENCES

Bryan Walsh, "Study: A Fairer Way to Cut Global CO_2 Emissions," *Time*, July 7, 2009, www.time.com on March 6, 2010; Douglas Fischer, "An Individual Carbon Cap for Every Man, Woman and Child?" *Daily Climate*, July 6, 2009, www.thedailygreen.com on March 6, 2010; "New Princeton Study May Help Allocate Carbon Emissions Responsibility among Nations," *Pollution Online*, July 13, 2009, www.pollutiononline.com on March 6, 2010; Shoibal Chakravarty et al., "Sharing Global CO_2 Emission Reductions among One Billion High Emitters," *Proceedings of the National Academy of Sciences*, vol. 106 (July 2009), www.pnas.org on March 6, 2010; Stuart Silverstein, "Teamwork, Not Rivalry, Marks New Era in Research," *Los Angeles Times*, November 3, 2004, www.artn.com on March 7, 2010; Stefan Wuchty et al., "The Increasing Dominance of Teams in Production of Knowledge," *Sciencexpress*, April 12, 2009, www.sciencexpress.org on March 7, 2010; "The Power of the Ivory Tower," *Horizon*, April 2005, www.sciencemag.org on March 6, 2010; Princeton University, "About the Carbon Mitigation Initiative," Carbon Mitigation Initiative, 2010, http://cmi.princeton.edu.

EXPERIENCING ORGANIZATIONAL BEHAVIOR

Team Problem Solving with the Fishbone Diagram

Introduction   The use of groups and teams is becoming more common in organizations throughout the world. The following exercise teaches you a problem-solving technique that can be effectively used by teams.

Instruction   Read "The Fishbone Instructions" that follow. Working in a small group, choose one of the topics for analysis. (Alternatively, your professor may assign topics to groups. You can also write your own topic but be sure that every student has some experience and understanding of the topic.) Perform the analysis and present your findings to the class.

Topics

a. Student parking on campus is inadequate.
b. Required courses are not offered at convenient, varied, or flexible times.
c. There are too few business elective courses offered.
d. There are not enough sections of required courses to meet student demand.
e. Some business courses have too many students in them to optimize leaning.
f. Faculty are not available for student assistance and office hours.
g. Students do not receive adequate counseling on academic matters and scheduling.

The structure of your completed fishbone diagram will look something like this.

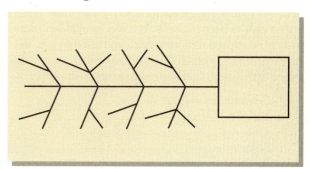

The Fishbone Instructions

1. Write the problem in the "head" of the fish.
2. Brainstorm the major causes of the problem and list them on the fish "bones."
3. Analyze each main cause and write in contributing factors on bone sub-branches.
4. Reach consensus on the one or two most important causes of the problem.
5. Explore ways to correct or remove the major cause(s).

Reference: Adapted from Linda Morable, *Exercises in Management,* Houghton Mifflin Company, Boston, Copyright © 2005, to accompany *Management,* 8th edition, by Ricky Griffin, Houghton Mifflin Company, Boston, Copyright © 2005.

BUILDING MANAGERIAL SKILLS

Exercise Overview   Groups and teams are becoming ever more important in organizations. This exercise will allow you to practice your conceptual skills as they apply to work teams in organizations.

   Exercise Background: A variety of highly effective groups exists outside the boundaries of typical business organizations. For example, each of the following represents a team:

1. A basketball team
2. An elite military squadron
3. A government policy group such as the presidential cabinet
4. A student planning committee

Exercise Task:

1. Identify an example of a real team, such as one just listed. Choose one team (1) that is not part of a normal business and (2) that you can argue is highly effective.
2. Determine the reasons for the team's effectiveness.
3. Determine how a manager could learn from this particular team and use its success determinants in a business setting.

SELF-ASSESSMENT EXERCISE

How Well Do You Add Up as a Team Member?

Think about a group or team that you've been a part of. Answer the following questions about the nature of your participation by selecting the option that's most accurate. There are no right or wrong answers. You may have to be "hypothetical" in responding to a few items, and in some cases, you might have to rely on "composite" answers reflecting your experience in more than one group or teamwork setting.

1. I offer information and opinions . . .
   a. Very Frequently
   b. Frequently
   c. Sometimes
   d. Rarely
   e. Never
2. I summarize what's happening in the group . . .
   a. Very Frequently
   b. Frequently
   c. Sometimes
   d. Rarely
   e. Never
3. When there's a problem, I try to identify what's happening . . .
   a. Very Frequently
   b. Frequently
   c. Sometimes
   d. Rarely
   e. Never
4. I start the group working . . .
   a. Very Frequently
   b. Frequently
   c. Sometimes
   d. Rarely
   e. Never
5. I suggest directions that the group can take . . .
   a. Very Frequently
   b. Frequently
   c. Sometimes
   d. Rarely
   e. Never

6. I listen actively . . .
   a. Very Frequently
   b. Frequently
   c. Sometimes
   d. Rarely
   e. Never
7. I give positive feedback to other members of the group . . .
   a. Very Frequently
   b. Frequently
   c. Sometimes
   d. Rarely
   e. Never
8. I compromise . . .
   a. Very Frequently
   b. Frequently
   c. Sometimes
   d. Rarely
   e. Never
9. I help relieve tension . . .
   a. Very Frequently
   b. Frequently
   c. Sometimes
   d. Rarely
   e. Never
10. I talk . . .
   a. Very Frequently
   b. Frequently
   c. Sometimes
   d. Rarely
   e. Never
11. I help to ensure that meeting times and places are arranged . . .
   a. Very Frequently
   b. Frequently
   c. Sometimes
   d. Rarely
   e. Never

12. I try to observe what's happening in the group . . .
   a. Very Frequently
   b. Frequently
   c. Sometimes
   d. Rarely
   e. Never
13. I try to help solve problems . . .
   a. Very Frequently
   b. Frequently
   c. Sometimes
   d. Rarely
   e. Never
14. I take responsibility for ensuring that tasks are completed . . .
   a. Very Frequently
   b. Frequently
   c. Sometimes
   d. Rarely
   e. Never
15. I like the group to be having a good time . . .
   a. Very Frequently
   b. Frequently
   c. Sometimes
   d. Rarely
   e. Never

How to score: Award yourself points according to the values shown in the following table. An answer of "b" on Question 5, for example, is worth 1 point, while a "b" on Question 6 is worth 3 points. To get your total score, add up all the numbers in your "Score" column.

Question	a	b	c	d	e	Score
1	1	2	3	2	1	
2	1	2	3	2	1	
3	1	2	3	2	1	
4	2	2	3	1	0	
5	0	1	3	1	0	
6	3	3	2	1	0	
7	3	3	2	1	0	
8	2	3	3	1	0	
9	1	2	3	1	0	
10	0	0	3	2	1	
11	2	3	3	1	0	
12	3	3	2	1	0	
13	2	3	3	1	0	
14	2	2	3	1	0	
15	1	1	2	1	1	
TOTAL						

41–45 = Very effective team person

35–40 = Effective team person

Under 35 = Person who probably needs to work on his or her teamwork skills

REFERENCE

Adapted from University of South Australia, "Test Your Effectiveness as a Team Member." *"Working in Teams" Online Workshop*. Handout: "Teamwork Skills Questionnaire." March 24, 2010 at www.unisanet.unisa.edu.au.

COMMUNICATION IN ORGANIZATIONS

CHAPTER LEARNING OBJECTIVES

After studying this chapter you should be able to:

- Discuss the nature of communication in organizations.
- Identify and describe the primary methods of communication.
- Describe the communication process.
- Note how information technology affects communication.
- Identify and discuss the basic kinds of communication networks.
- Discuss how communication can be managed in organizations.

While communication has always been an important process in organizations, the growing sophistication of both electronic communication and the internet have combined to make it more important than ever before. Indeed, information has become such a commodity that fact-checking firms like Snopes .com have sprung up to help people verify the truthfulness of information they pick up online.

You Can't Make This Stuff Up

"You can't make this stuff up. Well, I guess you could."

—BARBARA MIKKELSON, COFOUNDER OF SNOPES.COM

Let's say that there was a time when, like about 15 percent of all Americans, your connectivity needs required you to be on your cell phone for more than 1,000 minutes per month, or just over 30 minutes a day. Like just about everybody else in the same segment of the population, you were happy to report that both your business affairs and your personal life had improved significantly. Then you ran across an article in a British Internet magazine called *Wymsey Village*. Entitled "Weekend Eating: Mobile Cooking," it showed you how to cook an egg using

two cell phones. At first, you marveled at what they had in fact thought of next, but not long afterward, someone emailed you a copy of an article in which, complete with photographs, two Russian journalists explained how they'd replicated the process by propping a hard-boiled egg between two activated cell phones for an hour. This time, however, the article ended on an ominous note: "If the microwave radiation emitted by the mobile phones is capable of modifying the proteins in an egg," concluded the authors, "imagine what it can do to the proteins in our brains." At that point, you ditched your cell phone and had your landline reinstalled (although you routinely use the speakerphone and stay as far away as possible from the unit itself). Last but not least, you did your civic duty by forwarding both articles to everybody on your email list.

Perhaps you should have "Snopsed" the information that you were relying on when you abandoned your cell phone and urged everybody you knew to do the same. Had you queried the fact-checkers at Snopes.com—and a lot of people did—you would have found that the *Wymsey Village* article was a spoof and the article from the Russian tabloid a hoax. "The stories that rise the most," says Snopes cofounder David Mikkelson, "are those that pose a threat to readers....The things that take off have to hit a nerve we're all thinking about." It's not that hard to debunk them, Mikkelson adds, if you "start off with the thought that extraordinary claims require extraordinary proof," but even so, he admits, "most rumors never die completely." The *Wymsey Village* "article," for example, is still out there, and the unmasked author's only regret "is that I didn't get a dime for every hit on that page."

Snopes.com started out in 1995 as a hobby for David Mikkelson and his wife Barbara, who share a passion for urban legends. The site, which they operate from their California home, now attracts more than 6 million visitors a month. "We quickly became the place where people mailed anything that was questionable," explains David. "If they needed verification, they'd ask us." A tech columnist for the *New York Times* has called Snopes "the Internet's authority on emailed myths," and Richard Roeper, a film critic and amateur myth-buster, declares that "Snopes is like having your own army of fact-checkers sniffing out a million wacko leads."

"Most of what we deal with," says David Mikkelson, "exists outside traditional media," but he's quick to point out that traditional media sources could perform much the same service as Snopes. "Our approach," he explains, "is going to be that something outrageous is going to be a hoax. But that's unfortunately not what a lot of people in the media do. They say, 'This is real, and we'll see if there's proof it isn't.'" Take, for instance, the famous "Hunting for Bambi" case, in which a Las Vegas TV station did a four-part story on a local outfit offering hunters the chance to shoot paintballs at naked women for a fee of $10,000. "In this case," reports Mikkelson,

> we [said] is there anything that demonstrates it's real. The first thing you notice is that it's rather improbable that naked women wearing no protection whatsoever, not even helmets or goggles, will run around in front of guys with unmodified paintball guns with nothing more than a vague promise they won't shoot above the waist.

"You can't make this stuff up," adds Barbara Mikkelson, who pauses before adding, "Well, I guess you could. But if you do, I'm sure we'll get to the bottom of it."

The advent of the Internet, of course, is a key factor in the growth of the hoax and misinformation business—but the Internet, says David, "has made it easier to debunk hoaxes while at the same time making it easier to perpetrate them....Really widespread Internet-based hoaxes," he adds, "are fairly uncommon. Most of them are just, 'I'm going to put up this gag and see if anyone falls for it.' Having someone go through the time and effort to do a really thought-out hoax is pretty rare, maybe happening once or twice a year." Mikkelson admits that "there's a lot on the Internet that you can't trust," but he's also well aware that "there's a lot on your bookshelf and the library shelves that you can't trust either. . . . There's never been a medium that you could inherently trust. You still have to look at who's telling you this. . . . The concept hasn't changed. . . . Nothing's really changed but the technology."

Fortunately, the Mikkelsons aren't alone in the online fact-checking business. In October 2008, an email began circulating under the head "PLEASE READ!!!!!!! VERY IMOPRTANT—SNOPES EXPOSED." The anonymous emailer proceeded to reveal that Snopes was "owned by a flaming liberal . . . in the tank for Obama" and warned everyone receiving his urgent news that "you cannot and should not trust Snopes.com . . . for anything that remotely resembles the truth." In the spring of 2009, FactCheck.org, which describes itself as "a nonpartisan, nonprofit 'consumer advocate' for voters that aims to reduce the level of deception and confusion in U.S. politics," set out to investigate the allegations against Snopes. Researchers confirmed that Barbara Mikkelson is a nonvoting Canadian citizen and discovered that David Mikkelson, though now an independent, had last registered his party affiliation as Republican. The anti-Snopes email, concluded the FactCheck report, "contains a number of false claims about the urban-legend-busting Snopes.com and its proprietors," and, as for political bias, "we reviewed a sampling of their political offerings, including rumors about George W. Bush, Sarah Palin, and Barack Obama, and we found them to be utterly poker-faced."

It would appear, then, that it is indeed safe to do your fact checking at Snopes.com, where you'll continue to find thorough reviews of widely circulating information—and misinformation—of all kinds. For the record, the bad (but true) news is that Bill Gates is not giving away cash to anyone who forwards a certain email. The good (and true) news is that terrorists are not paying exorbitant prices on eBay for UPS uniforms to be used in some as-yet-unfathomed plot.

Hoaxes, of course, aren't the only source of online misinformation or mischief. Sometimes it's the result of what Snopes.com calls "slacktivism"—passing on rumors, particularly warnings, without checking to see if there's any truth to them. For an example, see the *Technology* box entitled "The Medical Uses of Viral Email: on page 312."

What Do You Think?

1. The Internet has clearly become a major source of information for many people. To what extent do you routinely "trust" that the information you obtain from the Internet is true?

2. Have you had any instances in which you have received or seen emails purporting to have a true inside story on something (such as the cell phone and egg story) only to discover they are false?

References: "Oeuf the Wall," *Snopes.com,* March 17, 2009, www.snopes.com on March 10, 2010; "Weekend Eating: Mobile Cooking," *Wymsey Weekend,* 2008, www.wymsey.co.uk on March 10, 2010; David Hochman, "Rumor Detectives: True Story or Online Hoax?" *Reader's Digest,* April 2009, www.rd.com on March 10, 2010; "For Snopes.com, Debunking the Bambi Hoax Was All in a Day's Work," *Online Journalism Review,* July 31, 2003, www.ojr.org on March 10, 2010; David Pogue, "Tech Tips for the Basic Computer User," *New York Times,* October 2, 2008, http://pogue.blogs.nytimes.com on March 11, 2010; Viveca Novak, "Snopes.com," *FactCheck.org,* April 10, 2009, www.factcheck.org on March 11, 2010.

Communication is something that most of us take for granted—we have been communicating for so long that we really pay little attention to the actual process. Even at work, we often focus primarily on doing our jobs and pay little attention to how we communicate about those jobs. However, since methods of communication play such a pervasive role in affecting behavior in organizations and represent another vital underpinning of interpersonal processes, we need to pay more attention to the processes that effectively link what we do to others in the organization.

In this chapter, we focus on interpersonal communication and information processing. First, we discuss the importance of communication in organizations and some important aspects of international communication. Next, we describe the methods of organizational communication and examine the basic communication process. Then we examine the potential effects of computerized information technology and telecommunications. Next, we explore the development of communication networks in organizations. Finally, we discuss several common problems of organizational communication and methods of managing communication.

THE NATURE OF COMMUNICATION IN ORGANIZATIONS

Communication is the social process in which two or more parties exchange information and share meaning. Communication has been studied from many perspectives. In this section, we provide an overview of the complex and dynamic communication process and discuss some important issues relating to international communication in organizations.

The Purposes of Communication in Organizations

Communication among individuals and groups is vital in all organizations. Some of the purposes of organizational communication are shown in Figure 11.1. The primary purpose is to achieve coordinated action.[1] Just as the human nervous system responds to stimuli and coordinates responses by sending messages to the various parts of the body, communication coordinates the actions of the parts of an organization. Without communication, an organization would be merely a collection of individual workers doing separate tasks. Organizational action would lack coordination and would be oriented toward individual rather than organizational goals.

Figure 11.1 THREE PURPOSES OF ORGANIZATIONAL COMMUNICATION

Achieving coordinated action is the prime purpose of communication in organizations. Sharing information properly and expressing emotions help achieve coordinated action.

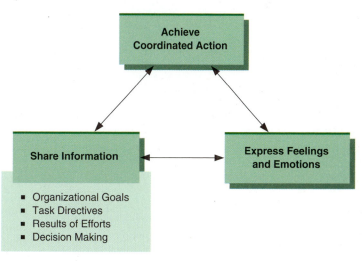

A second purpose of communication is information sharing. The most important information relates to organizational goals, which give members a sense of purpose and direction. Another information-sharing function of communication is to give

Communication is the social process in which two or more parties exchange information and share meaning.

specific task directions to individuals. Whereas information on organizational goals gives employees a sense of how their activities fit into the overall picture, task communication tells them what their job duties are (and are not). Employees must also receive information on the results of their efforts, as in performance appraisals.

Communication is essential to the decision-making process as well, as we discuss in Chapter 8. Information and information sharing are needed to define problems, generate and evaluate alternatives, implement decisions, and control and evaluate results. Finally, communication expresses feelings and emotions. Organizational communication is far from merely a collection of facts and figures. People in organizations, like people anywhere else, often need to communicate emotions such as happiness, anger, displeasure, confidence, and fear.

Communication Across Cultures

Communication is an element of interpersonal relations that obviously is affected by the international environment, partly because of language issues and partly because of coordination issues.

Language Differences in languages are compounded by the fact that the same word can mean different things in different cultures. For example, Chevrolet once tried to export a line of cars to Latin America that it called the "Nova" in the United States, but then found that "no va" means "doesn't go" in Spanish—not the best name for an automobile! Similarly, just as KFC was about to launch a major new advertising campaign in China a local manager pointed out that the firm's long-time American slogan "Finger Lickin' Good" meant "Eat Your Fingers Off" when translated directly into Chinese. Fortunately for KFC it had time to revise its slogan before the new advertising campaign was started. On a more positive note, Akio Morita and his business partner Masaru Ibuka named their firm "Sony" because their research found that the word has no specific meaning in any language.

Elements of nonverbal communication also vary across cultures. Colors and body language can convey quite a different message in one culture than in another. For example, the American sign for "OK" (making a loop with thumb and first finger) is considered rude in Spain and vulgar in Brazil. Managers should be forewarned that they can take nothing for granted in dealing with people from other cultures. They must take the time to become as fully acquainted as possible with the verbal and nonverbal languages of a culture. And indeed, new forms of communication technology such as email are actually changing language itself.

To see how eBay has encountered difficulties in translating the online-auction business into the consumer languages of other countries, go to the *Globalization* box on page 297.

JEFF MORGAN 10/ALAMY

The world of international business has provided numerous humorous examples of blunders associated with translating product names into a foreign language only to discover the foreign translation meant something quite different from what was intended. For instance, when Imperial Oil of Canada introduced its gasoline brand Esso in Japan, it quickly discovered that the word Esso could easily be misinterpreted as meaning "stalled car"—not a winning name for gas! When Akio Morita and his business partner Masaru Ibuka were launching their electronics firm, they carefully selected the name Sony because the word had no specific meaning in other languages.

GLOBALIZATION

eBay Communicates with the World

eBay communicates globally through 38 international websites, including countries from the Americas, Asia, and Europe. About $3.9 billion, or 51 percent of the firm's total sales, comes from outside of the United States. That number is up from just 15 percent in 2005.

International eBay websites look the same. On each site, the navigation toolbar lists categories of items. Categories are similar, including items such as computers, autos, and jewelry. In 2002, eBay purchased PayPal, which manages currency translation and money transfer for international buyers and sellers.

In other aspects, the websites are tailored to local communication needs—Bollywood memorabilia on eBay India, for example. While sites for Italy, Korea, and Argentina are translated into their country's primary language, sites for countries with numerous local languages, such as India and the Philippines, use English. Each site lists prices in local currency.

eBay is aggressively expanding overseas, but is not equally successful everywhere. In Japan, for example, eBay entered the online auction business late. "When we arrived, the 800-pound gorilla was already positioned," says former

> *"When we arrived, the 800-pound gorilla was already positioned."*
> —MERLE OKAWARA, PRESIDENT, EBAY JAPAN

eBay Japan president Merle Okawara. The company ceased Japanese operations in 2003. eBay is considering exiting China, a market dominated by competitor Yahoo! as well as dozens of local companies. And while eBay would like to enter large, untapped global markets in Indonesia, Vietnam, and Thailand, these countries have strong restrictions on online payments.

One of the difficulties may lie in the eBay top-management team. The heads of international eBay sites are often local managers. Yet the headquarters team in San Jose, California, responsible for overall company strategy and operations, has only one international member, Rajiv Dutta, the chief financial officer.

The online auction industry continues to attract a wide variety of strong competitors. Focusing on communication with diverse international users can lead eBay to increased success and competitive victory.

References: eBay, "Global Trade," "Welcome to eBay," www.ebay.com on April 20, 2005; Bambi Francisco, "All Eyes on eBay," *Market Watch*, www.marketwatch.com on April 20, 2005; "eBay Profits Miss the Mark," *CNN Money*, January 19, 2005, http://money.cnn.com on March 12, 2010; Ken Belson, "How Yahoo! Japan Beat eBay at Its Own Game," *BusinessWeek*, June 4, 2001, www.businessweek.com on March 12, 2010; Troy Wolverton, "eBay Readies Execs for Merger," *CNET News*, September 5, 2002, http://news.cnet.com on March 12, 2010.

Coordination　International communication is closely related to issues of coordination. For example, an American manager who wants to speak with his or her counterpart in Hong Kong, Singapore, Rome, or London must contend not only with language differences but also with a time difference of many hours. When the American manager needs to talk on the telephone, the Hong Kong executive may be home asleep. Consequently, organizations are employing increasingly innovative methods for coordinating their activities in scattered parts of the globe. Merrill Lynch, for example, has its own satellite-based telephone network to monitor and participate in the worldwide money and financial markets. And of course, the Internet makes it easier than ever to communicate across different parts of the world.

METHODS OF COMMUNICATION

The three primary methods of communicating in organizations are written, oral, and nonverbal. Often the methods are combined. Considerations that affect the choice of method include the audience (whether it is physically present), the nature of the message (its urgency or secrecy), and the costs of transmission.[2] Figure 11.2 shows various forms each method can take.

Written Communication

Organizations typically produce a great deal of written communication of many kinds. A letter is a formal means of communicating with an individual, generally someone outside the organization. Email is probably the most common form of written communication in organizations today. The office memorandum, or memo, is also still very common. Memos usually are addressed to a person or group inside the organization. They tend to deal with a single topic and are more impersonal (as they often are destined to reach more than one person) but less formal than letters. Most email is similar to the traditional memo, although it is even less formal.

Other common forms of written communication include reports, manuals, and forms. Reports generally summarize the progress or results of a project and often provide information to be used in decision making. Manuals have various functions in organizations. Instruction manuals tell employees how to operate machines; policy and procedures manuals inform them of organizational rules; operations manuals describe how to perform tasks and respond to work-related problems. Forms are standardized documents on which to report information. As such, they represent attempts to make communication more efficient and information more accessible. A performance appraisal form is an example. We should also note that although many of these forms of written communication have historically been used in a paper-based environment, they are increasingly being put on websites and intranets in many companies today.

Oral Communication

The most prevalent form of organizational communication is oral. Oral communication takes place everywhere—in informal conversations, in the process of doing work, in meetings of groups and task forces, and in formal speeches and presentations. Recent studies identified oral communication skills as the number one criterion for hiring new college graduates.[3] Business school leaders have also been urged by industry to develop better communication skills in their graduates.[4] Even in Europe, employers have complained that the number one problem with current graduates is

Figure 11.2 **METHODS OF COMMUNICATION IN ORGANIZATIONS**

The three methods of communication in organizations are related to each other. Each one supplements the other, although each can also stand alone.

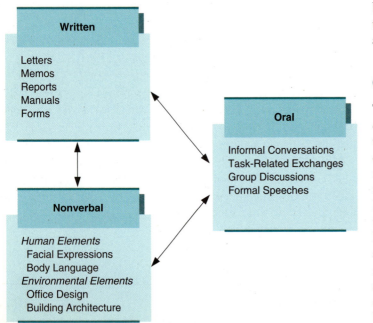

the lack of oral communication skills, citing cultural factors and changes in the educational process as primary causes.[5]

Oral forms of communication are particularly powerful because they include not only speakers' words but also their changes in tone, pitch, speed, and volume. As listeners, people use all of these cues to understand oral messages. Try this example with a friend or work colleague. Say this sentence several times, each time placing the emphasis on a different word: "The boss gave Joe a raise." See how the meaning changes depending on the emphasis! Moreover, receivers interpret oral messages in the context of previous communications and, perhaps, the reactions of other receivers. (Try saying another sentence before saying the phrase about the boss—such as "Joe is so lazy" or "Joe is such a good worker.") Quite often the top management of an organization sets the tone for oral communication throughout the organization.

The popular voice mail has all the characteristics of traditional verbal communication except that there is no feedback. The sender just leaves a message on the machine or network with no feedback or confirmation that the message was, or will be, received. With no confirmation, the sender does not know for sure whether the message will be received as he or she intended it. Therefore, it may be wise for the receiver of a voice mail to quickly leave a message on the sender's voice mail telling that the original message was received. But then the "great voice mail phone tag" is on at its worst! Also, the receiver then has an excuse in the event that something goes wrong later and can always say that a return message was left on the sender's voice mail! The receiver could also pass the blame by saying that no such voice message was received. The lack of confirmation (or two-way communication) can lead to several problems, as will be discussed in later sections of this chapter.

Nonverbal Communication

Nonverbal communication includes all the elements associated with human communication that are not expressed orally or in writing. Sometimes nonverbal communication conveys more meaning than words do. Human elements of nonverbal communication include facial expressions and physical movements, both conscious and unconscious. Facial expressions have been categorized as (1) interest-excitement, (2) enjoyment-joy, (3) surprise-startle, (4) distress-anguish, (5) fear-terror, (6) shame-humiliation, (7) contempt-disgust, and (8) anger-rage. The eyes are the most expressive component of the face.

Physical movements and "body language" are also highly expressive human elements. Body language includes both actual movement and body positions during communication. The handshake is a common form of body language. Other examples include making eye contact, which expresses a willingness to communicate; sitting on the edge of a chair, which may indicate nervousness or anxiety; and sitting back with arms folded, which may convey an unwillingness to continue the discussion.

Environmental elements such as buildings, office space, and furniture can also convey messages. A spacious office, expensive draperies, plush carpeting, and elegant furniture can combine to remind employees or visitors that they are in the office of the president and CEO of the firm. On the other hand, the small metal desk set in the middle of the shop floor accurately communicates the organizational rank of a first-line supervisor. Thus, office arrangements convey status, power, and prestige and create an atmosphere for doing business. The physical setting can also be instrumental in the development of communication networks because a centrally located person can more easily control the flow of task-related information.

As electronic communication has become more widespread, nonverbal elements are also commonly used there as well. For instance, adding electronic characters to indicate humor or unhappiness can help the receiver better appreciate the intended meaning of an email. An email that reads "You're fired," for example, followed quickly by a "smiley face" has a much different meaning than just the words alone.

THE COMMUNICATION PROCESS

Communication is a social process in which two or more parties exchange information and share meaning. The process is social because it involves two or more people. It is a two-way process and takes place over time rather than instantaneously. The communication process illustrated in Figure 11.3 shows a loop between the source and the receiver.[6] Note the importance of the feedback portion of the loop; upon receiving the message, the receiver responds with a message to the source to verify the communication. Each element of the basic communication process is important. If one part is faulty, the message may not be communicated as it was intended. A simple organizational example might be when a manager attempts to give direction to an employee regarding the order in which to perform two tasks. (We refer to this example again in later discussions.) The manager wants to send a message and have the employee understand precisely the meaning she intends. Each part of the communication process is described next.

Source

The **source** is the individual, group, or organization interested in communicating something to another party. In group or organizational communication, an individual may send the message on behalf of the organization. The source is responsible for preparing the message, encoding it, and entering it into the transmission medium. In some cases, the receiver chooses the source of information, as when a decision maker

> The **source** is the individual, group, or organization interested in communicating something to another party.

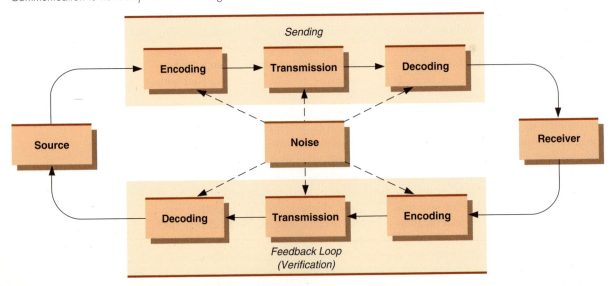

𝒥igure 11.3   THE COMMUNICATION PROCESS

The communication process is a loop that connects the sender and the receiver and operates in both directions. Communication is not complete until the original sender knows that the receiver understands the message.

seeks information from trusted and knowledgeable individuals.[7] The source in organizational communication is often the manager giving directions to employees.

Encoding

Encoding is the process by which the message is translated from an idea or thought into symbols that can be transmitted. The symbols may be words, numbers, pictures, sounds, or physical gestures and movements. In a simple example, the manager may use words in English as the symbols, usually spoken or written. The source must encode the message in symbols that the receiver can decode properly; that is, the source and the receiver must attach the same meaning to the symbols. When we use the symbols of a common language, we assume those symbols have the same meaning to everyone who uses them. However, the inherent ambiguity of symbol systems can lead to decoding errors. In verbal communication, for example, some words have different meanings for different people. Parents and children often use the same word, but the differences in their positions and ages may lead them to interpret words quite differently. If a manager only speaks Spanish and an employee only speaks German, the message is unlikely to be understood. The meanings of words used by the sender may differ depending on the nonverbal cues, such as facial expression, that the sender transmits along with them.

Transmission

Transmission is the process through which the symbols that carry the message are sent to the receiver. The **medium** is the channel, or path, of transmission. The medium for face-to-face conversation is sound waves. The same conversation conducted over the telephone involves not only sound waves but also electrical impulses and the lines that connect the two phones. To tell the employee in what order to perform tasks, the manager could tell the employee face-to-face or use the telephone, a memo, email, or voice mail.

Communications media range from interpersonal media, such as talking or touching, to mass media, such as newspapers, magazines, or television broadcasts. Different media have different capacities for carrying information. For example, a face-to-face conversation generally has more carrying capacity than a letter because it allows the transmission of more than just words. In addition, the medium can help determine the effect the message has on the receiver. Calling a prospective client on the telephone to make a business proposal is a more personal approach than sending a letter and is likely to elicit a different response. It is important that a sender choose the medium that is most likely to correspond to the type of message that needs to be sent and understood.

Decoding

Decoding is the process by which the receiver of the message interprets its meaning. The receiver uses knowledge and experience to interpret the symbols of the message; in some situations, he or she may consult an authority such as a dictionary or a code book. Up to this point, the receiver has been relatively inactive, but the receiver becomes more active in the decoding phase. The meaning the receiver attaches to the symbols may be the same as—or different from—the meaning intended by the source. If the meanings differ, of course, communication breaks down, and misunderstanding is likely. In our example, if the employee does not understand the language or a particular word, then the employee will not comprehend the same meaning as the sender (manager) and may do the tasks in the wrong order or not do them at all.

Encoding is the process by which the message is translated from an idea or thought into transmittable symbols.

Transmission is the process through which the symbols that represent the message are sent to the receiver.

The **medium** is the channel, or path, through which the message is transmitted.

Decoding is the process by which the receiver of the message interprets its meaning.

Receiver

The **receiver** of the message may be an individual, a group, an organization, or an individual acting as the representative of a group. The receiver decides whether to decode the message, whether to make an effort to understand it, and whether to respond. Moreover, the intended receiver may not get the message at all whereas an unintended receiver might get it, depending on the medium and the symbols used by the source and the attention level of potential receivers. Also, an employee may share the same language (know the symbols) used by the manager but may not want to get the sender's meaning.

The key skill for proper reception of the message is good listening. The receiver may not concentrate on the sender, the message, or the medium such that the message is lost. Listening is an active process that requires as much concentration and effort from the receiver as sending the message does for the sender. The expression of emotions by the sender and receiver enters into the communication process at several points. First, the emotions may be part of the message, entering into the encoding process. For example, if the manager's directions are encoded with a sense of emotional urgency—for example, if they are given with a high-pitched or loud voice—the employee may move quickly to follow the directions. However, if the message is urgent, but the manager's tone of voice is low and does not send urgent signals, employees may not engage in quick action. Second, as the message is decoded, the receiver may let his or her emotions perceive a message different from what the sender intended. Third, emotion-filled feedback from the intended receiver can cause the sender to modify her or his subsequent message.

Feedback

Feedback is the receiver's response to the message. Feedback verifies the message by telling the source whether the receiver received and understood the message. The feedback may be as simple as a phone call from the prospective client expressing interest in the business proposal, or as complex as a written brief on a complicated point of law sent from an attorney to a judge. In our example, the employee can respond to the manager's directions by a verbal or written response indicating that he or she does or does not understand the message. Feedback could also be nonverbal, as when, in our example, the employee does not do either task. With typical voice mail, the feedback loop is missing, which can lead to many communication problems.

Noise

Noise is any disturbance in the communication process that interferes with or distorts communication. Noise can be introduced at virtually any point in the communication process. The principal type, called **channel noise**, is associated with the medium.[8] Radio static and "ghost" images on television are examples of channel noise, as is an email virus. When noise interferes in the encoding and decoding processes, poor encoding and decoding can result. An employee may not hear the directions given by the manager owing to noisy machinery on the shop floor or competing input from other people. Emotions that interfere with an intended communication may also be considered a type of noise.

Effective communication occurs when information or meaning has been shared by at least two people. Therefore, communication must include the response from the receiver back to the sender. The sender cannot know if the message has been conveyed as intended if there is no feedback from the receiver, as when we leave voice mail.

The **receiver** is the individual, group, or organization that perceives the encoded symbols; the receiver may or may not decode them to try to understand the intended message.

Feedback is the process in which the receiver returns a message to the sender that indicates receipt of the message.

Noise is any disturbance in the communication process that interferes with or distorts communication.

Channel noise is a disturbance in communication that is primarily a function of the medium.

Both parties are responsible for the effectiveness of the communication. The evolution of new technology in recent years presents novel problems in ensuring that communications work as sender and receiver expect them to.

ELECTRONIC INFORMATION PROCESSING AND TELECOMMUNICATIONS

Communications-related changes in the workplace are occurring at a rapid clip. Many recent innovations are based on new technologies—computerized information processing systems, telecommunication systems, the Internet, organizational intranets and extranets, and various combinations of these technologies. Managers send and receive memos and other documents to and from one person or a group scattered around the world from their computers using the Internet, and they can do so in their cars or via their notebook computers and cellular phones on the commuter train. Wireless devices such as smart phones and Wi-Fi hotspots are making these activities even more commonplace. Indeed, many employees telecommute from home rather than going to the office every day. And whole new industries are developing around information storage, transmission, and retrieval that were not even dreamed of a few years ago.

The "office of the future" is here, but it just may not be in a typical office building. Every office now has a facsimile (fax) machine, a copier, and personal computers, most of them linked into a single integrated system and to numerous databases and electronic mail systems. Automobile companies advertise that their cars and trucks have equipment for your cellular telephone, computer, and fax machine. The electronic office links managers, clerical employees, professional workers, sales personnel—and often suppliers and customers as well—in a worldwide communication network that uses a combination of computerized data storage, retrieval, and transmission systems.

Noise is a disturbance in the communication process that interferes with or distorts communication. Increasingly, noise refers to things like dropped cell phone calls, misdirected emails, computer crashes, and network outages. But sometimes the traditional version of noise is still a problem. Take these two construction managers, for example. Background noise from construction equipment is making it difficult for them to talk. To compensate, they are standing close together, talking loudly, and using gestures to reinforce their verbal dialogue.

CHARLES THATCHER/STONE/GETTY IMAGES

In fact, the computer-integrated organization is becoming commonplace. Ingersol Milling Machine of Rockford, Illinois, boasts a totally computer-integrated operation in which all major functions—sales, marketing, finance, distribution, and manufacturing—exchange operating information quickly and continuously via computers. For example, product designers can send specifications directly to machines on the factory floor, and accounting personnel receive online information about sales, purchases, and prices instantaneously. The computer system parallels and greatly speeds up the entire process.[9]

Computers are facilitating the increase in telecommuting across the United States and reducing the number of trips people make to the office to get work done. Several years ago IBM provided many of its employees with notebook computers and told them not to come to the office but instead to use the computers to work out in the field and interface with the firm electronically.[10] Other companies, such as Motorola and AT&T, have also encouraged such telecommuting by employees. Employees report increased productivity, less fatigue caused by commuting, reduced commuting expenses, and increased personal freedom. In addition, telecommuting may reduce air pollution and overcrowding. Some employees have reported, however, that they miss the social interaction of the office. Some managers have also expressed concerns about the quantity and quality of the work telecommuting employees do when away from the office.

Research conducted among office workers using a new electronic office system indicated that attitudes toward the system were generally favorable. On the other hand, other research also suggests that a reduction of face-to-face meetings may depersonalize the office. Some observers are also concerned that companies are installing electronic systems with little consideration for the social structures of the office. As departments rely more heavily on computerized information systems, the activities of work groups throughout the organization are likely to become more interdependent, a situation that may alter power relationships among the groups. Most employees quickly learn the system of power, politics, authority, and responsibility in the office. A radical change in work and personal relationships caused by new office technology may disrupt normal ways of accomplishing tasks, thereby reducing productivity. A related problem may occur when an entire network goes out of service, causing most work in an organization to come to a halt. Other potential problems include information overload, loss of records in a "paperless" office, and the dehumanizing consequences of using electronic equipment. In effect, new information processing and transmission technologies mean new media, symbols, message transmission methods, and networks for organizational communication.

The real increases in organizational productivity due to information technology may come from the ability to communicate in new and different ways rather than from simply speeding up existing communication patterns. For example, to remain competitive in a very challenging global marketplace, companies will need to be able to generate, disseminate, and implement new ideas more effectively. In effect, organizations will become "knowledge-based" learning organizations that are continually generating new ideas to improve themselves. This can only occur when expert knowledge is communicated and available throughout the organization. FedEx credits its highly developed and integrated internal and external communications networks as being a cornerstone of its long-term success.[11]

One of these new ways of communicating is idea sharing, or knowledge sharing, by sharing information on what practices work best. A computer-based system is necessary to store, organize, and then make available to others the best practices from throughout the company.[12] For example, Eli Lilly, a large pharmaceutical company, uses a company-wide intranet for all of its sixteen thousand employees. This system makes available internal email, corporate policies, and corporate directories and enables information sharing throughout the organization.[13] Electronic information technology is, therefore, speeding up existing communication and developing new types of organizational communication processes with potential new benefits and problems for managers.

KEN SEET/FLAME/CORBIS

Technology has made it easier—and therefore much more common—for people to work remotely. Indeed, many people today routinely work from home and/or while they are commuting to or from their office. We check our email, text messages, and so forth as easily and casually as people once looked at their notebooks or address books. For instance, this man is checking his voice mail and text messages while waiting for his airplane to take off. Just a few years ago this communication capability did not exist.

COMMUNICATION NETWORKS

Communication links individuals and groups in a social system. Initially, task-related communication links develop in an organization so that employees can get the information they need to do their jobs and coordinate their work with that of others in the system. Over a long period, these communication relationships become a sophisticated social system composed of both small-group communication networks and a larger organizational network. These networks structure both the flow and the content of communication and support the organizational structure.[14] The pattern and content of communication also support the culture, beliefs, and value systems that enable the organization to operate. (We should also note that this discussion is based on theory and research associated with face-to-face group dynamics. Web-based social networking tools such as MySpace and Facebook also reflect networks as well, but these have not been studied in an organizational context.)

Small-Group Networks

To examine interpersonal communication in a small group, we can observe the patterns that emerge as the work of the group proceeds and information flows from some people in the group to others.[15] Four such patterns are shown in Figure 11.4. The lines identify the communication links most frequently used in the groups.

A **wheel network** is a pattern in which information flows between the person at the end of each spoke and the person in the middle. Those on the ends of the spokes do

Figure 11.4 SMALL-GROUP COMMUNICATION NETWORKS

These four types of communication networks are the most common in organizations. The lines represent the most frequently used communication links in small groups.

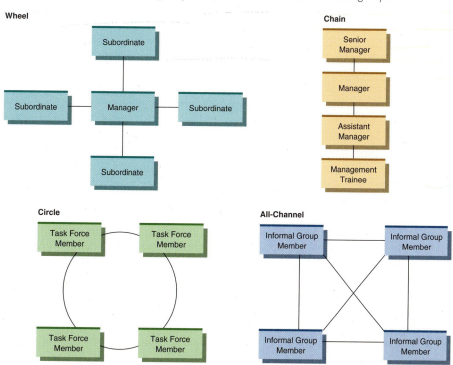

In a **wheel network,** information flows between the person at the end of each spoke and the person in the middle.

not directly communicate with each other. The wheel network is a feature of the typical work group, in which the primary communication occurs between the members and the group manager. In a **chain network**, each member communicates with the person above and below, except for the individuals on each end, who communicate with only one person. The chain network is typical of communication in a vertical hierarchy, in which most communication travels up and down the chain of command. Each person in a **circle network** communicates with the people on both sides but not with anyone else. The circle network often is found in task forces and committees. Finally, in an all-channel network, all members communicate with all the other members. The **all-channel network** often is found in informal groups that have no formal structure, leader, or task to accomplish.

Communication may be more easily distorted by noise when much is being communicated or when the communication must travel a great distance. Improvements in electronic communication technology, such as computerized mail systems and intranets, are reducing this effect. A relatively central position gives a person an opportunity to communicate with all of the other members, so a member in a relatively central position can control the information flow and may become a leader of the group. This leadership position is separate and distinct from the formal group structure, although a central person in a group may also emerge as a formal group leader over a long period.

Communication networks form spontaneously and naturally as interactions among workers continue. They are rarely permanent since they change as the tasks, interactions, and memberships change. The task is crucial in determining the pattern of the network. If the group's primary task is decision making, an all-channel network may develop to provide the information needed to evaluate all possible alternatives. If, however, the group's task mainly involves the sequential execution of individual tasks, a chain or wheel network is more likely because communication among members may not be important to the completion of the tasks.

The environment (the type of room in which the group works or meets, the seating arrangement, the placement of chairs and tables, the geographical dispersion, and other aspects of the group's setting) can affect the frequency and types of interactions among members. For example, if most members work on the same floor of an office building, the members who work three floors down may be considered outsiders and develop weaker communication ties to the group. They may even form a separate communication network.

Personal factors also influence the development of the communication network. These include technical expertise, openness, speaking ability, and the degree to which members are acquainted with one another. For example, in a group concerned mainly with highly technical problems, the person with the most expertise may dominate the communication flow during a meeting.

The group performance factors that influence the communication network include composition, size, norms, and cohesiveness. For example, group norms in one organization may encourage open communication across different levels and functional units whereas the norms in another organization may discourage such lateral and diagonal communication. These performance factors are discussed in Chapter 9.

Because the outcome of the group's efforts depends on the coordinated action of its members, the communication network strongly influences group effectiveness. Thus, to develop effective working relationships in the organization, managers need to make a special effort to manage the flow of information and the development of communication networks. Managers can, for example, arrange offices and work spaces to foster communication among certain employees. Managers may also attempt to involve members who typically contribute little during discussions by asking them

In a **chain network,** each member communicates with the person above and below, except for the individuals on each end, who communicate with only one person.

In a **circle network,** each member communicates with the people on both sides but with no one else.

In an **all-channel network,** all members communicate with all other members.

Communication networks form spontaneously and naturally as the interactions among workers continue over time.

direct questions such as "What do you think, Tom?" or "Maria, tell us how this problem is handled in your district." Methods such as the nominal group technique, also discussed in Chapter 9, can also encourage participation.

One other factor that is becoming increasingly more important in the development of communication networks is the advent of electronic groups fostered by electronic distribution lists, chat rooms, discussion boards, and other computer networking systems. This form of communication results in a network of people who may have little or no face-to-face communication but still may be considered a group communication network. For example, your professor is probably a member of a virtual group of other professors who share an interest in the topic of this course. Through the electronic group, they keep up with new ideas in the field.

Organizational Communication Networks

An organization chart shows reporting relationships from the line worker up to the CEO of the firm. The lines of an organization chart may also represent channels of communication through which information flows, yet communication may also follow paths that cross traditional reporting lines. Information moves not only from the top down—from CEO to group members—but also upward from group members to the CEO. In fact, a good flow of information to the CEO is an important determinant of the organization's success.

Several companies have realized that the key to their continuing success was improved internal communication. General Motors was known for its extremely formal, top-down communication system. But as the firm's performance suffered, the formality of its system came under fire from virtually all of its stakeholders. GM's response was to embark on a massive communication improvement program that included sending employees to public-speaking workshops, improving the more than 350 publications that it sends out, providing videotapes of management meetings to employees, and using satellite links between headquarters and field operations to establish two-way conversations around the world.

Downward communication generally provides directions whereas upward communication provides feedback to top management. Communication that flows horizontally or crosses traditional reporting lines usually is related to task performance. For example, a design engineer, a manufacturing engineer, and a quality engineer may communicate about the details of a particular product design, thus making it easy to manufacture and inspect. Horizontal communication often travels faster than vertical communication because it need not follow organizational protocols and procedures.

Organizational communication networks may diverge from reporting relationships as employees seek better information with which to do their jobs. Employees often find that the easiest way to get their jobs done or to obtain the necessary information is to go directly to employees in other departments rather than through the formal channels shown on the organization chart. Figure 11.5 shows a simple organization chart and the organization's real communication network. The communication network links the individuals who most frequently communicate with one another; the firm's CEO, for example, communicates most often with employee 5. (This does not mean that individuals who are not linked in the communication network never communicate, but only means that their communications are relatively infrequent.) Perhaps the CEO and the employee interact frequently outside of work, in church, in service organizations such as Kiwanis, or at sporting events. Such interactions may lead to close friendships that carry over into business relationships. The figure also shows that the group managers do not have important roles in the communication network, contrary to commonsense expectations.

Figure 11.5 COMPARISON OF AN ORGANIZATION CHART AND THE ORGANIZATION'S COMMUNICATION NETWORK

A single organization chart compared with actual communication patterns are quite different from the reporting relationships shown in the organization chart.

Organization Chart

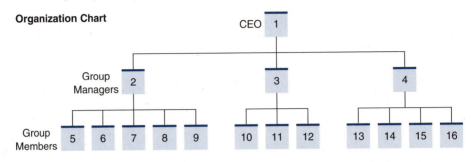

Communication Network of Most Frequent Communications for the Same Organization

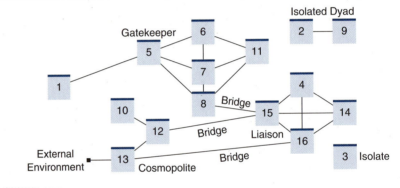

The roles that people play in organizational communication networks can be analyzed in terms of their contribution to the functioning of the network.[16] The most important roles are labeled in the bottom portion of Figure 11.5. A **gatekeeper** (employee 5) has a strategic position in the network that allows him or her to control information moving in either direction through a channel. A **liaison** (employee 15) serves as a bridge between groups, tying groups together and facilitating the communication flow needed to integrate group activities. Employee 13 performs the interesting function of **cosmopolite**, who links the organization to the external environment by, for instance, attending conventions and trade shows, keeping up with outside technological innovations, and having more frequent contact with sources outside the organization. This person may also be an opinion leader in the group. Finally, the **isolate** (employee 3) and the **isolated dyad** (employees 2 and 9) tend to work alone and have little interaction and communication with others.

Each of these roles and functions plays an important part in the overall functioning of the communication network and in the organization as a whole. Understanding these roles can help both managers and group members facilitate communication. For instance, the manager who wants to be sure that the CEO receives certain information is well advised to go through the gatekeeper. If the employee who has the technical knowledge necessary for a particular project is an isolate, the manager can take special steps to integrate the employee into the communication network for the duration of the project.

The **gatekeeper** has a strategic position in the network that allows him or her to control information moving in either direction through a channel.

The **liaison** serves as a bridge between groups, tying groups together and facilitating the communication flow needed to integrate group activities.

The **cosmopolite** links the organization to the external environment and may also be an opinion leader in the group.

The **isolate** and the **isolated dyad** tend to work alone and to interact and communicate little with others.

Managers should strive to communicate as effectively as possible. Sometimes, though, it seems like they are doing just the opposite. This manager, for example, is trying to make himself look good by using big words and long phrases instead of simple and short ones. Of course, his subordinate recognizes that the communication is just becoming less effective.

Dilbert: © Scott Adams/Distributed by United Feature Syndicate

Recent research has indicated some possible negative impacts of communication networks. Employee turnover has been shown to occur in clusters related to employee communication networks.[17] That is, employees who communicate regularly in a network may share feelings about the organization and thus influence one another's intentions to stay or quit. Communication networks therefore may have both positive and negative consequences.[18]

As we discuss in Chapter 16, a primary function of organizational structure is to coordinate the activities of many people doing specialized tasks. Communication networks in organizations provide this much-needed integration. In fact, in some ways, communication patterns influence organizational structure. Some companies are finding that the need for better communication forces them to create smaller divisions. The fewer managerial levels and improved team spirit of these divisions tend to enhance communication flows.

MANAGING COMMUNICATION

As simple as the process of communication may seem, messages are not always understood. The degree of correspondence between the message intended by the source and the message understood by the receiver is called **communication fidelity**. Fidelity can be diminished anywhere in the communication process, from the source to the feedback. Moreover, organizations may have characteristics that impede the flow of information.

Improving the Communication Process

To improve organizational communication, one must understand potential problems. Using the basic communication process, we can identify several ways to overcome typical problems.

Source   The source may intentionally withhold or filter information on the assumption that the receiver does not need it to understand the communication. Withholding information, however, may render the message meaningless or cause an erroneous

Communication fidelity is the degree of correspondence between the message intended by the source and the message understood by the receiver.

interpretation. For example, during a performance appraisal interview, a manager may not tell the employee all of the sources of information being used to make the evaluation, thinking that the employee does not need to know them. If the employee knew, however, he or she might be able to explain certain behaviors or otherwise alter the manager's perspective of the evaluation and thereby make it more accurate. Filtering may be more likely to occur in electronic communication such as email or voice mail since they carry an implied emphasis on brevity and conciseness. Selective filtering may cause a breakdown in communication that cannot be repaired, even with good follow-up communication.

To avoid filtering, the communicator needs to understand why it occurs. Filtering can result from a lack of understanding of the receiver's position, from the sender's need to protect his or her own power by limiting the receiver's access to information, or from doubts about what the receiver might do with the information. The sender's primary concern, however, should be the message. In essence, the sender must determine exactly what message he or she wants the receiver to understand, send the receiver enough information to understand the message but not enough to create an overload, and trust the receiver to use the information properly.

Encoding and Decoding   Encoding and decoding problems occur as the message is translated into or translated from the symbols used in transmission. Such problems can relate to the meaning of the symbols or to the transmission itself. Encoding and decoding problems include lack of common experience between source and receiver, problems related to semantics and the use of jargon, and difficulties with the medium.

Clearly, the source and the receiver must share a common experience with the symbols that express the message if they are to encode and decode them in exactly the same way. People who speak different languages or come from different cultural backgrounds may experience problems of this sort. But even people who speak the same language can misunderstand each other.

Semantics is the study of language forms, and semantic problems occur when people attribute different meanings to the same words or language forms. For example, J. Edgar Hoover, the legendary former director of the FBI, once jotted "watch the borders" on a memo he had received and sent it back to the senior agency manager who had written it. Only after dispatching several dozen agents to guard the border between the United States and Mexico did the agency manager learn what Hoover had actually meant—the margins on the memo were too narrow! Similarly, when discussing a problem employee, the division head may tell her assistant, "We need to get rid of this problem." The division head may have meant that the employee should be scheduled for more training or transferred to another division. However, the assistant may interpret the statement differently and fire the problem employee.

The specialized or technical language of a trade, field, profession, or social group is called **jargon**. Jargon may be a hybrid of standard language and the specialized language of a group. For example, experts in the computer field use terms such as "gigs," "megs," "RAM," and "bandwidth" that have little or no meaning to those unfamiliar with computers. The use of jargon makes communication within a close group of colleagues more efficient and meaningful, but outside the group it has the opposite effect. Sometimes a source person comfortable with jargon uses it unknowingly in an attempt to communicate with receivers who do not understand it, thus causing a communication breakdown. In other cases, the source may use jargon intentionally to obscure meaning or to show outsiders that he or she belongs to the group that uses the language.

Semantics is the study of language forms.

Jargon is the specialized or technical language of a trade, profession, or social group.

The use of jargon is acceptable if the receiver is familiar with it; otherwise, it should be avoided. Repeating a jargon-laden message in clearer terms should help the receiver understand it. In general, the source and the receiver should clarify the set of symbols to be used before they communicate. Also, the receiver can ask questions frequently and, if necessary, ask the source to repeat all or part of the message. The source must send the message through a medium appropriate to the message itself and to the intended receiver. For example, a commercial run on a traditional radio station will not have its intended effect if the people in the desired market segment listen primarily to satellite radio.

Largely influenced by the Enron debacle, many investors are increasingly beginning to scrutinize the financial reporting systems of larger companies. Coca-Cola, for instance, has recently seen its own accounting practices criticized in the media. These critics contend that the firm is using increasingly complex reporting methods to make its earnings seem higher than they would have been if simpler and more straightforward accounting practices had been used.[19]

Receiver Several communication problems originate in the receiver, including problems with selective attention, value judgments, source credibility, and overload. Selective attention exists when the receiver attends only to selected parts of a message—a frequent occurrence with oral communication. For example, in a college class, some students may hear only part of the professor's lecture as their minds wander to other topics. To focus receivers' attention on the message, senders often engage in attention-getting behaviors such as varying the volume, repeating the message, and offering rewards.

Value judgments are influenced by the degree to which a message reinforces or challenges the receiver's basic personal beliefs. If a message reinforces the receiver's beliefs, he or she may pay close attention and believe it completely, without examination. On the other hand, if the message challenges those beliefs, the receiver may entirely discount it. Thus, if a firm's sales manager predicts that the demand for new baby-care products will increase substantially over the next two years, he or she may be ignoring reports that the birthrate is declining.

The receiver may also judge the credibility of the source of the message. If the source is perceived to be an expert in the field, the listener may pay close attention to the message and believe it. Conversely, if the receiver has little respect for the source, he or she may disregard the message. The receiver considers both the message and the source in making value judgments and determining credibility. An expert in nuclear physics may be viewed as a credible source if the issue is building a nuclear power plant, yet the same person's evaluation of the birthrate may be disregarded, perhaps correctly. This is one reason that trial lawyers ask expert witnesses about their education and experience at the beginning of their testimony: to establish credibility.

A receiver experiencing communication overload is receiving more information than she or he can process. In organizations, this can happen very easily; a receiver can be bombarded with computer-generated reports and messages from superiors, peers, and sources outside the organization. It is not unusual for middle managers or telecommuters to receive one hundred email messages per day. Unable to take in all the messages, decode them, understand them, and act on them, the receiver may use selective attention and value judgments to focus on the messages that seem most important. Although this type of selective attention is necessary for survival in an information-glutted environment, it may mean that vital information is lost or overlooked.[20]

The *Technology* box on page 312 entitled "The Medical Uses of Viral E-Mail" shows how value judgments, particularly when combined with selective attention, can influence a receiver's assessment of message content regardless of the perceived credibility of the source.

TECHNOLOGY

The Medical Uses of Viral Email

Dr. William H. Parker, clinical professor of obstetrics and gynecology at the UCLA School of Medicine, says that there's a certain patient question which he answers almost every day. It concerns a blood test known as CA-125, which is used to monitor the status of the disease in women diagnosed with ovarian cancer. "I probably answer maybe five or six patients a week who come in saying, 'I read this email that says I'm supposed to get this test.'…I don't mind educating my patients," Parker explains, but the email "is based on bad information." When he investigated the online message that had spurred the concerns of so many patients, Parker discovered that it had been circulating for nearly 10 years.

It was written by a woman named Carolyn Benivegna, who'd had a bad experience with the diagnosis of a disease quite similar to ovarian cancer. Dissatisfied with the diagnosis of her symptoms by her first physician, Benivegna had persisted until a correct diagnosis was finally made through a CA-125 test. "Nobody had ever told me about the CA-125 test," Benivegna said later, "even though I was a high-risk patient for ovarian cancer…I knew very little about ovarian cancer, but I learned that they would have found my cancer many months earlier if I had been given a CA-125 test. Needless to say, I was upset when I wrote that…email." Dispatched in July 1998, Benivegna's chain letter emphasized that her cancer could have been treated more effectively if doctors had ordered the CA-125 test earlier in the lengthy diagnostic process. "Having gone through this ordeal," she explained, "I want to save others from the same fate," and she urged everyone

> *"So one day I thought to myself, 'I need to do what they did. I need to get an email out there that will take on a life of its own.'"*
>
> —DR. WILLIAM H. PARKER ON HOW TO COUNTER ONLINE MEDICAL MISINFORMATION

who received her message "to give it or send it via email to everybody you know." She also added: "Beware that their doctors might try to talk them out of it. Don't take no for an answer." Before long, Benivegna's warning was on a decade-long journey through cyberspace—"a full-blown viral message with seemingly unstoppable momentum," according to one medical journalist.

Hence Dr. Parker's dilemma. "To explain to [patients] why this test is not reliable, without brushing off their concerns," he says, "I have to launch into a 15-minute discussion about the science and why this email presents the wrong information. And," he adds, "I still have to quell their anxiety about it." Parker can, for example, explain, "the science" this way (and often does):

> *If 10,000 women aged 50–64 are screened with CA-125 testing for ovarian cancer yearly, 300 women will test positive and require further evaluation. Twenty-four of these women will need surgery, 20 of whom will not have ovarian cancer and, therefore, be subjected to unnecessary surgery with inherent risks and recovery. Only 4 of the 10,000 women will have ovarian cancer.*

Not surprisingly, however, Parker discovered that "the science" doesn't have nearly the impact of Benivegna's cautionary tale on the minds of those people who are most anxious about the early detection of a life-threatening disease.*

---

*When she learned in 2002 that she had inadvertently passed along potentially harmful misinformation, Benivegna hastened to circulate a corrective email. Unfortunately, the follow-up has never attained the popularity of the original. Benivegna died of ovarian cancer in September 2008.

"So one day," he says, "I thought to myself, 'I need to do what they did. I need to get an email out there that will take on a life of its own and be passed from woman to woman.'" With his first-round target audience the 6,000 members of the National Uterine Fibroids Foundation, a nonprofit women's health organization, Parker composed an anti-misinformation email and ran it by Carla Dionne, the Foundation's executive director. "It needed a lot of work," recalls Dionne. "It was extremely passive and written from the clinician's perspective. It was calm, educated and careful. The whole business of catching attention seemed somewhat offensive to him." Ironically, she advised Parker to consult Benivegna's original message to see how it should be done, and Parker came back with a revised version of his email message, charging it with some emotion and putting the important information up front. It promised to be much more effective. "The content of the message," explains Jeanne Jennings, an email marketing consultant in Washington, D.C., "has to be of intense interest to your target audience. Women, of course, are naturally looking out for each other. So if there's a health concern or a danger, they'll naturally pass it on to their network of friends and relatives." When it went out January 2008, Parker's email began like this:

HAVE YOU HEARD ABOUT THE CA-125 TEST FOR OVARIAN CANCER?

Did you know it is NOT an effective screening test for ovarian cancer?...

Why not? Because it doesn't work!

Many women have undergone unnecessary surgery (and anxiety) as a result of this test, while others have been falsely reassured by a normal result—while they actually had ovarian cancer.

It took a couple of weeks before a patient mentioned his email, but at least Parker knew that it was making the rounds. He keeps copies of it, along with a write-up in the *New York Times*, in his waiting room, and now, he says, "when patients ask about the test, I refer them to the email and the article. Then, if they have more questions, I talk to them. It just makes my life much easier this way."

References: John McCormack, "Rumor Control: How to Battle Online Misinformation," *American Medical News*, March 17, 2008, www.ama-assn.org on March 10, 2010; "CA-125 Screening for Ovarian Cancer," *BreakTheChain.org*, June 27, 2002/September 27, 2008, www.breakthechain.org on March 10, 2010; Laura Dolson, "The Truth about CA 125," *About.com*, 2001, www.baymoon.com on March 10, 2010; Tara Parker-Pope, "Doctors Take On a Notorious E-Mail," *New York Times*, January 18, 2008, http://well.blogs.nytimes.com on March 12, 2010; "CA-125," *Snopes.com*, March 11, 2009, www.snopes.com on March 12, 2010.

Feedback   The purpose of feedback is verification, in which the receiver sends a message to the source indicating receipt of the message and the degree to which it was understood. Lack of feedback can cause at least two problems: First, the source may need to send another message that depends on the response to the first; if the source receives no feedback, the source may not send the second message or may be forced to send the original message again. Second, the receiver may act on the unverified message; if the receiver misunderstood the message, the resulting act may be inappropriate.

Because feedback is so important, the source must actively seek it, and the receiver must supply it. Often it is appropriate for the receiver to repeat the original message as an introduction to the response, although the medium or symbols used may be different. Nonverbal cues can provide instantaneous feedback. These include body language and facial expressions such as anger and disbelief.

The source needs to be concerned with the message, the symbols, the medium, and the feedback from the receiver. Of course, the receiver is concerned with these things, too, but from a different point of view. In general, the receiver needs to be source oriented just as the source needs to be receiver oriented. Table 11.1 gives specific suggestions for improving the communication process.

Verification is the feedback portion of communication in which the receiver sends a message to the source indicating receipt of the message and the degree to which he or she understood the message.

Table 11.1 IMPROVING THE COMMUNICATION PROCESS

Focus	Source Question	Source Corrective Action	Receiver Question	Receiver Corrective Action
MESSAGE	What idea or thought are you trying to get across?	Give more information. Give less information. Give entire message.	What idea or thought does the sender want you to understand?	Listen carefully to the entire message, not just to part of it.
SYMBOLS	Does the receiver use the same symbols, words, jargon?	Say it another way. Employ repetition. Use receiver's language or jargon. Before sending, clarify symbols to be used.	What symbols are being used— for example, foreign language, technical jargon?	Clarify symbols before communication begins. Ask questions. Ask sender to repeat message.
MEDIUM	Is this a channel that the receiver monitors regularly? Sometimes? Never?	Use multiple media. Change medium. Increase volume (loudness).	What medium or media is the sender using?	Monitor several media.
FEEDBACK	What is the receiver's reaction to your message?	Pay attention to the feedback, especially nonverbal cues. Ask questions.	Did you correctly interpret the message?	Repeat message.

Improving Organizational Factors in Communication

Organizational factors that can create communication breakdowns or barriers include noise, status differences, time pressures, and overload. As previously stated, disturbances anywhere in the organization can distort or interrupt meaningful communication. Thus, the noise created by a rumored change in a firm's financial situation can disrupt the orderly flow of task-related information. For instance, rumors about a possible bankruptcy may cause a firm's stock to plummet (this actually happened once to retailer Kmart).[21] Similarly, rumors about a potential merger or acquisition can cause share prices to jump or fall, depending on the market's perceptions of the rumored new deal.

Status differences between source and receiver can cause some of the communication problems just discussed. For example, a firm's chief executive officer may pay little attention to communications from employees far lower on the organization chart, and employees may pay little attention to communications from the CEO. Both are instances of selective attention prompted by the organization's status system. Time pressures and communication overloads are also detrimental to communication. When the receiver is not allowed enough time to understand incoming messages, or when there are too many messages, he or she may misunderstand or ignore some of them. Effective organizational communication provides the right information to the right person at the right time and in the right form.

Reduce Noise   Noise is a primary barrier to effective organizational communication. A common form of noise is the rumor **grapevine**, an informal system of communication that coexists with the formal system. The grapevine usually transmits information faster than official channels do. Because the accuracy of this information often is quite low, however, the grapevine can distort organizational communication. Management can reduce the effects of the distortion by using the grapevine as an additional channel for disseminating information and by constantly monitoring it for accuracy.

Foster Informal Communication   Communication in well-run companies was once described as "a vast network of informal, open communications."[22] Informal communication fosters mutual trust, which minimizes the effects of status differences. Open communication can also contribute to better understanding between diverse groups in an organization. Monsanto Company created fifteen-member teams in its Agricultural Group, the primary objective being to increase communication and awareness among various diverse groups. Its Chemical Group set up diversity pairs of one supervisor and one worker to increase communication and awareness. In both cases, Monsanto found that increasing communication between people who were different paid handsome benefits for the organization.[23] Open communication also allows information to be communicated when it is needed rather than when the formal information system allows it to emerge. Some experts also describe communication in effective companies as chaotic and intense, supported by the reward structure and the physical arrangement of the facilities. This means that the performance appraisal and reward system, offices, meeting rooms, and work areas are designed to encourage frequent, unscheduled, and unstructured communication throughout the organization.

Develop a Balanced Information Network   Many large organizations have developed elaborate formal information networks to cope with the potential problems of information overload and time pressures. In many cases, however, the networks have created problems instead of solving them. Often they produce more information than managers and decision makers can comprehend and use in their jobs. The networks also often use only formal communication channels and ignore various informal lines of communication. Furthermore, they frequently provide whatever information the computer program is set up to provide—information that may not apply to the most pressing problem at hand. The result of all these drawbacks is loss of communication effectiveness.

Organizations need to balance information load and information-processing capabilities. In other words, they must take care not to generate more information than people can handle. It is useless to produce sophisticated statistical reports that managers have no time to read. In response to threes problems, many systems now use a view-at-a-glance "dashboard" to convey essential information in a logical and condensed manner. Furthermore, the new technologies that are making more information available to managers and decision makers must be unified to produce usable information. Information production, storage, and processing capabilities must be compatible with one another and, equally important, with the needs of the organization.

Some companies—for example, General Electric, Anheuser-Busch, and McDonald's—have formalized an upward communication system that uses a corporate "ombudsperson" position. A highly placed executive who is available outside the formal chain of command to hear employees' complaints usually holds this position. The system provides an opportunity for disgruntled employees to complain without fear of losing their jobs and may help some companies achieve a balanced communication system.

The **grapevine** is an informal system of communication that coexists with the formal system.

SYNOPSIS

Communication is the process by which two parties exchange information and share meaning. It plays a role in every organizational activity. The purposes of communication in organizations are to achieve coordinated action, to share information, and to express feelings and emotions.

People in organizations communicate through written, oral, and nonverbal means. Written communications include letters, memos, email, reports, and the like. Oral communication is the type most commonly used. Personal elements, such as facial expressions and body language, and environmental elements, such as office design, are forms of nonverbal communication.

Communication among individuals, groups, or organizations is a process in which a source sends a message and a receiver responds. The source encodes a message into symbols and transmits it through a medium to the receiver, who decodes the symbols. The receiver then responds with feedback, an attempt to verify the meaning of the original message. Noise—anything that distorts or interrupts communication—may interfere at virtually any stage of the process.

The fully integrated communication-information office system—the electronic office—links personnel in a communication network through a combination of computers and electronic transmission systems. The full range of effects of such systems has yet to be fully realized.

Communication networks are systems of information exchange within organizations. Patterns of communication emerge as information flows from person to person in a group. Typical small-group communication networks include the wheel, chain, circle, and all-channel networks.

The organizational communication network, which constitutes the real communication links in an organization, usually differs from the arrangement on an organization chart. Roles in organizational communication networks include those of gatekeeper, liaison, cosmopolite, and isolate.

Managing communication in organizations involves understanding the numerous problems that can interfere with effective communication. Problems may arise from the communication process itself and from organizational factors such as status differences.

DISCUSSION QUESTIONS

1. How is communication in organizations an individual process as well as an organizational process?

2. Discuss the three primary purposes of organizational communication.

3. Describe a situation in which you tried to carry on a conversation when no one was listening. Were any messages sent during the "conversation"?

4. A college classroom is a forum for a typical attempt at communication as the professor tries to communicate the subject to the students. Describe classroom communication in terms of the basic communication process outlined in the chapter.

5. Is there a communication network (other than professor-to-student) in the class in which you are using this book? If so, identify the specific roles that people play in the network. If not, why has no network developed? What would be the benefits of having a communication network in this class?

6. Why might educators typically focus most communication training on the written and oral methods and pay little attention to the nonverbal methods? Do you think that more training emphasis should be placed on nonverbal communication? Why or why not?

7. Is the typical classroom means of transferring information from professor to student an effective form of communication? Where does it break down? What are the communication problems in the college classroom?

8. Who is responsible to solve classroom communication problems: the students, the professor, or the administration?

9. Have you ever worked in an organization in which communication was a problem? If so, what were some causes of the problem?

10. What methods were used, or should have been used, to improve communication in the situation you described in question 9?

11. Would the use of advanced computer information processing or telecommunications have helped solve the communications problem you described in question 9?

12. What types of communication problems will new telecommunications methods probably be able to solve? Why?

13. What types of communications would NOT be appropriate to send by email? Or by voice mail?

14. Which steps in the communication process are usually left out, or at the very least, poorly done, when email and voice mail are used for communication?

ORGANIZATIONAL BEHAVIOR CASE FOR DISCUSSION

GETTING PEOPLE OFF THE WELFARE PHONE

By the time she was six months pregnant, Stacie Kelly had been trying long and hard to see a doctor. "It's just really hard to be excited about having a baby," she said, "when you're worried all the time. There are all kinds of medical tests that I should have had run." Kelly, 27, had no medical insurance and depended on Indiana's Family and Social Services Administration (FSSA) to process her application for Medicaid coverage. "I just wanted to go to the doctor. That's all," explains Kelly, who says that she'd submitted the required Medicaid application to FSSA two months earlier. "And then," she reports, "basically, they dropped off the face of the planet. …I haven't heard anything since then, and so I called my caseworker and left numerous messages. They don't return your calls."

"We don't call back because we're not getting paid for it," said George Thompson, a former employee at an FSSA call center. As an FSSA agent, Thompson worked not for the state of Indiana, but for Affiliated Computer Services (ACS), which had been contracted to handle calls from residents seeking such welfare benefits as food stamps and Medicaid coverage. "It [was] just about ACS making money," says Thompson, who adds that training for call center employees "was very substandard." Angie Kennaugh, another ex-ACS employee, agrees: "Your job," she told a local reporter, was "to get people off the phone. The people running the call centers came from Sprint and Taco Bell. They had absolutely no experience whatsoever." Scott Severns, an attorney representing thousands of Indiana residents in a class-action lawsuit against ACS, was just as harsh in assessing the company's approach to making a profit in the contract-call center business: "It's like a company that

> *"The people running the call centers came from Sprint and Taco Bell. They had absolutely no experience whatsoever."*
> —A FORMER EMPLOYEE AT A CONTRACT CALL CENTER FOR INDIANA'S FAMILY AND SOCIAL SERVICES ADMINISTRATION

produces a whole lot of junk," he said. "They can be proud of how fast they get it out, but it really doesn't matter if it isn't right."

ACS, a Dallas-based provider of business-process outsourcing, had been hired by IBM to handle calls from social-services applicants when IBM contracted with the state to manage approximately one-third of its welfare caseload. The $1.3 billion contract had been signed in December 2007, with Governor Mitch Daniels promising that privatizing the state's welfare and food stamp programs would save taxpayers $1 billion over the next decade. Serious problems, however, surfaced and multiplied over the next 18 months, concerning the performance not only of ACS but that of IBM itself. Both companies fell under mounting scrutiny from state officials and criticism from welfare-rights organizations, and in July 2009, both were put on notice by the Daniels administration that their contract with the state might be in jeopardy.

In August, IBM announced plans to fix such problems as "inaccurate and incomplete data gathering" and "incorrect communications to clients"—problems that critics boiled down to lengthy call center hold times and too many errors in processing applications (including loss of documents). "Too many seniors, people with disabilities, and other of our most vulnerable citizens," charged an official of AARP Indiana, "have endured monstrous challenges [to efforts] to address their basic healthcare, nutritional, and other daily necessities." A lawsuit filed by the American Civil Liberties Union cited the case of a mother of two who lost her food stamps and health care for her children because her tax form was missing one document.

"There are a thousand of these stories," says ACLU attorney Gavin Rose, who charges that all of the parties to the lawsuit had been denied benefits because FSSA was missing some document—a document that each applicant had, like Stacie Kelly, duly submitted. According to Rose, every applicant received a letter citing "failure to cooperate" as the reason for denial of services. "You cannot deny someone for 'failing to cooperate,' " says Rose, who points out that Medicaid and other federal rules bar "failure to cooperate" as a reason for dismissing claims. "[People] get this letter, and they have absolutely no idea what they did wrong. ... I'm sure there are cases out there where people are quite literally facing a life-or-death situation." One woman told a panel of state legislators that her husband had died of a heart ailment within a year of being denied Medicaid benefits by FSSA. "It's not right," said Nanceen Alexander. "He did his part, and now it's time for the system to do its part."

Many critics blamed the failure of the system, at least in part, on the elimination of individual caseworkers. Prior to privatization, each household was assigned a caseworker who monitored its eligibility for benefits and, when problems arose, intervened to make sure that applications were properly submitted and assessed. Under the privatized system, a household's welfare records were stored electronically for access by caseworkers located across the state. Testifying before a state administrative committee in September 2009, FSSA Secretary Anne Murphy admitted that greater personal contact between the agency and its clients might be beneficial but reaffirmed that individual caseworkers were a thing of the past. "If [clients] wish to stay at home and apply online," said Murphy, "they can do that. If they wish to apply by telephone, they can do that. I'm not saying there haven't been problems," she added, promising that IBM was in the process of fixing them.

The fix, however, did not come fast enough to suit exasperated state officials. In October, just 22 months after he'd authorized Indiana's privatized welfare system, Gov. Daniels fired IBM as its primary contractor. "The intended service improvements," explained the governor, "have not been delivered, and that's not acceptable."

In place of the failed system, Daniels announced a new "hybrid system" that would retain some of the best features of the privatized process while restoring some of the best elements of the traditional state-operated system. IBM would no longer be involved, but workers hired by certain contractors—including ACS—would stay on under state supervision.

CASE QUESTIONS

1. In what ways did Indiana's privatized social-services system fail to satisfy the three purposes of organizational communication—achieving coordinated action, sharing information, and expressing feelings and emotions?
2. What kinds of *noise* disturbed the flow of communications in the system described in the case? At what points did it appear to enter into the communication process?
3. One of IBM's jobs was to enhance the efficiency of the social-services system by further automating it. In your opinion, why did the introduction of added technology into the system decrease rather than increase its communications effectiveness?
4. Had you been called in to improve IBM's management of the FSSA communication system, which of the components of the communication process would you have focused on?

REFERENCES

"Medicaid Application Slowed by Inefficient System," *The IndyChannel .com*, July 8, 2009, www.theindychannel.com on March 13, 2010; Sandra Chapman, "Former ACS Workers Highlight Call Center Problems," *wthr.com*, August 10, 2009, www.wthr.com on March 13, 2010; "IBM Under Fire for Handling of Welfare System," *TheIndy-Channel.com*, September 25, 2009, www.theindychannel.com on March 13, 2010; "ACLU Lawsuit Targets Indiana Welfare Changes," *Chesterton* (Indiana) *Tribune*, May 20, 2008, http://chestertontribune .com on March 13, 2010; "IBM Details 36 Problems to Be Fixed," *TheIndyChannel.com*, September 25, 2009, www.theindychannel .com on March 13, 2010; Rick Callahan, "Ind. Panel Approves Ending Welfare Privatization," *ABC News*, December 14, 2009, http://abcnews.go.com on March 13, 2010; Leonard Gilroy, "Indiana Cancels IBM Welfare Modernization Contract," Reason Foundation, October 16, 2009, http://reason.org on March 13, 2010.

EXPERIENCING ORGANIZATIONAL BEHAVIOR

The Importance of Feedback in Oral Communication

Purpose This exercise demonstrates the importance of feedback in oral communication.

Format You will be an observer or play the role of either a manager or an assistant manager trying to tell a coworker where a package of important materials is to be picked up. The observer's role is to make sure the other two participants follow the rules and to observe and record any interesting occurrences.

Procedure The instructor will divide the class into groups of three. (Any extra members can be roving observers.) The three people in each group will take the roles of manager, assistant manager, and observer. In the second trial, the manager and the assistant manager will switch roles.

Trial 1: The manager and the assistant manager should turn their backs to each other so that neither can see the other. Here is the situation: The manager is in another city that he or she is not familiar with but that the assistant manager knows quite well. The manager needs to find the office of a supplier to pick up drawings of a critical component of the company's main product. The supplier will be closing for the day in a few minutes; the drawings must be picked up before closing time. The manager has called the assistant manager to get directions to the office. However, the connection is faulty; the manager can hear the assistant manager, but the assistant manager can hear only enough to know the manager is on the line. The manager has redialed once, but there was no improvement in the connection. Now there is no time to lose. The manager has decided to get the directions from the assistant without asking questions.

Just before the exercise begins, the instructor will give the assistant manager a detailed map of the city that shows the locations of the supplier's office and the manager. The map will include a number of turns, stops, stoplights, intersections, and shopping centers between these locations. The assistant manager can study it for no longer than a minute or two. When the instructor gives the direction to start, the assistant manager describes to the manager how to get from his or her present location to the supplier's office. As the assistant manager gives the directions, the manager draws the map on a piece of paper.

The observer makes sure that no questions are asked, records the beginning and ending times, and notes how the assistant manager tries to communicate particularly difficult points (including points about which the manager obviously wants to ask questions) and any other noteworthy occurrences.

After all pairs have finished, each observer "grades" the quality of the manager's map by comparing it with the original and counting the number of obvious mistakes. The instructor will ask a few managers who believe they have drawn good maps to tell the rest of the class how to get to the supplier's office.

Trial 2: In trial 2, the manager and the assistant manager switch roles, and a second map is passed out to the new assistant managers. The situation is the same as in the first trial except that the telephones are working properly and the manager can ask questions of the assistant manager. The observer's role is the same as in trial 1—recording the beginning and ending times, the methods of communication, and other noteworthy occurrences.

After all pairs have finished, the observers grade the maps, just as in the first trial. The instructor then selects a few managers to tell the rest of the class how to get to the supplier's office. The subsequent class discussion should center on the experiences of the class members and the follow-up questions.

Follow-up Questions

1. Which trial resulted in more accurate maps? Why?
2. Which trial took longer? Why?
3. How did you feel when a question needed to be asked but could not be asked in trial 1? Was your confidence in the final result affected differently in the two trials?

SOURCE

"Diagnosing Your Listening Skills," from Ethel C. Glenn and Elliott A. Pond, "Listening Self-Inventory," *Supervisory Management,* January 1989, pp. 12–15. Copyright 1989 by American Management Association(J) in the format Textbook via Copyright Clearance Center.

BUILDING MANAGERIAL SKILLS

Exercise Overview Communications skills refer to your ability to convey ideas and information to other people. The task, of course, is easier when the person to whom you're communicating is familiar with the same language as you are. In an increasingly diverse business environment, however, you won't always have the luxury of expressing yourself strictly on your own terms. This exercise asks you to communicate information by carefully crafting the terms in which you express yourself.

Exercise Background Because more than half the information in any face-to-face exchange is conveyed by nonverbal means, body language is a significant factor in any interpersonal communication. Consider, for example, the impact of a yawn or a frown (never mind a shaken fist!). At the same time, however, most people pay relatively little conscious attention to the nonverbal elements of an exchange, especially the more subtle ones. And if you misread the complete set of signals that someone is sending you, you're not likely to receive that person's message in the way that's intended.

In this exercise, you'll examine some interactions between two people from which we've eliminated sound; in other words, you'll have only visual clues to help you decipher the meaning of the messages being sent and received. Then you'll be asked to examine those same interactions with both visual and verbal clues intact.

Exercise Task
1. Observe a silent video segment (you can find it on the student website). For each segment, describe the nature of the relationship and interaction between the two individuals. What nonverbal clues did you rely on in reaching your conclusions?
2. Next, observe the same video segments with audio included. Describe the interaction again, this time indicating any verbal clues that you relied on.
3. How accurate were your assessments when you had only visual information? Explain why you were or were not accurate in your assessment of the situation.
4. What does this exercise show you about the role of nonverbal factors in interpersonal communication? What advice would you now give managers about the importance of these factors?

SELF-ASSESSMENT EXERCISE

Diagnosing Your Listening Skills

Introduction Good listening skills are essential for effective communication and are often overlooked when communication is analyzed. This self-assessment questionnaire examines your ability to listen effectively.

Instructions Go through the following statements, checking "Yes" or "No" next to each one. Mark each question as truthfully as you can in light of your behavior in the last few meetings or gatherings you attended.

Yes   No

____ ____   1. I frequently attempt to listen to several conversations at the same time.

____ ____   2. I like people to give me only the facts and then let me make my own interpretation.

____ ____   3. I sometimes pretend to pay attention to people.

____ ____   4. I consider myself a good judge of nonverbal communications.

____ ____   5. I usually know what another person is going to say before he or she says it.

____ ____   6. I usually end conversations that don't interest me by diverting my attention from the speaker.

____ ____   7. I frequently nod, frown, or in some other way let the speaker know how I feel about what he or she is saying.

____ ____   8. I usually respond immediately when someone has finished talking.

____ ____   9. I evaluate what is being said while it is being said.

____ ____ 10. I usually formulate a response while the other person is still talking.

____ ____ 11. The speaker's "delivery" style frequently keeps me from listening to content.

____ ____ 12. I usually ask people to clarify what they have said rather than guess at the meaning.

____ ____ 13. I make a concerted effort to understand other people's point of view.

____ ____ 14. I frequently hear what I expect to hear rather than what is said.

____ ____ 15. Most people feel that I have understood their point of view when we disagree.

Scoring: The correct answers according to communication theory are as follows:

No for statements 1, 2, 3, 5, 6, 7, 8, 9, 10, 11, and 14. Yes for statements 4, 12, 13, and 15.

If you missed only one or two responses, you strongly approve of your own listening habits, and you are on the right track to becoming an effective listener in your role as manager. If you missed three or four responses, you have uncovered some doubts about your listening effectiveness, and your knowledge of how to listen has some gaps. If you missed five or more responses, you probably are not satisfied with the way you listen, and your friends and coworkers may not feel you are a good listener, either. Work on improving your active listening skills.

Reference: "Diagnosing Your Listening Skills," from Ethel C. Glenn and Elliott A. Pond, "Listening Self-Inventory," *Supervisory Management*, January 1989, pp. 12–15. Reprinted with permission of American Management Association via Copyright Clearance Center.

12

CHAPTER

CHAPTER LEARNING OBJECTIVES

After studying this chapter you should be able to:

- Characterize the nature of leadership.
- Trace the early approaches to leadership.
- Discuss the emergence of situational theories and models of leadership.
- Describe the LPC theory of leadership.
- Discuss the path-goal theory of leadership.
- Describe Vroom's decision tree approach to leadership

TRADITIONAL MODELS FOR UNDERSTANDING LEADERSHIP

Coke Manages a Comeback

"I think Neville basically fixed the company and its culture. When Neville came in, people didn't like working at Coke. . . . He used the force of his own personality and style to provide leadership—give people confidence in the company again."

—JOHN SICHER, PUBLISHER AND EDITOR OF *BEVERAGE DIGEST*

In 1996, at the peak of Coca-Cola's dominance of the soft-drink industry, the company seemed invincible. As far as CEO Roberto Goizueta was concerned, chief rival PepsiCo was a casualty of the "Cola Wars," and many industry observers agreed with him. Goizueta assured stockholders that cola purchases would remain

Leadership failures caused serious problems at Coca-Cola. Neville Isdell, however, used his own brand of leadership to set things right and get the firm back on track.

ULRICH BAUMGARTEN/VARIO IMAGES GMBH & CO KG/ALAMY

steady through both thick and thin economic conditions and that cola drinkers would always be willing to pay a premium price for the number-one soft drink.

Goizueta died suddenly in 1997, however, and for the better part of a decade, the Coke story was a chronicle of poor strategy, weak leadership, shoddy implementation, and innovation failures. Just about everyone, for example, had failed to predict the backlash against soft drinks, with water and sports drinks replacing cola as the trendiest beverages, especially among the health-conscious. And lo and behold, Pepsi regrouped and recovered its morale, and investor perceptions of the two companies' strategic positions took dramatic turns: Between 2001 and 2006, Pepsi's stock price climbed by one-third while Coke's dropped by a third.

How did Coke fall so far so fast? The heart of the problem, it seems, was the lack of strong, consistent leadership. Between 1997 and 2004, for example, Coke ran through two CEOs. Upon Goizueta's death, Douglas Ivester inherited a well-oiled machine with excellent control systems that enabled Coke to manage far-flung global operations. Unfortunately, Ivester's analytical approach relied heavily on numbers while neglecting to motivate and develop employees. Coke insiders report that he distanced himself, ignoring the people side of the business, and he was ousted after just two years on the job. Next came Doug Daft, a good salesman but not—again— much of a "people" person. Daft focused on operational details but lacked both a long-term strategic vision and the necessary skills to communicate his managerial priorities. He stepped down after five troubled years.

It appears in retrospect that Daft and Ivester shared a reliance on numbers-oriented management principles that took precedence over alternative approaches to management—namely, approaches that focus on the behavior of people within the organization. Under their leadership, Coke developed superior technical and operational skills while vision, motivation, group processes, and culture received little attention. As a result, many capable managers and workers left Coke, and, what's worse, although the quantitative models did effectively pinpoint trouble spots, poor attitudes and strategic confusion led to weak implementation of corrective measures. Innovation suffered, too. Despite the rollout of two new low-calorie drinks, Diet Coke with Splenda and Coca-Cola Zero, Coke hadn't introduced a truly innovative beverage since the launch of Diet Coke in 1982.

In addition, upper management's inattention to behavioral details resulted in some serious problems, including the irruption of a culture of racism that culminated in a $192 million legal settlement in 2000. Both Daft and Ivester were also accused of ignoring the murders of union leaders at a Coke bottling plant in Colombia, South America. Indeed, the South American union alleged that the murders were part of a union-busting campaign undertaken with the company's implicit consent. Coke refused to compensate the workers' families for the deaths and now faces union conflicts, a boycott, and several lawsuits in U.S. courts.

When Daft retired in 2004, the Coke board turned unexpectedly to Neville Isdell, a former Coke executive who'd been in retirement for four years. The choice surprised both insiders and outside observers, but in just three years, Isdell managed to turn the floundering organization around. For one thing, he expanded the company's portfolio with products aimed at both new-growth and core markets. In 2007, for instance, Coke purchased Glaceau, whose line of enhanced waters, led by Vitaminwater and Smartwater, helped the company adjust to a U.S. market that was moving away from carbonated drinks. At the same time, Isdell championed Coke Zero, a no-calorie drink that's refreshed the company's core carbonated-beverage line since its introduction in 2005.

Perhaps more importantly, Isdell addressed lingering problems in the firm's culture, including morale. Having inherited a company that had cut 6,000 jobs in two years, Isdell commissioned a document called "Our Manifesto for Growth," whose purpose was to rebuild confidence in Coke's commitment to its employees. He then backed up his promise by presiding over two years of solid growth. In 2007, net income rose 18 percent, to $5.98 billion, and revenue 20 percent, to $28.9 billion. At $1.9 billion, net income for the third quarter of 2008, when Isdell stepped down as CEO, was up 14 percent over the same period in 2007, and revenue, at $8.4 billion, was up by 9 percent. (For the same quarter, Pepsi reported a drop in net income of 9.6 percent and announced that it would cut 3,300 jobs.)

"I think Neville basically fixed the company and its culture," says John Sicher, publisher of *Beverage Digest*. "When Neville came in, people didn't like working at Coke. ... He used the force of his own personality and style to provide leadership—give people confidence in the company again."

Before Isdell left, he did one more thing that his predecessors hadn't done—he named a successor whom he himself had prepared for the job. Former Coke president and chief operating officer Muhtar Kent embraced Isdell's commitment to the company's carbonated-beverage line (which remains stronger in international markets than in the U.S. market) by focusing on Coca-Cola Classic, Diet Coke, and Coke Zero, and he's also followed Isdell's lead in using acquisition as a means of strengthening other product lines.

Looking at the bigger picture, Kent also plans to increase Coke's revenues from its current $650 billion to more than $1 trillion by 2020. He's well aware of the fact that he's preparing to implement strategies for achieving that goal in the midst of a global economic crisis, but according to Kent, "turbulence is a time to focus on what matters most to your business..... It's a time when waste and duplication need to be shed, and it's a time ... for a marketing company like Coca-Cola to communicate with its customers."

The *Ethics* box on page 327 entitled "When Does Leading Entail Misleading?" discusses Muhtar Kent's actions in a situation requiring him to keep an eye on executive ethics while watching out for shareholder interests.

What Do You Think?

1. Based on the information presented, do you think Coca-Cola would have gone through so much turbulence if Robert Goizueta were still in charge? Why or why not?

2. As a potential investor, how much confidence do you have in Coke's current leadership? Why?

References: Betsy Morris, "Coke Gets a Jolt," *Fortune*, May 15, 2006, http://talkprof.com on March 16, 2010; Geri Smith, "Inside Coke's Labor Struggles," *BusinessWeek*, January 23, 2006, www.businessweek.com on March 16, 2010; Joe Guy Collier, "Coke's Winning Formula," *Atlanta Journal-Constitution*, February 14, 2008; Collier, "Departing CEO Isdell Awarded High Marks," *Atlanta Journal-Constitution*, July 2, 2008; Collier, "Coke Earnings Beat Expectations," *Atlanta Journal-Constitution*, October 15, 2008; Collier, "Coke's New Chief Makes Two Key Moves," *Atlanta Journal-Constitution*, September 3, 2008—www.ajc.com on March 18, 2010; "In the Global Crisis, Coke CEO Muhtar Kent Sees Headwinds—and Tailwinds," *Knowledge@Wharton*, November 26, 2008, http://knowledge.wharton.upenn.edu on March 16, 2010; Michael J. de la Merced, "Coke Confirms Purchase of a Bottling Unit," *New York Times*, February 26, 2010, www.nytimes.com on March 16, 2010.

The mystique of leadership makes it one of the most widely debated, studied, and sought-after properties of organizational life. Managers talk about the characteristics that make an effective leader and the importance of leadership to organizational success, while organizational scientists have extensively studied leadership and myriad related phenomena for decades. Paradoxically, however, while leadership is among the most widely studied concepts in the entire field of management, there remain many unanswered questions. Why, then, should we continue to study leadership? First, leadership is of great practical importance to organizations. Second, in spite of many remaining mysteries, researchers have isolated and verified some key variables that influence leadership effectiveness.[1]

This chapter, the first of two devoted to leadership, introduces the fundamental traditional models that are commonly used as a basis for understanding leadership. We start with a discussion of the meaning of leadership, including its definition and the distinctions between leadership and management. Then we turn to historical views of leadership, focusing on the trait and behavioral approaches. Next, we examine three contemporary leadership theories that have formed the basis for most leadership research: the LPC theory developed by Fiedler, the path-goal theory, and Vroom's decision tree approach to leadership. In our next chapter we explore several contemporary views of leadership.

THE NATURE OF LEADERSHIP

Because "leadership" is a term that is often used in everyday conversation, you might assume that it has a common and accepted meaning. In fact, just the opposite is true—like several other key organizational behavior terms such as "personality" and "motivation," "leadership" is used in a variety of ways. Thus, we first clarify its meaning as we use it in this book.

The Meaning of Leadership

We will define **leadership** in terms of both process and property.[2] As a process, leadership is the use of noncoercive influence to direct and coordinate the activities of group members to meet a goal. As a property, leadership is the set of characteristics attributed to those who are perceived to use such influence successfully.[3] **Influence**, a common element of both perspectives, is the ability to affect the perceptions, beliefs, attitudes, motivation, and/or behaviors of others. From an organizational viewpoint, leadership is vital because it has such a powerful influence on individual and group behavior.[4] Moreover, because the goal toward which the group directs its efforts is often the desired goal of the leader, it may or may not mesh with organizational goals.

Leadership involves neither force nor coercion. A manager who relies solely on force and formal authority to direct the behavior of subordinates is not exercising leadership. Thus, as discussed more fully in the next section, a manager or supervisor may or may not also be a leader. It is also important to note that on one hand, a leader may actually possess the characteristics attributed to him or her; on the other, the leader may merely be perceived as possessing them.

Leadership versus (U of C 8.167 as a preposition) Management

From these definitions, it should be clear that leadership and management are related, but they are not the same. A person can be a manager, a leader, both, or neither.[5] Some of the basic distinctions between the two are summarized in Table 12.1. On the

Leadership is both a process and a property. As a *process*, leadership involves the use of noncoercive influence. As a *property*, leadership is the set of characteristics attributed to someone who is perceived to use influence successfully.

Influence is the ability to affect the perceptions, beliefs, attitudes, motivation, and/or behaviors of others.

simultaneous support of Coke's franchise system and his intention to purchase its largest franchise. Legally speaking, executives cannot deny outright that they're engaged in negotiations, but they're also barred from mentioning negotiations in public: Such statements would amount to leaking inside information and might affect stock prices—in which case, investors who lost money when the market reacted to executives' statements could sue the company. For his part, Kent explained his actions as a matter of streamlining Coke's North American operations, not of a broader shift in strategy. "Part of this is the artful use of words," suggests Paul Lapides, director of the Corporate Governance Center at Kennesaw State University, who does not feel that Coke's leader was misleading his investors. "Shareholders would really like to know everything that management is thinking about," says Lapides, "but that's just bad business."

In this case, for example, hints of an imminent deal could have driven up the price that Coke would have had to pay for CCE. According to John Sicher, a former corporate lawyer who's now editor of *Beverage Digest*, Kent had skillfully walked a thin legal and ethical line. "He couldn't say too little or too much. His 'committed to the franchise system' message was accurate and an appropriate communication."

On the point that Kent saved money for Coke investors, even Gorham tends to agree: "If it involves telling a little white lie for a few months while negotiations are going on," he admits, "that's probably the best way to go about it."

References: The Coca-Cola Company, "Our Company: Bottler Web Sites," 2010, www.thecoca-colacompany.com on March 18, 2010; Coca-Cola Enterprises, "About Us: Overview," 2010, www.cokecce.com on March 18, 2010; Michael J. de la Merced, "Coke Confirms Purchase of a Bottling Unit," *New York Times*, February 26, 2010, www.nytimes.com on March 16, 2010; Jeremiah McWilliams, "Coca-Cola's Mixed Message Draws Critics," *Atlanta Journal-Constitution*, March 13, 2010, www.ajc.com on March 16, 2010; Brad Dorfman and Martinne Geller, "Coca-Cola Sales Rise, Led by Emerging Markets," Reuters, February 9, 2010, www.reuters.com on March 16, 2010.

authority may be quite effective at taking charge of a chaotic situation and directing others in how to deal with specific patient problems. Others in the emergency room may respond because they trust the nurse's judgment and have confidence in the nurse's decision-making skills.

And the head of pediatrics, supervising a staff of twenty other doctors, nurses, and attendants, may also enjoy the staff's complete respect, confidence, and trust. They readily take her advice and follow directives without question, and often go far beyond what is necessary to help carry out the unit's mission. Thus, being a manager does not ensure that a person is also a leader—any given manager may or may not also be a leader. Similarly, a leadership position can also be formal, as when someone appointed to head a group has leadership qualities, or informal, as when a leader emerges from the ranks of the group according to a consensus of the members. The chief of staff described earlier is a manager but not really a leader. The emergency-room nurse is a leader but not a manager. And the head of pediatrics is likely both.

Organizations need both management and leadership if they are to be effective. For example, leadership is necessary to create and direct change and to help the organization get through tough times.[6] And management is necessary to achieve coordination and systematic results and to handle administrative activities during times of stability and predictability. Management in conjunction with leadership can help achieve planned orderly change, and leadership in conjunction with management can keep the organization properly aligned with its environment. In addition, managers and leaders also play a major role in establishing the moral climate of the organization and in determining the role of ethics in its culture.[7] As you can see from the *Ethics* box on page 327 entitled "When Does Leading Entail Misleading?" maintaining one's ethical balance while discharging other leadership duties can sometimes require an executive to walk a fairly fine line.

EARLY APPROACHES TO LEADERSHIP

Although leaders and leadership have profoundly influenced the course of human events, careful scientific study of them began only about a century ago. Early studies focused on the traits, or personal characteristics, of leaders.[8] Later research shifted to examine actual leader behaviors.

Trait Approaches to Leadership

Lincoln, Napoleon, Joan of Arc, Hitler, and Gandhi are names that most of us know quite well. Early researchers believed that leaders such as these had some unique set of qualities or traits that distinguished them from their peers. Moreover, these traits were presumed to be relatively stable and enduring. Following this **trait approach**, these researchers focused on identifying leadership traits, developing methods for measuring them, and using the methods to select leaders.

Hundreds of studies guided by this research agenda were conducted during the first several decades of the twentieth century. The earliest writers believed that important leadership traits included intelligence, dominance, self-confidence, energy, activity, and task-relevant knowledge. The results of subsequent studies gave rise to a long list of additional traits. Unfortunately, the list quickly became so long that it lost any semblance of practical value. In addition, the results of many studies were inconsistent.

For example, one early argument was that effective leaders such as Lincoln tended to be taller than ineffective leaders. But critics were quick to point out that Hitler and Napoleon, both effective leaders in their own way, were not tall. Some writers have even tried to relate leadership to such traits as body shape, astrological sign, or handwriting patterns. The trait approach also had a significant theoretical problem in that it could neither specify nor prove how presumed leadership traits are connected to leadership per se. For these and other reasons, the trait approach was all but abandoned several decades ago.

In recent years, however, the trait approach has received renewed interest. For example, some researchers have sought to reintroduce a limited set of traits into the leadership literature. These traits include emotional intelligence, drive, motivation, honesty and integrity, self-confidence, cognitive ability, knowledge of the business, and charisma (which is discussed in Chapter 13).[9] Some people even believe that biological factors may play a role in leadership. Although it is too early to know whether these traits have validity from a leadership perspective, it does appear that a serious and scientific assessment of appropriate traits may further our understanding of the leadership phenomenon.

Behavioral Approaches to Leadership

In the late 1940s, most researchers began to shift away from the trait approach and started to look at leadership as an observable process or activity. The goal of the so-called **behavioral approach** was to determine what behaviors are associated with effective leadership.[10] The researchers assumed that the behaviors of effective leaders differed somehow from the behaviors of less effective leaders and that the behaviors of effective leaders would be the same across all situations. The behavioral approach to the study of leadership included the Michigan studies, the Ohio State studies, and the leadership grid.

The Michigan Studies   The **Michigan leadership studies** were a program of research conducted at the University of Michigan.[11] The goal of this work was to determine the pattern of leadership behaviors that results in effective group performance.

The **trait approach** to leadership attempted to identify stable and enduring character traits that differentiated effective leaders from nonleaders.

The **behavioral approach** to leadership tried to identify behaviors that differentiated effective leaders from nonleaders.

The **Michigan leadership studies** defined job-centered and employee-centered leadership as opposite ends of a single leadership dimension.

The trait approach to leadership suggests that certain stable and enduring traits differentiate leaders from nonleaders. Both Mohandas ("Mahatma") Gandhi (left) and Winston Churchill (right), for example, are often held up as exemplars of outstanding and strong leadership. The trait approach would suggest that the two shared some underlying set of commonalities that allowed them to be such great leaders.

From interviews with supervisors and subordinates of high- and low-productivity groups in several organizations, the researchers collected and analyzed descriptions of supervisory behavior to determine how effective supervisors differed from ineffective ones. Two basic forms of leader behavior were identified—job-centered and employee-centered—as shown in the top portion of Figure 12.1.

The leader who exhibits **job-centered leader behavior** pays close attention to the work of subordinates, explains work procedures, and is mainly interested in performance. The leader's primary concern is efficient completion of the task. The leader who engages in **employee-centered leader behavior** attempts to build effective work groups with high performance goals. The leader's main concern is with high performance, but that is to be achieved by paying attention to the human aspects of the group. These two styles of leader behavior were presumed to be at opposite ends of a single dimension. Thus, the Michigan researchers suggested that any given leader could exhibit either job-centered or employee-centered leader behavior, but not both at the same time. Moreover, they suggested that employee-centered leader behavior was more likely to result in effective group performance than was job-centered leader behavior.

The Ohio State Studies   The **Ohio State leadership studies** were conducted about the same time as the Michigan studies (in the late 1940s and early 1950s).[12] During this program of research, behavioral scientists at Ohio State University developed a questionnaire, which they administered in both military and industrial settings, to assess subordinates' perceptions of their leaders' behavior. The Ohio State studies identified several forms of leader behavior but tended to focus on the two most significant ones: consideration and initiating-structure.

When engaging in **consideration behavior**, the leader is concerned with the subordinates' feelings and respects subordinates' ideas. The leader-subordinate relationship is characterized by mutual trust, respect, and two-way communication. When using **initiating-structure behavior**, on the other hand, the leader clearly defines the leader-subordinate roles so that subordinates know what is expected of them. The leader also

Job-centered leader behavior involves paying close attention to the work of subordinates, explaining work procedures, and demonstrating a strong interest in performance.

Employee-centered leader behavior involves attempting to build effective work groups with high performance goals.

The **Ohio State leadership studies** defined leader consideration and initiating-structure behaviors as independent dimensions of leadership.

Consideration behavior involves being concerned with subordinates' feelings and respecting subordinates' ideas.

Initiating-structure behavior involves clearly defining the leader-subordinate roles so that subordinates know what is expected of them.

establishes channels of communication and determines the methods for accomplishing the group's task.

Unlike the employee-centered and job-centered leader behaviors, consideration and initiating structure were not thought to be on the same continuum. Instead, as shown in the bottom portion of Figure 12.1, they were seen as independent dimensions of the leader's behavioral repertoire. As a result, a leader could exhibit high initiating-structure behavior and low consideration or low initiating-structure behavior and high consideration. A leader could also exhibit high or low levels of each behavior simultaneously. For example, a leader may clearly define subordinates' roles and expectations but exhibit little concern for their feelings. Alternatively, she or he may be concerned about subordinates' feelings but fail to define roles and expectations clearly. But the leader might also demonstrate concern for performance expectations and employee welfare simultaneously.

The Ohio State researchers also investigated the stability of leader behaviors over time. They found that a given individual's leadership pattern appeared to change little as long as the situation remained fairly constant.[13] Another topic they looked at was the combinations of leader behaviors that were related to effectiveness. At first, they believed that leaders who exhibit high levels of both behaviors would be most effective. An early study at International Harvester (now Navistar Corporation), however, found that employees of supervisors who ranked high on initiating-structure behavior were higher performers but also expressed lower levels of satisfaction. Conversely, employees of supervisors who ranked high on consideration had lower performance ratings but also had fewer absences from work.[14] Later research showed that these conclusions were misleading because the studies did not consider all the important variables. Nonetheless, however, the Ohio State studies represented another important milestone in leadership research.[15]

Figure 12.1 **EARLY BEHAVIORAL APPROACHES TO LEADERSHIP**

Two of the first behavioral approaches to leadership were the Michigan and Ohio State studies. The results of the Michigan studies suggested that there are two fundamental types of leader behavior, job-centered and employee-centered, which were presumed to be at opposite ends of a single continuum. The Ohio State studies also found two similar kinds of leadership behavior, "consideration" and "initiating-structure," but this research suggested that these two types of behavior were actually independent dimensions.

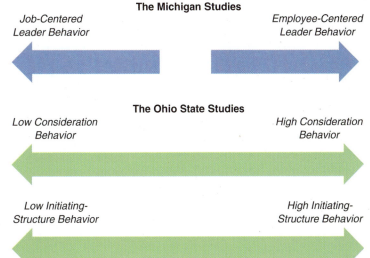

Leadership Grid®   Yet another behavioral approach to leadership is the Leadership Grid® (originally called the Managerial Grid).[16] The Leadership Grid® provides a means for evaluating leadership styles and then training managers to move toward an ideal style of behavior. The most current version of the Leadership Grid® is shown in Figure 12.2. The horizontal axis represents *concern for production* (similar to job-centered and initiating-structure behaviors), and the vertical axis represents *concern for people* (similar to employee-centered and consideration behavior). Note the five extremes of leadership behavior: the 1,1 manager (impoverished management) who exhibits minimal concern for both production and people; the 9,1 manager (authority-compliance) who is highly concerned about production but exhibits little concern for people; the 1,9 manager (country club management) who has the exact

𝓕igure 12.2   THE LEADERSHIP GRID

The Leadership Grid® is a method of evaluating leadership styles. The overall objective of an organization using the Grid® is to train its managers using organizational development techniques so that they are simultaneously more concerned for both people and production (9,9 style on the Grid®).

Source: The Leadership Grid Figure from *Leadership Dilemmas—Grid Solutions* by Robert R. Blake and Anne Adams McCanse. (Formerly the Managerial Grid by Robert R. Blake and Jane S. Mouton.) Houston: Gulf Publishing Company, p. 29. Copyright © 1997 by Grid International, Inc. Reproduced by permission of Grid International, Inc.

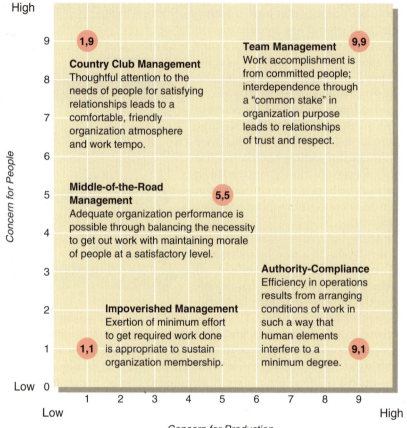

opposite concerns from the 9,1 manager; the 5,5 manager (middle of the road management) who maintains adequate concern for both people and production; and the 9,9 manager (team management) who exhibits maximum concern for both people and production.

According to this approach, the ideal style of leadership is 9,9. The developers of this model thus created a multiphase training and development program to assist managers in achieving this style of behavior. A.G. Edwards, Westinghouse, the FAA, Equicor, and other companies have used the Leadership Grid®, and anecdotal evidence seems to confirm its effectiveness in some settings. However, there is little published scientific evidence regarding its true effectiveness and the extent to which it applies to all managers and/or to all settings. Indeed, as we discuss next, such evidence is not likely to actually exist.

THE EMERGENCE OF SITUATIONAL LEADERSHIP MODELS

The leader-behavior theories have played an important role in the development of more realistic, albeit more complex, approaches to leadership. In particular, they urge us not to be so preoccupied with what properties may be possessed by leaders (the trait approach), but to instead concentrate on what leaders actually do (their behaviors). Unfortunately, these theories also make universal generic prescriptions about what constitutes effective leadership. When we are dealing with complex social systems composed of complex individuals, however, few if any relationships are consistently predictable, and certainly no formulas for success are infallible.

Yet, the behavior theorists tried to identify consistent relationships between leader behaviors and employee responses in the hope of finding a dependable prescription for effective leadership. As we might expect, they often failed. Other approaches to understanding leadership were therefore needed. The catalyst for these new approaches was the realization that although interpersonal and task-oriented dimensions might be useful to describe the behavior of leaders, they were not useful for predicting or prescribing it. The next step in the evolution of leadership theory was the creation of situational models.

Situational models assume that appropriate leader behavior varies from one situation to another. The goal of a situational theory, then, is to identify key situational factors and to specify how they interact to determine appropriate leader behavior. Before discussing the major situational theories, we first discuss an important early model that in many ways laid the foundation for these theories. In a seminal article about the decision-making process, Robert Tannenbaum and Warren H. Schmidt proposed a continuum of leadership behavior. Their model is much like the original Michigan framework.[17] Besides purely job-centered behavior (or "boss-centered" behavior, as they termed it) and employee-centered ("subordinate-centered") behavior, however, they identified several intermediate behaviors that a manager might consider. These are shown on the leadership continuum in Figure 12.3.

This continuum of behavior ranges from the one extreme of having the manager make the decision alone to the other extreme of having the employees make the decision with minimal guidance from the leader. Each point on the continuum is influenced by characteristics of the manager, subordinates, and the situation. Managerial characteristics include the manager's value system, confidence in subordinates, personal inclinations, and feelings of security. Subordinate characteristics include the subordinates' need for independence, readiness to assume responsibility, tolerance for ambiguity, interest in the problem, understanding of goals, knowledge, experience, and expectations. Situational characteristics that affect decision making include the type of organization, group effectiveness, the problem itself, and time pressures.

As we suggest in our opening story in Chapter 3, the remarkable success of Apple Computer reflects a complex interplay among several factors, including Steve Jobs's leadership personality, the eagerness of employees to participate in the pursuit of his vision for the company, and an organizational culture that values independence and creative input. The *Technology* box on page 335 follows up on this relationship, especially in showing how Jobs functions, both at Apple and at Pixar, as a leader much more than as a manager.

Hence, the leadership continuum acknowledged for the first time that leader behaviors represent a continuum rather than discrete extremes, and that various characteristics and elements of any given situation would affect the success of any given leadership style. Although this framework pointed out the importance of situational

be "mismatches." Recall that a basic premise of his theory is that leadership behavior is a personality trait. Thus, the mismatched leader cannot readily adapt to the situation and achieve effectiveness. Fiedler contends that when a leader's style and the situation do not match, the only available course of action is to change the situation through "job engineering."[19]

For example, Fiedler suggests that if a person-oriented leader ends up in a situation that is very unfavorable, the manager should attempt to improve matters by spending more time with subordinates to improve leader-member relations and by laying down rules and procedures to provide more task structure. Fiedler and his associates have also developed a widely used training program for supervisors on how to assess situational favorableness and to change the situation, if necessary, to achieve a better match.[20] Weyerhaeuser and Boeing are among the firms that have experimented with Fiedler's training program.

Evaluation and Implications

The validity of Fiedler's LPC theory has been heatedly debated because of the inconsistency of the research results. Apparent shortcomings of the theory are that the LPC measure lacks validity, the theory is not always supported by research, and Fiedler's assumptions about the inflexibility of leader behavior are unrealistic.[21] The theory itself, however, does represent an important contribution because it returned the field to a study of the situation and explicitly considered the organizational context and its role in effective leadership.

THE PATH-GOAL THEORY OF LEADERSHIP

Another important contingency approach to leadership is the path-goal theory. Developed jointly by Martin Evans and Robert House, the path-goal theory focuses on the situation and leader behaviors rather than on fixed traits of the leader.[22] In contrast to the LPC theory, the path-goal theory suggests that leaders can readily adapt to different situations.

Basic Premises

The path-goal theory has its roots in the expectancy theory of motivation discussed in Chapter 4. Recall that expectancy theory says that a person's attitudes and behaviors can be predicted from the degree to which the person believes job performance will lead to various outcomes (expectancy) and the value of those outcomes (valences) to the individual. The **path-goal theory of leadership** argues that subordinates are motivated by their leader to the extent that the behaviors of that leader influence their expectancies. In other words, the leader affects subordinates' performance by clarifying the behaviors (paths) that will lead to desired rewards (goals). Ideally, of course, getting a reward in an organization depends on effective performance. Path-goal theory also suggests that a leader may behave in different ways in different situations.

Leader Behaviors As Figure 12.4 shows, path-goal theory identifies four kinds of leader behavior: directive, supportive, participative, and achievement-oriented. With *directive leadership*, the leader lets subordinates know what is expected of them, gives specific guidance as to how to accomplish tasks, schedules work to be done, and maintains definitive standards of performance for subordinates. A leader exhibiting *supportive*

5

The **path-goal theory of leadership** suggests that effective leaders clarify the paths (behaviors) that will lead to desired rewards (goals).

leadership is friendly and shows concern for subordinates' status, well-being, and needs. With *participative leadership*, the leader consults with subordinates about issues and takes their suggestions into account before making a decision. Finally, *achievement-oriented leadership* involves setting challenging goals, expecting subordinates to perform at their highest level, and showing strong confidence that subordinates will put forth effort and accomplish the goals. Unlike the LPC theory, path-goal theory assumes that leaders can change their behavior and exhibit any or all of these leadership styles. The theory also predicts that the appropriate combination of leadership styles depends on situational factors.

Situational Factors   The path-goal theory proposes two types of situational factors that influence how leader behavior relates to subordinate satisfaction: the personal characteristics of the subordinates and the characteristics of the environment (see Figure 12.4).

Two important personal characteristics of subordinates are locus of control and perceived ability. Locus of control, discussed in Chapter 3, refers to the extent to which individuals believe that what happens to them results from their own behavior or from external causes. Research indicates that individuals who attribute outcomes to their own behavior may be more satisfied with a participative leader (since they feel their own efforts can make a difference) whereas individuals who attribute outcomes to external causes may respond more favorably to a directive leader (since they think their own actions are of little consequence). Perceived ability pertains to how people view their own ability with respect to the task. Employees who rate their own ability relatively high are less likely to feel a need for directive leadership (since they think they know how to do the job), whereas those who perceive their own ability to be relatively low may prefer directive leadership (since they think they need someone to show them how to do the job).

Important environmental characteristics are task structure, the formal authority system, and the primary work group. The path-goal theory proposes that leader behavior will motivate

Leaders need to carefully gauge situational factors when deciding how to most effectively lead others. The path–goal theory of leadership suggests that both personal characteristics of followers and environmental characteristics should be considered. This leader, for example, is making a formal presentation to a group of employees. If her style properly aligns with the situation, her followers will most likely rally to her message and work together to help meet the goals she is setting. But if her style isn't aligned properly, the followers will be less motivated by her agenda and goal achievement will be less likely

COMSTOCK/JUPITER IMAGES

subordinates if it helps them cope with environmental uncertainty created by those characteristics. In some cases, however, certain forms of leadership will be redundant, decreasing subordinate satisfaction. For example, when task structure is high, directive leadership is less necessary and therefore less effective; similarly, if the work group gives the individual plenty of social support, a supportive leader will not be especially attractive. Thus, the extent to which leader behavior matches the people and environment in the situation is presumed to influence subordinates' motivation to perform.

Figure 12.4   THE PATH-GOAL THEORY OF LEADERSHIP

The path-goal theory of leadership specifies four kinds of leader behavior: directive, supportive, participative, and achievement-oriented. Leaders are advised to vary their behaviors in response to such situational factors as personal characteristics of subordinates and environmental characteristics.

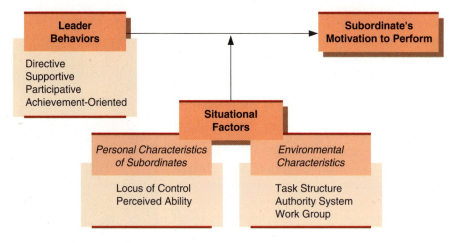

Evaluation and Implications

The path-goal theory was designed to provide a general framework for understanding how leader behavior and situational factors influence subordinate attitudes and behaviors. But the intention of the path-goal theorists was to stimulate research on the theory's major propositions, not to offer definitive answers. Researchers hoped that a more fully developed, formal theory of leadership would emerge from continued study. Further work actually has supported the theory's major predictions, but it has not validated the entire model. Moreover, many of the theory's predictions remain overly general and have not been fully refined and tested.

VROOM'S DECISION TREE APPROACH TO LEADERSHIP

The third major contemporary approach to leadership is **Vroom's decision tree approach**. The earliest version of this model was proposed by Victor Vroom and Philip Yetton and later revised and expanded by Vroom and Arthur Jago.[23] Most recently, Vroom has developed yet another refinement of the original model.[24] Like the path-goal theory, this approach attempts to prescribe a leadership style appropriate to a given situation. It also assumes that the same leader may display different leadership styles. But Vroom's approach concerns itself with only a single aspect of leader behavior: subordinate participation in decision making.

Basic Premises

Vroom's decision tree approach to leadership attempts to prescribe how much participation subordinates should be allowed in making decisions.

Vroom's decision tree approach assumes that the degree to which subordinates should be encouraged to participate in decision making depends on the characteristics of the situation. In other words, no one decision-making process is best for all situations.

After evaluating a variety of problem attributes (characteristics of the problem or decision), the leader determines an appropriate decision style that specifies the amount of subordinate participation.

Vroom's current formulation suggests that managers should use one of two different decision trees.[25] To do so, the manager first assesses the situation in terms of several factors. This assessment involves determining whether the given factor is "high" or "low" for the decision that is to be made. For instance, the first factor is decision significance. If the decision is extremely important and may have a major impact on the organization (i.e., choosing a location for a new plant), its significance is high. But if the decision is routine, and its consequences not terribly important (i.e., selecting a logo for the firm's softball team uniforms), its significance is low. This assessment guides the manager through the paths of the decision tree to a recommended course of action. One decision tree is to be used when the manager is primarily interested in making the decision on the most timely basis possible; the other is to be used when time is less critical, and the manager is interested in helping subordinates to improve and develop their own decision-making skills.

The two decision trees are shown in Figures 12.5 and 12.6. The problem attributes (situational factors) are arranged along the top of the decision tree. To use the model, the decision maker starts at the left side of the diagram and assesses the first problem attribute (decision significance). The answer determines the path to the second node on the decision tree, where the next attribute (importance of commitment) is assessed. This process continues until a terminal node is reached. In this way, the manager identifies an effective decision-making style for the situation.

The various decision styles reflected at the ends of the tree branches represent different levels of subordinate participation that the manager should attempt to adopt in a given situation. The five styles are defined as follows:

- *Decide*: The manager makes the decision alone and then announces or "sells" it to the group.

- *Delegate*: The manager allows the group to define for itself the exact nature and parameters of the problem and to then develop a solution.

- *Consult (Individually)*: The manager presents the program to group members individually, obtains their suggestions, and then makes the decision.

- *Consult (Group)*: The manager presents the problem to group members at a meeting, gets their suggestions, and then makes the decision.

- *Facilitate*: The manager presents the problem to the group at a meeting, defines the problem and its boundaries, and then facilitates group member discussion as members make the decision.

Vroom's decision tree approach represents a very focused but quite complex perspective on leadership. To compensate for this difficulty, Vroom has developed elaborate expert system software to help managers assess a situation accurately and quickly and then make an appropriate decision regarding employee participation. Many firms, including Halliburton Company, Litton Industries, and Borland International, have provided their managers with training in how to use the various versions of this model.

Evaluation and Implications

Because Vroom's current approach is relatively new, it has not been fully scientifically tested. The original model and its subsequent refinement, however, attracted a great deal of attention and were generally supported by research.[26] For example, there is some support for the idea that individuals who make decisions consistent

How had he risen through the ranks to become CEO? "Just luck," quips Barrett, who adds that "we were able to turn manufacturing around. That caught the eye of Andy [Grove] and Gordon Moore." As chief operating officer from 1993 and the company's fourth president from 1997, Barrett had also developed a working relationship with Grove, who remained with the company as chairman and senior advisor, much like the one that Grove had enjoyed earlier with Gordon Moore. And like Grove, Barrett credits the difference in leadership styles as a critical factor in his success in the top spot: "Andy and I," says Barrett, "are very different in style. … Andy has a pretty instantaneous opinion. … I'm more of a classic engineer and a data-driven guy. Faced with a problem, I wait for the data and analyze the problem. Andy probably gets frustrated with that approach because he wants to take action. That drove me to do my part of the equation a bit faster. It was very complementary."

Barrett turned over the CEO job to Paul Otellini in 2005. With a background in finance, Otellini is the first nonengineer to lead Intel, but he's had a lot of experience in computer hardware: From 1993 to 1996, as general manager of the Peripheral Components Operation and then of the Intel Architecture Group, he was responsible for chipset operations, microprocessor and chipset business strategies, and giving technical advice to Andy Grove. He served as COO from 2002 to May 2005, when he became CEO. He announced that he would "restructure, repurpose, and resize" the company and has since moved to eliminate redundant jobs, simplify operations by reducing the total number of products, and selling off noncore and unprofitable businesses. He's also initiated strategies designed to bring new products to market more quickly.

CASE QUESTIONS

1. Of the five profiled Intel CEOs, which would you characterize as the most *job-centered leader*? The least job-centered? The most *employee-centered leader*? The least employee-centered? Whose style most exemplifies *initiating-structure behavior*? Whose style least exemplifies it? Explain your thinking in each case.
2. Where would you place the style of each Intel CEO on the *leadership grid*? Explain your reasoning.
3. Characterize each of the Intel CEOs in terms of the *most* appropriate *leadership behavior—directive, supportive, participative,* or *achievement oriented.* Explain your thinking in each case.
4. Intel appears to rely heavily on mentoring and long-term leadership development from within. What are the pros and cons of such an approach? Intel also seems to have thrived on a pattern of alternating leadership styles. What are the pros and cons of this approach?

REFERENCES

Leslie Berlin, *The Man Behind the Microchip: Robert Noyce and the Invention of Silicon Valley* (New York: Oxford University Press, 2005), http://books.google.com on March 16, 2010; Cliff Edwards, "Inside Intel," *BusinessWeek*, January 9, 2006, www.businessweek.com on March 16, 2010; "Corporate Timeline: Our History of Innovation," "Moore's Law," "Intel's Tick-Tock Model," Intel website, 2010, www.intel.com on March 16, 2010; Richard S. Tedlow, "The Education of Andy Grove," *Fortune*, December 12, 2005, http://money.cnn.com on March 16, 2010; Dean Takahashi, "Exit Interview: Retiring Intel Chairman Craig Barrett on the Industry's Unfinished Business," *VentureBeat*, May 8, 2009, http://venturebeat.com on March 16, 2010; Cliff Edwards, "Craig Barrett's Mixed Record at Intel," *BusinessWeek*, January 23, 2009, www.businessweek.com on March 16, 2010; Adam Lashinsky, "Is This the Right Man for Intel?" *Fortune*, April 18, 2005, http://money.cnn.com on March 16, 2010.

EXPERIENCING ORGANIZATIONAL BEHAVIOR

Understanding Successful and Unsuccessful Leadership

Purpose   This exercise will help you better understand the behaviors of successful and unsuccessful leaders.

Format   You will be asked to identify contemporary examples of successful and unsuccessful leaders and then to describe how these leaders differ.

Procedure
1. Working alone, each student should list the names of ten people he or she thinks of as leaders in public life. Note that the names should not necessarily be confined to "good" leaders but instead should also identify "strong" leaders.

2. Next, students should form small groups and compare their lists. This comparison should focus on common and unique names as well as on the kinds of individuals listed (i.e., male or female, contemporary or historical, business or nonbusiness, and so on).
3. From all the lists, choose two leaders whom most people would consider very successful and two who would be deemed unsuccessful.
4. Identify similarities and differences between the two successful leaders and between the two unsuccessful leaders.

5. Relate the successes and failures to at least one theory or perspective discussed in the chapter.
6. Select one group member to report your findings to the rest of the class.

Follow-up Questions
1. What role does luck play in leadership?
2. Are there factors about the leaders you researched that might have predicted their success or failure before they achieved leadership roles?
3. What are some criteria of successful leadership?

BUILDING MANAGERIAL SKILLS

Exercise Overview　Conceptual skills refer to the manager's ability to think in the abstract. This exercise will enable you to apply your conceptual skills to better understanding the distinction between leadership and management.

Exercise Task　First, identify someone who currently occupies a management and/or leadership position. This individual can be a manager in a large business, the owner of a small business, the president of a campus organization, or any other similar kind of position. Next, interview this individual and ask them the following questions:

1. Name three recent tasks or activities that were primarily management in nature, requiring little or no leadership.

2. Name three recent tasks or activities that were primarily leadership in nature, requiring little or no management.
3. Do you spend most of the time working as a manager or a leader?
4. How easy or difficult is it to differentiate activities on the basis of them being management versus leadership?

Finally, after you have completed the interview, break up into small groups with your classmates and discuss your results. What have you learned about leadership from this activity?

SELF-ASSESSMENT EXERCISE

Are You Ready to Lead?

This exercise is designed to help you assess both your current readiness for leadership and your current preference in leadership style. The 10 statements in the table below reflect certain preferences in the nature of work performance. Indicate the extent to which you agree or disagree with each statement by circling the number in the appropriate column.

Statement of preference	Strongly agree				Strongly disagree
1. I like to stand out from the crowd.	1	2	3	4	5

2. I feel proud and satisfied when I influence others to do things my way.　1　2　3　4　5

3. I enjoy doing things as part of a group rather than achieving results on my own.　1　2　3　4　5

4. I have a history of becoming an officer or captain in clubs or organized sports.　1　2　3　4　5

5. I try to be the one who is most influential in tasks groups at school or work.　1　2　3　4　5

6. In groups, I care most about good relationships.
1   2   3   4   5

7. In groups, I most want to achieve task goals.
1   2   3   4   5

8. In groups, I always show consideration for the feelings and needs of others.
1   2   3   4   5

9. In groups, I always structure activities and assignments to help get the job done.
1   2   3   4   5

10. In groups, I shift between being supportive of others' needs and pushing task accomplishment.
1   2   3   4   5

How to score: Follow the instructions in the following table to enter the numbers that you've circled:

Leadership Readiness Score	Add the numbers that you circled on items 1–5: ___
Leadership Style Score	
Task Preference Score	Add the numbers that you circled on items 7 and 9: ___
Relationship Preference Score	Add the numbers that you circled on items 6 and 8: ___
	Difference between Task and Relationship scores: ___
	Check the higher score: Task ___ Relationship ___
Adaptability Score	Your score on item 10 ___

How to interpret your scores:

Leadership Readiness: If your total score on items 1–5 is 20 or more, you'll probably enjoy a leadership role. If your score is 10 or less, you're probably more interested in personal achievement—*at least at this point in your life.* If you've scored somewhere in the middle range, your leadership potential is still flexible—you could go either way, depending on circumstances.

Leadership Style: Your responses to items 6–10 reflect your leadership style, which may be *task oriented, relationship oriented,* or *flexible.* Your current *leadership-style preference* is determined by the higher of your two scores on the dimensions of task and relationship. The strength of your preference is indicated by the difference between your scores on the two dimensions.

Leadership Style Adaptability: A score of 4 or 5 on item 10 suggests that you're likely to adapt to circumstances as they arise.

Reference: Adapted from Phillip L. Hunsaker, *Management: A Skills Approach,* 2nd ed. (Upper Saddle River, NJ: Pearson Education, 2005), 419–20.

CONTEMPORARY VIEWS OF LEADERSHIP IN ORGANIZATIONS

CHAPTER LEARNING OBJECTIVES

After studying this chapter you should be able to:

- Identify and describe contemporary situational theories of leadership.
- Discuss leadership through the eyes of followers.
- Identify and describe alternatives to leadership.
- Describe the changing nature of leadership.
- Identify and discuss emerging issues in leadership.

Tips from the Top

"[Leadership is] a game of pinball, and you're the ball."

—U.S. SENATOR JOHN MCCAIN

It isn't easy leading a U.S. business these days. Leaving aside the global recession, the passion for "lean and mean" operations means that there are fewer workers to do more work. Globalization means keeping abreast of cross-cultural differences. Knowledge industries present unique leadership challenges requiring better communication skills and greater flexibility. Advances in technology have

OMAR SOBHANI/REUTERS /LANDOV

Arizona senator John McCain has provided numerous insights into the nature and meaning of contemporary leadership.

opened unprecedented channels of communication. Now more than ever, leaders must be able to do just about everything and, more of it. As U.S. Senator and former presidential candidate John McCain puts it, "[Leadership is] a game of pinball, and you're the ball." Fortunately, a few of Corporate America's veteran leaders have some tips for those who still want to follow their increasingly treacherous path.

First of all, if you think you're being overworked—if your hours are too long and your schedule's too demanding—odds are, you're right: Most people—including executives—*are* overworked. And in some industries, they're *particularly* overworked. U.S. airlines, for example, now service 100 million more passengers annually than they did just four years ago—with 70,000 fewer workers. "I used to manage my time," quips one airline executive. "Now I manage my energy." In fact, many high-ranking managers have realized that energy is a key factor in their ability to complete their tasks on tough schedules. Most top corporate leaders work 80 to 100 hours a week, and a lot of them have found that regimens which allow them to rebuild and refresh make it possible for them to keep up the pace.

Carlos Ghosn, who's currently president of Renault *and* CEO of Nissan, believes in regular respites from his workweek routine. "I don't bring my work home. I play with my four children and spend time with my family on weekends," says Ghosn. "I come up with good ideas as a result of becoming stronger after being recharged." Google VP Marissa Mayer admits that "I can get by on four to six hours of sleep," but she also takes a weeklong vacation three times a year. Many leaders report that playing racquetball, running marathons, practicing yoga, or just getting regular exercise helps them to recover from overwork.

Effective leaders also take control of information flow—which means managing it, not reducing the flow until it's as close to a trickle as you can get it. Like most executives, for example, Mayer can't get by without multiple sources of information: "I always have my laptop with me," she reports, and "I adore my cell phone." Starbucks CEO Howard Schultz receives a morning voice mail summarizing the previous day's sales results and reads three newspapers a day. Mayer watches the news all day, and Bill Gross, a securities portfolio manager, keeps an eye on six monitors displaying real-time investment data.

On the other hand, Gross stands on his head to force himself to take a break from communicating. When he's upright again, he tries to find time to concentrate. "Eliminating the noise," he says, "is critical. . . . I only pick up the phone three or four times a day. . . . I don't want to be connected—I want to be disconnected." Ghosn, whose schedule requires weekly intercontinental travel, uses bilingual assistants to screen and translate information—one assistant for information from Europe (where Renault is), one for information from Japan (where Nissan is), and one for information from the United States (where Ghosn often has to be when he doesn't have to be in Europe or Japan). Clothing designer Vera Wang also uses an assistant to filter information. "The barrage of calls is so enormous," she says, "that if I just answered calls I'd do nothing else. . . . If I were to go near email, there'd be even more obligations, and I'd be in [a mental hospital] with a white jacket on."

Not surprisingly, Microsoft chairman Bill Gates integrates the role of his assistant into a high-tech information-organizing system:

> On my desk I have three screens, synchronized to form a single desktop. I can drag items from one screen to the next. Once you have that large display area, you'll never go back, because it has a direct impact on productivity.

The screen on the left has my list of emails. On the center screen is usually the specific email I'm reading and responding to. And my browser is on the right-hand screen. This setup gives me the ability to glance and see what new has come in while I'm working on something and to bring up a link that's related to an email and look at it while the email is still in front of me.

At Microsoft, email is the medium of choice. . . . I get about 100 emails a day. We apply filtering to keep it to that level. Email comes straight to me from anyone I've ever corresponded with, anyone from Microsoft, Intel, HP, and all the other partner companies, and anyone I know. And I always see a write-up from my assistant of any other email, from companies that aren't on my permission list or individuals I don't know. . . .

We're at the point now where the challenge isn't how to communicate effectively with email—it's ensuring that you spend your time on the email that matters most. I use tools like "in-box rules" and search folders to mark and group messages based on their content and importance.

And since we brought it up, what about leading in a recession? For tips on leading employees during an economic crisis, see the *Change* box entitled "Tips for Tough Times" on page 359.

What Do You Think?

1. In what ways has information technology changed the work of leaders?

2. How do you think the work of leaders will change in the future?

References: Geoffrey Colvin, "Catch a Rising Star," *Fortune*, February 6, 2006, http://money.cnn.com on March 15, 2010; Bill Gates, "How I Work," *Fortune*, April 7, 2006, http://money.cnn.com on March 15, 2010; Colvin, "Star Power," *Fortune*, January 30, 2006, http://money.cnn.com on March 15, 2010; Jerry Useem, "Making Your Work Work for You," *Fortune*, March 15, 2006, http://money.cnn.com on March 15, 2010.

The three major situational theories of leadership discussed in Chapter 12 altered everyone's thinking about leadership. No longer did people feel compelled to search for the one best way to lead. Nor did they continue to seek universal leadership prescriptions or relationships. Instead, both researchers and practicing managers turned their attention to a variety of new approaches to leadership. These new approaches, as well as other current emerging leadership issues, are the subject of this chapter. We first describe two relatively new situational theories, as well as recent refinements to the earlier theories. We then examine leadership through the eyes of followers. Recent thinking regarding potential alternatives to traditional leadership are then explored. Next we describe the changing nature of leadership. We conclude this chapter with a discussion of several emerging issues in leadership.

to a transactional role and continues to lead the firm toward higher revenues, market share, and profits.[8]

At Walt Disney, however, the story was different. Michael Eisner took over the floundering company in the early 1990s at a time when it had become stagnant and was heading into decline. Relying on his transformational skills, he turned things around in dramatic fashion. Among many other things, he quickly expanded the company's theme parks, built new hotels, improved Disney's movie business, created a successful Disney cruise line, launched several other major new initiatives, and changed the company into a global media powerhouse. But when the firm began to plateau and needed some time to let all the changes settle in, Eisner was unsuccessful at changing his own approach from transformational leadership to transactional leadership, and was subsequently pressured into retiring.

ROBERT GALBRAITH/REUTERS /LANDOV

Charismatic leadership can be a powerful force in an organization. Charismatic leaders have an exceptional ability to inspire support and acceptance. Steve Jobs, legendary co-founder and long-time CEO of Apple, is widely recognized as a charismatic leader. His capabilities as a leader have helped Apple launch a string of major new innovative products, including the iPhone and the iPad.

Charisma is a form of interpersonal attraction that inspires support and acceptance.

Charismatic leadership is a type of influence based on the leader's personal charisma.

Charismatic Leadership

Perspectives based on charismatic leadership, like the trait theories discussed in Chapter 12, assume that charisma is an individual characteristic of the leader. **Charisma** is a form of interpersonal attraction that inspires support and acceptance. **Charismatic leadership** is accordingly a type of influence based on the leader's personal charisma. All else being equal, then, someone with charisma is more likely to be able to influence others than someone without charisma. For example, a highly charismatic supervisor will be more successful in influencing subordinate behavior than a supervisor who lacks charisma. Thus, influence is again a fundamental element of this perspective.[9]

Robert House first proposed a theory of charismatic leadership based on research findings from a variety of social science disciplines.[10] His theory suggests that charismatic leaders are likely to have a lot of self-confidence, firm confidence in their beliefs and ideals, and a strong need to influence people. They also tend to communicate high expectations about follower performance and to express confidence in their followers. Herb Kelleher, legendary CEO of Southwest Airlines (now retired), is an excellent example of a charismatic leader. Kelleher skillfully blended a unique combination of executive skill, honesty, and playfulness. These qualities attracted a group of followers at Southwest who were willing to follow his lead without question and to dedicate themselves to carrying out his decisions and policies with unceasing passion.[11] Other individuals who are or were seen as charismatic leaders include Barack Obama, Mary Kay Ash, Steve Jobs, Ted Turner, Martin Luther King, Jr., and Pope John Paul II. Unfortunately, however, charisma can also empower leaders in other directions. Adolf Hitler had strong charismatic qualities, for instance, as does Osama bin Laden.

Figure 13.3 portrays the three elements of charismatic leadership in organizations that most experts acknowledge today.[12] First, charismatic leaders are able to envision likely future trends and patterns, to set high expectations for themselves and for others, and to model behaviors consistent with meeting those expectations. Next, charismatic leaders are able to energize others by demonstrating personal excitement, personal confidence, and consistent patterns of success. Finally, charismatic leaders enable others by supporting them, empathizing with them, and expressing confidence in them.[13]

Charismatic leadership ideas are quite popular among managers today and are the subject of numerous books and articles.[14] Unfortunately, few studies have specifically

Figure 13.3   THE CHARISMATIC LEADER

The charismatic leader is characterized by three fundamental attributes. As illustrated here, these are behaviors resulting in envisioning, energizing, and enabling. Charismatic leaders can be a powerful force in any organizational setting.

Reference: David A. Nadler and Michael L. Tushman, "Beyond the Charismatic Leader: Leadership and Organizational Change," *California Management Review*, Winter 1990, pp. 70–97.

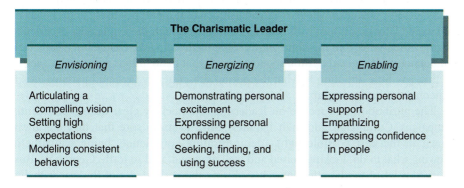

attempted to test the meaning and impact of charismatic leadership. Lingering ethical concerns about charismatic leadership also trouble some people. They stem from the fact that some charismatic leaders inspire such blind faith in their followers that they may engage in inappropriate, unethical, or even illegal behaviors just because the leader instructed them to do so. This tendency likely played a role in the unwinding of both Enron and Arthur Andersen as people followed orders from their charismatic bosses to hide information, shred documents, and mislead investigators. Taking over a leadership role from someone with substantial personal charisma is also a challenge. For instance, the immediate successors to very successful charismatic football coaches like Vince Lombardi (Green Bay Packers), Steve Spurrier (University of Florida), and Tom Osborne (University of Nebraska) each failed to measure up to his predecessor's legacy and was subsequently fired.

Attribution and Leadership

We discussed attribution theory back in Chapter 3 and noted then that people tend to observe behavior and then attribute causes (and hence meaning) to it. There are clear implications for attribution theory and leadership, especially when leadership is framed through the eyes of followers. Basically, then, the **attribution perspective** holds that when behaviors are observed in a context associated with leadership, others may attribute varying levels of leadership ability or power to the person displaying those behaviors.

For example, suppose we observe an individual behaving confidently and decisively; we also observe that others are paying close attention to what this person says and does and that they seem to defer to and/or consult with her on various things. We might subsequently conclude that this individual is a leader because of both her behavior and the behaviors of others. However, in a different setting we observe that a person seems to not be especially confident or decisive; we also observe that others seem relatively indifferent to what she has to say and that she is not routinely consulted about things. In this case we are more likely to assume that this person is not really a leader.

The attributions we make subsequently affect both our own behavior and the actual capacity of an individual to behave like a leader. For instance, suppose after observing

The **attribution perspective** on leadership holds when behaviors are observed in a context associated with leadership, then others may attribute varying levels of leadership ability or power to the person displaying those behaviors.

of crisis," he advises, "make sure your message reaches all levels, from the very lowest to the uppermost." Kip Tindell, who's been CEO of the Container Store since its founding in 1978, agrees. That's why his managers "run around like chickens relentlessly trying to communicate everything to every single employee at all times." He admits that it's an impossible task, but he's also convinced that the effort is more important than ever in times of crisis. He also contends that his company is in a better position to ride out the economic storm "because we're so dedicated to the notion that communication and leadership are the same thing." At the very least, he says, "we're fortunate to be minus the paranoia that goes with employees who feel they don't know what's going on."

References: Emily Thornton, "Managing through a Crisis: The New Rules," *BusinessWeek*, January 8, 2009, www.businessweek.com on March 15, 2010; Anthony Portuesi, "Leading in a Recession: An Interview with Jack Hayhow," *Driven Leaders*, February 24, 2009, http://drivenleaders.com on March 15, 2010; Jim Donald, "Guest Post: Former Starbucks CEO's Tips for Tough Times," *Fortune*, April 1, 2009, http://postcards.blogs.fortune.cnn.com on March 15, 2010; Ellen Davis, "Retail Execs Offer Insights on Leadership in Tough Economic Times," *NRF Annual 2009 Convention Blog*, January 15, 2009, http://blog.nrf.com on March 15, 2010.

Table 13.1
SUBSTITUTES AND NEUTRALIZERS FOR LEADERSHIP

Individual	Group
Individual professionalism	Group norms
Motivation	Group cohesiveness
Experience and training	
Indifference to rewards	

Job	Organization
Structured/automated	Rigid procedures and rules
Highly controlled	Explicit goals and objectives
Intrinsically satisfying	Rigid reward system
Embedded feedback	

stand around waiting for someone to take control and instruct them on what to do? The answer is obviously no—they are highly trained and well-prepared professionals who know how to respond, who to depend on, who to communicate with, how to work together as a team, and so forth. In short, they are fully capable of carrying out their jobs without someone playing the role of leader.

Individual ability, experience, training, knowledge, motivation, and professional orientation are among the characteristics that may substitute for leadership. Similarly, a task characterized by routine, a high degree of structure, frequent feedback, and intrinsic satisfaction may also render leader behavior unnecessary. Thus, if the task gives the subordinate enough intrinsic satisfaction, she or he may not need support from a leader.

Explicit plans and goals, rules and procedures, cohesive work groups, a rigid reward structure, and physical distance between supervisor and subordinate are organizational characteristics that may substitute for leadership. For example, if job goals are explicit, and there are many rules and procedures for task performance, a leader providing directions may not be necessary. Research has provided support for the concept of leadership substitutes, but additional research is needed to identify other potential substitutes and their impact on leadership effectiveness.[16]

Leadership Neutralizers

Leadership neutralizers are factors that render ineffective a leader's attempts to engage in various leadership behaviors.

In other situations, even if a leader is present and attempts to engage in various leadership behaviors, those behaviors may be rendered ineffective—neutralized—by various factors. These factors are referred to as **leadership neutralizers**. Suppose, for example, that a relatively new and inexperienced leader is assigned to a work group comprised of very experienced employees with long-standing performance norms and a high level of group cohesiveness. The norms and cohesiveness of the group may be so strong that there is nothing the new leader can do to change things. Of course, this pattern may also work in several different ways. The norms may dictate acceptable but not high performance, and the leader may be powerless to improve things because the group is so cohesive. Or, the norms may call for very high performance, and even a bungling and ineffective leader cannot cause any damage. In both cases, however, the process is the same—the leader's ability to alter the situation is neutralized by elements in that situation.

In addition to group factors, elements of the job itself may also limit a leader's ability to "make a difference." Consider, for example, employees working on a moving assembly line. Employees may only be able to work at the pace of the moving line, so performance quantity is constrained by the speed of the line. Moreover, if performance quality is also constrained (say, by simple tasks and/or tight quality control procedures), the leader may again be powerless to influence individual work behaviors.

Finally, organizational factors can also neutralize at least some forms of leader behavior. Suppose a new leader is accustomed to using merit pay increases as a way to motivate people. But in her or his new job, pay increases are dictated by union contracts and are based primarily on employee seniority and cost-of-living. Or suppose that an employee is already at the top of the pay grade for his or her job. In either case, the leader's previous approach to motivating people has been neutralized and so new approaches will have to be identified.

THE CHANGING NATURE OF LEADERSHIP

Various alternatives to leadership aside, though, many settings still call for at least some degree of leadership, although the nature of that leadership continues to evolve.[17] Among the recent changes in leadership that managers should recognize are the increasing role of leaders as coaches and gender and cross-cultural patterns of leader behavior.

Leaders as Coaches

We noted in Chapter 10 that many organizations today are using teams. And many other organizations are attempting to become less hierarchical—that is, to eliminate the old-fashioned command-and-control mentality often inherent in bureaucratic organizations and to motivate and empower individuals to work independently. In each case, the role of leaders is also changing. Whereas leaders were once expected to control situations, direct work, supervise people, closely monitor performance, make decisions, and structure activities, many leaders today are being asked to change how they manage people. Perhaps the best description of this new role is for the leader to become a **coach** instead of an overseer.[18]

Consider the metaphor from the standpoint of an actual coach of an athletic team. The coach plays a role in selecting the players for the team and deciding on the general direction to take (such as emphasizing offense versus defense). The coach also helps develop player talent, and teaches them how to execute specific plays. But at game time, the coach stays on the sideline; it's up to the players themselves to execute plays and get the job done. And while the coach may get some of the credit for the victory, he or she didn't actually score any of the points.

Likewise, then, from the standpoint of an organizational leader, a coaching perspective would call for the leader to help select team members and other new

Whereas leaders were once expected to control situations, direct work, supervise people, closely monitor performance, make decisions, and structure activities, many leaders today are being asked to change how they manage people—to become **coaches**.

As organizations make increasing use of work teams, the role of leader is also changing in those organizations. Whereas they previously supervised people, directed their work, and controlled their activities, leaders in team-based organizations generally need to adopt the role of coach. In this role the leader provides general direction and helps develop employee talent but then remains in the background, allowing the team to function on its own. In some ways, this role parallels that of the leader on a rowing team.

employees, to provide some general direction, to help train and develop the team and the skills of its members, and to help the team get the information and other resources it needs. The leader may also have to help resolve conflict among team members and mediate other disputes that arise. And coaches from different teams may need to play important roles in linking the activities and functions of their respective teams. But beyond these activities, the leader keeps a low profile and lets the group get its work done with little or no direct oversight from the leader.

Of course, some managers long accustomed to the traditional approach may have trouble changing to a coaching role. But others seem to make the transition with little or no difficulty. Moreover, companies such as Texas Instruments, Halliburton, and Yum! Brands have developed very successful training programs to help their managers learn how to become better coaches. Within the coaching role, some leaders have also excelled at taking on more responsibilities as a **mentor**—the role of helping a less-experienced person learn the ropes to better prepare himself or herself to advance within the organization. Texas Instruments, again, has maintained a very successful mentoring program for years.

Gender and Leadership

Another factor that is clearly changing the nature of leadership is the growing number of women advancing to higher levels in organizations. Given that most leadership theories and research studies have focused on male leaders, developing a better understanding of how females lead is clearly an important next step. For example, do women and men tend to lead differently? Some early research suggests that there are indeed fundamental differences in leadership as practiced by women and men.[19]

For instance, in contrast to original stereotypes, female leaders are not necessarily more nurturing or supportive than are male leaders. Likewise, male leaders are not systematically more harsh, controlling, or task focused than are female leaders. The one difference that does seem to arise in some cases is that women have a tendency to be slightly more democratic in making decisions, whereas men have a similar tendency to be somewhat more autocratic.[20]

There are two possible explanations for this pattern. One possibility is that women may tend to have stronger interpersonal skills than men and are hence able to better understand how to effectively involve others in making decisions. Men, on the other hand, may have weaker interpersonal skills and thus have a tendency to rely on their own judgment. The other possible explanation is that women may encounter more stereotypic resistance to their occupying senior roles. If this is the case, they may actively work to involve others in making decisions so as to help minimize any hostility or conflict. Clearly, however, much more work needs to be done in order to better understand the dynamics of gender and leadership. It is obvious, of course, that high-profile and successful female

Within the coaching role, some leaders have also excelled at taking on more responsibilities as a **mentor**—helping a less-experienced person learn the ropes to better prepare himself or herself to advance within the organization.

JENS UNGER/ISTOCKPHOTO

leaders such as Andrea Jung (CEO of Avon Products) and Condoleezza Rice (former Secretary of State) are demonstrating the effectiveness with which women can be truly exceptional leaders.

Cross-Cultural Leadership

Another changing perspective on leadership relates to cross-cultural issues. In this context culture is used as a broad concept to encompass both international differences and diversity-based differences within one culture. For instance, when a Japanese firm sends an executive to head up the firm's operation in the United States, that person will need to become acclimated to the cultural differences that exist between the two countries and consider changing his or her leadership style accordingly. Japan is generally characterized by collectivism, while the United States (U of C 15.34) is based more on individualism. The Japanese executive, then, will find it necessary to recognize the importance of individual contributions and rewards and the differences in individual and group roles that exist in Japanese and U.S. businesses.

Similarly, cross-cultural factors also play a growing role in organizations as their workforces become more and more diverse. Most leadership research, for instance, has been conducted on samples or case studies involving white male leaders (since until several years ago most business leaders were white males!). But as African Americans, Asian Americans, (U of C 8.42) Hispanics, and members of other ethnic groups achieve leadership positions, it may be necessary to reassess how applicable current theories and models of leadership are when applied to an increasingly diverse pool of leaders.

"Do you have any problem being fired by a woman?"

The role of gender in leadership has become an interesting topic in recent years. For example, some people think that women and men tend to lead in different ways. Similarly, as illustrated here, there is interest in the possibility that followers may respond differently to men versus women leaders. In reality, of course, both women and men have the capacity to be strong leaders.

PETER STEINER/CARTOONBANK.COM

EMERGING ISSUES IN LEADERSHIP

Finally, there are also three emerging issues in leadership that warrant discussion. These issues are strategic leadership, ethical leadership, and virtual leadership.

Strategic Leadership

Strategic leadership is a new concept that explicitly relates leadership to the role of top management.[21] We will define **strategic leadership** as the capability to understand the complexities of both the organization and its environment and to lead change in the organization so as to achieve and maintain a superior alignment between the organization and its environment. In some ways, then, strategic leadership may be seen as an extension of the transformational leadership role discussed earlier. However, this recent focus has more explicitly acknowledged and incorporated the importance of strategy and strategic decision making. That is, while both transformational and strategic leadership include the concept of change, transformational leadership

Strategic leadership is the capability to understand the complexities of both the organization and its environment and to lead change in the organization so as to achieve and maintain a superior alignment between the organization and its environment.

ALEX WONG/GETTY IMAGES

Ethical leadership has grown in importance in recent years. In some cases leaders like Ken Lay and Jeff Skilling, the two leaders who ran Enron, personify ethical misdeeds and are held directly accountable for their actions. But in other cases the ethical context of leadership may be less clear. Take Tony Hayward, for example. Hayward was CEO of BP when the oil firm's deep water rig exploded in the Gulf of Mexico in 2010, pumping thousands of gallons of oil into the water. While Hayward was never explicitly charged with wrongdoing, nevertheless his demeanor and attitude led many observers to believe he was covering up important facts during the investigation. Indeed, he was eventually pressured to resign from his position

Now more than ever high standards of **ethical conduct** are being held up as a prerequisite for effective leadership. Top managers are being called upon to maintain high ethical standards for their own conduct, to unfailingly exhibit ethical behavior, and to hold others in their organizations to the same standards.

Virtual leadership is emerging as an important issue for organizations.

implicitly emphasizes the ability to lead change as the central focus. Strategic leadership, on the other hand, puts greater weight on the leader's ability to think and function strategically.

To be effective in this role, a manager needs to have a thorough and complete understanding of the organization—its history, its culture, its strengths, and its weaknesses. In addition, the leader needs a firm grasp of the organization's environment. This understanding must encompass current conditions and circumstances as well as significant trends and issues on the horizon. The strategic leader also needs to recognize how the firm is currently aligned with its environment—where it relates effectively with that environment, and where it relates less effectively. Finally, looking at environmental trends and issues, the strategic leader works to improve not only the current alignment but also the future alignment.

Andrea Jung (CEO of Avon Products), Michael Dell (founder and CEO of Dell Computer), and A. G. (U of C 8.6) Lafley (former CEO of Procter & Gamble) have all been recognized as strong strategic leaders. Reflecting on the dramatic turnaround he led at Procter & Gamble, for instance, Lafley commented, "I have made a lot of symbolic, very physical changes so people understand we are in the business of leading change." On the other hand, Jurgen Schrempp (former CEO of DaimlerChrysler), Raymond Gilmartin (CEO of Merck), and Scott Livengood (CEO of Krispy Kreme) have been singled out for their poor strategic leadership.[22]

Ethical Leadership

Most people have long assumed that top managers are ethical people. But in the wake of recent corporate scandals at firms like Enron, Boeing, and WorldCom, faith in top managers has been shaken. Hence, perhaps now more than ever, high standards of **ethical conduct** are being held up as a prerequisite for effective leadership. More specifically, top managers are being called upon to maintain high ethical standards for their own conduct, to unfailingly exhibit ethical behavior, and to hold others in their organizations to the same standards.

The behaviors of top leaders are being scrutinized more than ever, and those responsible for hiring new leaders for a business are looking more and more closely at the backgrounds of those being considered. The emerging pressures for stronger corporate governance models are likely to further increase the commitment to select only those individuals with high ethical standards for leadership positions in business, and to hold them more accountable than in the past for both their actions and the consequences of those actions.[23]

Virtual Leadership

Finally, **virtual leadership** is also emerging as an important issue for organizations. In earlier times leaders and their employees worked together in the same physical location and engaged in personal (i.e., face-to-face) interactions on a regular basis. But in today's world both leaders and their employees may work in locations that are far from one another. Such arrangements might include people telecommuting from a home office one or two days a week to people actually living and working far from company headquarters and seeing one another in person only very infrequently.

How then do managers carry out leadership when they do not have regular personal contact with their followers? And how do they help mentor and develop others? Communication between leaders and their subordinates will still occur, of course, but it may be largely by telephone and email. Hence, one implication may be that leaders in these situations may simply need to work harder at creating and maintaining relationships with their employees that go beyond simply words on a computer screen. While nonverbal communication such as smiles and handshakes may not be possible online, managers can instead make a point of adding a few personal words in an email (whenever appropriate) to convey appreciation, reinforcement, or constructive feedback. Building on this, managers should then also take advantage of every single opportunity whenever they are in face-to-face situations to go further than they might have done under different circumstances to develop a strong relationship.

But beyond these simple prescriptions, there is no theory or research to guide managers functioning in a virtual world. Hence, as electronic communications continues to pervade the workplace, researchers and managers alike need to work together to first help frame the appropriate issues and questions regarding virtual leadership, and then collaborate to help address those issues and answer those questions.[24]

SYNOPSIS

There are two contemporary situation theories. The leader-member exchange model (LMX) of leadership stresses the importance of variable relationships between supervisors and each of their subordinates. Each superior-subordinate pair is referred to as a "vertical dyad." The Hersey and Blanchard model argues that appropriate leader behavior depends on the subordinate's degree of motivation, competence, experience, and interest in accepting responsibility. In addition to these somewhat newer models, the three dominant situational theories have also continued to undergo various refinements and revisions.

There are three primary approaches to leadership through the eyes of followers. Transformational leadership focuses on the basic distinction between leading for change and leading for stability. Perspectives based on charismatic leadership assume that charisma is an individual characteristic of the leader. Charisma is a form of interpersonal attraction that inspires support and acceptance. The attribution perspective holds that when behaviors are observed in a context associated with leadership, others may attribute varying levels of leadership ability or power to the person displaying those behaviors.

Another perspective on leadership that has received considerable attention in recent years has focused on alternatives to leadership. In some cases, circumstances

may exist that render leadership unnecessary or irrelevant. The factors that contribute to these circumstances are called leadership substitutes. In other cases, factors may exist that neutralize or negate the influence of a leader even when that individual is attempting to exercise leadership.

The nature of leadership continues to evolve. Among recent changes in leadership that managers should recognize is the increasing role of leaders as coaches. The most frequent instance of this arrangement is when an organization uses self-managing teams. Gender differences in leader behavior are also becoming more important, especially given the increasing numbers of women advancing up the organizational ladder. Cross-cultural patterns of leadership both between and within national boundaries are also taking on growing importance.

Finally, there are three emerging issues in leadership. Strategic leadership is a new concept that explicitly relates leadership to the role of top management. In addition, leaders in all organizations are being called upon to maintain high ethical standards for their own conduct, to unfailingly exhibit ethical behavior, and to hold others in their organizations to the same standards. And the growing importance of virtual leadership needs to be further studied.

3. In what ways was Anderson a *transformational leader*? In order to execute his strategy for Best Buy, how did he combine transformational with transactional leadership? In what ways did Anderson exhibit characteristics of a *charismatic leader*?

4. Assume that you've put in a year to 18 months working in the cell phone department at a Best Buy store. Apply the *Hersey and Blanchard model* of leadership to your situation: what must your superiors do in order to get you "ready" to make inventory-management and similar decisions?

REFERENCES

Matthew Boyle, "Best Buy's Giant Gamble," *Fortune*, April 3, 2006, http://money.cnn.com on March 15, 2010; Kristina Bell, "Q&A with Best Buy CEO Brad Anderson," *Time*, June 12, 2008, www.time .com on February 18, 2009; Matthew Boyle, "Q&A with Best Buy CEO Brad Anderson," *CNNMoney.com*, April 18, 2007, http://money .cnn.com on March 15, 2010; "How to Break Out of Commodity Hell," *BusinessWeek*, March 27, 2006, www.businessweek.com on March 15, 2010; Ken Cotrill, "Best Buy's Supply Chain Transformation," *Harvard Business School Working Knowledge*, January 23, 2006, http://hbswk.hbs.edu on March 15, 2010; Best Buy Inc., "Best Buy Reports December Revenue of $7.5 Billion, Continues Market Share Gains," news release, January 9, 2009, www.bestbuyinc.com on March 15, 2010.

EXPERIENCING ORGANIZATIONAL BEHAVIOR

Understanding Leadership Substitutes

Purpose This exercise will help you assess the possibilities and limitations of leadership substitutes in organizations.

Format Working in small groups, you will identify several factors that can substitute for and/or neutralize leadership in different settings.

Procedures Your instructor will divide the class into small groups of four to five members each. Working as a team, do the following:

1. Identify two jobs, one that is relatively simple (perhaps a custodian or a fast-food cook) and one that is much more complex (such as an airline pilot or software engineer).
2. For each job, identify as many potential leadership substitutes and neutralizers as possible.

3. Next, exchange one of your lists with one group and the other list with a different group.
4. Review the two new lists and look for areas where you agree or disagree.
5. Exchange lists once again to get back your original lists.
6. Discuss among yourselves if there is a discernable pattern as to the types of job groups in which leadership might be most easily substituted or neutralized.

Follow-up Questions

1. To what extent did your own experiences affect how you performed this exercise?
2. Are there some jobs for which there are no substitutes for leadership? Provide examples.
3. Should managers actively seek substitutes for leadership? Why or why not?

BUILDING MANAGERIAL SKILLS

Exercise Overview Interpersonal skills refer to a manager's ability to communicate with, understand, and motivate individuals and groups. This exercise will help you develop your interpersonal skills as they relate to leadership.

Exercise Background As noted in the chapter, virtual leadership is an emerging phenomenon about

which little is known. Begin this exercise by partnering three of your classmates (that is, create groups of four). Spend some time with your group members getting to know each other and exchanging email addresses.

Next, create a hypothetical work team. The team should identify one of you as the leader, and the other three as employees. Develop relatively detailed roles for yourselves—gender, age, work experiences, motivations and aspirations, and so forth, as well as some detail about a work project that the team has been assigned.

Between now and the next class meeting, you should all exchange numerous emails about your hypothetical work project. The leader should be especially active in the process and send a wide array of messages. Specifically, the leader should be sure to provide some encouragement, respond to questions, relay some information, provide some criticism, and so forth. The leader should also maintain a written log of what the intention was of each email that was sent. Employees can communicate among yourselves, but also be sure to communicate with your leader—ask questions, relay information, and so forth.

During the process of exchanging emails, it is virtually certain that you will need to "make up some things." Try to maintain realism, however, and try to be consistent with things that have already transpired. For example, an employee might "create" a problem and ask the leader's advice. However, the problem should be realistic, and it should be reasonable for the leader to be able to answer the question. For her or his part, the leader should also make a realistic effort to answer the question. Later during subsequent exchanges, remember to account for the question and the answer if and when appropriate. You can end the exercise whenever several exchanges have taken place and you sense that the group has "run out of steam."

Exercise Task At the next class meeting, reconvene with your team members and respond to the following questions:

1. The leader should first recount each email that was sent and then convey his or her intended meaning; the recipient(s) should then convey how the message was actually interpreted. Were there any differences between the intended message and how it was interpreted?
2. To what extent did interactions among those playing the roles of employees affect how they interpreted messages from the leader?
3. What, if anything, could the leader have done to improve communication?

SELF-ASSESSMENT EXERCISE

What Are Your Skills Leading Up To?

Now that you're more than half way through this book, you've probably come to recognize a number of interesting facts about today's organizations and the people who lead them. One of them is—or ought to be—the fact that conditions are in the process of changing rapidly: Hierarchies are flatter and more fluid. Teams are more vital though sometimes virtual. Workforces are accustomed to doing more with less, and workers want a more workable balance between work and nonwork life. Only when managers manage well under these conditions do organizations manage to operate effectively.

So here's an important question that you might want to ask yourself: Are you the kind of person who's likely to succeed in making the necessary adjustments for leading in the twenty-first century—or are you just gearing up to drive your grandfather's organization?

The following quiz—which is by no means exhaustive—is designed to provide you with a very informal answer to this question by assessing the degree to which you possess a few specific skills. On some items, you'll have to assess your personality and skills without the benefit of real-life experience, but you should know yourself fairly well by now. Remember: The more honest you are, the more useful the results will be.

For each of the 11 skill areas on the quiz, ask yourself *how others would characterize you* and put the *number* corresponding to the best answer in the appropriate blank space:

1. Do I have a **need to exceed**?
   Do I demonstrate a sustained passion to succeed? Willingly step up to significant challenges? Set high standards? Convey a sense of urgency? Hold myself accountable for adding value? Am I driven to achieve results?
   ____ A. This is not me (1)
   ____ B. Sometimes this is me (3)
   ____ C. This is definitely me (5)

2. Do I **help others succeed?**

Do I support others by providing constructive feedback or coaching? Do I provide developmental resources and try to see that others are developed?

____ A. This is not me (1)
____ B. Sometimes this is me (3)
____ C. This is definitely me (5)

3. Am I **courageous?**

Am I willing to stand up and be counted? Do I step forward to address difficult issues? Put myself on the line to deal with important problems? Stand firm when necessary? Am I willing to hold back nothing that needs to be said? Am I willing to take negative action when appropriate?

____ A. This is not me (1)
____ B. Sometimes this is me (3)
____ C. This is definitely me (5)

4. Do I **lead?**

Do I try to offer a vision and purpose that others buy into and share? Do I take actions that inspire confidence in my vision? Do I set clear and compelling goals that serve as a unifying focal point of joint efforts? Do I encourage team spirit? Do I believe that "good enough" never is?

____ A. This is not me (1)
____ B. Sometimes this is me (3)
____ C. This is definitely me (5)

5. Am I **customer focused?**

Do I try to create sustained partnerships with customers (internal and external) based on a thorough firsthand understanding of what creates value for them? Do I continually search for ways to increase customer satisfaction?

____ A. This is not me (1)
____ B. Sometimes this is me (3)
____ C. This is definitely me (5)

6. Am I a **relationship builder?**

Do I initiate and develop relationships with others as a key priority? Use informal networks to get things done? Rely more on ability than on hierarchical relationships to influence people?

____ A. This is not me (1)
____ B. Sometimes this is me (3)
____ C. This is definitely me (5)

7. Am I a **team builder?**

Do I champion teamwork? Do I try to create an environment in which teams are used appropriately, their development is supported, and they are generally successful? Do I foster collaboration among team members and among teams and create a feeling of belonging among members?

____ A. This is not me (1)
____ B. Sometimes this is me (3)
____ C. This is definitely me (5)

8. Am I **principled?**

Do I inspire trust through ethical behavior? Show consistency among my principles, values, and behavior? Consistently live, breathe, and express my principles in all that I do?

____ A. This is not me (1)
____ B. Sometimes this is me (3)
____ C. This is definitely me (5)

9. Am I a **change agent?**

Do I act as a catalyst for change and stimulate others to change? Challenge the status quo and champion new initiatives? Effectively manage the implementation of change?

____ A. This is not me (1)
____ B. Sometimes this is me (3)
____ C. This is definitely me (5)

10. Am I an **eager learner?**

Do I learn from experience? Learn quickly? Actively pursue learning and self-development? Am I a versatile learner?

____ A. This is not me (1)
____ B. Sometimes this is me (3)
____ C. This is definitely me (5)

11. Do I **value others?**.

Do I show and foster respect and appreciation for everyone, regardless of background, race, age, gender, values, or lifestyles? Do I make others feel valued for their ideas and contributions? Do I seek other people's point of view? Do I recognize the contributions of others and make them feel appreciated?

____ A. This is not me (1)
____ B. Sometimes this is me (3)
____ C. This is definitely me (5)

How to score: Add up all the numbers that you put in the blank spaces and compare your score to the following scale:

11 – 21 You're an **obsolete manager**.

If you're presently a manager, you're probably quite frustrated and yearn for the good old days. Sorry, but they weren't that good in the first place, and they aren't coming back. Have you considered a nonmanagerial position?

21 – 43 You're a **closet twenty-first-century manager**.

You may be torn between the impulse to hold on to the past and perpetuate the skills of your old masters and the desire to join your more progressive contemporaries. Sometimes you go one way, sometimes another. What you need is more consistency. Start by trusting yourself: You're at a fork in the road, but you know which way you need to go. Look for opportunities to sharpen your skills so that you can develop more confidence in relying on them.

45 – 55 You're a **twenty-first-century manager**.

Your skills should stand you in good stead in the future. Don't relax, however, and keep learning and adapting. You never know what the future has in store, but it's a pretty safe bet that it's going to be something different. Besides, a constant willingness to learn and adapt is a handy personality trait under any circumstances characterized by change.

Reference: Matt M. Starcevich, Center for Coaching and Mentoring, Inc., "Are You Ready to Manage in the 21st Century?" 2009, www.work911.com. Accessed June 1, 2010. Used by permission of Matt M. Starcevich, Ph.D.

CHAPTER 14

POWER, POLITICS, AND ORGANIZATIONAL JUSTICE

CHAPTER LEARNING OBJECTIVES

After studying this chapter you should be able to:

- Define and discuss influence in organizations.
- Describe the types and uses of power in organizations.
- Discuss politics and political behavior in organizations.
- Describe the various forms and implications of justice in organizations.

Facets of Jamie Dimon's Strategy at JPMorgan Chase & Co.

"[A large organization] can get arrogant and ... lose focus, like the Roman Empire."

—JAMIE DIMON, CEO, JPMORGAN CHASE & CO.

In October 2006, the head of the mortgage-servicing department, which collects payments on home loans, informed JPMorgan CEO Jamie Dimon that late payments were increasing at an alarming rate. When Dimon reviewed the report, he

The financial crisis of 2009–2010 led to thousands of mortgage foreclosures. Jamie Dimon, CEO of JPMorgan Chase & Co., used his power to create strong controls in his firm. These controls, in turn, helped keep his firm afloat.

FOTOG/TETRA IMAGES/JUPITER IMAGES

confirmed not only that late payments were a problem at Morgan, but that things were even worse for other lenders. "We concluded," recalls Dimon, "that underwriting standards were deteriorating across the industry." Shortly thereafter, Dimon was informed that the cost of insuring securities backed by subprime mortgages was going up even though ratings agencies persisted in rating them *AAA*. At the time, creating securities backed by subprime mortgages was the hottest and most profitable business on Wall Street, but by the end of the year, Dimon had decided to get out of it. "We saw no profit, and lots of risk," reports Bill Winters, co-head of Morgan's investment arm. "It was Jamie," he adds, "who saw all the pieces."

Dimon's caution—and willingness to listen to what his risk-management people were telling him—paid off in a big way. Between July 2007 and July 2008, when the full impact of the crisis hit the country's investment banks, Morgan recorded losses of $5 billion on mortgage-backed securities. That's a lot of money, but relatively little compared to the losses sustained by banks that didn't see the writing on the wall—$33 billion at Citibank, for example, and $26 billion at Merrill Lynch. Citi is still in business thanks to $45 billion in cash infusions from the federal government, but Merrill Lynch isn't—it was forced to sell itself to Bank of America. Morgan, though hit hard, weathered the storm and is still standing on its own Wall Street foundations. "You know," said President-elect Barack Obama as he surveyed the damage sustained by the U.S. banking industry in 2008, ". . . there are a lot of banks that are actually pretty well managed, J.P. Morgan being a good example. Jamie Dimon . . . is doing a pretty good job managing an enormous portfolio."

Ironically, Dimon had gotten his start at Citi, where, as a newly minted MBA, he worked closely with legendary CEO Sandy Weill for 12 years, helping to transform Citigroup into the largest financial institution in the United States. The relationship, however, eventually soured, and Dimon left in 1998. Taking over as CEO in 2000, he revitalized Bank One, then the country's fifth-largest bank, before selling it to J.P. Morgan Chase in 2004. In 2006, he became CEO and chairman of JPMorgan Chase, a financial services institution which includes J.P. Morgan Chase Bank, a commercial-retail bank, and J.P. Morgan Trust Company, an investment bank. With assets of $2.3 trillion, JPMorgan Chase boasts the largest market-capitalization and deposit bases in the U.S. financial industry.

Dimon came to JPMorgan Chase with a few ideas about how to manage an enormous portfolio. Shortly after he took over, he increased oversight and control of Bank One's operations and expenses, using cost-saving measures to free up $3 billion annually by 2007. He then used the cash to finance the expansion of JPMorgan Chase operations, including the installation of more ATM machines and the creation of new products. As improved fundamentals and expanded operations yielded greater revenues, the bank's stock price went up (at least until the subprime crisis hit), freeing up further funds for new growth. Once the basics are right, says Dimon, "you earn the right to do a deal," and he set about building a Citi-like financial empire, relying mostly on mergers to jumpstart growth in underserved regional and international markets.

Experience had shown Dimon that a large organization "can get arrogant and . . . lose focus, like the Roman Empire." In 2006, for example, JPMorgan Chase was enjoying high sales but spending a lot more than Dimon was used to spending at Bank One. Moreover, Dimon had inherited a company that had engineered multiple mergers without making much effort to integrate operations. The results included ho-hum profits and a loose collection of incompatible structures and systems. Financial results from different divisions, for instance, were simply being combined, and the upshot, according to CFO Michael Cavanagh, was that even though "strong businesses were subsidizing weak ones ... the numbers didn't jump out at you. With the results mashed together, it was easy for managers to hide."

Dimon thus set out to exercise more effective operational oversight, and his control practices currently extend to virtually every aspect of JPMorgan Chase operations:

- Every month, managers must submit 50-page reports showing financial ratios and results, product sales, and even detailed expenses for every worker. Then Dimon and his top executives spend hours combing through the data, with the CEO asking tough questions and demanding frank answers.

- Dimon prepares a detailed to-do list every week. "I make my list by business [and] by person [in order] to think about what I might be avoiding [and] what I have to do. It's hard to see the truth," he admits, "[and] even harder to do something about it."

- One of Dimon's top priorities is slashing bloated budgets. "Waste hurt[s] our customers," he reminds his management team. "Cars, phones, clubs, perks—what's that got to do with customers?" He's also eliminated such amenities as fresh flowers, lavish expense accounts, and oversized offices and closed the in-house gym. One time, he asked a line of limousine drivers outside company headquarters for the names of the executives they were waiting for. Then he called up each one, asking, "Too good for the subway?" or "Why don't you try walking?" Dimon denies the story, but limo service at JPMorgan Chase is way down.

- Dimon also takes a close look at compensation. Regional bank managers at JPMorgan Chase once earned $2 million a year, compared with Bank One's modest salary of $400,000. "I'd tell people they were way overpaid," says Dimon, and as he suspected, "they already knew it." He cut pay for most staff by 20 to 50 percent, but most people elected to stay with the company. Today, a strict pay-for-performance formula keeps compensation in line.

- "In a big company," Dimon advises, "it's easy for people to b.s. you. A lot of them have been practicing for decades." So he gathers outcome data from every manager, various forms of information from low-level staffers, and even candid performance critiques from suppliers. "If you just want to run your business on your own and report results," warns Steve Black, co-head of investment banking, "you won't like working for Jamie."

- Finally, Dimon is convinced that IT is critical to the bank's long-term strategy and once cancelled a long-running information-services contract with IBM. "When you're outsourcing," he explained, "... people don't care" about your performance. At JPMorgan Chase, "we want patriots, not mercenaries." Between 2007 and 2008, he invested $2 billion in technology developed in-house and considers it money well spent.

Dimon, however, doesn't like being thought of as a control freak. "It's offensive ... to be called a cost cutter," he complains, and besides, his long-run goal isn't merely control—it's growth. "It's [a] thousand-mile march," observes one JPMorgan analyst, "and not everyone will survive."

What Do You Think?

1. Describe the role of power and politics at JPMorgan Chase.

2. Do you think that issues associated with power and political behaviors exist in all organizations? Why or why not?

References: Felix Salmon, "Dimon in the Rough: How JPMorgan's CEO Manages Risk," *Seeking Alpha*, September 3, 2008, www.seekingalpha.com on March 26, 2010; Duff McDonald, "The Banker Who Saved Wall Street," *Newsweek*, September 11, 2009, www.newsweek.com on March 26, 2010; Shawn Tully, "How J.P. Morgan Steered Clear of the Credit Crunch," *CNNMoney.com*, September 2, 2008, http://money.cnn.com on March 26, 2010; Mara Der Hovanesian, "Dimon in the Rough," *BusinessWeek*, March 28, 2005, www.businessweek.com on March 26, 2010; Mara Der Hovanesian with Emily Thornton et al., "Dimon's Grand Design," *BusinessWeek*, March 28, 2005, www.businessweek.com on March 26, 2010; "Jamie Dimon, In His Own Words," *BusinessWeek*, March 28, 2005, www.businessweek.com on March 26, 2010; Jamie Dimon, "No More 'Too Big to Fail,'" *Washington Post*, November 13, 2009, www.washingtonpost.com on March 26, 2010.

As we learned in Chapters 12 and 13, leadership is a powerful, complex, and amorphous concept. This chapter explores a variety of forces and processes in organizations that are often related to—but at the same time distinct from—leadership. These forces and processes may precede, follow from, undermine, and/or reinforce a leader's ability to function effectively. They may also occur independently of leadership and its other associated activities.

We begin by briefly revisiting the concept of influence. While we introduced influence at the beginning of Chapter 12 as a basis for defining leadership, we now examine influence a bit more completely, and also describe a specific form of influence known as impression management. We then discuss power in its myriad forms in organizations. Politics and political behavior are then introduced and described in detail. Finally, we discuss organizational justice. (Some authors treat justice in the context of motivation, but given its close association with influence, power, and politics, it seems most reasonable to cover it here.)

INFLUENCE IN ORGANIZATIONS

Recall that in Chapter 12 we defined leadership (from a process perspective) as the use of noncoercive influence to direct and coordinate the activities of group members to meet goals. We then described a number of leadership models and theories based variously on leadership traits, behaviors, and contingencies. Unfortunately, most of these models and theories essentially ignore the influence component of leadership. That is, they tend to focus on the characteristics of the leader (traits, behaviors, or both) and the responses from followers (satisfaction, performance, or both, for instance) with little regard for how the leader actually exercises influence in an effort to bring about the desired responses from followers.

But influence should actually be seen as the cornerstone of the process of one person attempting to affect another. For instance, regardless of the leader's traits or behaviors, leadership only matters if influence actually occurs. That is, a person's effectiveness in affecting the behavior of others through influence is the ultimate determinant of whether she or he is really a leader. No one can truly be a leader without the ability to influence others. And if someone does have the ability to influence others, he or she clearly has the potential—at least—to become a leader.

PETER SERLING

Influence, the ability to affect the perceptions, attitudes, or behaviors of others, is a fundamental cornerstone of leadership. Childhood friends Rameck Hunt, Sampson Davis, and George Jenkins vowed to defy the limits of their inner-city upbringings and become doctors together. Throughout the rigors of college and medical school, the friends pushed each other to do their best. And there is little doubt in any of their minds that their mutual influence was the catalyst for each of them to succeed. Now they do their best to exert that same positive influence on others who face similar challenges.

The Nature of Influence

Influence is defined as the ability to affect the perceptions, attitudes, or behaviors of others.[1] If a person can make another person recognize that her working conditions are more hazardous than she currently believes them to be (change in perceptions), influence has occurred. Likewise, if an individual can convince someone else that the organization is a much better place to work than he currently believes it to be (change in attitude), influence has occurred. And if someone can get others to work harder or to file a grievance against their boss (change in behavior), influence has occurred.[2]

Influence can be dramatic or subtle. For instance, a new leader may be able to take a group of disenchanted employees working on a flawed and poorly conceived project and energize them to work harder while simultaneously enhancing the nature and direction of their project so as to make it much more worthwhile. As a result, the group will enjoy much greater success. In a different setting, however, a specific disgruntled employee may be very unhappy and on the verge of resigning. One morning a supervisor makes an innocuous comment that the unhappy employee perceives to be a criticism. That one comment, taken alone, might objectively be seen as very trivial. But on top of the employee's current feelings and attitudes, it's enough to prompt an immediate resignation.

We should also point out that both the source and the target of influence might be a person or group. For instance, the efforts and success of a work team might so inspire other teams as to cause them to work harder. Further, influence might be intentional or unintentional. If one employee starts coming to work dressed more casually than has been the norm, others might follow even though the actions of the first employee were not meant to influence others in any way, but only to be more comfortable.

Note, too, that influence can be used in ways that are beneficial or harmful. Someone can be influenced to help clean up a city park on the weekend as part of a community service program, for example. Operating employees can be influenced to work harder, engineers can be influenced to become more creative and innovative, and teams can be influenced to increase their efficiency. But people can also be influenced to use or sell drugs or to smoke. Employees can be influenced to care less about the quality of their work, engineers can be influenced to not explore or advocate new ideas, and teams can be influenced to be less efficient. Hence, influence is a major force in organizations that managers cannot afford to ignore.

Influence is the ability to affect the perceptions, attitudes, or behaviors of others.

Impression Management

Impression management is a special—and occasionally subtle—form of influence that deserves special mention. **Impression management** is a direct, intentional effort by someone to enhance his or her image in the eyes of others. People engage in impression management for a variety of reasons. For one thing, they may do so to further their own careers. By making themselves look good, they think they are more likely to receive rewards, attractive job assignments, and promotions. They may also engage in impression management to boost their own self-esteem. When people have a positive image in an organization, others make them aware of it through their compliments, respect, and so forth. Another reason people use impression management is to acquire more power and hence more control.

People attempt to manage how others perceive them through a variety of mechanisms. Appearance is one of the first things people think of. Hence, a person motivated by impression management will pay close attention to choice of attire, selection of language, and the use of manners and body posture. People interested in impression management are also likely to jockey to be associated only with successful projects. By being assigned to high-profile projects led by highly successful managers, a person can begin to link his or her own name with such projects in the minds of others.

In its most basic sense, of course, there is nothing wrong with impression management. After all, most people want to create a positive—and honest—image of themselves in the eyes of others. Sometimes, however, people motivated too strongly by impression management become obsessed by it and resort to dishonest or unethical means. For example, a person may start to take credit for the work of others in an effort to make herself or himself look better. People may also exaggerate or even falsify their personal accomplishments in an effort to enhance their image. Hence, while there is clearly nothing wrong with "putting your best foot forward," people should be cognizant of the impressions they are attempting to create and make sure they are not using inappropriate methods.

POWER IN ORGANIZATIONS

Influence is also closely related to the concept of power. Power is one of the most significant forces that exist in organizations. Moreover, it can be an extremely important ingredient in organizational success—or organizational failure. In this section we first describe the nature of power. Then we examine the types and uses of power.

The Nature of Power

Power has been defined in dozens of different ways; no one definition is generally accepted. Drawing from the more common meanings of the term, we define **power** as the potential ability of a person or group to exercise control over another person or group.[3] Power is distinguished from influence due to the element of control—the more powerful control the less powerful. Thus, power might be thought of as an extreme form of influence.

One obvious aspect of our definition is that it expresses power in terms of potential; that is, we may be able to control others but may choose not to exercise that control. Nevertheless, simply having the potential may be enough to influence others in some settings. We should also note that power may reside in individuals (such as managers

Impression management is a direct and intentional effort by someone to enhance his or her own image in the eyes of others.

Power is the potential ability of a person or group to exercise control over another person or group.

and informal leaders), in formal groups (such as departments and committees), and in informal groups (such as a clique of influential people). Finally, we should note the direct link between power and influence. If a person can convince another person to change his or her opinion on some issue, to engage in or refrain from some behavior, or to view circumstances in a certain way, that person has exercised influence—and used power.

Considerable differences of opinion exist about how thoroughly power pervades organizations. Some people argue that virtually all interpersonal relations are influenced by power, whereas others believe that the exercise of power is confined only to certain situations. Whatever the case, power is undoubtedly a pervasive part of organizational life. It affects decisions ranging from the choice of strategies to the color of the new office carpeting. It makes or breaks careers. And it enhances or limits organizational effectiveness.

Types of Power

Within the broad framework of our definition, there obviously are many types of power. These types usually are described in terms of bases of power and position power versus personal power. Table 14.1 identifies and summarizes the most common forms of power.

Bases of Power   The most widely used and recognized analysis of the bases of power is the classic framework developed by John R. P. French and Bertram Raven.[4] French and Raven identified five general bases of power in organizational settings: legitimate, reward, coercive, expert, and referent power.

Legitimate power, essentially the same thing as authority, is granted by virtue of one's position in an organization. Managers have legitimate power over their subordinates. The organization specifies that it is legitimate for the designated individual to direct the activities of others. The bounds of this legitimacy are defined partly by the formal nature of the position involved and partly by informal norms and traditions. For example, it was once commonplace for managers to expect their secretaries not only to perform work-related activities such as typing and filing but also to run personal errands such as picking up laundry and buying gifts. In highly centralized, mechanistic and bureaucratic organizations such as the military, the legitimate power inherent in each position is closely specified, widely known, and strictly followed. In more organic organizations, such as research and development labs and software firms, the lines of legitimate power often are blurry. Employees may work for more than one boss at the same time, and leaders and followers may be on a nearly equal footing.

Table 14.1   COMMON FORMS OF POWER IN ORGANIZATIONS

LEGITIMATE POWER	Power that is granted by virtue of one's position in the organization
REWARD POWER	Power that exists when one person controls rewards that another person values
COERCIVE POWER	Power that exists when one person has the ability to punish or physically or psychologically harm someone else
EXPERT POWER	Power that exists when one person controls information that is valuable to someone else
REFERENT POWER	Power that exists when one person wants to be like or imitates someone else
POSITION POWER	Power that resides in a position, regardless of who is filling that position
PERSONAL POWER	Power that resides in the person, regardless of the position being filled

Legitimate power is power that is granted by virtue of one's position in the organization.

Reward power is the extent to which a person controls rewards that are valued by another. The most obvious examples of organizational rewards are pay, promotions, and work assignments. If a manager has almost total control over the pay his or her subordinates receive, can make recommendations about promotions, and has considerable discretion to make job assignments, he or she has a high level of reward power. Reward power can extend beyond material rewards. As we noted in our discussions of motivation theory in Chapters 4 and 5, people work for a variety of reasons in addition to pay. For instance, some people may be motivated primarily by a desire for recognition and acceptance. To the extent that a manager's praise and acknowledgment satisfy those needs, that manager has even more reward power.

Coercive power exists when someone has the ability to punish or physically or psychologically harm another person. For example, some managers berate subordinates in front of their peers and colleagues, belittling their efforts and generally making their work lives miserable. Certain forms of coercion may also be more subtle than this example. In some organizations, a particular division may be notorious as a resting place for people who have no future with the company. Threatening to transfer someone to a dead-end branch or some other undesirable location is thus a form of coercion. Clearly, the more negative the sanctions a manager can bring to bear on others, the stronger is that manager's coercive power. At the same time, the use of coercive power carries a considerable cost in terms of employee resentment and hostility. It may also entail legal consequences, as you can see from the *Ethics* box on page 380, entitled "Judging Arrested Development in the Workplace."

Control over expertise or, more precisely, over information is another source of power in an organization. For example, to the extent that an inventory manager has information that a sales representative needs, the inventory manager has **expert power** over the sales representative. The more important the information and the fewer the alternative sources for getting it, the greater the power. Expert power can reside in many niches in an organization; it transcends positions and jobs.[5] Although legitimate, reward, and coercive power may not always correspond exactly to formal authority, they often do. Expert power, on the other hand, may be much less associated with formal authority. Upper-level managers usually decide on the organization's strategic agenda, but individuals at lower levels in the organization may have the expertise those managers need to do the tasks. A research scientist may have crucial information about a technical breakthrough of great importance to the organization and its strategic decisions. Or an assistant may take on so many of the boss's routine and mundane activities that the manager loses track of such details and comes to depend on the assistant to keep things running smoothly. In other situations, lower-level participants are given power as a way to take advantage of their expertise. For instance, some airlines have given their flight service managers more say over whether to delay a flight based on catering problems. The logic is that the flight attendants on board a plane may be in the best position to judge their ability to handle a shortage of, say, ice or beverage cups.

Referent power is power through identification. If Jose is highly respected by Adam, Jose has referent power over Adam. Like expert power, referent power does not

RON LEVINE/LIFESIZE/JUPITER IMAGES

Referent power is power through identification. When a person has referent power, others may begin to emulate how the person dresses, the hours the person works, and even the mannerisms the person displays. In this photo the older manager may have referent power over the younger manager. The younger manager is wearing a similar suit and tie, for instance. Their posture and mannerisms are also very similar.

Reward power is the extent to which a person controls rewards that another person values.

Coercive power is the extent to which a person has the ability to punish or physically or psychologically harm someone else.

Expert power is the extent to which a person controls information that is valuable to someone else.

Referent power exists when one person wants to be like or imitates someone else.

Airlines once had a very unpopular CEO named Frank Lorenzo; some employees routinely disobeyed his mandates as a form of protest against his leadership of the firm.

Table 14.3 suggests ways for leaders to use various kinds of power most effectively. By effective use of power we mean using power in the way that is most likely to engender commitment (or at the least compliance) and that is least likely to engender resistance. For example, to suggest a somewhat mechanistic approach, managers may enhance their referent power by choosing subordinates with backgrounds similar to their own. They might, for instance, build a referent power base by hiring several subordinates who went to the same college they did. A more subtle way to exercise referent power is through role modeling: The leader behaves as she or he wants subordinates to behave. As noted earlier, since subordinates relate to and identify with the leader with referent power, they may subsequently attempt to emulate that person's behavior.

Table 14.3 GUIDELINES FOR USING POWER

Basis of Power	Guidelines for Use
REFERENT POWER	Treat subordinates fairly Defend subordinates' interests Be sensitive to subordinates' needs, feelings Select subordinates similar to oneself Engage in role modeling
EXPERT POWER	Promote image of expertise Maintain credibility Act confident and decisive Keep informed Recognize employee concerns Avoid threatening subordinates' self-esteem
LEGITIMATE POWER	Be cordial and polite Be confident Be clear and follow up to verify understanding Make sure request is appropriate Explain reasons for request Follow proper channels Exercise power regularly Enforce compliance Be sensitive to subordinates' concerns
REWARD POWER	Verify compliance Make feasible, reasonable requests Make only ethical, proper requests Offer rewards desired by subordinates Offer only credible rewards
COERCIVE POWER	Inform subordinates of rules and penalties Warn before punishing Administer punishment consistently and uniformly Understand the situation before acting Maintain credibility Fit punishment to the infraction Punish in private

References: Yukl, Gary A., *Leadership in Organizations,* 5th ed., © 2002, pp. 144–152. Adapted by permission of Pearson Education, Inc., Upper Saddle River, NJ.

In using expert power, managers may subtly make others aware of their education, experience, and accomplishments as they apply to current circumstances. But to maintain credibility, a leader should not pretend to know things that he or she really does not know. A leader whose pretensions are exposed will rapidly lose expert power. A confident and decisive leader demonstrates a firm grasp of situations and takes charge when circumstances dictate. Managers should also keep themselves informed about developments related to tasks that are valuable to the organization and relevant to their expertise.

A leader who recognizes employee concerns works to understand the underlying nature of these issues and takes appropriate steps to reassure subordinates. For example, if employees feel threatened by rumors that they will lose office space after an impending move, the leader might ask them about this concern and then find out just how much office space there will be and tell the subordinates. Finally, to avoid threatening the self-esteem of subordinates, a leader should be careful not to flaunt expertise or behave like a "know-it-all."

In general, a leader exercises legitimate power by formally requesting that subordinates do something. The leader should be especially careful to make requests diplomatically if the subordinate is sensitive about his or her relationship with the leader. This might be the case, for example, if the subordinate is older or more experienced than the leader. But although the request should be polite, it should be made confidently. The leader is in charge and needs to convey his or her command of the situation. The request should also be clear. Thus, the leader may need to follow up to ascertain that the subordinate has understood it properly. To ensure that a request is seen as appropriate and legitimate to the situation, the leader may need to explain the reasons for it. Often subordinates do not understand the rationale behind a request and consequently are unenthusiastic about it. It is important, too, to follow proper channels when dealing with subordinates.

Suppose a manager has asked a subordinate to spend his day finishing an important report. Later, while the manager is out of the office, the manager's boss comes by and asks the subordinate to drop that project and work on something else. The subordinate will then be in the awkward position of having to choose which of two higher-ranking individuals to obey. Exercising authority regularly will reinforce its presence and legitimacy in the eyes of subordinates. Compliance with legitimate power should be the norm, because if employees resist a request, the leader's power base may diminish. Finally, the leader exerting legitimate power should attempt to be responsive to subordinates' problems and concerns in the same ways we outlined for using expert power.

Reward power is in some respects the easiest base of power to use. Verifying compliance simply means that leaders should find out whether subordinates have carried out their requests before giving rewards; otherwise, subordinates may not recognize the linkage between their performance and subsequent reward. The request that is to be rewarded must be both reasonable and feasible, of course, because even the promise of a reward will not motivate a subordinate who thinks a request should not or cannot be carried out.

The same can be said for a request that seems improper or unethical. Among other things, the follower may see a reward linked to an improper or unethical request, such as a bribe or other shady offering. Finally, if the leader promises a reward that subordinates know she or he cannot actually deliver, or if they have little use for a reward the manager can deliver, they will not be motivated to carry out the request. Further, they may grow skeptical of the leader's ability to deliver rewards that are worth something to them.

Coercion is in many ways the most difficult form of power to exercise. Because coercive power is likely to cause resentment and to erode referent power, it should

SIPRESS

"By the way, this isn't a robbery. It's just coercive borrowing."

Coercion may take a variety of forms. Sometimes, as shown here, an individual engaging in coercion may attempt to present it as something else altogether!

be used infrequently, if at all. Compliance is about all one can expect from using coercive power, and even that much can be expected only if the power is used in a helpful, nonpunitive way — that is, if the sanction is mild and fits the situation and if the subordinate learns from it. In most cases, resistance is the most likely outcome, especially if coercive power is used in a hostile or manipulative way.

The first guideline for using coercive power — that subordinates should be fully informed about rules and the penalties for violating them — will prevent accidental violations of a rule, which pose an unpalatable dilemma for a leader. Overlooking an infraction on the grounds that the perpetrator was ignorant may undermine the rule or the leader's legitimate power, but carrying out the punishment probably will create resentment. One approach is to provide reasonable warning before inflicting punishment, responding to the first violation of a rule with a warning about the consequences of another violation. Of course, a serious infraction such as a theft or violence warrants immediate and severe punishment.

The disciplinary action needs to be administered consistently and uniformly, because doing so shows that punishment is both impartial and clearly linked to the infraction. Leaders should obtain complete information about what has happened before they punish, because punishing the wrong person or administering uncalled-for punishment can stir great resentment among subordinates. Credibility must be maintained, because a leader who continually makes threats but fails to carry them out loses both respect and power. Similarly, if the leader uses threats that subordinates know are beyond his or her ability to impose, the attempted use of power will be fruitless. Obviously, too, the severity of the punishment generally should match the seriousness of the infraction. Finally, punishing someone in front of others adds humiliation to the penalty, which reflects poorly on the leader and makes those who must watch and listen uncomfortable as well.

POLITICS AND POLITICAL BEHAVIOR

Organizational politics are activities carried out by people to acquire, enhance, and use power and other resources to obtain their desired outcomes.

A concept closely related to power in organizational settings is politics, or political behavior. **Organizational politics** are activities people perform to acquire, enhance, and use power and other resources to obtain their preferred outcomes in a situation where there is uncertainty or disagreement. Thus, political behavior is the general means by which people attempt to obtain and use power. Put simply, the goal of such behavior is to get one's own way about things.[7]

The Pervasiveness of Political Behavior

One important survey provides some interesting insights into how managers perceive political behavior in their organizations.[8] Roughly one-third of the 428 managers who responded to this survey believed political behavior influenced salary decisions in their organizations, while 28 percent felt it affected hiring decisions. Moreover, three-quarters of them also believed political behavior to be more prevalent at higher levels of the organization than at lower levels. More than half believed that politics is unfair, unhealthy, and irrational but also acknowledged that successful executives must be good politicians and that it is necessary to behave politically to get ahead. The survey results suggest that managers see political behavior as an undesirable but unavoidable facet of organizational life.

Politics often are viewed as synonymous with dirty tricks or backstabbing and therefore as something distasteful and best left to others. But the results of the survey just described demonstrate that political behavior in organizations, like power, is pervasive. Thus, rather than ignoring or trying to eliminate political behavior, managers might more fruitfully consider when and how organizational politics can be used constructively.

Figure 14.2 presents an interesting model of the ethics of organizational politics.[9] In the model, a political behavior alternative (PBA) is a given course of action, largely political in character, in a particular situation. The model considers political behavior ethical and appropriate under two conditions: (1) if it respects the rights of all affected parties, and (2) if it adheres to the canons of justice (that is, to a commonsense judgment of what is fair and equitable). Even if the political behavior does not meet these tests, it may be ethical and appropriate under certain circumstances. For example, politics may provide the only possible basis for deciding which employees to let go during a recessionary period of cutbacks. In all cases where nonpolitical alternatives exist, however, the model recommends rejecting political behavior that abrogates rights or justice.

To illustrate how the model works, consider Susan Jackson and Bill Thompson, both assistant professors of English at a private university. University regulations stipulate that only one of the assistant professors may be tenured; the other must be let go (some universities actually follow this practice!). Both Susan and Bill submit their credentials for review. By most objective criteria, such as number of publications and teaching evaluations, the two faculty members' qualifications are roughly the same. Because he fears termination, Bill begins an active political campaign to support a tenure decision favoring him. For instance, he reminds the tenured faculty of his intangible contributions, such as his friendship with influential campus administrators, and points out his family ties to the university. Susan, on the other hand, decides to say nothing and let her qualifications speak for themselves. The department ultimately votes to give Bill tenure and let Susan go.

Was Bill's behavior ethical? Assuming that his comments about himself were accurate and that he said nothing to disparage Susan, his behavior did not affect her rights; that is, she had an equal opportunity to advance her own cause but chose not to do so. Bill's efforts did not directly hurt Susan but only helped himself. On the other hand, it might be argued that Bill's actions violated the canons of justice because clearly defined data on which to base the tenure decision were available. Thus, one could argue that Bill's calculated introduction of additional information into the decision was unjust.

This model has not been tested empirically. Indeed, its very nature may make it impossible to test. Further, as the preceding demonstrates, it often is difficult to give an

Figure 14.2 A MODEL OF ETHICAL POLITICAL BEHAVIOR

Political behavior can serve both ethical and unethical purposes. This model helps illustrate circumstances in which political behavior is most and least likely to have ethical consequences. By following the paths through the model, a leader concerned about the ethics of an impending behavior can gain insights into whether ethical considerations are really a central part of the behavior.

Reference: Gerald E. Cavanaugh, Dennis J. Moberg, and Manuel Velasques, "The Ethics of Organizational Politics," *Academy of Management Review,* July 1981, p. 368. Used with permission.

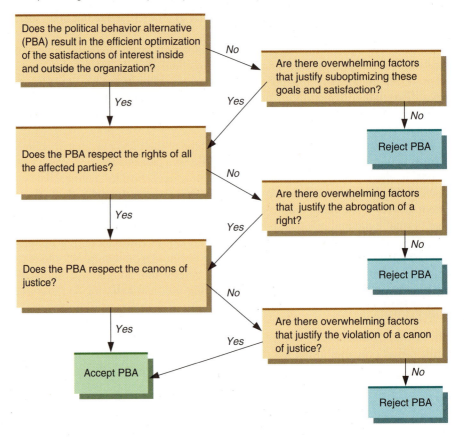

unequivocal yes or no answer to the questions, even under the simplest circumstances. Thus, the model serves as a general framework for understanding the ethical implications of various courses of action managers might take.

How, then, should managers approach the phenomenon of political behavior? Trying to eliminate political behavior will seldom, if ever, work. In fact, such action may well increase political behavior because of the uncertainty and ambiguity it creates. At the other extreme, universal and freewheeling use of political behavior probably will lead to conflict, feuds, and turmoil. In most cases, a position somewhere in-between is best: Recognizing its inevitability, the manager does not attempt to eliminate political activity, and may try to use it effectively, perhaps following the ethical model just described. At the same time, the manager can take certain steps to minimize the potential dysfunctional consequences of abusive political behavior.

Managing Political Behavior

Managing organizational politics is not easy. The very nature of political behavior makes it tricky to approach in a rational and systematic way. Success will require a basic understanding of three factors: the reasons for political behavior, common techniques for using political behavior, and strategies for limiting the effects of political behavior.

Reasons for Political Behavior   Political behavior occurs in organizations for five basic reasons: ambiguous goals, scarce resources, technology and environment, nonprogrammed decisions, and organizational change (see Figure 14.3).

Most organizational goals are inherently ambiguous. Organizations frequently espouse goals such as "increasing our presence in certain new markets" or "increasing our market share." The ambiguity of such goals provides an opportunity for political behavior, because people can view a wide range of behaviors as helping meet the goal. In reality, of course, many of these behaviors may actually be designed for the personal gain of the individuals involved. For example, a top manager might argue that the corporation should pursue its goal of entry into a new market by buying out another firm instead of forming a new division. The manager may appear to have the good of the corporation in mind—but what if his or her spouse owns some of the target firm's stock and stands to make money on a merger or acquisition?

Whenever resources are scarce, some people will not get everything they think they deserve or need. Thus, they are likely to engage in political behavior as a means of inflating their share of the resources. In this way, a manager seeking a larger budget might present accurate but misleading or incomplete statistics to inflate the perceived importance of her department. Because no organization has unlimited resources, incentives for this kind of political behavior are often present.

Technology and environment may influence the overall design of the organization and its activities. The influence stems from the uncertainties associated with nonroutine technologies and dynamic, complex environments. These uncertainties favor the use

𝒥igure 14.3   USES OF POLITICAL BEHAVIOR: REASONS, TECHNIQUES, AND POSSIBLE CONSEQUENCES

People choose to engage in political behavior for many reasons. Depending on the reasons and circumstances, a person interested in using political behavior can employ a variety of techniques, which will produce a number of intended—and possibly unintended—consequences.

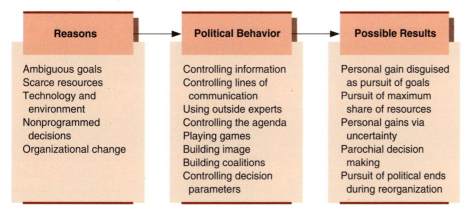

Reasons	Political Behavior	Possible Results
Ambiguous goals	Controlling information	Personal gain disguised as pursuit of goals
Scarce resources	Controlling lines of communication	Pursuit of maximum share of resources
Technology and environment	Using outside experts	Personal gains via uncertainty
Nonprogrammed decisions	Controlling the agenda	
Organizational change	Playing games	Parochial decision making
	Building image	Pursuit of political ends during reorganization
	Building coalitions	
	Controlling decision parameters	

MARTIN SIEPMANN/JUPITERIMAGES

Controlling information and controlling the agenda are two common techniques of political behavior. For instance, if one person, such as the manager shown here talking to a team of coworkers, retains vital information that others need but do not have, he can decide how and when to introduce that information into the discussion so as to promote his own goals. Likewise, if a manager can decide what issues the group will address, she can guide and direct the flow of discussion in order to promote her own agenda.

of political behavior, because in a dynamic and complex environment, it is imperative that an organization respond to change. An organization's response generally involves a wide range of activities, from purposeful activities to uncertainty to a purely political response. In the last case, a manager might use an environmental shift as an argument for restructuring his or her department to increase his or her own power base.

Political behavior is also likely to arise whenever many nonprogrammed decisions need to be made. Nonprogrammed-decision situations involve ambiguous circumstances that allow ample opportunity for political maneuvering. The two faculty members competing for one tenured position is an example. The nature of the decision allowed political behavior, and in fact, from Bill's point of view, the nonprogrammed decision demanded political action.

As we discuss in Chapter 19, changes in organizations occur regularly and can take many forms. Each such change introduces some uncertainty and ambiguity into the organizational system, at least until it has been completely institutionalized. The period during which this is occurring usually affords much opportunity for political activity. For instance, a manager worried about the consequences of a reorganization may resort to politics to protect the scope of his or her authority.

The Techniques of Political Behavior   Several techniques are used in practicing political behavior. Unfortunately, because these techniques have not been systematically studied, our understanding of them is based primarily on informal observation and inference.[10] To further complicate this problem, the participants themselves may not even be aware that they are using particular techniques. Figure 14.3 also summarizes the most frequently used techniques.[11]

One technique of political behavior is to control as much information as possible. The more critical the information and the fewer the people who have access to it, the larger the power base and influence of those who do. For example, suppose a top manager has a report compiled as a basis for future strategic plans. Rather than distributing the complete report to peers and subordinates, he shares only parts of it with the few managers who must have the information. Because no one but the manager has the complete picture, he has power and is engaging in politics to control decisions and activities according to his own ends.

Similarly, some people create or exploit situations to control lines of communication, particularly access to others in the organization. Administrative assistants frequently control access to their bosses. An assistant may put visitors in contact with the boss, send them away, delay the contact by ensuring that phone calls are not returned promptly, and so forth. People in these positions often find that they can use this type of political behavior quite effectively.

Using outside experts, such as consultants or advisers, can be an effective political technique. The manager who hires a consultant may select one whose views match her own. Because the consultant realizes that the manager was responsible for selecting him, he feels a certain obligation to her. Although the consultant truly attempts to be objective and unbiased, he may unconsciously recommend courses of action favored by the manager. Given the consultant's presumed expertise and neutrality, others in the organization accept his recommendations without challenge. By using an outside expert, the manager has ultimately gotten what she wants.

Controlling the agenda is another common political technique. Suppose a manager wants to prevent a committee from approving a certain proposal. The manager first tries to keep the decision off the agenda entirely, claiming that it is not yet ready for consideration, or attempts to have it placed last on the agenda. As other issues are decided, he sides with the same set of managers on each decision, building up a certain assumption that they are a team. When the controversial item comes up, he can defeat it through a combination of collective fatigue, the desire to get the meeting over with, and the support of his carefully cultivated allies. This technique, then, involves group polarization. A less sophisticated tactic is to prolong discussion of prior agenda items so that the group never reaches the controversial one. Or the manager may raise so many technical issues and new questions about the proposal that the committee decides to table it. In any of these cases, the manager will have used political behavior for his or her own ends.

"Game playing" is a complex technique that may take many forms. When playing games, managers simply work within the rules of the organization to increase the probability that their preferred outcomes will come about. Suppose a manager is in a position to cast the deciding vote on an upcoming issue but does not want to alienate either side by voting on it. One game she might play is to arrange to be called out of town on a crucial business trip when the vote is to take place. Assuming that no one questions the need for the trip, she will successfully maintain her position of neutrality and avoid angering either opposing camp.

Another game would involve using any of the techniques of political behavior in a purely manipulative or deceitful way. For example, a manager who will soon be making recommendations about promotions tells each subordinate, in "strictest confidence," that he or she is a leading candidate and needs only to increase his or her performance to have the inside track. Here the manager is using his control over information to play games with his subordinates. A power struggle at the W.R. Grace Company clearly illustrates manipulative practices. One senior executive fired the CEO's son and then allegedly attempted to convince the board of directors to oust the CEO and to give him the job. The CEO, in response, fired his rival and then publicly announced that the individual had been forced out because he had sexually harassed other Grace employees.[12]

The technique of building coalitions has as its general goal convincing others that everyone should work together to accomplish certain things. A manager who believes she does not control enough votes to pass an upcoming agenda item may visit with other managers before the meeting to urge them to side with her. If her preferences are in the best interests of the organization, this may be a laudable strategy for her to follow. But if she herself is the principal beneficiary, the technique is not desirable from the organization's perspective.

At its extreme, coalition building, which is frequently used in political bodies, may take the form of blatant reciprocity. In return for Roberta Kline's vote on an issue that concerns him, Jose Montemayor agrees to vote for a measure that does not affect his group at all but is crucial to Kline's group. Depending on the circumstances, this practice may benefit or hurt the organization as a whole.

The technique of controlling decision parameters can be used only in certain situations and requires much subtlety. Instead of trying to control the actual decision, the manager backs up one step and tries to control the criteria and tests on which the decision is based. This allows the manager to take a less active role in the actual decision but still achieve his or her preferred outcome. For example, suppose a district manager wants a proposed new factory to be constructed on a site in his region. If he tries to influence the decision directly, his arguments will be seen as biased and self-serving. Instead, he may take a very active role in defining the criteria on which the decision will be based, such as target population, access to rail transportation, tax rates, distance from other facilities, and the like. If he is a skillful negotiator, he may be able to influence the decision parameters such that his desired location subsequently appears to be the ideal site as determined by the criteria he has helped shape. Hence, he gets just what he wants without playing a prominent role in the actual decision.

Limiting the Effects of Political Behavior   Although it is virtually impossible to eliminate political activity in organizations, managers can limit its dysfunctional consequences. The techniques for checking political activity target both the reasons it occurs in the first place and the specific techniques that people use for political gain.

Open communication is one very effective technique for restraining the impact of political behavior. For instance, with open communication the basis for allocating scarce resources will be known to everyone. This knowledge, in turn, will tend to reduce the propensity to engage in political behavior to acquire those resources, because people already know how decisions will be made. Open communication also limits the ability of any single person to control information or lines of communication.

A related technique is to reduce uncertainty. Several of the reasons political behavior occurs—ambiguous goals, nonroutine technology, an unstable environment, and organizational change—and most of the political techniques themselves are associated with high levels of uncertainty. Political behavior can be limited if the manager can reduce uncertainty. Consider an organization about to transfer a major division from Florida to Michigan. Many people will resist the idea of moving north and may resort to political behavior to forestall their own transfer. However, the manager in charge of the move could announce who will stay and who will go at the same time that news of the change spreads throughout the company, thereby curtailing political behavior related to the move.

The adage "forewarned is forearmed" sums up one final technique for controlling political activity. Simply being aware of the causes and techniques of political behavior can help a manager check their effects. Suppose a manager anticipates that several impending organizational changes will increase the level of political activity. As a result of this awareness, the manager quickly infers that a particular subordinate is lobbying for the use of a certain consultant only because the subordinate thinks the consultant's recommendations will be in line with his own. Attempts to control the agenda, engage in game playing, build a certain image, and control decision parameters often are transparently obvious to the knowledgeable observer. Recognizing such behaviors for what they are, an astute manager may be able to take appropriate steps to limit their impact.

ORGANIZATIONAL JUSTICE

Organizational justice is an important phenomenon that has recently been introduced into the study of organizations. Justice can be discussed from a variety of perspectives, including motivation, leadership, and group dynamics. We choose to discuss it here

Figure 14.4 **FOUR BASIC FORMS OF ORGANIZATIONAL JUSTICE**

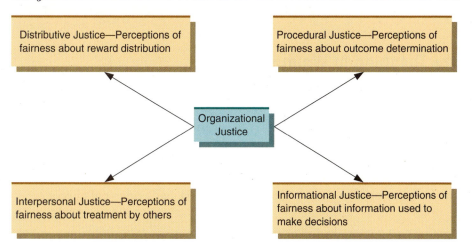

because it is also likely to be related to power and political behavior in organizations. Basically, **organizational justice** refers to the perceptions of people in an organization regarding fairness.[13] As illustrated in Figure 14.4, there are four basic forms of organizational justice.

Distributive Justice

Distributive justice refers to people's perceptions of the fairness with which rewards and other valued outcomes are distributed within the organization. Obviously related to the equity theory of motivation discussed back in Chapter 4, distributive justice takes a more holistic view of reward distribution than simply a comparison between one person and another. For instance, the compensation paid to top managers (especially the CEO), to peers and colleagues at the same level in an organization, and even to entry-level hourly workers can all be assessed in terms of their relative fairness vis-à-vis anyone else in the organization.

Perceptions of distributive justice affect individual satisfaction with various work-related outcomes such as pay, work assignments, recognition, and opportunities for advancement. Specifically, the more *just* people see rewards to be distributed, the more satisfied they will be with those rewards; the more *unjust* they see rewards to be distributed, the less satisfied they will be. Moreover, individuals who feel that rewards are not distributed justly may be inclined to attribute such injustice to misuse of power and/or to political agendas.

Procedural Justice

Another important form of organizational justice is *procedural justice*—individual perceptions of the fairness of the process used to determine various outcomes. For instance, suppose an employee's performance is evaluated by someone very familiar with the job being performed. Moreover, the evaluator clearly explains the basis for the evaluation and then discusses how that evaluation will translate in other outcomes such as promotions and pay increases. The individual will probably see this set of procedures as being fair and just. But if the evaluation is conducted by someone unfamiliar with

Organizational justice refers to the perceptions of people in an organization regarding fairness.

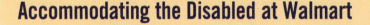

DIVERSITY

Accommodating the Disabled at Walmart

In 2008, Walmart settled a high-profile lawsuit brought by a disabled worker. However, it's not clear that Walmart was at fault. The case shows that enforcement of the ADA (Americans with Disabilities Act) is confusing and inconsistent.

Pam Huber earned $13 an hour filling grocery orders for Walmart in Arkansas. She hurt her arm at work in 2001 and was unable to do her job. She requested an open position as a router, a desk job that paid $12.90. Instead, Walmart managers told her she had to compete for it. In the end, Walmart hired someone with better qualifications, although Huber also had good qualifications. She became a janitor, working for $6.20 an hour.

Huber sued Walmart in 2004, claiming she should have been given the router position. An Arkansas judge ruled in favor of Huber. On appeal, the Eighth U.S. Circuit Court found in favor of Walmart. Yet around the country, other appeals courts have upheld claims similar to Huber's.

In December 2007, the Supreme Court agreed to hear the case. The issue is this: When the ADA includes job reassignment in the list of reasonable accommodations for disabled workers, does that mean the employer must give priority to disabled workers? Walmart argues that it always hires the most qualified worker. Huber's attorneys claim that the ADA would merely repeat that a disabled worker is free to compete when that's clearly already true.

> **"I am so grateful that Walmart was willing to give me another opportunity."**
> —STEVEN SANDERS, WALMART EMPLOYEE

Walmart settled Huber's claim out of court, stopping the Supreme Court's involvement. Now Walmart and other employers use the local circuit court's opinion to resolve disability issues. Procedural justice demands that laws protecting disabled workers be the same everywhere in the nation.

Steven Sanders, a disabled Walmart employee who was reinstated, says, "I am so grateful that Walmart was willing to give me another opportunity." But what about Huber? She's still at the janitorial job, although she now earns $7.90.

References: Equal Employment Opportunity Commission, "Comprehensive EEOC, Wal-Mart Settlement Resolves Disability Lawsuit," press release, December 17, 2001, www.eeoc.gov on April 8, 2010; Christopher S. Rugaber, "Supreme Court to Hear Wal-Mart Disability Case," *Washington Post*, December 8, 2007, www.washingtonpost.com on April 8, 2010; Marta Russell, "A Brief History of Wal-Mart and Disability Discrimination," *ZNet*, February 15, 2004, www.zcommunications.org on April 8, 2010; Jim Salter, "Wal-Mart Settles with Applicant with Disability," *AccessibilityGuy.com*, April 17, 2008, www.texasras.com on April 8, 2010.

the job who provides no explanation as to how the evaluation is being done nor what it will mean, the individual is likely to see that process as less fair and just.

When workers perceive a high level of procedural justice, they are somewhat more likely to be motivated to participate in activities, to follow rules, and to accept relevant outcomes as being fair. But if workers perceive more procedural injustice, they tend to withdraw from opportunities to participate, to pay less attention to rules and policies, and to see relevant outcomes as being unfair. In addition, perceptions of procedural injustice may be accompanied by interpretations based on the power and political behaviors of others.

In examining a case involving procedural justice at Walmart, the *Diversity* box above shows that employers and employees—not to mention judges—may have different ideas about organizational justice.

Interpersonal Justice

Interpersonal justice relates to the degree of fairness people see in how they are treated by others in their organization. For instance, suppose an employee is treated by his boss with dignity and respect. The boss also provides information on a timely basis, and is always open and honest in her dealings with the subordinate. The subordinate will express high levels of interpersonal justice. But if the boss treats her subordinate with disdain and a clear lack of respect, and withholds important information and is often ambiguous or dishonest in her dealings with the subordinate, he will experience more interpersonal injustice.

Perceptions of interpersonal justice will most affect how individuals feel about those with whom they interact and communicate. If they experience interpersonal justice, they are likely to reciprocate by treating others with respect and openness. But if they experience interpersonal injustice, they may be less respectful in turn, and may be less inclined to follow the directives of their leader. Power and political behaviors are also again likely to be seen as playing roles in interpersonal justice.

Informational Justice

Finally, *informational justice* refers to the perceived fairness of information used to arrive at decisions. If someone feels that a manager made a decision based on relatively complete and accurate information, and that the information was appropriately processed and considered, the person will likely experience informational justice even if they don't completely agree with the decisions. But if the person feels that the decision was based on incomplete and inaccurate information and/or that important information was ignored, the individual will experience less informational justice.

Power and political behaviors are likely to play an important role in perceptions of informational justice. Recall, for example, our earlier discussion of information control as a political tactic. To the extent that people believe that informational justice is lacking, they may very well attribute power and political behaviors as having played a major role in the decision-making process.[14]

SYNOPSIS

Influence can be defined as the ability to affect the perceptions, attitudes, or behaviors of others. Influence is a cornerstone of leadership. Impression management is a direct, intentional effort by someone to enhance his or her image in the eyes of others. People engage in impression management for a variety of reasons and use a variety of methods to influence how others see them.

Power is the potential ability of a person or group to exercise control over another person or group. The five bases of power are legitimate power (granted by virtue of one's position in the organization); reward power (control of rewards valued by others); coercive power (the ability to punish or harm); expert power (control over information that is valuable to the organization);

and referent power (power through personal identification). Position power is tied to a position regardless of the individual who holds it. Personal power is power that resides in a person regardless of position. Attempts to use power can result in commitment, compliance, or resistance.

Organizational politics are activities people perform to acquire, enhance, and use power and other resources to obtain their preferred outcomes in a situation where uncertainty or disagreement exists. Research indicates that most managers do not advocate use of political behavior but acknowledge that it is a necessity of organizational life. Because managers cannot eliminate political activity in the organization, they must learn to cope with it. Understanding how to manage political behavior requires understanding why it occurs, what techniques it employs, and strategies for limiting its effects.

Organizational justice refers to the perceptions of people in an organization regarding fairness. There are four basic forms of organizational justice: distributive, procedural, interpersonal, and informational. Power and political behaviors are likely to be attributed when any or all of these forms of justice are seen as being deficient.

DISCUSSION QUESTIONS

1. Can a person without influence be a leader? Does having influence automatically make someone a leader?
2. Have you ever engaged in impression management? What did you hope to accomplish?
3. What might happen if two people, each with significant, equal power, attempt to influence each other?
4. Cite examples based on a professor-student relationship to illustrate each of the five bases of organizational power.
5. Is there a logical sequence in the use of power bases that a manager might follow? For instance, should the use of legitimate power usually precede the use of reward power, or vice versa?
6. Cite examples in which you have been committed, compliant, and resistant as a result of efforts to influence you. Think of times when your attempts to influence others led to commitment, compliance, and resistance.
7. Do you agree or disagree with the assertion that political behavior is inevitable in organizational settings?
8. The term "politics" is generally associated with governmental bodies. Why do you think it has also come to be associated with the behavior in organizations described in this chapter?
9. Recall examples of how you have either used or observed others using the techniques of political behavior identified in the chapter. What other techniques can you suggest?
10. Recall an instance when you have experienced each of the four forms of organizational justice in either a positive or a negative manner.

ORGANIZATIONAL BEHAVIOR CASE FOR DISCUSSION

RULING OUT CORPORATE LUNACY

Recent research shows that 31 percent of female workers in the United States have been harassed at work—all of them by men. Forty-three percent identified the male harasser as a supervisor, 27 percent as an employee senior to them, and 19 percent as a coworker at the same level. In 2009, nearly 13,000 charges of sexual harassment were filed with the U.S. Equal Employment Opportunity Commission (EEOC), 84 percent of them by women.

Why does sexual harassment (mostly of women) occur in the workplace?

"Power," says researcher Debbie Dougherty, who conducted a study in conjunction with a large Midwestern healthcare organization. "It was the common answer.

> *"The 'equal opportunity abuser' defense is on the way out."*
> —EMPLOYMENT LAWYER FRANK STEINBERG

It came up repeatedly," says Dougherty, a specialist in communications and power in organizations. She also found that men and women understand the idea of *power* differently, and that difference in understanding, she reports, may play an important part in the persistence of harassing behavior in the workplace:

- For most men, power is something that belongs to superiors—managers and supervisors—who can harass because they possess the power to do so. By this definition's reasoning, a male coworker cannot actually harass a female coworker who's at the same level because he doesn't possess sufficient power over her.

- Women, on the other hand, see power as something that can be introduced into a relationship as it develops; it's something more than the mere formal authority built into the superior's job description. Harassment can be initiated by anyone who's able to create the perception of power.

According to Dougherty, gender differences in the perception of power may account, at least in part, for gender differences in perceptions of behavior. "If a man," she suggests, "thinks that sexual harassment only comes from a supervisor, he may feel free to make sexual comments to a female coworker," reasoning that because he holds no power over her, she won't perceive the behavior as harassment. She, however, probably regards power as something that can be sought and gained in a relationship and may therefore "see the sexual comments as a quest for power and label it as sexual harassment."

The findings of another recent study tend to support Dougherty's conclusions. Researchers from the University of Minnesota discovered that women in supervisory positions were 137 percent more likely to be harassed than women in nonsupervisory roles. Although many of the harassers were men in superior positions, a large number were coworkers in equivalent positions. It would seem, then, that male coworkers felt free to behave in a harassing manner because they believed that their female targets would not perceive their behavior as efforts to express power. As Dougherty predicts, however, they were wrong: The women perceived the harassing behaviors as power plays. "This study," says researcher Heather McLaughlin, "provides the strongest evidence to date supporting the theory that sexual harassment is less about sexual desire than about control and domination. ... Male coworkers ... and supervisors seem to be using harassment as an equalizer against women in power."

Not surprisingly, the perceptions of both women and men are influenced by the workplace environments in which they find themselves. Studies show, for example, that harassment of women is three times more likely in environments in which the use of obscenity is common and 3 to 7 times more likely in environments that tolerate sexual joking. Employers may be held liable for creating "hostile work environments" whether the harasser is a superior or a coworker, and that's one reason why 97 percent of U.S. companies have written sexual harassment policies. In order to determine sexual harassment, the law describes a *hostile environment* as a workplace in which sexual comments, offensive sexual materials, or unwelcome physical contact are regular occurrences. We specified the legal criteria for *sexual harassment* in the *Ethics* box entitled "Judging Arrested Development in the Workplace" and we'll add here that charges of a sexually hostile environment must meet two additional requirements: (1) the person(s) affected must find sexually oriented conduct abusive, and (2) the conduct in question must be sufficiently severe or pervasive for a reasonable person to find it abusive.

All of which brings us back to the case of Julie Gallagher, which we introduced in the *Ethics* box earlier in this chapter. Gallagher appealed the decision of the district court judge to the U.S. Court of Appeals for the Sixth Circuit, which delivered its opinion in May 2009. To appreciate fully the court's attention to detail, it will help to recall the four facts that, according to employee-rights attorney Ellen Simon, Gallagher had to establish in her suit against her former employer, C.H. Robinson Worldwide (italics added):

1. That she was a member of a *protected class* (female)
2. That she was subjected to harassment either through words or actions, *based on sex*
3. That the harassment had the effect of *unreasonably interfering with her work performance* and creating *an objectively intimidating, hostile, or offensive work environment*
4. That there existed some basis for *liability on the part of her employer*

As you'll recall, District Judge Dan A. Polster had rejected Gallagher's suit for three reasons. Here's a point-by-point summary of the appeals court's decision in *Gallagher v. C.H. Robinson Worldwide, Inc.*:

- First, the judges ruled that the conduct of Gallagher's coworkers was indeed "based on sex": Even though both men and women were exposed to the offensive conduct, that conduct, said the court, was "patently degrading and anti-female" in nature; thus "it stands to reason that women would suffer ... greater disadvantage in the terms and conditions of their employment than men."
- Second, the appeals court rejected the district judge's opinion that the harassment was not sufficiently severe or pervasive. Even if the offensive conduct was not directed specifically at Gallagher, the nature of the office layout meant that "she had no means of escaping [and] was unavoidably exposed to it." In addition, any "reasonable person" would have found the "vulgar language, demeaning conversations and images, and palpable

anti-female animus" of the C.H. Robinson office "objectively hostile"—in other words, just as hostile as Gallagher found it; her reaction, therefore, was not "unreasonable, exaggerated, or hypersensitive." Finally, the court deemed it reasonable to accept her claim that the abusive conduct "rendered her work more difficult."

- Third, the appeals court panel ruled that C.H. Robinson could be held liable for creating a sexually hostile workplace environment. The facts showed that the branch manager knew about the offensive behavior and about Gallagher's objections to it, and the law holds that a company is also aware of any situation which is known to "any supervisor or department head who has been authorized ... to receive and respond to or forward such complaints to management." Moreover, said the court, "a reasonable jury" should be given the opportunity to determine whether Robinson had responded to Gallagher's complaints "with manifest indifference."

The ruling of the district court judge was reversed and the case sent back to district court for reconsideration. It hasn't yet been settled, but many lawyers believe that the appeals court delivered a clear message to both employers and lower-court judges. According to Frank Steinberg, an attorney who handles sexual harassment and other employment-related cases, C.H. Robinson's conduct in the entire matter is an "illustration of self-destructive corporate lunacy. ... So if you run a business," he advises,

don't be lulled into a false sense of security by the fact that you curse at women and men with equal gusto. The "equal opportunity abuser" defense is on the way out. And don't think that the work environment is not hostile to women just because some women are acting like the boys.

CASE QUESTIONS*

1. Explain how each of the following forms of *power* was involved in Gallagher's situation: *legitimate*, *coercive*, *position*, and *personal*.
2. In your opinion, to what extent were *organizational politics* involved in Gallagher's situation?
3. Explain how Gallagher's rights to *procedural justice* were violated. How about her rights to *interpersonal justice*?
4. Experts estimate that only 5 to 15 percent of women who've been harassed in the workplace complain either to their employers or to such agencies as the EEOC. Why do you suppose this is so? If you were an employer, what steps would you take to improve this situation?

REFERENCES

"Sexual Harassment in the Workplace," *Sexual Harassment Support* (2009), sexualharassmentsupport.org on April 6, 2010; "Power and Sexual Harassment—Men and Women See Things Differently," *Science Daily*, April 6, 2007, www.sciencedaily.com on April 8, 2010; Ellen Simon, "Harassed Female Wins 'Locker Room' Hostile Environment Case," *Employee Rights Post*, June 2, 2009, www.employeerightspost .com on April 5, 2010; "Preventing Sexual Harassment: A Fact Sheet for Employees," *SexualHarassmentLawFirms.com*, November 17, 2004, www.sexualharassmentlawfirms.com on April 9, 2010; United States Court of Appeals for the Sixth Circuit, *Gallagher v. C.H. Robinson Worldwide, Inc.*, No. 08-3337, May 22, 2009, www.ca6.uscourts.gov on April 8, 2010; Frank Steinberg, "Sexual Harassment: Workplace Loaded with Pornography and Bad Language," *New Jersey Employment Law Blog*, June 24, 2009, http://employment.lawfirmnewjersey.com on April 9, 2010.

---

* The questions for this case require that you be familiar with the *Ethics* box entitled "Judging Arrested Development in the Workplace" on page 380 as well as with the *Organizational Behavior Case* itself.

EXPERIENCING ORGANIZATIONAL BEHAVIOR

Power Bases

Purpose   This exercise will give you practice in identifying power bases associated with various formal and informal positions in organizations.

Format   You will name and explain the power bases individually. Then you will meet in a small group or

as a class to discuss your responses and to answer the follow-up questions.

Procedure   For each of the following positions, decide which of the five power bases are present (legitimate, reward, coercive, referent, and expert power). There may be more than one power base for an occupation. Then for each power base that is present, write a sentence to explain or give a brief example.

- Top-performing salesperson
- Professor
- Popular campus athlete
- Small business owner
- Corporate CEO
- Research scientist heading corporate R&D
- Administrative assistant to a corporate CEO
- The U.S. president

Follow-up Questions

1. Did class members find it easy to agree on the answers? If not, why not?
2. To what extent would more knowledge of a specific individual change your answers? To what extent would more knowledge of a specific situation change your answers?
3. Based on each position's power base(s), what outcomes would a person in this position be likely to experience if they were acting as a leader?

BUILDING MANAGERIAL SKILLS

Exercise Overview Diagnostic skills help a manager visualize appropriate responses to a situation. One situation managers often face is whether to use power to solve a problem. This exercise will help you develop your diagnostic skills as they relate to using different types of power in different situations.

Exercise Background Several methods have been identified for using power. These include:

1. Legitimate request—The manager requests that the subordinate comply because the subordinate recognizes that the organization has given the manager the right to make the request. Most day-to-day interactions between manager and subordinate are of this type.
2. Instrumental compliance—In this form of exchange, a subordinate complies to get the reward the manager controls. Suppose that a manager asks a subordinate to do something outside the range of the subordinate's normal duties, such as working extra hours on the weekend, terminating a relationship with a long-standing buyer, or delivering bad news. The subordinate complies and, as a direct result, reaps praise and a bonus from the manager. The next time the subordinate is asked to perform a similar activity, that subordinate will recognize that compliance will be instrumental in her getting more rewards. Hence the basis of instrumental compliance is clarifying important performance-reward contingencies.

3. Coercion—This is used when the manager suggests or implies that the subordinate will be punished, fired, or reprimanded if he does not do something.
4. Rational persuasion—This is when the manager can convince the subordinate that compliance is in the subordinate's best interest. For example, a manager might argue that the subordinate should accept a transfer because it would be good for the subordinate's career. In some ways, rational persuasion is like reward power except that the manager does not really control the reward.
5. Personal identification—This is when a manager who recognizes that she has referent power over a subordinate can shape the behavior of that subordinate by engaging in desired behaviors: The manager consciously becomes a model for the subordinate and exploits personal identification.
6. Inspirational appeal—This is when a manager can induce a subordinate to do something consistent with a set of higher ideals or values through inspirational appeal. For example, a plea for loyalty represents an inspirational appeal.

Exercise Task With these ideas in mind, do the following:

1. Relate each of the uses of power listed above to the five types of power identified in the chapter. That is, indicate which type(s) of power are most closely associated with each use of power, which type(s)

may be related to each use of power, and which type(s) are unrelated to each use of power.

2. Is a manager more likely to be using multiple forms of power at the same time, or using a single type of power?

3. Identify other methods and approaches to using power.

4. What are some of the dangers and pitfalls associated with using power?

SELF-ASSESSMENT EXERCISE

How to Gain Power and Influence People

This exercise is designed to help you assess the ways in which your approach to your work will be effective in gaining power and influence. If you have a job, consider that your work; if you're a student, apply this exercise to your school work.

The 28 statements below reflect approaches that people can take toward their work, both personally and in their relationships with others. Using the following scale, indicate the extent to which, in your opinion, each statement is true of you.

1. Strongly disagree
2. Disagree
3. Slightly disagree
4. Slightly agree
5. Agree
6. Strongly agree

In a situation in which it is important to obtain more power:

____ 1. I strive to become highly proficient in my line of work.

____ 2. I express friendliness, honesty, and sincerity toward those with whom I work.

____ 3. I put forth more effort and take more initiative than expected in my work.

____ 4. I support organizational and ceremonial events and activities.

____ 5. I form a broad network of relationships with people at all levels throughout the organization.

____ 6. I send personal notes to others when they accomplish something significant or when I pass along important information to them.

____ 7. In my work, I strive to generate new ideas, initiate new activities, and minimize routine tasks.

____ 8. I try to find ways to be an external representative for my unit or organization.

____ 9. I am continually upgrading my skills and knowledge.

____ 10. I strive to enhance my personal appearance.

____ 11. I work harder than most of my coworkers.

____ 12. I encourage new members to support important organizational values by both their words and their actions.

____ 13. I gain access to important information by becoming central in communications networks.

____ 14. I strive to find opportunities to make reports about my work, especially to senior people.

____ 15. I maintain variety in the tasks that I perform.

____ 16. I keep my work connected to the central mission of the organization.

When trying to influence someone for a specific purpose:

____ 17. I emphasize reason and factual information.

____ 18. I feel comfortable using a variety of different influence techniques, matching them to specific circumstances.

____ 19. I reward others for agreeing with me, thereby establishing a condition of reciprocity.

____ 20. I use a direct, straightforward approach rather than an indirect or manipulative one.

____ 21. I avoid using threats or demands to impose my will on others.

When resisting an inappropriate influence attempt directed at me:

____ 22. I use resources and information I control to equalize demands and threats.

____ 23. I refuse to bargain with individuals who use high-pressure negotiation tactics.

____ 24. I explain why I can't comply with reasonable-sounding requests by pointing out how the consequences would affect my responsibilities and obligations.

When trying to influence those above me in the organization:

_____ 25. I help determine the issues to which they pay attention by effectively selling the importance of those issues.

_____ 26. I convince them that the issues on which I want to focus are compatible with the goals and future success of the organization.

_____ 27. I help them solve problems that they didn't expect me to help them solve.

_____ 28. I work as hard to make them look good and be successful as I do for my own success.

How to score: Add up the numbers that you put down in the left-hand column. The maximum possible score is 168. You should compare your score with the scores of other students in the class and with those of 1,500 business school students summarized as follows:

Score	Ranking
134.9	mean
145 or above	top quartile
136–144	second quartile
126–135	third quartile
125 or below	bottom quartile

Reference: David A. Whetten and Kim S. Cameron, *Developing Management Skills*, 7th ed. (Upper Saddle River, NJ: Prentice Hall, 2007), 284–85, 324.

15 CHAPTER

CHAPTER LEARNING OBJECTIVES

After studying this chapter you should be able to:

- Define and discuss the nature of conflict in organizations.
- Identify and describe the common forms and causes of conflict.
- Discuss the most frequent reactions to conflict in organizations.
- Describe how conflict can be managed.
- Define negotiation in organizations and discuss its underlying processes.

CONFLICT AND NEGOTIATION IN ORGANIZATIONS

Conflict of Interests

"I want the world to know what happened."

—EX-TOYOTA EMPLOYEE AND WHISTLE-BLOWER DIMITRIOS BILLER

"Mr. Biller's actions and the timing of his lawsuit do not support his claim that he is motivated by the public interest."

—TOYOTA MOTOR CORP.

Back in 2003, the Toyota Corolla in which Raul and Diana Lopez were driving with their young daughter was rear-ended by an SUV. The Lopezes sued Toyota, charging that the driver's seat recliner had failed, causing the seat to strike

Problems with alleged uncontrolled acceleration have plagued several Toyota products in recent years. The driver of this Prius claimed that his 2010 crash was caused when the car accelerator pedal became stuck and the car would not stop.

AP PHOTO/SETH WENIG

their daughter and leaving her blind in one eye. The Toyota defense team was led by Dimitrios Biller, the automaker's National Managing Counsel for accident litigation, who forced Todd Tracy, the Lopezes' attorney, to settle the suit in 2004. There was apparently no love lost between the two lawyers in the case. "He was hard-nosed, almost obsessive-compulsive, about cases," says Tracy, who'd faced Biller in court 25 times. "People on the plaintiff side," he adds, "thought that he was a mean-spirited bastard." Not so, responds Biller, who claims that he sometimes cried after winning personal-injury cases because he "just felt a lot of empathy" for the plaintiffs.

Biller remained with Toyota until he resigned in 2007, and it now appears that the parting was not exactly amicable. Suffering from psychiatric problems, Biller had taken a medical leave of absence in June and then left the company with a $3.7 million severance package in September. He also left with some 6,000 company documents related to vehicle safety defects and now says that he was "forced" to resign because he resisted the company's "calculated conspiracy to prevent the disclosure of damaging evidence" in about 300 personal-injury lawsuits. Biller claims that his superiors at Toyota had subjected him to "intimidation, harassment, and an uncertain future" and that he had suffered "a complete mental and physical breakdown." His severance package, he says, was "hush money," and he took the internal documents because of legal and ethical obligations to turn over "clearly discoverable material."

How did Biller intend to disclose this damaging evidence? In 2008, he went into business as Litigation Discovery and Trial Consulting (LDT), whose services include electronic discovery—the pretrial handling of evidence in electronic formats ranging from email and instant messaging to documents stored in accounting databases. Shortly thereafter, Toyota, alleging that internal company documents had surfaced through LTD, sued Biller, arguing that, in disclosing privileged information, the former in-house lawyer had violated the confidentiality clause of his severance agreement. "In our view," said Toyota, "Mr. Biller has repeatedly breached his ethical and professional obligations, both as an attorney and in his commitments to us, by violating attorney-client privilege."

In July 2009, Biller responded by filing a whistle-blower suit against Toyota and several of his former supervisors, claiming that they had acted to "stop, prevent, and delay" his efforts to "search, collect, preserve, review, and produce" documents for disclosure in litigation brought against the company. "I did as much as I could as a lawyer for a client" to prevent the client from breaking the law, says Biller. "I wrote email after email, memo after memo, explaining the legal obligations Toyota ... needed to fill." But Toyota, he charges, continued to engage in "improper and illegal activities, including concealing and destroying evidence, perjury, violation of court orders, obstructing justice, mail fraud, wire fraud, and conspiracy to commit crimes." He filed the suit, Biller says, because "I want the world to know what happened."

His former employer, however, was skeptical: Biller's "actions and the timing of his lawsuit," replied Toyota, "do not support his claim that he is motivated by the public interest. [His] actions have been motivated by his own personal financial interests." The company also reminded the court of public opinion that "Mr. Biller claims he ... has suffered from organic brain disease 'for most of his life.'" Biller acknowledges that he suffers from "serious depression" and told a legal journalist in October 2009 that "I'm heavily medicated, so I function on a day-to-day basis. ... I had some troubles [at Toyota] because of my mental condition," he admits but hastens to add that his former employer was the cause rather than the victim of his mental turmoil.

And what about those 6,000 documents that Biller took with him when he parted company with Toyota? What kind of information do they contain? "Trade secrets," says the automaker, but Biller maintains that "these documents can be used to establish liability against Toyota in product liability and negligence cases." Toyota secured a court order to keep the documents confidential and moved further to obtain permission to destroy them. At this point in the proceedings, Biller was joined by an unlikely ally in his battle to disclose his potentially incriminating evidence. In October 2009, Biller drove from his home in California all the way to Texas, where he personally turned over his cache of documents to a federal judge. It seems that Todd Tracy, spurred by the revelations promised in Biller's suit against Toyota, had decided to refile 17 of the personal-injury lawsuits that he'd originally lost to Biller, starting with the case of Raul and Diana Lopez. The documents provided by Biller, declared Tracy, clearly contained "information that Toyota does not want the public to see. . . . Toyota's accident victims need to see [this] information . . . to find out if the Japanese auto giant perverted the course of American justice."

Apparently, however, the course of American justice had indeed run smoothly. In December, Tracy announced that he was voluntarily withdrawing his petition to reopen his 17 cases. "After reviewing . . . the Biller documents," said Tracy, "I did not see any type of concealment, destruction, or pattern of discovery abuse that had affected my cases. . . . I did not see a smoking gun," Tracy added, "I didn't even see a smoldering gun." At the time, Tracy's defection was just the latest in a series of legal blows to Biller's case. In September, a federal judge had responded to Toyota's complaint that Biller had violated the terms of his severance agreement by referring Biller to the California State Bar for investigation. A month later, another federal judge dismissed his allegations against Toyota's in-house lawyers and sent the case to arbitration.

Then in March 2010, the strange case of *Dimitrios Biller vs. Toyota Motor Corp.* took yet another twist. Meeting to hear complaints of uncontrolled acceleration problems in Toyota vehicles, the Congressional Committee on Oversight and Government Reform had subpoenaed the documents in Biller's possession, and committee chairman Ed Towns apparently found them much more interesting than Todd Tracy had. "We have reviewed these documents," wrote Towns in a letter to Toyota officials, "and found evidence that Toyota deliberately withheld relevant electronic records that it was legally required to produce in response to discovery orders in litigation." In particular, the chairman cited a memo from in-house attorney Dimitrios Biller urging his supervisor to turn over electronic information relating to vehicle design flaws. "The Biller documents," Congressman Towns concluded, "indicate a systematic disregard for the law and routine violation of court discovery orders in litigation."

As of this writing, Dimitrios Biller's case against Toyota has not been settled. Toyota also faces nearly 100 lawsuits from plaintiffs blaming crashes on sudden acceleration and more than 130 class-action suits brought by owners claiming that recent recalls and negative publicity have triggered sharp drops in the value of their Toyota vehicles.

For another perspective on the complexities of whistle-blowing as a special form of legal conflict, read the *Change* box entitled "Whistle-blowing in the Dark" on page 408.

What Do You Think?

1. Do you think conflict is inevitable in a large organization? Why or why not?

2. In what ways might negotiation eventually play a role in settling the controversies facing Toyota?

References: Deborah Feyerick and Sheila Steffen, "Ex-Toyota Lawyer Says Documents Prove Company Hid Damaging Information," *CNN.com*, March 10, 2010, www.cnn.com on April 12, 2010; Zusha Elinson, "Ex-Toyota Lawyer Holds Tight to Whistleblower Suit," *Law.com*, October 22, 2009, www.law.com on April 12, 2010; Michelle Massey, "Tracy Refiles Toyota Suit as Whistleblower Faces Sanctions," *The Southeast Texas Record*, October 30, 2009, www.setexasrecord.com on April 14, 2010; Rob Riggs, "Toyota Whistleblower Supports Fraud Case with Insider Documents," *Articlesbase*, October 2, 2009, www.articlesbase.com on April 14, 2009; "Dallas Attorney Todd Tracy Dismisses Suit to Reopen Toyota Accident Cases," *EIN Presswire*, December 26, 2009, www.einpresswire.com on April 14, 2010; Jeremy Korzeniewski, "Report: Toyota 'Whistleblower' Documents Trouble House Panel," *Autoblog*, February 26, 2010, www.autoblog.com on April 15, 2010; Peter Valdes-Dapena, "Oversight Chief Says Toyota Withheld Documents," *CNNMoney*, February 26, 2010, http://money.cnn.com on April 12, 2010; Curt Anderson and Danny Robbins, "Toyota Has History of Evasive Legal Tactics, Review Finds," *Statesman.com*, April 11, 2010, www.statesman.com on April 15, 2010.

When people work together in organizational settings, myriad consequences can result. For instance, people may leave work each day feeling happy and energized for having done a great job; they can be frustrated and unhappy because of some problem they encountered; or they can feel stressed because of the pressures being imposed upon them. Another possible outcome that occurs with regularity is conflict, the subject of this chapter. We begin with a discussion of the nature of conflict. We then examine its most common forms and the things that cause it in the first place. We then discuss reactions to conflict and how it can be managed. We conclude with a discussion of a related organizational process, negotiation.

THE NATURE OF CONFLICT IN ORGANIZATIONS

Conflict is a common occurrence in organizations. While there are numerous definitions of **conflict**, we will define it as a process resulting in the perceptions of two parties that they are working in opposition to each other in ways that result in feelings of discomfort and/or animosity. There are several elements of this definition that warrant additional comment.

First, note that conflict is a process, not a singular event. It evolves over time and draws upon previous events. While it may emerge as a result of a specific event, more than likely it has been brewing for some time. Further, the parties have to actually perceive it to exist in order for conflict to be real. If an observer witnesses what appears to be an argument between two other individuals but those people do not perceive their dialog to be conflictual, then conflict does not really exist. Finally, discomfort or animosity must occur in order for the conflict to be real. For example, a group of friends who play each other in a friendly game of softball may be competing for victory but are not in conflict.

Conflict is a process resulting in the perceptions of two parties that they are working in opposition to each other in ways that result in feelings of discomfort and/or animosity.

Figure 15.1 THE NATURE OF ORGANIZATIONAL CONFLICT

Either too much or too little conflict can be dysfunctional for an organization. In either case, performance may be low. However, an optimal level of conflict that sparks motivation, creativity, innovation, and initiative can result in higher levels of performance. T. J. Rodgers, CEO of Cypress Semiconductor, maintains a moderate level of conflict in his organization as a way of keeping people energized and motivated.

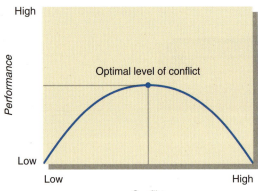

We should also note that the parties involved in conflict may be individuals, groups, and/or organizations. Hence, conflict may involve one person in opposition to another, one group in opposition to another, or one organization in opposition to another. Conflict may also exist across levels, for example when an individual is in conflict with a group. Conflict may also result from the anticipation of future problems. For example, a person may behave antagonistically toward another person whom he or she expects to pose obstacles to goal achievement.[1]

Although conflict often is considered harmful, and thus something to avoid, it can also have some benefits. A total absence of conflict can lead to apathy and lethargy. A moderate degree of focused conflict, on the other hand, can stimulate new ideas, promote healthy competition, and energize behavior. In some organizations, especially profit-oriented ones, many managers believe that conflict is dysfunctional. On the other hand, many managers in not-for-profit organizations often view conflict as beneficial and conducive to higher-quality decision making.[2] In many cases, the impact of conflict on performance may take the form shown in Figure 15.1. Either too little or too much conflict may result in low performance, while a moderate level of conflict may lead to higher performance.[3]

COMMON FORMS AND CAUSES OF CONFLICT

Conflict may take a number of forms. In addition, it may be caused by a wide array of factors in an organization.

Common Forms of Conflict

In general, there are three basic forms of conflict that exist within an organization. There are additional forms that can relate to conflict between organizations. **Task conflict** refers to conflict regarding the goals and content of the work. For instance, suppose one manager believes that the firm should strive to maximize profits and hence shareholder value. This individual will feel strongly that the organization should avoid social causes and instead focus its efforts on increasing revenues and/or lowering costs to the exclusion of most other activities. Another manager in the same firm, however, may believe the business should have a pronounced social agenda and be an active participant in relevant social programs. While this manager recognizes the importance of profits, he or she also sees the importance of corporate citizenship. To the extent that their differences lead to disagreements over substantive issues, it represents task conflict.

Process conflict occurs when the parties agree on the goals and content of work, but disagree on how to achieve the goals and actually do the work. For example, suppose the two executives noted above actually both believe in the importance of a social agenda and support the concept of sharing corporate profits with society. Hence, they have no task conflict. However, one thinks the best way to do this is to simply give a portion of the firm's profits to one or more social causes. The other, however, thinks

Task conflict refers to conflict regarding the goals and content of the work.

Process conflict occurs when the parties agree on the goals and content of work, but disagree on how to achieve the goals and actually do the work.

the company should be more active; for instance, she or he wants the firm to sponsor ongoing building projects through Habitat for Humanity. While they share the same goals, they see different processes being the best way to achieve those goals.

Relationship conflict occurs when the parties have interpersonal issues. For instance, suppose one person has very strict conservative religious beliefs. This person is offended by the use of vulgar language, believes strongly in the importance of regular church attendance, and has no qualms about voicing his or her beliefs to others. A co-worker, however, may frequently use off-color words and joke about the need to sleep late on weekends to recover from late nights in bars. While conflict between these two individuals is not certain, there is a reasonable likelihood that they will at least occasionally each let the other know that they value different things.

At a somewhat different level, **legal conflict** may arise when there are differences in perceptions between organizations. For instance, if one firm sees a competitor as engaging in predatory pricing practices or a supplier as failing to live up to the terms of a contract, it may bring legal action against the other firm. Needless to say, legal conflict may also involve government bodies. Take, for example, the case of *whistle-blowing*, which refers to the disclosure by an employee of illegal or unethical conduct on the part of an organization. By its very nature, whistle-blowing presupposes a significant level of process conflict between employee and employer; however, whistle-blowers are protected from retaliation by a variety of state and federal laws, and many companies have found themselves embroiled in legal conflicts resulting not only from activities disclosed by whistle-blowers, but from actions they've taken to retaliate against them. As we saw in our chapter opener, laws—and legal conflicts—can get complicated and acrimonious, both for employers and whistle-blowers. For another example of the legal complications that can plague legal conflict, see the *Change* box entitled "Whistle-blowing in the Dark."

Causes of Conflict

Interpersonal Conflict   Conflict between two or more individuals is almost certain to occur in any organization, given the great variety in perceptions, goals, attitudes, and so forth among its members. William Gates, founder and CEO of Microsoft, and Kazuhiko Nishi, a former business associate from Japan, ended a long-term business relationship because of interpersonal conflict. Nishi accused Gates of becoming too political, while Gates charged that Nishi became too unpredictable and erratic in his behavior.[4]

A frequent source of interpersonal conflict in organizations is what many people call a personality clash—when two people distrust each others' motives, dislike one another, or for some other reason simply can't get along.[5] Conflict also may arise between people who have different beliefs or perceptions about some aspect of their work or their organization. For example, one manager may want the organization to require that all employees use Microsoft Office software to promote standardization. Another manager may believe a variety of software packages should be allowed in order to recognize individuality. Similarly, a male manager may disagree with his female colleague over whether the organization is guilty of discriminating against women in promotion decisions. Former Defense Secretary Donald Rumsfeld frequently had conflicts with others because of his abrasive and confrontational style.[6]

Conflict also can result from excess competitiveness among individuals. Two people vying for the same job, for example, may resort to political behavior in an effort to gain an advantage. If either competitor sees the other's behavior as inappropriate, accusations are likely to result. Even after the "winner" of the job is determined, such conflict may continue to undermine interpersonal relationships, especially if the

Relationship conflict occurs when the parties have interpersonal issues.

Legal conflict may arise when there are differences in perceptions between organizations.

CHANGE

Whistle-Blowing in the Dark

In 2008, Joseph Burke, a former manager at the advertising firm Ogilvy & Mather (O&M), filed a complaint with the Occupational Safety and Health Administration (OSHA), which is responsible for enforcing the whistle-blower–protection provisions of the Sarbanes-Oxley Act (SOX). Burke charged that, in violation of SOX, he had been fired for cooperating with a federal investigation into his employer's billing practices. The story (at least so far) may seem straightforward, but already it raises two fairly obvious questions:

1. Why SOX? Enacted in 2002 in the wake of corporate scandals involving such companies as Enron and WorldCom, SOX protects people who blow the whistle on firms that are registered or required to file reports with the Securities and Exchange Commission (SEC). The law states in part that covered companies "may not discharge or in any manner retaliate against an employee because he or she … assisted in an investigation by … a federal regulatory or law enforcement agency."

2. Why OSHA? Under the direction of the U.S. Department of Labor (DOL), OSHA is responsible for enforcing the whistle-blowing statutes of SOX. A complaint like Joseph Burke's goes first to an OSHA official, where it may be upheld or dismissed. It may then be appealed to a DOL administrative law judge (ALJ) and again appealed to the DOL's Administrative Review Board (ARB).

Burke's complaint didn't get very far: It was dismissed by OSHA, whose decision was upheld by an ALJ. As it happens, Burke has a lot of company in his frustration. Since SOX was passed nearly a decade ago, the OSHA-

> *"Otherwise, a company that wants to do something shady could just do it in a subsidiary."*
> —U.S. SENATOR PATRICK LEAHY ON THE INTENDED SCOPE OF FEDERAL WHISTLE-BLOWER PROTECTION

DOL process has ultimately ruled in favor of only 21 corporate whistle-blowers—out of nearly 1,500 complaints. And almost 1,000 others have been dismissed before reaching an ALJ. Why this overwhelming preponderance in favor of corporate defendants? Under the Bush administration, DOL lawyers issued a directive declaring that there is "no legal basis for the argument that subsidiaries of covered corporations are automatically covered" by SOX; after all, said administration lawyers, the law nowhere "expressly" says "subsidiaries." Joseph Burke, as an employee of O&M, worked for a *nonpublic subsidiary* of publicly traded WPP Group Plc. Thus, his case, according to the ALJ who presided over it, fell short because "only employees of publicly traded companies are protected" and Burke had "not established, by a preponderance of evidence, that he is an employee of a company covered under" SOX.

Not surprisingly, many people, both in government and the legal profession, are opposed to the DOL's strict interpretation of SOX. At least one ALJ, recalling the era of unchecked corporate fraud under which the law was passed, has reminded his colleagues that "subsidiaries were the vehicles through which the fraud was facilitated or accomplished" in the first place. Also adamant about the broader intent of SOX is U.S. Senator Patrick Leahy, who coauthored the law's whistle-blowing provisions. Why *wouldn't* SOX cover subsidiaries? he asks. "Otherwise, a company that wants to do something shady could just do it in a subsidiary." In September 2008, Leahy and SOX coauthor Senator Charles Grassley sent a letter to Secretary of Labor Elaine Chao, in which they objected to the DOL's interpretation of their wording: "We want to point out, as clearly and emphatically as we can," said the lawmakers,

> that there is simply no basis to assert ... that employees of subsidiaries of the companies identified in the statute were intended to be excluded from its protections. Moreover, as the authors of this provision, we can clearly state that it was by no means our intention to restrict these important protections to a small minority of corporate employees or to give corporations a loophole.

As Congress subsequently moved to close the loophole, OSHA took apparent steps to enforce the whistle-blowing provisions of SOX more vigorously: In March 2010, the agency issued awards totaling more than $1.6 million, plus reinstatement, to two whistle-blowers. In April, the Senate Banking Committee issued legislation to amend SOX and close the subsidiary loophole: The new law would expressly cover any subsidiary or affiliate whose financial information is included in the consolidated financial statements of a covered company.

References: Jennifer Levitz, "Shielding the Whistleblower," *Wall Street Journal*, December 1, 2009, http://online.wsj.com on April 17, 2010; David Nolte, "DOL Continues to Ignore and Rewrite SOX's Whistleblower Law," *HGExperts.com*, 2010, www.hgexperts.com on April 17, 2010; Squire, Sanders & Dempsey L.L.P., "Sarbanes-Oxley Whistleblower Complaints against Non-Public Subsidiaries Routinely Dismissed by OSHA," *martindale.com*, October 16, 2008, www .martindale.com on April 17, 2010; Jennifer Levitz, "Whistleblowers Are Left Dangling," *Wall Street Journal*, September 4, 2008, http:// online.wsj.com on April 17, 2010; Occupational Safety and Health Administration, "OSHA Fact Sheet," December 2006, www.osha .gov on April 17, 2009; Senator Patrick Leahy and Senator Charles Grassley, United States Senate, Committee of the Judiciary, Letter to the Honorable Elaine Chao, Secretary of Labor, September 9, 2008, http://judiciary.senate.gov on April 17, 2010; Seyfarth Shaw LLP, "OSHA Steps Up Enforcement of Sarbanes-Oxley Whistleblower Claims," *Lexology*, March 24, 2010, www.lexology.com on April 17, 2010; Wolters Kluwer, "Senate Committee Mulls Bill to Increase Scope of Employers Subject to SOX's Whistleblower Protections," *CHH*, April 2, 2010, http://hr.cch.com on April 18, 2010.

reasons given in selecting one candidate are ambiguous or open to alternative explanation. Robert Allen had to resign as CEO of Delta Airlines because of his disagreement with other key executives over how best to reduce the carrier's costs. After he began looking for a replacement for one of his rivals without the approval of the firm's board of directors, the resultant conflict and controversy left him no choice but to leave.[7]

Intergroup Conflict Conflict between two or more organizational groups is also quite common. For example, the members of a firm's marketing group may disagree with the production group over product quality and delivery schedules. Two sales groups may disagree over how to meet sales goals, and two groups of managers may have different ideas about how best to allocate organizational resources.

At a J.C. Penney department store, conflict arose between stockroom employees and sales associates. The sales associates claimed that the stockroom employees were slow in delivering merchandise to the sales floor so that it could be priced and shelved. The stockroom employees, in turn, claimed that the sales associates were not giving them enough lead time to get the merchandise delivered and failed to understand that they had additional duties besides carrying merchandise to the sales floor.

Just like people, different departments often have different goals. Further, these goals may often be incompatible. A marketing goal of maximizing sales, achieved partially by offering many products in a wide variety of sizes, shapes, colors, and models, probably conflicts with a production goal of minimizing costs, achieved partially by long production runs of a few items. Reebok recently confronted this very situation. One group of managers wanted to introduce a new sportswear line as quickly as possible, while other managers wanted to expand more deliberately and cautiously. Because the two groups were not able to reconcile their differences effectively, conflict between the two factions led to quality problems and delivery delays that plagued the firm for months.

Competition for scarce resources can also lead to intergroup conflict. Most organizations—especially universities, hospitals, government agencies, and businesses

DAN D'ERRICO/PHOTOSHOT

Sales associates at this J.C. Penney store claimed that stockroom employees were too slow to deliver merchandise to the sales floor. The stockroom employees, for their part, argued that the sales associates were not giving them enough lead time. The store manager eventually helped resolve the conflict by establishing a rule about how much lead time was necessary to have merchandise delivered to the sales floor and creating procedures that helped stockroom employees understand how to best prioritize deliveries when they were performing multiple tasks.

in depressed industries—have limited resources. In one New England town, for example, the public works department and the library battled over funds from a federal construction grant. The Buick and Chevrolet divisions of General Motors have frequently fought over the rights to manufacture various new products developed by the company. And in some firms, such as Boeing, the corporate culture may breed competition to the point that conflict is an ever-present phenomenon.[8]

Conflict Between Organization and Environment Conflict that arises between one organization and another is called interorganizational conflict. A moderate amount of interorganizational conflict resulting from business competition is, of course, expected—but sometimes conflict becomes more extreme. For example, the owners of Jordache Enterprises, Inc. and Guess?, Inc. battled in court for years over ownership of the Guess label, allegations of design theft, and several other issues. Similarly, General Motors and Volkswagen went to court to resolve a bitter conflict that spanned more than four years. It all started when a key GM executive, Jose Ignacio Lopez de Arriortua, left for a position at Volkswagen. GM claimed that he took with him key secrets that could benefit its German competitor. After the messy departure, dozens of charges and countercharges were made by the two firms, and only a court settlement was able to put the conflict to an end.

Conflict can also arise between an organization and other elements of its environment. For example, a business organization may conflict with a consumer group over claims it makes about its products. McDonald's faced this problem a few years ago when it published nutritional information about its products that omitted details about fat content. A manufacturer might conflict with a governmental agency such as OSHA. For example, the firm's management may believe it is in compliance with OSHA regulations, while officials from the agency itself feel that the firm is not in compliance. Or a firm might conflict with a supplier over the quality of raw materials. The firm may think the supplier is providing inferior materials, while the supplier thinks the materials are adequate. Finally, individual managers may obviously have disagreements with groups of workers. For example, a manager may think her workers are doing poor quality work and that they are unmotivated. The workers, on the other hand, may believe they are doing a good job and that the manager is doing a poor job of leading them.

Task Interdependence Task interdependence can also result in conflict across any of the levels noted previously. The greater the interdependence between departments, the greater the likelihood that conflict will occur. There are three major forms of interdependence: pooled, sequential, and reciprocal.[9]

Pooled interdependence represents the lowest level of interdependence, and hence results in the least amount of conflict. Units with pooled interdependence operate with little interaction—the output of the units is pooled at the organizational level. The Gap clothing stores operate with pooled interdependence. Each store is considered a "department" by the parent corporation. Each has its own operating budget, staff, and so forth. The profits or losses from each store are "added together" at the organizational level. The stores are interdependent to the extent that the financial success or failure of one store affects the others, but they do not generally interact on a day-to-day basis.

In **sequential interdependence**, the output of one unit becomes the input for another in a sequential fashion. This creates a moderate level of interdependence and a somewhat higher potential for conflict. At Nissan, for example, one plant assembles engines and then ships them to a final assembly site at another plant where the cars are completed. The plants are interdependent in that the final assembly plant must have the engines from the engine assembly plant before it can perform its primary function of producing finished automobiles. But the level of interdependence is generally one-way—the engine plant is not necessarily dependent on the final assembly plant. In this example, though, if the engine assembly plant is constantly late with its deliveries, it will quickly encounter problems with managers at the final assembly plant.

Reciprocal interdependence exists when activities flow both ways between units. This form is clearly the most complex, and hence has the highest potential for conflict. Within a Marriott Hotel, for example, the reservations department, front-desk check-in, and housekeeping are all reciprocally interdependent. Reservations has to provide front-desk employees with information about how many guests to expect each day, and housekeeping needs to know which rooms require priority cleaning. If any of the three units does not do its job properly, the others will all be affected. And as a result, routine conflict is almost inevitable.

Another example is the reciprocal interdependence between the Hollywood studios, which produce and distribute movies and TV shows, and the guilds of artists who write, direct, and act in them. For some details on the most recent round of intergroup conflict in the entertainment industry, see the *Technology* box on page 412.

REACTIONS TO CONFLICT

The most common reactions to conflict are avoidance, accommodation, competition, collaboration, and compromise.[10] Whenever conflict occurs between groups or organizations, it is really the people who are in conflict. In many cases, however, people are acting as representatives of the groups to which they belong. In effect, they work together, representing their group as they strive to do their part in helping the group achieve its goals. Thus, whether the conflict is between people acting as individuals or people acting as representatives of groups, the five types of interactions can be analyzed in terms of relationships among the goals of the people or the groups they represent.

Reactions to conflict can be differentiated along two dimensions: how important each party's goals are to that party and how compatible the goals are, as shown in Figure 15.2. The importance of reaching a goal may range from very high to very low. The degree of **goal compatibility** is the extent to which the goals can be achieved simultaneously. In other words, the goals are compatible if one party can meet its goals without preventing the other from meeting its goals. The goals are incompatible

Pooled interdependence represents the lowest level of interdependence, and hence results in the least amount of conflict.

In **sequential interdependence**, the output of one unit becomes the input for another in a sequential fashion; this creates a moderate level of interdependence and a somewhat higher potential for conflict.

Reciprocal interdependence exists when activities flow both ways between units; this form has the highest potential for conflict.

The degree of **goal compatibility** is the extent to which the goals can be achieved simultaneously.

TECHNOLOGY

New Technology Impacts Entertainment Industry

Media technology is constantly evolving. The Internet and cellular technology are changing the entertainment industry, and with this comes conflict.

In 2008, the 13,000-member Directors Guild of America (DGA) and the 11,000-member Writers Guild of America (WGA) renegotiated their contracts. These artists wanted compensation for new media, including Internet downloading. The DGA renegotiated without much conflict, while the WGA called a strike—but for both unions, negotiations were complicated by the complexity of the technology.

For example, writers of dramatic scripts created for new media will be paid $618 for two minutes of material plus $309 for each extra minute. For comedy, variety, soap opera, or other products, the rates are less. Directors operate under a completely separate union contract. For paid downloads of television shows, directors receive 0.36 percent of the distributor's gross margin, rising to 0.70 percent when over 100,000 units are downloaded. Paid downloads of films have different charges, as does free ad-supported streaming. For both writers and directors, there are further clauses for traditional works that are reused in new media, advertising clips, cellular streaming, and downloaded rentals.

The negotiations were intense. Writers and directors settled for about one-third of their original demands, while studios doubled their original offers. The SAG is experiencing internal conflict because some members want to limit contract voting rights to those who work the most. Many actors feel this is undemocratic, including Ron Livingston, star of the movie *Office Space.* "It's not a collective agreement unless you agree to it collectively," Livingston states. "The strength of the union is not just the actor working the job, it's the other nine actors next to him who say, 'We'd love that job, too, but we're not going to take it unless you pay him what he's worth.'"

> *"It's not a collective agreement unless you agree to it collectively."*
> —RON LIVINGSTON, ACTOR AND SAG MEMBER

References: Writers Guild of America, West, "Summary of the Tentative 2008 WGA Theatrical and Television Basic Agreement," 2010, www.wga.org on April 17, 2010; Ronald Grover, "Writers' Strike: The Show Must Go On," *BusinessWeek*, November 7, 2007, www .businessweek.com on April 19, 2010; Ron Grover, "Directors' Deal May End Writers' Strike," *BusinessWeek*, January 18, 2008, www .businessweek.com on April 17, 2010; Peter Sanders, "Actors Guild Faces Drama in Its Ranks," *Wall Street Journal*, April 3, 2008, http:// online.wsj.com on April 17, 2010.

if one party's meeting its goals prevents the other party from meeting its goals. The goals of different groups may be very compatible, completely incompatible, or somewhere in between.

Avoidance   Avoidance occurs when an interaction is relatively unimportant to either party's goals, and the goals are incompatible, as in the bottom left corner of Figure 15.2. Because the parties to the conflict are not striving toward compatible goals, and the issues in question seem unimportant, the parties simply try to avoid interacting with one another. For example, one state agency may simply ignore another agency's requests for information. The requesting agency can then practice its own form of avoidance by not following up on the requests.

Avoidance occurs when an interaction is relatively unimportant to either party's goals, and the goals are incompatible.

Accommodation Accommodation occurs when the goals are compatible, but the interactions are not considered important to overall goal attainment, as in the bottom right corner of Figure 15.2. Interactions of this type may involve discussions of how the parties can accomplish their interdependent tasks with the least expenditure of time and effort. This type of interaction tends to be very friendly. For example, during a college's course scheduling period, potential conflict may exist between the marketing and management departments. Both departments offer morning classes. Which department is allocated the 9:00 A.M. time slot and which one the 10:00 A.M. time slot is not that important to either group. Their overall goal is that the classes are scheduled so that students will be able to take courses.

Competition Competition occurs when the goals are incompatible, and the interactions are important to each party's meeting its goals, as in the top left corner of Figure 15.2. If all parties are striving for a goal, but only one can reach the goal, the parties will be in competition. As we noted earlier, if a competitive situation gets out of control, as when overt antagonism occurs, and there are no rules or procedures to follow, then competition can result in conflict. Sometimes, however, conflict can also change to competition if the parties agree to rules to guide the interaction, and conflicting parties agree not to be hostile toward each other.

In one freight warehouse and storage firm, the first, second, and third shifts each sought to win the weekly productivity prize by posting the highest productivity record. Workers on the winning shift received recognition in the company newspaper. Because the issue was important to each group, and the interests of the groups were incompatible, the result was competition.

The competition among the shifts encouraged each shift to produce more per week, which increased the company's output and eventually improved its overall welfare (and thus the welfare of each group). Both the company and the groups benefited from the competition because it fostered innovative and creative work methods, which further boosted productivity. After about three months, however, the competition got out of control. The competition among the groups led to poorer overall performance as the groups started to sabotage other shifts and inflate records. The competition became too important, open antagonism resulted, rules were ignored, and the competition changed to open conflict, resulting in actual decreases in work performance.[11]

Collaboration Collaboration occurs when the interaction between groups is very important to goal attainment, and the goals are compatible, as in the top right corner of Figure 15.2. In the class scheduling situation mentioned earlier,

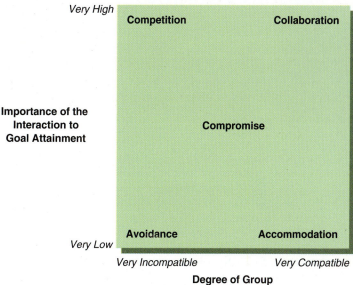

Figure 15.2 FIVE TYPES OF REACTIONS TO CONFLICT

The five types of reactions to conflict stem from the relative importance of interaction to goal attainment and the degree of goal compatibility.

Reference: Adapted from Kenneth Thomas, "Conflict and Conflict Management," in Marvin Dunnette (ed.), *Handbook of Industrial and Organizational Psychology* (Chicago: Rand McNally, 1976), pp. 889–935. Reprinted by permission.

Accommodation occurs when the goals are compatible, but the interactions are not considered important to overall goal attainment.

Competition occurs when the goals are incompatible, and the interactions are important to each party's meeting its goals.

Collaboration occurs when the interaction between groups is very important to goal attainment, and the goals are compatible.

JIM WEST/ALAMY

Contract negotiations between large businesses and their labor unions can be extremely complex and contentious. Successful negotiations usually involve compromises by each side. This photo illustrates the opening session of a contract negotiation between Ford Motor Company and the United Auto Workers union. Members of Ford's team, shown on the right, are dressed in formal business attire, while the UAW representatives are wearing their normal work clothes. These differences, along with the seating arrangements, help underscore for both sides the fact that they represent different interests.

conflict may arise over which courses to teach in the first semester and which ones in the second. Both departments would like to offer specific courses in the fall. However, by discussing the issue and refocusing their overall goals to match students' needs, the marketing and economics departments can collaborate on developing a proper sequence of courses. At first glance, this may seem to be simple interaction in which the parties participate jointly in activities to accomplish goals after agreeing on the goals and their importance. In many situations, however, it is no easy matter to agree on goals, their importance, and especially the means for achieving them. In a collaborative interaction, goals may differ but be compatible. Parties to a conflict may initially have difficulty working out the ways in which all can achieve their goals. However, because the interactions are important to goal attainment, the parties are willing to continue to work together to achieve the goals. Collaborative relationships can lead to new and innovative ideas and solutions to differences among the parties.

Compromise   Compromise occurs when the interactions are moderately important to goal attainment, and the goals are neither completely compatible nor completely incompatible. In a compromise situation, parties interact with others striving to achieve goals, but they may not aggressively pursue goal attainment in either a competitive or collaborative manner because the interactions are not that important to goal attainment. On the other hand, the parties may neither avoid one another nor be accommodating because the interactions are somewhat important. Often each party gives up something, but because the interactions are only moderately important, they do not regret what they have given up.

Contract negotiations between union and management are usually examples of compromise. Each side brings numerous issues of varying importance to the bargaining table. The two sides frequently give and take on the issues through rounds of offers and counteroffers. The complexity of such negotiations increases as negotiations spread to multiple plants in different countries. Agreements between management and labor in a plant in the United States may be unacceptable to either or both parties in Canada. Weeks of negotiations ending in numerous compromises usually result in a contract agreement between the union and management.

In summary, when groups are in conflict, they may react in several different ways. If the goals of the parties are very compatible, the parties may engage in mutually supportive interactions—that is, collaboration or accommodation. If the goals are very incompatible, each may attempt to foster its own success at the expense of the other, engaging in competition or avoidance.

Compromise occurs when the interactions are moderately important to goal attainment, and the goals are neither completely compatible nor completely incompatible.

MANAGING CONFLICT

Managers must know when to stimulate conflict and when to resolve it if they are to avoid its potentially disruptive effects.[12] As we noted earlier, too little conflict and too much conflict are each dysfunctional in their own ways. Hence, if there is too little conflict managers many need to stimulate a moderate degree of conflict. If conflict is excessive, however, it may need to be reduced. Figure 15.3 introduces some of the basic techniques for stimulating and resolving conflict.

Stimulating Conflict

A complete absence of conflict may indicate that the organization is stagnant and that employees are content with the status quo. It may also suggest that work groups are not motivated to challenge traditional and well-accepted ideas. **Conflict stimulation** is the creation and constructive use of conflict by a manager. Its purpose is to bring about situations in which differences of opinion are exposed for examination by all.

For example, if competing organizations are making significant changes in products, markets, or technologies, it may be time for a manager to stimulate innovation and creativity by challenging the status quo. Conflict may give employees the motivation and opportunity to reveal differences of opinion that they previously kept to themselves. When all parties to the conflict are interested enough in an issue to challenge other groups, they often expose their hidden doubts or opinions. These in turn allow the parties to get to the heart of the matter and often to develop unique solutions to the problem. Indeed, the interactions may lead the groups to recognize that a problem in fact does exist. Conflict, then, can be a catalyst for creativity and change in an organization.

Several methods can be used to stimulate conflict under controlled conditions. These include altering the physical location of groups to stimulate more interactions, forcing more resource sharing, and implementing other changes in relationships among groups. In addition, training programs can be used to increase employee awareness of potential problems in group decision making and group interactions. Adopting

Figure 15.3   CONFLICT MANAGEMENT ALTERNATIVES

Conflict management may involve resolution or stimulation of conflict, depending on the situation.

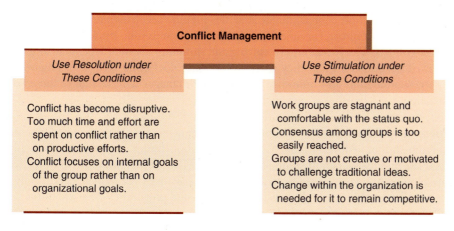

Conflict Management

Use Resolution under These Conditions	Use Stimulation under These Conditions
Conflict has become disruptive. Too much time and effort are spent on conflict rather than on productive efforts. Conflict focuses on internal goals of the group rather than on organizational goals.	Work groups are stagnant and comfortable with the status quo. Consensus among groups is too easily reached. Groups are not creative or motivated to challenge traditional ideas. Change within the organization is needed for it to remain competitive.

Conflict stimulation is the creation and constructive use of conflict by a manager.

the role of "devil's advocate" in discussion sessions is another way to stimulate conflict among groups. In this role, a manager challenges the prevailing consensus to ensure that all alternatives have been critically appraised and analyzed. Although this role is often unpopular, employing it is a good way to stimulate constructive conflict.

Conflict Resolution

When a potentially harmful conflict situation exists, however, a manager needs to engage in **conflict resolution**. Conflict needs to be resolved when it causes major disruptions in the organization and absorbs time and effort that could be used more productively. Conflict should also be resolved when its focus is on the group's internal goals rather than on organizational goals.

When attempting to resolve conflict, managers should first attempt to determine the source of the conflict. If the source of destructive conflict is a particular person or two, it might be appropriate to alter the membership of one or both groups. If the conflict is due to differences in goals, perceptions of the difficulty of goal attainment, or the importance of the goals to the conflicting parties, then the manager can attempt to move the conflicting parties into one of the five types of reactions to conflict, depending on the nature of the conflicting parties.

To foster collaboration, it might be appropriate to try to help people see that their goals are really not as different as they seem to be. The manager can help groups view their goals as part of a **superordinate goal** to which the goals of both conflicting parties can contribute. A superordinate goal is a goal of the overall organization and is more important to the well-being of the organization and its members than the more specific goals of the conflicting parties. If the goals are not really that important and are very incompatible, the manager may need to develop ways to help the conflicting parties avoid each other. Similarly, accommodation, competition, or compromise might be appropriate for the conflicting parties.

Using Structure to Manage Conflict

Beyond the methods noted above, managers can also rely heavily on elements of organization structure to manage conflict. Among the more common methods are the hierarchy, rules and procedures, liaison roles, and task forces.

The Managerial Hierarchy Organizations that use the hierarchy to manage conflict place one manager in charge of people, groups, or departments in conflict. In Walmart distribution centers, major activities include receiving and unloading bulk shipments from railroad cars and loading other shipments onto trucks for distribution to retail outlets. The two groups (receiving and shipping) are interdependent and may experience conflict in that they share the loading docks and some equipment. To ensure coordination and minimize conflict, one manager is in charge of the whole operation.

Rules and Procedures Routine conflict management can be handled via rules and standard procedures. In the Walmart distribution center, an outgoing truck shipment has priority over an incoming rail shipment. Thus, when trucks are to be loaded, the shipping unit is given access to all of the center's auxiliary forklifts. This priority is specifically stated in a rule. But, as useful as rules and procedures often are in routine situations, they are not particularly effective when coordination problems and conflict are complex or unusual.

Conflict resolution is a managed effort to reduce or eliminate harmful conflict.

A **superordinate goal** is a goal of the overall organization and is more important to the well-being of the organization and its members than the more specific goals of the conflicting parties.

Liaison Roles We introduce the liaison role of management in Chapter 1. As a device for managing conflict, a manager in a liaison role coordinates activities acting as a common point of contact. This individual may not have any formal authority over the groups but instead simply facilitates the flow of information between parties. Two engineering groups working on component systems for a large project might interact through a liaison. The liaison maintains familiarity with each group as well as with the overall project. She can answer questions and otherwise serve to integrate the activities of all the groups. Since the groups do not directly interact with one another, there is less chance of conflict.

Task Forces A task force may be created when the need for conflict management is acute. When interdependence is complex and several groups and/or individuals are involved, a single liaison person may not be sufficient. Instead, a task force might be assembled by drawing one representative from each group. The conflict management function is thus spread across several individuals, each of whom has special information about one of the groups involved. When the project is completed, task force members return to their original positions. For example, a college overhauling its degree requirements might establish a task force made up of representatives from each department affected by the change. Each person retains her or his regular departmental affiliation and duties but also serves on the special task force. After the new requirements are agreed on, the task force is dissolved.

Using Interpersonal Techniques to Manage Conflict

There are also several techniques that focus on interpersonal processes that can be used to manage conflict. These often fall under the heading of organization development, discussed in Chapter 19. Hence, we describe a few examples here.

Team Building Team-building activities are intended to enhance the effectiveness and satisfaction of individuals who work in groups or teams and to promote overall group effectiveness; consequently there should be less conflict among members of the team. Given the widespread use of teams today, these activities have taken on increased importance. Caterpillar used team building as one method for changing the working relationships between workers and supervisors from confrontational to cooperative. An interesting approach to team building involves having executive teams participate in group-cooking classes to teach them the importance of interdependence and coordination.[13]

Survey Feedback In survey feedback, each employee responds to a questionnaire intended to measure perceptions and attitudes (for example, satisfaction and supervisory style). Everyone involved, including the supervisor, receives the results of the survey. The aim of this approach is usually to change the behavior of supervisors by showing them how their subordinates view them. After the feedback has been provided, workshops may be conducted to evaluate results and suggest constructive changes.

Third-Party Peacemaking A somewhat more extreme form of interpersonal conflict management is third-party peacemaking, which is most often used when substantial conflict exists within the organization. Third-party peacemaking can be

Team-building activities are intended to enhance the effectiveness and satisfaction of individuals who work in groups or teams and to promote overall group effectiveness; consequently there should be less conflict among members of the team.

In **survey feedback**, each employee responds to a questionnaire intended to measure perceptions and attitudes (for example, satisfaction and supervisory style).

Third-party peacemaking, primarily used to address extreme conflict, involves bringing in an outsider to facilitate conflict resolution.

DAVID MADISON/IVY/CORBIS

Team building is a common method used by organizations to help overcome conflict and promote collaboration among employees. Outward Bound was a pioneer in developing unique and challenging outdoor exercises for teams. The idea is that by spending time together in demanding situations and having to rely on each other to accomplish their goals, team members will develop improved working relationships. That is, trust and respect developed during the outdoors exercises will (in theory, at least) carry over back at work. This group of professionals has just gone through team-building exercises as part of a hiking and camping excursion in Vermont.

appropriate on the individual, group, or organization level. A third party, usually a trained external facilitator, uses a variety of mediation or negotiation techniques to resolve problems or conflicts between individuals or groups.

Negotiated Conflict Management

Finally, conflict solutions are sometimes negotiated in advance. For instance, a labor agreement often spells out in detail how union members must report a grievance, how management must respond, and how the dispute will be resolved. Conflict is thus avoided by preestablishing exactly how it will be addressed. The following discussion of negotiation also has other implications for conflict management.

NEGOTIATION IN ORGANIZATIONS

Negotiation is the process in which two or more parties (people or groups) reach agreement on an issue even though they have different preferences regarding that issue. In its simplest form the parties involved may be two individuals who are trying to decide who will pay for lunch. A little more complexity is involved when two people, such as an employee and manager, sit down to decide on personal performance goals for the next year against which the employee's performance will be measured. Even more complex are the negotiations that take place between labor unions and the management

Negotiation is the process in which two or more parties (people or groups) reach agreement on an issue even though they have different preferences regarding that issue.

of a company or between two companies as they negotiate the terms of a joint venture. The key issues in such negotiations are that at least two parties are involved, their preferences are different, and they need to reach agreement.

Approaches to Negotiation

Interest in negotiation has grown steadily in recent years.[14] Four primary approaches to negotiation have dominated this study: individual differences, situational characteristics, game theory, and cognitive approaches. Each of these is briefly described in the following sections.

"A good negotiator can stand back and gain perspective."

Negotiators may get so personally involved in a bargaining process that their objectivity suffers. Many experts caution against this mistake, and some offer advice on how to remain objective. Of course, it is also possible for a person to become so far removed from the negotiation process that they lose touch with what is actually happening.
CARTOONBANK.COM

Individual Differences   Early psychological approaches concentrated on the personality traits of the negotiators.[15] Traits investigated have included demographic characteristics and personality variables. Demographic characteristics have included age, gender, and race, among others. Personality variables have included risk taking, locus of control, tolerance for ambiguity, self-esteem, authoritarianism, and Machiavellianism. The assumption of this type of research was that the key to successful negotiation was selecting the right person to do the negotiating, one who had the appropriate demographic characteristics or personality. This assumption seemed to make sense because negotiation is such a personal and interactive process. However, the research rarely showed the positive results expected because situational variables negated the effects of the individual differences.[16]

Situational Characteristics   Situational characteristics are the context within which negotiation takes place. They include such things as the types of communication between negotiators, the potential outcomes of the negotiation, the relative power of the parties (both positional and personal), the time frame available for negotiation, the number of people representing each side, and the presence of other parties. Some of this research has contributed to our understanding of the negotiation process. However, the shortcomings of the situational approach are similar to those of the individual characteristics approach. Many situational characteristics are external to the negotiators and beyond their control. Often the negotiators cannot change their relative power positions or the setting within which the negotiation occurs. So, although we have learned a lot from research on the situational issues, we still need to learn much more about the process.

Game Theory   Game theory was developed by economists using mathematical models to predict the outcome of negotiation situations (as illustrated in the Academy Award–winning movie A Beautiful Mind). It requires that every alternative and

Game theory was developed by economists using mathematical models to predict the outcome of negotiation situations.

outcome be analyzed with probabilities and numerical outcomes reflecting the preferences for each outcome. In addition, the order in which different parties can make choices and every possible move are predicted, along with associated preferences for outcomes. The outcomes of this approach are exactly what negotiators want: A predictive model of how negotiation should be conducted. One major drawback is that it requires the ability to describe all possible options and outcomes for every possible move in every situation before the negotiation starts. This is often very tedious, if possible at all. Another problem is that this theory assumes that negotiators are rational at all times. Other research in negotiation has shown that negotiators often do not act rationally. Therefore, this approach, although elegant in its prescriptions, is usually unworkable in a real negotiation situation.

Cognitive Approaches   The fourth approach is the cognitive approach, which recognizes that negotiators often depart from perfect rationality during negotiation; it tries to predict how and when negotiators will make these departures. Howard Raiffa's decision analytic approach focuses on providing advice to negotiators actively involved in negotiation.[17] Bazerman and Neale have added to Raiffa's work by specifying eight ways in which negotiators systematically deviate from rationality.[18] The types of deviations they describe include escalation of commitment to a previously selected course of action, overreliance on readily available information, assuming that the negotiations can produce fixed-sum outcomes, and anchoring negotiation in irrelevant information. These cognitive approaches have advanced the study of negotiation a long way beyond the early individual and situational approaches. Negotiators can use them to attempt to predict in advance how the negotiation might take place.

Figure 15.4   **THE PRAM MODEL OF NEGOTIATION**

The PRAM model shows the four steps in setting up negotiation so that both parties win.

Reference: Brian G. Long, Ph.D., and Ross R. Reck, Ph.D., The Win-Win Negotiator: How to Negotiate Favorable Agreements That Last. Copyright © 1985, 1987 by Brian G. Long and Ross R. Reck. Reprinted with permission of Ross R. Reck, Ph.D.

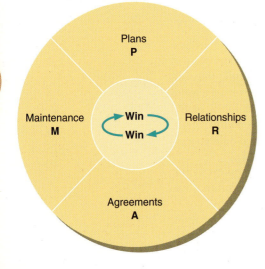

The **PRAM model** is four-step approach to negotiation that proposes that proper planning, building relationships, getting agreements, and maintaining the relationships are the key steps to successful negotiation.

Win-Win Negotiation

In addition to the approaches to negotiation previously described, a group of approaches proposed by consultants and advisors is meant to give negotiators a specific model to use in carrying out difficult negotiations. One of the best of these is the "Win-Win Negotiator" developed by Ross Reck and his associates.[19] The Win-Win approach does not treat negotiation as a game in which there are winners and losers. Instead, it approaches negotiation as an opportunity for both sides to be winners, to get what they want out of the agreement. The focus is on both parties reaching agreement such that both are committed to fulfilling their own end of the agreement and to returning for more agreements in the future. In other words, both parties want to have their needs satisfied. In addition, this approach does not advocate either a "tough guy" or a "nice guy" approach to negotiation, both of which are popular in the literature. It assumes that both parties work together to find ways to satisfy both parties at the same time.

The Win-Win approach is a four-step approach illustrated in the **PRAM model** shown in Figure 15.4. The PRAM four-step approach proposes that proper planning, building relationships, getting agreements, and maintaining the relationships are the key steps to successful negotiation.

Planning requires that each negotiator set his or her own goals, anticipate the goals of the other, determine areas of probable agreement, and develop strategies for reconciling areas of probable disagreement.

Developing Win-Win *relationships* requires that negotiators plan activities that enable positive personal relationships to develop, cultivate a sense of mutual trust, and allow relationships to develop fully before discussing business in earnest. The development of trust between the parties is probably the single most important key to success in negotiation.

Forming Win-Win *agreements* requires that each party confirm the other party's goals, verify areas of agreement, propose and consider positive solutions to reconcile areas of disagreement, and jointly resolve any remaining differences. The key in reaching agreement is to realize that both parties share many of the goals. The number of areas of disagreement is usually small.

Finally, Win-Win *maintenance* entails providing meaningful feedback based on performance, each of the parties holding up an end of the agreement, keeping in contact, and reaffirming trust between the parties. The assumption is that both parties want to keep the relationship going so that future mutually beneficial transactions can occur. Both parties must uphold their ends of the agreement and do what they said they would do. Finally, keeping in touch is as easy as making a telephone call or meeting for lunch.

SYNOPSIS

Conflict is a process resulting in the perceptions of two parties that they are working in opposition to each other in ways that result in feelings of discomfort and/or animosity. Although conflict often is considered harmful, and thus something to avoid, it can also have some benefits.

There are three basic forms of conflict that exist within an organization. Task conflict refers to conflict regarding the goals and content of the work. Process conflict occurs when the parties agree on the goals and content of work, but disagree on how to achieve the goals and actually do the work. Relationship conflict occurs when the parties have interpersonal issues. Legal conflict may arise when there are differences in perceptions between organizations.

Causes of conflict can include an array of interpersonal and intergroup issues. There may also be conflict between an organization and its environment. Task interdependence (pooled, sequential, and reciprocal) can also cause conflict.

The most common reactions to conflict are avoidance, accommodation, competition, collaboration, and compromise. Reactions to conflict can be differentiated along two dimensions: how important each party's goals are to that party and how compatible the goals are.

Managers must know when to stimulate conflict and when to resolve it if they are to avoid its potentially disruptive effects. There are a variety of methods that can be used to either stimulate or resolve conflict. Organization structure and various interpersonal methods may also be useful in managing conflict. Conflict resolution may also be negotiated in advance.

Negotiation is the process in which two or more parties (people or groups) reach agreement on an issue even though they have different preferences regarding that issue. Four primary approaches to negotiation focus on individual differences, situational characteristics, game theory, and cognitive approaches. The Win-Win approach does not treat negotiation as a game in which there are winners and losers. Instead, it approaches negotiation as an opportunity for both sides to be winners, to get what they want out of the agreement.

DISCUSSION QUESTIONS

1. Recall instances in which you have experienced each of the three primary forms of conflict.
2. In general, is one form of conflict likely to be more costly to an organization than the others? Why or why not?
3. Are certain forms of conflict more likely than others to be associated with each level of interdependence? In what way?
4. Have you ever been a party to conflict that had positive benefits? What were the details?
5. How comfortable are you personally in dealing with conflict?
6. What is the primary risk of trying to stimulate moderate levels of conflict in a situation characterized by lethargy?
7. Relate the various methods of resolving conflict to the primary forms of conflict. That is, for example, what conflict resolution methods are most likely to be useful in dealing with task conflict?
8. Describe various ways in which conflict and negotiations may be related.
9. Recall an instance in which you negotiated something and describe it in terms of the discussion of negotiation in this chapter.
10. Why don't people engaged in all negotiation situations try to adopt a win-win mentality?

ORGANIZATIONAL BEHAVIOR CASE FOR DISCUSSION

THE TROUBLE WITH FILLING SHOES AT NIKE

Sometimes a successful entrepreneur gets too attached to his brainchild, identifying himself so closely with the organization, its products, and its people that it becomes almost impossible to let go. Sometimes, of course, he or she lets go and then grabs hold again. That's what happened at Nike when founder Phil Knight forced out CEO William Perez just 13 months after handpicking the ex-head of S.C. Johnson to take over his job. In hiring Perez, Knight was making no less than his third effort to step back from direct supervision of the world's largest sneaker and athletic-apparel company.

> *"The message about filling shoes is that you can't. You've got to design new shoes."*
> —STEPHEN MADER, EXECUTIVE HEADHUNTER

It's "a predictable script," says Yale professor Jeffrey Sonnenfeld, who likens this recurring corporate drama to sagas of more universal import: "It's like Shakespeare or Greek tragedy or the Bible." Business journalists have even given the familiar scenario a suitably epic title— "The Return of the Founder." Knight, who'd chosen Perez to instill the sort of organizational and managerial discipline that had never been his own strong suit, put a fairly typical spin on the executive coup: Perez, he explained, had failed to grasp the company culture and had failed to deploy the proven management teams already in place.

Over the years, Nike insiders have invited a few outside superstars to join in their management ranks, but for the most part, the company's managerial talent has always been homegrown. The promote-from-within mentality, combined with a strong cross-training program for managers, lends itself to the kind of internal cohesiveness that Knight and Nike like. Because new executives broaden their experience by rotating through various departments, they develop connections with several senior people in the company, and Nike's matrix organization (see Chapter 17) means that they're working with several ranking managers at any given time. One result of this approach to managerial indoctrination has been the development of a culture that some observers regard as a little too insular. "People who don't get the culture," advises Don Murray, a management consultant who's worked closely with Knight and Nike for many years, "don't stick around very long. They know they don't fit. That's it."

And Bill Perez? He was shy and introspective— ironically, a lot like Knight—but even though he was a novice in the athletic wear and equipment industry, his experience at a giant consumer-products company with diverse product lines promised to be a significant asset at

Nike, which was in the process of expanding its offerings in both sports gear and apparel. Having overseen numerous acquisitions at S.C. Johnson, Perez also seemed well equipped to help Nike grow. "There will be a little bit of a bumpy period," Knight acknowledged at the time of the transition, but "I'm committed to making it work."

Unfortunately, Perez apparently ruffled feathers almost from day one. "[He] started asking questions of 20- to-30-year veterans that [had] never been asked before," says one executive. He also irked marketing executives by questioning award-winning ads and adopting an unfamiliar approach to evaluating campaigns. "He didn't have an intuitive sense of Nike as a brand," complained one marketing manager. "He relied more on the spreadsheet, analytical approach as opposed to having a good creative marketing sense." Before long, Perez had butted heads with numerous executives, including Mark Parker and Charlie Denson, two Nike lifers who'd competed for the CEO spot before Knight decided to go with Perez.

According to Perez, Nike insiders were unreasonably resistant to change, and Knight, he adds, complicated matters by interfering with his efforts to do his job. "From virtually the day I arrived," he recalls, "Phil was as engaged in the company as he ever was. He was talking to my direct reports. It was confusing for the people and frustrating for me." Knight responded by blaming Perez for his inability to work with Nike veterans. "I think the failure to … get his arms around this company and this industry," he said, "led to confusion on behalf of the management team." Knight also cited cultural incompatibility: "Basically," he told analysts and journalists, "the distance between the company Bill managed in the packaged-goods business and Nike and the kind of new athletic-equipment business was too great. The cultural leap," he concluded, "was really too great."

When the dust had cleared, Parker and Denson had been anointed president and CEO, respectively. Today, Parker holds both jobs while Knight continues to serve as chairman of the board. Many outside observers remain critical of Knight and the Nike board, particularly for perpetuating an insular culture that's apparently as inimical to fresh blood as it ever was. "It's almost like a death wish, coming into that company from outside," says Stephanie Joseph, an expert on corporate boards. Many observers also continue to fault the board for being unable to envision the company without its founder and to establish a firm plan of succession. Says Stephen Mader, an executive headhunter who believes that Nike needs not only better succession planning but an infusion of new ideas: "The message about filling shoes is that you can't. You've got to design new shoes."

CASE QUESTIONS

1. In what ways did William Perez encounter *process conflict* at Nike? How about *relationship conflict*?

2. In what respects does Nike's managerial hierarchy appear to be conducive to conflict?

3. Phil Knight has said: "It's been 40 years that the company has grown around my idiosyncrasies. They don't even know that they're idiosyncrasies anymore, and of course neither do I." If you were working with Phil Knight, what steps would you take to avoid *relationship* and *interpersonal conflict*?

4. "Nike's early management meetings," reports a writer familiar with the company, "were rowdy, drunken affairs. When fights broke out … Knight would rarely interrupt. He liked to see the passion." At what point does the strategy of *conflict stimulation* appear to break down at Nike? In your opinion, why does it break down? Does it have to break down?

REFERENCES

Amy Gunderson, "The Great Leaders Series: Phil Knight of Nike," *Inc.*, November 4, 2009, www.inc.com on March 26, 2010; Stanley Holmes, "Nike: Can Perez Fill Knight's Shoes?" *BusinessWeek*, November 19, 2004, www.businessweek.com on March 26, 2010; Holmes, "Inside the Coup at Nike," *BusinessWeek*, February 6, 2006, www.businessweek.com on March 26, 2010; Holmes, "Nike's CEO Gets the Boot," *BusinessWeek*, January 24, 2006, www.businessweek.com on March 26, 2010; Daniel Roth, "Can Nike Still Do It without Phil Knight?" *Fortune*, April 4, 2005, http://money.cnn.com on March 26, 2010.

EXPERIENCING ORGANIZATIONAL BEHAVIOR

Learning Negotiation Skills

Purpose This exercise will help you learn more about how to prepare for and participate in a negotiation.

Format You will participate in this exercise with one of your classmates. The two of you will attempt to negotiate an understanding regarding a hypothetical assignment.

Procedure Assume that your instructor has assigned the two of you an out-of-class project. The hypothetical project consists of the following activities:

1. You are to interview a total of five managers in your local community. Each interview should last about an hour. The purpose of the interviews is to learn more about the nature and substance of managerial work. You will ask each manager a set of predetermined questions about their jobs.
2. The results of the interviews are to be synthesized into a single discussion of what managers do. Detailed analyses of the responses to each question are to be carefully studied and integrated into a single overall description.
3. The description is to be written up in the form of a paper of approximately 10 pages. In addition to its content, issues such as language, grammar, spelling, and format will all be considered when the paper is graded.
4. Finally, the content of the paper must also be organized for an in-class presentation. The presentation needs to be of professional quality, make use of Power Point slides and other visual aids, and be formally presented to a group of visiting executives.
5. Your instructor is indifferent as to how the assignment is completed. That is, you and your partner can divide the work up in any way that you see fit. However, you will each receive the same overall grade on the project regardless of what you each do.

Now, you and your partner should negotiate what you will each do. Be as specific as possible when deciding how to divide up the work involved in completing the project.

Follow-up Questions
1. What factors did you consider as you reached agreement on how to divide up the work?
2. How comfortable were you with the final division of labor?
3. If this were a real assignment, what concerns would you have about having a successful outcome? What steps, if any, might you use to offset those concerns?

BUILDING MANAGERIAL SKILLS

Exercise Overview A manager's interpersonal skills refer to her or his ability to understand how to motivate individuals and groups. Clearly, then, interpersonal skills play a major role in determining how well a manager can interact with others in a group setting. This exercise will allow you to practice your interpersonal skills in relation to just such a setting.

Exercise Background You have just been transferred to a new position supervising a group of five employees. The business you work for is fairly small and has few rules and regulations. Unfortunately, the lack of rules and regulations is creating a problem that you must now address.

Specifically, two of the group members are nonsmokers. They are becoming increasingly more vocal about the fact that two other members of the group smoke at work. These two workers feel that the secondary smoke in the workplace is endangering their health and want to establish a no-smoking policy like those of many large businesses today.

The two smokers, however, argue that since the firm did not have such a policy when they started working there, it would be unfair to impose such a policy now. One of them, in particular, says that he turned down an attractive job with another company because he wanted to work in a place where he could smoke.

The fifth worker is also a nonsmoker but says that she doesn't care if others smoke. Her husband smokes at home anyway, she says, so she is used to being around smokers. You suspect that if the two vocal nonsmokers are not appeased, they may leave. At the same time, you also think that the two smokers will leave if you mandate a no-smoking policy. All five workers do good work, and you do not want any of them to leave.

Exercise Task With this information as context, do the following:

1. Explain the nature of the conflict that exists in this work group.
2. Develop a course of action for dealing with the situation.

SELF-ASSESSMENT EXERCISE

What Do You Do When Interests Conflict?

This exercise is designed to help you assess your level of competency in managing conflict. If you have a job, consider that your work; if you're a student, apply this exercise to your school work.

The 24 statements below reflect approaches that people can take toward managing workplace conflict. Using the following scale, indicate the extent to which, in your opinion, each statement is true of you.

1. Strongly disagree
2. Disagree
3. Slightly disagree
4. Slightly agree
5. Agree
6. Strongly agree

When I see someone doing something that needs correcting:

_____ 1. I avoid making personal accusations and attributing self-serving motives to the other person.

_____ 2. I present my concerns as my problems.

_____ 3. I succinctly describe problems in terms of the behavior that occurred, its consequences, and my feelings about it.

_____ 4. I specify the expectations and standards that have been violated.

_____ 5. I make a specific request, detailing a more acceptable solution.

_____ 6. I persist in explaining my point of view until it is understood by the other person.

_____ 7. I encourage two-way interaction by inviting the respondent to express his or her perspective and to ask questions.

_____ 8. I approach multiple concerns incrementally, starting with the simple and easy issues and then progressing to those that are more complex and difficult.

When someone complains about something that I've done:

_____ 9. I look for our common areas of agreement.

_____ 10. I show genuine concern and interest, even when I disagree.

_____ 11. I avoid justifying my actions and becoming defensive.

_____ 12. I seek additional information by asking questions that provide specific and descriptive information.

_____ 13. I focus on one issue at a time.

_____ 14. I find some aspects of the complaint with which I can agree.

_____ 15. I ask the other person to suggest more acceptable actions.

_____ 16. I reach agreement on a remedial plan of action.

When two other people are in conflict and I'm the mediator:

_____ 17. I acknowledge that conflict exists and treat it as serious and important.

_____ 18. I help to create an agenda for a problem-solving meeting by identifying the issues to be discussed, one at a time.

_____ 19. I don't take sides, but remain neutral.

_____ 20. I help focus the discussion on the impact of the conflict on work performance.

_____ 21. I keep the interaction focused on problems instead of personalities.

_____ 22. I make certain that neither party dominates the conversation.

_____ 23. I help the parties generate multiple alternatives.

_____ 24. I help the parties find areas on which they agree.

How to score: Add up the numbers that you put down in the left-hand column. The maximum possible score is 144. You should compare your score with the scores of other students in the class and with those of 1,500 real-world managers and business school students:

Score	Ranking
113.20	mean
122 or above	top quartile
114–121	second quartile
105–113	third quartile
104 or below	bottom quartile

Reference: David A. Whetten and Kim S. Cameron, *Developing Management Skills*, 7th ed. (Upper Saddle River, NJ: Prentice Hall, 2007), 378–79, 438–39.

PART 3
INTEGRATIVE RUNNING CASE

"PH.D'S FOR A DOLLAR AN HOUR" AND OTHER REASONS WHY NETFLIX RELISHES TECHNOLOGICAL CHANGE

In addition to an efficient workforce, Netflix's strategies for enhancing customer satisfaction depend heavily on its *organizational technology*—the sum of mechanical and intellectual processes that it uses to transform inputs (such as information on consumer wants and needs) into profitable outputs (numbers of subscribers and fulfilled rental requests) (see Chapter 17). According to CEO Reed Hastings, most of this technology (much of which has been developed in-house) is designed to provide each customer with "the most personalized website in the world. If the Starbucks secret is a smile when you get your latte," he says, "ours is that the website adapts to the individual's taste."

A high-tech inventory system, for example, is essential to Netflix operations. "Ten years ago," recalls Hastings, ". . . it was just a bunch of us sitting around card tables, stuffing and licking envelopes. Then we added bar coding and got better with our automation." Sophisticated bar coding, for instance, is crucial for tracking the location and availability of the nearly 90 million DVD discs owned by Netflix and directing them to the company's 12 million-plus subscribers. On a more personal level, the Netflix inventory system automatically scans the DVD that you've just returned, updates your queue and account information, and sends you an email confirming that your returned DVD has in fact arrived. The system then matches your queue information with system-wide inventory data (e.g., what discs are available and where they're located) and—if you haven't exceeded your monthly rental allotment—tells shipping-center employees what movie to send you next. Meanwhile, a machine much like the one used by the U.S. Postal Service (USPS) sorts by ZIP code all incoming titles that have been requested by other subscribers. Once that's been done, a machine called "The Stuffer" puts all of these outgoing discs into envelopes, seals them, and labels them by laser. The system handles about 30,000 discs an hour and currently allows Netflix to ship 2.2 million DVDs (through the USPS) every day. (The billionth disc was shipped on February 25, 2007.)

Another critical component of Netflix's organizational technology is its *recommender system*—software that analyzes patterns in a subscriber's rental choices. It's important because it can help to predict other movies that the subscriber might like—and thus maximize the number of movies that the subscriber rents. Detecting patterns and generating recommendations wasn't so important when Netflix stocked only about 1,000 movies, but as its catalog of titles grew, an effective recommender system became a must. "Once you get beyond 1,000 choices," explains Hastings, "a recommendation system becomes critical. People have limited cognitive time they want to spend on picking a movie." In 2000, Netflix thus introduced a system called "Cinematch," which, as Hastings recalls, didn't work very well at first, turning out "a mix of insightful and boneheaded recommendations." Programmers, however, improved the system over the next few years, until it was able to make some pretty surprising connections—who would have guessed that people who liked the heartwarming drama *Play It Forward* would also like the high-tech thriller *I, Robot?*

In 2006, when Netflix programmers had reached the point of diminishing returns in their efforts to enhance the system, Hastings came up with the idea of offering a $1 million prize to anyone who could improve the accuracy of Cinematch by 10 percent. It took three years (and a couple of interim "Progress Prizes"), but by September 2009, there was finally a winner: a team of researchers from Austria and the United States who'd started out as competitors but joined forces as the competition grew more complex and more intense. ("You need to think outside the box," says one member of the winning team, "and the only way to do that is find someone else's box.") As a result of its million-dollar tweaking, reports *New York Times* science writer Clive Thompson, Cinematch now functions as a sort of "video-store roboclerk" whose suggestions drive nearly 60 percent of all Netflix rentals. And that's why improving Cinematch was worth $1 million to Netflix: "Getting to 10 percent would certainly be worth well in excess of $1 million," commented Hastings at the outset of the contest, and when it was over, he added that it had also been extremely cost effective: "You look at the cumulative hours, and you're getting Ph.D.'s for a dollar an hour."

To get a better idea of how its well-tuned recommender technology can contribute to customer satisfaction, and customer satisfaction to profitability, consider

Netflix's success in renting out films from its "backlist," which includes older, independent, and foreign movies—just about everything that doesn't fall into the category of big-studio blockbusters. Netflix subscribers rent backlist movies because they show up on their recommendation lists and, more importantly, because they've come to trust Netflix's recommender system to make a high percentage of reliable recommendations.

Back in 2006, for example, even before the Cinematch-enhancement contest, Netflix boasted a library of 60,000 titles. On a typical day, between 35,000 and 40,000 of those titles were rented at least once. In other words, almost two-thirds of all movies available from Netflix (which is pretty much two-thirds of all movies ever put on DVD) were rented by Netflix customers, and that total obviously included a lot of backlist movies. "Americans' tastes are really broad," concludes Hastings, and the data continue to bear him out: Today, about 70 percent of all Netflix rentals are backlist titles—compared to about 20 percent for traditional video stores. In other words, Netflix depends on blockbusters for only about 30 percent of its rental business, while brick-and-mortar outlets (which obviously can't carry much backlist inventory) depend on popular new-release hits for about 80 percent of all rentals. The difference is significant because revenue-sharing agreements with the studios that produce new movies take a much bigger chunk out of the rental company's profit than do backlist movies.

Recommender systems, however, typically don't know much about demographics—about customers themselves and their individual or collective tastes. Netflix knows that its average customer is a woman over 35 with a family income of $75,000 or less, but beyond such bare-bones data, it doesn't make much use of demographic information in trying to predict customer preferences. Some critics, however—and even some experts in recommender-system technology—think that the human factor should play a bigger role in designing systems. In fact, says Matt Turck, whose TripleHop Technologies builds recommender engines, "the best results are achieved from powerful technology and human intervention."

Gavin Potter agrees. Potter, a retired British management consultant with a degree in psychology, finished 17th in the Netflix Cinematch contest. "The fact that [Netflix movie] ratings were made by human beings," he suggested shortly after the contest had reached the halfway point, "seems to me to be an important piece of

> *"Ten years ago ... it was just a bunch of us sitting around card tables, stuffing and licking envelopes. Then we added bar coding and got better with our automation."*
> —REED HASTINGS, COFOUNDER AND CEO OF NETFLIX

information that should be and needs to be used." He argued that the computer scientists among the entrants suffered from a form of *groupthink* (see Chapter 9) because they all focused on mathematical approaches to a solution while making room for only "crude" psychological models. "If you use a computerized system based on [the] ratings," he adds, "you'll tend to get very relevant but safe answers. If you go with a movie-store clerk, you'll get more unpredictable but potentially more exciting recommendations."

Pattie Maes, a professor of media arts and sciences at MIT, agrees with Potter. She thinks that computerized reasoning will eventually be less useful to online retailers than the sort of social-networking tools, which, like Facebook, tap into customers' socially influenced behavior. As for Reed Hastings, he likes the fact that "human beings are very quirky and individualistic and wonderfully idiosyncratic," but those very qualities, he adds, "make it hard to figure out what they like." Like Maes, he suspects that social-networking tools will become more important to Netflix in the future, but so far, he points out, they haven't proved nearly as valuable as computerized intelligence gathering.

In 2004 Netflix had in fact launched a website feature called "Friends," which allowed users to see how their friends rated a movie, find out what movies they were renting, and leave one another personal notes. The feature, however, was removed by 2010, although the company's method of communicating the news to customers—simply phasing out the original feature amidst a series of website redesigns—wasn't exactly optimal. Fans of the "Friends" feature were angry, and in no uncertain terms—for example:

> *I have always been a HUGE proponent of Netflix and have brought a few customers onto the service. One of the reasons I NEVER considered switching to a different service (until now!) was because of all my Netflix friends. Now there's nothing holding me back from going somewhere else.*

Todd Yellin, VP of product management, blogged an apology that focused on miscommunication—"We apologize for not being more upfront earlier"—and explained that only about 2 percent of subscribers used the "Friends" feature. That 2 percent, however, proved to be among the most avid users of the Netflix site and among the company's most vocal stakeholders,

16 CHAPTER

FOUNDATIONS OF ORGANIZATION STRUCTURE

CHAPTER LEARNING OBJECTIVES

After studying this chapter, you should be able to:

- Define organization structure and discuss its purpose.
- Describe the classic views of organization structure.
- Describe structural configuration and summarize its four basic dimensions.
- Discuss two structural policies that affect operations.
- Explain the dual concepts of authority and responsibility.

Authority & Function at A&F

"How does a store look? How does it feel? How does it smell? That's what I'm obsessed with."

—ABERCROMBIE & FITCH CEO MICHAEL JEFFRIES

Along with American Eagle and Aéropostale, Abercrombie & Fitch (A&F) is one of the "Three A's" of retailing for younger consumers—the three largest specialty retailers catering to young adults ages 18 to 22 (and up). Look around

This store clerk is ringing up a sale to what is hopefully a satisfied shopper. The store is attractive, brightly lighted up, with merchandise easy to see and approach. Abercrombie & Fitch has a formula for store layout and atmosphere that attracts a certain type of customer. This creation is intentional and closely controlled from top management all the way to the store clerk. The functional structure seems to be having the desired result.

KUMAR SRISKANDAN/ALAMY

your college classroom and you will probably spy at least one A&F item—a cap, a shirt, a pair of jeans. Abercrombie & Fitch, a line of "casual luxury" apparel and other products, is actually one of five brands owned by Ohio-based A&F Corporation. The company's other brands include abercrombie ("classic cool" for preteens), Hollister ("SoCal" for teenagers), RUEHL 925 (a higher-priced brand for post-collegiates 22 to 30), and Gilly Hicks (Australian-themed lounge- and under-wear for women). Obviously, A&F's businesses are related, and although its overall corporate strategy is designed to take advantage of this linkage, it does not reflect the *divisionalized form* of organization favored by most companies that operate multiple related businesses (see Chapter 17). Rather, A&F relies on a design based on *functional* departments—that is, groups responsible for specific company or management functions.

Interestingly, some form of divisionalized structure is preferred by most firms that pursue strategies of related diversification. Limited Brands, for example, a close competitor (and onetime parent) of A&F, uses a divisional structure to coordinate such well-known brands as the Limited, Victoria's Secret, and Bath and Body Works. Each unit is empowered to make autonomous decisions but can also access companywide staff support in areas such as logistics, information technology, real estate, and store design. At A&F, on the other hand, every employee is assigned to one of eight basic business functions, such as planning, purchasing, distribution, or stores, each of which is headed by a president. Why this design? Basically, A&F wants every employee to develop highly specialized skills within a functional area. In addition, this design is obviously more effective in coordinating activities within a function.

The company's history also accounts in part for its choice of a functional structure. From its founding in 1892 until a bankruptcy in 1977, Abercrombie & Fitch was a high-end sporting-goods retailer. In 1978, Oshman's, a Houston-based sporting-goods chain, purchased the company brand and trademark and for 11 years operated a combination retail chain and catalog company selling an eclectic line of products ranging from tweed jackets to exercise machines. Limited Brands purchased the brand in 1988, putting it in preppy, upscale clothing for young adults. Nine years later, Limited sold 16 percent of the company through a public stock sale, and when the remaining shares were sold to the public in 1998, A&F became an independent company. In its current incarnation, then, A&F started out as a division of a larger firm, and so it makes sense that its structure would be much like that of one division in a multidivisional corporation.

It is also interesting to note that, even before the spinoff from Limited, A&F had begun to establish its own culture and its own pattern of growth. Michael Jeffries, a retail-industry veteran, became president in 1992 and undertook to transform the company into the retailer of choice for younger consumers. Jeffries quickly managed to attach the brand to an ideal lifestyle, emphasizing apparel that complemented youth, good looks, and good times. The transformation turned out to be highly profit-able, with sales increasing from $85 million in 1992 to $165 million in just two years. During the same period, the number of stores in the chain grew from 36 to 67, and in 1999, with 212 stores nationwide, A&F topped $1 billion in sales. In the same year, A&F started its abercrombie division for children and preteens, and a year later, it launched Hollister, the first of its "lifestyle" chains. By the end of 2002, the multidivision company was running 485 A&F stores, 144 abercrombie shops, and 32 Hollister outlets. Sales for the year were just under $1.4 billion. RUEHL opened in 2004 and Gilly Hicks in 2008. Today, A&F Corporation operates nearly 1,100 stores.

And yet, A&F is still organized as if it were one big company with one big brand. As we have already seen, the main advantage of this choice can be explained as a desire to exercise top-down control over each brand by separating and controlling all the functions on which every brand—that is, every store type—depends. Regardless of how A&F is organized and managed, one thing is clear: things are the way they are because that is the way CEO Jeffries wants it. Jeffries took over a company that was losing $25 million a year, declared that survival depended on becoming a "young, hip, spirited company," and engineered a reversal of fortunes by turning it into something completely new—a retailer that celebrates what one observer calls "the vain, highly constructed male" (A&F has had much less influence on women's fashion). And Jeffries himself, suggests Benoit Denizet-Lewis, demonstrates his own brand of brand loyalty by gleefully playing the role of the vain, highly constructed male. Although he is now in his sixties, he dies his hair blond and dresses for work in torn A&F jeans, A&F muscle polo shirts, and A&F flip-flops. The Jeffries outfit is more or less a uniform among employees at the company's "campus" in New Albany, Ohio, where the CEO has designed everything to foster what Denizet-Lewis characterizes as "a cultlike immersion in his brand identity."

The A&F brand may be a direct extension of Jeffries' eccentric image of the contemporary young American male, but as Denizet-Lewis puts it, Jeffries has made it "the most dominant and imitated lifestyle-based brand for young men in America." The key to his success seems to be his determination to control every aspect of his brands and his business. Jeffries spends much of the time in his office (which is actually a conference room with big windows from which he can see the whole campus) discussing new products and new ideas with designers and much of the time outside his office overseeing the details of store layouts, down to the fixtures and mannequins. "How does a store look? How does it feel? How does it smell? That's what I'm obsessed with," admits Jeffries. On the Ohio campus, there are models of all four A&F store types (RUEHL closed in 2009), and it is not unusual to find Jeffries making sure that everything is just the way he wants it. When it is, pictures are taken and sent to stores so that everything can be perfectly replicated. "It's so rare to find someone who's brilliant at both the creative and the business sides," says a former coworker at Jeffries' previous employer. "But Jeffries is both. He is good at thinking in broad terms, but he is also obsessed with details."

By the end of fiscal 2008, Jeffries had also delivered 56 straight quarters of increased revenues (except for one quarter in 2004). "To me," says investment analyst Robert Buchanan, "it's the most amazing record . . . in U.S. retailing, period." (Fiscal 2009 was another matter, but we will get to that.) As the company's earnings record suggests, there does not seem to be much wrong with the way A&F has been run, but it stands to reason that, given the thoroughness of his hands-on approach—in addition to an organizational structure that is conducive to the exercise of top-down authority—Michael Jeffries must be held responsible for the firm's debits as well as its credits. We continue our story in the *Change* box entitled "With Authority Comes Responsibility" on page 453, in which we discuss A&F's fortunes during the recession that hit the global economy in 2008.

What Do You Think?

1. Do you think the organization structure of Abercrombie & Fitch is working for them? Why or why not?

2. Would you like to work for Abercrombie & Fitch? Why or why not?

References: Robert Berner, "Flip-Flops, Torn Jeans—and Control," *BusinessWeek*, May 30, 2005, www.businessweek .com on April 20, 2010; Jess Cartner-Morley, "History of Abercrombie & Fitch: Tracing a Line from JFK's Blazer," *The Guardian*, June 24, 2009, www.guardian.com on April 20, 2010; Benoit Denizet-Lewis, "The Man behind Abercrombie & Fitch," *Salon.com*, January 24, 2006, www.salon.com on April 20, 2010; Andria Cheng, "Abercrombie & Fitch Clothed in Green," *MarketWatch*, February 13, 2009, www.marketwatch.com on March 17, 2010

An organization changing its structure is not unusual among businesses these days as they struggle to remain competitive in a rapidly changing world. A& F, on the other hand, has maintained its functional structure for many years. This chapter introduces many of the key concepts of organization structure and sets the stage for understanding the many aspects of developing the appropriate organization design, which is discussed in Chapter 17.

THE NATURE OF ORGANIZATION STRUCTURE

In other chapters we discuss key elements of the individual and the factors that tie the individual and the organization together. In a given organization, these factors must fit together within a common framework: the organization's structure.

Organization Defined

An organization is a goal-directed social entity with deliberate processes and systems.[1] In other words, an organization is a collection of people working together to accomplish something better than they could working separately.[2] Organizations are social actors, influencing and being influenced by their environments, and affecting the behaviors of individuals in them. As social actors organizations are different from two other entities, those being individuals and the government or state. Organizations influence and are influenced by other organizations, as well as individuals and the state.[3] Top management determines the direction of the organization by defining its purpose or mission, establishing goals to meet that purpose, and formulating strategies to achieve the goals.[4] The definition of its purpose gives the organization reason to exist; in effect, it answers the question "What business are we in?"

Establishing goals converts the defined purpose into specific, measurable performance targets. Organizational goals are objectives that management seeks to achieve in pursuing the purpose of the firm. Goals motivate people to work together. Although each individual's goals are important to the organization, it is the organization's overall goals that are most important. Goals keep the organization on track by focusing the attention and actions of the members. They also give the organization a forward-looking

An **organization** is a goal-directed social entity with deliberate processes and systems.

Organizational goals are objectives that management seeks to achieve in pursuing the firm's purpose.

AP PHOTO/STEVE POPE

Kenyan Florence Wambugu has developed genetically modified foods, such as bananas and sweet potatoes, to help the starving people of her homeland. However, some governments in Africa object to genetically altered food, and people are starving despite the availability of the controversial crops. Wambugu has created a new organization, Africa Harvest Biotech Foundation International, to serve as a pan-African voice on the issue. With the organizational goal of increasing the availability of genetically modified crops in Africa, the organization will be better able to stay on track and continue its forward momentum.

orientation. They do not address past success or failure; rather, they force members to think about and plan for the future.

Finally, strategies are specific action plans that enable the organization to achieve its goals and thus its purpose. Pursuing a strategy involves developing an organization structure and the processes to do the organization's work.

Organization Structure

Organization structure is the system of task, reporting, and authority relationships within which the work of the organization is done. Thus, structure defines the form and function of the organization's activities. Structure also defines how the parts of an organization fit together, as is evident from an organization chart.

The purpose of an organization's structure is to order and coordinate the actions of employees to achieve organizational goals. The premise of organized effort is that people can accomplish more by working together than they can separately. The work must be coordinated properly, however, if the potential gains of collective effort are to be realized. Consider what might happen if the thousands of employees at Dell Computers worked without any kind of structure. Each person might try to build a computer that he or she thought would sell. No two computers would be alike, and each would take months or years to build. The costs of making the computers would be so high that no one would be able to afford them. To produce computers that are both competitive in the marketplace and profitable for the company, Dell must have a structure in which its employees and managers work together in a coordinated manner. When Intel changed its organization structure from a product-centered structure to a customer-focused model, it did so to better coordinate its efforts to serve its customers better.[5]

The task of coordinating the activities of thousands of workers to produce microprocessors and computers that do the work expected of them and that are guaranteed and easy to maintain may seem monumental. Yet whether the goal is to mass-produce computers or to make soap, the requirements of organization structure are similar. First, the structure must identify the various tasks or processes necessary for the organization to reach its goals. This dividing of tasks into smaller parts is often called "division of labor." Even small organizations (those with fewer than one hundred employees) use a division of labor.[6] Second, the structure must combine and coordinate the divided tasks to achieve a desired level of output. The more interdependent the divided tasks,

Organization structure is the system of task, reporting, and authority relationships within which the organization does its work.

the more coordination is required.[7] Every organization structure addresses these two fundamental requirements.[8] The various ways of approaching these requirements are what make one organization structure different from another.

In this chapter we first describe three of the classical views of organizations that strongly influence how organizations are still viewed today. Then, we break down the various components of organization structure. Organization structure can be analyzed in three ways: First, we can examine its configuration—that is, its size and shape—as depicted on an organization chart. Second, we can analyze its operational aspects or characteristics, such as separation of specialized tasks, rules and procedures, and decision making. Finally, we can examine responsibility and authority within the organization. In this chapter, we describe organization structure from all three points of view.

CLASSIC VIEWS OF STRUCTURE

The earliest views of organization structure have often been called "classical organization theory" and include Max Weber's concept of the ideal bureaucracy, the classic organizing principles of Henri Fayol, and the human organization view of Rensis Likert. All three approaches attempt to describe an organization structure that is universally applicable across organizations, and thus are called universal approaches, yet their concerns and structural prescriptions differ significantly.

Ideal Bureaucracy

In the early 1900s, Max Weber, a German sociologist, proposed a "bureaucratic" form of structure that he believed would work for all organizations. Weber's **ideal bureaucracy** was an organizational system characterized by a hierarchy of authority and a system of rules and procedures that, if followed, would create a maximally effective system for large organizations. Weber, writing at a time when organizations were inherently inefficient, claimed that the bureaucratic form of administration is superior to other forms of management with respect to stability, control, and predictability of outcomes.[9]

Weber's ideal bureaucracy had seven essential characteristics: rules and procedures, division of labor, a hierarchy of authority, technical competence, separation of ownership, rights and property differentiation, and documentation, as shown in Table 16.1. As you can see, these characteristics utilize several of the building blocks discussed in this chapter. Weber intended these characteristics to ensure order and predictability in relationships among people and jobs in the bureaucracy. But it is easy to see how the same features can lead to sluggishness, inefficiency, and red tape. The administrative system can easily break down if any of the characteristics are carried to an extreme or are violated. For example, if endless arrays of rules and procedures bog down employees who must find the precise rule to follow every time they do something, responses to routine client or customer requests may slow to a crawl. Moreover, subsequent writers have said that Weber's view of authority is too rigid and have suggested that the bureaucratic organization may impede creativity and innovation and result in a lack of compassion for the individual in the organization.[10] In other words, the impersonality that is supposed to foster objectivity in a bureaucracy may result in serious difficulties for both employees and the organization. However, some organizations retain some characteristics of a bureaucratic structure while remaining innovative and productive.

Paul Adler has recently countered the currently popular movements of "bureaucracy busting" by noting that large-scale, complex organizations still need some of the basic characteristics that Weber described—hierarchical structure, formalized procedures,

Weber's **ideal bureaucracy** is characterized by a hierarchy of authority and a system of rules and procedures designed to create an optimally effective system for large organizations.

Table 16.1
**ELEMENTS OF WEBER'S
IDEAL BUREAUCRACY**

Elements	Comments
1. RULES AND PROCEDURES	A consistent set of abstract rules and procedures should exist to ensure uniform performance.
2. DISTINCT DIVISION OF LABOR	Each position should be filled by an expert.
3. HIERARCHY OF AUTHORITY	The chain of command should be clearly established.
4. TECHNICAL COMPETENCE	Employment and advancement should be based on merit.
5. SEGREGATION OF OWNERSHIP	Professional managers rather than owners should run the organization.
6. RIGHTS AND PROPERTIES OF THE POSITION	These should be associated with the organization, not with the person who holds the office.
7. DOCUMENTATION	A record of actions should be kept regarding administrative decisions, rules, and procedures.

and staff expertise—in order to avoid chaos and ensure efficiency, quality products and services, and timeliness. Adler further proposes a second type of bureaucracy that essentially serves an enabling function in organizations.[11] The need for bureaucracy is not relegated to the past. Bureaucracy, or at least some of its elements, is still critical for designing effective organizations.

The Classic Principles of Organizing

Also at the beginning of the twentieth century, Henri Fayol, a French engineer and chief executive officer of a mining company, presented a second classic view of the organization structure. Drawing on his experience as a manager, Fayol was the first to classify the essential elements of management—now usually called **management functions**—as planning, organizing, command, coordination, and control.[12] In addition, he presented fourteen principles of organizing that he considered an indispensable code for managers (see Table 16.2).

Fayol's principles have proved extraordinarily influential; they have served as the basis for the development of generally accepted means of organizing. For example, Fayol's "unity of command" principle means that employees should receive directions from only one person, and "unity of direction" means that tasks with the same objective should have a common supervisor. Combining these two principles with division of labor, authority, and responsibility results in a system of tasks and reporting and authority relationships that is the very essence of organizing. Fayol's principles thus provide the framework for the organization chart and the coordination of work.

The classic principles have been criticized on several counts. First, they ignore factors such as individual motivation, leadership, and informal groups—the human element in organizations. This line of criticism asserts that the classic principles result in a mechanical organization into which people must fit, regardless of their interests, abilities, or motivations. The principles have also been criticized for their lack of operational specificity in that Fayol described the principles as universal truths but did not specify the means of applying many of them. Finally, Fayol's principles have been discounted because they were not supported by scientific evidence; Fayol presented them as universal principles, backed by no evidence other than his own experience.[13]

The **management functions** set forth by Henri Fayol include planning, organizing, command, coordination, and control.

Principle	Fayol's Comments
1. DIVISION OF WORK	Individuals and managers work on the same part or task.
2. AUTHORITY AND RESPONSIBILITY	Authority—right to give orders; power to exact obedience; goes with responsibility for reward and punishment.
3. DISCIPLINE	Obedience, application, energy, behavior. Agreement between firm and individual.
4. UNITY OF COMMAND	Employee receives orders from one superior.
5. UNITY OF DIRECTION	One head and one plan for activities with the same objective.
6. SUBORDINATION OF INDIVIDUAL INTEREST TO GENERAL INTEREST	Objectives of the organization come before objectives of the individual.
7. REMUNERATION OF PERSONNEL	Pay should be fair to the organization and the individual; discussed various forms.
8. CENTRALIZATION	Proportion of discretion held by the manager compared to that allowed to subordinates.
9. SCALAR CHAIN	Line of authority from lowest to top.
10. ORDER	A place for everyone and everyone in his or her place.
11. EQUITY	Combination of kindness and justice; equality of treatment.
12. STABILITY OF TENURE OF PERSONNEL	Stability of managerial personnel; time to get used to work.
13. INITIATIVE	Power of thinking out and executing a plan.
14. ESPRIT DE CORPS	Harmony and union among personnel is strength.

Table 16.2
FAYOL'S CLASSIC PRINCIPLES OF ORGANIZING

Reference: From *General and Industrial Management*, by Henri Fayol. Copyright © Lake Publishing 1984, Belmont, CA 94002. Used with permission.

Human Organization

In the 1960s Rensis Likert developed an approach to organization structure he called human organization.[14] Because Likert, like others, had criticized Fayol's classic principles for overlooking human factors, it is not surprising that his approach centered on the principles of supportive relationships, employee participation, and overlapping work groups.

The term "supportive relationships" suggests that in all organizational activities, individuals should be treated in such a way that they experience feelings of support, self-worth, and importance. By "employee participation," Likert meant that the work group needs to be involved in decisions that affect it, thereby enhancing the employee's sense of supportiveness and self-worth. The principle of "overlapping work groups" means that work groups are linked, with managers serving as the "linking pins." Each manager (except the highest ranking) is a member of two groups: a work group that he or she supervises and a management group composed of the manager's peers and their supervisor. Coordination and communication grow stronger when the managers perform the linking function by sharing problems, decisions, and information both upward and downward in the groups to which they belong. The **human organization** concept rests on the assumption that people work best in highly cohesive groups oriented toward

Rensis Likert's **human organization** approach is based on supportive relationships, participation, and overlapping work groups.

organizational goals. Management's function is to make sure the work groups are linked for effective coordination and communication.

Likert described four systems of organizing, which he called management systems, whose characteristics are summarized in Table 16.3. System 1, the exploitive authoritative system, can be characterized as the classic bureaucracy. System 4, the

Table 16.3
CHARACTERISTICS OF LIKERT'S FOUR MANAGEMENT SYSTEMS

Characteristic	System 1: Exploitive Authoritative	System 2: Benevolent Authoritative	System 3: Consultative	System 4: Participative Group
LEADERSHIP				
• Trust in subordinates	None	None	Substantial	Complete
• Subordinates' ideas	Seldom used	Sometimes used	Usually used	Always used
MOTIVATIONAL FORCES				
• Motives tapped	Security, status	Economic, ego	Substantial	Complete
• Level of satisfaction	Overall dissatisfaction	Some moderate satisfaction	Moderate satisfaction	High satisfaction
COMMUNICATION				
• Amount	Very little	Little	Moderate	Much
• Direction	Downward	Mostly downward	Down, up	Down, up, lateral
INTERACTION-INFLUENCE				
• Amount	None	None	Substantial	Complete
• Cooperative teamwork	None	Virtually none	Moderate	Substantial
DECISION MAKING				
• Locus	Top	Policy decided at top	Broad policy decided at top	All levels
• Subordinates involved	Not at all	Sometimes consulted	Usually consulted	Fully involved
GOAL SETTING				
• Manner	Orders	Orders with comments	Set after discussion	Group participation
• Acceptance	Covertly resisted	Frequently resisted	Sometimes resisted	Fully accepted
CONTROL PROCESSES				
• Level	Top	None	Some below top	All levels
• Information	Incomplete, inaccurate	Often incomplete, inaccurate	Moderately complete, accurate	Complete, accurate
PERFORMANCE				
• Goals and Training	Mediocre	Fair to good	Good	Excellent

Reference: Adapted from Rensis Likert, *New Patterns of Management* (New York: McGraw-Hill, 1961), pp. 223–233; and Rensis Likert, *The Human Organization* (New York: McGraw-Hill, 1967), pp. 197, 198, 201, 203, 210, and 211.

participative group, is the organization design Likert favored. System 2, the benevolent authoritative system, and system 3, the consultative system, are less extreme than either system 1 or system 4.

Likert described all four systems in terms of eight organizational variables: leadership processes, motivational forces, communication processes, interaction-influence processes, decision-making processes, goal-setting processes, control processes, and performance goals and training. Likert believed that work groups should be able to overlap horizontally as well as vertically where necessary to accomplish tasks. This feature is directly contrary to the classic principle that advocates unity of command. In addition, rather than the hierarchical chain of command, Likert favored the linking-pin concept of overlapping work groups for making decisions and resolving conflicts.

Research support for Likert's human organization emanates primarily from Likert and his associates' work at the Institute for Social Research at the University of Michigan. Although their research has upheld the basic propositions of the approach, it is not entirely convincing. One review of the evidence suggested that although research has shown characteristics of system 4 to be associated with positive worker attitudes and, in some cases, increased productivity, it is not clear that the characteristics of the human organization "caused" the positive results.[15] It may have been that positive attitudes and high productivity allowed the organization structure to be participative and provided the atmosphere for the development of supportive relationships. Likert's design has also been criticized for focusing almost exclusively on individuals and groups and not dealing extensively with structural issues. Overall, the most compelling support for this approach is at the individual and work-group levels. In some ways, Likert's system 4 is much like the team-based organization popular today.

Thus, the classic views of organization embody the key elements of organization structure. Each view, however, combined these key elements in different ways and with other management elements. These three classic views are typical of how the early writers attempted to prescribe a universal approach to organization structure that would be best in all situations. In the following sections we break down the various elements of organization structure to examine how they contribute to coordinating the tasks and people who perform those tasks toward goal accomplishment.

STRUCTURAL CONFIGURATION

The structure of an organization is most often described in terms of its organization chart. See Figure 16.1 for an example. A complete **organization chart** shows all people, positions, reporting relationships, and lines of formal communication in the organization. (However, as we discussed in Chapter 11, communication is not limited to these formal channels.) For large organizations, several charts may be necessary to show all positions. For example, one chart may show top management, including the board of directors, the chief executive officer, the president, all vice presidents, and important headquarters staff units. Subsequent charts may show the structure of each department and staff unit. Figure 16.1 depicts two organization charts for a large firm; top management is shown in the upper portion of the figure and the manufacturing department in the lower portion. Notice that the structures of the different manufacturing groups are given in separate charts.

An organization chart depicts reporting relationships and work-group memberships and shows how positions and small work groups are combined into departments, which together make up the configuration, or shape, of the organization. The **configuration** of organizations can be analyzed in terms of how the two basic requirements of structure — division of labor and coordination of the divided tasks — are fulfilled.

An **organization chart** is a diagram showing all people, positions, reporting relationships, and lines of formal communication in the organization.

The **configuration** of an organization is its shape, which reflects the division of labor and the means of coordinating the divided tasks.

Figure 16.1   EXAMPLES OF ORGANIZATIONAL CHARTS

These two charts show the similarities between a top-management chart and a department chart. In each, managers have four other managers or work groups reporting to them.

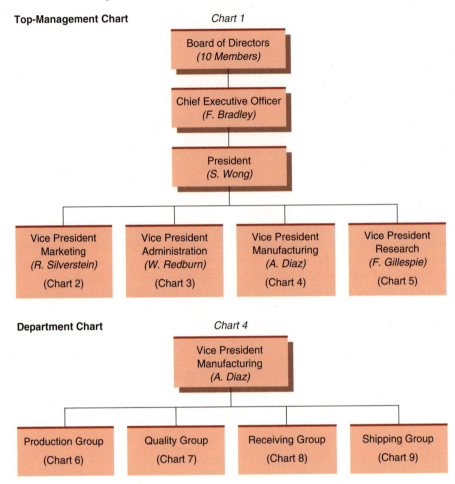

Top-Management Chart

Chart 1

Board of Directors
(10 Members)

Chief Executive Officer
(F. Bradley)

President
(S. Wong)

Vice President
Marketing
(R. Silverstein)
(Chart 2)

Vice President
Administration
(W. Redburn)
(Chart 3)

Vice President
Manufacturing
(A. Diaz)
(Chart 4)

Vice President
Research
(F. Gillespie)
(Chart 5)

Department Chart

Chart 4

Vice President
Manufacturing
(A. Diaz)

Production Group
(Chart 6)

Quality Group
(Chart 7)

Receiving Group
(Chart 8)

Shipping Group
(Chart 9)

Division of Labor

Division of labor is the extent to which the organization's work is separated into different jobs to be done by different people and is often referred to as **specialization**, which we discuss in Chapter 5 on motivation and work design. The more people become divided doing different tasks, the more differentiated they become, thus requiring more coordination. **Differentiation** is the process of establishing the division of labor and tasks throughout the organization. While division of labor is one of the seven primary characteristics of structuring described by Max Weber[16] discussed earlier in this chapter, the concept can be traced back to eighteenth-century economist Adam Smith, who used a study of pin making to promote the idea of dividing production work to increase productivity.[17] Division of labor grew more popular as large organizations became more prevalent in a manufacturing society. This trend has continued, and most research indicates that large organizations usually have more division of labor than smaller ones.[18] Division of labor has been found to have both advantages and disadvantages (see Table 16.4). Modern managers and organization theorists are

Division of labor is the way the organization's work is divided into different jobs to be done by different people. Division of labor is often referred to as **specialization**.

Differentiation is the process of establishing the division of labor and tasks throughout the organization.

Table 16.4   ADVANTAGES AND DISADVANTAGES OF DIVISION OF LABOR

Advantages	Disadvantages
Efficient use of labor	Routine, repetitive jobs
Reduced training costs	Reduced job satisfaction
Increased standardization and uniformity of output	Decreased worker involvement and commitment
Increased expertise from repetition of tasks	Increased worker alienation
	Possible incompatibility with computerized manufacturing technologies

still struggling with the primary disadvantage: division of labor often results in repetitive, boring jobs that undercut worker satisfaction, involvement, and commitment.[19] In addition, extreme division of labor may be incompatible with new, integrated computerized manufacturing technologies that require teams of highly skilled workers.[20]

However, division of labor need not result in boredom. Visualized in terms of a small organization such as a basketball team, it can be quite dynamic. A basketball team consists of five players, each of whom plays a different role on the team. In professional basketball the five positions typically are center, power forward, small forward, shooting guard, and point guard. The tasks of the players in each position are quite different, so players of different sizes and skills are on the floor at any one time. The teams that win championships, such as the San Antonio Spurs and the Los Angeles Lakers, use division of labor by having players specialize in doing specified tasks, and doing them impeccably. Similarly, organizations must have specialists who are highly trained and know their specific jobs very well.

Coordinating the Divided Tasks

Divided tasks need to be properly coordinated in order to achieve the potential productivity gains expected from specialization of task. The problem of differentiation must be balanced with proper integration. **Integration** is the process of coordinating the various tasks and roles to achieve goal accomplishment. Three basic mechanisms are used to help coordinate the divided tasks: departmentalization, span of control, and administrative hierarchy. These mechanisms focus on grouping tasks in some meaningful manner, creating work groups of manageable size, and establishing a system of reporting relationships among supervisors and managers. When companies reorganize, they are usually changing the ways in which the divided labor is coordinated. To some people affected by reorganization, it may seem that things are still just as disorganized as they were before. But there really is a purpose for such reorganization efforts. Top management expects that the work will be better coordinated under the new system.

Departmentalization   **Departmentalization** is the manner in which divided tasks are combined and allocated to work groups. It is a consequence of the division of labor if coordinated action is to be achieved. Because employees engaged in specialized activities can lose sight of overall organizational goals, their work must be coordinated to ensure that it contributes to goal accomplishment for the organization.

Integration is the process of coordinating the various tasks and roles in the organization to achieve goal accomplishment.

Departmentalization is the manner in which divided tasks are combined and allocated to work groups.

Figure 16.2   DEPARTMENTALIZATION BY BUSINESS FUNCTION AND BY PROCESS

These two charts compare departmentalization by business function and by process. "Functions" are the basic business functions whereas "processes" are the specific categories of jobs that people do.

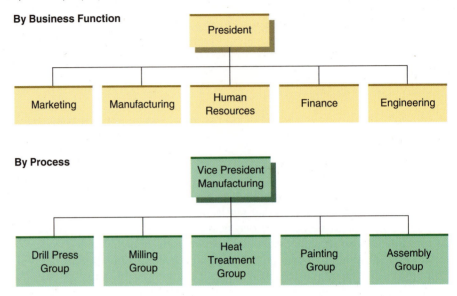

There are many possible ways to group, or departmentalize, tasks. The five groupings most often used are business function, process, product or service, customer, and geography. The first two, function and process, derive from the internal operations of the organization; the others are based on external factors. Most organizations tend to use a combination of methods, and departmentalization often changes as organizations evolve.[21]

Departmentalization by business function is based on traditional business functions such as marketing, manufacturing, and human resource administration (see Figure 16.2). In this configuration, employees most frequently associate with those engaged in the same function, a situation that helps in communication and cooperation. In a functional group, employees who do similar work can learn from one another by sharing ideas about opportunities and problems they encounter on the job. Unfortunately, functional groups lack an automatic mechanism for coordinating the flow of work through the organization.[22] In other words, employees in a functional structure tend to associate little with those in other parts of the organization. The result can be a narrow focus that limits the coordination of work among functional groups, as when the engineering department fails to provide marketing with product information because it is too busy testing materials to think about sales.

Departmentalization by process is similar to functional departmentalization except that the focus is much more on specific jobs grouped according to activity. Thus, as Figure 16.2 illustrates, the firm's manufacturing jobs are divided into certain well-defined manufacturing processes: drilling, milling, heat treatment, painting, and assembly. Hospitals often use process departmentalization, grouping the professional employees such as therapists according to the types of treatment they provide.

Process groupings encourage specialization and expertise among employees, who tend to concentrate on a single operation and share information with departmental colleagues. A process orientation may develop into an internal career path and managerial hierarchy within the department. For example, a specialist might become the "lead" person for that specialty—that is, the lead welder or lead designer. As in functional grouping, however, narrowness of focus can be a problem. Employees in a process group may become so absorbed in the requirements and execution of their operations that they disregard broader considerations such as overall product flow.[23]

Departmentalization by product or service occurs when employees who work on a particular product or service are members of the same department regardless of their business function or the process in which they are engaged. In the late 1980s, IBM reorganized its operations into five autonomous business units: personal computers, medium-size office systems, mainframes, communications equipment, and components.[24] Although the reorganization worked for a while, the company took quite a downturn in the early 1990s. Then, facing the Internet age at the beginning of the new century, IBM reorganized again by adding several new divisions: a global computer services group to provide computing services; an Internet division to develop, manufacture, and distribute products for the new Internet age; and the Personal Computing Division to develop strategies centered on devices, software, and services that make the Internet accessible anywhere, anytime. These new divisions continued IBM's departmentalization by product or service.

Departmentalization according to product or service obviously enhances interaction and communication among employees who produce the same product or service and may reduce coordination problems. In this type of configuration, there may be less process specialization but more specialization in the peculiarities of the specific product or service. The disadvantage is that employees may become so interested in their particular product or service that they miss technological improvements or innovations developed in other departments.

In contrast, Intel reorganized away from product lines by creating five new customer-oriented divisions. Their new organization chart at the executive level is shown in Figure 16.3. In the past, Intel's corporate structure reflected the product-centered business model, with departments focused on microprocessors, networking equipment,

Figure 16.3   DEPARTMENTALIZATION BY CUSTOMER

Intel changed its departmentalization scheme by creating five new product groups. They expect the new structure will group together complementary business segments and improve the way technology is used.

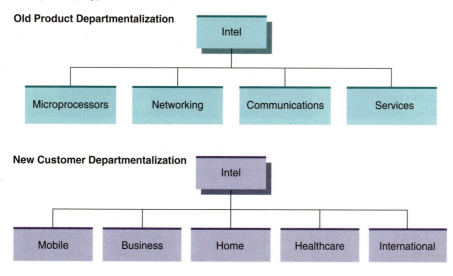

This team meeting is one example of how employees participate in decision making in organizations today. People from different levels and functional areas often meet to discuss alternatives and make decisions that increases their sense of involvement in and commitment to the organization.

Age" was that all employees throughout the organization would have more information and would therefore be able to participate more in decisions affecting their work, thus creating more decentralized organizations. However, some have suggested that all of this new information in organizations has had the opposite effect by enabling top managers to have more information about the organization's operations and keep decision making to themselves, thus creating more centralized organizations.[42]

Formalization

Formalization is the degree to which rules and procedures prescribe employees' jobs and activities. The purpose of formalization is to predict and control how employees behave on the job.[43] Rules and procedures can be both explicit and implicit. Explicit rules are set down in job descriptions, policy and procedures manuals, or office memos. Implicit rules may develop as employees become accustomed to doing things in a certain way over a period of time.[44] Though unwritten, these established ways of getting things done become standard operating procedures and have the same effect on employee behavior as written rules.

We can assess formalization in organizations by looking at the proportion of jobs that are governed by rules and procedures and the extent to which those rules permit variation. More formalized organizations have a higher proportion of rule-bound jobs and less tolerance for rule violations.[45] Increasing formalization may affect the design of jobs throughout the organization,[46] as well as employee motivation[47] and work group interactions.[48] The specific effects of formalization on employees are still unclear, however.[49]

Organizations tend to add more rules and procedures as the need for control of operations increases. Some organizations have become so formalized that they have rules for how to make new rules! One large state university created such rules in the form of a three-page document entitled "Procedures for Rule Adoption" that was added to the four-inch-thick *Policy and Procedures Manual*. The new policy first defines terms such as "university," "board," and "rule" and lists ten exceptions that describe when this policy on rule adoptions does not apply. It then presents a nine-step process for adopting a new rule within the university.

Other organizations are trying to become less formalized by reducing the number of rules and procedures employees must follow. In this effort, Chevron cut the number of its rules and procedures from over four hundred to eighteen. Highly detailed procedures for hiring were eliminated in favor of letting managers make hiring decisions based on common sense.[50]

Another approach to organizational formalization attempts to describe how, when, and why good managers should bend or break a rule.[51] Although rules exist in some form in almost every organization, how strictly they are enforced varies significantly from one organization to another and even within a single organization. Some managers argue that "a rule is a rule" and that all rules must be enforced to control employee behaviors and prevent chaos in the organization. Other managers act as if "all rules are made to be broken" and see rules as stumbling blocks on the way to effective action.

Formalization is the degree to which rules and procedures prescribe the jobs and activities of employees.

AVAVA/ISTOCKPHOTO.COM

Neither point of view is better for the organization; rather, a more balanced approach is recommended.

The test of a good manager in a formalized organization may be how well he or she uses appropriate judgment in making exceptions to rules. A balanced approach to making exceptions to rules should do two things. First, it should recognize that individuals are unique and that the organization can benefit from making exceptions that capitalize on exceptional capabilities. For example, suppose an engineering design department with a rule mandating equal access to tools and equipment acquires a limited amount of specialized equipment such as new computers with cutting-edge design software. The department manager decides to make an exception to the equal-access rule by assigning the computers to the designers the manager believes will use them the most and with the best results instead of making them available for use by all. Second, a balanced approach should recognize the commonalities among employees. Managers should make exceptions to rules only when there is a true and meaningful difference between individuals rather than base exceptions on features such as race, sex, appearance, or social factors.

RESPONSIBILITY AND AUTHORITY

Responsibility and authority are related to both configurational and operational aspects of organization structure. For example, the organization chart shows who reports to whom at all levels in the organization. From the operational perspective, the degree of centralization defines the locus of decision-making authority in the organization. However, often there is some confusion about what responsibility and authority really mean for managers and how the two terms relate to each other.

Responsibility

Responsibility is an obligation to do something with the expectation that some act or output will result. For example, a manager may expect an employee to write and present a proposal for a new program by a certain date; thus, the employee is responsible for preparing the proposal. Responsibility ultimately derives from the ownership of the organization. The owners hire or appoint a group, often a board of directors, to be responsible for managing the organization, making the decisions, and reaching the goals set by the owners. A downward chain of responsibility is then established. The board hires a chief executive officer (CEO) or president to be responsible for running the organization. The CEO or president hires more people and holds them responsible for accomplishing designated tasks that enable her or him to produce the results expected by the board and the owners. Jack Welch became famous for the way he ran GE for twenty years. Over the years he hired many managers

STEFAN KLEIN/ISTOCKPHOTO.COM

This organization chart shows the President/CEO reporting to the Board of Directors indicating the CEO is responsible to the Board for everything that happens in the organization. Does responsibility stop there? To whom is the Board responsible? Certainly the President/ CEO has a lot of authority based on the position shown, but the organization chart does not reveal much about that authority and how it is used or delegated.

Responsibility is an obligation to do something with the expectation of achieving some act or output.

and assigned responsibility for running various parts of the business. However, in the end, Jack Welch was responsible for all of the activities of the organization.

The chain extends throughout the organization because each manager has an obligation to fulfill: to appropriately employ organizational resources (people, money, and equipment) to meet the owners' expectations. Although managers can assign responsibility to others and expect them to achieve results, each manager is still held responsible for the outputs of those to whom he or she assigns the tasks.

A manager responsible for a work group assigns tasks to members of the group. Each group member is then responsible for doing his or her task, yet the manager still remains responsible for each task and for the work of the group as a whole. This means that managers can take on the responsibility of others but cannot shed their own responsibility onto those below them in the hierarchy.

Authority

Authority is power that has been legitimized within a specific social context.[52] (Power is discussed in Chapter 14.) Only when power is part of an official organizational role does it become authority. Authority includes the legitimate right to use resources to accomplish expected outcomes. As we discussed in the previous section, the authority to make decisions may be restricted to the top levels of the organization or dispersed throughout the organization.

Like responsibility, authority originates in the ownership of the organization. The owners establish a group of directors who have the authority to utilize certain resources and are responsible for managing the organization's affairs. The directors, in turn, authorize people in the organization to make decisions and to use organizational resources. Thus, they delegate authority, or power in a social context, to others.

Authority is linked to responsibility because a manager responsible for accomplishing certain results must have the authority to use resources to achieve those results.[53] The relationship between responsibility and authority must be one of parity; that is, the authority over resources must be sufficient to enable the manager to meet the output expectations of others.

But authority and responsibility differ in significant ways. Responsibility cannot be delegated down to others (as discussed in the previous section), but authority can. One complaint often heard from employees is that they have too much responsibility but not enough authority to get the job done. This indicates a lack of parity between responsibility and authority. Managers usually are quite willing to hold individuals responsible for specific tasks but are reluctant to delegate enough authority to do the job. In effect, managers try to rid themselves of responsibility for results (which they cannot do), yet they rarely like to give away their cherished authority over resources.

The *Change* box on page 453, entitled "With Authority Comes Responsibility," continues the story begun in our chapter-opening feature, showing how the exercise of authority by the CEO of a well-known company goes hand in hand with his responsibility to the firm's shareholders.

Delegation is the transfer to others of authority to make decisions and use organizational resources. Delegation of authority to lower-level managers to make decisions is common in organizations today. The important thing is to give lower-level managers authority to carry out the decisions they make. Managers typically have difficulty in delegating successfully. In the Self-Assessment Exercise at the end of this chapter, you will have a chance to practice delegation.

Authority is power that has been legitimized within a particular social context.

Delegation is the transfer to others of authority to make decisions and use organizational resources.

CHANGE

With Authority Comes Responsibility

Approval of Michael Jeffries' performance as CEO of Abercrombie & Fitch—the subject of our chapter-opening story on page 430—is neither unanimous nor unmixed. In fact, A. G. Edwards investment analyst Robert Buchanan, while impressed by Jeffries' streak of revenue increases in 55 out of 56 consecutive quarters, goes so far as to say that "Abercrombie's biggest weakness is that it's all about Mike." Jeffries' long tenure, though distinguished by outstanding financial success, has in fact been marred by periodic controversy.

Perhaps most serious, at least from a strictly business standpoint, are rumblings of dissatisfaction among A&F shareholders. In particular, investigations of shareholder complaints have indicated possible problems with Jeffries' control over his board of directors. In 2005, for instance, a suit filed by shareholders charged that Jeffries' pay was excessive. Although no one admitted any wrongdoing, Jeffries agreed to cut in half (from $12 million to $6 million) a bonus he was awarded for staying in his job. He also agreed to add more outside directors to the board at a time when two of its six outside members, including the head of the compensation committee, were receiving substantial fees for business conducted with the company. In addition, he agreed to make the heads of the firm's five retail divisions presidents of the company (up until then they had been executive or senior vice presidents). In January 2009, Jeffries reached an agreement to remain as chairman and CEO until 2014, with his compensation to remain pretty much the same: an annual base salary of $1.5 million plus bonuses up to a maximum of 240 percent of base salary.

> *"Abercrombie's biggest weakness is that it's all about Mike."*
>
> —INVESTMENT ANALYST ROBERT BUCHANAN ON A&F CEO MICHAEL JEFFRIES

Pensions, stock options, and perks had inflated Jeffries' total compensation to $71.8 million in 2008—a year in which A&F's net income was down 42 percent from the previous year. In the fourth quarter alone, which Jeffries called "a catastrophe for the retail industry," net profit had plummeted by 68 percent. Over the course of the year, the company's stock had lost 74 percent of its value, and although the global economy was obviously the primary factor, analysts and investors questioned the wisdom of Jeffries' persistent refusal both to discount prices and to engage in high-profile promotional activity as a means of countering the plunge in consumer spending. One analyst, for example, disagreed strongly with "Jeffries' stubborn position not to run sales promotions in the midst of the worst retail environment in decades." Jeffries replied that "promotions are a short-term solution with dreadful long-term effects" and insisted on avoiding any strategy that would compromise the long-term value of the company's brands.

He had taken the same stance during the post-9/11 economic slump of 2001–2002, emerging with his streak of increasingly profitable quarters intact and confirming his conviction that A&F's customers would pay premium prices for the brands they regarded as worth the money. "I don't care what anyone other than our target customer thinks," said Jeffries, but this time around, his target customers apparently worried more about the value of their money than that of their apparel. In 2009, A&F netted a grand total of $254 *thousand*—a figure that makes the take of $272 *million* in 2008 look like a spectacular windfall. Between the beginning of 2008 and the end of 2009, the company's

Continued

7. How might the impact of formalization differ for research scientists, machine operators, and bank tellers?
8. How might centralization or decentralization affect the job characteristics specified in job design?
9. When a group makes a decision, how is responsibility for the decision apportioned among the members?
10. Why do employees typically want more authority and less responsibility?
11. Consider the job you now hold or one that you held in the past. Did your boss have the authority to direct your work? Why did he or she have this authority?
12. Describe at least four features of organization structure that were important parts of the classic view of organizing.

ORGANIZATIONAL BEHAVIOR CASE FOR DISCUSSION

DELAYERING AS A DEFENSE MECHANISM

In October 2009, Anglo American PLC, the world's fourth-largest diversified mining company, announced that it was *delayering*—eliminating a layer of organizational structure. A review of its "operating model," reported the company (referring to itself as "the Group"), had "resulted in an organizational simplification and delayering across the Group, with the divisional co-ordinating level across . . . Coal and Ferrous Metals being removed." Previously, the company had been organized into two global divisions—Coal and Ferrous Metals, each with its own CEO, both of whom reported directly to the CEO of Anglo American. Below the divisional level were Anglo's various global business operations, each dealing with a different commodity (e.g., coal, platinum, iron ore) and each headed by its own CEO and functional support staff. The CEOs of these units reported directly to the CEO of his or her respective division.

As a result of "simplification and delayering," these businesses have been reorganized into seven "commodity business units" (BUs), each of which is to be "profit accountable"—that is, responsible for its own performance. The major criteria for this reorganization were geography and asset status. The platinum unit, for example, is to be headquartered in South Africa (which is also home to the parent company), the copper unit in Chile, and the metallurgical-coal unit in Australia. In addition, BUs have been established only for Anglo's *core assets*—operations that are essential to producing revenue, cash flow, or profit. Going hand in hand with the company's delayering strategy is thus a strategy to divest its non-core assets: having already shed its interests in gold and aluminum, Anglo has announced that it also intends to sell its holdings in such commodities as phosphates and zinc and a company that manufactures steel products for the construction industry. The

decision to delayer and divest, says Anglo chairman Sir John Parker, "represents an important step in creating a more streamlined business, with enhanced focus on operational effectiveness. ... We have a truly world-class portfolio of assets, and these initiatives further improve our ability to deliver its full potential."

Streamlining and efficiency, of course, are common and viable reasons for restructuring an organization, but if we look a little more closely at the recent history of Anglo American, we find that these strategies can also play a key role in a much more complicated game of corporate competition and, perhaps, even survival.

The year 2009 had already been a hectic one for Anglo. In February, CEO Cynthia Carroll had admitted that the organization, like many companies, had begun to feel the impact of the global recession: "The breadth and severity of the global downturn [is] difficult to understate," she said in announcing that Anglo would cut 19,000 jobs—about a tenth of its workforce—and suspend dividend payments accrued in 2008. Carroll also reported that earnings per share had fallen from $4.40 to $4.36 and that operating profit had dropped by 0.3 percent. The slippage was hardly catastrophic, but analysts had predicted an increase of 13 percent in earnings per share and had expected operating profit to at least remain flat.

When she was made CEO of Anglo in 2007, Carroll's appointment was a shock to many people in what the *Times of London* calls "an irredeemably macho industry." Not only was she not a man, she was neither a mining industry veteran nor a South African (she is an American). When her appointment was announced, Anglo's stock immediately dropped about $0.80 per share. The dice, observed the *Times*, were "probably loaded against her from the start," and to make her job even more difficult, she was soon forced to embark upon a $2 billion efficiency program involving a number of changes guaranteed to rile the old guard of the 91-year-old company. Her whirlwind campaign to cut costs by $450 million in the first half of 2009 earned her the nickname "Cyclone Cynthia," and many analysts and investors were unimpressed by the savings themselves: Because the entire industry was struggling with high costs during the recession, Carroll's cost-cutting was seen simply as the logical and obvious strategy to pursue.

Then in June 2009, the Swiss-British mining company Xstrata proposed a merger with Anglo—a move that would create a $68 billion firm to compete with industry giants like BHP Billiton, Vale, and Rio Tinto. Xstrata said in a statement that it was seeking "a merger of equals that would realize significant value for both companies' shareholders" and cited "substantial operational synergies," which could amount to savings of $1 billion a year in combined costs. For Anglo, there were drawbacks to the deal (its portfolio was worth more than Xstrata's and would be diluted by a merger of the two), but the appeal to Anglo shareholders was clear: depending on how the new company distributed the cost savings among its investors, Anglo shareholders stood to realize an increase in the market value of their holdings of 26 to 37 percent.

Carroll and the Anglo board, however, quickly rejected Xstrata's offer as "totally unacceptable," and in August, Carroll presented both Anglo's mid-year financial results and its argument for remaining independent. Once again, however, the numbers were underwhelming: because of the global economy, profits were off 69 percent and revenues 38 percent. Anglo investors wanted to know what management was doing to deliver the kind of returns promised by the Xstrata merger, and an analyst at Barclays Capital, Britain's biggest investment bank, announced that, "in our view, Anglo American has not yet presented a strong argument as to why a merger with Xstrata is not strategically sensible and value-creating for its shareholders." "Frankly," replied Carroll,

> I know what it is that we need to do. ... We have a strategy, we have clear goals, we have tremendous assets . . . in the most attractive commodities in the world. The opportunities are massive. ... We're well aware of what Xstrata does, but I'm very confident of what we can do in the future.

In October, Xstrata withdrew its offer in the face of resistance from the Anglo board. Anglo, said a company spokesman, "can now move forward and run our business without further distraction." One analyst predicted that

Anglo "will likely show a renewed sense of urgency . . . and pull out all the stops to win shareholders over," and exactly one week later, Carroll announced her "simplification and delayering" strategy. In making the announcement, she asked shareholders for more time to develop the company's assets and prove its value as an independent company. "The portfolio changes we have announced," she argued, ". . . will position Anglo American well for sustained, profitable growth in the commodities we have identified as being the most attractive."

CASE QUESTIONS

1. Based on what you can tell from the case, make a quick chart of Anglo's organization prior to Carroll's changes. Then make a similar chart of its organization after those changes. Be prepared to explain the key differences highlighted by your two charts, as well as the advantages that Carroll sees in her changes.

2. Describe the results of Anglo's changes to its organizational structure in terms of configuration, operational aspects, and responsibility and authority.

3. In addition to seven business units, Anglo's restructuring creates five functional groups— Finance, Mining & Technology, Business Performance & Projects, HR & Communications, and Strategy & Business Development. Describe some of the ways in which these new functional groups will interact with the company's new business units.

4. In your opinion, has Carroll done a good job so far of balancing her responsibility with her authority? What does she now have to do in order to sustain or improve that balance and to ensure that her strategy is successful?

REFERENCES

Jeffrey Sparshott, "Miner Anglo to Sell Assets in Shake-Up," *Wall Street Journal*, October 22, 2009, http://online.wsj.com on April 22, 2010; Kate Holton et al., "Xstrata Seeks $68 Billion Merger with Anglo," Reuters, June 21, 2009, www.reuters.com on April 23, 2010; Dana Cimilluca and Jeffrey Sparshott, "Miner Xstrata Seeks Merger with Anglo to Cut Costs," *Wall Street Journal*, June 22, 2009, http://online .wsj.com on April 23, 2010; Martin Waller and David Robinson, "Business Big Shot: Cynthia Carroll of Anglo American," *Times* (London) *Online*, August 1, 2009, http://business.timesonline.co.uk on April 23, 2010; Andrew Cave, "Cynthia Carroll Digs Deep for Anglo," *Telegraph*, August 1, 2009, www.telegraph.co.uk on April 22, 2010; Carli Lourens and Brett Foley, "Xstrata Drops Proposed $48 Billion Hostile Takeover Bid for Anglo American," *Industry-News*, October 15, 2009, http://industry-news.org on April 23, 2010.

EXPERIENCING ORGANIZATIONAL BEHAVIOR

Understanding Organization Structure

Purpose This exercise will help you understand the configurational and operational aspects of organization structure.

Format You will interview at least five employees in different parts of either the college or university you attend or a small- to medium-sized organization and analyze its structure. (You may want to coordinate this exercise with the exercise in Chapter 17.)

Procedure If you use a local organization, your first task is to find one with fifty to five hundred employees. The organization should have more than two hierarchical levels, but it should not be too complex to understand in a short period of study. You may want to check with your professor before contacting the company. Your initial contact should be with the highest-ranking manager, if possible. Be sure that top management is aware of your project and gives its approval.

If you use your local college or university, you could talk to professors, secretaries, and other administrative staff in the admissions office, student services department, athletic department, library, or many other areas. Be sure to represent a variety of jobs and levels in your interviews.

Using the material in this chapter, interview employees to obtain the following information on the structure of the organization:

1. The type of departmentalization (business function, process, product, customer, geographic region)
2. The typical span of control at each level of the organization

3. The number of levels in the hierarchy
4. The administrative ratio (ratio of managers to total employees and ratio of managers to production employees)
5. The degree of formalization (to what extent are rules and procedures written down in job descriptions, policy and procedures manuals, and memos?)
6. The degree of decentralization (to what extent are employees at all levels involved in making decisions?)

Interview three to five employees of the organization at different levels and in different departments. One should hold a top-level position. Be sure to ask the questions in a way that is clear to the respondents; they may not be familiar with the terminology used in this chapter.

Students should produce a report with a paragraph on each configurational and operational aspect of structure listed in this exercise as well as an organization chart of the company, a discussion of differences in responses from the employees interviewed, and any unusual structural features (for example, a situation in which employees report to more than one person or to no one). You may want to send a copy of your report to the company's top management.

Follow-up Questions
1. Which aspects of structure were the hardest to obtain information about? Why?
2. If there were differences in the responses of the employees you interviewed, how do you account for them?

BUILDING MANAGERIAL SKILLS

Exercise Overview Managers typically inherit an existing organization structure when they are promoted or hired into a position as manager. Often, however, after working with the existing structure for a while, they feel the need to rearrange the structure to increase the productivity or performance of the organization. This exercise provides you with the opportunity to restructure an existing organization.

Exercise Background Recall the analysis you did in the "Experiencing Organizational Behavior" exercise above in which you analyzed the structure of an existing organization. In that exercise you described the configurational and operational aspects of the structure of a local organization or a department at your college or university.

Exercise Task   Develop a different organization structure for that organization. You may utilize any or all of the factors described in this chapter. For example, you could alter the span of control, the administrative hierarchy, and the method of departmentalization as well as the formalization and centralization of the organization. Remember, the key to structure is to develop a way to coordinate the divided tasks. You should draw a new organization chart and develop a rationale for your new design.

Conclude by addressing the following questions:

1. How difficult was it to come up with a different way of structuring the organization?
2. What would it take to convince the current head of that organization to go along with your suggested changes?

SELF-ASSESSMENT EXERCISE

Making Some Sense of Yourself

As we saw in Chapter 5, *participation* and *empowerment* go hand in hand as techniques for motivating employees by getting them involved in an organization's decision-making processes. We also pointed out that both may be regarded as extensions of job design because both fundamentally affect how employees perform their jobs.

This exercise is designed to help you determine how much empowerment you feel in your own work, whether at a job or in school. If you have a job, consider that your work; if you are a student, apply this exercise to your school work.

The 20 statements below reflect attitudes that people can have toward their work. Using the following scale, indicate the extent to which, in your opinion, each statement is true of you.

1. Very strongly disagree
2. Strongly disagree
3. Disagree
4. Neutral
5. Agree
6. Strongly agree
7. Very strongly agree

_____ 1. The work that I do is very important to me.
_____ 2. I am confident about my ability to do my work.
_____ 3. I have significant autonomy in determining how I do my work.
_____ 4. I have significant impact on what happens in my work unit.
_____ 5. I trust my coworkers to be completely honest with me.
_____ 6. My work activities are personally meaningful to me.
_____ 7. My work is within the scope of my competence and capabilities.

_____ 8. I can decide how to go about doing my own work.
_____ 9. I have a great deal of control over what happens in my work unit.
_____ 10. I trust my coworkers to share important information with me.
_____ 11. I care about what I do in my work.
_____ 12. I am confident about my capabilities to perform my work successfully.
_____ 13. I have considerable opportunity for independence and freedom in how I do my work.
_____ 14. I have significant influence over what happens in my work unit.
_____ 15. I trust my coworkers to keep the promises they make.
_____ 16. The work I do has special meaning and importance to me.
_____ 17. I have mastered the skills necessary to do my work.
_____ 18. I have a chance to use personal initiative in carrying out my work.
_____ 19. My opinion counts in my work unit's decision making.
_____ 20. I believe that my coworkers care about my well-being.

How to score: Each of the 20 statements in this exercise falls into one of five skill areas. You will therefore be calculating your score in each of these areas. Scoring requires two steps:

1. Total up your scores for the 4 items in each skill area.
2. Divide your total score in each area by 4 in order to find your mean score.

Scoring Key

Skill Area	Statements	Mean (Total ÷ 4)
Self-efficacy—your sense of personal competence	2, 7, 12, 17	
Self-determination—your sense of personal choice	3, 8, 13, 18	
Personal consequence—your sense of having impact	4, 9, 14, 19	
Meaningfulness—your sense of value in your activities	1, 6, 11, 16	
Trust—your sense of security	5, 10, 15, 20	

Once you have determined your mean scores, you can compare them to the findings recorded in the following table, which reflect the scores of about 3,000 U.S. middle managers.

Comparison Data

Skill Area	Mean	Top Third	Bottom Third
Self-efficacy	5.76	>6.52	>5.00
Self-determination	5.50	>6.28	>4.72
Personal consequence	5.49	>6.34	>4.64
Meaningfulness	5.88	>6.65	>5.12
Trust	5.33	>60.3	>4.73

Reference: David A. Whetten and Kim S. Cameron, *Developing Management Skills*, 7th ed. (Upper Saddle River, NJ: Prentice Hall, 2007), 445–46, 451, 489–90.

ORGANIZATION DESIGN

CHAPTER LEARNING OBJECTIVES

After studying this chapter, you should be able to:

- Describe the basic premise of contingency approaches to organization design.
- Discuss how strategy and the structural imperatives combine to affect organization design.
- Summarize five types of organization designs.
- Explain several contemporary approaches to organization design.

Some Keys to Making a Steinway

"The payback is . . . when you get the celebrity treatment for building a Steinway."

—GINO ROMANO, SENIOR SUPERVISOR AT STEINWAY & SONS

Everybody knows what a grand piano looks like, although it is hard to describe its contour as anything other than "piano shaped." From a bird's-eye view, you might recognize a shape sort of like a big holster. The *case*—the curved lateral surface that runs around the whole instrument—appears to be a single

The hands of a pianist are only one pair of the many hands that go into making the beautiful music that comes from a Steinway piano. Steinway & Sons uses a combination of highly skilled crafts men and women and complex technology to build their superb instruments.

WAECHTER/CARO/ALAMY

continuous piece of wood, but it is not. If you examine the case of a piano built by Steinway & Sons, you will actually be looking at a remarkable composite of raw material, craftsmanship, and technology. The process by which this component is made—like most of the processes for making a Steinway grand—is a prime example of a *technical*, or *task*, *subsystem* at work in a highly specialized factory.

The *case* starts out as a *rim*, which is constructed out of separate slats of wood, mostly maple (Eastern rock maple, to be precise). Once raw boards have been cut and planed, they are glued along their lengthwise edges to the width of 12½ inches. These composite pieces are then glued and jointed end-to-end to form slats 22 feet long—the measure of the piano's perimeter. Next, a total of 18 separate slats—14 layers of maple and 4 layers of other types of wood—are glued and stacked together to form a *book*—one (seemingly) continuous "board" 3¼ inches thick. Then comes the process that is a favorite of visitors to the Steinway factory tour—bending this rim into the shape of a piano. Steinway still does it pretty much the same way that it has for more than a century—by hand and all at once. Because the special glue is in the process of drying, a crew of six has just 20 minutes to wrestle the book, using block and tackle and wooden levers and mallets, into a *rim-bending press*—"a giant piano-shaped vise," as Steinway describes it—which will force the wood to "forget" its natural inclination to be straight and assume the familiar contour of a grand piano.

Visitors report the sound of splintering wood, but factory personnel assure them that the specially cured wood is not likely to break nor is the specially mixed glue likely to lose its grip. Does a case *ever* break? "Nobody can understand how you can bend this wood," says Steinway PR executive Leo F. Spellman, who once asked the same question of a veteran factory foreman. He likes to quote the foreman's answer: " 'I've been here for over 30 years, and in my time, we've broken no more than three.' … It doesn't really happen a lot," Spellman concludes, and it is a good thing, both because the wood is expensive and because the precision Steinway process cannot afford much wasted effort. The company needs 12 months, 12,000 parts, 450 craftspeople, and countless hours of skilled labor to produce a grand piano. Today, the New York factory turns out about 10 pianos a day, or 2,500 a year—fewer than it averaged about 100 years ago. (A mass-producer might build 2,000 pianos a week.) The result of this painstaking task system, according to one business journalist, is "both impossibly perfect instruments and a scarcity," and that is why Steinways are so expensive—currently, somewhere between $45,000 and $110,000.

But Steinway pianos, the company reminds potential buyers, have always been "built to a standard, not to a price." Approximately 90 percent of all concert pianists prefer the sound of a Steinway, and the company's attention to manufacturing detail reflects the fact that when a piano is being played, the entire instrument vibrates— and thus affects its sound. In other words—and not surprisingly—the better the raw materials, design, and construction, the better the sound. That is one of the reasons why Steinway craftsmen put so much care into the construction of the piano's case: it is a major factor in the way the body of the instrument resonates. The maple wood for the case, for example, arrives at the factory with water content of 80 percent. It is then dried, both in the open air and in kilns, until the water content is reduced to about 10 percent—suitable for both strength and pliability. To ensure that these quali-ties remain stable, the slats must be cut so they are horizontally grained and arranged with the "inside" of one slat—the side that grew toward the center of the tree—facing the "outside" of the next one in the book. The case is removed from the press after one day and then stored for 10 weeks in a humidity-controlled *rim-bending room*. Afterwards, it is ready to be sawed, planed, and sanded to specification—a process called *frazing*. A black lacquer finish is added, and only then is the case ready to be installed as a component of a grand piano in progress.

Stability also contributes to durability. When asked about the life expectancy of the family product, Henry Steinway, the great grandson of the company's founder, used to tell people to ask him again in 50 years. Steinway, who died at 93 in 2008, explained that he did not have enough evidence to make a long-range forecast because no piano was more than 150 years old at the time. "It's a product," says Spellman, "that in some sense speaks to people and will have a legacy long after we're gone. What [Steinway] craftsmen work on today will be here for another 50 or 100 years." In 50 or 100 years, your Steinway is also likely to be worth much more than you paid for it. If you had bought a Steinway concert grand for $25,000 in 1975, you could get more than 4 times your original retail cost today. The oldest Steinways command as much as 13 times their original prices.

The Steinway process also puts a premium on skilled workers. Steinway has always been an employer of immigrant labor, beginning with the German craftsmen and laborers hired by founder Heinrich Steinweg in the 1860s and 1870s. Today, many Steinway employees are fairly recent immigrants, and it still takes time to train them. It takes about a year, for instance, to train a case maker, and "when you lose one of them for a long period of time," says Gino Romano, a senior supervisor hired in 1964, "it has a serious effect on our output." Romano recalls one year in mid-June when a case maker was injured in a car accident and unable to work for an extended period of time. Romano's whole department fell behind schedule, and it was September before he could find a suitable replacement (an experienced case maker in Florida who happened to be a relative of another Steinway worker).

The company's employees do not necessarily share Spellman's sense of the company's history, but many of them are well aware of the brand recognition commanded by the products they craft. "The payback," says Romano,

> is not in [the factory]. The payback is outside, when you get the celebrity treatment for building a Steinway—when you meet somebody for the first time and they ooh and ahh: "You build Steinways? Wow." You're automatically put on a higher level, and you go, "I didn't realize I was that notable."

Although Steinway still uses many traditional techniques, there have been a few advances in the making of its largely handcrafted products. We discuss some of these methods in the *Technology* box entitled "A Marriage of Technique and Technology" on page 477.

What Do You Think?

1. What is unusual about the manufacturing process at Steinway?
2. Would like to work at Steinway? Why or why not?

References: Steinway & Sons, "Online Factory Tour," "A Sound Investment," 2009, www.steinway.com on April 29, 2010; Public Broadcasting Service, "Note by Note: The Making of Steinway L1037," 2009, www.pbs.org on April 28, 2010; Maya Roney, "Steinway: Worth Much More Than a Song," *Bloomberg Businessweek*, March 6, 2007, www.businessweek.com on April 28, 2010; James Barron, "88 Keys, Many Languages, One Proud Name," *New York Times*, October 6, 2003, www.nytimes.com on April 29, 2010; Michael Lenehen, "K 2571: The Making of a Steinway Grand," *Atlantic Monthly*, August 1982, www.sherwinbeach.com on April 28, 2010; Rick Rogers, "Steinway Builds a Legacy with Distinctive Pianos," *Daily Oklahoman* (Oklahoma City), December 2000, www.richardhuggins.com on April 28, 2010.

Steinway has a unique manufacturing process that requires a very specific set of skills and work relationships. Because of its long history and stability it may not have changed its organization structure very often. Most organizations, however, struggle to find the best organizational design in order to survive in an ever-changing environment. Many companies are constantly reorganizing to try to increase their performance, productivity, and response times—or just to survive. The primary issue is how to determine which organizational form is right for a given organization at this point in time. In this chapter we describe several approaches to organization design.

CONTINGENCY APPROACHES TO ORGANIZATION DESIGN

Organization designs vary from rigid bureaucracies to flexible matrix systems. Most theories of organization design take either a universal or a contingency approach. A **universal approach** is one whose prescriptions or propositions are designed to work in any situation. Thus, a universal design prescribes the "one best way" to structure the jobs, authority, and reporting relationships of the organization, regardless of factors such as the organization's external environment, the industry, and the type of work to be done. The classical approaches discussed in Chapter 16 are all universal approaches: Weber's ideal bureaucracy, Fayol's classic principles of organizing, and Likert's human organization. A **contingency approach**, on the other hand, suggests that organizational efficiency and effectiveness can be achieved in several ways. In a contingency design, specific conditions such as the environment, technology, and the organization's workforce determine the structure. Figure 17.1 shows the distinction

In the **universal approach** to organization design, prescriptions or propositions are designed to work in any circumstances.

Under the **contingency approach** to organization design, the desired outcomes for the organization can be achieved in several ways.

𝒥igure 17.1 UNIVERSAL AND CONTINGENCY APPROACHES TO ORGANIZATIONAL DESIGN

The universal approach looks for the single best way to design an organization regardless of situational issues. The contingency approach designs the organization to fit the situation.

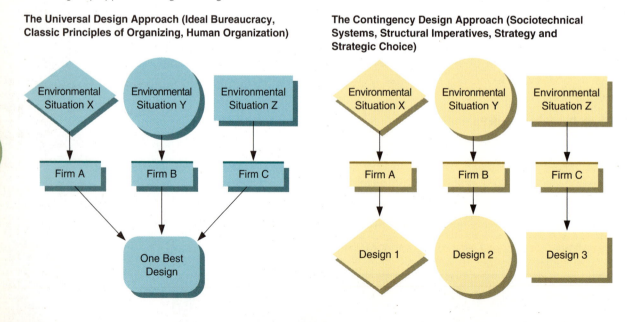

The Universal Design Approach (Ideal Bureaucracy, Classic Principles of Organizing, Human Organization)

The Contingency Design Approach (Sociotechnical Systems, Structural Imperatives, Strategy and Strategic Choice)

between the universal and contingency approaches. This distinction is similar to the one between universal and contingency approaches to motivation (Chapter 4), job design (Chapter 5), and leadership (Chapters 12 and 13). Although no one particular form of organization is generally accepted, the contingency approach most closely represents current thinking.

Weber, Fayol, and Likert (see Chapter 16) each proposed an organization design that is independent of the nature of the organization and its environment. Although each of their approaches contributed to our understanding of the organizing process and the practice of management, none has proved to be universally applicable. In this chapter we turn to several contingency designs, which attempt to specify the conditions, or contingency factors, under which they are likely to be most effective. The contingency factors include such things as the strategy of the organization, its technology, the environment, the organization's size, and the social system within which the organization operates.

The contingency approach has been criticized as being unrealistic because managers are expected to observe a change in one of the contingency factors and then to make a rational structural alteration. On the other hand, Lex Donaldson has argued that it is reasonable to expect organizations to respond to lower organizational performance, which may result from a lack of response to some significant change in one or several contingency factors.[1]

STRATEGY, STRUCTURAL IMPERATIVES, AND STRATEGIC CHOICE

The decision about how to design the organization structure is based on numerous factors. In this section, we present several views of the determinants of organization structure and integrate them into a single approach. We begin with the strategic view.

Strategy

A **strategy** is the set of plans and actions necessary to achieve organizational goals.[2] Every organization tries to develop a strategy that will enable it to meet its goals. Kellogg, for example, has attempted to be the leader in the ready-to-eat cereal industry by pursuing a strategy that combines product differentiation and market segmentation. Over the years, Kellogg has successfully introduced new cereals made from different grains in different shapes, sizes, colors, and flavors in its effort to provide any type of cereal the consumer might want.[3] McDonald's has been one of the leaders in the fast-food industry but has struggled lately to find the right strategy in a changing environment.[4]

After studying the history of seventy companies, Alfred Chandler drew certain conclusions about the relationship between an organization's structure and its business strategy.[5] Chandler observed that a growth strategy to expand into a new product line is usually matched with some type of decentralization, a decentralized structure being necessary to deal with the problems of the new product line.

Chandler's "structure follows strategy" concept seems to appeal to common sense. Management must decide what the organization is to do and what its goals are before deciding how to design the organization structure, which is how the organization will meet those goals. This perspective assumes a purposeful approach to designing the structure of the organization.

Strategy is the set of plans and actions necessary to achieve organizational goals.

Figure 17.2 THE STRUCTURAL-IMPERATIVES APPROACH

Organizational size, environment, and technology determine how an organization should be structured to be effective.

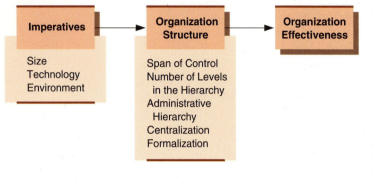

Structural Imperatives

The structural-imperatives approach to organization design probably has been the most discussed and researched contingency perspective of the last thirty years. This perspective was not formulated by a single theorist or researcher, and it has not evolved from a systematic and cohesive research effort. Rather, it gradually emerged from a vast number of studies that sought to address the question "What are the compelling factors that determine how the organization must be structured to be effective?" As Figure 17.2 shows, the three factors that have been identified as **structural imperatives** are size, technology, and environment.

Size The size of an organization can be gauged in many ways. Usually it is measured in terms of total number of employees, value of the organization's assets, total sales in the previous year (or number of clients served), or physical capacity. The method of measurement is very important, although the different measures usually are correlated.[6]

Generally, larger organizations have a more complex structure than smaller ones. Peter Blau and his associates concluded that large size is associated with greater specialization of labor, a larger span of control, more hierarchical levels, and greater formalization.[7] These multiple effects are shown in Figure 17.3. Increasing size leads to more specialization of labor within a work unit, which increases the amount of differentiation among work units and the number of levels in the hierarchy, resulting in a need for more intergroup formalization. With greater specialization within the unit, there is less need for coordination within groups; thus, the span of control can be larger. Larger spans of control mean fewer first-line managers, but the need for more intergroup coordination may require more second- and third-line managers and staff personnel to coordinate them. Large organizations may therefore be more efficient because of their

Structural imperatives—size, technology, and environment—are the three primary determinants of organization structure.

Figure 17.3 IMPACT OF LARGE SIZE ON ORGANIZATION STRUCTURE

As organizations grow larger, their structures usually change in predictable ways. Larger organizations tend to have more complex structures, larger spans of control, and more rules and procedures.

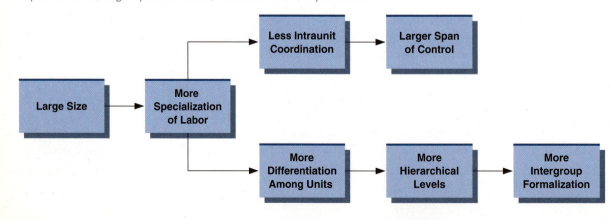

large spans of control and reduced administrative overhead; however, the greater differentiation among units makes the system more complex. Studies by researchers associated with the University of Aston in Birmingham, England, and others have shown similar results.[8]

Economies of scale are another advantage of large organizations. In a large operation, fixed costs—for example, plant and equipment—can be spread over more units of output, thereby reducing the cost per unit. In addition, some administrative activities such as purchasing, clerical work, and marketing can be accomplished for a large number of units at the same cost as for a small number. Their cost can then be spread over the larger number of units, again reducing unit cost.

Companies such as W. L. Gore, AT&T Technologies, General Electric's Aircraft Engines products group, and S. C. Johnson & Son have gone against the conventional wisdom that larger is always better in manufacturing plants. They cite as their main reasons the smaller investment required for smaller plants, the reduced need to produce a variety of products, and the desire to decrease organizational complexity (that is, reduce the number of hierarchical levels and shorten lines of communication). In a number of instances, smaller plants have resulted in increased team spirit, improved productivity, and higher profits.[9] Other studies have found that the relationship between size and structural complexity is less clear than the Blau results indicate. These studies suggest that size must be examined in relation to the technology of the organization.[10]

Traditionally, as organizations have grown, several layers of advisory staff have been added to help coordinate the complexities inherent in any large organization. However, even in good times, some organizations have gone through significant staff reductions. Known as **organizational downsizing** and discussed briefly in Chapter 16, this popular trend is aimed primarily at reducing the size of corporate staff and middle management to reduce costs. Companies such as NYNEX, Eastman Kodak, and RJR Nabisco have made cutbacks with disastrous results, and NYNEX had to hire back hundreds of employees who had taken an early retirement program to try to build back its reputation for customer service. NYNEX Corporation, the telephone company in the northeastern region of the United States in the 1980s and early 1990s had made massive cutbacks and layoffs in order to survive. At one point the New York Public Service Commission ordered NYNEX to rebate $50 million to 5 million customers because it had fallen behind in responding to problems due to its staff reductions. Eventually, NYNEX merged with Bell Atlantic in 1997, which merged with GTE in 1998 and eventually became Verizon in 2000. Eastman Kodak is paying more for contract workers who are doing the work that laid-off workers used to do. In addition, Kodak rehired some of those laid-off workers at increased salaries and incurred the costs of recruiting and rehiring.

In sales, cutting costs can be disastrous. Following a merger, RJR Nabisco decided to merge sales forces for its foods group—which handles Grey Poupon Mustard and Milkbone dog biscuits—with the Planters Life Savers Company, which makes gums, candies, and nuts. Problems arose when the lack of compatibility in product

HANS NELEMAN/THE IMAGE BANK/GETTY IMAGES

Whether due to recession or downsizing or some other reason, the impact of layoffs on workers is the same—packing up personal materials and heading for the door. There are also significant effects on those colleagues left behind as they have lost a coworker and may be concerned about how all the work will get done with that coworker gone, as well as wonder if they may be the next to go.

Organizational downsizing is a popular trend aimed at reducing the size of corporate staff and middle management to reduce costs.

types and in outlets began to surface. Sales representatives had trouble covering the much broader array of products and selling to twice as many outlets. As a result, customers were not called on promptly, and sales suffered significantly. Initially, profit margins did improve, but the next year operating earnings fell to 25 percent of their former levels.[11]

The results of downsizing have been mixed, with some observers noting that indiscriminate across-the-board cuts may leave the organization weak in certain key areas. However, positive results often include quicker decision making because fewer layers of management must approve every decision. One review of research on organizational downsizing found that it had both psychological and sociological impacts. Studies suggest that in a downsizing environment, size affects organization design in very complex ways.[12]

In difficult economic periods as recently experienced worldwide, many companies have been forced to reduce the number of employees throughout the organization through large-scale layoffs. Several years ago during a significant economic downturn, sales for Honeywell International, Inc. fell 11 percent in two years. Honeywell responded with massive layoffs of more than 31,000 employees and canceled plans for many new products and other global expansion plans. Executives now claim those moves were disastrous for the company when the economy turned around. During the most recent recession, when their sales fell 15 percent and profits dropped 23 percent, Honeywell took a more measured response by limiting layoffs to 6,000 and using benefit cuts and furloughs to reduce expenses.[13] This time they expect to be ready for the rebound with hundreds of new products and a full workforce.

Technology   **Organizational technology** consists of the mechanical and intellectual processes that transform raw materials into products and services for customers. For example, the primary technology employed by major oil companies transforms crude oil (input) into gasoline, motor oil, heating oil, and other petroleum-based products (outputs). Prudential Insurance uses actuarial tables and information-processing technologies to produce its insurance services. Of course, most organizations use multiple technologies. Oil companies use research and information-processing technologies in their laboratories, where new petroleum products and processes are generated.

Although there is general agreement that organizational technology is important, the means by which this technology has been evaluated and measured have varied widely. Five approaches to examining the technology of the organization are shown in Table 17.1. For convenience, we have classified these approaches according to the names of their proponents.

In an early study of the relationship between technology and organization structure, Joan Woodward categorized manufacturing technologies by their complexity: unit or small-batch, large-batch or mass production, and continuous process.[14] Tom Burns and George Stalker proposed that the rate of change in technology determines the best method of structuring the organization.[15] Charles Perrow developed a technological continuum, with routine technologies at one end and nonroutine technologies at the other, and claimed that all organizations could be classified on his routine-to-nonroutine continuum.[16] Thompson claimed that all organizations could be classified into one of three technological categories: long-linked, mediating, and intensive.[17] Finally, a group of English researchers at the University of Aston developed three categories of technology based on the type of workflow involved: operations, material, and knowledge.[18] These perspectives on technology are somewhat similar in that all (except the Aston typology) address the adaptability of the technological system to change. Large-batch or mass production, routine, and long-linked technologies are not very adaptable to change. At the opposite end of the continuum, continuous-process, nonroutine, and intensive technologies are readily adaptable to change.

Organizational technology refers to the mechanical and intellectual processes that transform inputs into outputs.

Table 17.1   SUMMARY OF APPROACHES TO TECHNOLOGY

Approach	Classification of Technology	Example
WOODWARD (1958 AND 1965) (CIT. NO. 14)	Unit or small-batch	Customized parts made one at a time
	Large-batch or mass production	Automobile assembly line
	Continuous process	Chemical plant, petroleum refinery
BURNS AND STALKER (1961) (CIT. NO. 15)	Rate of technological change	Slow: large manufacturing; rapid: computer industry
PERROW (1967) (CIT. NO. 16)	Routine	Standardized products (Procter & Gamble, General Foods)
	Nonroutine	New technology products or processes (computers, telecommunications)
THOMPSON (1967) (CIT. NO. 17)	Long-linked	Assembly line
	Mediating	Bank
	Intensive	General hospital
ASTON STUDIES: HICKSON, PUGH, AND PHEYSEY (1969) (CIT. NO. 18)	Workflow integration; operations, materials, and knowledge technologies	Technology differs in various parts of the organization

The effect of technology in organizations often is a function of the extent to which the technology creates or demands that tasks be interdependent in order to be accomplished. The more interdependent the tasks, the more coordination is required. Conversely, when the technology allows tasks to be more independent, less coordination is required. This effect may seem to be most pronounced in knowledge work where engineers or analysts may appear to work independently; however, a closer examination reveals that their tasks are highly interdependent and require very close coordination.[19]

One major contribution of the study of organizational technology is the recognition that organizations have more than one important "technology" that enables them to accomplish their tasks. Instead of examining technology in isolation, the Aston group recognized that size and technology are related in determining organization structure.[20] They found that in smaller organizations, technology had more direct effects on the structure. In large organizations, however, they, like Blau, found that structure depended less on the operations technology and more on size considerations such as the number of employees. In large organizations, each department or division may have a different technology that determines how that department or division should be structured. In short, in small organizations the structure depended primarily on the technology, whereas in large organizations the need to coordinate complicated activities was the most important factor. Thus, both organizational size and technology are important considerations in organization design.

Global technology variations come in two forms: variations in available technology and variations in attitudes toward technology. The technology available affects how organizations can do business. Many developing countries, for example, lack electric power sources, telephones, and trucking equipment, not to mention computers and robots. A manager working in such a country must be prepared to deal with many frustrations. Some Brazilian officials convinced a U.S. company to build a high-tech plant in their country. Midway through construction, however, the government of Brazil decided it would not allow the company to import some highly accurate measuring instruments that it needed to produce its products. The new plant was abandoned before it opened.[21]

Attitudes toward technology also vary across cultures. Surprisingly, Japan only began to support basic research in the 1980s. For many years, the Japanese government encouraged its companies to take basic research findings discovered elsewhere (often in the United States) and figure out how to apply them to consumer products (applied research). In the mid-1980s, however, the government changed its stance and started to encourage basic research as well.[22] Most Western nations have a generally favorable attitude toward technology whereas until the 1990s, China and other Asian countries (with the exception of Japan) did not.

Despite all of the emphasis on technology's role as a primary determinant of structure, there is some support for viewing it from the perspective that the strategy and structure of the organization determine what types of technology are appropriate. For example, Walmart and Dell Computers are careful to only use new information technology in ways that support their strategy and structure. Walmart's information systems keep track of its inventory from receipt to shelf placement to purchase, and Dell uses technology to optimize its manufacturing processes. Because both companies started with low-tech processes and then adopted new technologies over time, the technology clearly was a result of each firm's structure and strategy, and not the other way around.[23]

Environment   The organizational environment includes all of the elements— people, other organizations, economic factors, objects, and events—that lie outside the boundaries of the organization. The environment is composed of two layers: the general environment and the task environment. The **general environment** includes all of a broad set of dimensions and factors within which the organization operates, including political-legal, social, cultural, technological, economic, and international factors. The **task environment** includes specific organizations, groups, and individuals who influence the organization. People in the task environment include customers, suppliers, donors, regulators, inspectors, and shareholders. Among the organizations in the task environment are competitors, legislatures, and regulatory agencies. Economic factors in the task environment might include interest rates, international trade factors, and the unemployment rate in a particular area. Objects in the task environment include such things as buildings, vehicles, and trees. Events that may affect organizations include weather, elections, or war.

It is necessary to determine the boundaries of the organization to understand where the environment begins. These boundaries may be somewhat elusive, or at least changeable, and thus difficult to define. Many companies are spinning off some business units but then continuing to do business with them as suppliers. Therefore, one day a manager may be a member of an organization and the next day might be a part of that organization's environment. But for the most part, we can say that certain people, groups, or buildings are either in the organization or in the environment. For example, a college student shopping for a personal computer is part of the environment of HP, Dell, IBM, and other computer manufacturers. However, if the student works for one of these computer manufacturers, he or she is not part of that company's environment but is within the boundaries of the organization.

This definition of organizational environment emphasizes the expanse of the environment within which the organization operates. It may give managers the false impression that the environment is outside their control and interest. But because the environment completely encloses the organization, managers must be constantly concerned about it. Most managers these days are aware that the environment is changing rapidly. The difficulty for most is to determine how those changes affect the company.

The **organizational environment** is everything outside an organization and includes all elements — people, other organizations, economic factors, objects, and events — that lie outside the boundaries of the organization.

The **general environment** includes the broad set of dimensions and factors within which the organization operates, including political-legal, sociocultural, technological, economic, and international factors.

The **task environment** includes specific organizations, groups, and individuals who influence the organization.

The manager, then, faces an enormous, only vaguely specified environment that somehow affects the organization. Managing the organization within such an environment may seem like an overwhelming task. The alternatives for the manager are to (1) ignore the environment because of its complexity and focus on managing the internal operations of the company, (2) exert maximum energy in gathering information on every part of the environment and in trying to react to every environmental factor, and (3) pay attention to specific aspects of the task environment, responding only to those that most clearly affect the organization.

To ignore environmental factors entirely and focus on internal operations leaves the company in danger of missing major environmental shifts such as changes in customer preferences, technological breakthroughs, and new regulations. To expend large amounts of energy, time, and money exploring every facet of the environment may take more out of the organization than the effort may return.

The third alternative—to carefully analyze segments of the task environment that most affect the organization and to respond accordingly—is the most prudent course. The issue, then, is to determine which parts of the environment should receive the manager's attention. In the remainder of this section, we examine two perspectives on the organizational environment: the analysis of environmental components and environmental uncertainty.

Forces in the environment have different effects on different companies. For example, all organizations in the healthcare industry in the United States are quite concerned about the direction of the government's involvement in health care. It is not that various individuals and organizations are for or against any given proposal; their primary concern is how the various proposals will affect their operations. In fact, many industry leaders have been involved in consulting and lobbying activities in efforts to influence the final outcome. In effect, these organizations are trying to change the relevant environment, and will then have to determine how their organizations will be affected. It is most likely that it will take several years for organizations to fully adapt to new regulations. Quite different environmental forces, on the other hand, affect McDonald's—consumer demand, disposable income, the cost of meat and bread, and gasoline prices. Thus, the task environment, the specific set of environmental forces that influence the operations of an organization, varies among organizations.

The one environmental characteristic that brings together all of these different environmental influences and appears to have the most effect on the structure of the organization is uncertainty. **Environmental uncertainty** exists when managers do not have sufficient information about environmental factors, and thus they have difficulty predicting the impact of these factors on the organization.[24] Uncertainty has been described as resulting from complexity and dynamism in the environment. **Environmental complexity** is the number of environmental components that impinge on organizational decision making. **Environmental dynamism** is the degree to which important environmental components change.

In a low-uncertainty environment, there are few important components, and they change infrequently. A company in the cardboard container industry might have a highly certain environment when demand is steady, manufacturing processes are stable, and government regulations have remained largely unchanged. In contrast, in highly uncertain environments there are many important components involved in decision making that often change. The environment of health care in the United States is now highly uncertain with the new healthcare bill and the likelihood of continuing changes in the future. The toy industry also is in a highly uncertain environment. As they develop new toys, toy companies must stay in tune with movies, television shows, and cartoons, as well as with public sentiment. Between 1983 and 1988, Saturday

Environmental uncertainty exists when managers have little information about environmental events and their impact on the organization.

Environmental complexity is the number of environmental components that impinge on organizational decision making.

Environmental dynamism is the degree to which environmental components that impinge on organizational decision making change.

ROB KIM/EVERETT/PHOTOSHOT

Many toys are now based on movies. Children see the movie and then beg their parents to buy the action figures based on the movies. The Toy Story movies have spawned huge sales of the Jessie doll and other action figures for Mattel. Barbie and Ken have even found new life with Toy Story 3 and you can have the Barbie and Ken gift set for only $24.99!

morning cartoons were little more than animated stories about children's toys. Recently, however, due to the disappointing sales of many toys presented in cartoons designed to promote them, most toy companies have left the toy-based cartoon business. Many toys that are now sold are based on movies.[25]

Environmental characteristics and uncertainty have been important factors in explaining organization structure, strategy, and performance. For example, the characteristics of the environment affect how managers perceive the environment, which in turn affects how they adapt the structure of the organization to meet environmental demands.[26] The environment has also been shown to affect the degree to which a firm's strategy enhances its performance.[27] That is, a certain strategy will enhance organizational performance to the extent that it is appropriate for the environment in which the organization operates. Finally, the environment is directly related to organizational performance.[28] The environment and the organization's response to it are crucial to success.

An organization attempts to continue as a viable entity in a dynamic environment. The environment completely encloses the organization, and managers must be constantly concerned about it. The organization as a whole, as well as departments and divisions within it, are created to deal with different challenges, problems, and uncertainties. James Thompson suggested that organizations design a structure to protect the dominant technology of the organization, smooth out any problems, and keep down coordination costs.[29] Thus, organization structures are designed to coordinate relevant technologies and protect them from outside disturbances. Structural components such as inventory, warehousing, and shipping help buffer the technology used to transform inputs into outputs. For instance, demand for products usually is cyclical or seasonal and is subject to many disturbances, but warehousing inventory helps the manufacturing system function as if the environment accepted output at a steady rate, maximizing technological efficiency and helping the organization respond to fluctuating demands of the market. On the other hand, warehousing inventory costs money, so managers must balance costs of inventory with costs of shipping, labor costs, and many other factors.

Organizations with international operations must contend with additional levels of complexity and dynamism, both within and across cultures. Many cultures have relatively stable environments. For example, the economies of Sweden and the United States are fairly stable. Although competitive forces within each country's economic system vary, each economy remains strong. In contrast, the environments of other countries are much more dynamic. For example, France's policies on socialism versus private enterprise tend to change dramatically with each election. At present, far-reaching changes in the economic and management philosophies of most European countries make their environments far more dynamic than that of the United States. Managers of global corporations have experienced even more concerns as the worldwide recession in recent years has had many differential effects around the globe.

Environments also vary widely in terms of their complexity. The Japanese culture, which is fairly stable, is also quite complex. Japanese managers are subject to an array of cultural norms and values that are far more encompassing and resistant to change than those that U.S. managers face. India, too, has an extremely complex environment that continues to be influenced by its old caste system—in contrast to India's outstanding educational system, which produces a wealth of excellent engineering talent. Although the business potential is great in China, the many environmental uncertainties faced by foreign firms who want to do business there make it a difficult proposition. Infrastructure problems, language and cultural differences, governmental regulations, inconsistent suppliers, customs issues, and irregular copyright protection make it a difficult environment at best.[30]

In some cases, extremely low levels of income in a business environment make it understandably difficult to design productive organizations and operations. The *Globalization* box on page 474 shows how the phone maker Nokia overcame some of these barriers to doing business in Africa's economic environment.

Strategic Choice

The previous two sections described how structure is affected by the strategy of the organization and by the structural imperatives of size, technology, and environment. These approaches may seem to contradict each other since both approaches attempt to specify the determinants of structure. This apparent clash has been resolved by refining the strategy concept to include the role of the top management decision maker in determining the organization's structure.[31] In effect, this view inserts the manager as the decision maker who evaluates the imperatives and the organization strategy and then designs the organization structure.

The importance of the role of top management can be understood by comparing Figure 17.4 with Figure 17.2. Figure 17.4 shows structural imperatives as contextual factors—within which the organization must operate—that affect the purposes and goals of the organization. The manager's choices for organization structure are affected by the organization's strategy (purposes and goals), the imperatives (contextual factors), and the manager's personal value system and experience.[32] Organizational effectiveness depends on the fit among the size, the technology, the environment, the strategies, and the structure.

Another perspective on the link between strategy and structure is that the relationship may be reciprocal; that is, the structure may be set up to implement the strategy, but the structure may then affect the process of decision making, influencing such matters as the centralization or decentralization of decision making and the formalization of rules and procedures.[33] Thus, strategy determines structure, which in turn affects strategic decision making. A more complex view, suggested by Herman Boschken, is that strategy is a determinant of structure and long-term performance, but only when the subunits doing the planning have the ability to do the planning well.[34]

The relationship between strategic choice and structure is actually more complicated than the concept that "structure follows strategy" conveys. However, this relationship has received less research attention than the idea of structural imperatives. And, of course, some might view strategy simply as another imperative, along with size, technology, and environment. But the strategic-choice view goes beyond the imperative perspective because it is a product of both the analyses of the imperatives and the

GLOBALIZATION

Building Economies, One Phone at a Time

Grace Wachira, a Kenyan clothing maker, used to walk several hours to meet customers. Today, she uses a cell phone to set up appointments before leaving her village. "I'm saving time, I'm saving money," she says. Around the globe, Grace and millions of others are prospering thanks to cellular technology.

Cell phones improve communications and even provide financial services. By purchasing and transferring phone cards, people in remote areas trade airtime and obtain cash. "This turns anyone who has a mobile phone into an ATM machine," says Jan Chipchase, an anthropologist with Nokia.

Mobile communications improve living standards for the world's poor in unexpected ways. "The cell phone is the single most transformative technology for development," says professor Jeffrey Sachs. Telephone kiosks, where users share a phone, are a booming industry and even the smallest villages have at least one kiosk. The phones are used for many purposes, from summoning medical help to accessing agricultural training on the Internet.

To develop products for this market niche, Nokia first sends a team of anthropologists who conduct surveys, meet casually with many individuals, and live in the country for weeks. The scientists report to Nokia designers located in nine global design studios. The designers

> **"The cell phone is the single most transformative technology for development."**
> —ECONOMIST JEFFREY SACHS

tailor a product for a particular market. In India, for example, phones are often shared, so the Nokia 1200 phones feature multiple address books. The 1200s are dust- and heat-proof as well and have a built-in flashlight—handy during power failures.

Nokia's organization structure, with three divisions devoted to markets, devices, and services, supports intense customization. That is a good thing for Nokia because the company is facing very different consumer needs in developed and developing countries. Low levels of centralization and formalization support flexibility and creativity, as does the relatively flat organization hierarchy.

Nokia enjoyed sales increases of 22 percent in 2009, and as the economies of developing countries grow, so should sales of Nokia cell phones and other handheld devices. Africa's gross domestic product is expected to grow by 4.5 percent in 2010, and that is good news for both Nokia and 1 billion people whose median household income is about $1 a day.

References: Sara Corbett, "Can the Cellphone Help End Global Poverty?" *New York Times*, April 13, 2008, www.nytimes.com on April 30, 2010; Nandini Lakshman, "Nokia's Global Design Sense," *Bloomberg Businessweek*, August 10, 2007, www.businessweek.com on April 30, 2010; Jessi Hempel, "Nokia's Design Research for Everyone," *Bloomberg Businessweek*, March 14, 2007, www.businessweek.com on April 30, 2010; Jack Ewing, "Upwardly Mobile in Africa," *Bloomberg Businessweek*, September 24, 2007, www.businessweek.com on April 30, 2010.

organization's strategy. As an example, when Daimler-Benz merged with Chrysler, Daimler CEO Juergen Schrempp claimed it was a merger of equals. Very quickly, however, it became clear that was not accurate as Chrysler became just another division of the German automaker. Mr. Schrempp finally admitted that this was the structure he wanted all along.[35] Within only a few years, Chrysler was sold by Daimler to an investment group, went bankrupt, and was subsequently picked up by Fiat, the Italian automotive giant.[36]

Figure 17.4   **THE STRATEGIC CHOICE APPROACH TO ORGANIZATION DESIGN**

The integration of the structural imperative approach to organization design with the strategic choice approach takes into account the role of the manager, whose perspective on contextual factors and the organization, along with personal preferences, values, and experience, help determine the structure of the organization.

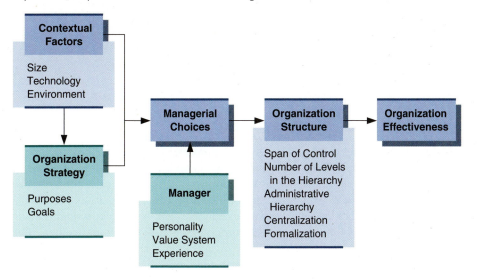

ORGANIZATIONAL DESIGNS

The previous section described several factors that determine how organizations are structured. In this section we present several different organizational designs that have been created to adapt organizations to the many contingency factors they face. We discuss mechanistic and organic structures, the sociotechnical system perspective, Mintzberg's designs, matrix designs, and virtual organizations.

Mechanistic and Organic Designs

As we discussed in the previous section, most organizational scholars believe that organizations need to be able to adapt to changes in the technology of that organization. For example, if the rate of change in technology is slow, the most effective design is bureaucratic or, to use Burns and Stalker's term, "mechanistic." As summarized in Table 17.2, a **mechanistic structure** is primarily hierarchical in nature, interactions and communications are mostly vertical, instructions come from the boss, knowledge is concentrated at the top, and continued membership requires loyalty and obedience.

But if the technology is changing rapidly, the organization needs a structure that allows more flexibility and faster decision making so that it can react quickly to change. This design is called "organic." An **organic structure** resembles a network— interactions and communications are more lateral, knowledge resides wherever it is most useful to the organization, and membership requires a commitment to the tasks of the organization. An organic organization is generally expected to be faster at reacting to changes in the environment.

A **mechanistic structure** is primarily hierarchical; interactions and communications typically are vertical, instructions come from the boss, knowledge is concentrated at the top, and loyalty and obedience are required to sustain membership.

An **organic structure** is set up like a network; interactions and communications are horizontal, knowledge resides wherever it is most useful to the organization, and membership requires a commitment to the organization's tasks.

Table 17.2
MECHANISTIC AND ORGANIC
ORGANIZATION DESIGNS

Characteristic	Mechanistic	Organic
STRUCTURE	Hierarchical	Network based on interests
INTERACTIONS, COMMUNICATION	Primarily vertical	Lateral throughout
WORK DIRECTIONS, INSTRUCTIONS	From supervisor	Through advice, information
KNOWLEDGE, INFORMATION	Concentrated at top	Throughout
MEMBERSHIP, RELATIONSHIP WITH ORGANIZATION	Requires loyalty, obedience	Commitment to task, progress, expansion

Sociotechnical Systems Designs

The foundation of the sociotechnical systems approach to organizing is systems theory, discussed in Chapter 1. There we defined a system as an interrelated set of elements that function as a whole. A system may have numerous subsystems, each of which, like the overall system, includes inputs, transformation processes, outputs, and feedback. An open system is one that interacts with its environment. A complex system is made up of numerous subsystems in which the outputs of some are the inputs to others. The sociotechnical systems approach views the organization as an open system structured to integrate the two important organizational subsystems: the technical (task) subsystem and the social subsystem.

The technical (task) subsystem is the means by which inputs are transformed into outputs. The transformation process may take many forms. In a steel machine shop, it would entail the way steel is formed, cut, drilled, chemically treated, and painted. In an insurance company or financial institution, it would be the way information is processed. Often, significant scientific and engineering expertise is applied to these transformation processes to get the highest productivity at the lowest cost. The transformation process usually is regarded as technologically and economically driven; that is, whatever process is most productive and costs the least is generally the most desirable.

As we saw in our opening vignette, however, a few products—such as Steinway pianos—are built to standards rather than prices. The *Technology* box entitled "A Marriage of Technique and Technology" on page 477 shows how Steinway applies modern time- and labor-saving technology to a transformation process geared toward traditional standards of quality.

The social subsystem includes the interpersonal relationships that develop among people in organizations. Employees learn one another's work habits, strengths, weaknesses, and preferences while developing a sense of mutual trust. The social relationships may be manifested in personal friendships and interest groups. Communication, about both work and employees' common interests, may be enhanced by friendship or hampered by antagonistic relationships. The Hawthorne studies, conducted between 1927 and 1932 at Western Electric's Hawthorne plant near Chicago, were the first serious studies of the social subsystems in organizations.[37]

The sociotechnical systems approach was developed by members of the Tavistock Institute of England as an outgrowth of a study of coal mining. The study concerned new mining techniques that were introduced to increase productivity but failed because they entailed splitting up well-established work groups.[38] The Tavistock researchers concluded that the social subsystem had been sacrificed to the technical subsystem. Thus, improvements in the technical subsystem were not realized because of problems in the social subsystem.

A **system** is an interrelated set of elements that function as a whole.

An **open system** is a system that interacts with its environment.

The **sociotechnical systems approach** to organization design views the organization as an open system structured to integrate the technical and social subsystems into a single management system.

A **technical (task) subsystem** is the means by which inputs are transformed into outputs.

A **social subsystem** includes the interpersonal relationships that develop among people in organizations.

TECHNOLOGY

A Marriage of Technique and Technology

Steinway & Sons was founded by a German cabinet maker and apprentice organ builder named Heinrich Steinweg, who had built his first grand piano in the kitchen of his home in a town called Seesen. He came to America in 1851 and, along with his four sons, worked for various piano makers until 1853, when he founded Steinway & Sons in Manhattan. By 1867, Steinway pianos had won prestigious prizes at such showcases as the New York Industrial Fair and the Universal Exposition in Paris. In 1883, the great composer and piano virtuoso Franz Liszt wrote Heinrich Steinweg (now Henry Steinway) to say that "the new Steinway grand is a glorious masterpiece in power, sonority, singing quality, and perfect harmonic effects, affording delight even to my old piano-weary fingers."

In particular, Liszt was impressed by the Steinway method of fashioning the piano's case, with "the vibrating body being bent into form out of one continuous piece." He also had good things to say about the piano's *scale*—basically, the arrangement of its strings. In 1859, Henry Steinway Jr. had patented a technique for scaling called *overstringing*: instead of running the bass strings parallel to the piano's treble strings, he fanned them diagonally over the trebles to create a second tier of strings. As a result, he was able to improve the instrument's tone by using longer strings with superior vibratory quality.

Another feature developed by Steinway in the mid-nineteenth century made it possible to use strings that were also bigger—and thus louder. If you look under a piano, you will see a cast-iron plate. This component was once made of wood and sometimes fortified by metal braces, but Steinway had made the cast-iron plate a regular feature by the 1840s. The

> *"We're talking about wood here."*
> —ANDREW HORBACHEVSKY, DIRECTOR
> OF MANUFACTURING, STEINWAY & SONS

metal plate, of course, is much stronger and allowed the piano maker to apply much greater tension to the strings; in turn, the ability to increase string tension made it possible to tune the piano to more exacting standards of pitch. (Bear in mind that there are more than 320 wires in a grand piano and that they can exert a tremendous amount of tension—collectively 45,373 pounds' worth in a modern Steinway.) Steinway was the first piano maker to combine the cast-iron plate with the technique of overstringing, and very little has changed in the construction of a grand piano since these and a few other facets of traditional technology were introduced.

This is not to say, however, that you will not find any modern technology in the present Steinway factory. Take, for example, the soundboard, which you can see if you open up a grand piano and look inside. A solid wooden "diaphragm" located between the strings and the metal plate, the *soundboard* is a marvel of deceptively simple design, which vibrates in order to amplify the sound of the strings while withstanding the 1,000 pounds of pressure that they place on it. Because they are constructed by hand, no two soundboards are exactly the same size. In fact, no two cases are the same size, either. "We're talking about wood here," says Andrew Horbachevsky, Steinway's director of manufacturing. "This [case] could be 1/16th [thicker than] that one." The important thing is that the case is fitted—and fitted *precisely*—to a soundboard. "We don't want...a foundation that twists," explains Horbachevsky.

Because the soundboard is measured first and the case then fitted to it, there is only one case for each soundboard. To ensure a satisfactory fit between case and soundboard, the case (as we saw in our opening story) must

Continued

be *frazed*—sawed and planed to specification. Back in 1997, the author of *88 Keys: The Making of a Steinway Piano* was highly skeptical about the possibility of performing the frazing process by machine: "Even the fanciest, well-programmed, computerized, laser-guided, diamond-tipped cutting machine," said Miles Capin, "would have to be instructed by a human as to just how much wood to remove to make a perfect fit between two pieces with as many curvilinear surfaces as a soundboard and a piano rim." Performed by hand, this task took 14 hours, but today it is done in 1½ hours by a CNC (for *computer numerically controlled*) milling machine—a system in which a computerized storage medium issues programmed commands to a variety of specialized tools.

Granted, CNC technology is fairly new at Steinway—the million-dollar milling machine, along with several other pieces of CNC technology, were introduced between 2000 and 2005. Most of Steinway's CNC tools are highly specialized, and the company custom-built several of them. One machine, for example, does nothing but fabricate *action parts*—the

components that make a *hammer* hit one or more strings every time the pianist strikes a key. There are 58 parts involved in every such *action*, and some of them must be made to very tight tolerances—say, 3–4 thousandths of an inch. Once upon a time—and not so long ago—this was all done by hand, but today a special Steinway CNC machine does all the shaping and drilling with the same painstaking attention to detail as artisans working by hand.

Obviously, such technology leads to a lot of labor saving, but Steinway officials are adamant about the role of technology in maintaining Steinway tradition: Some people, says Director of Quality Robert Berger, "think that Steinway is automating to save on labor costs or improve productivity. But these investments are all about quality. We're making a few specific technology investments in areas where we can improve the quality of our product."

References: Steinway & Sons, "Online Factory Tour," www.steinway .com on April 29, 2010; Victor Verney, "88 Keys: The Making of a Steinway Piano," *All About Jazz*, June 18, 2006, www.allaboutjazz .com on April 28, 2010; Public Broadcasting Service, "Note by Note: The Making of Steinway L1037," 2009, www.pbs.org on April 28, 2010; M. Eric Johnson, Joseph Hall, and David Pyke, "Technology and Quality at Steinway & Sons," Tuck School of Business at Dartmouth, May 13, 2005, http://mba.tuck.dartmouth.edu on May 2, 2010.

The Tavistock group proposed that an organization's technical and social subsystems could be integrated through autonomous work groups. The aim of **autonomous work groups** is to make technical and social subsystems work together for the benefit of the larger system. These groups are developed using concepts of task design—particularly job enrichment—and ideas about group interaction, supervision, and other characteristics of organization design. To structure the task, authority, and reporting relationships around work groups, organizations should delegate to the groups themselves decisions regarding job assignments, training, inspection, rewards, and punishments. Management is responsible for coordinating the groups according to the demands of the work and task environment. Autonomous work groups often evolve into self-managing teams, as was discussed in Chapter 10.

Organizations in turbulent environments tend to rely less on hierarchy and more on the coordination of work among autonomous work groups. Sociotechnical systems theory asserts that the role of management is twofold: to monitor the environmental factors that impinge on the internal operations of the organization and to coordinate the social and technical subsystems. Although the sociotechnical systems approach has not been thoroughly tested, it has been tried with some success in the General Foods plant in Topeka, Kansas; the Saab-Scania project in Sweden; and the Volvo plant in Kalmar, Sweden.[39] The development of the sociotechnical systems approach is significant in its departure from the universal approaches to organization design and in its emphasis on jointly harnessing the technical and human subsystems. The popular

Autonomous work groups are used to integrate an organization's technical and social subsystems for the benefit of the larger system.

movements in management today include many of the principles of the sociotechnical systems design approach. The development of cross-functional teams to generate and design new products and services is a good example (see Chapter 10).

Mintzberg's Designs

In this section we describe five specific organization designs proposed by Henry Mintzberg. The universe of possible designs is large, but fortunately we can divide designs into a few basic forms. Mintzberg proposed that the purpose of organizational design was to coordinate activities, and he suggested a range of coordinating mechanisms that are found in operating organizations.[40] In Mintzberg's view, organization structure reflects how tasks are divided and then coordinated. He described five major ways in which tasks are coordinated: by mutual adjustment, by direct supervision, and by standardization of worker (or input) skills, work processes, or outputs (see Figure 17.5). These five methods can exist side by side within an organization.

Coordination by mutual adjustment (1 in Figure 17.5) simply means that workers use informal communication to coordinate with one another, whereas *coordination by direct supervision* (2 in Figure 17.5) means that a manager or supervisor coordinates the actions of workers. As noted, *standardization* may be used as a coordination

$\mathcal{Figure}$ *17.5* **MINTZBERG'S FIVE COORDINATING MECHANISMS**

Mintzberg described five methods of coordinating the actions of organizational participants. The dashed lines in each diagram show the five different means of coordination: (1) mutual adjustment, (2) direct supervision, and standardization of (3) input skills, (4) work processes, and (5) outputs.

Reference: Henry Mintzberg, The Structuring of Organizations: A Synthesis of the Research, © 1979, p. 4. Reprinted by permission of Prentice Hall, Inc., Upper Saddle River, NJ.

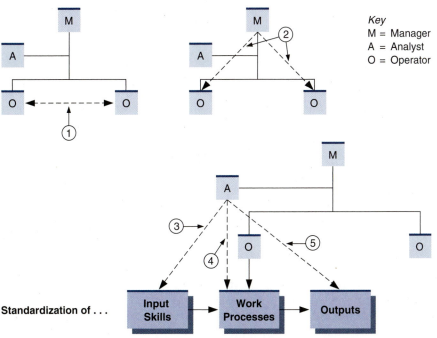

mechanism in three different ways: (1) We can standardize the *input skills* (3 in Figure 17.5)—that is, standardize the worker skills that are inputs to the work process; (2) we can standardize the *work processes* themselves (4 in Figure 17.5)—that is, standardize the methods workers use to transform inputs into outputs; and (3) we can standardize the *outputs* (5 in Figure 17.5)—that is, standardize the products or services or the performance levels expected of workers. Standardization usually is developed by staff analysts and enforced by management such that skills, processes, and output meet predetermined standards.

Mintzberg further suggested that the five coordinating mechanisms roughly correspond to stages of organizational development and complexity. In the very small organization, individuals working together communicate informally, achieving coordination by mutual adjustment. As more people join the organization, coordination needs become more complex, and direct supervision is added. For example, two or three people working in a small fast-food business can coordinate the work simply by talking to each other about the incoming orders for hamburgers, fries, and drinks. However, direct supervision becomes necessary in a larger restaurant with more complex cooking and warming equipment and several shifts of workers.

In large organizations, standardization is added to mutual adjustment and direct supervision to coordinate the work. The type of standardization depends on the nature of the work situation—that is, the organization's technology and environment. Standardization of work processes may achieve the necessary coordination when the organization's tasks are fairly routine. Thus, the larger fast-food outlet may standardize the making of hamburger patties: the meat is weighed, put into a hamburger press, and compressed into a patty. McDonald's is well known for this type of standardized process. Analysis of the success of McDonald's shows that some part of its success is due to the degree of standardization.

In other complex situations, standardization of the output may allow employees to do the work in any appropriate manner as long as the output meets specifications. Thus, the cook may not care how the hamburger is pressed, only being concerned that the right amount of meat is used and that the patty is the correct diameter and thickness. In other words, the worker may use any process as long as the output is a standard burger.

A third possibility is to coordinate work by standardizing worker skills. This approach is most often adopted in situations in which processes and outputs are difficult to standardize. In a hospital, for example, each patient must be treated as a special situation; the hospital process and output therefore cannot be standardized. Similar diagnostic and treatment procedures may be used with more than one patient, but the hospital relies on the skills of the physicians and nurses (which are standardized through their professional training) to coordinate the work. Organizations may have to depend on workers' mutual adjustment to coordinate their own actions in the most complex work situations or when the most important elements of coordination are the workers' professional training and communication skills. In effect, mutual adjustment can be an appropriate coordinating mechanism in both the simplest and the most complex situations.

Mintzberg pointed out that the five methods of coordination could be combined with the basic components of structure to develop five structural forms: the simple structure, the machine bureaucracy, the professional bureaucracy, the divisionalized form, and the adhocracy. Mintzberg called these structures pure or ideal types of designs.

Simple Structure   The simple structure characterizes relatively small, usually young organizations in a simple, dynamic environment. The organization has little specialization and formalization, and its overall structure is organic. Power and decision making are concentrated in the chief executive, often also the owner-manager, and the

The **simple structure**, typical of relatively small or new organizations, has little specialization or formalization; power and decision making are concentrated in the chief executive.

flow of authority is from the top down. The primary coordinating mechanism is direct supervision. The organization must adapt quickly to survive because of its dynamic and often hostile environment. Most small businesses—a car dealership, a locally owned retail clothing store, or a candy manufacturer with only regional distribution—have a simple structure.

Machine Bureaucracy   The **machine bureaucracy** is typical of large, well-established companies in simple, stable environments. Work is highly specialized and formalized, and decision making is usually concentrated at the top. Standardization of work processes is the primary coordinating mechanism. This highly bureaucratic structure does not have to adapt quickly to changes because the environment is both simple and stable. Examples include large mass-production firms such as Container Corporation of America, large meatpacking companies, and providers of services to mass markets, such as insurance companies.

GREG SMITH/CORBIS

Here Tyson Foods employees are processing chickens as they move along the assembly line. Coordination is achieved by standardizing the work processes and employees do the same things to every chicken along the line. Tyson Foods Inc. would most likely be characterized as a machine bureaucracy because work is highly specialized and formalized and decision making is most likely centralized.

Professional Bureaucracy   Usually found in a complex and stable environment, the **professional bureaucracy** relies on standardization of skills as the primary means of coordination. There is much horizontal specialization by professional areas of expertise but little formalization. Decision making is decentralized and takes place where the expertise is. The only means of coordination available to the organization is standardization of skills—those of the professionally trained employees.

Although it lacks centralization, the professional bureaucracy stabilizes and controls its tasks with rules and procedures developed in the relevant profession. Hospitals, universities, and consulting firms are examples.

Divisionalized Form   The **divisionalized form** is characteristic of old, very large firms operating in a relatively simple, stable environment with several diverse markets. It resembles the machine bureaucracy except that it is divided according to the various markets it serves. There is some horizontal and vertical specialization between the divisions (each defined by a market) and headquarters. Decision making is clearly split between headquarters and the divisions, and the primary means of coordination is standardization of outputs. The mechanism of control required by headquarters encourages the development of machine bureaucracies in the divisions.

The classic example of the divisionalized form is General Motors, which, in a reorganization during the 1920s, adopted a design that created divisions for each major car model.[41] Although the divisions have been reorganized and the cars changed several times, the concept of the divisionalized organization is still very evident at GM.[42] General Electric uses a two-tiered divisionalized structure, dividing its numerous businesses into strategic business units, which are then further divided into sectors.[43]

Adhocracy   The **adhocracy** is typically found in young organizations engaged in highly technical fields in which the environment is complex and dynamic. Decision making is spread throughout the organization, and power is in the hands of experts. There is horizontal and vertical specialization but little formalization, resulting in a

In a **machine bureaucracy**, which typifies large, well-established organizations, work is highly specialized and formalized, and decision making is usually concentrated at the top.

A **professional bureaucracy** is characterized by horizontal specialization by professional areas of expertise, little formalization, and decentralized decision making.

The **divisionalized form**, typical of old, very large organizations, is divided according to the different markets served; horizontal and vertical specialization exists between divisions and headquarters, decision making is divided between headquarters and divisions, and outputs are standardized.

In an **adhocracy**, typically found in young organizations in highly technical fields, decision making is spread throughout the organization, power resides with the experts, horizontal and vertical specialization exists, and there is little formalization.

very organic structure. Coordination is by mutual adjustment through frequent personal communication and liaison. Specialists are not grouped together in functional units but are instead deployed into specialized market-oriented project teams.

The typical adhocracy is usually established to foster innovation, something to which the other four types of structures are not particularly well suited. Numerous U.S. organizations— Whole Foods, W.L. Gore, and Google, for example—are known for their innovation and constant stream of new products.[44] These companies have minimal hierarchies, are built around teams, and are known as some of the most innovative companies in the world.

Mintzberg believed that fit among parts is the most important consideration in designing an organization. Not only must there be a fit among the structure, the structural imperatives (technology, size, and environment), and organizational strategy, but the components of structure (rules and procedures, decision making, specialization) must also fit together and be appropriate for the situation. Mintzberg suggested that an organization could not function effectively when these characteristics are not put together properly.[45]

Matrix Organization Design

One other organizational form deserves attention here: the matrix organization design. Matrix design is consistent with the contingency approach because it is useful only in certain situations. One of the earliest implementations of the matrix design was at TRW Systems Group in 1959.[46] Following TRW's lead, other firms in aerospace and high-technology fields created similar matrix structures.

The **matrix design** attempts to combine two different designs to gain the benefits of each. The most common matrix form superimposes product or project departmentalization on a functional structure (see Figure 17.6). Each department and project has a manager; each employee, however, is a member of both a functional department and a project team. The dual role means that the employee has two supervisors, the department manager and the project leader.

A matrix structure is appropriate when three conditions exist:

1. There is external pressure for a dual focus, meaning that factors in the environment require the organization to focus its efforts equally on responding to multiple external factors and on internal operations.

2. There is pressure for a high information-processing capacity.

3. There is pressure for shared resources.[47]

In the aerospace industry in the early 1960s, all these conditions were present. Private companies had a dual focus: their customers, primarily the federal government, and the complex engineering and technical fields in which they were engaged. Moreover, the environments of these companies were changing very rapidly. Technological sophistication and competition were increasing, resulting in growing environmental uncertainty and an added need for information processing. The final condition stemmed from the pressure on the companies to excel in a very competitive environment despite limited resources. The companies concluded that it was inefficient to assign their highly professional—and highly compensated—scientific and engineering personnel to just one project at a time.

Built into the matrix structure is the capacity for flexible and coordinated responses to internal and external pressures. Members can be reassigned from one project to another as demands for their skills change. They may work for a month on one project, be assigned to the functional home department for two weeks, and then

The **matrix design** combines two different designs to gain the benefits of each; typically combined are a product or project departmentalization scheme and a functional structure.

Figure 17.6 A MATRIX ORGANIZATION DESIGN

A matrix organization design superimposes two different types of departmentalization onto each other—for example, a functional structure and a project structure.

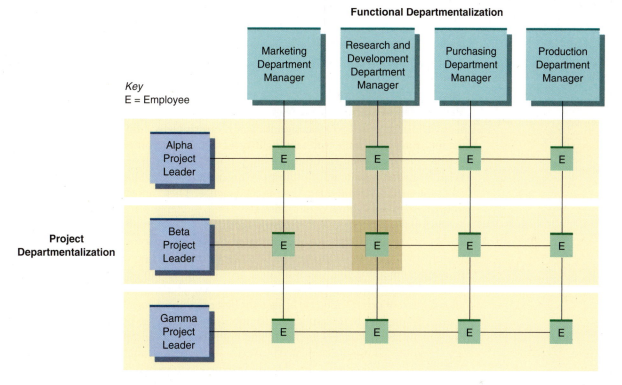

be reassigned to another project for the next six months. The matrix form improves project coordination by assigning project responsibility to a single leader rather than dividing it among several functional department heads. Furthermore, it improves communication because employees can talk about the project with members of both the project team and the functional unit to which they belong. In this way, solutions to project problems may emerge from either group. Many different types of organizations have used the matrix form of organization, notably large-project manufacturing firms, banks, and hospitals.[48]

The matrix organizational form thus provides several benefits for the organization. It is not, however, trouble-free. Typical problems include the following:

1. The dual reporting system may cause role conflict among employees.

2. Power struggles may occur over who has authority on which issues.

3. Matrix organization often is misinterpreted to mean that a group must make all decisions; as a result, group decision-making techniques may be used when they are not appropriate.

4. If the design involves several matrices, each laid on top of another, there may be no way to trace accountability and authority.[49]

Only under the three conditions listed earlier is the matrix design likely to work. In any case, it is a complex organizational system that must be carefully coordinated and managed to be effective.

Virtual Organizations

There are multiple meanings for the term "virtual organizations." The earliest usage, which we call the **virtual organization**, meant a relatively temporary alliance or network created by two or more organizations who agree to work together to complete a specific venture. A second usage of the term, which we call the **virtual company**, has come to refer any organization where everyone telecommutes to work from different places rather than go to work at a central office space. This allows workers to work from a coffee shop, from home, from a park somewhere, or a different country, yet stay in touch with coworkers via electronic telecommunications technology. In this section we describe the organizational issues involved in both types of virtual organizations, starting with the earlier usage.

Virtual Organizations as Networks   Some companies do one or two things very well, such as sell to government clients, but struggle with most others, such as manufacturing products with very tight precision. Other companies might be great at close-tolerance manufacturing but lousy at reaching out to certain types of clients. What is needed is some way for those two organizations to get together to utilize each other's strengths, yet still retain their independence. They can, and many are doing so in what are called "virtual organizations."

A virtual organization in this sense is a relatively temporary alliance or network created by two or more organizations who agree to work together to accomplish a specific venture. Each partner contributes to the partnership what it does best. The opportunity is usually something that needs a quick response to maximize the market opportunity. A slow response will probably result in losses. Therefore, a virtual organization allows different organizations to bring their best capabilities together without worrying about learning how to do something that they have never done before. Thus, the reaction time is faster, mistakes are fewer, and profits are quicker. Sharing of information among partners is usually facilitated by electronic technology such as computers, faxes, and electronic mail systems, thereby avoiding the expenses of renting new office space for the venture or costly travel time between companies.

There are no restrictions on how large or small organizations or projects need to be to take advantage of this type of alliance. In fact, some very small organizations are working together quite well. In Phoenix, Arizona, a public relations firm, a graphic design firm, and a management consulting firm are working together on projects that have multiple requirements beyond those offered by any single firm. Rather than turn down the business or try to hire additional staff to do the extra work, the three firms work together to better serve client needs. The clients like the arrangement because they get high-quality work and do not have to shop around for someone to do little pieces of work. The networking companies feel that the result is better creativity, more teamwork, more efficient use of resources, and better service for their clients.

More typically, however, large companies create virtual organizations. Corning is involved in nineteen partnerships on many different types of projects, and it is pleased with most of its ventures and plans to do more. Intel worked with two Japanese organizations to manufacture flash memory chips for computers. One of the Japanese companies was not able to complete its part of the project, leaving Intel with a major product-delivery problem. Intel's chairman at the time, Andrew Grove, was not too happy about that venture.[50]

The virtual organization is not just another management fad. It has become one way to deal with the rapid changes brought about by evolving technology and global competition. Management scholars have mixed opinions on the effectiveness of such arrangements. Although it may seem odd, this approach can produce substantial benefits in some situations.

A **virtual organization** is a temporary alliance formed by two or more organizations to pursue a specific venture or to exploit a specific opportunity.

The **virtual company** is an organization that allows employees the freedom to do their work anywhere they want or can, relaxing the requirement that employees go to the same location every day.

The Virtual Company as Telecommuters with No Office

In this alternate use of the term, the virtual company is an organization that allows employees the freedom to do their work anywhere they want or can, relaxing the requirement that employees go to the same location every day. With social networking tools, many different types of group/team software, instant messaging, videoconferencing and teleconferencing, cloud computing, as well as the standard email, it has become very common for employees to not have to go to "the office" every day to complete their work. Many companies allow individual employees in certain types of jobs to work from home one or a few days per week, requiring them to be at the office the other days. However, the fullest extension of this model is one where there is no office and all employees work from home. Many knowledge workers, such as designers, writers, professors who teach online, software developers, and numerous others have the capability of working this way.

The Star Alliance is an alliance, or a virtual organization, of 28 commercial airlines serving 1,172 airports in 181 countries. The airlines remain separate but cooperate in ticketing and reservations through a code-sharing system. As a result, all airlines increase their access to passengers and fly closer to capacity, thereby saving money and providing better services.

The company considering becoming a virtual company needs to examine many issues. Other than the obvious reductions in the cost of office space, reduced utilities, and reduced computer/server costs, the company needs to consider the culture of the organization, the role of collaboration (which may be a necessary part of what makes the company and its products/services unique and have value), and the type of employees and their relationships with each other. Managers often have difficulty giving up the sense of control they may have by being able to visually observe their employees at work.

One interesting example of the fully virtual company is the editorial staff of *Inc.* magazine, which did an experiment in which the editorial staff and writers did not go to the office for an entire month, doing their work from home, coffee shops, and other non-office places.[51] A summary of what they learned in shown in Table 17.3. The virtual company may be the wave of the future as communication technologies improve, fuel costs go higher, and concern for the environment becomes more intense. There is no clear mandate that all companies can or should "go virtual." The benefits, however, could be great for some companies.

CONTEMPORARY ORGANIZATION DESIGN PROCESSES

The current proliferation of design theories and alternative forms of organization gives practicing managers a dizzying array of choices. The task of the manager or organization designer is to examine the entity and its situation and to design a form of organization that meets its needs. A partial list of contemporary alternatives includes such approaches as downsizing, rightsizing, reengineering the organization, team-based organizations, and the virtual organization. These approaches often make use of total quality management, employee empowerment, employee involvement and participation, reduction in force, process innovation, and networks of alliances. Practicing managers must deal with the new terminology, the temptation to treat such new approaches as fads, and their own organizational situation before making

Table 17.3
LESSONS LEARNED FROM A MONTH AS A VIRTUAL COMPANY

For the Company
• Lower costs for office space and utilities.
• Company may have increased cost for computer equipment, software, and video/tele conferencing, but employees may already have the basics at home.
• Company may save on costs of telephone switching, servers, and expensive enterprise-software licensing.
• Potential loss of culture and standard ways of doing things.
• May be an asset in recruiting efforts.
• Loss of positive benefits of collaboration, depending on the nature of the project.

For Employees
• Save the costs of commuting, time, fuel, bus/train fares, eating out for lunch, and laundry.
• Can be at home for important family time and events, birthdays, and piano practice.
• Work-life balance has to be readjusted.
• Some forgot to eat lunch, while others ate all the time.
• May work more hours (no commuting) and no defined "leave the office and work at 6 P.M." rule.
• Must set up rules for when is family time and when is work time.
• May have to upgrade the office chair for better ergonomics.
• Loss of face-to-face relationships.
• Workers can stay focused for longer periods with fewer interruptions.
• Loss of stimulation created by collaborative work.

Source: Max Chafkin, "The Case, and the Plan, for the Virtual Company," *Inc.com*, April 1, 2010, accessed online April 25, 2010 at http://www.inc.com/magazine/20100401/the-case-and-the-plan-for-the-virtual-company.html.

major organization design shifts. In this section we describe two currently popular approaches—reengineering and rethinking the organization—as well as global organization structure and design issues. We conclude with a summary of the dominant themes in contemporary organization design.

Reengineering the Organization

Reengineering is the radical redesign of organizational processes to achieve major gains in cost, time, and provision of services. It forces the organization to start from scratch to redesign itself around its most important, or core, processes rather than beginning with its current form and making incremental changes. It assumes that if a company had no existing structure, departments, jobs, rules, or established ways of doing things, reengineering would design the organization as it should be for future success. The process starts with determining what the customers actually want from the organization and then developing a strategy to provide it. Once the strategy is in place, strong leadership from top management creates teams of people to design an organizational system to achieve the strategy.[52] The aim of reengineering is to fundamentally change the way everybody in the organization conceives his or her role. Rather than view their role as a position in a hierarchy, reengineering creates a horizontal flow of teams that focus on core processes that deliver the product or service. Throughout a decade of reengineering, the forces of change have been intensified by information technology—the Internet—that has accelerated all of these processes. This has led to what some have called "X-engineering," which takes these same reengineering processes across organizational boundaries, searching for new efficiencies from suppliers to distributors.[53]

Reengineering is the radical redesign of organizational processes to achieve major gains in cost, time, and provision of services.

Rethinking the Organization

Also currently popular is the concept of rethinking the organization. **Rethinking** the organization is also a process for restructuring that throws out traditional assumptions that organizations should be structured with boxes and horizontal and vertical lines. Robert Tomasko makes some suggestions for new organizational forms for the future.[54] He suggests that the traditional pyramid shape of organizations may be inappropriate for current business practices. Traditional structures, he contends, may have too many levels of management arranged in a hierarchy to be efficient and to respond to dynamic changes in the environment.

Rethinking organizations might entail thinking of the organization structure as a dome rather than a pyramid, the dome being top management, which acts as an umbrella, covering and protecting those underneath but also leaving them alone to do their work. Internal units underneath the dome would have the flexibility to interact with each other and with environmental forces. Companies such as Microsoft Corporation and Royal Dutch Petroleum have some of the characteristics of this dome approach to organization design. American Express Financial Advisors restructured from a vertical organization into a horizontal organization as a result of its rethinking everything about the ways it needed to meet customers' needs.[55]

Global Organization Structure and Design Issues

Managers working in an international environment must consider not only similarities and differences among firms in different cultures but also the structural features of multinational organizations.

Between-Culture Issues   "Between-culture issues" are variations in the structure and design of companies operating in different cultures. As might be expected, such companies have both differences and similarities. For example, one study compared the structures of fifty-five U.S. and fifty-one Japanese manufacturing plants. Results suggested that the Japanese plants had less specialization, more "formal" centralization (but less "real" centralization), and taller hierarchies than their U.S. counterparts. The Japanese structures were also less affected by their technology than the U.S. plants.[56]

Many cultures still take a traditional view of organization structure not unlike the approaches used in this country during the days of classical organization theory. For example, Tom Peters, a leading U.S. management consultant and coauthor of *In Search of Excellence,* spent some time lecturing to managers in China. They were not interested in his ideas about decentralization and worker participation, however. Instead, the most frequently asked question concerned how a manager determined the optimal span of control.[57] However, managers in global companies may have to understand the differential interaction patterns among employees in different countries and not draw the wrong conclusions from culturally based interactions.[58]

In contrast, many European companies are increasingly patterning themselves after successful U.S. firms, a move stemming in part from corporate raiders in Europe emulating their U.S. counterparts and partly from the managerial workforce becoming better educated. Together, these two factors have caused many European firms to become less centralized and to adopt divisional structures by moving from functional to product departmentalization.[59]

Multinational Organization   More and more firms have entered the international arena and have found it necessary to adapt their designs to better cope with different cultures.[60] For example, after a company has achieved a moderate level of

Rethinking the organization means looking at organization design in totally different ways, perhaps even abandoning the classic view of the organization as a pyramid.

international activity, it often establishes an international division, usually at the same organizational level as other major functional divisions. Levi-Strauss uses this organization design. One division, Levi-Strauss International, is responsible for the company's business activities in Europe, Canada, Latin America, and Asia.

For an organization that has become more deeply involved in international activities, a logical form of organization design is the international matrix. This type of matrix arrays product managers across the top. Project teams headed by foreign-market managers cut across the product departments. A company with three basic product lines, for example, might establish three product departments (of course, it would include domestic advertising, finance, and operations departments as well). Foreign-market managers can be designated for, say, Canada, Japan, Europe, Latin America, and Australia. Each foreign-market manager is then responsible for all three of the company's products in his or her market.[61]

Finally, at the most advanced level of multinational activity, a firm might become an international conglomerate. Nestlé and Unilever N.V. fit this type. Each has an international headquarters (Nestlé in Vevey, Switzerland, and Unilever in Rotterdam, the Netherlands) that coordinates the activities of businesses scattered around the globe. Nestlé has factories in fifty countries and markets its products in virtually every country in the world. Over 96 percent of its business is done outside of Switzerland, and only about 7,000 of its 160,000 employees reside in its home country.

Dominant Themes of Contemporary Designs

The four dominant themes of current design strategies are (1) the effects of technological and environmental change, (2) the importance of people, (3) the necessity of staying in touch with the customer, and (4) the global organization. Technology and the environment are changing so fast and in so many unpredictable ways that no organization structure will be appropriate for long. The changes in electronic information processing, transmission, and retrieval alone are so vast that employee relationships, information distribution, and task coordination need to be reviewed almost daily.[62] The emphasis on productivity through people that was energized by Thomas Peters and Robert Waterman Jr. in the 1980s continues in almost every aspect of contemporary organization design.[63] In addition, Peters and Nancy Austin further emphasized the importance of staying in touch with customers at the initial stage in organization design.[64] Superimposed over these four dominant themes are the rapid changes in technology, competition, and globalization. Organizations must be adaptive to new circumstances in order to survive.[65]

These popular contemporary approaches and the four dominant factors argue for a contingency design perspective. Unfortunately, there is no "one best way." Managers must consider the impact of multiple factors—sociotechnical systems, strategy, the structural imperatives, changing information technology, people, global considerations, and a concern for end users—on their particular organization, and then design the organization structure accordingly.

SYNOPSIS

Universal approaches to organization design attempt to specify the one best way to structure organizations for effectiveness. Contingency approaches, on the other hand, propose that the best way to design organization structure depends on a variety of factors. Important contingency approaches to organization design center on the organizational strategy, the determinants of structure, and strategic choice.

Initially, strategy was seen as the determinant of structure: the structure of the organization was designed to implement its purpose, goals, and strategies. Taking managerial choice into account in determining organization structure is a modification of this view. The manager designs the structure to accomplish organizational goals, guided by an analysis of the contextual factors, the strategies of the organization, and personal preferences.

The structural imperatives are size, technology, and environment. In general, large organizations have more complex structures and usually more than one technology. The structures of small organizations, on the other hand, may be dominated by one core operations technology. The structure of the organization is also established to fit with the environmental demands and buffer the core operating technology from environmental changes and uncertainties.

Organization designs can take many forms. A mechanistic structure relies on the administrative hierarchy for communication and directing activities. An organic design is structured like a network; communications and interactions are horizontal and diagonal across groups and teams throughout the organization.

In the sociotechnical systems view, the organization is an open system structured to integrate two important subsystems: the technical (task) subsystem and the social subsystem. According to this approach, organizations should structure the task, authority, and reporting relationships around the work group, delegating to the group decisions on job assignments, training, inspection, rewards, and punishments. The task of management is to monitor the environment and coordinate the structures, rules, and procedures.

Mintzberg's ideal types of organization design were derived from a framework of coordinating mechanisms. The five types are simple structure, machine bureaucracy, professional bureaucracy, divisionalized form, and adhocracy. Most organizations have some characteristics of each type, but one is likely to predominate. Mintzberg believed that the most important consideration in designing an organization is the fit among parts of the organization.

The matrix design combines two types of structure (usually functional and project departmentalization) to gain the benefits of each. It usually results in a multiple command and authority system. Benefits of the matrix form include increased flexibility, cooperation, and communication and better use of skilled personnel. Typical problems are associated with the dual reporting system and the complex management system needed to coordinate work.

Virtual organizations are temporary alliances between several organizations that agree to work together on a specific venture. Reaction time to business opportunities can be very fast with these types of alliances. In effect, organizations create a network of other organizations to enable them to respond to changes in the environment. A virtual company is an organization that allows employees the freedom to do their work anywhere they want or can, relaxing the requirement that employees go to the same location everyday.

Contemporary organization design is contingency oriented. Currently popular design strategies are reengineering the organization and rethinking the organization. Four factors influencing design decisions are the changing technological environment, concern for people as valued resources, the need to keep in touch with customers, and global impacts on organizations.

DISCUSSION QUESTIONS

1. What are the differences between universal approaches and contingency approaches to organization design?
2. Define "organizational environment" and "organizational technology." In what ways do these concepts overlap?
3. Identify and describe some of the environmental and technological factors that affect your college or university. Give specific examples of how they affect you as a student.
4. How does organization design usually differ for large and small organizations?
5. What might be the advantages and disadvantages of structuring the faculty members at your college or university as an autonomous work group?
6. What do you think are the purposes, goals, and strategies of your college or university? How are they reflected in its structure?
7. Which of Mintzberg's pure forms is best illustrated by a major national political party (Democratic or

Republican)? A religious organization? A football team? The U.S. Olympic Committee?

8. In a matrix organization, would you rather be a project leader, a functional department head, or a highly trained technical specialist? Why?

9. Discuss what you think the important design considerations will be for organization designers in the year 2020.

10. How would your college or university be different if you rethought or reengineered the way in which it is designed?

ORGANIZATIONAL BEHAVIOR CASE FOR DISCUSSION

CODESHARING THE WEALTH

Put yourself in the role of a businessperson in New York who needs to fly to Hong Kong. Logging on to Orbitz, you find that American Airlines offers a nonstop round-trip flight for $2,692. That is a lot of money, you say to yourself, but after all, it is a long way to go. Besides, Orbitz recommends that you "Act fast! Only 1 ticket left at this price!" So you buy your ticket online and arrive on your departure date at the American Airlines ticket desk, only to be referred to the Cathay Pacific Airways counter. Your flight, the ticket agent informs you, is actually operated by Cathay, and as if to chide you for ignoring a bargain that you have made with the devil, she points to the four-digit "codeshare number" on your ticket. Bewildered but fairly confident that you are still booked on a flight to Hong Kong, you hustle to the Cathay counter, where your ticket is in fact processed. Settled into your seat a few hours later, you decide to get on your laptop and see if you can figure out why you were confused. Going back to Orbitz, you find that, like American, Cathay does indeed offer a nonstop round-trip flight to and from its home city of Hong Kong—for $1,738. It dawns on you that if you had bought your ticket directly from Cathay, you would be sitting in the same seat on the same airplane for $954 less.

If this scenario sounds confusing, that is because, even to veteran flyers, it is. What is confusing about it is the practice of *codesharing*. American Airlines (AMR) once attempted to define the term as

> *an interline partnership where one carrier markets service and places its code on another carrier's flights. This offers carriers an opportunity to provide service to destinations not in their route structure. These schedules are considered online bookings for most situations. An exception could*

be the minimum connecting time, which is sometimes equal to the off-line connection time.

To put it more simply, codesharing works like this: You buy a ticket from Airline A for a flight operated by Airline B on a route that Airline A does not otherwise serve. This practice is possible if both airlines, like AMR and Cathay, belong to the same *airline alliance* (in this case, Oneworld).

On the surface, the advantages to the airlines may seem mostly a matter of perception: an airline seems to be serving given markets that it does not actually serve and flying given routes more frequently than it actually does. The networks formed by codesharing agreements, however, are real, and the breadth of an airline's network is a real factor in attracting high-margin corporate travelers. AMR is not new to such agreements, having joined with Australia's Qantas Airways back in 1990 to service a number of cities in both home countries. The spread of the practice has since led to the formation of much larger "alliances" of carriers who cooperate on a substantial level, including codesharing and shared frequent-flyer programs. The three largest airline alliances are the Star Alliance, which includes United Airlines, US Airways, Air Canada, Air China, and Scandinavian Airlines; SkyTeam, which includes Delta, Airfrance, Alitalia, and Dutch-based KLM; and Oneworld, which includes AMR, Cathay, Qantas, British Airways, and Japan's JAL.

An airline alliance is a good example of a *virtual organization*—a temporary alliance formed by two or more organizations to pursue a specific venture or to exploit a specific opportunity. Although each member remains an independently owned and managed organization, alliance members can save money by sharing sales, maintenance,

> *"American helped originate the whole idea of alliances and partnerships. If somebody should be good at it, you could make the argument they should be."*
> —INVESTMENT ANALYST GEORGE VAN HORN

and operational facilities and operational staff (such as check-in, boarding, and other on-the-ground personnel), and they can also cut costs on purchases and investments by negotiating volume discounts. The chief advantages, however, are breadth of service and geographical reach—in short, size (both perceived and real). Star Alliance, for example, operates 21,200 daily flights to 1,172 airports in 181 countries. According to the most recent annual figures, its members carried 627.52 million passengers for a total of more than a trillion *revenue passenger kilometers* (1 *rpk* means that 1 paying passenger was flown 1 kilometer). Based on *rpk* (which is really a measure of sales volume), Star commands 28 percent of global market share in the airline industry—greater than the combined market share of all airlines that don't belong to any of the three major alliances.

Note that our definition of a *virtual organization* indicates a "*temporary* alliance," and shifts by members of airline alliances are not unheard of. In January 2009, for example, a few months after merger talks had broken down with United Airlines, Continental Airlines, a member of SkyTeam since 2004, announced that it was joining United in the Star Alliance. According to one analyst, the move, which took effect in October 2009, "was obviously a precursor to a full-blown merger," and, sure enough, Continental and United announced in May 2010 that they had ironed out the wrinkles in their merger agreement and would join to become the largest U.S. airline by the end of the year. The new airline would remain a member of the Star Alliance.

The merger was particularly bad news for both AMR, a member of Oneworld and the country's largest stand-alone airline, and US Airways Group, a member of SkyTeam and the sixth-largest U.S. carrier. With the merger of Continental and United, says Vaughn Cordle, chief analyst at Airline Forecasts and a specialist in industry investment research, "the odds of … bankruptcy for US Airways and American increase because it will be too difficult, if not impossible, for them to remain viable as stand-alone businesses. … [W]ithout a new strategic direction and significant changes in the industry's structure," Cordle predicts, AMR and US Airways "will continue on the slow … path to failure."

Cordle recommends consolidation, and many analysts say that AMR management had been considering the possibilities even before the Continental-United merger. The best strategy, adds George Van Horn, an analyst at the research firm IBISWorld, need not be a merger but could involve some kind of looser alliance. Who are the likely partners if AMR decides to consolidate? John Kasarda, an aviation expert at the University of North Carolina's Kenan-Flagler Business School,

thinks that an AMR-US Airways merger is not out of the question: "It would be more out of necessity," he admits, but both airlines have been "asleep at the switch" and can expect their respective shareholders to demand some kind of action. A merger, however, would require US Airways to leave the Star Alliance, and US Airways says that "we highly value our membership in Star and maintain that it's the strongest alliance." Another candidate is JetBlue, which is already working with AMR on a passenger-sharing agreement. "We are open to having that conversation," said a JetBlue spokesperson, "but we have no specific plans at this moment."

In any case, observers agree that AMR needs to make some kind of strategic move. Once the world's largest airline, it is now number 3, behind the new Continental-United and Delta Airlines. Among U.S. airlines, AMR has the lowest margins and highest costs, and as of this writing, it is also the only U.S. airline likely to lose money in 2010. IBISWorld's Van Horn points out, however, that AMR has considerable experience at the kind of deal making in question: American, he reminds potential investors, "helped originate the whole idea of alliances and partnerships. If somebody should be good at it, you could make the argument they should be."

CASE QUESTIONS

1. Have you ever been on a flight that involved a *codesharing* arrangement? Did you notice then—or do you realize now—that there were advantages to the practice of codesharing? Based on what you know about airline travel, list a few of the possible advantages of codesharing for passengers.
2. In what ways might the *divisionalized forms* of most airlines lend themselves to the requirements of alliance membership? In what ways might they be compatible with the organizational needs of the alliances themselves?
3. In what ways does an airline alliance reflect each of the four dominant themes of current design strategy?
4. According to one industry analyst, "in a scale business … size does matter." What does he mean by "a scale business"? Why is the airline industry "a scale business"? Once you've thought about these two questions, how would you describe the "specific opportunity" which, as *virtual organizations*, airline alliances are designed to exploit?

REFERENCES

"Orbitz: Flights," *Orbitz.com*, May 3, 2010, www.orbitz.com on May 3, 2010; David Grossman, "The Anomalies of Code Share," *USA Today*, June 23, 2006, www.usatoday.com on May 3, 2010; "What the Heck Is a Codeshare, Anyway?" *ABC News*, June 21, 2005, http://abcnews.go.com on May 3, 2010; Star Alliance, "Facts and Figures," December 2009, www.staralliance.com on May 4, 2010; Ben Mutzabaugh, "Continental: SkyTeam Membership Ends Oct. 24," *USA Today*, January 30, 2009, http://blogs.usatoday.com on May 4, 2010; "Weighing United-Continental Merger's Impact on US Air-ways," *Charlotte* (North Carolina) *Business Journal*, May 4, 2010, www.bizjournals.com on May 4, 2010; Susanna Ray, "AMR May Seek Alliances as Mergers Erase Lead in Size," *Bloomberg Businessweek*, May 3, 2010, www.businessweek.com on May 3, 2010.

EXPERIENCING ORGANIZATIONAL BEHAVIOR

Studying a Real Organization

Purpose This exercise will help you understand the factors that determine the design of organizations.

Format You will interview at least five employees in different parts of the college or university that you attend or employees of a small- to medium-sized organization and analyze the reasons for its design. (You may want to coordinate this exercise with the "Experiencing Organizational Behavior" exercise in Chapter 16.)

Procedure If you use a local organization, your first task is to find one with between fifty and five hundred employees. If you did the exercise for Chapter 16, you can use the same company for this exercise. The organization should have more than two hierarchical levels, but it should not be too complex to understand with a short period of study. You may want to check with your professor before contacting the company. Your initial contact should be with the highest-ranking manager you can reach. Make sure that top management is aware of your project and gives its approval.

If you use your local college or university, you could talk to professors, secretaries, and other administrative staff in the admissions office, student services department, athletic department, library, and many others. Be sure to include employees from a variety of jobs and levels in your interviews.

Using the material in this chapter, you will interview employees to obtain the following information on the structure of the organization:

1. What is the organization in business to do? What are its goals and its strategies for achieving them?
2. How large is the company? What is the total number of employees? How many work full-time? How many work part-time?
3. What are the most important components of the organization's environment?
4. Is the number of important environmental components large or small?
5. How quickly or slowly do these components change?
6. Would you characterize the organization's environment as certain, uncertain, or somewhere in-between? If in-between, describe approximately how certain or uncertain.
7. What is the organization's dominant technology; that is, how does it transform inputs into outputs?
8. How rigid is the company in its application of rules and procedures? Is it flexible enough to respond to environmental changes?
9. How involved are employees in the daily decision making related to their jobs?
10. What methods are used to ensure control over the actions of employees?

Interview at least five employees of the college or company at different levels and in different departments. One should hold a top-level position. Be sure to ask the questions in a way the employees will understand; they may not be familiar with some of the terminology used in this chapter.

The result of the exercise should be a report describing the technology, environment, and structure of the company. You should discuss the extent to which the structure is appropriate for the organization's strategy, size, technology, and environment. If it does not seem appropriate, you should explain the reasons. If you also used this company for the exercise in Chapter 16, you can comment further on the organization chart and its appropriateness for the company. You may want to send a copy of your report to the cooperating company.

Follow-up Questions

1. Which aspects of strategy, size, environment, and technology were the most difficult to obtain information about? Why?
2. If there were differences in the responses of the employees you interviewed, how do you account for them?

3. If you were the president of the organization you analyzed, would you structure it in the same way? Why or why not? If not, how would you structure it differently?

4. How did your answers to questions 2 and 3 differ from those in the exercise in Chapter 16?

BUILDING MANAGERIAL SKILLS

Exercise Overview When organizations utilize a matrix organizational structure (see Figure 17.6), every employee and manager in the system has dual reporting relationships, a situation that puts additional pressure on the managerial skills of everybody in the system. This exercise provides you with an opportunity to analyze some of the managerial requirements for success in a matrix organizational structure.

Exercise Background The matrix organizational structure was initially established to overcome the inadequacies of traditional structures when the environment and technology of certain organizations required additional information-processing capabilities. It has been hailed as a great innovation in certain situations, but it has also caused some problems when utilized in other organizations.

Exercise Task Working alone, look again at the managerial roles and critical managerial skills described in Chapter 2. See if you can describe how each of these

managerial roles and skills is affected when an organization uses a matrix structure. Go through each role and each skill, first listing each one along with a simple one-sentence description. Then, reread the section on matrix organizations in this chapter and write a description of the roles and skills required of managers in a matrix structure.

Exchange papers with a classmate or share papers in a small group. Make notes about how others saw the roles and skills differently than you did. Discuss the differences and similarities that you find.

Conclude by addressing the following questions:

1. To what extent does the matrix organization structure put additional pressure on managers?
2. What should organizations using a matrix structure do to help their managers be prepared for those additional pressures?
3. Would you like to work in a matrix organizational structure? Why or why not?

SELF-ASSESSMENT EXERCISE

Finding Your Comfort Level

This exercise is designed to help you determine whether you'd be more comfortable working in an organization with a mechanistic structure or one with an organic structure. The 15 statements below reflect preferences that people can have in workplace structure and environment. Using the following scale, indicate the extent to which each statement accurately describes your preference:

5 Strongly agree

4 Agree somewhat

3 Undecided

2 Disagree somewhat

1 Strongly disagree

I prefer to work in an organization in which:

_____ 1. Goals are defined by those at higher levels.

_____ 2. Work methods and procedures are specified.

_____ 3. Top management makes important decisions.

_____ 4. My loyalty counts as much as my ability to do the job.

_____ 5. Clear lines of authority and responsibility are established

_____ 6. Top management is decisive and firm.

_____ 7. My career is pretty well planned out for me.

_____ 8. I can specialize.

_____ 9. My length of service is almost as important as my level of performance.

____ 10. Management is able to provide the information I need to do my job well.

____ 11. The chain of command is well established.

____ 12. Rules and procedures are adhered to equally by everyone.

____ 13. People accept the authority of a leader's position.

____ 14. People do as they've been instructed.

____ 15. People clear things with their bosses before going over their heads.

How to score: Find your score by adding the numbers that you assigned to the 15 statements. Interpret your score as follows:

- The higher your score, the more comfortable you are with a mechanistic structure.

- The lower your score *below* 48, the more comfortable you are with an organic structure.

- Scores between 48 and 64 can go either way.

Reference: John F. Veiga and John N. Yanousa, *The Dynamics of Organization Theory: Gaining a Macro Perspective* (St. Paul, MN: West, 1979).

ORGANIZATION CULTURE

CHAPTER LEARNING OBJECTIVES

After studying this chapter, you should be able to:

- Define organization culture, explain how it affects employee behavior, and understand its historical roots.
- Describe how to create organization culture.
- Describe two different approaches to culture in organizations.
- Identify emerging issues in organization culture.
- Discuss the important elements of managing the organizational culture.

Goldman Sachs Banks on Cultural Capital

*"Doing a good job will get you nowhere.
Doing a superb job will get you noticed."*

—A FORMER GOLDMAN SACHS VP ON CLIMBING THE COMPANY'S CORPORATE LADDER

By the fall of 2008, Wall Street had been decimated by the financial storm that first hit the U.S. subprime-mortgage market in 2006. The investment bank Goldman Sachs had been buffeted by the same choppy seas, but, as the *New York Times* pointed out, Goldman had "sailed through with relatively minor bumps." How had Goldman managed to stay afloat during a storm that swamped some of its rivals in a sea of debt and beached others on the shoals of insolvency? Needless

AP PHOTO/RICHARD DREW

A specialist and a trader work on the floor of the New York Stock Exchange Monday, April 19, 2010. The stock market ended mixed after investors set aside some of their concerns about the government's case against Goldman Sachs. The Goldman Sachs culture may have been the key component that helped it survive the investment banking disaster and the recent economic downturn. The Goldman Sachs culture is rooted in two seemingly contradictory core values—fierce internal competition and dedication to teamwork.

to say, the reasons are both numerous and complex, but many observers are inclined to look at Goldman's culture. Both Goldman's profitability and its durability, according to *Fortune* magazine, "are a testament to its culture, an impossible-to-replicate mix of extreme aggression, deep paranoia, individual ambition, and robot-like teamwork."

Goldman Sachs went public in 1999, but to many people on Wall Street, it is still "The Partnership." Goldman's partners remain among its chief owners, and they still comprise its highest-level management teams. Full partners account for the top one percent of a firm populated entirely by overachievers. They reap the greatest rewards when the firm is managed at the highest level of profitability, and they stand to lose the most when the company falters. As a rule, they tend to invest their own money in Goldman for decades, and, not surprisingly, they manage the company's assets for the long term. Goldman Sachs has always epitomized a high-risk, high-return culture, but its history shows that, despite a few missteps in the past seven decades, heavily vested senior executives tend to value the difference between high-risk investing and overly risky adventuring.

Since the mid-1970s, says Lisa Endlich, a former trader and VP at Goldman, there has been "no greater prize on Wall Street" than a Goldman Sachs partnership. She adds, however, that "rising through the ranks at Goldman Sachs is one of the steepest and most challenging corporate climbs," and getting to the top means mastering a culture "which on its face is rife with contradictions. . . . You'll be immersed in one of the world's most competitive environments. . . . Doing a good job will get you nowhere. Doing a superb job will get you noticed," but you will not make much progress at all unless you are willing to demonstrate a resolute commitment to upward mobility, including "hefty hours at the office and . . . a travel schedule that includes missing more than a few bedtime stories." You have to win every head-to-head contest with everybody else in the company who wants what you want, but—and here is one of those troublesome contradictions—"nothing will derail you faster than not being a team player." At Goldman, reports Endlich, the right competitive mixture of individual ambition and intramural team play means that

> you must make your accomplishments well known to the partner you work for, the partnership committee, and the management committee, while never once bragging. . . . [And] you must make the time . . . to advise and guide those coming up behind you, even if you feel you barely have a minute to breathe.

In a sense, then, going in the right direction at Goldman Sachs means communicating in all directions at once. Charles D. Ellis, a business-strategy consultant who has worked with Goldman executives for 30 years, attributes the company's "decisive advantage in management" to "the speed, accuracy, and extent of communication inside the company. . . . Goldman Sachs culture works," adds Ellis, because it thoroughly integrates two of the firm's core strengths: the loyalty of its employees and its approach to recruiting.

"You constantly feel there's more you can do at work," says Liz Beshel, who is now the firm's global treasurer, "because that's the kind of people Goldman hires—we're all perfectionists." According to Ellis, Goldman recruits only the top five percent of job candidates in the industry and typically lands most of them because the company's top executives get involved in the process. "By and large," he adds, "Goldman Sachs people . . . do not come with silver spoons. More often, they come from the wrong side of the tracks. They are upwardly mobile with a drive to succeed." The firm's strategy, suggests Ellis, is based on the theory that if you come from a working-class background, you will be hungrier for the kind of success that a job at Goldman makes possible.

Unfortunately, Goldman has recently been forced to cut more than 3,000 of those coveted jobs, or about 10 percent of its workforce. What happened? Ultimately, Goldman got caught in the undertow of the global financial crisis, and although executives tried to reassure investors that it was in no danger of going under, nervous shareholders began selling off shares, until the company's stock price had fallen about 50 percent from a peak of $247.92. In September 2008, Goldman succumbed to the pressure and announced that it was transforming itself from an investment bank into a holding-company bank. It will now be able to take deposits and buy other banks, but it will also be subject to much stricter federal regulation. It will not be nearly as profitable, and it will no longer enjoy the agility and creativity that had fostered a high-risk, high-return culture. "No matter how good it was," muses a Wall Street executive, Goldman "was not impervious to the fortunes of fate." One analyst, however, sees Goldman's self-engineered transformation as another sign of the agility that has helped it to survive seven decades of ups and downs in financial markets: "They change to fit their environment," he observes. "When it was good to go public, they went public. . . . Now that it's good to be a bank, they became a bank."

In the most recent chapter in the Goldman story, the Securities and Exchange Commission charged the bank with illegally manipulating mortgage investments. In July 2010, Goldman agreed to pay $550 million to settle the government's claims, and although the figure will scarcely create a wrinkle on Goldman's balance sheet, its vaunted reputation suffered serious damage during the highly publicized investigation.

In the *Change* box entitled "How to Make Change at an Investment Bank" on page 516, we'll examine better days at Goldman. In particular, we'll take a closer look at the process by which some key executives navigated the currents of the company's culture in successful efforts to effect critical changes at the firm.

What Do You Think?

1. What do you think it would be like to work for Goldman Sachs?
2. Would you like to work there? Why or why not?

References: Lisa Endlich, *Goldman Sachs: The Culture of Success* (New York: Alfred A. Knopf, 1999); George Anders, "Rich Bank, Poor Bank," *New York Times*, October 12, 2008, www.nytimes.com on May 7, 2010; Julie Creswell and Ben White, "Wall Street, R.I.P.: The End of an Era, Even at Goldman," *New York Times*, September 28, 2008, www.nytimes.com on May 7, 2010; Bethany McLean, "Top 20 Most Admired Companies: Goldman Sachs Group," *Fortune*, March 3, 2008, http://money.cnn.com on May 7, 2010; Ben White and Louise Story, "Last Two Big Investment Banks Reinvent Their Businesses," *New York Times*, September 23, 2008, www.nytimes.com on May 7, 2010; Miriam Marcus, "Goldman Sachs Eyes Ax," *Forbes.com*, October 23, 2008, www.forbes.com on May 7, 2010; Jenny Anderson, "As Goldman Thrives, Some Say an Ethos Has Faded," *New York Times*, December 16, 2009, www.nytimes.com on May 7, 2010; Louise Story and Gretchen Morgenson, "S.E.C. Accuses Goldman of Fraud in Housing Deal," *New York Times*, April 16, 2010, www.nytimes.com on May 7, 2010; "Goldman Sachs Group Inc.," *New York Times*, July 16, 2010, www.nytimes.com on August 22, 2010.

THE NATURE OF ORGANIZATION CULTURE

In the early 1980s, organization culture became a central concern in the study of organizational behavior. Hundreds of researchers began to work in this area. Numerous books were published, important academic journals dedicated entire issues to the discussion of culture, and, almost overnight, organizational behavior textbooks that omitted culture as a topic of study became obsolete.

Interest in organization culture was not limited to academic researchers. Businesses expressed a far more intense interest in culture than in other aspects of organizational behavior. *Business Week, Fortune,* and other business periodicals published articles that touted culture as the key to an organization's success and suggested that managers who could manage through their organization's culture almost certainly would rise to the top.[1]

The study of organization culture remains important, although the enthusiasm of the early 1980s has waned somewhat. The assumption is that organizations with a strong culture perform at higher levels than those without a strong culture.[2] For example, studies have shown that organizations with strong cultures that are strategically appropriate and that have norms that permit the organization to change actually do perform well.[3] Other studies have shown that different functional units may require different types of cultures.[4] The research on the impact of culture on organizational performance is mixed, however, depending on how the research is done and what variables are measured.

Many researchers have begun to weave the important aspects of organization culture into their research on more traditional topics. Now there are fewer headline stories in the popular business press about culture and culture management, but organization culture can have powerful effects on organizational performance, as the opening case about Goldman Sachs illustrates. The enormous amount of research on culture completed in the last twenty years has fundamentally altered the way both academics and managers look at organizations. Some of the concepts developed in the analysis of organization culture have become basic parts of the business vocabulary, and the analysis of organization culture is one of the most important specialties in the field of organizational behavior.

What Is Organization Culture?

A surprising aspect of the recent rise in interest in organization culture is that the concept, unlike virtually every other concept in the field, has no single widely accepted definition. Indeed, it often appears that authors feel compelled to develop their own definitions, which range from very broad to highly specific. For example, T. E. Deal and A. A. Kennedy define a firm's culture as "the way we do things around here."[5] This very broad definition presumably could include the way a firm manufactures its products or creates its service, pays its bills, treats its employees, and performs any other organizational operation. More specific definitions include those of E. H. Schein ("the pattern of basic assumptions that a given group has invented, discovered, or developed in learning to cope with its problems of external adaptation and internal integration"[6]) and Tom Peters and Robert Waterman ("a dominant and coherent set of shared values conveyed by such symbolic means as stories, myths, legends, slogans, anecdotes, and fairy tales"[7]). Table 18.1 lists these and other important definitions of organization culture.

Despite the apparent diversity of these definitions, a few common attributes emerge. First, all the definitions refer to a set of values held by individuals in an organization. These values define good or acceptable behaviors and bad or unacceptable

Table 18.1
**DEFINITIONS
OF ORGANIZATION CULTURE**

Definition	Source
"A belief system shared by an organization's members"	J. C. Spender, "Myths, Recipes and Knowledge-Bases in Organizational Analysis" (Unpublished manuscript, Graduate School of Management, University of California at Los Angeles, 1983), p. 2.
"Strong, widely shared core values"	C. O'Reilly, "Corporations, Cults, and Organizational Culture: Lessons from Silicon Valley Firms" (Paper presented at the Annual Meeting of the Academy of Management, Dallas, Texas, 1983), p. 1.
"The way we do things around here"	T. E. Deal and A. A. Kennedy, *Corporate Cultures: The Rites and Rituals of Corporate Life* (Reading, MA: Addison-Wesley, 1982), p. 4.
"The collective programming of the mind"	G. Hofstede, *Culture's Consequences: International Differences in Work-Related Values* (Beverly Hills, CA: Sage, 1980), p. 25.
"Collective understandings"	J. Van Maanen and S. R. Barley, "Cultural Organization: Fragments of a Theory" (Paper presented at the Annual Meeting of the Academy of Management, Dallas, Texas, 1983), p. 7.
"A set of shared, enduring beliefs communicated through a variety of symbolic media, creating meaning in people's work lives"	J. M. Kouzes, D. F. Caldwell, and B. Z. Posner, "Organizational Culture: How It Is Created, Maintained, and Changed" (Presentation at OD Network National Conference, Los Angeles, October 9, 1983).
"A set of symbols, ceremonies, and myths that communicates the underlying values and beliefs of that organization to its employees"	W. G. Ouchi, *Theory Z: How American Business Can Meet the Japanese Challenge* (Reading, MA: Addison-Wesley, 1981), p. 41.
"A dominant and coherent set of shared values conveyed by such symbolic means as stories, myths, legends, slogans, anecdotes, and fairy tales"	T. J. Peters and R. H. Waterman Jr., *In Search of Excellence: Lessons from America's Best-Run Companies* (New York: Harper & Row, 1982), p. 103.
"The pattern of basic assumptions that a given group has invented, discovered, or developed in learning to cope with its problems of external adaptation and internal integration"	E. H. Schein, "The Role of the Founder in Creating Organizational Culture," *Organizational Dynamics*, Summer 1985, p. 14.

behavior. In some organizations, for example, it is unacceptable to blame customers when problems arise. Here the value "the customer is always right" tells managers what actions are acceptable (not blaming the customer) and what actions are not acceptable (blaming the customer). In other organizations, the dominant values might support blaming customers for problems, penalizing employees who make mistakes, or treating employees as the organization's most valuable assets. In each case, values help members of an organization understand how they should act.

A second attribute common to many of the definitions in Table 18.1 is that the values that make up an organization's culture are often taken for granted; that is, they are basic assumptions made by the firm's employees rather than prescriptions written in a book or made explicit in a training program. It may be as difficult for an organization to articulate these basic assumptions as it is for people to express their personal beliefs and values. Several authors have argued that organization culture is a powerful influence on individuals in organizations precisely because it is not explicit but instead becomes an implicit part of employees' values and beliefs.[8]

Some organizations have been able to articulate the key values in their cultures. Some have even written down these values and made them part of formal training procedures. Whole Foods Market stands out from the rest of the supermarket industry. In 2004, the 160-store chain earned $137 million, while Kroger, the nation's largest supermarket chain, lost $100 million. Whole Foods has a unique organization culture, described by CEO John Mackey as "a fast-breaking basketball team. We're driving down the court, but we don't exactly know how the play is going to evolve." Many experts attribute the differences in performance to its unique organization culture that is democratic, participative, egalitarian, innovative, team-based, and transparent.[9]

Even when organizations can articulate and describe the basic values that make up their cultures, however, the values most strongly affect actions when people in the organization take them for granted. An organization's culture is not likely to influence behavior powerfully when employees must constantly refer to a handbook to remember what the culture is. When the culture becomes part of them—when they can ignore what is written in the book because they already have embraced the values it describes—the culture can have an important impact on their actions.

Would this be fun—to drive a Formula One race car on a track with your coworkers? This is a great way to spend the day with coworkers, racing Formula One cars and getting a feel for what working faster really means!

The final attribute shared by many of the definitions in Table 18.1 is an emphasis on the symbolic means through which the values in an organization's culture are communicated. Although, as we noted, companies sometimes could directly describe these values, their meaning is perhaps best communicated to employees through the use of stories, examples, and even what some authors call "myths" or "fairy tales." Stories typically reflect the important implications of values in an organization's culture. Often they develop a life of their own. As they are told and retold, shaped and reshaped, their relationship to what actually occurred becomes less important than the powerful impact the stories have on the way people behave every day. Nike uses a group of technical representatives called "Ekins" ("Nike" spelled backwards) who run a nine-day training session for large retailers, telling them stories about Nike's history and traditions, such as the stories about CEO Phil Knight selling shoes from the trunk of his car and cofounder Bill Bowerman using the family's waffle iron to create the first waffle-soled running shoe.[10]

Some organization stories have become famous. At E*Trade, CEO Christos Cotsakos has done many things that have since become famous around the company because he did not follow the rules for the typical investment company. To make people move faster, he organized a day of racing in Formula One cars at speeds of around 150 miles per hour. To create a looser atmosphere around the office, he had employees carry around rubber chickens or wear propeller beanies. To bond the employees together, he organized gourmet-cooking classes.[11] The stories of these incidents and others are told to new employees and are spread throughout the company, thus affecting the behavior of many more people than those who actually took part in each event.

We can use the three common attributes of definitions of culture just discussed to develop a definition with which most authors probably could agree: **Organization culture** is the set of shared values, often taken for granted, that help people in an organization understand which actions are considered acceptable and which are considered unacceptable. Often these values are communicated through stories and other symbolic means.

Historical Foundations

Although research on organization culture exploded onto the scene in the early 1980s, the antecedents of this research can be traced to the origins of social science. Understanding the contributions of other social science disciplines is particularly important in the case of organization culture because many of the dilemmas and debates that continue in this area reflect differences in historical research traditions.

Anthropological Contributions   Anthropology is the study of human cultures.[12] Of all the social science disciplines, anthropology is most closely related to the study of culture and cultural phenomena. Anthropologists seek to understand how the values and beliefs that make up a society's culture affect the structure and functioning of that society. Many anthropologists believe that to understand the relationship between culture and society, it is necessary to look at a culture from the viewpoint of the people who practice it—from the "native's point of view."[13] To reach this level of understanding, anthropologists immerse themselves in the values, symbols, and stories that people in a society use to bring order and meaning to their lives. Anthropologists usually produce book-length descriptions of the values, attitudes, and beliefs that underlie the behaviors of people in one or two cultures.[14]

Whether the culture is that of a large, modern corporation or a primitive tribe in New Guinea or the Philippines, the questions asked are the same: How do people in this culture know what kinds of behavior are acceptable and what kinds are unacceptable? How is this knowledge understood? How is this knowledge communicated to new members? Through intense efforts to produce accurate descriptions, the values and beliefs that underlie actions in an organization become clear. However, these values can be fully understood only in the context of the organization in which they developed. In other words, a description of the values and beliefs of one organization is not transferable to those of other organizations; each culture is unique.

Sociological Contributions   Sociology is the study of people in social systems such as organizations and societies. Sociologists have long been interested in the causes and consequences of culture. In studying culture, sociologists have most often focused on informal social structure. Émile Durkheim, an important early sociologist, argued that the study of myth and ritual is an essential complement to the study of structure and rational behavior in societies.[15] By studying rituals, Durkheim argued, we can understand the most basic values and beliefs of a group of people.

Many sociological methods and theories have been used in the analysis of organization cultures. Sociologists use systematic interviews, questionnaires, and other quantitative research methods rather than the intensive study and analysis of anthropologists. Practitioners using the sociological approach generally produce a fairly simple typology of cultural attributes and then show how the cultures of a relatively large number of firms can be analyzed with this typology.[16] The major pieces of research on organization culture that later spawned widespread business interest—including Ouchi's *Theory Z*, Deal and Kennedy's *Corporate Cultures*, and Peters and Waterman's *In Search of Excellence*[17]—used sociological methods. Later in this chapter, we review some of this work in more detail.

Organization culture is the set of values that helps the organization's employees understand which actions are considered acceptable and which are unacceptable.

CREATING THE ORGANIZATION CULTURE

To the entrepreneur who starts a business, creating the culture of the company may seem secondary to the basic processes of creating a product or service and selling it to customers or clients. However, as the company grows and becomes successful, it usually develops a culture that distinguishes it from other companies and that is one of the reasons for its success. In other words, a company succeeds as a result of what the company does (its strategy), and how the company does it (its culture). The culture is linked to the strategic values, whether one is starting up a new company or trying to change the culture of an existing company.[28] The process of creating an organization culture is really a process of linking its strategic values with its cultural values, much as the structure of the organization is linked to its strategy, as we described in Chapter 17. The process is shown in Table 18.2.

Establish Values

The first two steps in the process involve establishing values. First, management must determine the strategic values of the organization. **Strategic values** are the basic beliefs about an organization's environment that shape its strategy. They are developed following an environmental scanning process and strategic analysis that evaluate economic, demographic, public policy, technological, and social trends to identify needs in the marketplace that the organization can meet. Strategic values, in effect, link the organization with its environment. Dell Computer believed that customers would, if the price was right, buy computers from a catalogue rather than go to computer stores as the conventional wisdom dictated they would. A $6.8 billion business resulted.[29] The second set of required values are the cultural values of the organization. **Cultural values** are the values employees need to have and to act on for the organization to carry out its strategic values. They should be grounded in the organization's beliefs about how and why the organization can succeed. Organizations that attempt to develop cultural values that are not linked to their strategic values may end up with an empty set of values that have little relationship to their business. In other words, employees need to value work behaviors that are consistent with and support the organization's strategic values: low-cost production, customer service, or technological innovation. Herb Kelleher, former CEO and one of the early leaders of Southwest Airlines, believed that the culture, the "esprit de corps," was the most valuable asset of the company.[30]

Tony Hsieh (pronounced *Shay*) starting selling shoes online (Zappos.com) in 1999 and booked $1 billion in sales in 2008, but he believes the business is about one thing: happiness. He simply wanted to make customers and employees feel really, really good. His strategic values were that he believed shoes could be sold online

Table 18.2 CREATING ORGANIZATION CULTURE

Step 1—Formulate Strategic Values
Step 2—Develop Cultural Values
Step 3—Create Vision
Step 4—Initiate Implementation Strategies
Step 5—Reinforce Cultural Behaviors

with free shipping and free returns. Zappos now has ten core values that include "Be humble," "Create fun and a little weirdness," and "Deliver WOW through service." Hsieh's basic cultural value is to make everyone happy.[31]

Create Vision

After developing its strategic and cultural values, the organization must establish a vision of its direction. This "vision" is a picture of what the organization will be like at some point in the future. It portrays how the strategic and cultural values will combine to create the future. For example, an insurance company might establish a vision of "protecting the lifestyles of 2 million families by the year 2020." In effect, it synthesizes both the strategic and cultural values as it communicates a performance target to employees. The conventional wisdom has been that the vision statement is written first, but experience suggests that, for the vision to be meaningful, the strategic and cultural values must be established first. Mr. Hsieh, of Zappos, envisions big things for his company as long as he can provide a service that makes people happy. He is creating an outsourcing service to handle customer service, selling and shipping for other companies, and has initiated a website to provide training and education for small businesses.[32]

Initiate Implementation Strategies

The next step, initiating implementation strategies, builds on the values and initiates the action to accomplish the vision. The strategies cover many factors, from developing the organization design to recruiting and training employees who share the values and will carry them out. Consider a bank that has the traditional orientation of handling customer loans, deposits, and savings. If the bank changes, placing more emphasis on customer service, it may have to recruit a different type of employee, one who is capable of building relationships. The bank will also have to commit to serious, long-term training of its current employees to teach them the new service-oriented culture. The strategic and cultural values are the stimuli for the implementation practices.

Zappos fully implemented its cultural values in many ways. Zappos hires people who fit the culture, pays them average wages, and provides them lots of training on topics ranging from the initial two-week orientation to current business books, how to Twitter, public speaking, and financial planning—all intended to help people grow and think and be ready to be a senior leader in the company. Sales from the previous day are on a chart in the lobby of the headquarters building with a computer printout in the hallway showing how many shoes are in the warehouse. Call center reps are left to make decisions on their own, do not read from scripts, do not have their call times recorded, and are encouraged to create personal emotional connections (PEC) with customers. Managers are required to spend 10–20 percent of their time goofing off with the people they manage, and "hanging out with your people" is highly encouraged.

Reinforce Cultural Behaviors

The final step is to reinforce the behaviors of employees as they act out the cultural values and implement the organization's strategies. Reinforcement can take many forms. First, the formal reward system in the organization must reward desired behaviors in ways that employees value. Second, stories must be told throughout the organization about employees who engaged in behaviors that epitomize the cultural values. Third, the organization must engage in ceremonies and rituals that emphasize employees doing the things that are critical to carrying out the organization's vision. In effect, the organization must "make a big deal out of employees doing the right things." For example, if parties are held only for retirement or to give out longevity and service pins, the employees get the message that retirement and length of service are the only things that matter. On the other hand, holding a ceremony for a group of employees who provided exceptional customer service reinforces desirable employee behaviors. Reinforcement practices are the final link between the strategic and cultural values and the creation of the organization culture. Zappos reinforces the culture every single day as employees come to work happy, leave happy, and often go out with their coworkers and managers after work. It becomes a way of life for them.[33]

APPROACHES TO DESCRIBING ORGANIZATION CULTURE

The models discussed in this section provide valuable insights into the dimensions along which organization cultures vary. No single framework for describing the values in organization cultures has emerged; however, several frameworks have been suggested. Although these frameworks were developed in the 1980s, their ideas about organization culture are still influential today. Some of the "excellent" companies that they described are not as highly lauded today, but the concepts are still in use in companies all over the world. Managers should evaluate the various parts of the frameworks described and use the parts that fit the strategic and cultural values of their own organizations.

The Ouchi Framework

One of the first researchers to focus explicitly on analyzing the cultures of a limited group of firms was William G. Ouchi. Ouchi analyzed the organization cultures of three groups of firms, which he characterized as (1) typical U.S. firms, (2) typical Japanese firms, and (3) **Type Z** U.S. firms.[34]

Through his analysis, Ouchi developed a list of seven points on which these three types of firms can be compared. He argued that the cultures of typical Japanese firms and Type Z U.S. firms are very different from those of typical U.S. firms, and that these differences explain the success of many Japanese firms and Type Z U.S. firms as well as the difficulties faced by typical U.S. firms. The seven points of comparison developed by Ouchi are presented in Table 18.3.

Commitment to Employees According to Ouchi, typical Japanese and Type Z U.S. firms share the cultural value of trying to keep employees. Thus, both types of firms lay off employees only as a last resort. In Japan, the value of "keeping employees on" often takes the form of lifetime employment, although some Japanese companies, reacting to the economic troubles of the past few years, are challenging this value. A person who begins working at some Japanese firms usually has a virtual guarantee that he or she will never be fired. In Type Z U.S. companies, this cultural value is manifested in a commitment to what Ouchi called "long-term employment." Under the Japanese system of lifetime employment, employees usually cannot be fired. Under the U.S. system, workers and managers can be fired, but only if they are not performing acceptably.

The **Type Z firm** is committed to retaining employees; evaluates workers' performance based on both qualitative and quantitative information; emphasizes broad career paths; exercises control through informal, implicit mechanisms; requires that decision making occur in groups and be based on full information sharing and consensus; expects individuals to take responsibility for decisions; and emphasizes concern for people.

Cultural Value	Expression in Japanese Companies	Expression in Type Z U.S. Companies	Expression in Typical U.S. Companies
COMMITMENT TO EMPLOYEES	Lifetime employment	Long-term employment	Short-term employment
EVALUATION	Slow and qualitative	Slow and qualitative	Fast and quantitative
CAREERS	Very broad	Moderately broad	Narrow
CONTROL	Implicit and informal	Implicit and informal	Explicit and formal
DECISION MAKING	Group and consensus	Group and consensus	Individual
RESPONSIBILITY	Group	Individual	Individual
CONCERN FOR PEOPLE	Holistic	Holistic	Narrow

Table 18.3
THE OUCHI FRAMEWORK

Ouchi suggested that typical U.S. firms do not have the same cultural commitment to employees that Japanese firms and Type Z U.S. firms do. In reality, U.S. workers and managers often spend their entire careers in a relatively small number of companies. Still, there is a cultural expectation that if there is a serious downturn in a firm's fortunes, a change of ownership, or a merger, workers and managers will be let go. For example, when Wells Fargo Bank bought First Interstate Bank in Arizona, it expected to lay off about 400 employees in Arizona and 5,000 in the corporation as a whole. However, eight months after the purchase, Wells Fargo had eliminated over 1,000 employees in Arizona alone and had laid off a total of 10,800 workers. Wells Fargo already had a reputation as a vicious job cutter following takeovers and seemed to be living up to it.[35]

Evaluation   Ouchi observed that in Japanese and Type Z U.S. companies, appropriate evaluation of workers and managers is thought to take a very long time—up to ten years—and requires the use of qualitative as well as quantitative information about performance. For this reason, promotion in these firms is relatively slow, and promotion decisions are made only after interviews with many people who have had contact with the person being evaluated. In typical U.S. firms, on the other hand, the cultural value suggests that evaluation can and should be done rapidly and should emphasize quantitative measures of performance. This value tends to encourage short-term thinking among workers and managers.

Careers   Ouchi next observed that the careers most valued in Japanese and Type Z U.S. firms span multiple functions. In Japan, this value has led to very broad career paths, which may lead to employees' gaining experience in six or seven distinct business functions. The career paths in Type Z U.S. firms are somewhat narrower.

However, the career path valued in typical U.S. firms is considerably narrower. Ouchi's research indicated that most U.S. managers perform only one or two different business functions in their entire careers. This narrow career path reflects, according to Ouchi, the value placed on specialization that is part of so many U.S. firms.

Control   All organizations must exert some level of control to achieve coordinated action. Thus, it is not surprising that firms in the United States and Japan have developed cultural values related to organizational control and how to manage it. Most Japanese and Type Z U.S. firms assume that control is exercised through informal, implicit mechanisms. One of the most powerful of these mechanisms is the organization's

Appropriate Cultures

Much of the literature on organization culture has focused on describing the concept of organization culture, linking culture to performance, and then creating an organizational culture. For example, the Peters and Waterman framework described eight attributes that successful firms all had, the implication being that those same attributes would be desirable in all organizations. But one need only examine a few successful organizations—such as Southwest Airlines, General Electric, and Microsoft, all with vastly different cultures—to legitimately question the appropriateness of one culture for all organizations. Rob Goffee and Gareth Jones have questioned the idea that there is one best organization culture and instead propose that there are only "appropriate cultures."[45] After all, flying airplanes and moving people from one place to another at the lowest possible cost is vastly different from writing new software for personal computers. Goffee and Jones suggest that the nature of the value chain and the dynamism of the environment are two factors that may determine what type of culture is appropriate for a particular organization. The determining factors may prove to be quite elusive, however, as nobody has been able to successfully copy Southwest Airlines, although many have tried. Much more research is needed on the prospect of a contingency theory of organization culture.

Whole Foods Markets has created a culture that is right for it and quite different from the rest of the commercial food retail industry. Starting with a small natural food store in Austin, Texas, founder and CEO John Mackey studied Japanese management techniques and created a culture that is democratic, participative, egalitarian, innovative, team-based, and transparent. It is democratic in that employees created their "Declaration of Interdependence" and vote on whether or not new employees get to join the team.

At Whole Foods team members in each section make decisions regarding what products to make available for customers and how to display them. In this photo two team members in the Fresh & Wild section are preparing dishes for display. John Anderson mixes a Bowery Berry Goat Cheese salad in the Fresh & Wild section with Majory Louis, left, at the new Whole Foods Market location on Houston St. in the SoHo neighborhood of New York City. The strong performance and team-oriented culture separates Whole Foods from other competitors in the industry.

BLOOMBERG/GETTY IMAGES

It is participative in that decisions regarding store design, selection of products that will sell in the local store, and price setting are made by the people who have to implement the decisions. It is egalitarian in that average pay is respectable, no executive can make more than 19 times the average hourly wage, and employees get stock options, 93 percent of which go to nonexecutive personnel. It is innovative in that everyone is encouraged to experiment without asking permission. Store managers can spend up to $100,000 a year to try new ideas. It is team-based because each department is a team with the right to run their area, vote on new members to the team, and be responsible for team profit, to which team pay is tied. It is transparent because the company releases almost all financial data to everyone in the company and everyone knows how their team performed compared to all other teams and how much everyone in the company gets paid.[46] This culture of Whole Foods works for it and is counter to the rest of the industry. In other words, it is appropriate and fits Whole Foods.

MANAGING ORGANIZATION CULTURE

The work of Ouchi, Peters and Waterman, and many others demonstrates two important facts. First, organization cultures differ among firms; second, these different organization cultures can affect a firm's performance. Based on these observations, managers have become more concerned about how to best manage the cultures of their organizations. The three elements of managing organization culture are (1) taking advantage of the existing culture, (2) teaching the organization culture, and (3) changing the organization culture.

Taking Advantage of the Existing Culture

Most managers are not in a position to create an organization culture; rather, they work in organizations that already have cultural values. For these managers, the central issue in managing culture is how best to use the existing cultural system. It may be easier and faster to alter employee behaviors within the culture in place than it is to change the history, traditions, and values that already exist.[47]

To take advantage of an existing cultural system, managers must first be fully aware of the culture's values and what behaviors or actions those values support. Becoming fully aware of an organization's values usually is not easy, however. It involves more than reading a pamphlet about what the company believes in. Managers must develop a deep understanding of how organizational values operate in the firm—an understanding that usually comes only through experience.

This understanding, once achieved, can be used to evaluate the performances of others in the firm. Articulating organizational values can be useful in managing others' behaviors. For example, suppose a subordinate in a firm with a strong cultural value of "sticking to its knitting" develops a business strategy that involves moving into a new industry. Rather than attempting to argue that this business strategy is economically flawed or conceptually weak, the manager who understands the corporate culture can point to the company's organizational value: "In this firm, we believe in sticking to our knitting."

Senior managers who understand their organization's culture can communicate that understanding to lower-level individuals. Over time, as these lower-level managers begin to understand and accept the firm's culture, they will require less direct supervision. Their understanding of corporate values will guide their decision making.

As we saw in our opening vignette, the custodians of the culture at Goldman Sachs—and the stakeholders who stand to gain the most from its continuing profitability—are the partners who run the company. The *Change* box entitled "How to Make Change at an Investment Bank" on page 516 shows how Goldman's culture favors consensus building among the partners as a means of making major decisions.

Teaching the Organization Culture: Socialization

Socialization is the process through which individuals become social beings.[48] As studied by psychologists, it is the process through which children learn to become adults in a society—how they learn what acceptable and polite behavior is and what is not, how they learn to communicate, how they learn to interact with others, and so on. In complex societies, the socialization process takes many years.

Organizational socialization is the process through which employees learn about their organization's culture and pass their knowledge and understanding on to others. Employees are socialized into organizations, just as people are socialized into societies;

Socialization is the process through which individuals become social beings.

Organizational socialization is the process through which employees learn about the firm's culture and pass their knowledge and understanding on to others.

CHANGE

How to Make Change at an Investment Bank

The organization of Goldman Sachs is basically *flat*: it is run by committees composed of partners, and all of these committees operate on roughly the same level and exercise roughly the same wide span of administrative responsibility. Perhaps the most important consequence of this structure is the fact that making major decisions is almost invariably an exercise in consensus building—getting a group of people to agree on a course of action. Taking the company public in 1999, for example, was a nearly 15-year process that culminated when co-CEOs Jon Corzine and Hank Paulson were able to build a consensus of the partners on not only financial but cultural grounds.

> *"Goldman did what it has always done in the face of rapidly changing events: it turned on a dime."*
> —THE *NEW YORK TIMES* ON GOLDMAN SACHS' RESPONSE TO EARLY SIGNS OF TROUBLE IN THE HOME-MORTGAGE MARKET

Financially, the decision was a no-brainer: payouts from the IPO of $5 billion–$6 billion would enrich many of the firm's 188 general partners by $50 million to $100 million each.

The cultural angle, however, was a harder sell, with many of the company's partners expressing the legitimate concern that its closely knit culture—including the ties that bound its leadership—would come unraveled if the firm turned itself over to a random assemblage of outside owners (that is, shareholders). Ultimately, Goldman responded with an IPO, which, as one analyst put it, made it "the most *private* public company in America": the partners agreed that all power would remain in the hands of a small group of managing directors who (according to the prospectus) would continue to "control the management and policies of the Company and ... determine the outcome of any corporate transaction." Just as importantly, the firm's flat structure, with its open lines of communication, also remained intact.

The company's structure and culture were again critical in 2006, when another major change decision was necessary. Late in the year, CEO Lloyd C. Blankfein and CFO David Viniar convened a meeting of top-level executives to inform them that a storm was brewing on the investment horizon. We now know how turbulent that storm really was, but to avoid going into unnecessary detail, we will focus on the threat posed by heavy investments in ultra-risky home-mortgage loans. At Goldman (as at its rival banks), profits from mortgage-backed investment "products" depended on a hale and hearty home-mortgage market and robust mortgage prices, and at the 2006 meeting, it was Viniar's unpleasant task to be the bearer of bad tidings—namely, that the home-mortgage market was showing symptoms of rapidly declining health. Whatever each of the assembled partners may have thought about the market for mortgage-backed investment vehicles, they all knew that it had been generating massive industry-wide profits for about three years. Goldman itself was getting ready to announce fourth-quarter earnings of $3.2 billion—a whopping 93 percent increase over the previous year. And now Blankfein and Viniar were proposing that the bank hedge its bets by staking money *against* another year of phenomenal earnings in the home-mortgage market—that it play to limit its losses rather than to maximize its profits. It was hardly the sort of high-risk, high-return strategy to which Goldman Sachs partners had become accustomed—and which had just generated $16.5 billion in fiscal-year salaries and bonuses.

Blankfein and Viniar needed a consensus, they needed it quickly, and they got it: by April 2007, Goldman had hedging and other risk-reduction strategies in place and had begun to dispose of mortgage-backed securities. As Viniar had predicted, housing prices began to decline in late 2006 and went into free fall through 2007. While most of its Wall Street rivals sustained the heavy losses under which at least three major investment banks collapsed, Goldman survived. In fact, it made money—as much as a billion dollars a quarter from its hedge bets on a floundering home-mortgage market.

The success of the Blankfein-Viniar gambit may well bear out *Fortune* magazine's assessment that "the firm's culture has kept it as nimble as a start-up." Goldman Sachs, suggests another journalist, escaped the fate of its industry rivals because of a culture that enabled it to do "what it has always done in the face of rapidly changing events: it turned on a dime."*

References: Lisa Endlich, *Goldman Sachs: The Culture of Success* (New York: Alfred A. Knopf, 1999); Charles D. Ellis, *The Partnership: The Making of Goldman Sachs* (New York: Penguin Press, 2008); George Anders, "Rich Bank, Poor Bank," *New York Times,* October 12, 2008, www.nytimes.com on May 7, 2010; Julie Creswell and Ben White, "Wall Street, R.I.P.: The End of an Era, Even at Goldman," *New York Times,* September 28, 2008, www.nytimes.com on May 7, 2010; Allan Sloan, "Junk Mortgages under the Microscope," *CNNMoney.com,* October 16, 2007, http://money.cnn.com on May 7, 2010; Jody Shenn and Bob Ivry, "Abacus Let Goldman Shuffle Mortgage Risk Like Beads," *Bloomberg Businessweek,* April 17, 2010, www.businessweek .com on May 7, 2010.

*As we indicated at the close of our opening vignette, by April 2010 Goldman may have found itself sitting precariously on another dime: some of its hedging strategies are at the center of fraud charges filed against the bank by the Securities and Exchange Commission.

that is, they come to know over time what is acceptable in the organization and what is not, how to communicate their feelings, and how to interact with others. They learn both through observation and through efforts by managers to communicate this information to them. Research into the process of socialization indicates that for many employees, socialization programs do not necessarily change their values, but instead they make employees more aware of the differences between personal and organization values and help them develop ways to cope with the differences.[49]

A variety of organizational mechanisms can affect the socialization of workers in organizations. Probably the most important are the examples that new employees see in the behavior of experienced people. Through observing examples, new employees develop a repertoire of stories they can use to guide their actions. When a decision needs to be made, new employees can ask, "What would my boss do in this situation?" This is not to suggest that formal training, corporate pamphlets, and corporate statements about organization culture are unimportant in the socialization process. However, these factors tend to support the socialization process based on people's close observations of the actions of others.

In some organizations, the culture described in pamphlets and presented in formal training sessions conflicts with the values of the organization as they are expressed in the actions of its people. For example, a firm may say that employees are its most important asset but treat employees badly. In this setting, new employees quickly learn that the rhetoric of the pamphlets and formal training sessions has little to do with the real organization culture. Employees who are socialized into this system usually come to accept the actual cultural values rather than those formally espoused.

Changing the Organization Culture

Much of our discussion to this point has assumed that an organization's culture enhances its performance. When this is the case, learning what an organization's cultural values are and using those values to help socialize new workers and managers is very important, for such actions help the organization succeed. However, as Ouchi's and Peters and Waterman's research indicates, not all firms have cultural values that are consistent with high performance. Ouchi found that Japanese firms and Type Z U.S. firms have performance-enhancing values. Peters and Waterman identified performance-enhancing values associated with successful companies. By implication, some firms not included in Peters and Waterman's study must have had performance-reducing values. What should a manager who works in a company with performance-reducing values do?

The answer to this question is, of course, that top managers in such firms should try to change their organization's culture. However, this is a difficult thing to do.[50] Organization culture resists change for all the reasons that it is a powerful influence on behavior—it embodies the firm's basic values, it is often taken for granted, and it is typically most effectively communicated through stories or other symbols. When managers attempt to change organization culture, they are attempting to change people's basic assumptions about what is and is not appropriate behavior in the organization. Changing from a traditional organization to a team-based organization (discussed in Chapter 10) is one example of an organization culture change. Another is the attempt by 3M to change from its low-cost and efficiency culture to return to its roots as an innovative culture.[51]

Despite these difficulties, some organizations have changed their cultures from performance-reducing to performance-enhancing.[52] This change process is described in more detail in Chapter 19. The earlier section on creating organization culture describes the importance of linking the strategic values and the cultural values in creating a new organization culture. We briefly discuss other important elements of the cultural change process in the following sections.

Managing Symbols   Research suggests that organization culture is understood and communicated through the use of stories and other symbolic media. If this is correct, managers interested in changing cultures should attempt to substitute stories and myths that support new cultural values for those that support old ones. They can do so by creating situations that give rise to new stories.

Suppose an organization traditionally has held the value "employee opinions are not important." When management meets in this company, the ideas and opinions of lower-level people—when discussed at all—are normally rejected as foolish and irrelevant. The stories that support this cultural value tell about subordinate managers who tried to make a constructive point only to have that point lost in personal attacks from superiors.

An upper-level manager interested in creating a new story, one that shows lower-level managers that their ideas are valuable, might ask a subordinate to prepare to lead a discussion in a meeting and follow through by asking the subordinate to take the lead when the topic arises. The subordinate's success in the meeting will become a new story, one that may displace some of the many stories suggesting that the opinions of lower-level managers do not matter.

The Difficulty of Change   Changing a firm's culture is a long and difficult process. A primary problem is that upper-level managers, no matter how dedicated they are to implementing some new cultural value, may sometimes inadvertently revert to old patterns of behavior. This happens, for example, when a manager dedicated to implementing the value that lower-level employees' ideas are important vehemently attacks a subordinate's ideas.

This mistake generates a story that supports old values and beliefs. After such an incident, lower-level managers may believe that although the boss seems to want employee input and ideas, in fact, nothing could be further from the truth. No matter what the boss says or how consistent his/her behavior is in the future, some credibility has been lost, and cultural change has been made more difficult.

The Stability of Change   The processes of changing a firm's culture starts with a need for change and moves through a transition period in which efforts are made to adopt new values and beliefs. In the long run, a firm that successfully changes its culture will find that the new values and beliefs are just as stable and influential as the old ones. Value systems tend to be self-reinforcing. Once they are in place, changing them requires an enormous effort. Thus, if a firm can change its culture from performance-reducing to performance-enhancing, the new values are likely to remain in place for a long time.

SYNOPSIS

Organization culture has become one of the most discussed subjects in the field of organization behavior. It burst on the scene in the 1980s with books by Ouchi, Peters and Waterman, and others. Interest has not been restricted to academics, however. Practicing managers are also interested in organization culture, especially as it relates to performance.

There is little agreement about how to define organization culture. A comparison of several important definitions suggests that most have three things in common: They define culture in terms of the values that individuals in organizations use to prescribe appropriate behaviors; they assume that these values are usually taken for granted; and they emphasize the stories and other symbolic means through which the values are typically communicated.

Current research on organization culture reflects various research traditions. The most important contributions have come from anthropology and sociology. Anthropologists have tended to focus on the cultures of one or two organizations and have used detailed descriptions to help outsiders understand organization culture from the "natives' point of view." Sociologists typically have used survey methods to study the cultures of larger numbers of organizations. Two other influences on current work in organization culture are social psychology, which emphasizes the manipulation of symbols in organizations, and economics. The economics approach sees culture both as a tool used to manage and as a determinant of performance.

Creating organization culture is a four-step process. It starts with formulating strategic and cultural values for the organization. Next, a vision for the organization is created, followed by the institution of implementation strategies. The final step is reinforcing the cultural behaviors of employees.

Although no single framework for describing organization culture has emerged, several have been suggested. The most popular efforts in this area have been Ouchi's comparison of U.S. and Japanese firms and Peters and Waterman's description of successful firms in the United States. Ouchi and Peters and Waterman suggested several important dimensions along which organization values vary, including treatment of employees, definitions of appropriate means for decision making, and assignment of responsibility for the results of decision making.

Emerging issues in the area of organization culture include innovation, employee empowerment, and appropriate cultures. Innovation is the process of creating and doing new things that are introduced into the marketplace as products, processes, or services. The organization culture can either help or hinder innovation. Employee empowerment, in addition to being similar to employee participation as a motivation technique, is now viewed by some as a type of organization culture. Empowerment occurs when employees make decisions, set their own work goals, and solve problems in their own area of responsibility. Finally, experts are beginning to suggest that there are cultures that are appropriate for particular organizations rather than there being any one best type of culture. Managing the organization culture requires attention to three factors. First, managers can take advantage of cultural values that already exist and use their knowledge to help subordinates understand them. Second, employees need to be properly socialized, or trained, in the cultural values of the organization, either through formal training or by experiencing and observing the actions of higher-level managers. Third, managers can change the culture of the organization through managing the symbols, addressing the extreme difficulties of such a change, and relying on the durability of the new organization culture once the change has been implemented.

DISCUSSION QUESTIONS

1. A sociologist or anthropologist might suggest that the culture in U.S. firms simply reflects the dominant culture of the society as a whole. Therefore, to change the organization culture of a company, one must first deal with the inherent values and beliefs of the society. How would you respond to this claim?

2. Psychology has been defined as the study of individual behavior. Organizational psychology is the study of individual behavior in organizations. Many of the theories described in the early chapters of this book are based in organizational psychology. Why was this field not identified as a contributor to the study of organization culture along with anthropology, sociology, social psychology, and economics?

3. Describe the culture of an organization with which you are familiar. It might be one in which you currently work, one in which you have worked, or one in which a friend or family member works. What values, beliefs, stories, and symbols are significant to employees of the organization?

4. Discuss the similarities and differences between the organization culture approaches of Ouchi and Peters and Waterman.

5. Describe how organizations use symbols and stories to communicate values and beliefs. Give some examples of how symbols and stories have been used in organizations with which you are familiar.

6. What is the role of leadership (discussed in Chapters 12 and 13) in developing, maintaining, and changing organization culture?

7. Review the characteristics of organization structure described in earlier chapters and compare them with the elements of culture described by Ouchi and Peters and Waterman. Describe the similarities and differences, and explain how some characteristics of one may be related to characteristics of the other.

8. Discuss the role of organization rewards in developing, maintaining, and changing the organization culture.

9. Describe how the culture of an organization can affect innovation.

ORGANIZATIONAL BEHAVIOR CASE FOR DISCUSSION

INTERIOR DESIGNS: A TALE OF SEX, DRUGS, AND RECKLESS MANAGEMENT

In June 2007, about a year after his confirmation as Secretary of the Interior in the Bush administration, Dirk Kempthorne unveiled an initiative to turn his scandal-ridden agency into "a model of an ethical workplace." In an email sent to all department employees, he announced the implementation of 60 out of 80 targeted "best ethics practices" and the completion of "an action plan to implement the remaining 20 practices." In July, encouraged by the agency's newly declared commitment to openness, the nonprofit organization Public Employees for Environmental Responsibility (PEER) asked to see Kempthorne's action plan. In November, the Interior

"[MMS is] a dysfunctional organization . . . riddled with conflicts of interest, unprofessional behavior, and a free-for-all atmosphere. . . ."

—THE *NEW YORK TIMES* ON THE MINERALS MANAGEMENT SERVICE OF THE U.S. DEPT. OF THE INTERIOR

Department denied the request, explaining that the document was still in a "pre-decisional" state.

Fortunately, however, a wealth of information about department ethics was soon to become available from the office of the Interior Inspector General. In late 2006, Inspector General Earl E. Devaney launched an investigation into the actions of Julie A. MacDonald, Interior Department deputy director for Fish and Wildlife and Parks. Devaney's report, issued in March 2007, cited MacDonald for improperly removing wildlife from the endangered-species list and handing over internal department documents to lobbyists for the oil industry. Ron Wyden, a

U.S. senator from Oregon, cited the Inspector General's report as evidence of "how one person's contempt for the public trust can infect an entire agency." Other officials blamed the episode on an agency-wide "culture of fear" fostered by MacDonald and other senior managers. MacDonald resigned in May 2007, just weeks after her bosses had rewarded her efforts with cash bonuses. In three short years, according to Senator Wyden, she had not only done "significant harm to the integrity of the Endangered Species Act" but had wasted hundreds of thousands of taxpayers' dollars.

Inspector General Devaney's services were required again in late 2008, when he was called upon to investigate accusations of wrongdoing by employees of the Interior Department's Minerals Management Service (MMS), which collects royalties paid by organizations that extract oil and gas from public lands. Through its royalty-in-kind program, the agency also accepts oil and gas as royalty payments and then sells them on the open market. Among other things, Devaney discovered that program officials were in the habit of allowing buyers of agency-sold gas and oil to revise their bids downward after they had been awarded purchase contracts. The cost to taxpayers amounted to about $4.4 million.

Perhaps much more interesting—at least in this day and age, when we like to take our hard news with a hint of the unsavory and all-too-human—is the report's revelation of "a culture of substance abuse and promiscuity" within MMS. The nature of their jobs, observed the *New York Times*, exposes agency employees to "the expense-account–fueled world of oil and gas executives," but the Devaney report, said the paper, portrayed "a dysfunctional organization that has been riddled with conflicts of interest, unprofessional behavior, and a free-for-all atmosphere for much of the Bush administration's watch." The report itself concludes that MMS officials "frequently consumed alcohol at industry functions, had used cocaine and marijuana, and had sexual relationships with oil and gas company representatives." In the process of developing cozy professional relationships, about one third of the staff of the royalty-in-kind program also took inappropriate gifts from industry contacts. Socializing with industry representatives, explained employees, was simply a function of their involvement in industry culture, and they assured investigators that such relationships had no effect on the performance of their official duties. Skeptical investigators suggested that "sexual relationships with prohibited sources cannot, by definition, be arms' length" and concluded that the whole agency "appeared to be devoid of both ethical standards and internal controls sufficient

to protect the integrity of this vital revenue-producing program."

Then in January 2009, the *Washington Post* reported that Secretary Kempthorne had spent $235,000 in taxpayer money to refurbish the bathroom in his office. According to Inspector General Devaney, the project had been okayed by the General Services Administration (the federal agency that supports government functions) because aging plumbing needed be replaced anyway. Department officials admitted, however, that much of the money was spent on lavish floor tiling and floor-to-ceiling wood paneling. Kempthorne also installed a new shower, a new refrigerator, and a new freezer and furnished the bathroom with monogrammed towels—all just a few months before he was scheduled to leave office to make way for the Obama administration's new appointee, Ken Salazar (who had no use for his predecessor's monogrammed bath accessories).

During *his* first month in office, Salazar announced his goal "to restore the public's trust, to enact meaningful reform … to uphold the law, and to ensure that all of us—career public servants and political appointees—do our jobs with the highest level of integrity." It so happens that, three months later, MMS, which also oversees offshore oil-drilling activities, approved a plan for drilling in the Gulf of Mexico submitted by petroleum giant BP. Normally, such plans must undergo detailed environmental review before they are accepted, but in this case, MMS declared BP's application "categorically excluded" from environmental analysis. In a letter dated April 9, 2010, BP affirmed that environmental damage from any spill at the site would probably be "minimal or nonexistent." Eleven days later, a giant oil rig exploded, killing 11 workers at the newly approved BP facility and pouring oil into the Gulf of Mexico. As summarized in its drilling application, BP's worst-case scenario had predicted total spillage of 1,500 to 4,600 barrels, and escaping oil, according to the company, would dissipate before reaching land. Nineteen days after the explosion (the day of this writing), the leak was still discharging 5,000 barrels (1 million gallons) *a day* into the Gulf, and an oil slick the size of Puerto Rico was lapping at the coast of Louisiana. It will be quite some time before anyone is able to estimate the cost of the catastrophe on the environment.

Critics have been quick to point out that the oil and gas industry spent $169 million in lobbying expenses in 2009—$15.9 million of it by BP—and MMS, not surprisingly, is back in the news. "Secretary Salazar," charges Kierán Suckling, executive director of the Center for Biological Diversity, *has utterly failed to reform the Mineral Management Service. Instead of protecting the public interest by conducting environmental reviews, his agency rubber-stamped BP's drilling plan, just as it does hundreds of others every year. ... The Minerals Management Service has gotten worse, not better, under Salazar's watch.*

"My favorite agency," adds Senator Bill Nelson of Florida. "Remember in the Bush administration, these were the guys having sex orgies and pot parties and weren't showing up for work."

CASE QUESTIONS

1. Review the various definitions of *organization culture* in Table 18.1. If you were analyzing the culture at the Department of the Interior, which of these definitions would you use to explain what its *organization culture* is? Feel free to select more than one definition or to craft your own, but be sure to explain your choice.
2. The case mentions two explanations of the dysfunctional culture at the division of Fish and Wildlife and Parks: (a) it shows "how one person's contempt for the public trust can infect an entire agency"; (b) it reflects a "culture of fear" fostered by certain senior managers. In your opinion, which of these explanations is a better place to start in analyzing and changing the division's culture?
3. How would you describe the *strategic values* at the Department of the Interior in general and the

Minerals Management Service in particular? What changes would you recommend at MMS? In your opinion, what *cultural values* must the agency develop in order to implement your recommended strategic values?
4. Review the section in the chapter entitled "Changing the Organization Culture." How would you go about changing the culture at MMS? How would you manage its *symbols* for change? How would you identify and handle *difficulties* that you're bound to encounter? How will you know if your changes are beginning to *stabilize* the agency's culture?

REFERENCES

Public Employees for Environmental Responsibility, "Interior Ethics Initiative Evaporates behind Closed Doors," news release, December 18, 2007, www.peer.org on May 10, 2010; Derek Kravitz, "Report: Interior Office Meddled with Endangered Species Act," *Washington Post*, December 15, 2008, http://voices.washingtonpost.com on May 10, 2010; Public Employees for Environmental Responsibility, "Interior Ethics Scandals Involve More Than 'A Few,' " news release, September 11, 2008, www.peer.org on May 10, 2010; Charlie Savage, "Sex, Drug Use and Graft Cited in Interior Department," *New York Times*, September 11, 2008, www.nytimes.com on May 10, 2010; Center for Biological Diversity, "Interior Department Exempted BP Drilling from Environmental Review," press release, May 5, 2010, www.biologicaldiversity.org on May 10, 2010; Juliet Eilperin, "U.S. Exempted BP's Gulf of Mexico Drilling from Environmental Impact Study," *Washington Post*, May 5, 2010, www.washingtonpost.com on May 10, 2010; Alan Fram and Sharon Theimer, "BP Spends Big in Washington, But Will That Help It Survive during Gulf Oil Spill Crisis?" *Los Angeles Times*, May 10, 2010, www.latimes.com on May 10, 2010.

EXPERIENCING ORGANIZATIONAL BEHAVIOR

Culture of the Classroom

Purpose   This exercise will help you appreciate the fascination as well as the difficulty of examining culture in organizations.

Format   The class will divide into groups of four to six. Each group will analyze the organization culture of a college class. Students in most classes that use this book will have taken many courses at the college they attend and therefore should have several classes in common.

Procedure   The class is divided into groups of four to six on the basis of classes the students have had in common.

1. Each group should first decide which class it will analyze. Each person in the group must have attended the class.
2. Each group should list the cultural factors to be discussed. Items to be covered should include
   a. Stories about the professor
   b. Stories about the exams
   c. Stories about the grading
   d. Stories about other students
   e. The use of symbols that indicate the students' values
   f. The use of symbols that indicate the instructor's values

g. Other characteristics of the class as suggested by the frameworks of Ouchi and Peters and Waterman.

3. Students should carefully analyze the stories and symbols to discover their underlying meanings. They should seek stories from other members of the group to ensure that all aspects of the class culture are covered. Students should take notes as these items are discussed.

4. After twenty to thirty minutes of work in groups, the instructor will reconvene the entire class and ask each group to share its analysis with the rest of the class.

Follow-up Questions

1. What was the most difficult part of this exercise? Did other groups experience the same difficulty?
2. How did your group overcome this difficulty? How did other groups overcome it?
3. Do you believe your group's analysis accurately describes the culture of the class you selected? Could other students who analyzed the culture of the same class come up with a very different result? How could that happen?
4. If the instructor wanted to try to change the culture in the class you analyzed, what steps would you recommend that he or she take?

BUILDING MANAGERIAL SKILLS

Exercise Overview Typically, managers are promoted or selected to fill jobs in an organization with a given organization culture. As they begin to work, they must recognize the culture and either learn how to work within it or figure out how to change it. If the culture is a performance-reducing one, managers must figure out how to change the culture to a performance-enhancing one. This exercise will give you a chance to develop your own ideas about changing organization culture.

Exercise Background Assume that you have just been appointed to head the legislative affairs committee of your local student government. As someone with a double major in business management and government, you are eager to take on this assignment and really make a difference. This committee has existed at your university for several years, but it has done little because the members use the committee as a social group and regularly throw great parties. In all the years of its existence, the committee has done nothing to impact the local state legislature in relation to the issues important to

university students, such as tuition. Since you know that the issue of university tuition will come before the state legislature during the current legislative session, and you know that many students could not afford a substantial raise in tuition, you are determined to use this committee to ensure that any tuition increase is as small as possible. However, you are worried that the party culture of the existing committee may make it difficult for you to use it to work for your issues. You also know that you cannot "fire" any of the volunteers on the committee and can add only two people to the committee.

Exercise Task Using this information as context, do the following:

1. Design a strategy for utilizing the existing culture of the committee to help you impact the legislature regarding tuition.
2. Assuming that the existing culture is a performance-reducing culture, design a strategy for changing it to a performance-enhancing culture.

SELF-ASSESSMENT EXERCISE

Refining Your Sense of Culture

This exercise is designed to help you assess what you now know about organization culture. The 10 statements in the following table reflect certain opinions about the nature of work performed in the context of organization culture. Indicate the extent to which you agree or disagree with each opinion by circling the number in the appropriate column.

Statement of opinion		Strongly agree				Strongly disagree
1. If a person can do well in one organization, he or she can do well in any organization.	1	2	3	4	5
2. Skills and experience are all that really matter; how a job candidate will "fit in" is not an important factor in hiring.	1	2	3	4	5
3. Members of an organization explicitly tell people how to adhere to its culture.	1	2	3	4	5
4. After appropriate study, astute managers can fairly quickly change a corporate culture.	1	2	3	4	5
5. A common culture is important for unifying employees but does not necessarily affect the firm's financial health.	1	2	3	4	5
6. Conscientious workers are not really influenced by an organization's culture.	1	2	3	4	5
7. Strong organization cultures are not necessarily associated with high organization performance.	1	2	3	4	5
8. Members of a subculture share the common values of the subculture but not those of the dominant organization culture.	1	2	3	4	5
9. Job candidates seeking to understand a prospective employer's culture can do so by just asking the people who interview them.	1	2	3	4	5
Your total score						

How to score: To get your total score, add up the values of the numbers that you have circled. You can then interpret your score as follows:

Your score	
40-50	You have excellent instincts about organization cultures and how people respond to them.
30-39	You show average or above-average awareness of the principles of organization culture.
20-29	You have some sense of how cultures affect workers, but you need to improve your knowledge.
0-19	You definitely need to bolster your knowledge before thinking further about assessing or modifying an organization culture.

REFERENCE

Phillip L. Hunsaker, *Management: A Skills Approach*, 2nd ed. (Upper Saddle River, NJ: Pearson Education, 2005), 303–04.

19

CHAPTER

ORGANIZATION CHANGE AND DEVELOPMENT

CHAPTER LEARNING OBJECTIVES

After studying this chapter, you should be able to:

- Summarize the dominant forces for change in organizations.
- Describe the process of planned organization change.
- Discuss several approaches to organization development.
- Explain resistance to change.
- Identify the keys to managing successful organization change and development.

Shifting Gears in the Auto Industry

"This is one of the few times that an auto company has hired talent from outside, and ... his unconventional approach has revolutionized the culture in a way that will keep the company competitive in the long term."

—AUTO INDUSTRY ANALYST ON CEO SERGIO MARCHIONNE'S TURNAROUND AT FIAT

The year 1983 was a good one for Chrysler. In August, legendary CEO Lee Iacocca presented a check to the U.S. government for a little over $800 million: the final repayment—7 years ahead of schedule—of $1.2 billion in guaranteed loans

RAVEENDRAN/AFP/GETTY IMAGES

CEO of the Fiat group, Sergio Marchionne (right), looks at the launch of the new Fiat Grande Punto and the Alfa Romeo Del at the Auto Expo 2006 in New Delhi. Following the revolutionary turnaround of Fiat, CEO Marchionne plans to do the same with Chrysler by introducing new engineering design processes and high-technology manufacturing. The new Fiat 500 models should show up in Chrysler showrooms in 2011.

that had allowed the company to stave off bankruptcy. In the same year, Chrysler introduced the phenomenally successful minivan, and within 4 years, its stock was selling for over $52 per share—up from $1.50 at its lowest point.

On the other hand, 1983 was not so good for the Italian automaker Fiat, which was forced to abandon the American market just 4 years after its U.S. sales had reached an all-time high. The main problem was a notorious reputation for unreliability—for many American car buyers, *Fiat* stood for "Fix it again, Tony." In 1994, Fiat pulled its Alfa Romeo sports car from the U.S. market and was shut out of the U.S. auto industry until 2000, when it entered a joint venture to share platforms with General Motors. Five years later, GM was only too happy to buy its way out of the venture for $2 billion rather than face the prospect of having to take over Fiat, which was wallowing in debt after accumulated losses of $14 billion.

Now flip the calendar forward to late 2008. In November, Chrysler cut 25 percent of its workforce and acknowledged that U.S. sales had dropped 35 percent in 12 months. CEO Robert Nardelli also admitted that the company could survive only by means of an alliance with another automaker and an infusion of government cash. In December, Chrysler announced that it would shut down all production through January 2009, that it planned to file for bankruptcy, and that it ultimately expected to cease production permanently. Federal aid to both Chrysler and GM was authorized in the same month and had topped $17 billion by March 2009, when the Obama administration gave Chrysler 30 days to finalize a previously announced merger agreement with Fiat or face the loss of another $6 billion in government subsidies.

Fiat? It seems that things had gone a little better for Fiat than they had for Chrysler since the ignominious end of its ill-fated venture with GM in 2005. A year later, Fiat had actually shown a profit—its first since 2000—and its stock price had doubled. It is now Europe's third-largest car company, behind only Volkswagen and Peugeot Citroën and ahead of Renault, Daimler (Mercedes Benz), and BMW, and now No. 8 in the world, producing more cars than Hyundai, Mitsubishi, or Chrysler.

The credit for this remarkable turnaround in Fiat's fortunes goes to Sergio Marchionne, an Italian-born executive with dual Italian and Canadian citizenship. In 2004, Fiat named Marchionne, an accountant and industry outsider, as its fifth CEO in two years. His hiring, observes Billie Blair, a consultant specializing in corporate change management, "was one of the few times when an auto company has hired talent from outside," and she reports that Marchionne brought an "unconventional approach" to the task of managing a car company in the twenty-first century. In the process, she says—citing Marchionne's own explanation of his success at Fiat—he "revolutionized the [Fiat] culture in a way that will keep the company competitive in the long term." Adds David Johnston, whose Atlanta-based marketing company has worked with Chrysler: Marchionne "has been able to garner respect for Fiat again after its down years and reestablish it as a business leader."

What was Marchionne's "unconventional approach"? It is the same approach that he plans to take at Chrysler. Taking over Fiat after nearly 15 years of continuously poor performance (during which the company's share of the Italian market had dropped from 52 to 28 percent), Marchionne was forced to lay off employees, but he also focused his job-cutting strategy on longer-term goals: he cut 10 percent of the company's white-collar workforce of about 20,000, stripping away layers of management and making room for a younger generation of managers with experience in brand marketing rather than engineering. Refocusing the company on market-driven imperatives, he cut the design-to-market process from 4 years to 18 months, and even more importantly, he spurred the introduction of a slew of new products. The Grande Punto, launched in mid-2005, was the best-selling subcompact in Western Europe a year later and spearheaded the firm's resurgence. The Fiat Nuova 500, a subcompact with a distinctive retro look (think Volkswagen New Beetle), was first introduced in 2007. Both the car and its marketing launch were designed with heavy customer involvement, and the 500, like the Grande Punto, was an immediate success, with first-year sales outstripping Fiat's original target by 160 percent.

Under the merger agreement reached with Fiat in June 2009, the 500 is one of at least seven Fiat vehicles that Chrysler will begin building and selling in the United States by 2014. Slated to come out in four versions—hatchback, sporty hatchback, convertible, and station wagon—the U.S. adaptation of the 500 will start selling in early 2011, and Marchionne is convinced that, with a full range of body styles, "the 500 . . . will be a smash if we do it right." Strategically, Marchionne knows that he has to reposition Chrysler from a maker of clunky gas-guzzlers to a marketer of stylish energy-efficient technology, and the 500, which one marketing association in Japan has declared "the sexiest car in the world," has been designated the flagship in Fiat Chrysler's new North American fleet.

Many analysts, however, are skeptical about Marchionne's prospects for turning Chrysler around even if the 500 turns out to be a "smash." "It's a cute car," says Oliver Hazimeh of the consulting firm PRTM, ". . . but I don't think it's a game changer. . . . They need at least one or two what I would call 'home runs'—really 9 out of 10 strong 'buy' recommendations by Consumer Reports. And they need to have two or three additional, also very strong, product offerings." As of 2009, however, Consumer Reports had rated Chrysler's aging, truck-heavy product line "woefully uncompetitive," and in April 2010, analysts at the investment research firm Bernstein remained "unconvinced that Chrysler will survive in its current form despite Marchionne's blood, sweat, and tears."

The issue may come down to a matter of time. According to Marchionne's five-year plan for reviving Chrysler, its American partner will depend on Fiat platforms for 56 percent of its production volume by 2014, but as we have seen, the company's first new product—the Fiat 500—will not be in showrooms until 2011. The big question, then, is whether "New Chrysler" (officially Chrysler Group LLC) can hang on financially until projected new-product revenues start filling the company coffers. Marchionne says it can: he estimates that, at least for the present, Chrysler needs a 9 percent market share on industry sales of 10 million units in order to break even—and at the end of 2009, Chrysler was holding on to a 9.2 percent share in an industry that had sold 10.9 million units. Chrysler sales, Marchionne added in March 2010, were ahead of internal targets, and he was more confident about the prospects for a turnaround than he had been a year earlier, when the merger plans were being drawn up. "We've been sticking to our guns," he told reporters, "and it's worked well so far."

And if there is a long run for Fiat Chrysler in the U.S. market, what are Marchionne's long-term plans? For at least part of the answer to this question, see the *Technology* box entitled "Fiat's Designs on the U.S. Car Market" on page 539.

What Do You Think?

1. What kinds of behavioral changes do you foresee for the Chrysler employees under the new management?

2. Do you think the employees who remain at Chrysler will resist the changes required by the new management? Why or why not?

References: Dale Buss, "Fiat CEO Marchionne Has Led Unlikely Turnaround," *Edmunds Auto Observer*, January 21, 2009, www.autoobserver.com on May 17, 2010; Leslie Wayne, "Sergio Marchionne," *New York Times*, May 1, 2009, http://topics.nytimes.com on May 17, 2010; Gail Edmondson, "GM Leaves Fiat in the Dust," *BusinessWeek*, February 15, 2005, www.businessweek.com on May 17, 2010; Joann Muller, "Obama Takes the Wheel in Detroit," *Forbes.com*, March 30, 2009, www.forbes.com on May 17, 2010; James R. Healey, "7 New Fiat Models Bound for U.S.; 9 Chryslers to Go Abroad," *USA Today*, April 21, 2010, www.usatoday.com on May 20, 2010; Chris Poole, "2011 Fiat 500 Review and Prices," *Consumer Guide Automotive*, August 2, 2009, http://consumerguideauto.howstuffworks.com on May 20, 2010; "Analyst: Chrysler Unlikely to Survive As Is: Do You Agree?" *Motor Trend*, April 17, 2010, http://wot.motortrend.com on May 20, 2010; Soyoung Kim, "Chrysler Rescue under Fiat Still Uncertain," Reuters, April 20, 2010, www.reuters.com on May 17, 2010.

Chrysler and Fiat are typical of the predicament in which many organizations find themselves. They have a good business model that works and makes them a lot of money, possibly for many years. Then, the environment changes and the former business model no longer works. Companies that change appropriately can continue as viable businesses. Those that do not make the right changes cease to exist by going out of business or by being gobbled up by a larger organization. This chapter is about how organizations need to face the prospect of change and develop processes to ensure their viability in a complex, ever-changing global environment. The chapter begins with a discussion of some of the forces that create pressures for change followed by a detailed explanation of the complex change process. Then, we describe organization development and sources of resistance to change, finishing with a summary view of how to manage change in organizations.

FORCES FOR CHANGE

An organization is subject to pressures for change from far too many sources than can be discussed here. Moreover, it is difficult to predict what types of pressures for change will be most significant in the next decade because the complexity of events and the rapidity of change are increasing. However, it is possible—and important—to discuss the broad categories of pressures that probably will have major effects on organizations. The four areas in which the pressures for change appear most powerful involve people, technology, information processing and communication, and competition. Table 19.1 gives examples of each of these categories.

People

Approximately 56 million people were born in the United States between 1945 and 1960. These baby boomers differed significantly from previous generations with respect to education, expectations, and value systems.[1] As this group has aged, the median age of the U.S. population has gradually increased, passing 32 for the first time in 1988[2] and further increasing to 36.8 in 2008.[3] The special characteristics of baby boomers

Category	Examples	Type of Pressure for Change
People	Generation X, Y, Millennials Global Labor Supplies Senior citizens Workforce diversity	Demands for different training, benefits, workplace arrangements, and compensation systems
Technology	Manufacturing in space Internet Global design teams	More education and training for workers at all levels, more new products, products move faster to market
Information Processing and Communication	Computer, satellite communications Global Sourcing Videoconferencing Social Networking	Faster reaction times, immediate responses to questions, new products, different office arrangements, telecommuting, marketing, advertising, recruiting on social networking sites
Competition	Global markets International trade agreements Emerging nations	Global competition, more competing products with more features and options, lower costs, higher quality

Table 19.1
PRESSURES FOR ORGANIZATION CHANGE

show up in distinct purchasing patterns that affect product and service innovation, technological change, and marketing and promotional activities.[4] Employment practices, compensation systems, promotion and managerial succession systems, and the entire concept of human resource management are also affected.

Other population-related pressures for change involve the generations that sandwich the baby boomers: the increasing numbers of senior citizens and those born after 1960. The parents of the baby boomers are living longer, healthier lives than previous generations, and today they expect to live the "good life" that they missed when they were raising their children. The impact of the large number of senior citizens is already evident in part-time employment practices, in the marketing of everything from hamburgers to packaged tours of Asia, and in service areas such as healthcare, recreation, and financial services. The post-1960 generation of workers—often called Generation X, who entered the job market in the 1980s— was different from the baby-boom generation. Sociologists and psychologists have identified a new group, often called Millennials, born from roughly between 1980 and 2000 (experts differ on start and end dates from as early as 1977 to as late as 2002), who seem to be experiencing a distinct and separate life stage in between adolescence and adulthood in which young people may jump from job to job and relationship to relationship, often living at home with few responsibilities and experimenting with life. Millennials are putting off marriage, childbearing, home purchases, and most adult responsibilities.[5] However, they seem to be much more group oriented, celebrate diversity, are optimistic, assimilate technology, and multitask very fast.[6] These changes in demographics extend to the composition of the workforce, family lifestyles, and purchasing patterns worldwide.

The increasing diversity of the workforce in coming years will mean significant changes for organizations. This increasing diversity was discussed in some detail in Chapter 2. In addition, employees are facing a different work environment in the twenty-first century. The most descriptive word for this new work environment is "change." Employees must be prepared for constant change. Change is occurring in organizations' cultures, structures, work relationships, and customer relationships, as well as in the actual jobs that people do. People will have to be completely adaptable to new situations while maintaining productivity under the existing system.[7]

Technology

Not only is technology changing, but the rate of technological change is also increasing. In 1970, for example, all engineering students owned slide rules and used them in almost every class. By 1976, slide rules had given way to portable electronic calculators. In the mid-1980s, some universities began issuing personal computers to entering students or assumed that those students already owned them. In 1993, the Scholastic Aptitude Test (SAT), which many college-bound students take to get into college, allowed calculators to be used during the test. Today students cannot make it through the university without owning or at least having ready access to a personal computer in the form of a laptop, notebook, or iPad. Residence halls at most universities are wired for direct computer access for email and class assignments and for connection to the Internet. Many buildings at many universities are set up for wireless access for faculty, students, staff, and campus guests. With 3G and 4G technology people have Internet access from just about anywhere. Technological development is increasing so rapidly in almost every field that it is quite difficult to predict which products will dominate ten years from now. DuPont is an example of a company that is making major changes due to new technological developments. Although its business had been based on petrochemicals since the end of the nineteenth century, DuPont changed its basic business strategy as new technology developed in the life sciences.

It reorganized its eighty-one business units into only three and invested heavily in agrichemicals and the life sciences. Realizing that a biotechnology-based business changes much more rapidly than a petrochemical-based business, DuPont's former chairman from 1998 to 2008, Chad Holliday, had to make cultural changes as well as structural ones in order to make the strategy work.[8]

Interestingly, organization change is self-perpetuating. With the advances in information technology, organizations generate more information, and it circulates faster. Consequently, employees can respond more quickly to problems, so the organization can respond more quickly to demands from other organizations, customers, and competitors. Toyota, long known as a leader in developing and using new technologies in its plants, has introduced new advanced robots, "kokino robotto," in its efforts improve efficiency in its plants and reduce its costs to the level of China.[9]

New technology will affect organizations in ways we cannot yet predict. Gesture technology may eliminate all controls in your home, from your AV system remote to your thermostat, and replace them with your own gestures with your own hands and fingers. HP's TouchSmart

AP PHOTO/DAMIAN DOVARGANES

The HP TouchSmart PC is displayed at the HP booth at the 2007 International Consumer Electronics Show (CES) in Las Vegas, Nevada. The HP TouchSmart PC has a 19-inch touchscreen, AMD Turion 64 X 2 dual core TL-52 processor, 2GB SDRAM, 320GB drive, NVIDIA GeForce Go 7600, WiFi, Bluetooth, integrated 1.3 megapixel camera, integrated FM and ATSC HDTV tuners, a DVDRW / DVD-RAM burner with LightScribe, Pocket Media Drive bay, wireless keyboard, mouse, stylus, front media reader. The TouchSmart runs Windows Vista. HP TouchSmart 300 PC features Roxio CinemaNow, an application that enables users to rent or buy more than 12,000 movies. And that was 2007. Developers have now created an entire touchless wall that serves as the display using nine HDTVs and two infrared cameras.

technology allows people to touch things without actually touching them, and could drive innovations in medicine and education in a decade. Sensawaft technology will allow people to control devices such as smart phones and ATMs using exhaled breath—which could dramatically increase mobility and control for people with limited mobility.[10]

Several companies are developing systems to manufacture chemicals and exotic electronic components in space. The Internet, the World Wide Web, and cloud computing are changing the way companies and individuals communicate, market, buy, and distribute faster than organizations can respond. Thus, as organizations react more quickly to change, change occurs more rapidly, which in turn necessitates more rapid responses.

Information Processing and Communication

Advances in information processing and communication have paralleled each other. A new generation of computers, which will mark another major increase in processing power, is being designed. Satellite systems for data transmission are already in use. Today people carry a device in their pocket that serves as their portable computer, e-reader, pocket-size television, camera, video recorder, music player, and their personal communication device (telephone), all in one device. And they work all over the world.

Social networking may be the most radical and fastest-growing aspect of the advances in information processing and communication. Through such sites as MySpace, Facebook, Twitter, LinkedIn, NING, Bebo, Viadeo, and many others, people are networking with others exploring common interests. People are spending hours reading about others and updating their own sites. Business uses of this phenomenon include advertising, marketing, market research and test marketing, recruiting, and more. And everyone looking for a job starts with Monster.com, Jobing.com, and similar sites.[11]

In the future, people may not need offices as they work with computers and communicate through new data transmission devices. Work stations, both inside and outside of offices, will be more electronic than paper and pencil. For years, the capability has existed to generate, manipulate, store, and transmit more data than managers could use, but the benefits were not fully realized. Now the time has come to utilize all of that information-processing potential, and companies are making the most of it. Typically, companies received orders by mail in the 1970s, by toll-free telephone numbers in the 1980s, by fax machine in the late 1980s and early 1990s, and by electronic data exchange in the mid-1990s. Orders used to take a week; now they are placed instantaneously, and companies can and must be able to respond immediately, all because of changes in information processing and communication.[12] Zappos.com (discussed in more detail in Chapter 18) can ship a pair of shoes in as little as eight minutes from receiving an order.[13] Suppliers and end users in some industries now have the parts systems integrated so closely that new parts shipments sometimes are not even ordered—they just show up at the receiving dock when they are needed.

Competition

Although competition is not a new force for change, competition today has some significant new twists. First, most markets are global because of decreasing transportation and communication costs and the increasing export orientation of business.[14] The adoption of trade agreements such as the North American Free Trade Agreement (NAFTA) and the presence of the World Trade Organization (WTO) have changed the way business operates. In the future, competition from industrialized countries such as Japan and Germany will take a back seat to competition from the booming industries of developing nations such as China and India. The Internet is creating new competitors overnight in ways that could not have been imagined five years ago. Companies in developing nations may soon offer different, newer, cheaper, or higher-quality products while enjoying the benefits of low labor costs, abundant supplies of raw materials, expertise in certain areas of production, and financial protection from their own governments that may not be available to firms in older industrialized states.

Consider, for example, the market for cell phones or smart phones. Once consumers simply compared calling plans and phone costs and chose a phone available from a provider with the best deal and coverage in their primary area of usage. Currently, the choices are far more complex as we now have platforms, as well as manufacturers and carriers or service providers. Manufacturers include Apple, Blackberry, Motorola, Samsung, Sony Ericsson, HTC, LG, Nokia, Palm, Toshiba, and others. Carriers include Verizon, T-Mobile, AT&T, Sprint, Alltel, Bell, Orange, O2, Vodafone, and others. Platforms include Android, MacOS, Java, Linux, Palm OS, Symbian, Windows Mobile, and others. For consumers the choices are seemingly endless and extremely confusing. Manufacturers have to develop new equipment and software combinations to work on various platforms for a variety of carriers. Carriers must decide which instruments and platform combinations to offer to subscribers. And platform developers must show their platform can do more things, simpler and with fewer errors, with maximum flexibility. And every month there are new combinations of all three to further confuse consumers, as well as industry experts.

PROCESSES FOR PLANNED ORGANIZATION CHANGE

External forces may impose change on an organization. Ideally, however, the organization will not only respond to change but will also anticipate it, prepare for it through planning, and incorporate it in the organization strategy. Organization change can be viewed from a static point of view, such as that of Lewin (see next section), or from a dynamic perspective.

Lewin's Process Model

Planned organization change requires a systematic process of movement from one condition to another. Kurt Lewin suggested that efforts to bring about planned change in organizations should approach change as a multistage process.[15] His model of planned change is made up of three steps—unfreezing, change, and refreezing—as shown in Figure 19.1.

Figure 19.1 **LEWIN'S PROCESS OF ORGANIZATION STRUCTURE**

In Lewin's three-step model, change is a systematic process of transition from an old way of doing things to a new way. Inclusion of an "unfreezing" stage indicates the importance of preparing for the change. The "refreezing" stage reflects the importance of following up on the change to make it permanent.

Unfreezing is the process by which people become aware of the need for change. If people are satisfied with current practices and procedures, they may have little or no interest in making changes. The key factor in unfreezing is making employees understand the importance of a change and how their jobs will be affected by it. The employees who will be most affected by the change must be made aware of why it is needed, which in effect makes them dissatisfied enough with current operations to be motivated to change. Creating in employees the awareness of the need for change is the responsibility of the leadership of the organization.[16] Following the recent deep recession with so much downsizing, layoffs, restructuring, and takeovers, employees may be weary of the constant pressure and uncertainties of their position and/or organization. Top managers and change agents are urged to make the effort to empathize with employees, acknowledge the difficulties of the past and uncertainties of the present, and provide forums for employees to vent a little, followed up with workshops for information sharing and training. After making the emotional connection with employees, top management can make the intellectual connection and make the business case by sharing economic and marketing data and the short- and long-term visions for the organization, and by involving employees at all levels in translating organizational goals into division, department, and work unit goals.[17]

Change itself is the movement from the old way of doing things to a new way. Change may entail installing new equipment, restructuring the organization, or implementing a new performance appraisal system—anything that alters existing relationships or activities.

Refreezing makes new behaviors relatively permanent and resistant to further change. Examples of refreezing techniques include repeating newly learned skills in a training session and then role playing to teach how the new skill can be used in a real-life work situation. Refreezing is necessary because without it, the old ways of doing things might soon reassert themselves while the new ways are forgotten. For example, many employees who attend special training sessions apply themselves diligently and resolve to change things in their organizations. But when they return to the workplace, they find it easier to conform to the old ways than to make waves. There usually are few, if any, rewards for trying to change the organizational status quo. In fact, the personal sanctions against doing so may be difficult to tolerate. Learning theory and reinforcement theory (see Chapter 4) can play important roles in the refreezing phase.

The Continuous Change Process Model

Perhaps because Lewin's model is very simple and straightforward, virtually all models of organization change use his approach. However, it does not deal with several important issues. A more complex, and more helpful, approach is illustrated in Figure 19.2. This approach treats planned change from the perspective of top management and indicates that change is continuous. Although we discuss each step as if it were separate and distinct from the others, it is important to note that as change becomes continuous in organizations, different steps are probably occurring simultaneously throughout the organization. The model incorporates Lewin's concept into the implementation phase.

In this approach, top management perceives that certain forces or trends call for change, and the issue is subjected to the organization's usual problem-solving and decision-making processes (see Chapter 8). Usually, top management defines its goals in terms of what the organization or certain processes or outputs will be like after the change. Alternatives for change are generated and evaluated, and an acceptable one is selected.

Unfreezing is the process by which people become aware of the need for change.

Refreezing is the process of making new behaviors relatively permanent and resistant to further change.

Figure 19.2 CONTINUOUS CHANGE PROCESS MODEL
OF ORGANIZATION CHANGE

The continuous change process model incorporates the forces for change, a problem-solving process, a change agent, and transition management. It takes a top-management perspective and highlights the fact that in organizations today, change is a continuous process.

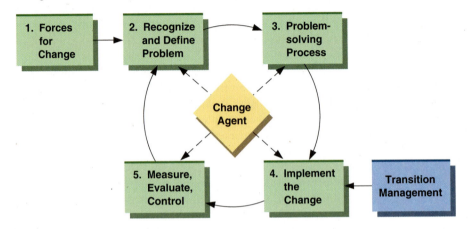

Early in the process, the organization may seek the assistance of a **change agent**— a person who will be responsible for managing the change effort. The change agent may also help management recognize and define the problem or the need for the change and may be involved in generating and evaluating potential plans of action. The change agent may be a member of the organization, an outsider such as a consultant, or even someone from headquarters whom employees view as an outsider. An internal change agent is likely to know the organization's people, tasks, and political situations, which may be helpful in interpreting data and understanding the system; but an insider may also be too close to the situation to view it objectively. (In addition, a regular employee would have to be removed from his or her regular duties to concentrate on the transition.) An outsider, then, is often received better by all parties because of his or her assumed impartiality. Under the direction and management of the change agent, the organization implements the change through Lewin's unfreeze, change, and refreeze process.

The final step is measurement, evaluation, and control. The change agent and the top management group assess the degree to which the change is having the desired effect; that is, they measure progress toward the goals of the change and make appropriate changes if necessary. The more closely the change agent is involved in the change process, the less distinct the steps become. The change agent becomes a "collaborator" or "helper" to the organization as she or he is immersed in defining and solving the problem with members of the organization. When this happens, the change agent may be working with many individuals, groups, and departments within the organization on different phases of the change process. When the change process is moving along from one stage to another, it may not be readily observable because of the total involvement of the change agent in every phase of the project. Throughout the process, however, the change agent brings in new ideas and viewpoints that help members look at old problems in new ways. Change often arises from the conflict that results when the change agent challenges the organization's assumptions and generally accepted patterns of operation.

A **change agent** is a person responsible for managing a change effort.

In this cartoon, the new "bungee boss" is like the change agent who sweeps in announcing many changes and then disappears. Clearly, little change will be accomplished with the "bungee boss"–type of change agent because employees never know what is happening next or when the "bungee boss" will reappear. This illustrates the importance of having a change agent who is intimately involved in the entire change process.

Through the measurement, evaluation, and control phase, top management determines the effectiveness of the change process by evaluating various indicators of organizational productivity and effectiveness or employee morale. It is expected the organization will be better after the change than before. However, the uncertainties and rapid changes in all sectors of the environment make constant organization change a given for most organizations.

Transition management is the process of systematically planning, organizing, and implementing change, from the disassembly of the current state to the realization of a fully functional future state within an organization.[18] No matter how much planning precedes the change and how well it is implemented, because people are involved there will always be unanticipated and unpredictable things that happen along the way.[19] One key role of transition management is to deal with these unintended consequences. Once change begins, the organization is in neither the old state nor the new state, yet business must go on. Transition management also ensures that business continues while the change is occurring; therefore, it must begin before the change occurs. The members of the regular management team must take on the role of transition managers and coordinate organizational activities with the change agent. An interim management structure or interim positions may be created to ensure continuity and control of the business during the transition. Communication about the changes to all involved, from employees to customers and suppliers, plays a key role in transition management.[20]

ORGANIZATION DEVELOPMENT

On one level, organization development is simply the way organizations change and evolve. Organization change can involve personnel, technology, competition, and other areas. Employee learning and formal training, transfers, promotions, terminations, and retirements are all examples of personnel-related changes. Thus, in the broadest sense, organization development means organization change.[21] The term as used here, however, means something more specific. Over the past forty

Transition management is the process of systematically planning, organizing, and implementing change.

years, organization development has emerged as a distinct field of study and practice. Experts now substantially agree as to what constitutes organization development in general, although arguments about details continue.[22] Our definition of organization development is an attempt to describe a very complex process in a simple manner. It is also an attempt to capture the best points of several definitions offered by writers in the field.

Organization Development Defined

"**Organization development** (OD) is a system-wide application of behavioral science knowledge to the planned development and reinforcement of organizational strategies, structures, and processes for improving an organization's effectiveness."[23] Three points in this definition make it simple to remember and use. First, organization development involves attempts to plan organization changes, which excludes spontaneous, haphazard initiatives. Second, the specific intention of organization development is to improve organization effectiveness. This point excludes changes that merely imitate those of another organization, are forced on the organization by external pressures, or are undertaken merely for the sake of changing. Third, the planned improvement must be based on knowledge of the behavioral sciences such as organizational behavior, psychology, sociology, cultural anthropology, and related fields of study rather than on financial or technological considerations. Under this definition, the replacement of manual personnel records with a computerized system would not be considered an instance of organization development. Although such a change has behavioral effects, it is a technology-driven reform rather than a behavioral one. Likewise, alterations in record keeping necessary to support new government-mandated reporting requirements are not a part of organization development because the change is obligatory and the result of an external force. The three most basic types of techniques for implementing organization development are system-wide, task and technological, and group and individual.

At one time in the 1960s and 1970s organization development was treated as a field of study and practiced by specially trained OD professionals. However, as organization change became the order of the day in progressive organizations around the world, it became clear that all organizational leaders needed to become leaders and teachers of change throughout their organizations if their organizations were going to survive. Excellent examples of organizations that have embraced OD are the U.S. Army, General Electric, and Royal Dutch Shell.[24]

System-wide Organization Development

The most comprehensive type of organization change involves a major reorientation or reorganization—usually referred to as a **structural change** or a system-wide rearrangement of task division and authority and reporting relationships. A structural change affects performance appraisal and rewards, decision making, and communication and information-processing systems. As we discussed in Chapter 17, reengineering and rethinking the organizations are two contemporary approaches to system-wide structural change. Reengineering can be a difficult process, but it has great potential for organizational improvement. It requires that managers challenge long-held assumptions about everything they do and set outrageous goals and expect that they will be met. An organization may change the way it divides tasks into jobs, combines jobs into departments and divisions, and arranges authority and reporting relationships among positions. It may move from functional departmentalization to a system based on products or geography, for example, or from a conventional linear design to

Organization development is a system-wide application of behavioral science knowledge to the planned development and reinforcement of organizational strategies, structures, and processes for improving organizational effectiveness.

Structural change is a system-wide organization development involving a major restructuring of the organization or instituting programs such as quality of work life.

a matrix or a team-based design. Other changes may include dividing large groups into smaller ones or merging small groups into larger ones. In addition, the degree to which rules and procedures are written down and enforced, as well as the locus of decision-making authority, may be altered. Supervisors may become "coaches" or "facilitators" in a team-based organization. The organization will have transformed both the configurational and the operational aspects of its structure if all of these changes are made.

No system-wide structural change is simple.[25] A company president cannot just issue a memo notifying company personnel that on a certain date they will report to a different supervisor and be responsible for new tasks and expect everything to change overnight. Employees have months, years, and sometimes decades of experience in dealing with people and tasks in certain ways. When these patterns are disrupted, employees need time to learn the new tasks and to settle into the new relationships. Moreover, they may resist the change for a number of reasons; we discuss resistance to change later in this chapter. Therefore, organizations must manage the change process.

Ford Motor Company is pretty typical of organizations that have had to make major organization-wide and worldwide changes. Over the years, Ford had developed several regional fiefdoms, such as Ford of Europe, Ford United States, and Ford Australia, which all operated relatively independently. When Jacques Nasser was named CEO, he set out to tear down those regionally based organizations and to create a truly globally integrated car manufacturer. As his plan was unfolding, however, Ford continued to lose market share, so on October 30, 2001, Nasser was replaced as CEO by Ford family member William Clay (Bill) Ford Jr., who is continuing to develop the global integration of the design, development, and manufacture of Ford automobiles. In the years under the leadership of Alan Mulally, Ford has made a stunning turnaround. [26]

Another system-wide change is the introduction of quality-of-work-life programs. J. Lloyd Suttle defined **quality of work life** as the "degree to which members of a work organization are able to satisfy important personal needs through their experiences in the organization."[27] Quality-of-work-life programs focus strongly on providing a work environment conducive to satisfying individual needs. The emphasis on improving life at work developed during the 1970s, a period of increasing inflation and deepening recession. The development was rather surprising because an expanding economy and substantially increased resources are the conditions that usually induce top management to begin people-oriented programs. However, top management viewed improving life at work as a means of improving productivity.

Any movement with broad and ambiguous goals tends to spawn diverse programs, each claiming to be based on the movement's goals, and the quality-of-work-life movement is no exception. These programs vary substantially, although most espouse a goal of "humanizing the workplace." Richard Walton divided them into the eight categories shown in Figure 19.3.[28] Obviously, many types of programs can be accommodated by the categories, from changing the pay system to establishing an employee bill of rights that guarantees workers the rights to privacy, free speech, due process, and fair and equitable treatment. The Defense Information Systems Agency (DISA) has a QWL program that includes options for a compressed work schedule, in which employees can work 80 hours in nine work days over a two week period, and a "telework" option in which eligible employees may telework at an alternative worksite such as a telework center, at home, or at a satellite office, on a regular and recurring schedule for a maximum of three days per week. The program is designed to promote a more beneficial lifestyle for employees personally, as well as professionally.[29]

Total quality management, which was discussed in several earlier chapters, can also be viewed as a system-wide organization development program. In fact, some might consider total quality management as a broad program that includes structural

Quality of work life is the extent to which workers can satisfy important personal needs through their experiences in the organization.

Figure 19.3 WALTON'S CATEGORIZATION OF QUALITY-OF-WORK-LIFE PROGRAMS

Quality-of-work-life programs can be categorized into eight types. The expected benefits of these programs are increased employee morale, productivity, and organizational effectiveness.

Reference: Adapted from Richard E. Walton, "Quality of Work Life: What Is It?" *Sloan Management Review,* Fall 1973, pp. 11–21, by permission of the publisher. Copyright © 1973 by the Sloan Management Review Association. All rights reserved.

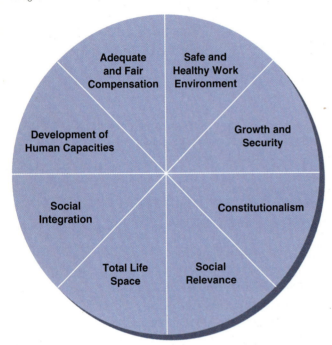

change as well as quality of work life. It differs from quality of work life in that it emphasizes satisfying customer needs by making quality-oriented changes rather than focusing on satisfying employee needs at work. Often, however, the employee programs are very similar to it.

The benefits gained from quality-of-work-life programs differ substantially, but generally they are of three types. A more positive attitude toward the work and the organization, or increased job satisfaction, is perhaps the most direct benefit.[30] Another is increased productivity, although it is often difficult to measure and separate the effects of the quality-of-work-life program from the effects of other organizational factors. A third benefit is increased effectiveness of the organization as measured by its profitability, goal accomplishment, shareholder wealth, or resource exchange. The third gain follows directly from the first two: if employees have more positive attitudes about the organization and their productivity increases, everything else being equal, the organization should be more effective.

Task and Technological Change

Another way to bring about system-wide organization development is through changes in the tasks involved in doing the work, the technology, or both. The direct alteration of jobs usually is called "task redesign." Changing how inputs are transformed into outputs is called "technological change" and also usually results in task changes. Strictly speaking, changing the technology is typically not part of organization development whereas task redesign usually is. However, even with a typical technology-based change, OD techniques are often used to facilitate the technological changes. At the "New Chrysler," for example, Fiat intends to enhance the product line by introducing a number of new technologies, many of them essential to the development of smaller, more fuel-efficient cars. As you can see from the *Technology* box entitled "Fiat's Designs on the U.S. Car Market" on page 539, this long-range plan entails changes not only in the product line, but also in the organization's perception of consumer preferences as well.

The structural changes discussed in the preceding section are explicitly system-wide in scope. Those we examine in this section are more narrowly focused and may not seem to have the same far-reaching consequences. It is important to remember, however, that their impact is felt throughout the organization. The discussion of task design in Chapter 5 focused on job definition and motivation and gave little attention to implementing changes in jobs. Here we discuss task redesign as a mode of organization change.

Several approaches to introducing job changes in organizations have been proposed. One is by a coauthor of this book, Ricky W. Griffin. Griffin's approach is an integrative framework of nine steps that reflect the complexities of the interfaces between individual

TECHNOLOGY

Fiat's Designs on the U.S. Car Market

"Sexy" used to refer to something that aroused plain old sexual interest, but not any more. Today, it can mean *appealing, attractive, exciting* (though not necessarily in the plain old sexual sense), or even—if you are a marketer or a marketing-sensitive consumer—*trendy*. A quick Google survey, for example, leaves no doubt that the extremely desirable iPod is "sexy"—as is just about everything designed to come into functional contact with it. If you want to enhance the sound from your iPod, you can get a "sexy iPod speaker station" from Sony. If you just want to stand it up on a shelf, all you need is a "sexy iPod dock" from Finite Elemente. You can put your iPod in a "Sexy Hard Case" from Speck Products, and if that is not quite as sexy as you had in mind, you can opt for a "sexy Bikini-shaped" case from Gamila and Pacific Design.

According to a blogger who signs herself/ himself "Sexylicious" (and who may thus be biased), "sexy is what makes a person do a double take. A person who is sexy turns heads, demands attention. A sexy car," he or she explains, "can have the same effect," and this otherwise casual analogy brings us back to the Fiat 500, which we introduced in our chapter-opening story: in the opinion of many people who pay attention to the relative arousal effects of automobiles, the 500 is a sexy car. In fact, *Top Gear*, England's best-selling automotive magazine, declared the 500 the "Sexiest Car in the World" (it "advertises nothing about its owner except that it's someone who doesn't need to try"). And that was *before* Fiat introduced the *Nuova 500* (i.e., *New 500*), which was promptly anointed the sexiest car of 2008 by evecars.com, a British women's car-buying website. Survey feedback, reports

> *"It's a highly technical product, but it has a purity and honesty to it. I want to ... get that kind of design language back into the product at Fiat."*
>
> —AUTOMOTIVE DESIGNER FRANK STEPHENSON ON THE IPOD

editor Alex Jenner-Furst, revealed "that women feel incredibly sexy when they drive this vehicle. ... It's fun to drive and looks the business," and size, apparently, is not all that important: the 140-inch 500 "may be small," adds Jenner-Furst, "but it's perfectly formed."

If all these cross-gender consumer plaudits are not enough to confirm that Fiat had sexy in mind when it designed the 500, consider the fact that CEO Sergio Marchionne calls the 500 "our iPod" and has encouraged executives at both Fiat and Chrysler to benchmark Apple's approach to product design and branding. Marchionne oversaw the development of the 500 as a key component of his strategy for turning Fiat around, and his main challenge in doing the same for Chrysler, says Carlo Carnevale, an Italian strategic-management expert, is to move the American carmaker "into 'pop' products, full of cool environmental technology." In Carnevale's view, Marchionne wants to do in the automotive industry what Steve Jobs has done in high tech (see the opening story in Chapter 3), and that, he explains, is why both Marchionne and Frank Stephenson, who designed the Fiat 500, are fond of "the iPod metaphor." Stephenson characterizes the iPod as "simplicity that's beautiful. ... It's so simple, but it's just right. ... It's a highly technical product, but it has a purity and honesty to it. I want to ... get that kind of design language back into the product at Fiat."

Stephenson reminds us that "sexy" usually entails a blend of design and high tech, and it is important to remember that when it comes to Fiat's award-winning innovations in "design," we are talking about more than just the creative fashion sense that makes the 500 "retro-cute."

Continued

According to Consumer Guide Automotive, an online buyer's resource, the Fiat 500 is "a thoroughly modern car" because it combines "retro-chic styling" with "premium engineering," including a small turbo-charged diesel engine with which Fiat hopes to balance out Chrysler's product line, which is currently weighed down with fuel-inefficient trucks and SUVs.

Fiat engine designs are also eco-friendly. Its cars carry some of the lowest carbon dioxide-emissions ratings on the market—a significant factor in Chrysler's eagerness to ally itself with the Italian carmaker. Fiat has already unveiled all-electric and hybrid versions of the 500 and plans to introduce both into the U.S. market in 2012. In February 2009, the Obama administration had made it clear that if Chrysler wanted a federal bailout, it was going to have to get a lot greener: "Industry financial analysts and industry experts," declared a presidential task force on the auto industry, "are nearly unanimous in their views that, to be competitive in the decades to come, auto companies will need to transform their processes and products to improve efficiency, reduce costs, and offer a higher-quality, more fuel-efficient fleet." Responding in April to the announcement of the Chrysler-Fiat merger, President Obama thus applauded "a partnership that will give Chrysler a chance not only to survive, but to thrive in a global auto industry. Fiat," he explained, "has demonstrated that it can build the clean, fuel-efficient cars that are the future of the industry."

References: "What Does Sexy Mean?" *The Sexy Side of Life*, June 17, 2007, http://sexy-side-of-life.blogspot.com on May 21, 2010; Ben Farmer, "Fiat 500 Is Britain's Sexiest Car," *Telegraph*, September 5, 2008, www.telegraph.co.uk on May 22, 2010; Peter Gumbel, "Chrysler's Sergio Marchionne: The Turnaround Artista," *Time*, www.time.com on May 20, 2010; "Online Extra: Fiat's Sexy Designs on Success," *BusinessWeek*, January 16, 2006, www.businessweek.com on May 20, 2010; Chris Poole, "2011 Fiat 500 Review and Prices," *Consumer Guide Automotive*, July 2, 2009, http://consumerguideauto.howstuffworks.com on May 20, 2010; Shawn Langlois, "Style and Substance," *MarketWatch*, December 3, 2009, www.marketwatch.com on May 24, 2010; Brian Merchant, "Obama to Automakers: Make Greener American Cars or Go Under," *TreeHugger.com*, March 30, 2009, www.treehugger.com on May 24, 2010.

jobs and the total organization.[31] The process, shown in Table 19.2, includes the steps usually associated with change such as recognizing the need for a change, selecting the appropriate intervention, and evaluating the change. But Griffin's approach inserts four additional steps into the standard sequence: diagnosis of the overall work system and context, including examination of the jobs, workforce, technology, organization design, leadership, and group dynamics; evaluating the costs and benefits of the change; formulating a redesign strategy; and implementing supplemental changes.

Diagnosis includes analysis of the total work environment within which the jobs exist. It is important to evaluate the organization structure, especially the work rules and decision-making authority within a department, when job changes are being considered.[32] For example, if jobs are to be redesigned to give employees more freedom in choosing work methods or scheduling work activities, diagnosis of the present system must determine whether the rules will allow that to happen. Diagnosis must also include evaluation of the work group and teams, as well as the intragroup dynamics (discussed in Chapters 9 and 10). Furthermore, it must determine whether workers have or can easily obtain the new skills to perform the redesigned task.

It is extremely important to recognize the full range of potential costs and benefits associated with a job redesign effort. Some are direct and quantifiable; others are indirect and not quantifiable. Redesign may involve unexpected costs or benefits; although these cannot be predicted with certainty, they can be weighed as possibilities. Factors such as short-term role ambiguity, role conflict, and role overload can be major stumbling blocks to a job redesign effort.

Implementing a redesign scheme takes careful planning, and developing a strategy for the intervention is the final planning step. Strategy formulation is a four-part process. First, the organization must decide who will design the

Step 1: Recognition of a need for a change
Step 2: Selection of task redesign as a potential intervention
Step 3: Diagnosis of the work system and context
    a. Diagnosis of existing jobs
    b. Diagnosis of existing workforce
    c. Diagnosis of technology
    d. Diagnosis of organization design
    e. Diagnosis of leader behavior
    f. Diagnosis of group and social processes
Step 4: Cost-benefit analysis of proposed changes
Step 5: Go/no-go decision
Step 6: Formulation of the strategy for redesign
Step 7: Implementation of the task changes
Step 8: Implementation of any supplemental changes
Step 9: Evaluation of the task redesign effort

Table 19.2
INTEGRATED FRAMEWORK FOR IMPLEMENTATION OF TASK REDESIGN IN ORGANIZATIONS

Reference: Ricky W. Griffin, *Task Design: An Integrative Framework* (Glenview, IL: Scott, Foresman, 1982), p. 208. Used by permission.

changes. Depending on the circumstances, the planning team may consist of only upper-level management or may include line workers and supervisors. Next, the team undertakes the actual design of the changes based on job design theory and the needs, goals, and circumstances of the organization. Third, the team decides the timing of the implementation, which may require a formal transition period during which equipment is purchased and installed, job training takes place, new physical layouts are arranged, and the bugs in the new system are worked out. Fourth, strategy planners must consider whether the job changes require adjustments and supplemental changes in other organizational components such as reporting relationships and the compensation system.

Group and Individual Change

Groups and individuals can be involved in organization change in a vast number of ways. Retraining a single employee can be considered an organization change if the training affects the way the employee does his or her job. Familiarizing managers with the leadership grid or the Vroom decision tree (Chapter 12) in order to improve the way they lead or involve subordinate participation in decision making is an attempt at change. In the first case, the goal is to balance management concerns for production and people; in the second, the goal is to increase the participation of rank-and-file employees in the organization's decision making. In this section, we present an overview of four popular types of people-oriented change techniques: training, management development programs, team building, and survey feedback.

Training   Training generally is designed to improve employees' job skills. Employees may be trained to run certain machines, taught new mathematical skills, or acquainted with personal growth and development methods. Stress management programs are becoming popular for helping employees, particularly executives, understand organizational stress and develop ways to cope with it.[33] Training may also be used in conjunction with other, more comprehensive organization changes. For instance, if an organization is implementing a management-by-objectives program, training in establishing goals and reviewing goal-oriented performance is probably needed. One important type of training that is becoming increasingly more common is training people to work in other countries. Companies such as Motorola give extensive training

Training can take many forms, from in-class sessions to simulation drills and practice. China International Search and Rescue (CISAR) teams take part in a search and rescue training exercise at an earthquake training base outside of Beijing February 26, 2010. CISAR is primarily responsible for implementing domestic search and rescue operations and international humanitarian missions for victims of natural disasters. During a disaster there is little time to train teams as lives may be at stake. Therefore, they use simulations and drills to train search and recovery teams

programs to employees at all levels before they start an international assignment. Training includes intensive language courses, cultural courses, and courses for the family.

Among the many training methods, the most common are lecture, discussion, a lecture-discussion combination, experiential methods, case studies, films or videotapes, and the increasingly popular online training modules. Training can take place in a standard classroom, either on company property or in a hotel, at a resort, at a conference center, or online from anywhere. On-the-job training provides a different type of experience in which the trainee learns from an experienced worker. Most training programs use a combination of methods determined by the topic, the trainees, the trainer, and the organization.

A major problem of training programs is transferring employee learning to the workplace. Often an employee learns a new skill or a manager learns a new management technique, but upon returning to the normal work situation, he or she finds it easier to go back to the old way of doing things. As we discussed earlier, the process of refreezing is a vital part of the change process, and some way must be found to make the accomplishments of the training program permanent.

Management Development Programs   Management development programs, like employee training programs, attempt to foster certain skills, abilities, and perspectives. Often, when a highly qualified technical person is promoted to manager of a work group, he or she needs training in how to manage or deal with people. In such cases, management development programs can be important to organizations, both for the new manager and for his or her subordinates.

Typically, management development programs use the lecture-discussion method to some extent but rely most heavily on participative methods such as case studies and role-playing. Participative and experiential methods allow the manager to experience the problems of being a manager as well as the feelings of frustration, doubt, and success that are part of the job. The subject matter of this type of training program is problematic, however, in that management skills, including communication, problem diagnosis, problem solving, and performance appraisal, are not as easy to identify or to transfer from a classroom to the workplace as the skills required to run a machine. In addition, rapid changes in the external environment can make certain managerial skills obsolete in a very short time. As a result, some companies are approaching the development of their management team as an ongoing, career-long process and require their managers to periodically attend refresher courses.

Jack Welch was so committed to making cultural changes within GE that he created the now famous Crotonville NY training facility to develop an army of change leaders. GE put more than 10,000 managers a year through a three-step workshop series called the Change Acceleration Program (CAP). Leadership was redefined as a teaching activity in which leaders taught their direct reports how to change the way they did their jobs. In order to make the system-wide changes Welch thought were needed, he turned to individual OD.[34]

As corporate America invests hundreds of millions of dollars in management development, certain guiding principles are evolving: (1) management development is a multifaceted, complex, and long-term process to which there is no quick or simple approach; (2) organizations should carefully and systematically identify their unique developmental needs and evaluate their programs accordingly; (3) management development objectives must be compatible with organizational objectives; and (4) the utility and value of management development remain more an article of faith than a proven fact.[35]

Team Building   When interaction among group members is critical to group success and effectiveness, team development, or team building, may be useful. Team building emphasizes members working together in a spirit of cooperation and generally has one or more of the following goals:

1. To set team goals and priorities
2. To analyze or allocate the way work is performed
3. To examine how a group is working—that is, to examine processes such as norms, decision making, and communications
4. To examine relationships among the people doing the work[36]

Total quality management efforts usually focus on teams, and the principles of team building must be applied to make them work. Team participation is especially important in the data-gathering and evaluation phases of team development. In data gathering, the members share information on the functioning of the group. The opinions of the group thus form the foundation of the development process. In the evaluation phase, members are the source of information about the effectiveness of the development effort.[37]

Like total quality management and many other management techniques, team building should not be thought of as a one-time experience, perhaps something undertaken on a retreat from the workplace; rather, it is a continuing process. It may take weeks, months, or years for a group to learn to pull together and function as a team. Team development can be a way to train the group to solve its own problems in the future. Research on the effectiveness of team building as an organization development tool so far is mixed and inconclusive. For more details on developing teams in organizations, please refer to Chapter 10.

Survey Feedback   Survey feedback techniques can form the basis for a change process. In this process, data are gathered, analyzed, summarized, and returned to those who generated them to identify, discuss, and solve problems. A survey feedback process is often set in motion either by the organization's top management or by a consultant to management. By providing information about employees' beliefs and attitudes, a survey can help management diagnose and solve an organization's problems. A consultant or change agent usually coordinates the process and is responsible for data gathering, analysis, and summary. The three-stage process is shown in Figure 19.4.[38]

The use of survey feedback techniques in an organization development process differs from their use in traditional attitude surveys. In an organization development process, data are (1) returned to employee groups at all levels in the organization and (2) used by all employees working together in their normal work groups to identify and solve problems. In traditional attitude surveys, top management reviews the data and may or may not initiate a new program to solve problems the survey has identified.

Figure 19.4 THE SURVEY FEEDBACK PROCESS

The survey feedback process has three distinct stages, which must be fully completed for the process to be most effective. As an organization development process, its purpose is to fully involve all employees in data analysis, problem identification, and development of solutions.

In the data-gathering stage, the change agent interviews selected personnel from appropriate levels to determine the key issues to be examined. Information from these interviews is used to develop a survey questionnaire, which is distributed to a large sample of employees. The questionnaire may be a standardized instrument, an instrument developed specifically for the organization, or a combination of the two. The questionnaire data are analyzed and aggregated by group or department to ensure that respondents remain anonymous.[39] Then the change agent prepares a summary of the results for the group feedback sessions. From this point on, the consultant is involved in the process as a resource person and expert.

The feedback meetings generally involve only two or three levels of management. Meetings are usually held serially, first with a meeting of the top management group, which is then followed by meetings of employees throughout the organization. The group manager rather than the change agent typically leads sessions to transfer "ownership" of the data from the change agent to the work group. The feedback consists primarily of profiles of the group's attitudes toward the organization, the work, the leadership, and other topics on the questionnaire. During the feedback sessions, participants discuss reasons for the scores and the problems that the data reveal.

In the process analysis stage, the group examines the process of making decisions, communicating, and accomplishing work, usually with the help of the consultant. Unfortunately, groups often overlook this stage as they become absorbed in the survey data and the problems revealed during the feedback sessions. Occasionally, group managers simply fail to hold feedback and process analysis sessions. Change agents should ensure that managers hold these sessions and that they are rewarded for doing so. The process analysis stage is important because its purpose is to develop action plans to make improvements. Several sessions may be required to discuss the process issues fully and to settle on a strategy for improvements. Groups often find it useful to document the plans as they are discussed and to appoint a member to follow up on implementation. Generally, the follow-up assesses whether communication and communication processes have actually been improved. A follow-up survey can be administered several months to a year later to assess how much these processes have changed since they were first reported.

The survey feedback method is probably one of the most widely used organization change and development interventions. If any of its stages are compromised or omitted, however, the technique becomes less useful. A primary responsibility of the consultant or change agent, then, is to ensure that the method is fully and faithfully carried through.

RESISTANCE TO CHANGE

Change is inevitable; so is resistance to change. Paradoxically, organizations both promote and resist change. As an agent for change, the organization asks prospective customers or clients to change their current purchasing habits by switching to the company's products or services, asks current customers to change by increasing their purchases, and asks suppliers to reduce the costs of raw materials. The organization resists change in that its structure and control systems protect the daily tasks of producing a product or service from uncertainties in the environment. The organization must have some elements of permanence to avoid mirroring the instability of the environment, yet it must also react to external shifts with internal change to maintain currency and relevance in the marketplace.

A commonly held view is that all resistance to change needs to be overcome, but that is not always the case. Resistance to change can be used for the benefit of the organization and need not be eliminated entirely. By revealing a legitimate concern that a proposed change may harm the organization or that other alternatives might be better, resistance may alert the organization to reexamine the change.[40] For example, an organization may be considering acquiring a company in a completely different industry. Resistance to such a proposal may cause the organization to examine the advantages and disadvantages of the move more carefully. Without resistance, the decision might be made before the pros and cons have been sufficiently explored. Some have suggested that change agents may contribute to resistance through their mismanagement of the change process or miscommunication throughout the process.[41]

Resistance may come from the organization, the individual, or both. Determining the ultimate source is often difficult, however, because organizations are composed of individuals. Table 19.3 summarizes various types of organizational and individual sources of resistance.

Organizational Sources	Examples
OVERDETERMINATION	Employment system, job descriptions, evaluation and reward system, organization culture
NARROW FOCUS OF CHANGE	Structure changed with no concern given to other issues, e.g., jobs, people
GROUP INERTIA	Group norms
THREATENED EXPERTISE	People move out of area of expertise
THREATENED POWER	Decentralized decision making
RESOURCE ALLOCATION	Increased use of part-time help
Individual Sources	**Examples**
HABIT	Altered tasks
SECURITY	Altered tasks or reporting relationships
ECONOMIC FACTORS	Changed pay and benefits
FEAR OF THE UNKNOWN	New job, new boss
LACK OF AWARENESS	Isolated groups not heeding notices
SOCIAL FACTORS	Group norms

Table 19.3
ORGANIZATIONAL AND INDIVIDUAL SOURCES OF RESISTANCE

Overdetermination, or **structural inertia**, occurs because numerous organizational systems are in place to ensure that employees and systems behave as expected to maintain stability.

Organizational Sources of Resistance

Daniel Katz and Robert Kahn have identified six major organizational sources of resistance: overdetermination, narrow focus of change, group inertia, threatened expertise, threatened power, and changes in resource allocation.[42] Of course, not every organization or every change situation displays all six sources.

Overdetermination   Organizations have several systems designed to maintain stability. For example, consider how organizations control employees' performance. Job candidates must have certain specific skills so that they can do the job the organization needs them to do. A new employee is given a job description, and the supervisor trains, coaches, and counsels the employee in job tasks. The new employee usually serves some type of probationary period that culminates in a performance review; thereafter, the employee's performance is regularly evaluated. Finally, rewards, punishment, and discipline are administered, depending on the level of performance. Such a system is said to be characterized by overdetermination, or structural inertia,[43] in that one could probably have the same effect on employee performance with fewer procedures and safeguards. In other words, the structure of the organization produces resistance to change because it was designed to maintain stability. Another important source of overdetermination is the culture of the organization. As discussed in Chapter 18, the culture of an organization can have powerful and long-lasting effects on the behavior of its employees.

Narrow Focus of Change   Many efforts to create change in organizations adopt too narrow a focus. Any effort to force change in the tasks of individuals or groups must take into account the interdependence among organizational elements such as people, structure, tasks, and the information system. For example, some attempts at redesigning jobs fail because the organization structure within which the jobs must function is inappropriate for the redesigned jobs.[44]

Group Inertia   When an employee attempts to change his or her work behavior, the group may resist by refusing to change other behaviors that are necessary complements to the individual's altered behavior. In other words, group norms may act as a brake on individual attempts at behavior change.

Threatened Expertise   A change in the organization may threaten the specialized expertise that individuals and groups have developed over the years. A job redesign or a structural change may transfer responsibility for a specialized task from the current expert to someone else, threatening the specialist's expertise and building his or her resistance to the change.

Threatened Power   Any redistribution of decision-making authority, such as with reengineering or team-based management, may threaten an individual's power relationships with others. If an organization is decentralizing its decision making, managers who wielded their decision-making powers in return for special favors from others may resist the change because they do not want to lose their power base.

Resource Allocation   Groups that are satisfied with current resource allocation methods may resist any change they believe will threaten future allocations. Resources in this context can mean anything from monetary rewards and equipment to additional seasonal help to more computer time.

These six sources explain most types of organization-based resistance to change. All are based on people and social relationships. Many of these sources of resistance can be traced to groups or individuals who are afraid of losing something—resources, power, or comfort in a routine.

Individual Sources of Resistance

Individual sources of resistance to change are rooted in basic human characteristics such as needs and perceptions. Researchers have identified six reasons for individual resistance to change: habit, security, economic factors, fear of the unknown, lack of awareness, and social factors (see Table 19.3).[45]

Habit   It is easier to do a job the same way every day if the steps in the job are repeated over and over. Learning an entirely new set of steps makes the job more difficult. For the same amount of return (pay), most people prefer to do easier rather than harder work.

Security   Some employees like the comfort and security of doing things the same old way. They gain a feeling of constancy and safety from knowing that some things stay the same despite all the change going on around them. People who believe their security is threatened by a change are likely to resist the change.

Economic Factors   Change may threaten employees' steady paychecks. Workers may fear that change will make their jobs obsolete or reduce their opportunities for future pay increases.

Fear of the Unknown   Some people fear anything unfamiliar. Changes in reporting relationships and job duties create anxiety for such employees. Employees become familiar with their bosses and their jobs and develop relationships with others within the organization, such as contact people for various situations. These relationships and contacts help facilitate their work. Any disruption of familiar patterns may create fear because it can cause delays and foster the belief that nothing is getting accomplished.

Lack of Awareness   Because of perceptual limitations such as lack of attention or selective attention, a person may not recognize a change in a rule or procedure and thus may not alter his or her behavior. People may pay attention only to things that support their point of view. As an example, employees in an isolated regional sales office may not notice—or may ignore—directives from headquarters regarding a change in reporting procedures for expense accounts. They may therefore continue the current practice as long as possible.

Social Factors   People may resist change for fear of what others will think. As we mentioned before, the group can be a powerful motivator of behavior. Employees may believe change will hurt their image, result in ostracism from the group, or simply make them "different." For example, an employee who agrees to conform to work rules established by management may be ridiculed by others who openly disobey the rules.

HANS NELEMAN/THE IMAGE BANK/GETTY IMAGES

Change often threatens the power base of many people throughout the organization. This lady looks happy while the man is less so – this time somebody won and somebody lost. While it may not always mean managers lose their offices, it may mean they lose power and influence within the organization. Thus, they may do everything they can to resist the change for fear of losing their power.

MANAGING SUCCESSFUL ORGANIZATION CHANGE AND DEVELOPMENT

In conclusion, we offer seven keys to managing change in organizations. They relate directly to the problems identified earlier and to our view of the organization as a comprehensive social system. Each can influence the elements of the social system and may help the organization avoid some of the major problems in managing the change. Table 19.4 lists the points and their potential impacts.

Consider Global Issues

One factor to consider is how global issues dictate organization change. As we have already noted, the environment is a significant factor in bringing about organization change. Given the additional environmental complexities multinational organizations face, it follows that organization change may be even more critical to them than it is to purely domestic organizations. Dell Computer, for example, owes much of its success to its original strategy of selling directly to consumers. Since 2006, however, it has expanded its distribution activities to include retail sales, and the *Globalization* box on page 549 shows how this significant system-wide change has eased the company's entry into some key foreign markets.

A second point to remember is that acceptance of change varies widely around the globe. Change is a normal and accepted part of organization life in some cultures. In other cultures, change causes many more problems. Managers should remember that techniques for managing change that have worked routinely back home may not work at all and may even trigger negative responses if used indiscriminately in other cultures.[46]

Table 19.4 KEYS TO MANAGING SUCCESSFUL ORGANIZATION CHANGE AND DEVELOPMENT

Key	Impact
Consider global issues.	Keeps in touch with the latest global developments and how change is handled in different cultures
Take a holistic view of the organization.	Helps anticipate the effects of change on the social system and culture
Start small.	Works out details and shows the benefits of the change to those who might resist
Secure top management support.	Gets dominant coalition on the side of change: safeguards structural change, heads off problems of power and control
Encourage participation by those affected by the change.	Minimizes transition problems of control, resistance, and task redefinition
Foster open communication.	Minimizes transition problems of resistance and information and control systems
Reward those who contribute to change.	Minimizes transition problems of resistance and control systems

GLOBALIZATION

Dell Moves Beyond Direct Sales

Computer maker Dell was founded on a simple concept, says the company's website: "selling computer systems directly to customers, we could best understand their needs and efficiently provide the most effective computing solutions to meet those needs." The direct sales model lets Dell eliminate wholesaling and retailing while allowing the company to grow at its own pace. Direct sales eliminates inventory and helps introduce new technology rapidly. Direct sales are the cornerstone of Dell's strategy, so it came as a shock when the company started selling through bricks-and-mortar shops.

Within the United States, Dell now offers Inspiron laptops and desktops through Walmart, which also offers PCs from HP and Compaq. In the United Kingdom and Japan, Dell partners with local chains. So far, the retailers' sales of Dell computers are insignificant. A much bigger change is Dell's new sales model for the developing world.

In China, for example, products are sold through Gome, the country's largest electronics seller. China is an important PC market, the second largest after the United States. Chinese consumers are expected to buy 50 million personal computers in 2010 and 60 million in 2011. Dell, however, currently holds less than a 10 percent share of that market. The Chinese, like buyers in many developing nations, prefer to buy directly, not online. Among the problems are unreliable delivery service and a cultural preference for shopping in person. In Russia, another important developing market, Dell has retail stores in shopping malls. This model works well in Eastern Europe, where PC sales are growing by 50 percent annually. In India, where annual growth is 60 percent, Dell still uses the direct model. "At present, we are not into retail operations in India, but that's going to change," says Dell India general manager Rajan Anandan.

"At present, we are not into retail operations in India, but that's going to change."

—RAJAN ANANDAN, GENERAL MANAGER, DELL INDIA

Dell is undergoing system-wide organization change. The company's experimentation with different sales channels may provide the key to staying competitive and restoring profitability.

References: Dell Inc., "Dell Sees Unrivalled Opportunity in Connected Era and Fast Growing Economies," press release, April 10, 2008, www.dell.com on May 26, 2010; Jack Ewing, "Where Dell Sells with Brick and Mortar," *BusinessWeek*, October 8, 2007, www.businessweek.com on May 26, 2010; "Dell Says Sales in India Grew to $700 Million," *Wall Street Journal*, March 25, 2008, www.wsj.com on April 26, 2008; Bruce Einhorn, "Dell Goes Retail in China with Gome," *BusinessWeek*, September 24, 2007, www.businessweek.com on May 26, 2010; "Microsoft Sees China PC Sales Growing 20% in 2011," *MarketWatch*, March 18, 2010, www.marketwatch.com on August 22, 2010.

Take a Holistic View

Managers must take a holistic view of the organization and the change project. A limited view can endanger the change effort because the subsystems of the organization are interdependent. A holistic view encompasses the culture and dominant coalition as well as the people, tasks, structure, and information subsystems.

Start Small

Peter Senge claims that every truly successful, system-wide change in large organizations starts small.[47] He recommends that change start with one team, usually an executive team. One team can evaluate the change, make appropriate adjustments along the way, and most importantly, show that the new system works and gets desired results. If the change makes sense, it begins to spread to other teams, groups, and divisions throughout the system. Senge described how at Shell and Ford, significant changes started small, with one or two parallel teams, and then spread as others recognized the benefits of the change. When others see the benefits, they automatically drop their inherent resistance and join in. They can voluntarily join and be committed to the success of the change effort.

Secure Top Management Support

The support of top management is essential to the success of any change effort. As the organization's probable dominant coalition, it is a powerful element of the social system, and its support is necessary to deal with control and power problems. For example, a manager who plans a change in the ways in which tasks are assigned and responsibility is delegated in his or her department must notify top management and gain its support. Complications may arise if disgruntled employees complain to high-level managers who have not been notified of the change or do not support it. The employees' complaints may jeopardize the manager's plan—and perhaps her or his job.

Encourage Participation

Problems related to resistance, control, and power can be overcome by broad participation in planning the change. Allowing people a voice in designing the change may give them a sense of power and control over their own destinies, which may help to win their support during implementation.

Foster Open Communication

Open communication is an important factor in managing resistance to change and overcoming information and control problems during transitions. Employees typically recognize the uncertainties and ambiguities that arise during a transition and seek information on the change and their place in the new system. In the absence of information, the gap may be filled with inappropriate or false information, which may endanger the change process. Rumors tend to spread through the grapevine faster than accurate information can be disseminated through official channels. A manager should always be sensitive to the effects of uncertainty on employees, especially during a period of change; any news, even bad news, seems better than no news.

Reward Contributors

Although this last point is simple, it can easily be neglected. Employees who contribute to the change in any way need to be rewarded. Too often, the only people acknowledged after a change effort are those who tried to stop it. Those who quickly grasp new work assignments, work harder to cover what otherwise might not get done during the transition, or help others adjust to changes deserve special credit—perhaps a mention in a news release or the internal company newspaper, special consideration in a performance appraisal, a merit raise, or a promotion. From a behavioral perspective, individuals need to benefit in some way if they are to willingly help change something that eliminates the old, comfortable way of doing the job.

In the current dynamic environment, managers must anticipate the need for change and satisfy it with more responsive and competitive organization systems. These seven keys to managing organization change may also serve as general guidelines for managing organizational behavior because organizations must change or face elimination.

SYNOPSIS

Change may be forced on an organization, or an organization may change in response to the environment or an internal need. Forces for change are interdependent and influence organizations in many ways. Currently, the areas in which the pressures for change seem most powerful involve people, technology, information processing and communication, competition, and social trends.

Planned organization change involves anticipating change and preparing for it. Lewin described organization change in terms of unfreezing, the change itself, and refreezing. In the continuous change process model, top management recognizes forces encouraging change, engages in a problem-solving process to design the change, and implements and evaluates the change.

Organization development is the process of planned change and improvement of organizations through the application of knowledge of the behavioral sciences. It is based on a systematic change process and focuses on managing the culture of the organization. The most comprehensive change involves altering the structure of the organization through reorganization of departments, reporting relationships, or authority systems.

Quality-of-work-life programs focus on providing a work environment in which employees can satisfy individual needs. Task and technological changes alter the way the organization accomplishes its primary tasks. Along with the steps usually associated with change, task redesign entails diagnosis, cost-benefit analysis, formulation of a redesign strategy, and implementation of supplemental changes.

Frequently used group and individual approaches to organization change are training and management development programs, team building, and survey feedback techniques. Training programs are usually designed to improve employees' job skills, to help employees adapt to other organization changes (such as a management-by-objectives program), or to develop employees' awareness and understanding of problems such as workplace safety or stress. Management development programs attempt to foster in current or future managers the skills, abilities, and perspectives important to good management. Team-building programs are designed to help a work team or group develop into a mature, functioning team by helping it define its goals or priorities, analyze its tasks and the way they are performed, and examine relationships among the people doing the work. As used in the organization development process, survey feedback techniques involve gathering data, analyzing and summarizing them, and returning them to employees and groups for discussion and to identify and solve problems.

Resistance to change may arise from several individual and organizational sources. Resistance may indicate a legitimate concern that the change is not good for the organization and may warrant a reexamination of plans.

To manage change in organizations, international issues must be considered, and managers should take a holistic view of the organization and start small. Top management support is needed, and those most affected by the change must participate. Open communication is important, and those who contribute to the change effort should be rewarded.

DISCUSSION QUESTIONS

1. Is most organization change forced on the organization by external factors or fostered from within? Explain.
2. What broad category of pressures for organization change other than the four discussed in the chapter can you think of? Briefly describe it.
3. Which sources of resistance to change present the most problems for an internal change agent? For an external change agent?
4. Which stage of the Lewin model of change do you think is most often overlooked? Why?
5. What are the advantages and disadvantages of having an internal change agent rather than an external change agent?
6. How does organization development differ from organization change?
7. How and why would organization development differ if the elements of the social system were not interdependent?
8. Do quality-of-work-life programs rely more on individual or organizational aspects of organizational behavior? Why?
9. Describe how the job of your professor could be redesigned. Include a discussion of other subsystems that would need to be changed as a result.
10. Which of the seven keys for successfully managing an organizational change effort seem to be the most difficult to manage? Why?

ORGANIZATIONAL BEHAVIOR CASE FOR DISCUSSION

ACTING ON A VISION OF CHANGE

Video-game maker Activision was founded in 1979 by an ex–music industry executive and four disgruntled programmers from Atari, a pioneer in arcade games and home video-game consoles. In part, the company was established as a haven for game developers unhappy with prevailing industry policy at the end of the 1970s. At the time, systems providers like Atari hired developers to create games only for their own systems; in-house developers were paid straight salaries and denied credit for individual contributions, and there was no channel at all for would-be independents. Positioning itself as the industry's first third-party developer, Activision began promoting creators as well as games. It went public in 1983 and successfully rode the crest of a booming market until the mid-1980s.

Its struggles began in 1986, when it entered an ill-advised merger with Infocom, a software firm founded to develop interactive-fiction games. The relationship was rocky from the first, and Activision closed down Infocom operations in 1989, after three years of mismanagement and escalating losses. Meanwhile, Activision had also begun to branch out from video games into other types of software and, in order to underscore its new commitment to a broader product line, changed its name to Mediagenic. By this time, however, competition in the video-game market had increased substantially, and the decision to expand into areas beyond its distinctive competence turned out to be a major strategic blunder. By 1991, Mediagenic was bankrupt.

This is the point at which Robert Kotick happened upon Activision/Mediagenic—"a company," as *Forbes* magazine put it, "with a sorry balance sheet but a storied history." Kotick, a serial entrepreneur with no particular passion for video games, bought one-third of the firm for $440,000 and looked immediately to industry leader Electronic Arts (EA) for a survey of best practices in the industry. What he discovered, however, was a competitor whose culture was beset by internal conflict—namely, between managers motivated by productivity and profit and developers driven by independence and imagination. But EA also sold a lot of video games, and to Kotick, the

> *"EA has tried to commoditize development. We won't absorb [developers] into a big Death Star culture."*
> —ACTIVISION CEO ROBERT KOTICK

basic tension in EA culture was not entirely surprising: clearly the business of making and marketing video games succeeded when the creative side of the enterprise was supported by financing and distribution muscle, but it was equally true that a steady stream of successful games came from a company's creative people. The key to getting Activision/Mediagenic back in the game, Kotick decided, was managing this complex of essential resources better than his competition—notably EA—did.

So the next year, Kotick raised $40 million through a stock offering, moved the company (rechristened Activision) from Silicon Valley to Los Angeles, and began to recruit the people who could furnish the resources that he needed most—creative expertise and a share of the passion that its customers brought to the video-game industry. Activision, he promised prospective developers, would not manage its human resources the way that EA did: EA, he argued, "has commoditized development. We won't absorb you into a big Death Star culture."

Between 1997 and 2003, Kotick proceeded to buy no fewer than nine studios, but his concept of a video-game studio system was quite different from that of EA, which was determined to make production more efficient by centralizing groups of designers and programmers into regional offices. Kotick allowed his studios keep their own names, often let them stay where they were, and further encouraged autonomy by providing seed money for Activision alumni who wanted to launch out on their own. He still conducts market research out of the company's L.A. headquarters but does not use the results to put pressure on his creative teams; rather, he shares the data with his studios and lets them draw their own conclusions. Each studio issues its own financial statements and draws on its own bonus pool, and the paychecks of studio heads reflect both company-wide profits and losses.

Kotick's strategy has paid off big time. In 1999, Activision's Neversoft studio came up with *Tony Hawks' Pro Skater*, which broke through the monotony of sports games by letting players proceed at their own pace through a virtual landscape. Activision's next blockbuster franchise—the World War II game *Call of Duty*—came in 2003 from a group of developers who had left EA to found a studio called Infinity Ward. In 2006, Kotick paid $100 million for a company called Harmonix, which had developed a game revolving around a guitar-shaped peripheral: the *Guitar Hero* franchise has revolutionized not only video games but the relationship between video games and popular music and, as of this writing, has generated more than $2 billion in revenue.

By this time, Activision had built or developed games for every lucrative product category in the market except one—the so-called "massively multiplayer" games in which players pay monthly subscription fees to enter online worlds and build characters over the course of months or even years. The attractiveness of the category is obvious: Whereas a console game might command a one-shot retail price of $40, an online multiplayer game might charge $15 a month to each of several million players. In December 2007, therefore, Activision announced a strategic move that would immediately transform it into a major player (so to speak) in the multiplayer category—a merger with the game-making unit of the French entertainment conglomerate Vivendi. Vivendi was big, but it had only one blockbuster game—the world's number-one online multiplayer franchise, called *World of Warcraft*. Developed by a Vivendi-owned California studio called Blizzard, *World of Warcraft* had 11 million subscribers and, with $1.1 billion in annual sales, was perhaps the most profitable video game ever invented. The merger, according to Kotick, was Activision's best strategy for making a critical move in an industry increasingly dominated by Internet-based innovations: "We looked every which way to figure out how to participate in what Blizzard had created. We couldn't find a way to duplicate it, but we could acquire the expertise," explained Kotick, who added that acquiring *World of Warcraft* and the know-how of Blizzard had saved Activision another $150 million in development costs.

The new company, known as Activision Blizzard, generated combined revenues of $3.8 billion for calendar year 2007—just enough to squeeze past EA's $3.7 billion and sneak into the top spot as the best-selling video-game publisher in the world not affiliated with a maker of game consoles (such as Nintendo and Microsoft). Today, Activision Blizzard's market capitalization of $13.3 billion is nearly twice that of EA. Kotick has attributed the firm's success to a "focus on a select number of proven franchises and genres where we have proven development expertise. … We look for ways to broaden the footprints of our franchises, and where appropriate, we develop innovative business models like subscription-based online gaming."

CASE QUESTIONS

1. As a force for change in the video-game industry, how has *technology* affected Kotick's strategy at Activision? How about *competition*?
2. In what ways has Robert Kotick acted as a *change agent* at Activision?
3. Apply *Lewin's process model* of organization change to the measures that Kotick has taken to effect change at Activision. Be sure to examine each step in the Lewin model, noting where the model applies particularly well and where it does not. Are there any points at which the *continuous change process model* provides a better description of the strategy at Activision?
4. To what extent can the changes at Activision be seen as aspects of *organization development*? In what areas do the three criteria for determining organization development apply particularly well? In what areas are other models more accurate in describing Kotick's change strategies?

REFERENCES

Peter C. Beller, "Activision's Unlikely Hero," *Forbes*, February 2, 2009, www.forbes.com on June 6, 2010; Matt Richtel, "Vivendi to Acquire Activision," *New York Times*, December 3, 2007, www.nytimes.com on June 6, 2010; "Activision Beats EA as Top Third Party Publisher in U.S.," *Gamasutra*, July 24, 2007, www.gamasutra.com on June 6, 2010; "Activision Posts 92% Revenue Increase in Record Year," *Gamasutra*, May 8, 2008, www.gamasutra.com on February 13, 2009; "Activision's 'Focus' Drives Revenue Past Estimates," *Gamasutra*, February 12, 2009, www.gamasutra.com on June 6, 2010; Activision Blizzard Inc., *2009 Annual Report*, 2010, http://investor.activision.com on June 6, 2010.

EXPERIENCING ORGANIZATIONAL BEHAVIOR

Planning a Change at the University

Purpose   This exercise will help you understand the complexities of change in organizations.

Format   Your task is to plan the implementation of a major change in an organization.

Procedure

Part 1

The class will divide into five groups of approximately equal size. Your instructor will assign each group one of the following changes:

1. A change from the semester system to the quarter system (or the opposite, depending on the school's current system)
2. A requirement that all work—homework, examinations, term papers, problem sets—be done on computers and submitted via computers
3. A requirement that all students live on campus
4. A requirement that all students have reading, writing, and speaking fluency in at least three languages, including English and Japanese, to graduate
5. A requirement that all students room with someone in the same major

First, decide what individuals and groups must be involved in the change process. Then decide how the change will be implemented using Lewin's process of organization change (Figure 19.1) as a framework. Consider how to deal with resistance to change, using Tables 19.3 and 19.4 as guides. Decide whether a change agent (internal or external) should be used. Develop a realistic timetable for full implementation of the change. Is transition management appropriate?

Part 2

Using the same groups as in Part 1, your next task is to describe the techniques you would use to implement the change described in Part 1. You may use structural changes, task and technology methods, group and individual programs, or any combination of these. You may need to go to the library to gather more information on some techniques.

You should also discuss how you will utilize the seven keys to successful change management discussed at the end of the chapter.

Your instructor may make this exercise an in-class project, but it is also a good semester-ending project for groups to work on outside of class. Either way, the exercise is most beneficial when the groups report their implementation programs to the entire class. Each group should report on which change techniques are to be used, why they were selected, how they will be implemented, and how problems will be avoided.

Follow-up Questions
Part 1

1. How similar were the implementation steps for each change?
2. Were the plans for managing resistance to change realistic?
3. Do you think any of the changes could be successfully implemented at your school? Why or why not?

Part 2

1. Did various groups use the same technique in different ways or to accomplish different goals?
2. If you did outside research on organization development techniques for your project, did you find any techniques that seemed more applicable than those in this chapter? If so, describe one of them.

BUILDING MANAGERIAL SKILLS

Exercise Overview   Diagnostic skills, which enable a manager to visualize the most appropriate response to a situation, are especially important during periods of organizational change.

Exercise Background   You are the general manager of a hotel situated along a beautiful stretch of beach on a tropical island. One of the oldest of six large resorts in the immediate area, your hotel is owned by a group of foreign investors. For several years, it has been operated as a franchise unit of a large international hotel chain, as are all of the other hotels on the island.

For the past few years, the hotel's franchisee-owners have been taking most of the profits for themselves and putting relatively little back into the hotel. They have also let you know that their business is not in good financial health and that the revenue from the hotel is being used to offset losses incurred elsewhere. In contrast, most of the other hotels on the island have recently been refurbished, and plans for two brand-new hotels have been announced for the near future.

A team of executives from franchise headquarters has just visited your hotel. They are quite disappointed in the property, particularly because it has failed to keep pace with other resorts on the island. They have informed you that if the property is not brought up to standards, the franchise agreement, which is up for review in a year, will be revoked. You realize that this move would be a potential disaster because you cannot afford to lose the franchisor's brand name or access to its reservation system.

Sitting alone in your office, you identified several seemingly viable courses of action:

1. Convince the franchisee-owners to remodel the hotel. You estimate that it will take $5 million to meet the franchisor's minimum standards and another $5 million to bring the hotel up to the standards of the top resort on the island.
2. Convince the franchisor to give you more time and more options for upgrading the facility.
3. Allow the franchise agreement to terminate and try to succeed as an independent hotel.
4. Assume that the hotel will fail and start looking for another job. You have a pretty good reputation, but are not not terribly happy about the possibility of having to accept a lower-level position (say, as an assistant manager) with another firm.

Exercise Task   Having mulled over your options, do the following:

1. Rank-order your four alternatives in terms of probable success. Make any necessary assumptions.
2. Identify alternatives other than those that you have identified above.
3. Ask yourself: Can more than one alternative be pursued simultaneously? Which ones?
4. Develop an overall strategy for trying to save the hotel while protecting your own interests.

SELF-ASSESSMENT EXERCISE

Support for Change

Introduction   The following questions are designed to help people understand the level of support or opposition to change within an organization. Scores on this scale should be used for classroom discussion only.

Instructions   Think of an organization for which you have worked in the past or an organization to which you currently belong and consider the situation when a change was imposed at some point in the recent past. Then circle the number that best represents your feeling about each statement or question.

1. Values and Vision
   (Do people throughout the organization share values or vision?)

1	2	3	4	5	6	7
Low						High

2. History of Change
   (Does the organization have a good track record in handling change?)

1	2	3	4	5	6	7
Low						High

3. Cooperation and Trust
   (Do they seem high throughout the organization?)

1	2	3	4	5	6	7
Low						High

4. Culture
   (Is it one that supports risk taking and change?)

1	2	3	4	5	6	7
Low						High

5. Resilience
(Can people handle more?)

1	2	3	4	5	6	7

Low   High

6. Rewards
(Will this change be seen as beneficial?)

1	2	3	4	5	6	7

Low   High

7. Respect and Face
(Will people be able to maintain dignity and self-respect?)

1	2	3	4	5	6	7

Low   High

8. Status Quo
(Will this change be seen as mild?)

1	2	3	4	5	6	7

Low   High

A Guide to Scoring and explanation is available in the *Instructor's Resource Manual.*

Reference: From Rick Maurer, *Beyond the Wall of Resistance*, 1996 (Austin, TX: Bard Press), pp. 104–105. Used by permission of Bard Press.

PART 4
INTEGRATIVE RUNNING CASE

"THE COMPANY IS CALLED NETFLIX, NOT DVD-BY-MAIL," AND OTHER REASONS WHY NETFLIX RELISHES CHANGE

In June 2003, Netflix received a patent on several of the basic features of its business model, including the technology on which its online movie-rental process depended. In particular, the protection covered the processes by which customers set up their rental lists and the company delivered DVD discs. In theory, Netflix would be able to challenge other companies wanting to enter its market or at least require them to license Netflix-patented technology. Incumbent competitors, however, were not terribly concerned about the development. "We can't imagine that there's a patent out there that will keep us from serving our customers as best we can," said a spokesperson for Blockbuster. Observers also noted that patents are not supposed to cover something that is "obvious" and that Netflix's methods for handling customer subscriptions and the flow of DVDs to and from users were pretty obvious to anyone interested in running a movie-rental-by-mail business.

One analyst even suggested that its new patents might make Netflix a more likely buyout target for one of the bigger players in the market—say, Blockbuster or Wal-Mart, both of whom had sizable advantages in capital, customer bases, and brand recognition (remember, this was back in 2003). "If Wal-Mart wanted," said another analyst, "they could send their big guns out and bury Netflix." We discussed the Netflix-Blockbuster competition for dominance of the movie-rental business in Part 1 of this case, but the foray of Wal-Mart (now Walmart) into the market is another episode altogether—and one that is particularly relevant to the final installment of our study. Wal-Mart (at that time a $244-billion-a-year retailing giant) rolled out its own movie-rental business in June 2003, offering just about the same features as Netflix, including price, selection, and even special envelopes. Its advantages—in addition to money, customers, and name recognition—also included the ability to process and ship DVDs from existing facilities and the ability to advertise directly to about 100 million weekly shoppers (compared to Netflix's subscriber base of 1 million).

Some of these advantages, however, turned out to be less competitive than many experts originally believed. Wal-Mart's expertise in efficient distribution, for example, focused on getting products to warehouses and from warehouses to retail outlets—not directly to individual customers. Netflix, on the other hand, had spent five years developing internal processes designed not only to deliver movies to its customers but to enhance their satisfaction in selecting movies. Months after the launch of its service, Wal-Mart was still trying to get the bugs out of its software. During one week, customers who ordered any of the five movies featured on the Walmart.com rental home page were forced to wait more than two weeks for three of these movies and more than a month for a fourth. All five were immediately available at Netflix.

Wal-Mart had also, it seems, overestimated the power of its customer base and its name recognition. For one thing, *when it came specifically to movie rentals*—which was, after all, the market in question—Netflix had developed significant leads in both areas. For another, Wal-Mart's reputation rested on its track record in selling low-priced retail products out of brick-and-mortar stores, not renting movies (or anything else) through online channels. In fact, Wal-Mart's efforts to *sell* products online had not exactly taken off, and by early 2004, Netflix CEO Reed Hastings was optimistic about his chances of fending off the Wal-Mart challenge in the movie-rental market:

> We look at it and say, "Online, their brand has not extended. Their core area is selling goods—i.e., competing with Amazon. And they have not beaten Amazon or come anywhere close to it. So how much focus are they going to put on online rental subscriptions, an area that's not their specialty?" "Not much" is our answer. So we look at it and say, "If they ever beat Amazon, then we'll have real issues."

In May 2005, Wal-Mart abruptly retreated from the field of battle—or, perhaps more accurately, shifted from one side to the other by moving to back up Netflix's position. Wal-Mart, explained Hastings, "realized it had such a huge opportunity to sell DVDs that a rental service didn't make much sense. I had dinner with the CEO of Walmart.com, and eventually we came to an arrangement where basically [our] companies promoted one another." The deal called for Wal-Mart to help its

Chapter 14

1 Robert W. Allen and Lyman W. Porter (eds.), *Organizational Influence Processes* (Glenview, IL: Scott, Foresman, 1983).

2 Alan L. Frohman, "The Power of Personal Initiative," *Organizational Dynamics*, Winter 1997, pp. 39–48; see also James H. Dulebohn and Gerald R. Ferris, "The Role of Influence Tactics in Perceptions of Performance Evaluations' Fairness," *Academy of Management Journal*, 1999, vol. 42, no. 3, pp. 288–303.

3 For reviews of the meaning of power, see Henry Mintzberg, *Power In and Around Organizations* (Englewood Cliffs, NJ: Prentice-Hall, 1983); Jeffrey Pfeffer, *Power in Organizations* (Marshfield, MA: Pitman Publishing, 1981); John Kenneth Galbraith, *The Anatomy of Power* (Boston: Houghton Mifflin, 1983); Gary A. Yukl, *Leadership in Organizations*, 3rd ed. (Englewood Cliffs, NJ: Prentice-Hall, 1994).

4 John R. P. French and Bertram Raven, "The Bases of Social Power," in Darwin Cartwright (ed.), *Studies in Social Power* (Ann Arbor, MI: University of Michigan Press, 1959), pp. 150–167. See also Philip M. Podsakoff and Chester A. Schriesheim, "Field Studies of French and Raven's Bases of Power: Critique, Reanalysis, and Suggestions for Future Research," *Psychological Bulletin*, 1985, vol. 97, pp. 387–411.

5 See Sze-Sze Wong, Violet Ho, and Chay Hoon Lee, "A Power Perspective to Interunit Knowledge Transfer: Linking Attributes to Knowledge Power and the Transfer of Knowledge," *Journal of Management*, 2008, vol. 34, no. 1, pp. 127–150.

6 Yukl, *Leadership in Organizations*, Chapter X.

7 See Darren Treadway, Wayne Hochwarter, Charles Kacmar, and Gerald Ferris, "Political Will, Political Skill, and Political Behavior," *Journal of Organizational Behavior*, 2005, vol. 26, pp. 229–245.

8 Victor Murray and Jeffrey Gandz, "Games Executives Play: Politics at Work," *Business Horizons*, December 1980, pp. 11–23. See also Jeffrey Gandz and Victor Murray, "The Experience of Workplace Politics," *Academy of Management Journal*, June 1980, pp. 237–251.

9 Gerald F. Cavanaugh, Dennis J. Moberg, and Manuel Valasquez, "The Ethics of Organizational Politics," *Academy of Management Review*, July 1981, pp. 363–374.

10 Pfeffer, *Power in Organizations*; Mintzberg, *Power In and Around Organizations*.

11 The techniques are based on Pfeffer, *Power in Organizations*; Mintzberg, *Power In and Around Organizations*; and Galbraith, *Anatomy of Power*.

12 "How the 2 Top Officials of Grace Wound Up in a Very Dirty War," *Wall Street Journal*, May 18, 1995, pp. A1, A8.

13 See Jerald Greenberg and Jason Colquitt, *Handbook of Organizational Justice* (Mahwah, NJ: Lawrence Erlbaum Associates, 2004) for a comprehensive discussion and review of the literature on justice in organizations. See also James Lavelle, Deborah Rupp, and Joel Brockner, "Taking a Multifoci Approach to the Study of Justice, Social Exchange, and Citizenship Behavior," *Journal of Management*, 2007, vol. 33, no. 6, pp. 841–866, and Joel Brockner, *A Contemporary Look at Organizational Justice* (New York: Routledge, 2010), for recent updates.

14 See Russell Cropanzano, David Bowen, and Stephen Gilliland, "The Management of Organizational Justice," *Academy of Management Perspectives*, 2007, vol. 21, no. 4, pp. 34–48.

Chapter 15

1 See Stephen P. Robbins, *Managing Organizational Conflict* (Englewood Cliffs, NJ: Prentice Hall, 1974), for a classic review.

2 Charles R. Schwenk, "Conflict in Organizational Decision Making: An Exploratory Study of Its Effects in For-Profit and Not-for-Profit Organizations," *Management Science*, April 1990, pp. 436–448.

3 See Carsten K.W. De Dreu, "The Virtue and Vice of Workplace Conflict: Food for (Pessimistic) Thought," *Journal of Organizational Behavior*, 2008, vol. 29, no. 1, pp. 5–18 and Dean Tjosvold, "The Conflict-Positive Organization: It Depends on Us," *Journal of Organizational Behavior*, 2008, vol. 29, no. 1, pp. 19–28 for discussions of negative and positive perspectives on conflict.

4 "How 2 Computer Nuts Transformed Industry Before Messy Breakup," *The Wall Street Journal*, August 27, 1996, pp. A1, A10.

5 Bruce Barry and Greg L. Stewart, "Composition, Process, and Performance in Self-Managed Groups: The Role of Personality," *Journal of Applied Psychology*, vol. 82, no. 1, 1997, pp. 62–78.

6 "Rumsfeld's Abrasive Style Sparks Conflict With Military Command," *USA Today*, December 10, 2002, pp. 1A, 2A.

7 "Delta CEO Resigns After Clashes With Board," *USA Today*, May 13, 1997, p. B1.

8 "Why Boeing's Culture Breeds Turmoil," *Business Week*, March 21, 2005, pp. 34–36.

9 James Thompson, *Organizations in Action* (New York: McGraw-Hill, 1967). For a more recent discussion, see Bart Victor and Richard S. Blackburn, "Interdependence: An Alternative Conceptualization," *Academy of Management Review*, July 1987, pp. 486–498.

10 Kenneth Thomas, "Conflict and Conflict Management," in Marvin Dunnette (ed.), *Handbook of Industrial and Organizational Psychology* (Chicago: Rand McNally, 1976), pp. 889–935.

11 Alfie Kohn, "How to Succeed Without Even Vying," *Psychology Today*, September 1986, pp. 22–28.

12 See Carsten K. W. De Dreu and Annelies E. M. Van Vianen, "Managing Relationship Conflict and the Effectiveness of Organizational Teams," *Journal of Organizational Behavior*, 2001, vol. 22, pp. 309–328; see also Kristin Behfar, Randall Peterson, Elizabeth Mannix, and William Trochim, "The Critical Role of Conflict Resolution in Teams: A Close Look at the Links Between Conflict Type, Conflict Management Strategies, and Team Outcomes," *Journal of Applied Psychology*, 2008, vol. 93, no. 1, pp. 170–188.

13 "Memo To the Team: This Needs Salt!" *The Wall Street Journal*, April 4, 2000, pp. B1, B14.

14 See Kimberly Wade-Benzoni, Andrew Hoffman, Leigh Thompson, Don Moore, James Gillespie, and Max Bazerman, "Barriers to Resolution in Ideologically Based Negotiations: The Role of Values and Institutions," *Academy of Management Review*, 2002, vol. 27, no. 1, pp. 41–57; see also Leigh Thompson, Jiunwen Wang, and Brian Gunia, "Negotiation," in Susan Fiske, Daniel Schacter, and Robert Sternberg, (eds.), vol. 61, *Annual Review of Psychology* (Palo Alto: Annual Reviews, 2010), pp. 491–516.

15 J. Z. Rubin and B. R. Brown, *The Social Psychology of Bargaining and Negotiation* (New York: Academic Press, 1975).

16 R. J. Lewicki and J. A. Litterer, *Negotiation* (Homewood, IL: Irwin, 1985).

17 Howard Raiffa, *The Art and Science of Negotiation* (Cambridge, MA: Belknap, 1982).

18 K. H. Bazerman and M. A. Neale, *Negotiating Rationally* (New York: Free Press, 1992).

19 Ross R. Reck and Brian G. Long, *The Win-Win Negotiator* (Escondido, CA: Blanchard Training and Development, 1985).

Chapter 16

1 See Richard L. Daft, *Organization Theory and Design*, 8th ed. (Mason, OH: South-Western, 2004), p.11, for further discussion of the definition of *organization*.

2 Gareth R. Jones, *Organizational Theory, Design, and Change*, 9th ed. (Upper Saddle River, New Jersey; Pearson Prentice Hall, 2007), p. 4.

3 Brayden G. King, Teppo Felin, and David A. Whetten, "Perspective—Finding the Organization in Organizational Theory: A Meta-Theory of the Organization as a Social Actor." *Organization Science*, January–February 2010, pp. 290–305, ©2010 INFORMS

4 Charles W. L. Hill and Gareth R. Jones, *Strategic Management: An Integrated Approach*, 9th ed. (Mason, Ohio: South-Western Cengage Learning, 2010), p. 12. See also John R. Montanari, Cyril P. Morgan, and Jeffrey S. Bracker, *Strategic Management* (Hinsdale, IL: Dryden Press, 1990), pp. 1–2.

5 "Intel Aligns Around Platforms," "Intel Corporation in Summary," Intel website, appzone.intel.com on February 8, 2005.

6 A. Bryman, A. D. Beardworth, E. T. Keil, and J. Ford, "Organizational Size and Specialization," *Organization Studies*, September 1983, pp. 271–278.

7 Joseph L. C. Cheng, "Interdependence and Coordination in Organizations: A Role System Analysis," *Academy of Management Journal*, March 1983, pp. 156–162.

8 Henry Mintzberg, *The Structuring of Organizations* (Englewood Cliffs, NJ: Prentice Hall, 1979), for further discussion of the basic elements of structure.

9 Max Weber, *The Theory of Social and Economic Organization*, trans. A. M. Henderson and Talcott Parsons (New York: Free Press, 1947).

10 For more discussion of these alternative views, see John B. Miner, *Theories of Organizational Structure and Process* (Hinsdale, IL: Dryden Press, 1982), p. 386.

11 Paul S. Adler, "Building Better Bureaucracies," *Academy of Management Executive*, November 1999, pp. 36–46.

12 This summary of the classic principles of organizing is based on Henri Fayol, *General and Industrial Management*, trans. Constance Storrs (London: Pittman, 1949); Miner, *Theories of Organizational Structure and Process*, pp. 358–381; and the discussions in Arthur G. Bedeian, *Organizations: Theory and Analysis*, 2nd ed. (Chicago: Dryden, 1984), pp. 58–59.

13 Miner, *Theories of Organizational Structure and Process*, pp. 358–381.

14 See Rensis Likert, *New Patterns of Management* (New York: McGraw-Hill, 1961), and Rensis Likert, *The Human Organization: Its Management and Value* (New York: McGraw-Hill, 1967), for a complete discussion of the human organization.

15 Miner, *Theories of Organizational Structure and Process*, pp. 17–53.

16 Weber, *The Theory of Social and Economic Organization*.

17 Adam Smith, *An Inquiry into the Nature and Causes of the Wealth of Nations* (London: Dent, 1910).

18 Nancy M. Carter and Thomas L. Keon, "The Rise and Fall of the Division of Labour, the Past 25 Years," *Organization Studies*, 1986, pp. 54–57.

19 Glenn R. Carroll, "The Specialist Strategy," *California Management Review*, Spring 1984, pp. 126–137.

20 "Management Discovers the Human Side of Automation," *Business Week*, September 29, 1986, pp. 70–75.

21 See Robert H. Miles, *Macro Organizational Behavior* (Santa Monica, CA: Goodyear, 1980), pp. 28–34, for a discussion of departmentalization schemes.

22 Mintzberg, *The Structuring of Organizations*, p. 125.

23 Miles, *Macro Organizational Behavior*, pp. 122–133.

24 "Big Blue Wants to Loosen Its Collar," *Fortune*, February 29, 1988, p. 8; "Inside IBM: Internet Business Machines," *Business Week*, December 13, 1999, pp. EB20– EB28.

25 "Performance Inside: 2007 Annual Report," "Intel Aligns Around Platforms," "Intel Corporation in Summary," Intel website, www.intel.com on April 21, 2008; Ephraim Schwartz, "The Age of the Industry-Specific PC," *InfoWorld*, January 28, 2005, www.infoworld.com on February 8, 2005; Gary Rivlin and John Markoff, "Can Mr. Chips Transform Intel?" *New York Times*, September 12, 2004, pp. BU1, BU4 (quote); "Intel Corporation," *Hoover's*, www.hoovers.com on March 6, 2005; "Intel Shuffles Key Management Roles," *TechWeb*, October 10, 2000, www.techweb.com on February 8, 2005.

26 Peggy Leatt and Rodney Schneck, "Criteria for Grouping Nursing Subunits in Hospitals," *Academy of Management Review*, March 1984, pp. 150–165.

27 "Fact Sheets,""Organizational Structure," Deutsche Bank website, group.deutsche-bank.de on June 7, 2002; Marcus Walker, "Lean New Guard at Deutsche Bank Sets Global Agenda—But Cultural Rifts Prevent More-Aggressive Cost Cuts—The Traditionalists Haven't Gone Quietly," *Wall Street Journal*, February 14, 2002. www.wsj.com on April 4, 2002; Stephen Graham, "Deutsche Bank Says 2001 Profit Plummeted, Proceeds with Management Shake-Up," *National Business Stream*, January 31, 2002; "Deutsche Bank Names Next CEO, Continuity Seen," *National Business Stream*, September 21, 2000.

28 Lyndall F. Urwick, "The Manager's Span of Control," *Harvard Business Review*, May–June 1956, pp. 39–47.

29 Dan R. Dalton, William D. Tudor, Michael J. Spendolini, Gordon J. Fielding, and Lyman W. Porter, "Organization Structure and Performance: A Critical Review," *Academy of Management Review*, January 1980, pp. 49–64.

30 Mintzberg, *The Structuring of Organizations*, pp. 133–147.

31 See David Van Fleet, "Span of Management Research and Issues," *Academy of Management Journal*, September 1983, pp. 546–552, for an example of research on span of control.

32 John R. Montanari and Philip J. Adelman, "The Administrative Component of Organizations and the Rachet Effect: A Critique of Cross-Sectional Studies," *Journal of Management Studies*, March 1987, pp. 113–123.

33 D. A. Heenan, "The Downside of Downsizing," *Journal of Business Strategy*, November–December 1989, pp. 18–23.

34 Wayne F. Cascio, "Downsizing: What Do We Know? What Have We Learned?" *Academy of Management Executive*, February 1993, pp. 95–104.

35 James P. Guthrie and Deepak K. Datta: "The Impact of Downsizing on Firm Performance," *Organization Science*, January–February 2008, pp. 108–123, ©2008 INFORMS

36 Dalton et al., "Organization Structure and Performance."

37 See John Child, *Organization: A Guide to Problems and Practice*, 2nd ed. (New York: Harper & Row, 1984), pp. 145–153, for a detailed discussion of centralization.

38 Richard H. Hall, *Organization: Structure and Process*, 3rd ed. (Englewood Cliffs, NJ: Prentice Hall, 1982), pp. 87–96.

39 "Can Jack Smith Fix GM?" *Business Week*, November 1, 1993, pp. 126–131; John McElroy, "GM's Brand Management Might Work," *Automotive Industries*, September 1996, p. 132.

40 Daniel R. Denison, "Bringing Corporate Culture to the Bottom Line," *Organizational Dynamics*, Autumn 1984, pp. 4–22.

41 Leonard W. Johnson and Alan L. Frohman, "Identifying and Closing the Gap in the Middle of Organizations," *Academy of Management Executive*, May 1989, pp. 107–114.

42 Michael Schrage, "I Know What You Mean, and I Can't Do Anything About It," *Fortune*, April 2, 2001, p. 186.

43 Mintzberg, *The Structuring of Organizations*, pp. 83–84.

44 Arthur P. Brief and H. Kirk Downey, "Cognitive and Organizational Structures: A Conceptual Analysis of Implicit Organizing Theories," *Human Relations*, December 1983, pp. 1065–1090.

45 Jerald Hage, "An Axiomatic Theory of Organizations," *Administrative Science Quarterly*, December 1965, pp. 289–320.

46 Gregory Moorhead, "Organizational Analysis: An Integration of the Macro and Micro Approaches," *Journal of Management Studies*, April 1981, pp. 191–218.

47 J. Daniel Sherman and Howard L. Smith, "The Influence of Organizational Structure on Intrinsic Versus Extrinsic Motivation," *Academy of Management Journal*, December 1984, pp. 877–885.

48 John A. Pearce II and Fred R. David, "A Social Network Approach to Organizational Design-Performance," *Academy of Management Review*, July 1983, pp. 436–444.

49 Eileen Farihurst, "Organizational Rules and the Accomplishment of Nursing Work on Geriatric Wards," *Journal of Management Studies*, July 1983, pp. 315–332.

50 "Chevron Corp. Has Big Challenge Coping with Worker Cutbacks," *Wall Street Journal*, November 4, 1986, pp. 1, 25.

51 Neil F. Brady, "Rules for Making Exceptions to Rules," *Academy of Management Review*, July 1987, pp. 436–444.

52 See Jeffrey Pfeiffer, *Power in Organizations* (Boston: Pittman, 1981), pp. 4–6, for a discussion of the relationship between power and authority.

53 John B. Miner, *Theories of Organizational Structure and Process*, p. 360.

54 Chester Barnard, *The Functions of the Executive* (Cambridge, MA: Harvard University Press, 1938), pp. 161–184.

55 Pfeiffer, *Power in Organizations*, pp. 366–367.

Chapter 17

1 Lex Donaldson, "Strategy and Structural Adjustment to Regain Fit and Performance: In Defense of Contingency Theory," *Journal of Management Studies*, January 1987, pp. 1–24.

2 John R. Montanari, Cyril P. Morgan, and Jeffrey Bracker, *Strategic Management* (Hinsdale, IL: Dryden Press, 1990), p. 114.

3 See Arthur A. Thompson Jr. and A. J. Strickland III, *Strategic Management*, 3rd ed. (Plano, TX: Business Publications, 1984), pp. 19–27.

4 David Stires, "Fallen Arches," *Fortune*, April 26, 1999, pp. 146–152.

5 Alfred D. Chandler, *Strategy and Structure: Chapters in the History of the American Industrial Enterprise* (Cambridge, MA: MIT Press, 1962).

6 John R. Kimberly, "Organizational Size and the Structuralist Perspective: A Review, Critique, and Proposal," *Administrative Science Quarterly*, December 1976, pp. 571–597.

7 Peter M. Blau and Richard A. Schoenherr, *The Structure of Organizations* (New York: Basic Books, 1971).

8 The results of these studies are thoroughly summarized in Richard H. Hall, *Organizations: Structure and Process*, 3rd ed. (Englewood Cliffs, NJ: Prentice Hall, 1982), pp. 89–94. For another study in this area, see John H. Cullen and Kenneth S. Anderson, "Blau's Theory of Structural Differentiation Revisited: A Theory of Structural Change or Scale?" *Academy of Management Journal*, June 1986, pp. 203–229.

9 "Small Is Beautiful Now in Manufacturing," *Business Week*, October 22, 1984, pp. 152–156.

10 Richard H. Hall, J. Eugene Haas, and Norman Johnson, "Organizational Size, Complexity, and Formalization," *American Sociological Review*, December 1967, pp. 903–912.

11 Catherine Arnst, "Downsizing: Out One Door and In Another," *Business Week*, January 22, 1996, p. 41; Peter Elstrom, "Dial A for Aggravation," *Business Week*, March 11, 1996, p. 34; Alex Markels and Matt Murray, "Call It Dumbsizing: Why Some Companies Regret Cost-Cutting," *Wall Street Journal*, May 14, 1996, pp. A1, A5.

12 James P. Guthrie and Deepak K. Datta: "The Impact of Downsizing on Firm Performance," *Organization Science*, January–February 2008, pp. 108–123, ©2008 INFORMS; and Robert I. Sutton and Thomas D'Anno, "Decreasing Organizational Size: Untangling the Effects of Money and People," *Academy of Management Review*, May 1989, pp. 194–212.

13 Scott Thurm, "Recalculating the Cost of Big Layoffs," *Wall Street Journal*, May 5, 2010, accessed online, May 6, 2010.

14 Joan Woodward, *Management and Technology: Problems of Progress in Industry*, no. 3 (London: Her Majesty's Stationery Office, 1958); Joan Woodward, *Industrial Organizations: Theory and Practice* (London: Oxford University Press, 1965).

15 Tom Burns and George M. Stalker, *The Management of Innovation* (London: Tavistock, 1961).

16 Charles B. Perrow, "A Framework for the Comparative Analysis of Organizations," *American Sociological Review*, April 1967, pp. 194–208.

17 James D. Thompson, *Organizations in Action* (New York: McGraw-Hill, 1967).

18 David J. Hickson, Derek S. Pugh, and Diana C. Pheysey, "Operations Technology and Organization Structure: An Empirical Reappraisal," *Administrative Science Quarterly*, September 1969, pp. 378–397.

19 Diane E. Bailey, Paul M. Leonardi, and Jan Chong, "Minding the Gaps: Understanding Technology Interdependence and Coordination in Knowledge Work," *Organization Science, Articles in Advance*, September 25, 2009, pp. 1–18. INFORMS.

20 Ibid.

21 Andrew Kupfer, "How to Be a Global Manager," *Fortune*, March 14, 1988, pp. 52–58.

22 "Going Crazy in Japan—In a Break from Tradition, Tokyo Begins Funding a Program for Basic Research," *Wall Street Journal*, November 10, 1986, p. D20.

23 "About Wal-Mart," "Wal-Mart Stores, Inc., at a Glance," Wal-Mart website, www.walmartstores.com on June 12, 2002; "Dell at a Glance," "Dell Worldwide," Dell website, www.dell.com on June 12, 2002; Brian Dumaine, "What Michael Dell Knows That You Don't," *Fortune*, June 3, 2002. www.fortune.com on June 12, 2002; Andy Serwer, "Dell Does Domination," *Fortune*, January 21, 2002, pp. 71–75; Eryn Brown, "America's Most Admired Companies," *Fortune*, March 1, 1999, pp. 68–73 (quotation on p. 70).

24 Richard L. Daft, *Organization Theory and Design*, 8th ed. (South-Western, a division of Thomson Learning, 2004), p. 141.

25 "Toy Makers Lose Interest in Tie-Ins with Cartoons," *Wall Street Journal*, April 28, 1988, p. 29.

26 Masoud Yasai-Ardekani, "Structural Adaptations to Environments," *Academy of Management Review*, January 1986, pp. 9–21.

27 John E. Prescott, "Environments as Moderators of the Relationship Between Strategy and Performance," *Academy of Management Journal*, June 1986, pp. 329–346.

28 Timothy M. Stearns, Alan N. Hoffman, and Jan B. Heide, "Performance of Commercial Television Stations as an Outcome of Interorganizational Linkages and Environmental Conditions," *Academy of Management Journal*, March 1987, pp. 71–90.

29 Thompson, *Organizations in Action*, pp. 51–82.

30 Lori Ioannou, "American Invasion," *Fortune*, May 13, 2002, www.fortune. com on June 12, 2002; Jesse Wong, "How to Start a Business Without a Road Map," *Fortune*, April 1, 2002, www.fortune.com on June 12, 2002; Camilla Ojansivu, "Strategy for a Stronger Market Economy: Corporate Restructuring the PRC," *Business Beijing*, November, 2001, pp. 38–39.

31 For more information on managerial choice, see John Child, "Organizational Structure, Environment, and Performance: The Role of Strategic Choice," *Sociology*, January 1972, pp. 1–22; John R. Montanari, "Managerial Discretion: An Expanded Model of Organizational Choice," *Academy of Management Review*, April 1978, pp. 231–241.

32 H. Randolph Bobbitt and Jeffrey D. Ford, "Decision Maker Choice as a Determinant of Organizational Structure," *Academy of Management Review*, January 1980, pp. 13–23.

33 James W. Frederickson, "The Strategic Decision Process and Organization Structure," *Academy of Management Review*, April 1986, pp. 280–297.

34 Herman L. Boschken, "Strategy and Structure: Reconceiving the Relationship," *Journal of Management*, March 1990, pp. 135–150.

35 "Kerkorian Sues Daimler," *CNN Money*, November 28, 2000, cnnmoney. com on March 10, 2005; Stephen Graham, "DaimlerChrysler to Trim Management," *Detroit Free Press*, February 1, 2003, www.freep.com on March 10, 2005; Danny Hakim, "You Say 'Takeover.' I Say 'Merger of Equals.'" *New York Times*, December 21, 2003, pp. BU 1, BU10; Jeffrey K. Liker, "What Was Daimler Thinking?" *Across the Board*, January/February 2005, pp. 12–13.

36 Jerry Flint, "Is Fiat Helping Chrysler—Or Fiat," *Forbes.com*, November 3, 2009, http://www.forbes.com/2009/11/02/chrysler-fiat-automobiles-jerry-flint-business-autos-backseat.html on May 2, 2010.

37 Elton Mayo, *The Human Problems of an Industrial Civilization* (New York: Macmillan, 1933); F. J. Roethlisberger and W. J. Dickson, *Management and the Worker* (Cambridge, MA: Harvard University Press, 1939).

38 Eric L. Trist and K. W. Bamforth, "Some Social and Psychological Consequences of the Longwall Method of Coal-Getting," *Human Relations*, February 1951, pp. 3–38.

39 Richard E. Walton, "How to Counter Alienation in the Plant," *Harvard Business Review*, November–December 1972, pp. 70–81; Pehr G. Gyllenhammar, "How Volvo Adapts Work to People," *Harvard Business Review*, July–August 1977, pp. 102–113; Richard E. Walton, "Work Innovations at Topeka: After Six Years," *Journal of Applied Behavioral Science*, July–August–September 1977, pp. 422–433.

40 Henry Mintzberg, *The Structuring of Organizations: A Synthesis of the Research* (Englewood Cliffs, NJ: Prentice Hall, 1979).

41 See Harold C. Livesay, *American Made: Men Who Shaped the American Economy* (Boston: Little, Brown, 1979), pp. 215–239, for a discussion of Alfred Sloan and the development of the divisionalized structure at General Motors.

42 Anne B. Fisher, "GM Is Tougher Than You Think," *Fortune*, November 10, 1986, pp. 56–64.

43 Thompson and Strickland, *Strategic Management*, p. 212.

44 Gary Hamel with Bill Breen, *The Future of Management* (Boston: Harvard Business School Press, 2007).

45 Henry Mintzberg, "Organization Design: Fashion or Fit," *Harvard Business Review*, January–February 1981, pp. 103–116.

46 Harvey F. Kolodny, "Managing in a Matrix," *Business Horizons*, March–April 1981, pp. 17–24.

47 Stanley M. Davis and Paul R. Lawrence, *Matrix* (Reading, MA: Addison-Wesley, 1977), pp. 11–36.

48 Lawton R. Burns, "Matrix Management in Hospitals: Testing Theories of Matrix Structure and Development," *Administrative Science Quarterly*, September 1989, pp. 355–358.

49 Ibid., pp. 129–154.

50 "The Virtual Corporation," *Business Week*, February 8, 1993, pp. 98–102; William H. Carlile, "Virtual Corporation a Real Deal," *Arizona Republic*, August 2, 1993, pp. E1, E4.

51 Max Chafkin, "The Case, and the Plan, for the Virtual Company," *Inc. com*, April 1, 2010, accessed online April 25, 2010 at http://www.inc.com/magazine/20100401/the-case-and-the-plan-for-the-virtual-company.html. See the following website for a more complete listing of the pros and cons of teleworking: http://www.teleworker.com/pro-con.html.

52 Thomas A. Stewart, "Reengineering: The Hot New Managing Tool," *Fortune*, August 23, 1993, pp. 41–48.

53 James A. Champy, "From Reengineering to X-Engineering," in *Organization 21C: Someday All Organizations Will Lead This Way*, Subir Chowdhury, ed. (Upper Saddle River, NJ: Financial Times Prentice Hall, 2003), pp. 93–95.

54 Robert Tomasko, *Rethinking the Corporation* (New York: AMA-COM, 1993).

55 Rahul Jacob, "The Struggle to Create an Organization for the 21st Century," *Fortune*, April 3, 1995, pp. 90–99; Gene G. Marcial, "Don't Leave Your Broker Without It?" *Business Week*, February 5, 1996, p. 138; Jeffrey M. Laderman, "Loading Up on No-Loads," *Business Week*, May 27, 1996, p. 138.

56 James R. Lincoln, Mitsuyo Hanada, and Kerry McBride, "Organizational Structures in Japanese and U.S. Manufacturing," *Administrative Science Quarterly*, September 1986, pp. 338–364.

57 "The Inscrutable West," *Newsweek*, April 18, 1988, p. 52.

58 Michael W. Morris, Joel Podolny, and Bilian Ni Sullivan, "Culture and Coworker Relations: Interpersonal Patterns in American, Chinese, German, and Spanish Divisions of a Global Retail Bank," *Organization Science*," July–August 2008, pp. 517–532.

59 Richard I. Kirkland Jr., "Europe's New Managers," *Fortune*, September 29, 1980, pp. 56–60; Shawn Tully, "Europe's Takeover Kings," *Fortune*, July 20, 1987, pp. 95–98.

60 Henry W. Lane and Joseph J. DiStefano, *International Management Behavior* (Ontario: Nelson, 1988).

61 William H. Davison and Philippe Haspeslagh, "Shaping a Global Product Organization," *Harvard Business Review*, July–August 1982, pp. 125–132.

62 John Child, *Organizations: A Guide to Problems and Practice* (New York: Harper & Row, 1984), p. 246.

63 Thomas J. Peters and Robert H. Waterman Jr., *In Search of Excellence: Lessons from America's Best-Run Companies* (New York: Harper & Row, 1982), pp. 235–278.

64 Thomas J. Peters and Nancy K. Austin, "A Passion for Excellence," *Fortune*, May 13, 1985, pp. 20–32.

65 Michael Beer, "Building Organizational Fitness" in *Organization 21C: Someday All Organizations Will Lead This Way*, Subir Chowdhury, ed. (Upper Saddle River, NJ: Financial Times Prentice Hall, 2003), pp. 311–312.

Chapter 18

1 See "Corporate Culture: The Hard-to-Change Values That Spell Success or Failure," *Business Week*, October 27, 1980, pp. 148–160; Charles G. Burck, "Working Smarter," *Fortune*, June 15, 1981, pp. 68–73.

2 Charles A. O'Reilly and Jennifer A. Chatman, "Culture as Social Control: Corporations, Cults, and Commitment," in vol. 18, *Research in Organizational Behavior*, Barry M. Staw and L. L. Cummings, eds., pp. 157–200 (Stamford, CT: JAI Press, 1996).

3 J. P. Kotter and J. L. Heskett, *Corporate Culture and Performance* (New York: Free Press, 1992).

4 Michael Tushman and Charles A. O'Reilly, *Staying on Top: Managing Strategic Innovation and Change for Long-Term Success* (Boston: Harvard Business School Press, 1996).

5 T. E. Deal and A. A. Kennedy, *Corporate Cultures: The Rites and Rituals of Corporate Life* (Reading, MA: Addison-Wesley, 1982), p. 4.

6 E. H. Schein, "The Role of the Founder in Creating Organizational Culture," *Organizational Dynamics*, Summer 1983, p. 14.

7 Thomas J. Peters and Robert H. Waterman Jr., *In Search of Excellence: Lessons from America's Best-Run Companies* (New York: Harper & Row, 1982), p. 103.

8 See M. Polanyi, *Personal Knowledge* (Chicago: University of Chicago Press, 1958); E. Goffman, *The Presentation of Self in Everyday Life* (New York: Doubleday, 1959); and P. L. Berger and T. Luckman, *The Social Construction of Reality* (Garden City, NY: Anchor Books, 1967).

9 "Declaration of Interdependence," Whole Foods Market website, www.wholefoodsmarket.com on May 1, 2005; "David B. Dillon," *Forbes*, www.forbes.com on April 29, 2005; "The Kroger Co.," *Hoover's*, www.hoovers.com on April 29, 2005; Charles Fischman, "The Anarchist's Cookbook," *Fast Company*, July 2004, pp. 70–78; Evan Smith, "John Mackey," *Texas Monthly*, March 2005, pp. 122–132 (quotation); Amy Tsao, "Whole Foods' Natural High," *Business Week*, July 17, 2003, www.businessweek.com on April 30, 2005.

10 Eric Ransdell, "The Nike Story? Just Tell It!" *Fast Company*, January–February 2000, pp. 44–46 (quotation on p. 46); Claude Solnik, "Co-Founder of Nike Dies Christmas Eve," *Footwear News*, January 3, 2000, p. 2; Rosemary Feitelberg, "Bowerman's Legacy Runs On," *WWD*, December 30, 1999, p. 8.

11 Louise Lee, "Tricks of E*Trade," *Business Week E.Biz*, February 7, 2000, pp. EB18–EB31.

12 A. L. Kroeber and C. Kluckhohn, "Culture: A Critical Review of Concepts and Definitions," in *Papers of the Peabody Museum of American Archaeology and Ethnology*, vol. 47, no. 1 (Cambridge, MA: Harvard University Press, 1952).

13 C. Geertz, *The Interpretation of Cultures* (New York: Basic Books, 1973).

14 See, for example, B. Clark, *The Distinctive College* (Chicago: Aldine, 1970).

15 E. Durkheim, *The Elementary Forms of Religious Life*, trans. J. Swain (New York: Collier, 1961), p. 220.

16 See William G. Ouchi, *Theory Z: How American Business Can Meet the Japanese Challenge* (Reading, MA: Addison-Wesley, 1981); and Peters and Waterman, *In Search of Excellence*.

17 See Ouchi, *Theory Z*; Deal and Kennedy, *Corporate Cultures*; and Peters and Waterman, *In Search of Excellence*.

18 E. Borgida and R. E. Nisbett, "The Differential Impact of Abstract vs. Concrete Information on Decisions," *Journal of Applied Social Psychology*, July–September 1977, pp. 258–271.

19 J. Martin and M. Power, "Truth or Corporate Propaganda: The Value of a Good War Story," in Pondy et al., *Organizational Symbolism* (Greenwich, CT: JAI), 1983, pp. 93–108.

20 W. G. Ouchi, "Markets, Bureaucracies, and Clans," *Administrative Science Quarterly*, March 1980, pp. 129–141; A. Wilkins and W. G. Ouchi, "Efficient Cultures: Exploring the Relationship Between Culture and Organizational Performance," *Administrative Science Quarterly*, September 1983, pp. 468–481.

21 Peters and Waterman, *In Search of Excellence*.

22 J. B. Barney, "Organizational Culture: Can It Be a Source of Sustained Competitive Advantage?" *Academy of Management Review*, July 1986, pp. 656–665.

23 Michelle Conlin, "Is Wal-Mart Hostile to Women?" *Business Week*, July 16, 2001. www.businessweek.com on June 21, 2002.

24 Kate Linebaugh, Dionne Searcey and Norihiko Shirouzu, "Secretive Culture Led Toyota Astray," *The Wall Street Journal*, February 8, 2010, accessed online, February 13, 2010.

25 Daniel R. Denison, "What Is the Difference Between Organizational Culture and Organizational Climate? A Native's Point of View on a Decade of Paradigm Wars," *Academy of Management Review*, July 1996, pp. 619–654.

26 S. G. Isaksen and G. Ekvall, *Assessing the Context for Change: A Technical Manual for the Situational Outlook Questionnaire* (Orchard Park, NY: The Creative Problem Solving Group, 2007).

27 O'Reilly and Chatman, "Culture as Social Control."

28 Richard L. Osborne, "Strategic Values: The Corporate Performance Engine," *Business Horizons*, September–October 1996, pp. 41–47.

29 See Osborne, "Strategic Values: The Corporate Performance Engine"; and Gary McWilliams, "Dell's Profit Rises Slightly, As Expected," *Wall Street Journal*, February 11, 2000, p. A3.

30 "The Jack and Herb Show," *Fortune*, January 11, 1999, p. 166.

31 Max Chafkin, "The Zappos Way of Managing," *Inc.com*, May 1, 2009, accessed online www.inc.com, April 25, 2010.

32 Ibid.

33 Ibid.

34 Ouchi, *Theory Z*.

35 Catherine Reagor, "Wells Fargo Riding Roughshod in State, Some Say," *Arizona Republic*, September 8, 1996, pp. D1, D4; Catherine Reagor, "Wells Fargo to Cut 3,000 Additional Jobs," *Arizona Republic*, December 20, 1996, pp. E1, E2.

36 O'Reilly and Chatman, "Culture as Social Control."

37 John E. Sheridan, "Organizational Culture and Employee Retention," *Academy of Management Journal*, December 1992, pp. 1036–1056; Lisa A. Mainiero, "Is Your Corporate Culture Costing You?" *Academy of Management Executive*, November 1993, pp. 84–85.

38 Peters and Waterman, *In Search of Excellence*.

39 Watts S. Humphrey, *Managing for Innovation: Leading Technical People* (Englewood Cliffs, NJ: Prentice Hall, 1987).

40 Brian O'Reilly, "Secrets of the Most Admired Corporations: New Ideas and New Products," *Fortune*, March 3, 1997, pp. 60–64.

41 Laurie K. Lewis and David R. Seibold, "Innovation Modification During Intraorganizational Adoption," *Academy of Management Review*, April 1993, vol. 10, no. 2, pp. 322–354.

42 Brian Hindo, "3M's Culture of Innovation, *"Business Week,"* June 11, 2007, www.businessweek.com on April 25, 2008; Brian Hindo, "At 3M, A Struggle Between Efficiency and Creativity," *Business Week*, June 11, 2007, www.businessweek.com on January 18, 2008; Brian Hindo, "3M Chief Plants a Money Tree," *Business Week*, June 11, 2007, www.businessweek.com on April 25, 2008.

43 For more discussion of W. L. Gore & Associates, see Gary Hamel (with Bill Breen) *The Future of Management* (Boston: Harvard Business School Press, 2007), pp. 83–100.

44 Oren Harari, "Stop Empowering Your People," *Management Review*, November 1993, pp. 26–29.

45 Rob Goffee and Gareth Jones, "Organizational Culture," in *Organization 21C: Someday All Organizations Will Lead This Way*, Subir Chowdhury, ed. (Upper Saddle River, NJ: Financial Times Prentice Hall, 2003), pp. 273–290.

46 "Declaration of Interdependence," Whole Foods Market website, www.wholefoodsmarket.com on May 1, 2005 ; Amy Tsao, "Whole Foods' Natural High," *Business Week*, July 18, 2003, www.businessweek.com on April 30, 2005; Charles Fischman, "The Anarchist's Cookbook," *Fast Company*, July 2004, pp. 70–78; "David B. Dillon," *Forbes*, www.forbes.com on April 29, 2005; Evan Smith, "John Mackey," *Texas Monthly*, March 2005, pp. 122–132.

47 See Warren Wilhelm, "Changing Corporate Culture—Or Corporate Behavior? How to Change Your Company," *Academy of Management Executive*, November 1992, pp. 72–77.

48 "Socialization" has also been defined as "the process by which culture is transmitted from one generation to the next." See J. W. M. Whiting, "Socialization: Anthropological Aspects," in vol. 14, *International Encyclopedia of the Social Sciences*, D. Sils, ed. (New York: Free Press, 1968), p. 545.

49 J. E. Hebden, "Adopting an Organization's Culture: The Socialization of Graduate Trainees," *Organizational Dynamics*, Summer 1986, pp. 54–72.

50 J. B. Barney, "Organizational Culture: Can It Be a Source of Sustained Competitive Advantage?" *Academy of Management Review*, July 1986, pp. 656–665.

51 Brian Hindo, "3M's Culture of Innovation."

52 James R. Norman, "A New Teledyne," *Forbes*, September 27, 1993, pp. 44–45.

Chapter 19

1 "Baby Boomers Push for Power," *Business Week*, July 2, 1984, pp. 52–56.

2 "Americans' Median Age Passes 32," *Arizona Republic*, April 6, 1988, pp. A1, A5.

3 "Population Estimates Program," Population Division, U.S. Census Bureau, Washington, DC, (www.census.gov/popest/national/asrh/ NC-EST2008-sa May 23, 2010).

4 Geoffrey Colvin, "What the Baby Boomers Will Buy Next," *Fortune*, October 15, 1984, pp. 28–34.

5 Lev Grossman, "Grow Up? Not So Fast," *Time*, January 24, 2005, p. 42.

6 Diane Thielfoldt and Devon Scheef, "Generation X and The Millennials: What You Need to Know About Mentoring the New Generations," *Law Practice Today*, August 2004, www.abanet.org/lm/lpt/articles/nosearch/ mgt08044_print.html on March 11, 2008.

7 John Huey, "Managing in the Midst of Chaos," *Fortune*, April 5, 1993, pp. 38–48.

8 "DuPont Adopts New Direction in China," Xinhua News Agency, September 7, 1999, p. 1008250h0104; Alex Taylor III, "Why DuPont Is Trading Oil for Corn," *Fortune*, April 26, 1999, pp. 154–160; Jay Palmer, "New DuPont: For Rapid Growth, an Old-Line Company Looks to Drugs, Biotechnology," *Barron's*, May 11, 1998, p. 31.

9 "Toyota to Employ Robots," News24.com website, January 6, 2005, www.news24.com on May 4, 2005; "Toyota's Global New Body Line," Toyota Motor Manufacturing website, www.toyotageorgetown.com on May 4, 2005; Burritt Sabin, "Robots for Babies—Toyota at the Leading Edge," Japan.com website, www.japan.com on May 5, 2005.

10 Stephanie Schomer, "Body Language," *Fast Company*," May 2010, pp. 61–66.

11 Tarmo Virki, "Professional Social Networking Booming," bx.businessweek.com, May 18, 2010; and Eric Tsai, "How to Integrate Email Marketing, SEO, and Social Media," bx.businessweek.com, May 20, 2010, accessed May 24, 2010.

12 Thomas A. Stewart, "Welcome to the Revolution," *Fortune*, December 13, 1993, pp. 66–80.

13 Max Chafkin, "The Zappos Way of Managing," *Inc.com*, May 1, 2009, www.inc.com, accessed online April 25, 2010.

14 See Thomas L. Friedman, *The World Is Flat 3.0, A Brief History of the Twenty-First Century* (New York: Farrar, Straus & Giroux, 2007), for an excellent account of the impact of globalization and technology.

15 Kurt Lewin, *Field Theory in Social Science* (New York: Harper & Row, 1951).

16 W. Warner Burke, "Leading Organizational Change," in *Organization 21C: Someday All Organizations Will Lead This Way*, Subir Chowdhury, ed. (Upper Saddle River, NJ: Financial Times Prentice Hall, 2003), pp. 291–310.

17 Mitchell Lee Marks, "In With the New," *Wall Street Journal*, May 24, 2010, online.wsj.com, accessed online May 24, 2010.

18 Linda S. Ackerman, "Transition Management: An In-Depth Look at Managing Complex Change," *Organizational Dynamics*, Summer 1982, pp. 46–66; David A. Nadler, "Managing Transitions to Uncertain Future States," *Organizational Dynamics*, Summer 1982, pp. 37–45.

19 Burke, "Leading Organizational Change."

20 Noel M. Tichy and David O. Ulrich, "The Leadership Challenge—A Call for the Transformational Leader," *Sloan Management Review*, Fall 1984, pp. 59–68.

21 W. Warner Burke, *Organization Development: Principles and Practices* (Boston: Little, Brown, 1982).

22 Michael Beer, *Organization Change and Development* (Santa Monica, CA: Goodyear, 1980); Burke, *Organization Development*.

23 Cummings and Worley, *Organization Development and Change*, 6th ed. (South-Western Publishing, 1997), p. 2.

24 Noel M. Tichy and Christopher DeRose, "The Death and Rebirth of Organizational Development," in *Organization 21C: Someday All Organizations Will Lead This Way*, Subir Chowdhury, ed. (Upper Saddle River, NJ: Financial Times Prentice Hall, 2003), pp. 155–177.

25 Danny Miller and Peter H. Friesen, "Structural Change and Performance: Quantum Versus Piecemeal-Incremental Approaches," *Academy of Management Journal*, December 1982, pp. 867–892.

26 Sharon Silke Carty, "Bill Ford Carries on Family Name with Grace," *USA Today*, February 27, 2005, http://www.usatoday.com/money/ autos/2005-02-27-ford-ceo-usat_x.htm on March 12, 2008; "Ford Enters New Era of E-Communication: New Web Sites Connect Dealers, Consumer, Suppliers," *PR Newswire*, January 24, 2000, p. 7433; Suzy Wetlaufer, "Driving Change," *Harvard Business Review*, March–April 1999, pp. 77–85; "Ford's Passing Fancy," *Business Week*, March 15, 1999, p. 42; Bill Saporito, "Can Alan Mulally Keep Ford in the Fast Lane?" *Time*, August 9, 2010, http://www.time.com/time/magazine/ article/0,9171,2007401,00.html, August 19, 2010.

27 J. Lloyd Suttle, "Improving Life at Work—Problems and Prospects," in *Improving Life at Work: Behavioral Science Approaches to Organizational Change*, J. Richard Hackman and J. Lloyd Suttle, eds. (Santa Monica, CA: Goodyear, 1977), p. 4.

28 Richard E. Walton, "Quality of Work Life: What Is It?" *Sloan Management Review*, Fall 1983, pp. 11–21.

29 DISA website, www.disa.mil/careers/worklife, on May 23, 2010.

30 Daniel A. Ondrack and Martin G. Evans, "Job Enrichment and Job Satisfaction in Greenfield and Redesign QWL Sites," *Group & Organization Studies*, March 1987, pp. 5–22.

31 Ricky W. Griffin, *Task Design: An Integrative Framework* (Glenview, IL: Scott, Foresman, 1982).

32 Gregory Moorhead, "Organizational Analysis: An Integration of the Macro and Micro Approaches," *Journal of Management Studies*, April 1981, pp. 191–218.

33 James C. Quick and Jonathan D. Quick, *Organizational Stress and Preventive Management* (New York: McGraw-Hill, 1984).

34 Tichy and DeRose, "The Death and Rebirth of Organizational Development."

35 Kenneth N. Wexley and Timothy T. Baldwin, "Management Development," *1986 Yearly Review of Management of the Journal of Management*, in the *Journal of Management*, Summer 1986, pp. 277–294.

36 Richard Beckhard, "Optimizing Team-Building Efforts," *Journal of Contemporary Business*, Summer 1972, pp. 23–27, 30–32.

37 Bernard M. Bass, "Issues Involved in Relations Between Methodological Rigor and Reported Outcomes in Evaluations of Organizational Development," *Journal of Applied Psychology*, February 1983, pp. 197–201; William M. Vicars and Darrel D. Hartke, "Evaluating OD Evaluations: A Status Report," *Group & Organization Studies*, June 1984, pp. 177–188.

38 Beer, Organization Change and Development.

39 Jerome L. Franklin, "Improving the Effectiveness of Survey Feedback," *Personnel*, May–June 1978, pp. 11–17.

40 Paul R. Lawrence, "How to Deal with Resistance to Change," *Harvard Business Review*, May–June 1954, reprinted in *Organizational Change and Development*, Gene W. Dalton, Paul R. Lawrence, and Larry E. Greiner, eds. (Homewood, IL: Irwin, 1970), pp. 181–197.

41 Jeffrey D. Ford, Laurie W. Ford, and Angelo D'Amelio, "Resistance to Change: The Rest of the Story," *Academy of Management Review*, 2008, pp. 362–377.

42 Daniel Katz and Robert L. Kahn, *The Social Psychology of Organizations*, 2nd ed. (New York: John Wiley and Sons, 1978), pp. 36–68.

43 See Michael T. Hannah and John Freeman, "Structural Inertia and Organizational Change," *American Sociological Review*, April 1984, pp. 149–164, for an in-depth discussion of structural inertia.

44 Moorhead, "Organizational Analysis: An Integration of the Macro and Micro Approaches."

45 G. Zaltman and R. Duncan, *Strategies for Planned Change* (New York: John Wiley and Sons, 1977); David A. Nadler, "Concepts for the Management of Organizational Change," *Perspectives on Behavior in Organizations*, 2nd ed., J. Richard Hackman, Edward E. Lawler III, and Lyman W. Porter, eds. (New York: McGraw-Hill, 1983), pp. 551–561.

46 Alfred M. Jaeger, "Organization Development and National Culture: Where's the Fit?" *Academy of Management Review*, January 1986, pp. 178–190.

47 Alan M. Webber, "Learning for a Change," *Fast Company*, May 1999, pp. 178–188.

NAME INDEX

COMPANY INDEX

SUBJECT INDEX